IRISH ARTS REVIEW YEARBOOK

SPONSORED BY

GLEN DIMPLEX

Foreword

By

The Executive Chairman of Glen Dimplex

Sponsors of Irish Arts Review Yearbook 2000

Once again we are delighted to support the *Irish Arts Review*. This edition, the sixteenth, follows on from the inspiration of past editions and provides a distinctive and wide ranging view of the arts. It celebrates the best of Irish and we are proud to be associated with it.

Martin Naughton
Executive Chairman, Glen Dimplex

IRISH ARTS REVIEW YEARBOOK

IRISH ARTS REVIEW YEARBOOK

Volume 16
2000

Irish Arts Review Limited

SPONSORED BY GLEN DIMPLEX

IRISH ARTS REVIEW

PO Box 3500, Dublin 4. Ireland
Tel/Fax: +353-1-670 3503 Email: editorial@irishartsreview.com Website: www.irishartsreview.com

YEARBOOK 2000: VOLUME 16

PUBLISHER : ANN REIHILL

EDITOR : HOMAN POTTERTON
EDITORIAL ASSISTANT : HELEN O'CONNELL
ADMINISTRATOR : BREDA CONWAY
ADVERTISING MANAGER : VERA FINNEGAN
ART DIRECTOR : JOHN POWER

COVER ILLUSTRATION

Irish Tweed Coat by Sybil Connolly.
Photographed by Norman Parkinson for *Vogue,* March 1954, and modelled by Wenda Parkinson.

FRONTISPIECE

TERRYBAUN POTTERY *A selection of jugs.* Earthenware by Grattan and Madeleine Freyer c.1960.

British Library Cataloguing in Publication Data
A catalogue record for this book is available from the British Library
Irish Arts Review Yearbook is indexed in *BHA: Bibliography of the History of Art*

ISBN 0 9536510 1 0 (hardback); 0 9536510 0 2 (paperback); ISSN 0791-3540

IRISH ARTS REVIEW is published annually in November.
Price: IR£40 (hardback): IR£26 (paperback)

Three-year subscription prices (inclusive of postage):
IR£95 (US IR£107) hardback; IR£60 (US IR£80) paperback
Address for subscriptions: PO Box 3500, Dublin 4

IRISH ARTS REVIEW receives grants from the Arts Council of Northern Ireland;
the Irish Arts Council/An Chomhairle Ealaíon The Arts Council An Chomhairle Ealaíon; assistance from the
Cultural Relations Committee of the Irish Department of Foreign Affairs; and support from the
Commissioners of Public Works in the form of office accommodation in Dublin Castle.

IRISH ARTS REVIEW is published for Ann Reihill by Irish Arts Review Limited, PO Box 3500, Dublin 4, Ireland

Typeset by Pat Brennan
Colour reproduction by Typeform Repro
Printed in Ireland by Betaprint

Contents

Irish Arts Review Yearbook 2000: Vol 16

Contents

Irish Arts Review Yearbook 2000: Vol 16

List of Subscribers

Subscribers must register their order for *Irish Arts Review Yearbook* by 15th August in the year of publication to have their name included on this list

Acorn Gallery
Mrs Acton
Sheila M Adair
Mrs L Adams
Jean Agnew
Fergus Ahern
Professor Anders Ahlqvist
Alexandra College, Dublin
Mrs Caroline Aliaga-Kelly
William Aliaga-Kelly
R. Ivan Allen
Muriel J Allison
St Andrew's College, Library
Christopher Anthony
Mrs Amelia Archer
Armagh Public Library
Diana Armytage
David Arnold
Phyllis Arnold Gallery Antiques
Lady A Arnott
ARTbibliographies, Oxford
Christopher Ashe
Ashmolean Library, Oxford

Backwater Artists Group
Giles Baily
Beatrice Baird
The Ballinglen Arts Foundation
Bridge Primary School, Banbridge
Vivienne Barber
John Barry & Jean Barry
Peter Barry
Rosemary Beasley
Olive Beaumont
Belfast Public Libraries
Prof Christopher Bell
Nelson & Clover Bell
Lord Belmore
Douglas Bennett
Dr Síghle Bhreathnach-Lynch
Dorcas Birthistle
T A Birthistle MD
Eileen Black
Miss A F C Blackmore
Nin Bligh
David Boles
Anne Bolger
Jackie Bolger
Ron Bolger
Marieke Booth
Boston College, Irish Studies Programme
Dr Josephine Borchert-Ansinger
Marie Bourke
Grace Bouton Magan
Mr & Mrs Mary & Ray Bowe
Pamela Bowell
Michael Boyd
Barra Boydell
Mrs Mary Boydell
Mrs Mary Boylan
Dr Peter Boylan
J F Bradley
Dr & Mrs Aidan M Brady
Mrs Máire Brady
Siobhan Brady
Ciarán Breathnach
Ulli de Breffny
Colin Brennan
G M Brennan
Mr Neil J Brennan
P J Brennan
Daniel J Breslin
Donal M Brooks FRCS
Sir Charles Brett
Viscountess Bridgeman
Gary Britton
Galer Britton Barnes
The Hon G D Browne
Gerard & Fidelma Browne
Malcolm & Jane Brush
Emer Buckley

Frank X Buckley
Michael Buckley
Ann Budd
Dr A M Bulbulia
Rev R J Bunday
F H J van Bunningen
Burke-Kennedy Doyle Architects
Burlington Dental Clinic
Mr & Mrs Brian P Burns
Niamh Burns
Richard Burrows
Mari Colleen Bush
Butler Gallery
Patricia Butler
Thomas C Butler
Norrie Buxton
Helen Byrne
Mrs Joyce Byrne
Kevin Byrne

Fabian P Cadden
Professor Kevin M Cahill
Stephen Cahill
Hugh & Jean Campbell
Julian Campbell
Mrs Noëlle Cantwell
Margarita Cappock
Edmond A Carberry
Mary Carberry-Sharma
Paul Carey
Eugenie Carr
Gemma Carton
Dr Austin T Carty
Carolyn Caruth
Barry Carville
Frank & Alison Casey
Glynis & Pat Casey
Joseph T Casey
Dr Noelle Casey
Marion Cashman
Mr Tom Cavanagh
Grainne B Cella
Celtic Ross Hotel
John Chambré
Ann Charles
Stella Cherry
Mr Dermot Chichester
Mr Robert Edward Christie
Mr Carey Clarke
Eithne Clarke
Frank Clarke
Leo Clarke
Thomas J Clarke
Henry J Cleeve
Mrs Mavis Cleggett
Mr Vernon Cluff
Robert Clyde
Mr Patrick Coakley
Pauline Coakley
Alec Cobbe
Lady H Cochrane
Timothy Cochrane
Dr Ellen Cody
James J Coleman
John C Coleman
John & Patricia Coleman
Norman Colfer
Mrs A M Collins
Jane Collins
Vera Collins
Helen Conlan
Gary R Connolly Dip RA of Fine Arts
John & Brideen Connolly
Joseph F Connolly
Thurloe & Jacqueline Conolly
Alan Conroy

Deirdre Conroy
Dr John G Cooney
Caroline Corballis
Mrs John Corcoran
Cork Public Museum
Edmund P B Corrigan
Michael Corrigan
Mrs Finbar Costello
Finola Costello
Joyce Costello
Seamus A Costello
Catherine Cotter
Christopher & Deirdre Coughlan
Frances & John Coulter
Timothy B. Counihan
Courtauld Institute of Art
(University of London)
Marianne Court
Fergus Courtney
Maurice F Cowhey
Jill Cox
Brian Coyle FRICS
Rose Mary Craig
Craigavon Museum Project
Crawford Municipal Art Gallery
G A Creedon
Helen Crilly
Deirdre Crofts
Pat Crowley
William Crozier
Clare Cryan
Ann Cullen
Dr Fintan Cullen
L M Cullen
Oriole Cullen
William Cullen
Eve-Anne Cullinan
James J Curran Jr
Mr Kevin Curry
Mrs Helen Curtain
Elizabeth Cusack
Igor Cusack

Adele M Dalsimer
Patrick H Daly
V Daly
Peter & Maureen Danby-Smith
Christine Davies
Sir David Davies
Sir Robert & Lady Davis-Goff
Jackie Dawson
Angélique Day
Mary Deegan
Joan & Michael Deeny
Geraldine Deering
Mrs Ida Delamer
Moya Delaney
Olivia Delaney
Mrs H G Denniston
Derry City Council,
Heritage & Museum Service
Maurice Desmond
Polly Devlin
Christopher & Jane Dick
Eoin & Hilary Dickie
Dr Jakob Diehn
Jean M Dillon
Mr Val Dillon
Anne Dillon Carrigan
Patrick & Lynda Dillon-Malone
Thomas Dillon Redshaw Ph.D
Mrs Celia Dineen
Wallace Dinsmore
Dr T Dixon
Dr Arthur M Dolan
Margo Dolan/Peter Maxwell

Philo Dolan
John Donahue
Mary Rita Donleavy
Elizabeth A Donnelly
Jacqueline M Donnelly
Otto Donner
Joseph A Donohoe V
Patrick & Hanneluise Doran
Amanda Douglas
Daniel Dowling
Jim Dowling
Paul G Dowling
Edward R Downe Jnr
Margaret Downes
Áine Doyle
Bridget Doyle
Helen M Doyle
Mrs Kay Doyle
Mary Doyle
Lee F Driscoll Jr
Duff Tisdall Ltd
Dr Illona Duffy
Mr R R Dunbar
Dundalk Urban District Council, Arts Office
Mairead Dunlevy
Peter Dunne
John Dunn Gallagher
Mr & Mrs Roger Dunwoody
Patrick & Mary-Clare Durcan

Robert Earle
B J Eastwood
Fiona Eastwood
Stephen T C Eastwood
June Eiffe
A C Elias Jr
Acheson & Margaret Elliott
John M Elliot

Mrs Ruth Faehndrich
Deirdre Fagan
Juliet Fairfax Crone
Conor & Nancy Fallon
William & Catherine Fanning
Anne & Adrian Farrelly
John Farrington/Thomas Dobson
Margaret Farrington
Jane Fenlon
Loraine Fennelly & Simon McAleese
Noleen & Vincent Ferguson
T N Fewer
Dr Nicola Figgis
Judith Finlay
Ann Marie Fitzgerald
Mrs B Fitzgerald
Dr Eddie Fitzgerald
Patricia Fitzgerald
Mrs R Fitzjohn
Mr & Mrs William E Flaherty
Rory Flanagan
Dr J Flood
Leo Flynn
Streeter B Flynn Jr
Rev Thomas Flynn
Maire & Maurice Foley
V Rev W Forde
Robin Forrester
Roy Foster
Four Courts Press
Joan & Eddie Fox
Mary P Fox
Eleanor J Franklin
Edward J Frayne
Ann Fuller
Mairead Furlong

Patrick Gageby SC
John T Gallagher FRCOG
Michael Galvin
Galway Arts Centre
Catherine Gaynor

List of Subscribers

Georgian Antiques
James Gilligan
Margaret Gilligan
David F Gilvarry
W D Girvan
Ann Gleasure
Glucksman Ireland House
Cathal Goan
John Godson
Sir Robert & Lady Sheelagh Goff
Rosemary Goodbody
Leo Goodstadt
Mr Angus E Gordon
Mr Richard J Gordon
Sir Josslyn Gore-Booth Bt
Nancy C Gorman
Viscount Gormanston
Anne Gormley
Paul Gormley
John P Greely
Godfrey D H Greene
Niall Greene
Dr M J Gregan
Brendan Grimes
Jason A Groarke
Desmond Guinness
Patrick Guinness

Rosalind Hadden
Colin G Haddick
Dickon Hall
Hamilton Osborne King
Frank Hamill
Hugh Hamill
Eamonn Hannan
Bernard Hanratty
Dr Peter Harbison
Kitty Harney
Mrs Maeve Hart
Norah Hart
Denis J Hartnett
Ros Harvey
Joseph Hassett
Philip C Haughey
Mrs Ivy Hawkes
John R Hayes
Sam Hazlett
J Healy SC
Patricia A Healy
John G Hearne
Charles Hennessy
John Herlihy
The Heritage Council,
An Chomhairle Oidhreachta
Iolanda Herron
Dorinda Hickey
Josephine Hickey
Ted Hickey
Niall P Higgins
Jeremy Hill
Robert Charles Hill QC SC
History Ireland
Anne Hodge
Arlene Hogan
Mr Mike Hogan
Mary Holian
Michael Holland
Maya Homburger
Thomas E Honan
John M Hood FRCS
Noel & Margaret Horgan
Mrs Irene Houlihan
Mr Roy Thomas Houston
Ms Elizabeth Howell
Mr & Mrs Frank Hughes
Rita Hughes
Roland Hulme-Beaman
The Hunt Museum
Mary Hunter
Bernardine Hurley
Paulyne Hurley

Derry Hussey
Dr Robin Hyndman

Makoto Imura
Aideen Ireland
Irish American Cultural Institute
Irish Architectural Archive
Irish College for the Humanities
Irish Linen Centre and Lisburn Museum
James C Irwin
Stephen Irwin
Professor Hiro Ishibashi
Embassy of Israel

Philip & Brigid Jacob
Kurt Jaeger
Dr Bernard Jaffa
Gerald W Jennings
The Jesuit Library, Milltown
Frank Johnson
Ms Norma Johnson
Eva Johnston
Jennifer Johnston
Cecily Joyce
John P Joyce

Eileen Kane
Mrs E Kato
Mark Kavanagh
Robert J Kavanagh
Cornelius Keane
Frank X Keane
John Kerry Keane
Dr J B Kearney
Geoffrey Keating
The Keatley Trust
Raymond Keaveney
James Kehoe
Mrs Susan Kellett
Anne Kelly
Bill Kelly
Mrs Delphine Kelly
John Kelly
Mr Thomas Cyril Kenefick FRCS
Brian P Kennedy
Roisin Kennedy
Dr S B Kennedy
Charles M Kenny
William E Keohane
David Ker Esq
K C Keville
Kildare Street & University Club
Eden Kilgallen
William B Kilmurray
Patrick Kilroy
Brendan Kilty
Danny Kinahan
Felicity King & David Fitzpatrick
Heather A King
Nicholas King
The Honorable Society of King's Inns
Dr Claudia Kinmonth
V Reverend T Kinsella
James Kirwan
Dr Richard E Kistler
Mr & Mrs Fred A Krehbiel

William Laffan
Dr Bruce Lambert
Gordon Lambert
James S Lamont
Sonja Landweer
Oonagh Lane-O'Kelly
Dr Gabrielle Langdon Ph D
Stephen Lanigan-O'Keeffe
Helen Lanigan Wood
Dr & Mrs John E Larkin Jr
Christine Lavelle
Patrick & Frances Lawlor
Mr R J Lawrence
Richard & Marie Lawton

Louis le Brocquy
Beatrice Leahy
Fionola Leane
James A Lenehan
Robert Lennon
V Revd John Leonard
Myles Leonard
Celia Lepere
Rev D A Levistone Cooney
Geoffrey Lewis
Limerick County Council
Anne Loane
Rolf Loeber
Mrs Joan Logan
Alan Logue
London Library
Nora Liddy
Gena Lynam
Mr Brendan Lynch
Frances Lynch
Padraig Lynch
Fidelma Lyons
Lorcan Lyons
Oliver & Patricia Lyons

Very Revd Dr R B MacCarthy
Roisin MacDougald
Patrick MacEntee SC QC
Uinseann MacEoin
Dr Myles MacEvilly
Rupert MacHenry
Alastair MacKeown
Daniel MacLaughlin
Camilla McAleese
Michael B McAuley
Martin & Janet McAuley
R John McBratney
Mr W & Mrs C McCabe
Mr Pat McCaffrey
H McCalmont
Neil McCann
T McCann
Mrs Breda McCarthy
Derry & Valerie McCarthy
Michael A McCarthy
Dr Michael McCarthy
Manus McClafferty
George & Maura McClelland
Jeannie & James Lyle McCollum
Professor K McConkey
Dr John McCormack
Simon McCormick
Mairtín McCullough
Augusta Josefine McDermott
Enda McDonagh
Gérard A C McDonnell
Helen McDonnell
James Paul McDonnell
Jim & Ceri McDonnell
Mrs McDonnell
Paul McDonnell
Petria McDonnell
Anne McElree
Muriel McEntagart
Dr Philip McEvansoneya
Dermot & Kay McEvilly
Evanna McGilligan
Jacquline McGlade
Eoin McGonigal SC
Dr P W McGrath
Margery McGuckian
James McGuire
John F McGuire
Margaret McGuire
Mary McInerney
Cyril McKeon
Gerard C McKeown
Margaret McKilty
Robert McKinstry
Joan McLaughlin
Kyran McLaughlin

Robert McLaughlin
Anna Maria McMahon
K McMahon
Olivia McManus-Gross
Michael McMorrow
Susanne McNab
Donald McNamara
Eileen A McNulty
Edward McParland
Mrs K Macauley Tomson
Suzanne Macdougald
Maureen Macken
Patrick P Mackie
Bernadette Madden
David Madden
Johnny Madden
Croine Magan
Denis M Magee
Susan Magnier
Mrs Mary Mahon
Stella Mahon
Mr Eamon Mallie
Mr Joseph Mallon
Jacqueline Maloney
Simone Mancini
Walter Maros
Josephine Marr
E & M Martin
Valerie Syms Martin
Jan Martin & Neil Armstrong
Maureen Mason
Sheena Masterson
Margaret Mathews
Mrs Patricia Mathews
Judith Matthews
Nicola Matthews
Mrs Avice Maughan
Mr Christy Maye
Mrs Joan M Maynard
National Centre for Liturgy, St Patrick's
College, Maynooth
Barry Meagher
John Meagher
Judith Meagher
Niall Meagher
Richard Meagher
George & Fonsie Mealy
Barbara Meata
Dr C H B Mee
The Paul Mellon Centre
for Studies in British Art
Mercer Library,
Royal College of Surgeons in Ireland
Jane Meredith
Sue Miller
Maura Miskell
Cara Mary Moloney
Tom Moloney
Miss Victoria Moltke
Mrs Anna E Montgomery
Mrs Claire Moore
Mrs Jacqueline Moore
Mary Moore
Patrick T Moore
D Moore-Gwyn, Sothebys
Roxane Moorhead Antiques Ltd
Gerard Moran
Una Moran
Thomas M Morgan
Profs Donald E Morse/Csilla Bertha
Linn Morton
Mrs Roderick Morton
P T Moyer
Ulrike Muehle
Rosemarie Mulcahy
Claire Mulholland
Mary Mullery
Patricia Mullen
Mullingar Arts Centre
Noel & Dolores Mulvin
Nuala Murnaghan

List of Subscribers

Francis D Murnaghan Jr
Denis J Murphy
Mrs Elizabeth Murphy
Finuala Murphy
J Brien Murphy
Joan Murphy
Joseph M Murphy
Margaret Murphy
Norman Murphy
Paula Murphy
Patrick & Antoinette Murphy
Richard Murphy Architects
James Murray
Dr Sean & Nancy Murray
Le Musée Schwatschke
E M Myers
Robert S Myerscough

National Council for
Educational Awards
National Gallery of Ireland
National Irish Visual Arts Library,
NCAD
Martin & Carmel Naughton
Mr Kevin P Neary
Dermot J Neilan
Maura Neligan
Miss Rosemary Nelson -
Christie's Furniture Dept
Mrs Worth Newenham
Ruth Ferguson - Newman House
Peter T W Nicholl
Finnuala Nicholson
David M Nolan
Mr J C M Nolan
Rossa Nolan
Catherine J Noonan
Mr James Noonan
Dr Patricia Noone
Richard S Noone

Aidan O'Boyle
Ciaran O'Brien
Colm O'Brien
Dr Conor O'Brien
Damian O'Brien
Mrs David O'Brien
Donal O'Brien
Professor Eoin O'Brien
Jacqueline O'Brien
James P O'Brien
John J O'Brien
John O'Callaghan
Martha O'Callaghan
Aindrias Ó Caoimh
Fr Tomás Ó Caoimh
Gerry & Jasone O'Carroll
Cormac O'Cléirigh
Adrian & Patricia O'Connell
Louis O'Connell
Alec Fitzgerald O'Connor FRCS
Ann V O'Connor
Conseulo & Brian O'Connor
Cynthia O'Connor Gallery
Eugene O'Connor
Gillian O'Connor
Hubert S O'Connor
Norhild O'Connor
Rose T O'Connor
Séamus O'Connor
Sylvia O'Connor
Rev Sean O'Doherty
Adrienne O'Donnell
Dr J R O'Donnell
John O'Donnell
Claire O'Donoghue
Rory St J O'Donoghue
Finbarr & Moyra O'Donovan
The O'Donovan &
Madam O'Donovan
Fachtna O'Driscoll

James O'Driscoll
John & Catherine O'Driscoll
Dr Frederick O'Dwyer
Canon J O'Farrell OBE
Niall O'Farrell
Pádraig Ó Flannabhra
Mrs C O'Flynn
Claire O'Gara Grimes
Ronnie P O'Gorman
Dr Barbara O'Hanlon
Mr & Mrs Brian O'Hara
Niall Ó hUadhaigh
Padraig O hUiginn
Mr & Mrs Arthur F O'Leary
Dr Denis O'Leary
Sean O'Lubaigh
Ann O'Malley
Connor O'Malley
Dept. Arts, Heritage, Gaeltacta,
& The Islands
Cormac K H O'Malley
Mary Pat O'Malley
Tony & Jane O'Malley
William T O'Malley
Alphonsus M O'Mara
Diarmuid Ó Mathúna
Des & Joan O'Meara
Dominique O'Meara
Dr J O'Meara
John O'Meara
Anne O'Neill
Brian O'Neill
Christine O'Neill
James M O'Neill
Karina O'Neill
Rose O'Neill
Mafra O'Reilly
Miriam O'Riordan
Fionnuala O'Rourke
John O'Shea
Kevin O'Sullivan
Kilian O'Sullivan
Raymond Oakes
Speer Ogle
M Phyllis Ohlandt
Oisín Gallery
Christian Brothers
Grammar School, Omagh
Caroline Orr
M B Owen

St Patrick's College Library, Drumcondra
Noel Pearson
Dr Colette Pegum
Ann & Mark Pery-Knox-Gore
Celestine & Bill Phelan
Mrs Linda C Pilaro
Gerald Plunkett
Mr Larry Powell
Mr B J Power
Mary P Purdy
Hilary Pyle-Carey
Grace Pym

Phillippa Quinlan
Lochlann & Brenda Quinn
Mr Cornelius V Quirke
Gillian Quirke

Colin Rafferty
Brian Ranalow
P J Rankin
Dr K Rankin
Rathdown School
John R Redmill
Regina Mundi College
Zita Reihill
B K Reilly
T J Rice
Michael Rich
Celia Richards

Professor John Riely
Mary Rigney
J M Ritchie
Fred Robinson
Dr K Robinson
Kate Robinson
Nicholas Robinson
Renate Roche-Webster
John Rochford
Mr John Ronan
John B Ronan
Michael J Ronayne
Roscommon County Library
The Earl of Rosse
William M Roth
Grellan D Rourke
I G Rowan
Royal Hibernian Academy, The President
Kent dur Russell & Aisling Gaughan
John A Ryan
Maureen Ryan
Mrs Odile Ryan
Richard Ryan
Thomas Ryan RHA
Dabheoc Rynne

Justin Sadleir
Mrs Mary Sandford
T A Satterfield
Mr & Mrs C G Saunders-Davies
Timothy J Scannell
Prof Pierre Schlevogt
Professor David Scott
Patrick Scott
Peter G W Scott
Robert H & Kenneth R Scott
SELB Library Headquarters
Prof A C Sella
Marcella Senior
Kenneth Severens
Robert L Shafer
Patrick Shaffrey
Canice W Sharkey
Margaret Sheehy
Catherine Sheridan
Fr Christopher Sheridan
Marie Sheridan
Leonard Silke
Mr Brendan Sinnott
William Skelton
Lydia Skinner
Tom Skuse
Liam Slattery
Alistair Smith
Pat Smith
Paul Smith
Gaby Smyth
Mrs Maureen Smyth
Mrs Patricia Smyth
Peter E Smyth
Colin Smythe
Mervyn Solomon
Mrs S M G Somerville
Sotheby's British Painting Department
T D Spearman
Arthur Spears
Mary Spillane
Mary Spollen
Daniel Spring & Co
Philip Stafford
Roger Stalley
Dr Joseph Stanley
Antoinette Staunton
Ronnie & Lyla Steele
John H Stewart
Trevor & Nora Pat Stewart
Hilda van Stockum Marlin
Canon & Mrs A E Stokes
Richard & Eilish Stokes
Sheila Stott
Elizabeth Strong

Barry Sullivan
Ivan Sutton
Frank Swift

The Taylor Gallery Ltd
Mrs E Temple
Temple Auctions Ltd
Gareth V Thomas
Joe Thomas
Shirley Thompson
Mrs Mary Thornton
Maura Thorogood
John & Fedelma Tierney
Miss Tara Tierney
Kathleen & John Timmes
Dr Martin Tinney
Tipperary SR County Council
Tipperary SR County Museum
Brendan & Nuala Toal
Stella Tobin-Long
Diane Tomlinson
Rachel Treacy
Mrs Chenevix Trench
Trinity College, History of Art
Department
Ronald E Tucker
Mary Turner
Liam Tuite
Mark Tully
Michael Tully
Peter J Tuohy
Mary Turner
John Turpin
Veith Turske
Misses L & V Twiss
Marie Twomey
P J Tynan

University College Dublin,
Dept of History of Art
University of Limerick, President's Office
Sandra Vernon
The Viscount de Vesci
Tim Vignoles

Mrs Lygia Waller
Pauline Walley
Mrs Clair Walsh
J Brian Walsh
Mrs Maureen Walsh
Dr Niall & Breda Walsh
Mr & Mrs Frank Warren
Margaret Warren
Gerry Watson
Geraldine Watts
Mrs Iris M Weaver
Mrs Donna Weir
Dr Hugh W L & The Hon Mrs Weir
Dr Herman Wheeler
Anthony Whelan
Kevin Whelan
Ben Whitaker - Director Calouste
Gulbenkian Foundation
David White
Dr James White
Peter S White
Richard J White
Wicklow County Council Arts Officer
Jane Williams
Jeremy Williams
Jackie Wilson
Mrs Jean G Wilson
Primrose Wilson
Robert W Wilson
Judge Desmond P H Windle
Siobhan M Windle
Franz & Carmel Winkelmann
Stephen Wood
Joe Woods
Mr P Woods
Dr Michael Wynne

Limerick City Gallery of Art

Achill Head
Paul Henry

View of Kinsale
Patrick Hennessy

Limerick City Gallery of Art, a part of Limerick Corporation, was founded in 1948 as an addition to the Carnegie Library and Museum of 1906, a Neo-Hiberno-Romanesque style building adjacent to the People's Park and on the 19th century Georgian styled Pery Square in Limerick, Ireland's third largest city.

Since 1985 LCGA has occupied the complete two story Carnegie Building which has just undergone major renovation and expansion.

LCGA offers its audiences a Permanent Collection, and a Programme of Exhibitions, Concerts and other art related events throughout the year.

The Permanent Collection consists of some 500 works in a wide variety of media and styles dating from the 18th century to contemporary practice, and is mostly Irish or Irish related in origin with exceptional examples of work by leading Irish artists of all periods.

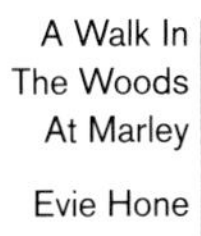

A Walk In The Woods At Marley
Evie Hone

Powerscourt
George Barret

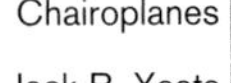

Chairoplanes
Jack B. Yeats

Details shown of all above works

The Permanent Collection also houses the National Collection of Contemporary Drawing with a published catalogue, and the Michael O'Connor Poster Collection, which consists of 3,800 works of international graphic design.

The Temporary Exhibition Programme offers a wide selection of works in all media, styles and periods. Over 40 exhibitions are offered on an annual basis.

LCGA is also home base for the annual Exhibition of Visual$^+$ Art, known as EV$^+$A, Ireland's leading contemporary art exhibition.

For current and ongoing exhibition details contact administration at:
Telephone +353 61 310633
Facsimile +353 61 415266
Email lcgartzz@iol.ie

Opening hours:
Monday - Friday 10am to 6pm
Thursday 10am to 7pm
Saturday 10am to 1pm

Exhibition of Visual$^+$ Art

EV$^+$A 99

EV$^+$A began in 1977 as a way of bringing contemporary artists and audiences into mutual close encounters through works of art, so that, together, sense and meaning can be made in and of the world we share.

EV$^+$A – now Ireland's premier annual exhibition of contemporary art – offers a wide-ranging programme of events that integrate local, national and international communities in the celebration of contemporary art and culture.

OPEN EV$^+$A, the original approach, is an annual open-submission exhibition in which all artists are encouraged to enter their work for adjudication by an internationally renowned curator who single-handedly decides the character, selection and layout of the exhibition.

YOUNG EV$^+$A, begun in 1986, annually brings together young adults and contemporary artists in a three-month series of workshops leading to an exhibition of their work-in-progress. 'Artists in the Gallery' features artists selected for Open EV$^+$A in day-long encounters with audiences young and old.

INVITED EV$^+$A, begun in 1994, is a biennial event in which the Open EV$^+$A adjudicator of that year personally invites the participation of artists of international status, and curates and places their work in Limerick City and environs, setting up a counterpart to the Open EV$^+$A selection.

EV$^+$A COLLOQUIES, begun in 1997, is a biennial event devoted to the ongoing attempt to make sense and meaning out of the ways contemporary art and culture engage us.

Installation shots above: details from EV$^+$A 1999

LOUISE KENNEDY
56 Merrion Square, Dublin 2
Monday - Saturday 9.30 - 6pm. Tel: 662 0056

JANUS
ANTIQUES
& INTERIORS

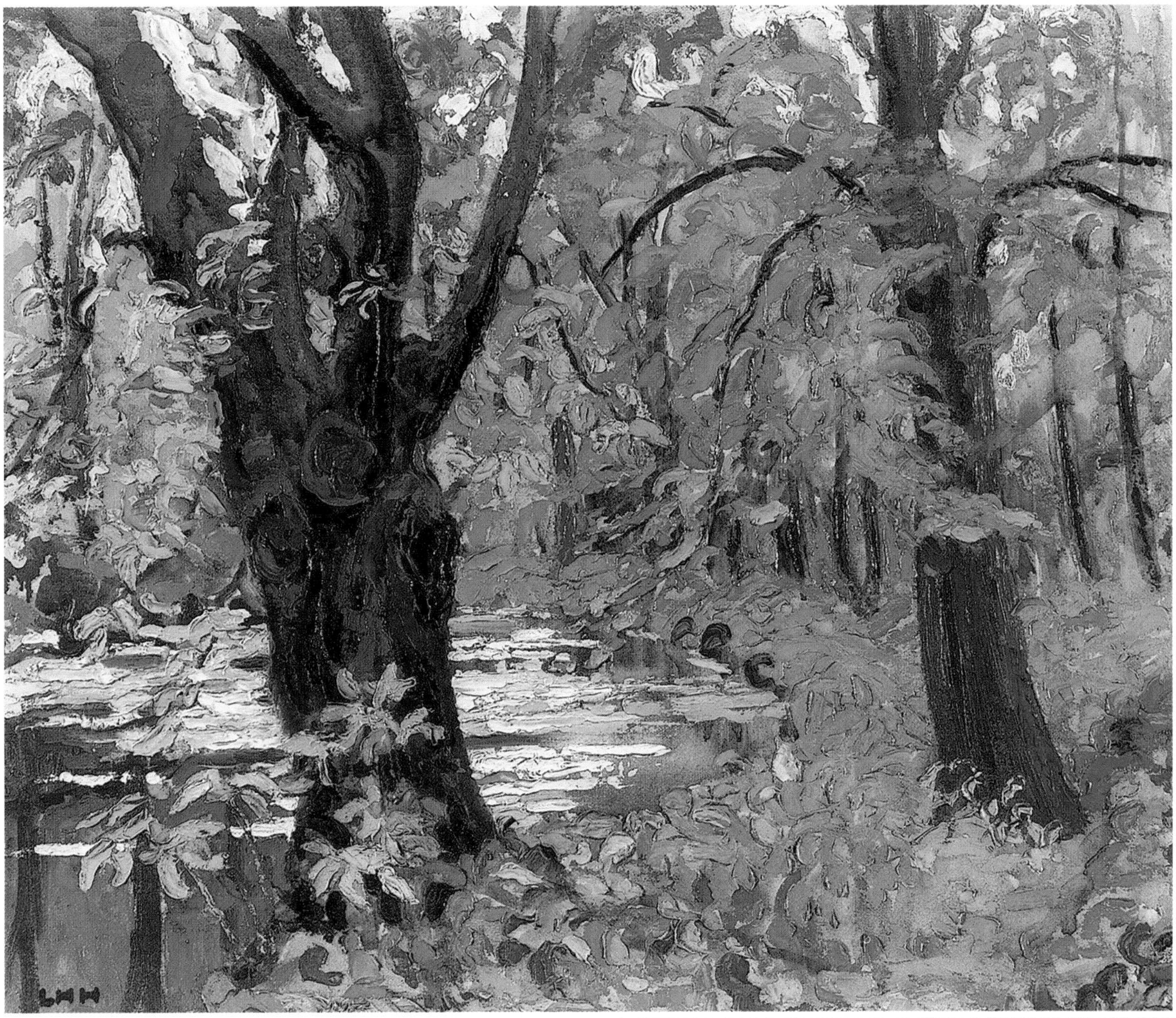

Letitia M. Hamilton RHA 1878 - 1964 *Autumn on the Liffey*
Oil on canvas on board 19 1/2" x 23 3/4"

JORGENSEN FINE ART

18th, 19th and 20th Century Irish and other European paintings and drawings.

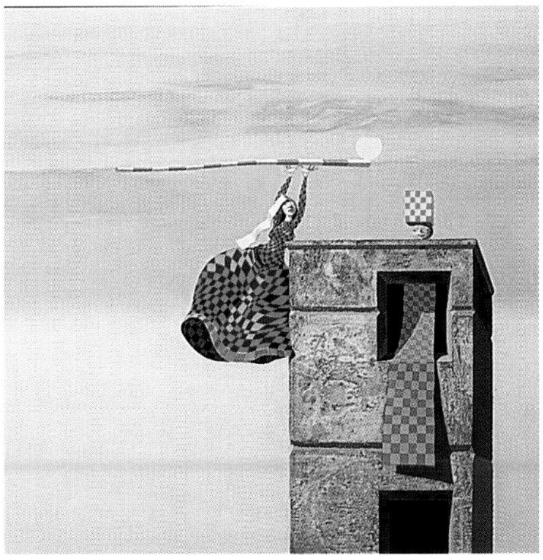

Colin Middleton RHA (1910 - 1983)
"Game of Chance, Wilderness Series No. 1
Oil on board 24" x 24"

Open 9 - 5.30pm Mon-Fri.

9:30 - 2pm Sat.

29 Molesworth St., Dublin 2

Tel: 661 9758/59

Fax: 661 9760

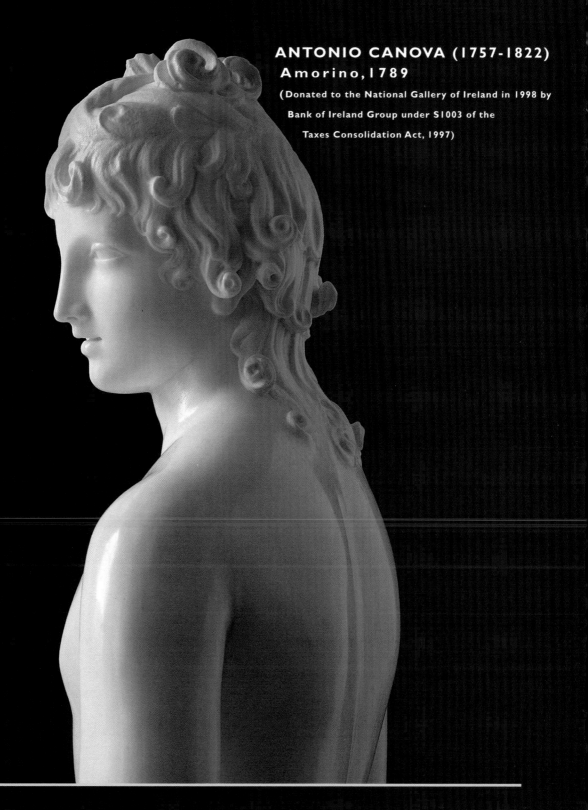

THE BASEMENT GALLERY
TOWN HALL, DUNDALK
bg
THE BASEMENT GALLERY IS PROGRAMMED AND MANAGED BY THE ARTS OFFICE OF DUNDALK U.D.C.
TEL 042 - 9332276

John Farrington Antiques
Specialists in Fine Antique Jewellery & Gilt Mirrors
32 Drury Street, Dublin 2 Tel: 01-679 1899

MONT BLANC
75 years Meisterstück
Montblanc® Meisterstück®
PASSION AND
75 years of passion and soul
Only passion can create a piece of eternity like the Montblanc Meisterstück. This timeless classic has been unchanged for 75 years. And will remain so in future. In a unique and exclusive tribute to this year's 75th anniversary, Montblanc is honouring the legendary Meisterstück by creating a special edition featuring a gold-plated cap ring engraved with the anniversary motto "75 years of passion and soul" and embellished by a superb diamond. The precious Montblanc Anniversary Edition includes writing instruments, watches, jewellery and leather items available from Montblanc Boutiques, selected jewellers and specialist retailers.
Montblanc Retailer
The Pen Corner Ltd, 12 College Green, Dublin 2. Tel: 01-679 3641

Republic of Ireland

European Gold Portrait Award of the Year

Maidin de Luain, Castlemartyr College, Co Cork.

Pádraig Ó Flannabhra, Winner

Photoart Studio • Connolly Street • Nenagh • Co Tipperary • Éire. Tel: +353 (0)67 32766

ART IN STATE BUILDINGS
1970 - 1985
EPISODES FROM THE PASSION
ART IN STATE BUILDINGS
1985 – 1995
OPW

A superb mahogany serving table, the rectangular and shaped top with gadroon and leaf-carved moulded edge fitted with a brass gallery centred by a pierced scale-trellis panel below an anthemion flanked by leaf scrolls, the uprights with engine turned collars and urn finials. The frieze inlaid with ebony stringing, gathered scroll and lozenges, on acanthus leaf carved, scrolled legs with paw feet, c.1820-30.

UPPER COURT MANOR, FRESHFORD, CO KILKENNY, IRELAND. TEL: 056-32174. FAX: 056-32325
54 HANOVER SQUARE, FRANCIS STREET, DUBLIN 8. TEL: 01-473 0037

NUMBER
TWENTY NINE

0044
Irish Artists in Britain
0946846 243 Crawford Gallery, 1999
27x23cm 176pp 80c+60b illus
£25 hb

CRAWFORD ART GALLERY
Illus. Summary Catalogue
Crawford Gallery, 1992 24x22cm
xii+276pp 24c+1,400b illus
1874756 007 £35 hb / 015 £25 pb

EDGE TO EDGE – O'Connell, Prendergast, Roche
0946641 129 Gandon Editions, 1991
27x24cm 50pp 25c+12b illus
£7.50 pb

EUROPEAN LARGE-FORMAT PRINTMAKING
0946641 20X Gandon / BCPS, 1991
21x21cm 68pp 13c+43b illus
£4.95 pb

EV+A 96
Exhibition of Visual+ Art 96
adjudicator: Guy Tortosa
09517352 5X EV+A, 1996 23x23cm
100pp 28c+11b illus £7.50 pb

IRISH STEEL
0946641 595 Gandon / Model Arts Centre, 1995 24x17cm 64pp
27c+13b illus £7.50 pb

LIVING LANDSCAPE 1987-1996
0946641 773 Gandon / WCAC, 1996
23x23cm 48pp 17c illus £4.95 pb

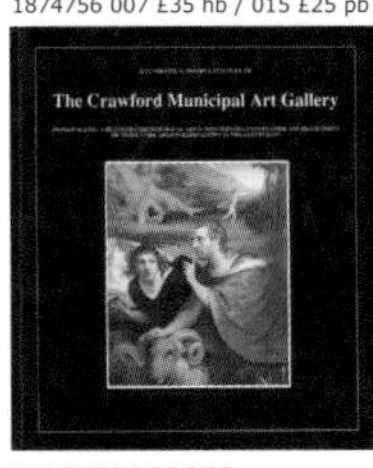

MASTERPIECES
from the Crawford Gallery
1874756 023 Crawford Gallery, 1992
24x22cm 36pp 25c+4b illus
£4.95 pb

National Collection of CONTEMPORARY DRAWING
0946641 714 Limerick City Gallery, 1996 23x23cm 144pp 73c illus
£20 hb

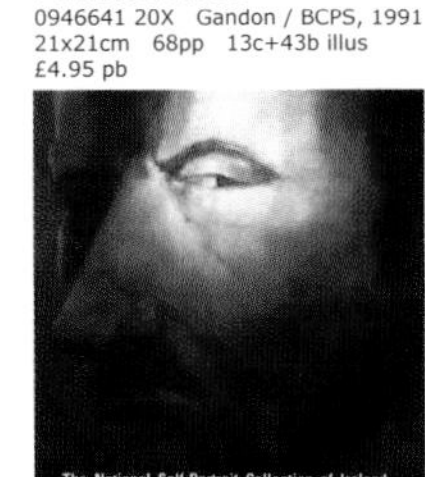

NATIONAL SELF-PORTRAIT COLLECTION – vol.1
0950342 777 Uni. of Limerick, 1989
24x22cm 260pp 126c illus
£15 pb

NATIONAL SELF-PORTRAIT COLLECTION – vol.2
Uni. of Limerick, Nov 1999 24x22cm
360pp 170c illus
0946846 332 £25 hb / 340 £15 pb

Irish Artists

LOUIS LE BROCQUY
The Head Image
0946641 587 Gandon Editions, 1996
30x24cm 184pp 82c illus £25 hb

LOUIS LE BROCQUY
The Irish Landscape
Gandon Editions, 1992 24x30cm
100pp 39c illus
0946641 293 £25 hb / 285 £100 hb*

LOUIS LE BROCQUY
Paintings 1939-1996
1873654 464 IMMA, 1996 28x22cm
112pp 47c+69b illus £15 pb

LOUIS LE BROCQUY
Procession
0946641 447 Gandon Editions, 1994
24x30cm 84pp 30c illus £25 hb

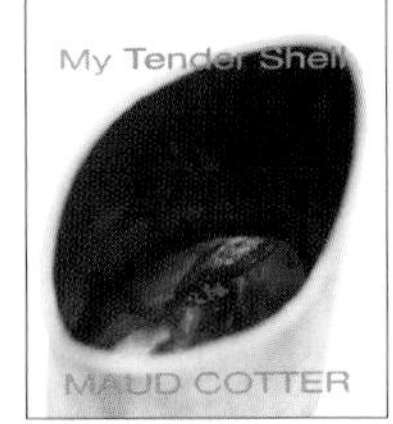

MAUD COTTER
My Tender Shell
0946641 218 Gandon Editions, 1991
24x22cm 36pp 15c+10b illus
£4.95 pb

ALASTAIR MacLENNAN
Coming to Meet
1872493 092 Project Press, 1996
24x16cm 32pp 24c illus £3 pb

CARMEL MOONEY
0946846 227 Gandon Editions, 1999
23x23cm 48pp 21c+6b illus
£7.50 pb

EILÍS O'CONNELL
0946641 366 Gandon / Gallery John Jones, London, 1993 28x22cm 64pp
50c+4b illus £9.95 pb

HELEN HOOKER O'MALLEY ROELOFS
1874653 216 Uni. of Limerick, 1993
21x21cm 48pp b/w illus £4.95

PATRICK SWIFT 1927-1983
PS ... of course
0946641 374 Gandon Editions, 1993
24x17cm 274pp 50c+ 110b illus
£25 hb

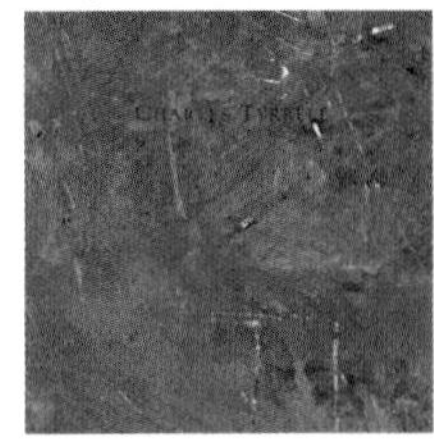

CHARLES TYRRELL
Paintings 1993-1994
0946641 439 Gandon / Austin-Desmond, London, 1994 23x21cm
36pp 18c+ 3b illus £4.95 pb

Profile 5
MARY LOHAN
0946641 889 Gandon Editions, 1998
23x23cm 48pp 21c+1b illus
£7.50 pb

Profile 6
ALICE MAHER
0946641 935 Gandon Editions, 1998
23x23cm 48pp 23c+6b illus
£7.50 pb

Profile 7
CHARLES HARPER
0946846 111 Gandon Editions / Sligo Art Gallery, 1998 23x23cm 48pp
19c+5b illus £7.50 pb

Profile 8
MAUD COTTER
0946641 073 Gandon Editions, 1998
23x23cm 48pp 24c+6b illus
£7.50 pb

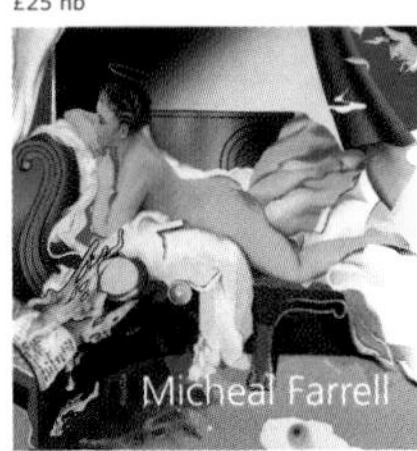

Profile 9
MICHEAL FARRELL
0946846 138 Gandon Editions, 1998
23x23cm 48pp 25c+8b illus
£7.50 pb

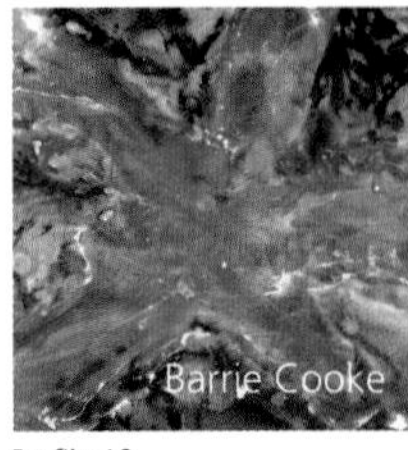

Profile 10
BARRIE COOKE
0946846 170 Gandon Editions, 1998
23x23cm 48pp 25c+4b illus
£7.50 pb

Works 3
PATRICK HICKEY
0946641 153 Gandon Editions, 1991
20x15cm 32pp 10c+14b illus
£3.95 pb

Works 4
ANDREW FOLAN
0946641 161 Gandon Editions, 1991
20x15cm 32pp 11c+13b illus
£3.95 pb

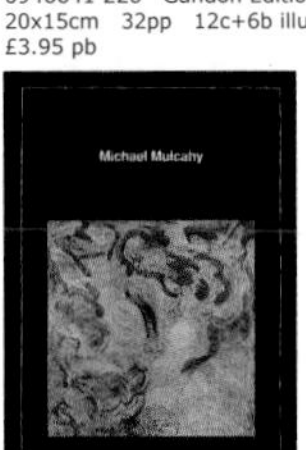

Works 5
PATRICK GRAHAM
0946641 226 Gandon Editions, 1992
20x15cm 32pp 12c+6b illus
£3.95 pb

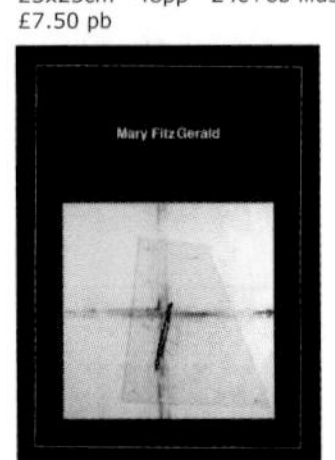

Works 6
MARY FITZGERALD
0946641 234 Gandon Editions, 1992
20x15cm 32pp 15c+7b illus
£3.95 pb

Works 7
MICHAEL CULLEN
0946641 242 Gandon Editions, 1992
20x15cm 32pp 12c+5b illus
£3.95 pb

Works 8
THE IRISH PAVILION
0946641 250 Gandon Editions, 1992
20x15cm 32pp 14c+5b illus
£3.95 pb

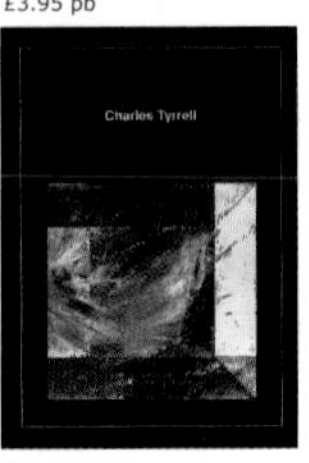

Works 15
CHARLES TYRRELL
0946641 412 Gandon Editions, 1994
20x15cm 32pp 16c+2b illus
£3.95 pb

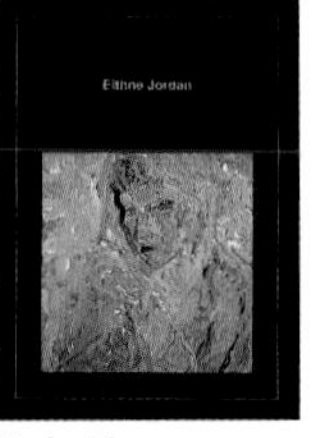

Works 16
EITHNE JORDAN
0946641 420 Gandon Editions, 1994
20x15cm 32pp 16c+1b illus
£3.95 pb

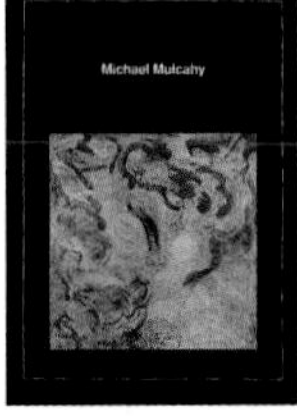

Works 17
MICHAEL MULCAHY
0946641 471 Gandon Editions, 1995
20x15cm 32pp 16c+1b illus
£3.95 pb

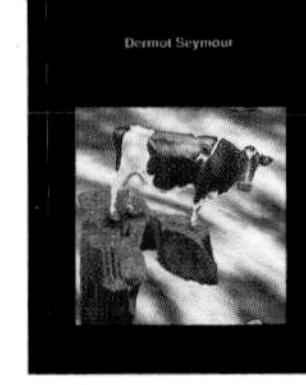

Works 18
DERMOT SEYMOUR
0946641 48X Gandon Editions, 1995
20x15cm 32pp 16c+1b illus
£3.95 pb

Works 19
MARTIN GALE
0946641 498 Gandon Editions, 1995
20x15cm 32pp 16C+1b illus
£3.95 pb

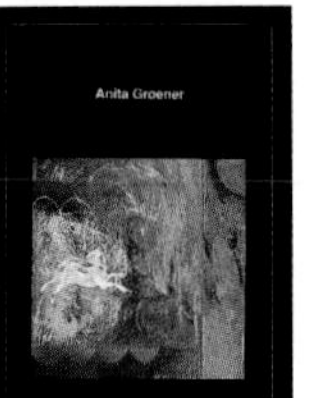

Works 20
ANITA GROENER
0946641 501 Gandon Editions, 1995
20x15cm 32pp 16c+2b illus
£3.95 pb

EV+A 98 – Circus ZZ
Exhibition of Visual+ Art 98
adjudicator: Paul M O'Reilly
0946846 189 EV+A, 1998 23x25cm
168pp 114c+3b illus £10 pb

EV+A 99 – Reduced
Exhibition of Visual+ Art 99
adjud.: Jeanne Greenberg Rohatyn
0946846 26X EV+A, 1999 23x23cm
164pp 89c+3b illus £10 pb

EV+A COMPENDIUM
Exhibition of Visual+ Art
Invited EV+A 94/96/98, Colloquies 97
0946846 278 EV+A, 1999 23x23cm
216pp 118c+22b illus £10 pb

THE GUIDE TO EXHIBITION VENUES IN IRELAND
0906627 605 Arts Council, 1994
21x15cm 172pp illus £5.95 pb

HANDBOOKS
Handle with Care!
0906627 443 Arts Co, 1991 £3 pb
Organising an Exhibition
0906627 435 Arts Co, 1991 £3 pb

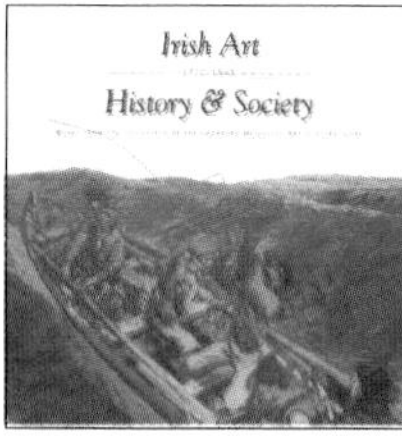

IRISH ART 1770-1995
History and Society
0946641 897 Crawford Gallery, 1997
30x30cm 108pp 46c+ 10b illus
£20 hb

ONLOOKERS IN FRANCE
Crawford Gallery, 1993 23x25cm
36pp 30c+4b illus £4.95 pb

ORMONDE COLLECTION
Paintings at Kilkenny Castle
Dúchas, Nov 1999 30x24cm 112pp
25c+100b illus
0946846 375 £25 hb / 383 £15 pb

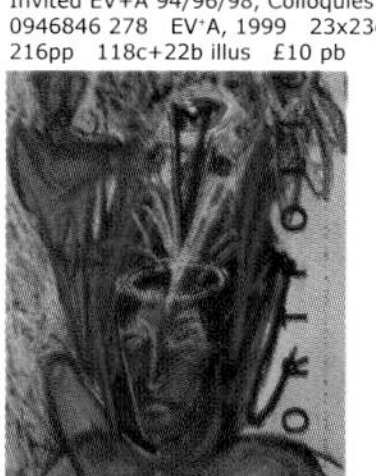

PORTFOLIO 1
Art + Architecture Review
Gandon Editions, 1991 30x24cm
148pp 57c+128b illus
0946641 17X £25 hb / 188 £15 pb

TEMPLE BAR
The Power of An Idea
Temple Bar Properties, 1996
30x24cm 224pp 173c+196b illus
0946641 811 £25 hb

THINKING LONG
Contemporary Art in the N. Ireland
by Liam Kelly 0946641 668
Gandon Editions, 1996 27x24cm
248pp 170c+ 142b illus £25 hb

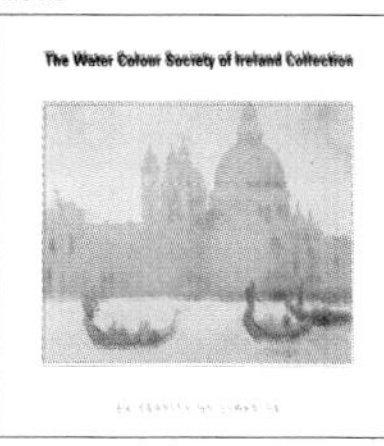

WATER COLOUR SOCIETY OF IRELAND COLLECTION
1874653 208 Uni. of Limerick, 1993
21x21cm 48pp 1c+98b illus
£4.95 pb

Monograph
CONOR FALLON
0946641 692 Gandon Editions, 1996
27x24cm 72pp 36c+10b illus
£20 hb

TOM FITZGERALD
Ephemeral Lexicon
0946641 684 Project / LCGA, 1995
23x25cm 24pp 10c+3b illus £3 plt

PATRICK GRAHAM
The Lark in the Morning
0907660 509 DHG / Crawford, 1994
24x28cm 40pp 23c+ 11b illus
£4.95 pb

GAVIN HOGG
Freedom within Discipline
0946641 765 Gandon Editions, 1996
23x23cm 24pp 10c illus £3 pb

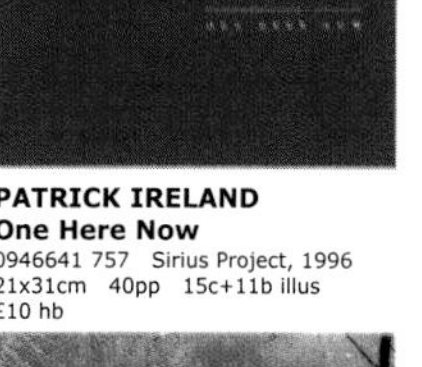

PATRICK IRELAND
One Here Now
0946641 757 Sirius Project, 1996
21x31cm 40pp 15c+11b illus
£10 hb

BRIAN KENNEDY
The Lagganstown Prints
0946641 730 Crawford Gallery, 1996
21x31cm 32pp 11c+ 2b illus
£10 hb

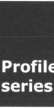

MICHAEL WARREN
Places
0946641 358 Gandon / Galerie Der Spiegel, Köln, 1993 21x21cm 40pp
24c illus £4.95 pb

THE ESSENTIAL REFERENCE SERIES ON CONTEMPORARY IRISH ARTISTS
(series editor: John O'Regan)

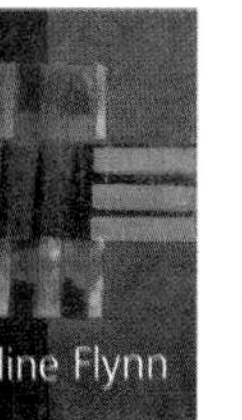

Profile 1
PAULINE FLYNN
0946641 722 Gandon Editions, 1996
23x23cm 48pp 19c+3b illus
£7.50 pb

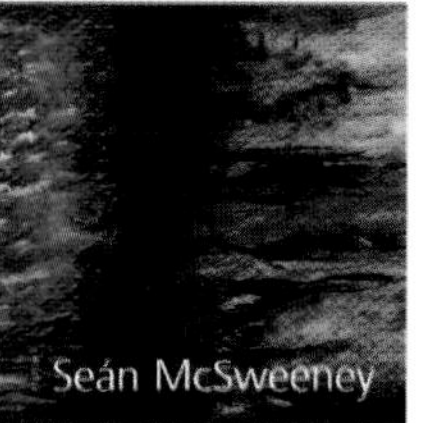

Profile 2
SEÁN McSWEENEY
0946641 617 Gandon Editions, 1996
23x23cm 48pp 17c+6b illus
£7.50 pb

Profile 3
EILÍS O'CONNELL
0946641 870 Gandon Editions / Butler Gallery, 1997 23x23cm 48pp
27c+8b illus £7.50 pb

Profile 4
SIOBHÁN PIERCY
0946641 900 Gandon Editions, 1997
23x23cm 48pp 32c+6b illus
£7.50 pb

Profile 11
VIVIENNE ROCHE
0946846 235 Gandon Editions, Oct 1999 23x23cm 48pp col illus
£7.50 pb

Profile 12
CAMILLE SOUTER
0946641 560 Gandon Editions, Spring 2000 23x23cm 48pp
col illus £7.50 pb

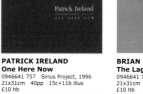

Profile 13
JAMES SCANLON
0946641 579 Gandon Editions, Spring 2000 23x23cm 48pp
col illus £7.50 pb

A MINI-LIBRARY OF CONTEMPORARY IRISH ART
(series editor: John O'Regan)

Works 1
JAMES SCANLON – Sneem
0946641 536 Gandon Editions (2nd rev ed), 1995 20x15cm 32pp
20c+4b illus £3.95 pb

Works 2
VIVIENNE ROCHE
0946641 145 Gandon Editions, 1991
20x15cm 32pp 9c+14b illus
£3.95 pb

Works 9
CHARLES BRADY
0946641 307 Gandon Editions, 1993
20x15cm 32pp 17c+1b illus
£3.95 pb

Works 10
MICHAEL SCOTT 1905-1989
0946641 315 Gandon Editions, 1993
20x15cm 32pp 27 illus £3.95 pb

Works 11
JOHN T DAVIS
0946641 323 Gandon Editions, 1993
20x15cm 32pp 17 illus £3.95 pb

Works 12
PATRICK HALL
0946641 331 Gandon Editions, 1993
20x15cm 32pp 16c+1b illus
£3.95 pb

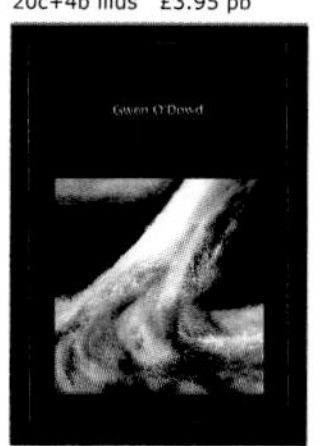

Works 13
GWEN O'DOWD
0946641 390 Gandon Editions, 1994
20x15cm 32pp 16c+2b illus
£3.95 pb

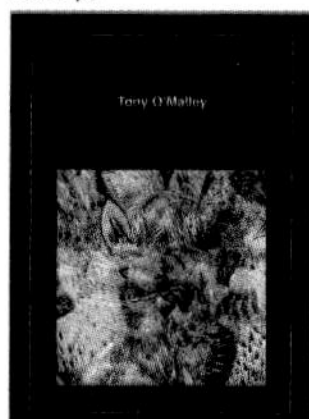

Works 14
TONY O'MALLEY
0946641 404 Gandon Editions, 1994
20x15cm 32pp 17c+3b illus
£3.95 pb

ORDER FORM

We can only show a selection of our ART books above; we also have an extensive range of ARCHITECTURE books. Our full range of books is detailed in our colour catalogue and on our web-site.

- books can be ordered from any good bookshop or direct from us
- order by phone / fax / e-mail / from web-site with credit card; or order by post enclosing cheque in Ir£ /stg £
- advance orders recorded; standing orders accepted on all series
- p&p free within Ireland; same-day dispatch of books in stock
- p&p outside Ireland at cost – tick: ❑ economy / ❑ priority

❑ cheque / PO enclosed for Ir£ / stg£ ________ ❑ charge to my
❑ Eurocard / ❑ Laser / ❑ Mastercard / ❑ Visa – exp __ __ / __ __

a/c no. ___ ___ ___ ___

order: ___ x ________________
___ x ________________
___ x ________________
PRINT DETAILS (continue order on additional sheet if necessary)

name ________________

address ________________

________________ date ________

TRADE – order from Gandon by phone / fax / e-mail / web-site / post / TeleOrdering (distributor key: 10384660). All books S/R.
order no. ____________ contact ____________

Send completed order form to: Gandon Editions, Oysterhaven, Kinsale, Co Cork, Ireland

tel: +353 (0)21-770830 / fax: +353 (0)21-770755
e-mail: gandon@eircom.net

visit our web-site at www.gandon-editions.com

Gandon Editions
BOOKS ON IRISH ART + ARCHITECTURE

'Mother & Child' 1997, oil on board, Colin Watson

A Proposal for the Millennium

Maurice Craig

makes a case for the recreation of some lost Irish treasures

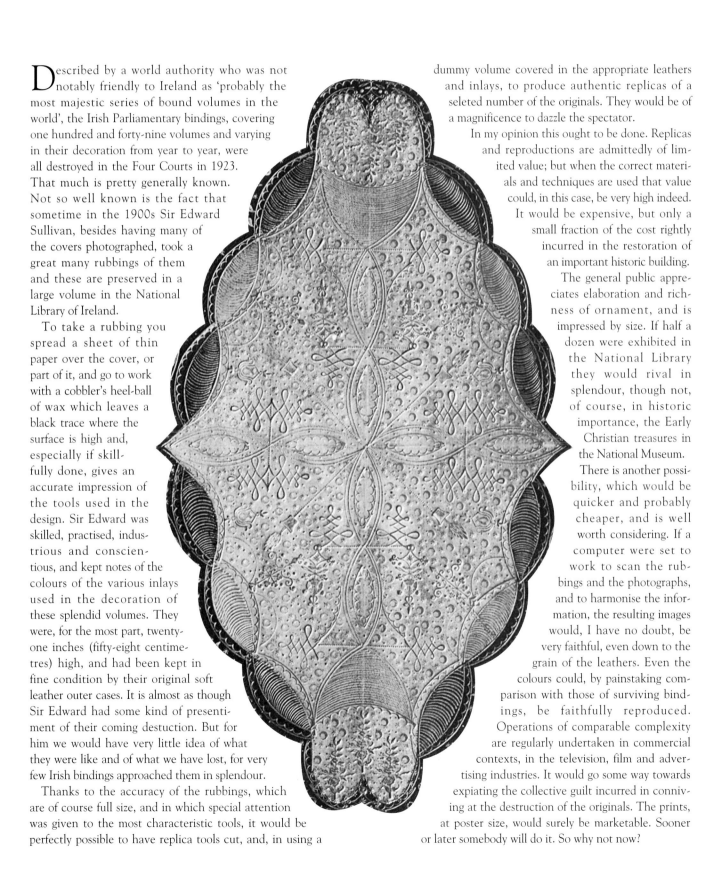

Described by a world authority who was not notably friendly to Ireland as 'probably the most majestic series of bound volumes in the world', the Irish Parliamentary bindings, covering one hundred and forty-nine volumes and varying in their decoration from year to year, were all destroyed in the Four Courts in 1923. That much is pretty generally known. Not so well known is the fact that sometime in the 1900s Sir Edward Sullivan, besides having many of the covers photographed, took a great many rubbings of them and these are preserved in a large volume in the National Library of Ireland.

To take a rubbing you spread a sheet of thin paper over the cover, or part of it, and go to work with a cobbler's heel-ball of wax which leaves a black trace where the surface is high and, especially if skillfully done, gives an accurate impression of the tools used in the design. Sir Edward was skilled, practised, industrious and conscientious, and kept notes of the colours of the various inlays used in the decoration of these splendid volumes. They were, for the most part, twenty-one inches (fifty-eight centimetres) high, and had been kept in fine condition by their original soft leather outer cases. It is almost as though Sir Edward had some kind of presentiment of their coming destuction. But for him we would have very little idea of what they were like and of what we have lost, for very few Irish bindings approached them in splendour.

Thanks to the accuracy of the rubbings, which are of course full size, and in which special attention was given to the most characteristic tools, it would be perfectly possible to have replica tools cut, and, in using a dummy volume covered in the appropriate leathers and inlays, to produce authentic replicas of a seleted number of the originals. They would be of a magnificence to dazzle the spectator.

In my opinion this ought to be done. Replicas and reproductions are admittedly of limited value; but when the correct materials and techniques are used that value could, in this case, be very high indeed. It would be expensive, but only a small fraction of the cost rightly incurred in the restoration of an important historic building.

The general public appreciates elaboration and richness of ornament, and is impressed by size. If half a dozen were exhibited in the National Library they would rival in splendour, though not, of course, in historic importance, the Early Christian treasures in the National Museum.

There is another possibility, which would be quicker and probably cheaper, and is well worth considering. If a computer were set to work to scan the rubbings and the photographs, and to harmonise the information, the resulting images would, I have no doubt, be very faithful, even down to the grain of the leathers. Even the colours could, by painstaking comparison with those of surviving bindings, be faithfully reproduced. Operations of comparable complexity are regularly undertaken in commercial contexts, in the television, film and advertising industries. It would go some way towards expiating the collective guilt incurred in conniving at the destruction of the originals. The prints, at poster size, would surely be marketable. Sooner or later somebody will do it. So why not now?

1. Commons Journal 1751. Destroyed in the conflagration of the Four Courts, 1922. Red goatskin with coloured and marbled inlays, gold-tooled, about 53.3 cm high. Photograph taken about 1904 (National Library of Ireland). The now-destroyed 18th-century bindings of the *Common Journals* were particularly splendid examples of the bookseller's craft. This photograph was taken for Sir Edward Sullivan who also made rubbings of the bindings and from these rubbings it would be possible to recreate the bindings today.

A Diary of the Art Year in Ireland

Paul Spellman & Margarita Cappock
chronicle noteworthy exhibitions and events between
September 1998 and August 1999

September

Ian Breakwell at the Temple Bar Gallery

■ The *Temple Bar Galleries* mounted an impressive series of stone sculptures by Cork sculptor, **Michael Quane**, which combined animal and human figures, the artist creating a great weightiness to the figures. Running concurrently at the same venue in studio 8 was an audio-visual work, 'The Rose', by **Ian Breakwell**. Based on the theme of 'The Dance of Death' the artist used images of skeletons within the design of an illuminated rose window, making reference to the transitory nature of life. This macabre theme was echoed in the accompanying soundtrack by **Ron Geesin**.

■ To coincide with the 17th Biennial Congress of the International Institute of Conservation, the *National Gallery of Ireland* mounted an interesting exhibition entitled 'The Deeper Picture'. This looked at 17 paintings in the Gallery's collection from the point of conservation, setting out both the principles and the processes used. All types of media were looked at, from large Old Masters by **Goya** and **Rubens** to delicate works on paper. The exhibition also featured a painting, 'Head of an Old Man' which the Gallery believe to be an original **Rembrandt**, a possibility which is currently being investigated by the Rembrandt Research Project.

■ **Martine Frank** visited Tory Island with Derek Hill in 1993, and displayed the resulting photographs at the *Gallery of Photography, Temple Bar*. These were seen by Aidan Dunne as 'well composed documentary images of the Island and its people with informative captions.' Also in Temple Bar, the *Arthouse* hosted a very different exhibition of photographs by **John Byrne** and **Sean Hillen** called 'Among Your Own'. By digitally distorting images and superimposing text, the artists made a hard-hitting commentary upon their experience of growing up in Northern Ireland.

■ Derry artist, **Willie Doherty**, was given the honour of being the first artist to have a solo exhibition in the newly refurbished *Tate Gallery in Liverpool*. Under the title 'Somewhere Else', this was Doherty's largest show to date with ten years of output included. Included were his large photographic works dealing with the two conflicting views people have of his hometown; a naturally beautiful landscape and yet a place associated with the troubles. In more recent work, as in the exhibition title piece, Doherty made use of audio-visual installations to good effect.

■ Showing at the *Taylor Galleries* during September were two shows: **Mary Lohan's** 'Sea met Sky' and **Janet Pearse's** 'Ceanalas'. These were very different in style. Lohan applied thickly-impastoed horizontal bands of paint to create lush seascapes whereas Pearse used thin layers of watercolour to suggest imaginary landscapes which were inspired by Scotland and the sean-nós singing of Donegal's Mairhread Ní Dhomhnaill.

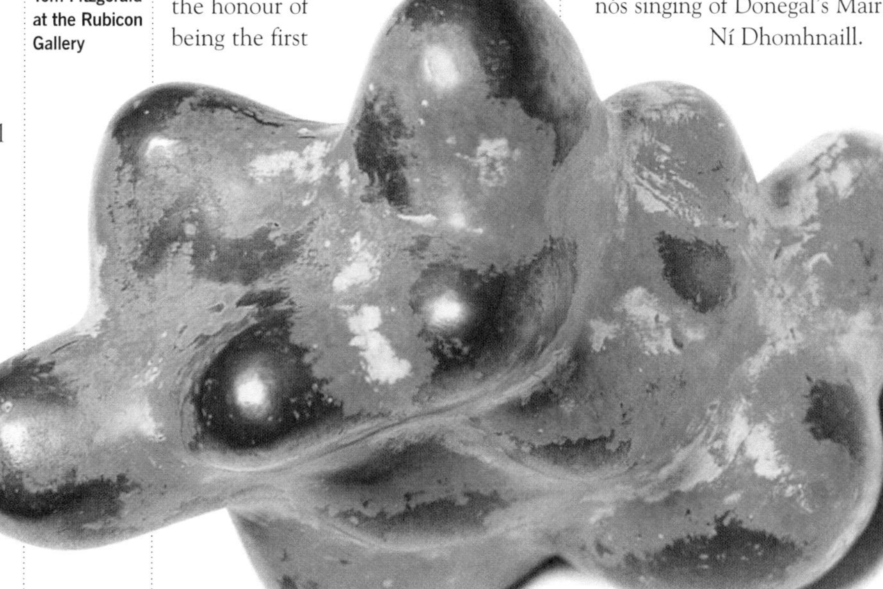

Tom Fitzgerald at the Rubicon Gallery

■ Southampton-born **Derek Hill**, founder of the **Tory Island** painters, received formal recognition of his contribution to the arts in Ireland over the last 40 years by being awarded honorary Irish citizenship. The announcement of the award coincided with a large retrospective of the artist's work at the *RHA Gallagher Gallery*. This comprehensive show of 120 paintings demonstrated Hill's ability both as a perceptive portraitist and a sensitive landscape painter. Hill's contact with many well-known figures in Ireland and abroad made for some interesting portrait subjects such as the Duchess of Abercorn, Dr Garret Fitzgerald, Prof Anne Crookshank, Seamus Heaney and John Hume.

■ Two emerging artists, **Corrina Earlie** and **Paul Doran,** were on show at the *Kilcock Art Gallery*. Both artists sold extremely well. At the *Rubicon Gallery*, sculpture by **Tom Fitzgerald** attracted attention.

■ At the *Green on Red Gallery*, **Michael Coleman** showed new paintings which varied in style from squares of pure colour to darker images of colour breaking through a layer of black paint, the picture surface often marked and scratched subsequently. A series of Carborundum prints completed what was seen as a strong showing by the artist. Also in Dublin, the *Kerlin Gallery* showed a modestly-sized exhibition of recent work by **Willie McKeown**. A series of seven canvases, each painted a particular shade of grey, off-white or in the case of one, vivid yellow, hung very well together as an installation against the white-washed space of the gallery.

■ The annual *Claremorris Open Exhibition* celebrated its 21st year by changing the format slightly. The committee of COE '98 invited artists to exhibit work in spaces and sites located around the town of Claremorris rather than centrally. All forms of art were exhibited including painting, printmaking, photography, sculpture, installation, video, soundpieces, performance and multi-media.

Top: Janet Pearse at the Taylor Galleries
Below: Corinna Earlie at the Kilcock Art Gallery

■ Dutch-born **Marianne Heemskerk**, a founder member of *The Project Arts Centre*, exhibited a good mix of colour etchings, gouache and oils under the title 'Myths and other Animals' at the *Logan Gallery, Galway*. Through a series of themes such as 'sheela-na gig' and 'Mad March Hares', the artist explored the relationship between the landscape and various myths associated with it.

October

■ The *9th RHA Banquet* exhibition took place at the *RHA Gallagher Gallery* under the title 'Academy Without Walls: Artists' View'. Out of a total 117 exhibits, 40 were by RHA members including **John Behan, Peter Collis, John Coyle, John Kelly, Martin Gale, Michael O'Dea, Tony O'Malley**, and **Walter Verling.** The remainder of the show was comprised of contemporary work chosen by five well-known artists; **Cathy Carman, William Crozier, Diarmuid Delargy, Felim Egan**, and **Joan O'Connor**, who each presented their 'ideal academy'. Popular choices were **Mick Cullen, Barrie Cooke, Chung Eun-Mo, Graham Gingles, Anne Madden, Stephen McKenna,** and **Gwen O'Dowd** who were all selected by more than two of the adjudicators.

■ The *22nd EV+A* open submission event in Limerick broke with its tradition of foreign-based adjudicators by appointing **Paul M O'Reilly** of Limerick City Gallery of Art. This year the adjudicator's guiding principle in choosing work was the presence and the extent of the commitment that contemporary artists give to lens/screen based media in making their work. Works by about 100 artists were selected from the open submission and a further 50 artists, mainly foreign, were invited to show among 30 venues. Among the screen-based artists who featured strongly were **Paul Gray, Jonathan Horowitz, Paddy Jolley, Bernard Smyth,** and the Swiss pair **Peter Fischli** and **David Weiss**. There was also room made for painters, **Hazel Walker, Richard Gorman, Ciaran Lennon,** printmakers, **Grainne Buckley, Catherine Lynch, Collette Nolan,** and sculptors, **Corban Walker** and **Tom FitzGerald.**

■ An unusual and colourful exhibition of Mexican art entitled 'Behind the Mask: Mexican Devotions' was held at the *Douglas Hyde Gallery* in conjunction with the Embassy of Mexico. This exhibition demonstrated how much of Mexican popular art is inspired by pre-christian rituals and the Catholic Church. Exhibits included pottery, banners, brightly coloured skeletons, and religious souvenirs. During the course of the exhibition two Mexican artists, **Eugenio Reyes Eustaquio** and **Tiburcio Soteno Fernandez**, used the gallery as a studio.

■ **Brian Maguire** was Ireland's representative at the *XXIV Bienal de Sao Paolo* in Brazil, the overall theme of which was the concept of density and anthropophagy. Maguire spent ten weeks in Sao Paolo prior to the exhibition, making drawings and photographs of the people of Favlea Prudente, a shanty town on the outskirts of the city. At the exhibition, Maguire showed an impressive and moving series of photographs of the children of Casa da Caltura in their homes together with their portraits which had been presented to them by the artist.

Oliver Comerford at the Hallward Gallery

■ The *Kerlin Gallery* hosted an exhibition of paintings and drawings by **William Scott** which included good examples of his sparse still-lifes and landscapes which followed on from the large-scale retrospective held at the *Irish Museum of Modern Art* earlier in the year. An exhibition of paintings and drawing by **Hughie O'Donoghue** spanning 15 years took place at the *IMMA* under the title 'Corp'. The show included 25 paintings with emphasis on the human figure and included the large-scale charcoal drawing 'Crossing the Rapido'.

Martin Gale at the RHA Banquet Exhibition

■ 'Bogland and Shoreline Sligo' was the title of a superb collection of recent paintings by **Sean McSweeney** at the *Taylor Galleries*. While the imagery was familiar, his handling of subjects such as 'Shoreline Doneel' demonstrated McSweeney's continued mastery of the Irish landscape. Meanwhile at the *Hallward Gallery*, **Oliver Comerford** showed an impressive exhibition, 'Talk to Me', a series of photo realist images inspired by a recent trip to Iceland. At the *Solomon Gallery*, **Patrick O'Reilly** displayed a series of witty sculptures which combined found objects with sculpted bronze figures.

■ The *Ormeau Baths Gallery* in Belfast hosted its first annual open exhibition, Perspective '98, which featured 17 artists selected from 270 submissions. All forms of contemporary art were included. The first prize of £6,000 was awarded to **Dan Shipsides** for his performance piece 'The Stone Bridge'. Other artists included in the show were established painters, **Dermot Seymour, Theo Sims, Anne Ryan, Fiona Larkin**, and **Mary Kelly**.

■ 'When Time Began to Rant and Rage: Figurative Painting from Twentieth Century Ireland' was the title of a comprehensive survey of Irish figurative painting over the last 100 years which opened at the *Walker Gallery, Liverpool* and travelled to the University of California *Berkeley Art Museum*, the *Gray Art Gallery*, New York, and finally the *Barbican Art Gallery* in London. The catalogue of the exhibition is reviewed in this issue.

■ 'Out of Denmark,' a Danish cultural programme initiated by the Danish Embassy, was launched in Dublin. The visual arts featured well among the events with the *National Gallery* hosting **PS Kroyer** and the Artist's Colony at Skagen. This show highlighted the development at the end of the last century of a school of French-inspired *plein air* painters at Skagen, Jutland. There were some fine examples of Kroyer's work such as 'Self Portrait' and 'Girl on Strand' with works by lesser artists such as **Michael Ancher**, his wife **Anna Ancher**, and **Carl Locher** seeming only ordinary in comparison. Printmakers from Dublin, Belfast, Cork, Berlin, Bilbao, Marseilles, Stoke-on-Trent, and Venice represented the city they lived in. Janet Preston, John Gerrard, and Paul Green showed examples of new techniques such as photo-etching and digital prints, while more traditional methods were employed by Stephen Vaughan, Tracy Staunton, and Colin Martin. A truly international flavour was maintained throughout the show with large prints by Enzo Cucchi, Maurizio Pellegrin and Paco Polan.

Brian Maguire a the Sao Paolo Bienal

Michael Warren at EV+A

■ 'Talking about Artists' Sketchbooks' was the title of an original exhibition organised by the *Lavitt Gallery Cork* in association with Cork County Library Service. It travelled to Cobh, Charleville, Bandon, Bantry and elsewhere. The beautiful catalogue reported conversations with six artists about their use of sketchbooks: **Janet Mullarney, Tony O'Malley, Brian Bourke, Katherine Boucher Beug, Megan Eustace,** and **Aoife Desmond. Charles Quain** had a one-man show at the Lavitt Gallery to mark his retirement as administrator of the Gallery.

■ An exhibition of sculptural work, 'The Perfect Family' by **Janet Mullarney**, was shown at the *Hugh Lane Gallery*. This show featured carved wooden figures with many pieces borrowing from and subverting Italian religious iconography, an outstanding example being the Madonna and Child piece, 'Red-handed'. Religious and animal imagery featured throughout the show with the artist making commentary upon oppressive forces in people's life, be it religious dogma, social structures or natural inhibitions.

■ The *National Gallery of Ireland* mounted the exhibition, 'The La Touche Amorino: Canova and his fashionable Irish Patrons', showing the extent of art patronage by the La Touche family since the 18th century. The centrepiece of this exhibition was a marble statue of 'Cupid' (Amorino) by the Italian neo-classical sculptor, Antonio Canova, donated to the Gallery by the *Bank of Ireland* under section 1003 of the Consolidated Taxes Act, 1997. This piece was originally commissioned by John David La Touche, son of the first Governor of the Bank of Ireland, and brought to Ireland in 1792. Its whereabouts since the mid-19th century was unknown until it turned up in England in recent years.

November

■ Among the nine new members elected to Aosdána were painters **Rosaleen Davey** and **Stephen McKenna**, and sculptors **Janet Mullarney** and **Michael Quane**. The *Arts Council* launched 'Contemporary Art'; an exhibition of works by 13 artists from their own collection, at five centres around Dublin. The *Arthouse* hosted the majority with works by **Micky Donnelly, Karl Grimes, Aidan Linehan, Fergus Feehily, Phelan/McLoughlin, Caroline McCarthy** and **Grace Weir**. On show at the *Hugh Lane Municipal Gallery* were **Kathy Prendergast** and **Finola Jones**. Recent acquisitions by **Paul Seawright** and **Willie Doherty** were

Pat Murphy at the Dyehouse Gallery

to be seen at the *Gallery of Photography*. **Dorothy Cross** and **Ciarán Lennon** gave an unusual modern look to the *National Gallery of Ireland* while the Arts Council Offices displayed a second work by some of the artists.

■ As part of the *Belfast Festival* the *Ormeau Baths Gallery* held solo exhibitions by two artists better known for their work in popular music, **Yoko Ono** and **David Byrne**. Ono displayed a survey of her work since the 1960s, encompassing a variety of media from painting to installation and performance work under the title 'Have you seen the horizon lately?' David Byrne presented two photographic projects, 'Strange Ritual' and 'Sleepless Nights', in the gallery. Coinciding with this was a series of billboard posters by Byrne at sites across Belfast entitled 'Better Living through Chemistry' which appeared like advertisement photos yet superimposed drug paraphernalia and motivational phraseology. Also as part of the festival, **Bill Viola** showed a disturbing video piece 'Nantes Triptych' at the *Portview Trade Centre*, Belfast.

■ The *Kerlin Gallery* capitalised on the continuing popularity of **Andy Warhol**, as evidenced by last year's hugely successful *IMMA* show, by mounting a collection of his silkscreen prints dating from the 1960s to the '80s. Well-known images such as 'Marilyn', 'Superman', 'Lenin', 'Mao', JFK' and 'Grace Kelly' comprised an impressive show. Many of these original prints were on sale with a percentage going to the Ireland Funds.

■ **John Keating** showed 'Works on Paper and Recent Edition Prints' at the *South Tipperary Art Centre*. Included in the show were examples of the artist's subtle figurative work with a variety of textures achieved through the use of watercolour, charcoal and mixed media.

■ Work by Scottish-born, **William Crozier,** featured in two simultaneous shows in Dublin. 'A Greater Garden' at the *Taylor Galleries* included paintings and watercolours while the *Graphic Studio Gallery* in Temple Bar showed a selection of Carborundum prints. Both shows featured Crozier's distinctive, strongly-coloured images of landscape and garden plant life.

■ As part of the Ford Spirit of Life Awards in association with the Sunday Independent, **Brian Maguire** was awarded the Painter of the Year award while **John Behan** won the Sculpture Award. The prize winners at the 144th *Watercolour Society of Ireland* exhibition held at the RDS were the following: **Patrick Cahill, Rosita Manahan, Pamela Leonard, Carey Clarke,** and **Elizabeth O'Brien**.

■ The London architect, **Ian Ritchie**, was announced as the winner of the competition to design a 'Millennium Monument' to be erected on the old site of Nelson's Pillar in *O'Connell Street*. His proposed construction of a 394 foot stainless steel spike tapering to an illuminated apex received a mixed reaction. **Joan O'Connor**, of the Royal Institute of Architects in Ireland, saw it as 'a wonderful wand ... a beautiful illuminated spire.' However, Labour councillor, Eamonn O'Brien, saw it as 'a huge hypodermic needle, an eternal eyesore and a symbol of a drug city.' A public exhibition of all competition entries went on view at the *RIAI Architectural Centre*.

■ At the *Green on Red Gallery*, prints by **Peter Jones** who lectures at the DIT School of Art and Design were on show. In Waterford, at the *Dyehouse Gallery*, drawings and mixed media compositions by local artist, **Pat Murphy**, attracted considerable attention. Small self-portraits, studies of plants, and a range of works inspired by Waterford itself made up the show.

Janet Mullarney at the Hugh Lane Gallery

December

Arthur Gibney at the 144th Watercolour Society of Ireland exhibition.

■ At the *Temple Bar Gallery and Studios* in Temple Bar, **Annabel Konig** displayed her audio-visual piece 'Generation' which is an ongoing project to record short moments or memories from the lives of 2,000 people. These incidents varied from a dramatic moment told in one sentence to an event told over a minute. At the *RHA Gallagher Gallery*, the **Barry Castle** retrospective included over 100 works displaying the artist's meticulous technique and imaginative subject-matter.

■ The Russian installation artists **Ilya and Emilia Kabakov** transformed the east wing of the *Irish Museum of Modern Art* into a series of mock-hospital wards as part of their installation 'The Children's Hospital'. Combining hospital furniture with puppet theatre and music, the artists attempted to convey the atmosphere of a real hospital, triggering off memories in the viewer.

■ The Belfast-born painter **Martin Mooney** was featured at the *Solomon Gallery* in a show which included bright architectural paintings of Morocco alongside more tonal Irish landscapes and Dutch-inspired still-life pieces. Also in Dublin, the *Frederick Gallery* mounted an interesting exhibition devoted entirely to drawings, etchings and engravings. With over 300 pieces to choose from, there were interesting small-scale sketchbook-type works by **Dermod O'Brien, John Butler Yeats, Walter Osborne, Alexander Williams, Samuel C Taylor, Mainie Jellet**, and **Evie Hone** among others.

Peter Jones at the Green on Red Gallery

■ The *Arthouse* in Dublin mounted 'Freeze: Winter Projection Festival' which showcased projection works by over 33 artists from Ireland, Europe, America and Asia. The projections changed on a weekly basis and took the form of abstract slides, light based sculpture, Super 8 installations, live projections, and shadow puppetry. Nearby at the *Temple Bar Gallery*, a memorial exhibition was mounted in honour of the painter, **Gerry Caffrey** (1947-1997), who occupied a studio in *Temple Bar* for a number of years.

■ The *RHA* marked the opening of the new Members Gallery within the *RHA Gallagher Gallery* by mounting a 'Small Works Christmas Exhibition' featuring works by academicians. At the same venue was an interesting and successful show entitled 'Absolut Secret', sponsored by Absolut Vodka. Well-known Irish artists were invited to submit works of art on a standard postcard-sized piece of card. The exhibits were only signed on the reverse of the cards, the identity of the artists only revealed to the purchaser at the end of the exhibition, with the proceeds going to the *National College of Art and Design* Research and Development Project.

■ Along a similar vein, the *Sligo Art Gallery* continued its tradition of inviting 26 artists to submit one artwork each in a medium of their choice on a small piece of MDF board supplied by the Gallery.

Lorraine Christie at Jorgenson Fine Art

■ A retrospective of the work of **Hilda Roberts** was organised by Waterford's *Newtown School* for its Bicentenary Celebrations and later travelled to the *RHA Gallagher Gallery*. Roberts, who was instrumental in promoting the arts in Waterford during the 1930s, was shown to be an interesting and varied figurative painter with some fine portraits included among the eighty works. At the same venue was an exhibition of landscapes and figures by **Brian Bourke** entitled 'Dip-Trip-Quadrip-Pentap-Polyp-tych'.

■ At the *Douglas Hyde Gallery*, Swiss Photographer, **Annelies Strba**, showed a collection of photographs in the form of 3 simultaneous slide projections changing at 11 second intervals, with urban domestic scenes dominating the imagery. Alongside, Strba's husband, **Bernhard Schobinger**, displayed a piece called 'The Heart Sutra on a Gold Bangle', which consisted of ancient Buddhist text engraved on a ring of gold.

■ The *Kerlin Gallery* mounted an exhibition of abstract work by **Richard Gorman** which consisted of large expanses of impeccably-applied oil and tempera in muted colours. This show coincided with a prestigious retrospective exhibition spanning over ten years of the artist's work at the *Itami City Gallery of Art*, Osaka which later travelled to the *Mitaka City Art Foundation* in Tokyo.

■ The *Ormeau Baths Gallery* in Belfast hosted 'Tête à Tête', a touring exhibition of the work of the renowned photographer, **Henri Cartier-Bresson**, in celebration of his 90th birthday. This exhibition, consisting of 110 photos spanning 60 years, included portraits of French artists and intellectuals such as Matisse, Colette and Sartre, American icons, Marilyn Monroe, Martin Luther King and British subjects, Francis Bacon and Tony Hancock.

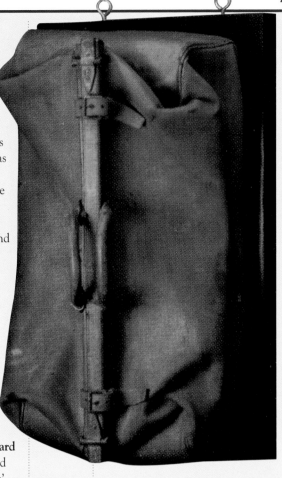

Patrick O'Reilly at the Triskel Arts Centre

■ 'Human Images: early and recent work on paper' at the *Taylor Galleries* consisted of a mini-retrospective of **Louis le Brocquy**'s works on paper since 1961. Watercolour versions of his well-known 'heads' series of portraits of Joyce, Beckett, W B Yeats and Federico Garcia Lorca, were included alongside his 'being' series of human figures.

■ Two solo exhibitions were mounted at the *Triskel Arts Centre* in Cork. Dublin artist **Ciaran O'Cearnaigh** showed 'The Age of Reason', sculpture and photographs which distorted everyday objects while **Patrick O'Reilly** showed installation-type sculpture under the title 'A Not So Still Life'.

■ The first in a series of five portraits of prominent Irish people, sponsored by *Irish Life*, was unveiled at the *National Gallery*. The double portrait of **Mary and Nicholas Robinson** by the Belfast artist, **Mark Shields**, is part of a series to be commissioned over the next 10 years which will be added to the Gallery's portrait collection.

■ At the *Belltable* in Limerick, 'Quadrant '98' featured work by four emerging artists selected by **Dorothy Walker**. Included were paintings by **Cian Donnelly** and **Shane Sinnott**, light boxes by **Namara Lindsey** and a slide sequence by **Clare Gilmour**.

Liam O'Neill at the Greenlane Gallery

William Conor at the Ulster Museum

■ An exhibition by **Mary Theresa Keown** and **Margaret Hamill** entitled 'The Cutting Rooms' was mounted in Beflast. Hamill died last October, aged fifty, and left behind many writings and collages in preparation for this exhibition which Keown subsequently used as inspiration for a series of Baconesque paintings. Also in Belfast at the *Fenderesky Gallery* at the Cresent was an exhibition of paintings and works on paper featuring established painters **David Crone, Diarmuid Delargy, Felim Egan, Ciaran Lennon, Clement McAleer, Stephen McKenna, Michael Mulcahy,** and **Dermot Seymour.**

■ Showing at the *Ulster Museum* were a number of exhibitions including 'The Legacy of Raphael: The Influence of Raphael on European Painting', '**William Conor** 1881-1968: The People's Painter' and 'A Land of Heart's Desire: 300 Years of Irish Painting.' Meanwhile the *Orchard Gallery* in Derry showed 'New Media Works' by **Nigel Rolfe, Ana Katrina Dolvin, Marie Jo Lafontaine, Dorothy Cross,** and **Tacita Dean.**

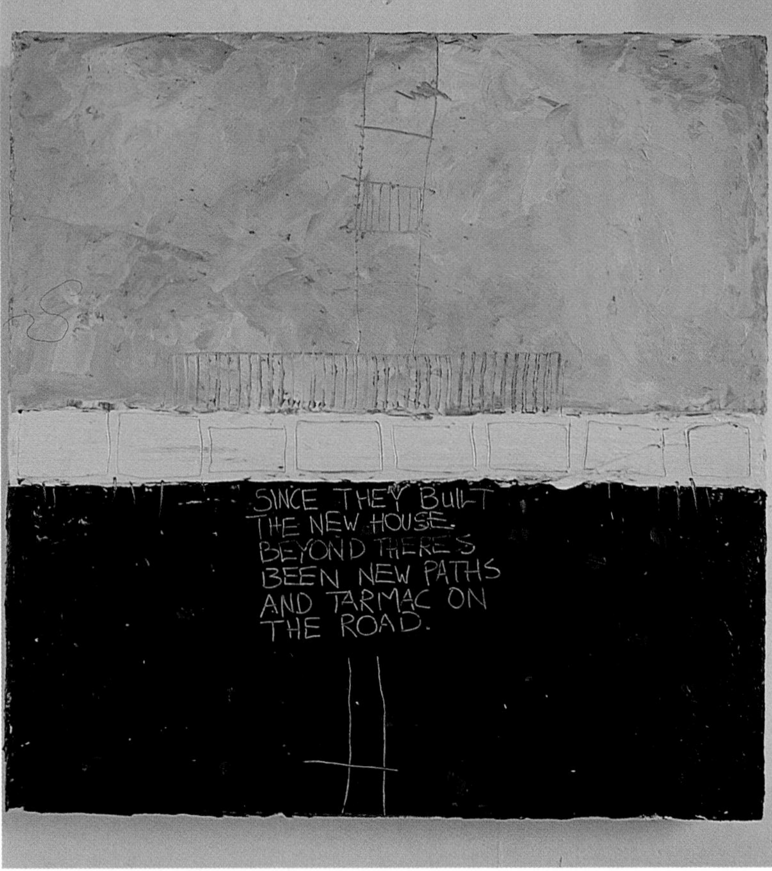

Kathy Herbert at the TristAnn's Gallery

Colin Davidson at the Solomon Gallery

January

■ The *RHA Gallagher Gallery* mounted 'Episodes from the Passion', a series of 21 monumental paintings by **Hughie O'Donoghue.** Over the last 12 years, O'Donoghue has been working on a series of paintings, drawings and prints on the theme of the Passion of Christ which have been commissioned by Craig Baker, an American collector. An agreement was made between Mr Baker and the Commissioners of Public Works in Ireland to make an extended loan of the paintings to the people of Ireland. The intention is to display this impressive body of work at various locations and abroad in advance of creating a permanent architectural space in Ireland for the collection.

■ To coincide with the launch of its Website, *IMMA* mounted a selection of exhibits from their growing permanent collection in the West Wing of the gallery under the title 'A Collection in the Making'. Among the artists included were **Marina Abramovic, Gilbert and George, Mark Joyce, Nick Miller, Colin**

Middleton, Paul Henry, Patrick Hennessy, Maria Simons-Gooding, Rachel Whiteread, and **Bill Woodrow**.

■ The *Hallward Gallery* showed 'Icons from the House of the Tragic Poet', a series of mixed media works by **Christopher Banahan**. The young Belfast painter, **Colin Davidson,** showed paintings of landscapes, cityscapes and boatscenes at the *Solomon Gallery*.

■ *The National Gallery of Ireland* opened 'Twentieth Century Irish Portraits', a new display of portraits of Irish men and women who have contributed to Irish life. Selections from the gallery's permanent collection were exhibited under various groups such as Statesmen and Politicians, the Church, the World of Theatre, Literary Portraits, the Art World, the Business World. Included were paintings by **Sean O'Sullivan, William Orpen, Muriel Brandt, James le Jeune, Edward McGuire**, along with work by living artists such as **Derek Hill, Hilda van Stockum, Robert Ballagh, Barrie Cooke**, and **Mark Shields**.

■ From more than 70 nominations, four artists were shortlisted for the £15,000 *Glen Dimplex Artists Award 1999*. These were Irish video and sound artist, **Orla Barry**, Belfast sculptor and installation artist, **Susan MacWilliam**, Japanese photographic artist, **Hiroshi Sugimoto** and British photographic and video artist, **Catherine Yass**. All four will exhibit at *IMMA* in May.

■ London-based **Elizabeth Magill** showed a strong collection of paintings at the *Kerlin Gallery*, many having a mysterious mood achieved by subdued lighting effects.

■ 'Landmarks', Kathy Herbert's exhibition involving a unique representation of what it feels like to live in Ireland in the 1990s was at *TristAnn's Gallery*, Dundalk.

February

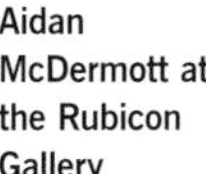

Aidan McDermott at the Rubicon Gallery

■ In Dublin the *Hallward Gallery* showed 'Details' an exhibition of painting by **Sarah Durcan** which included imagery of domestic utensils and furniture painted in pale decorative colours. At the *Rubicon* **Aidan McDermott** showed 'Morphic Heads', a series of paintings based on clay models of grotesquely-distorted heads. **Mike Nelson**'s 'Tourist Hotel' at the *Douglas Hyde* featured architectural drawings of a modern hotel alongside an installation which recreated a hotel as part of an exploration of western and Islamic cultures.

■ 'Pony Kids' at the *Hugh Lane Gallery* featured recent work by well-known fashion photographer, **Perry Ogden**. His subjects were the people and ponies of Smithfield Market set against a white background in formal portraits. These large-scale photographs were seen as a celebration of the suburban Dublin horse culture yet also received some criticism for not confronting the inherent dangers to both people and animals.

■ The *Paul Kane Gallery* mounted a show of two young artists with subdued abstracts by **Ita Freeney** and impressive abbey interiors by **Deirdre O'Brien**. The *Solomon Gallery* showed recent work by Northern artist, **Hector McDonnell,** which consisted of street and market scenes of Manhattan where the artist has lived for the last two years. At the *Gallery of Photography* **Michael Boran** showed 'The Palace of Bubbles', a catalogue of bubble types captured on film.

■ 'Highlights from the Print Collection' was a selection of old masters and modern prints on display at the *National Gallery of Ireland*. Subjects included portraits, caricatures, landscapes, genre scenes, copies from old masters and modern works and included **William Hogarth, James McArdell, Stanley Hayter** and **Henri Matisse**.

■ At the *Bourne Vincent Gallery* in the University of Limerick was an exhibition of book illustration, paintings and sculpture by the famous surrealist **Max Ernst**. In Cork at *Tig Fili*, **Niamh Lawlor** mounted the show 'Her Sopa Del Dia' which employed glass in sculptural pieces concerned with the exploitation of the female form in advertising.

■ Winner of the 1998-1999 *Nissan Art Project*, **Dorothy Cross**' 'Ghost Ship' was finally set afloat in Scotsman's Bay, *Dún Laoghaire* after a delay due to the complex nature of the piece. Intended as a tribute to the now decommissioned lightships which once dotted the coast, one such ship was painted vivid green which illuminated and faded in 8 minute cycles for three hours every night during the month.

■ New works by the Dublin-born artist, **Paddy Lennon**, who is currently resident in Wexford, were at the *Dyehouse Gallery*, Waterford.

■ At the *Logan Gallery* in Galway, **Dermot Seymour** showed a series of seven works under the title 'Consuming Units', Euro-speak for cows. This show included much of Seymour's typical bovine subjects together with enigmatic titles which challenged our way of seeing familiar imagery.

■ To mark the Joyce Centennial, the *Taylor Galleries* in collaboration with the George Moore Society presented the exhibition 'Joycesight' which featured nine artists who have been inspired by the writings of Joyce. Portraits of Joyce were included in works by **Brian Bourke, Conor Fallon, Michael Farrell, Brian King,** and **Louis le Brocquy**. Landscapes inspired by Joycean themes featured in works by **Basil Blackshaw, Barrie Cooke, Anne Donnelly**, and **Camille Souter**.

■ The *RHA Gallagher Gallery* mounted 'First Look', a display of work by 11 emerging Irish artists. Photography featured in the work of **John Halpin, Eoin McCarthy** and **Clare Langan. Andrew Boyle** showed etchings, while **Megan Eustace** and **Billy Foley** displayed drawings. **David Timmons** created industrial-style painted steel sculpture. **Niamh Lawlor** showed pieces of glass cast in the shape of pillows. **Seamus O'Rourke** used acrylic, eggshell and beeswax to create abstract work. **Alan Lambert** painted on wooden panels and subsequently sanded the surface while **Mary Keown** showed oils on canvas.

Dorothy Cross in Scotsman's Bay, Dún Laoghaire

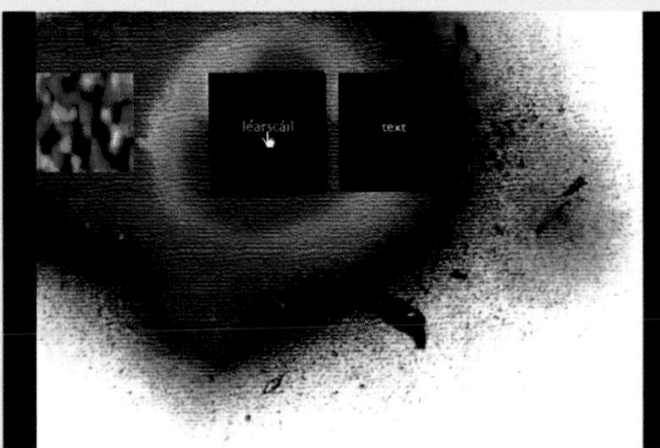

Sarah McConkey at the Arthouse

■ The *Triskel Arts Centre* in Cork featured two artists as part of a continuing commitment to highlighting local talent. **Helen Farrell** showed 'Grounded', a series of paintings, drawings and prints exploring the male figure. **Emma Mahony** used video in an installation, 'Going Nowhere', exploring the notion of travelling in time and space.

■ At *Arthouse* in Dublin, **Sara McConkey** showed an installation entitled 'Territory' using sound, image and text which commented on the historical segregation of Belfast. The *Arthouse* in Dublin and the *Engine Room* in Belfast were linked by means of a website which allowed audience interaction between the two venues.

March

■ The *Frederick Gallery* held a spring exhibition of Irish art with fine works by artists such as **Sean Keating, Charles Lamb, Jack Yeats, George Campbell, Mildred Anne Butler, and William Leech,** to name but a few. Highlights of the Spring Exhibition at *Jorgensen Fine Art* included **William Scott's** 'Still Life, Ochre, 1957' and **Colin Middleton's** 'Game of Chance'. Attractive works by **Letitia Hamilton, Dan O'Neill, Evie Hone,** and **Dermod O'Brien** also featured. *Jorgensen Fine Art* was also the venue for the first solo exhibition of Dublin artist, **Conor Walton,** who adhered to a realist style in the abundant still lifes on show.

■ *The Pallas Studios* in Foley Street was the venue for the third group exhibition of a number of young artists for whom the space is used as both a studio and an exhibition space. 'PreMillenial Tension: Where's My Brief?' consisted of a miscellany of media and styles with a film installation by **Sarah Carroll**, foam sculptures by **Gavin Corcoran** and abstracted landscapes by **Orla Whelan**. Other exhibitors included **Clodagh Emoe, Katie Holten, David Timmons, Sandra Meehan** and **Mark Cullen.**

Sean Keating at the Frederick Gallery

■ Dún Laoghaire Rathdown County Council launched 'How to Butterfly a Leg of Lamb' by **Abigail O'Brien** and **Mary Kelly,** the first in a series of installations in the concourse space of their revamped *County Hall*. A kitchen area was placed in the centre of the concourse with a small television on the worktop. On screen, Elaine Hartigan demonstrated how to butterfly a leg of lamb with some gruesome close-up views of tearing tissue.

■ At the *Solomon Gallery*, an exhibition of recent sculpture by **Catherine Greene,** took place. Greene works mainly in bronze and her work is based on the figurative image loosely drawn from strands of the mythological and historical. According to the artist her work 'is evocative of a pilgrimage, a journey or inner voyage. The pilgrim sets out to create a vision of the future...encompassing all human experience from the contemporary to the ancient world.'

■ The highlight of this month was the opening of the Yeats Museum at the *National Gallery of Ireland*. The museum is dedicated primarily to the work of **Jack B Yeats** with an excellent selection of oil paintings, watercolours and drawings by the artist on show. The museum also includes works by other members of the family with a sizeable number of portraits by **John Butler Yeats**, a watercolour of a small boy by **William Butler Yeats,** a watercolour of Jack B Yeats's studio by **Elizabeth Corbet (Lolly)**, and two embroideries of landscapes by **Susan Mary (Lily)**. Also included in the museum are two oil paintings by **Anne Yeats**, 'Women and washing, Sicily' and 'Green cloth floating', the latter presented to the Gallery by the Friends of the National Collections of Ireland. The Gallery already had the most important single collection of paintings by Jack B Yeats, but with the acquisition of the Yeats Archive, generously donated by Anne Yeats, the Gallery has now become the repository of his personal memorabilia. *Yeats: Portrait of an Artistic Family*, a recent publication by Dr Hilary Pyle, Curator of the Yeats Collection, provides a comprehensive commentary on the Gallery's collection with illustrated reference to the 100 items on display in the museum.

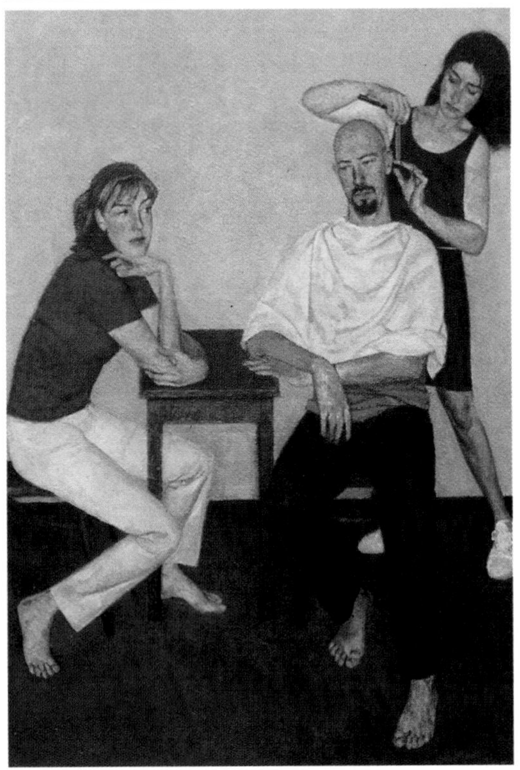

Colin Watson at the Elaine Somers Gallery

■ At the *Cavehill Gallery*, in Belfast, the work of four landscape artists was on show. In this exhibition, painters, **Siobhan Magee, Simon McKinstry** and **Tracey Quinn**, and textile artist, **Helen Kerr**, reflected their differing perceptions of the Irish countryside.

■ At the *Graphic Studio Gallery* in Temple Bar, contemporary prints by the renowned British artist, **Ken Kiff,** featured. These etchings, woodcuts and monotypes, produced in London and New York in recent years, bore testimony to Kiff's highly individual approach. The subject matter of Kiff's prints (smiling suns, symbolic trees and fantastical creatures) conveyed a sense of a dreamlike and mystical inner world while possessing more sinister overtones. At the *Temple Bar Gallery and Studios*, **Cathy Carman's** 'Homage to my Mother', an intensely personal body of sculptural work dedicated to the artist's mother who died six years ago, was on show. Working in white plaster, the artist produced ghostly, life-size figures with sinister fishheads eating their way out of the bodies. This was followed by an exhibition of the work of **Angela Fewer** and **Rachel Joynt** at the same venue. While Fewer's work consisted of oil on canvas paintings, charcoal drawings and some oil stick works on paper, Joynt's 'Feed' was a site specific kinetic installation which filled the void that rises through the Gallery and Studios building. A continuous stream of fine white sand flowed from a large steel funnel and percolated its way down through perforated tray-like structures. The streams of sand created a multi-tiered system of sandscapes which evolved and eroded in a rhythmical manner.

■ Landscape was the subject of three divergent exhibitions held during this month at the *Guinness Gallery in Foxrock*. Scottish-born **Jean Duncan** exhibited a series of paintings and prints based on a visit to an Andalusian village in which Duncan accurately captured the textures, light and shade of her surrounding scenery. **Breeda Mooney's** 'Petrified' at the *Droichead Arts Centre* consisted of a series of large scale photographs of the Petrified Forests of Namibia and Arizona. In contrast, Danish photographer, **Kirsten Klein,** at the *Bank of Ireland Arts Centre*, showed more photographs of the west of Ireland. Despite the conventional nature of the subject matter, Aidan Dunne, art critic for *The Irish Times*, wrote '...she is a wonderful photographer, and images that might have been hackneyed and superficial are subtly, beautifully observed.'

■ 'Edaín', an exhibition of work by **Mick O'Dea**, took place in the *Ashford Gallery* at the *Royal Hibernian Academy*. It consisted of thirty drawings and paintings of figurative painter, Edaín O'Donnell, who, in this instance, acted as model. O'Dea has a high regard for O'Donnell's work and the dynamics of the relationship between an artist and model were re-evaluated in that the artist was engaging with another artist.

■ At the *Taylor Galleries* in Dublin, paintings and etchings by French artist, **Jean Dometti,** were on show. In what appeared to be a reciprocal agreement, recent work by **Michael Mulcahy** was the subject of an exhibition at the Galerie Médiart in Paris, where the artist is now based.

■ The *Museum of Pont-Aven* in France held a retrospective exhibition of the prints of **Roderic O'Conor (1860-1940)**. While living in Brittany, the artist developed a close friendship with the French printmaker, Armand Seguin, who introduced O'Conor to the technique of etching. O'Conor's prints are extremely rare as he chose not to publish them as editions and only 43 prints from his hand have been traced and identified. Many of these works draw their motifs from the coastal environment at Le Pouldu, an isolated community to the south of Pont-Aven. This exhibition was accompanied by a beautifully-produced catalogue *raisonné* written by Roy Johnston.

Gladys Maccabe at the Leinster Gallery

■ Photos of the rich and famous by **Anton Corbijn** were projected nightly at *Meeting House Square* in Temple Bar. These highly-staged, black and white and later, sepia and blue images of Naomi Campbell, Luciano Pavaortti and Jodie Foster were highly atmospheric. At the *Gallery of Photography*, the collaborative work of writer, **Judy Kravis,** and artist, **Peter Morgan,** featured in 'Lives Less Ordinary'.

■ At the *Rubicon Gallery*, drawings by Waterford artist **Tom Molloy** were on show. This, his fourth solo exhibition with the Dublin gallery, consisted of three sets of pencil drawings. The Seven Photocopies series, based on a photocopy of Caravaggio's 'Basket of Fruit', played on the optical illusion created by both the original painting and its reproduction. In this intriguing play of reproductions and copies, the photocopy is transposed into an original. 'Oak' consisted of ninety-two beautifully-rendered drawings of individual leaves from a red oak tree.

■ Elsewhere in Dublin, at the *Green On Red Gallery*, new work by **Fergus Martin** was on show. **Sean Shanahan's** sparse paintings on MDF and pre-painted steel, filled the *Kerlin Gallery*. **Carmel Mooney's show**, 'From The Dark Earth', at the *Hallward Gallery*, reflected the artist's continuing interest in volcanoes. 'Still Life' at the *Paul Kane Gallery*, featured the work of **MJ Lahaye, Meriel Nicoll, Lidia de Lange** and **Deirdre Nolan.**

■ A selection of work from the collection of the Arts Council of Ireland was on show at the *Ormeau Baths Gallery* in Belfast. It included the work of well-known contemporary artists including **Micky Donnelly, Willie Doherty, Aidan Linehan, Caroline McCarthy, Phelan McLoughlin, Kathy Prendergast, Ciaran Lennon, Fergus Feehily, Karl Grimes, Finola Jones, Paul Seawright, Dorothy Cross** and **Grace Weir**. 'Be Prepared', a new sequence of large scale colour images by photographer, **John Duncan**, was also on show at the Gallery. Although his work is not overtly political, he is concerned with the politics of urban representation. At *Catalyst Arts* in Belfast, the fruits of **Gerard Byrne** and **Mark Orange's** sojourn in New York, on the PS1 scholarship were on display. The annually-awarded scholarship is one of the most prestigious prizes for Irish artists. Byrne showed four large photoworks of dormant spaces, such as offices between working hours, while Orange showed a video installation and small framed screenprint. Also in Belfast, on a more conventional note, the *Ulster Museum* held an impressive exhibition, 'Reflections of a Golden Age: Dutch Art of the Seventeenth Century'.

■ To mark the International Year of Older Persons, the *Irish Museum of Modern Art* showed some 60 artworks created by a group of older people from the Inchicore area of Dublin. The exhibition celebrated older people's creativity and their engagement with contemporary visual art through the Museum.

■ 'Side-by-Side' at the *Elaine Somers Gallery*, Holywood, Co Down showed the work of two artists, **Noel Murphy** and **Colin Watson**.

■ Two interesting exhibitions took place at the *Sligo Art Gallery* during this month. 'Kaleidoscope', an exhibition of recent paintings and prints by **Audrey Irwin** was followed by **Cormac O'Leary's** show, 'Night Crossing'. **Alice Maher** and **Tim Davies** work was on show at the Triskel Arts Centre in Cork.

April

Siobhan Magee at the Cavehill Gallery

■ *The Royal Hibernian Academy's* 169th Annual Exhibition opened at the *RHA Gallagher Gallery*. Approximately 460 exhibits were chosen by the Selection Committee as a broad representation of the best works submitted. The selection included invited work from artists such as **Colin Harrison, William Crozier, Cathy Carman, Brian Bourke, Philip Flanagan, Barry Flanagan, Terry Frost RA, Michael Kenny RA, Eithne Jordan, Pat Harris, Stephen McKenna, Sean McSweeney, Simon McWilliams, Nick Miller, Janet Mullarney, Patrick O'Reilly, Michael Warren** and **Kate Wilson**.

■ Dazzling new works by **Tony O'Malley** filled the spaces at the *Taylor Galleries*. The works spanned the last four years and included some of the largest compositions ever produced by the artist. **O'Malley** is now based near his home-town of Callan in Co. Kilkenny, having spent many years in Cornwall and also in the Bahamas. Works such as 'The Sun in the Pond' 'Hallowe'en' and 'Yellow Pond' reflected the richness and inventiveness of his work since his return to Ireland. At *Jorgensen Fine Art*, an exhibition of recent work by **Gordon Bryce** took place.

Tarquin Landseer at the Kennedy Gallery

Peter Behan at the Origin Gallery

■ The Dublin-born artist, **Peter Behan**, who lives and works in Italy and who has exhibited very widely internationally showed new works at the *Origin Gallery*, Dublin.

■ To celebrate the bicentenary of the death of Lord Charlemont, the Royal Irish Academy held an exhibition of manuscripts and works of art associated with him. A symposium on Lord Charlemont and his Circle was held at the *National Gallery of Ireland* to mark the publication of Cynthia O'Connor's book, *The Pleasing Hours: James Caulfield, 1st Earl of Charlemont, Traveller, Connoisseur and Art Patron.*

■ In Dublin, the *Frederick Gallery* presented a selection of new works by Wexford-based artist, **Mark O'Neill**. At the *Solomon Gallery*, an exhibition of important contemporary Scottish art took place. Attractive works by **John Houston, David Michie, June Redfern, John Bellany, Elizabeth Blackadder, Bob Lynn** and **Marj Bond** featured. *The Hallward Gallery* was the venue for an exhibition of new works by artist, **Robert Armstrong**. 'Still', new paintings and drawings by **Samuel Walsh,** filled the space of the *Rubicon Gallery*. At the *Bank of Ireland Arts Centre*, artist, **Promilla Luthra Shaw** presented 'Journey Within II'.

■ The first solo exhibition in Ireland of the work of Belgian artist, **Luc Tuymans**, was held at the *Douglas Hyde Gallery*. Tuymans is widely considered to be one of the most significant figurative painters of the past decade. Nine new pieces, all on the theme of the Passion, featured in this show. The detached, remote quality of his work was particularly evident in works such as 'Mirror' and 'Gas Chamber'.

■ The Temple Bar area of Dublin was the venue for a number of interesting exhibitions during this month. 'A Welcome Exchange', an exhibition of work by sixteen painters from *The Painting Center, New York* took place in the Atrium space at the *Temple Bar Gallery and Studios*. This formed one component of an arrangement between the American Gallery and the Irish one whereby exhibitions are arranged in both venues. Sixteen American artists, including **Melissa Chaney, Greg Decker, Laura Taylor,** and **Mark Kloth**, exhibited in Dublin and the following month, the *Painting Center* hosted an exhibition of work by Irish artists, **Robert Armstrong, Michael Dempsey,** and **Mary-Avril Gillan**. This exhibition was followed by a show of new work by **Michael Beirne.** Also in Temple Bar, new works by **Sarah Horgan** featured at the *Original Print Gallery* in Dublin. Working in lino etching, her prints were subtle, evocative and elegant. Temple Bar Properties staged an open-air screening of **Matthew Barney's** 'Cremaster 5', the artist's most ambitious project to date, in *Meeting House Square*, Temple Bar. Barney established his reputation with an arresting video installation at the *Barbara Gladstone Gallery* in New York in 1991. It featured the artist, naked except for a climbing harness, working his way up the wall and across the ceiling of the gallery supported by titanium ice screws. His Irish show was a bizarre mix of filmed opera and was recommended by *The Irish Times* art critic, Aidan Dunne, who wrote, 'It's the first time Barney's work will be shown publicly in Ireland and love it or loathe it, it is well worth seeing. Don't miss it.'

■ A collaborative exhibition by sculptor, **Vivienne Roche,** and composer, **John Buckley**, filled four rooms at the *Hugh Lane Municipal Gallery*. The thematic focus for this collaboration was the relationship between the sea and human emotions. The exhibition title 'Tidal Erotics' was taken from the first section of the exhibition which consisted of a series of small two-part wall sculptures, varying in scale. These were cast in bronze from seaweed encased in wax. The thematic concerns of the show were further explored in a series of drawings in graphite on tracing paper. Buckley's composition for percussion, piano, horn, flute and cello, was relayed through a series of sound sources located within the exhibition. Both art forms formed complimentary responses to the common theme. As Roche stated of this exhibition, 'I see it as a set of visual and aural forms meeting in time and space.' Also at the *Hugh Lane Gallery*, 'Knot', an exhibition of drawings curated by Irish artist, **Alice Maher,** took place. This exhibition originated from the Gallery's invitation to Maher to curate an exhibition from the permanent collection of works on paper. 'Knot' presented the artist's chosen works from the collection with 'Coma Berenices', a suite of her own monumental charcoal drawings of coils of hair realised in direct response to two works in particular: 'Sleep' by **Keith Henderson** and 'Anima errante' by **Paul Klee**. Exquisite works by 39 artists, in total, including **Camille Corot, Jean-Francois Millet, Keith Henderson, Simeon Solomon, Jack B Yeats** and **Patrick Tuohy** were presented.

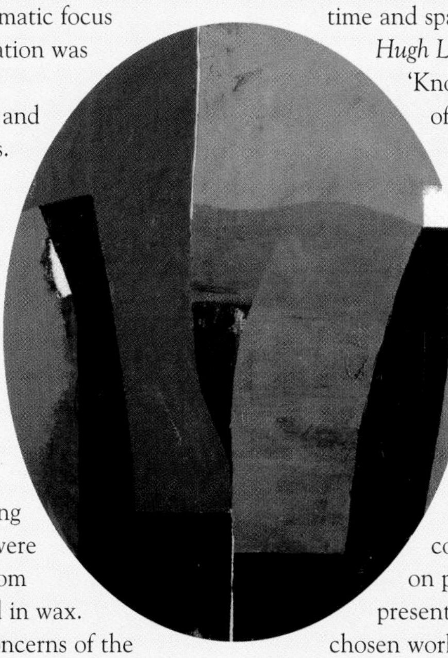

Richard Gorman in Japan

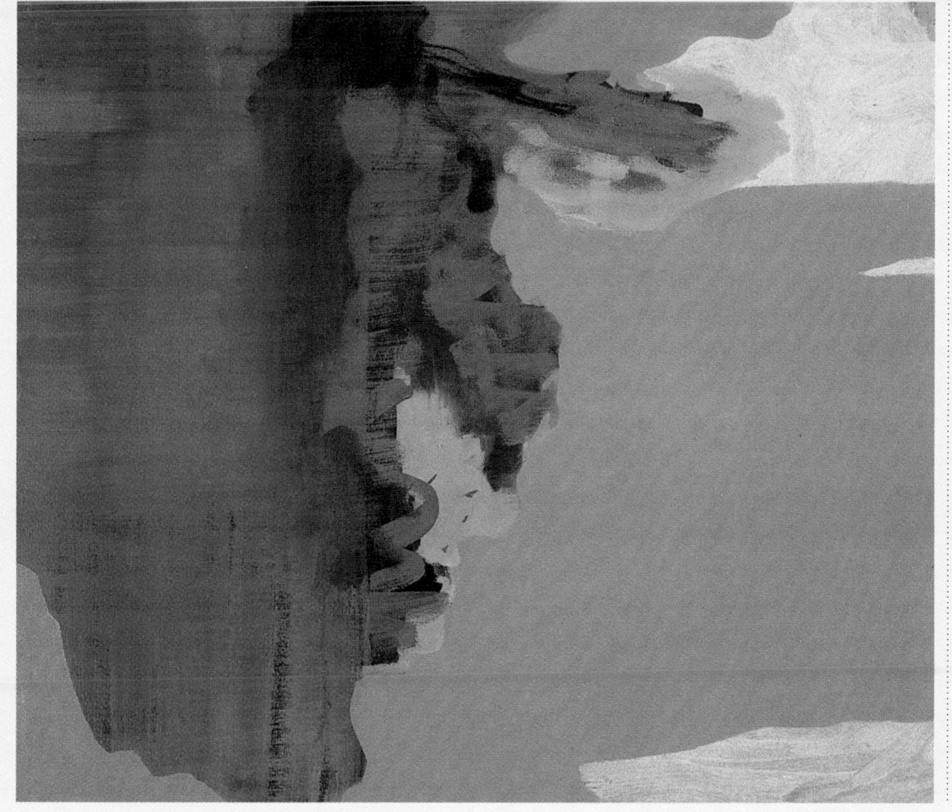

Sinéad Aldridge at the Sligo Art Gallery

■ At the *Kennedy Gallery* 'Heartland' was the title of **Tarquin Landseer's** exhibition of paintings based on his Mexican Experiences.

■ At the *Graphic Studio Gallery*, lithographs and prints portraying 'the city and the self' featured. These were the work of **Yoko Akino** and **Joy Gerrard.** *The Grosvenor Room Gallery* on Ormond Quay showed a series of atmospheric landscapes and portraits by Northern Irish artist, **Mark Shields.**

■ An exhibition of new works by **Felix Anaut** was held at the Belfast Waterfront Hall. Organised in association with the *Elaine Somers Gallery*, the show consisted of mammoth paper tapestries concentrating on female heads and hands. A series of bronze sculptures by Anaut complemented these works. At the **Ormeau Baths Gallery**, two divergent shows dominated the Gallery spaces. These were **Brian Maguire's** 'Casa da Cultura Prejudicial Portraits' and drawing and sculpture by Dutch artists, **Arno Kramer, Helen Frik** and **Tjibbe Hooghiemstra**. Maguire's exhibition included elements of his work for the Sao Paolo Bienial as well as new works specifically commissioned for the Belfast Gallery and developed through a period of residency in Belfast.

■ Further afield, an exhibition of the work of Irish artist, **Richard Gorman,** was held at the *Mitaka City Gallery of Art* in Japan.

■ 'The Light Sleep of Space', an exhibition of the work of **Sinead Aldridge,** was held at the *Sligo Art Gallery*. At the *Galway Arts Centre*, figurative studies and skull drawing sequences by **Brian Bourke** were on display.

Eoin McCarthy at the Butler Gallery

Peter Curling at the Molesworth Gallery

■ 'From Cookstown to the Colosseum' was the novel title for a major exhibition at the *Ulster Museum* to celebrate the acquisition of a portrait of James Stewart (1742-1821) by **Pompeo Batoni** (1708-1787). Stewart who was from Killymoon in Northern Ireland went on the Grand Tour for a two year period from 1766 to 1768. In the spring of 1767, Stewart posed for Batoni in Rome and the resulting portrait, which was acquired by the *Ulster Museum* in 1997, forms the centre-piece of this exhibition which also featured Italian and Irish portraits and landscapes on loan from various collections.

■ A wide variety of exhibitions took place in Dublin during this month. New work by **John Kelly RHA** was on show at the ***Hallward Gallery***. This was followed by an exhibition of the work of **Sarah Walker**. *The Solomon Gallery* mounted a show of new landscape paintings by established artist **Trevor Geoghegan.** *Jorgensen Fine Art* showed paintings by **John Long**. At the *Graphic Print Studio,* the work of printmakers **Niall Naessens** and **Pauline Macey** was on show. The Equestrian Show, including works by **Peter Curling, Peter Deighan, Michael Jeffery, Gemma Guihan,** and **Patrick Cahill**, filled the space at the *Molesworth Gallery*. **Michael Kane's** show, the 'Humours of Zeus', took place in the *Rubicon Gallery*. At *Dublin Castle,* the Values Foundation, Bulgaria presented an exhibition of painting and sculpture from that country.

■ A group exhibition of contemporary photography by **Uta Barth, Oliver Boberg, Jeff Burton, Esko Mannikko,** and **Walter Niedermayr** was held at the *Kerlin Gallery* and was reflective of current trends in international contemporary photography. A series of photographic installations also featured at the *Temple Bar Gallery and Studios* in 'Other World' by Irish-born artist, **Peter Hendrick**. Currently based in New York, Hendrick combined photographs taken in the year of his birth with others taken during his residency at the *Temple Bar Gallery and Studios.*

■ A retrospective exhibition of the work of two of Ireland's finest painters, **Nano Reid** and **Camille Souter**, was held at the *Droichead Arts Centre* in Drogheda, Reid's home town, and then travelled to the *Linenhall Arts Centre* in Castlebar. While the artists have little in common, Reid's darker and more tonal works provided a delicate counterpoint to Souter's delicate and subtle handling of colour.

■ 'First look', a group show of the work of eleven young artists, took place at the *Butler Gallery* in Kilkenny. It was curated by Patrick . Murphy, Director of the RHA.

■ The Pastel Society of Ireland held its Annual Exhibition in Dublin for the first time since its formation some ten years ago. The Society had held previous exhibitions at venues across Northern Ireland but with membership increasing throughout Ireland the Society felt it was time to widen its horizons to the viewing public. The exhibition was held at the *Kennedy Gallery.*

■ The *Sligo Art Gallery* had a busy exhibitions programme during this month. **Siobán Piercy's** show, 'Palimpsest' featured striking screenprints and this was followed by an exhibition of prints by **Tony and Jane O'Malley.** A collaborative exhibition between painter, **Catherine McWilliams,** and poet, **Tom Morgan,** followed. A strong sense of place was apparent in this show, 'Ballintrillick in the light of Ben Wiskin' which was a visual and poetic response to the Sligo landscape.

■ The *Paul Kane Gallery* showed examples of the work of **Margaret O'Sullivan** and **Fintan O'Byrne**. O'Sullivan's small coastal studies were fresh vigorous responses to landscape while O'Byrne offered a more distant, abstracted consideration of landscape, with an oriental influence evident in his subtle watercolours.

Joseph Beuys at the Irish Museum of Modern Art

■ **Katie Holten** used her experiences abroad as a basis for an exhibition in the *Basement Gallery*, Dundalk

■ As part of the programming policy for the Atrium space at *Temple Bar Gallery & Studios*, there is an opportunity for artists to curate exhibitions and group exchanges are regularly facilitated. 'PastPresentFuture' was the title of a show organised with Parking Space, Liverpool, an artist-led initiative. Featuring new mixed media, 'PastPresentFuture' showcased the work of ten emerging artists, including **Simon Armstrong, Jane Anderson, Peter Bonnell, Lucienne Cole,** and **Nicholas Fox.** Artists from *Temple Bar Gallery & Studios* will exhibit at Liverpool's *Static Gallery* early in the new year. The intention of these exhibitions is to explore and develop relations between the twinned cities of Liverpool and Dublin by hosting reciprocal shows.

■ The *Taylor Galleries* was the venue for two interesting exhibitions during this month. **James O'Connor's** show, 'Immanence and Trascendence', showed the fruits of several years of the artist's work on paper. **Paki Smith's** 'The Holy Shiver' followed this and this show featured both his paintings and notebooks from 1994 to 1999. It also marked the publication of the artist's book, *The Rose Hedge*.

■ The new commercial space at the RHA, the *Ashford Gallery* was the venue for an engaging exhibition of the work of Irish artist, **Anne Donnelly**, 'Light in Wings'.

■ The Glen Dimplex Artists Award exhibition, now in its sixth year, opened at the *Irish Museum of Modern Art.* The £15,000 award is intended to mark a level of achievement in the work and practice of exhibiting artists of any age, using any medium. As in previous years, the artists (text, sound and video artist Orla Barry, sculptor and installation artist **Susan MacWilliam,** photographic artist **Hiroshi Sugimoto** and **Catherine Yass**) were allocated individual spaces at the Museum in which to represent their work.

■ A major exhibition of multiples, or works produced in editions, by the legendary German artist, **Joseph Beuys** (1921-1986), opened at the *Irish Museum of Modern Art.* This show was the largest exhibition of Beuys's work seen in Ireland to-date and was also one of the most important showings of his multiples ever organised, including many of his best known and most influential works. For Beuys his multiples represented a vehicle for communication, a means of disseminating his ideas across time and space. From 1965 to 1985, he produced almost 600 multiples in a variety of media, including graphic works, found objects, photographs, audio tapes and films. Each one encapsulated a specific moment in Beuys's life or work: an idea, a performance, a lecture, an exhibition. Some 300 works were shown at IMMA and included many of Beuys's most famous works, such as 'Sled' (1969), 'Felt Suit' (1970) and 'Rose for Direct Democracy' (1973). Works were arranged thematically based on key ideas explored by Beuys, such as nature, healing, communication and political activism.

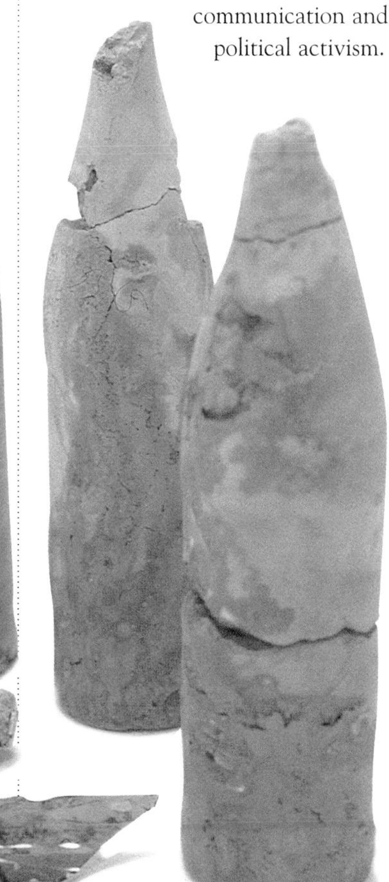

Katie Holten at the Basement Gallery Dundalk

Callum Innes at the Irish Museum of Modern Art

Tom Carr at the Taylor Gallery, Belfast

June

■ Installations featured prominently during this month with **Mary Avril Gillan**'s 'Virtual Belonging' at the *Temple Bar Gallery* and **Jaki Irvine**'s 'The Hottest Sun, The Darkest Hour' at the **Douglas Hyde Gallery**. Both Irvin and Gillan employed a number of multiple projections to create an overall atmosphere, although both exhibitions were entirely different. Gillan's video installation, composed of three simultaneous projections in a darkened room, was highly effective. All three videos represented a journey across the United States on an interstate bus, following in a broad sense the path of colonisation across America from east to west. They played with experience of landscape, motion and time and made for an engaging encounter for the viewer. Gillan combined this ambitious video installation with a series of paintings based on the vision of landscape as viewed from a car. This was Gillan's third solo exhibition and sees the artist going from strength to strength. Irvine's show consisted of five 6mm films, of varying length, projected simultaneously. Irvine developed these films over the last year in Rome, where she was in residence at the British School. The five short films that comprise this piece are individually entitled, 'Marco, One Afternoon', 'Fireflies at 3am?' 'Dani and Diego', 'Portrait of Daniela', and 'The Take Off'. Rather than being an obvious narrative development from one to the other, a sense of time and place was slowly built up in the films.

■ At the *National Gallery of Ireland* an exhibition of fifty works by **Richard 'Dickie' Doyle** (1824-83), one of the best known illustrators of the 19th century, was staged in the Print Gallery. This show consisted of watercolours, drawings, and illustrations for well-known publications, such as *Punch* magazine, where Doyle worked until 1850. Works by Doyle's father, 'H13', also featured. The exhibition covered imaginative subjects such as 'A Fairy Pageant' as well as illustrations for children and a selection of landscape watercolours of the artist's favourite views. Also at the *National Gallery*, '*Parau na te Varua ino*' (Words of the Devil) by **Paul Gauguin**, went on display. Currently on loan from the **National Gallery of Art** in Washington DC, this stunning work was painted by Gaughin in 1892 during his first stay in Tahiti. The work was flanked by works by Irish artists, **Roderic O'Conor** and **Mary Swanzy**, both of whom were influenced by the great Post-Impressionist master.

■ 'A Land of Heart's Desire', a celebration of the richness and diversity of Irish painting, over the last 300 years, opened in the newly-refurbished temporary exhibition gallery of the *Ulster Museum* in Belfast. This stunning collection of the finest painting from the Museum's permanent collection focused on the theme of landscape and the exhibition traced the evolution of Irish painting from its origins in topographic views to the international art of the present day. **George Garret, William Ashford, Sir John Lavery, Sir William Orpen, Jack Yeats, William Conor, Dan O'Neill, William Scott, Tony O'Malley** and **Basil Blackshaw** were some of the artists whose work featured in this show.

■ New paintings by **Chung Eun-Mo** were on view at the *Kerlin Gallery*. Born and educated in Korea, Chung Eun-Mo moved to New York in the mid-1960s and has been based in Italy and Ireland since the late 1980s. In this new work, she increasingly used rounded forms and rich, luminous tones. Principally concerned with the planar distribution of colour, something she attributes to the influence of Korean and Italian architecture, the artist juxtaposes different colours, shapes and shades of light to great effect.

■ The National College of Art and Design Fine Art MA students' show filled the space at the *Douglas Hyde Gallery*. The format was quite traditional with four painters out of a total of six graduates. Some of the most striking pieces were Catherine Kelly's 'Safe as House', a gigantic house of cards, which functioned as a metaphor for the role of chance in life and Tafina Flood's expressive use of colour and texture in her prints.

■ 'In', a mixed media installation by New York-based Irish artist, **Catherine Owens**, incorporated drawing, sculpture, animation, sound and photography, and filled the exhibition rooms at the *Hugh Lane Municipal Gallery of Modern Art*. The show brought together many of the elements and ideas that have been the focus of Owens's work over the last few years and was a response to the blurred definitions between the worlds of art, entertainment, technology, and fashion. The installation was accompanied by a haunting acapella soundtrack by Northern Irish singer, Brian Kennedy.

■ An exhibition of the work of Scottish artist, **Callum Innes**, took place at the *Irish Museum of Modern Art*. Internationally recognised as having made a significant contribution to the field of contemporary abstract painting, Innes works mostly in monochrorne. This show consisted of a specially-selected body of new and recent work, including paintings from the 'Exposed and Resonance' series and watercolours. Also during this month, the *Irish Museum of Modern Art* marked the contribution of the distinguished art collector, Gordon Lambert, to the Museum by dedicating part of its exhibition space to him. Lambert has donated more than 300 works to the Museum, including works by international artists such as **Victor Vaserely, Bridget Riley**, and Irish artists, **Patrick Collins, Robert Ballagh and Michael Farrell**. *The Gordon Lambert Galleries*, on the west ground floor of the building, were officially dedicated by the Minister for Arts, Heritage, Gaeltacht and the Islands, Sile de Valera.

■ *The Green on Red Gallery* showed a number of **Eilis O'Connell's** recent sculptures in what the *Irish Times* art critic, Aidan Dunne, described as 'an outstanding show'. Her brilliant use of woven stainless steel cable in works as 'Carapace', demonstrate the sculptor's preoccupation with the finish of her works.

■ In France, a major exhibition of Irish artists in Brittany, curated by Dr Julian Campbell, took place at *Musée de Pont-Aven*. Key works by **Augustus Burke, Norman Garstin, Nathaniel Hone, Aloysius O'Kelly, Roderic O'Conor, Henry Jones Thaddeus,** and **Helen Mabel Trevor** were on show.

■ A diverse range of exhibitions took place in a number of Dublin galleries during this month. Mixed media paintings by *Leonard Sheil* filled the rooms at the *Paul Kane Gallery*. 'Paper Tigers, Stalking-Horses' was the intriguing title of **James Hanley**'s exhibition at the *Hallward Gallery*. A sense of unease and menace permeates a lot of Hanley's work and this show did not disappoint in that regard. The artist employed a variety of media including conte and graphite, indian ink, oil and graphite and gouache and works such as 'Post Modernist Redcoat' and 'Speechless' were particularly noteworthy. Elsewhere in Dublin, **Aoife Harrington**'s work at the *Rubicon Gallery*, concentrated on a single abstract motif. At the *Kevin Kavanagh Gallery*, 'Flesh and Air', the work of **Beth O'Halloran**, explored the contingency of experience in a number of Iyrical, airy works. Recent paintings by **James MacKeown** featured at the *Solomon Gallery*. At *Jorgensen Fine Art*, the first solo exhibition in Dublin of **Fred Cuming RA** took place.

■ Islands' at the *Taylor Galleries*, showed **Michael Mulcahy** returning to more familiar terrain with a number of paintings largely inspired by the Skelligs. This theme is reminiscent of the series of works of Brendan the Navigator which Mulcahy painted in the early 1980s. In these he celebrated Irish mythology and although Mulcahy has been based in Paris for several years, his painting expresses the mystery attached to this remote, yet sublime, location for a religious settlement. Established artist, **Charles Tyrell**, also exhibited at the *Taylor Galleries* during this month.

Melanie Le Brocquy at the RHA Gallery

Vincent Sheridan at the Lambay House Contemporary Art Gallery

■ At the *RHA* a well-deserved retrospective exhibition of the work of sculptor, **Melanie le Brocquy,** took place. She could never be described as a prolific artist and this modestly-sized show spanned her work from the 1930s to the present day. The tactile surface of her work was a constant quality in most of the pieces on display and the theme of the family was ever present.

■ In Limerick, 'EV+A reduced' celebrated the reopening of *Limerick City Gallery of Art* after its extension and refurbishment. Photography, video, installations, and work that emphasised a contemporary concern for the minimal, were the order of the day. The works were selected by American curator, Jeanne Greenberg Rohatyn. Work by artists **Robert Janz, Sandra Meehan, Amanda Coogan, Oliver Comerford, Michael Canning, Margaret Corcoran, Diana Copperwhite, Carissa Farrell, Mark Orange, Fiona Mulholland, Colin Carters** and many others were on display. At *Éigse Carlow Arts Festival*, **Pauline Flynn, Sean Henry, Anthony Whishaw, Darragh Hogan, Helen Gaynor** were among the exhibitors.

■ 'Attitudes' was the title of an exhibition at the *Lambay House Gallery*, Howth of works by **Vincent Sheridan** who spent some years in the Canadian High Arctic and who draws his subject matter from the animal kingdom.

■ The attractive summer exhibition at the *Taylor Gallery*, Belfast included works by **Tom Carr, Markey Robinson, Colin Middleton, James Humbert Craig** and other Irish artists.

■ The Fine Art Degree Show of the National College of Art and Design took place at the *RHA Gallagher Gallery* and it reflected the range of work being produced by contemporary Irish artists. A wide range of works featured. One of the most striking, installations was **Eilish O'Toole's** 'Sky Room', and among the painters, the work of **Suzette Tackney** and **Saralene Tapley** stood out.

■ To the delight of some and the chagrin of others, the plan for the 'Monument of Light' or the 'spike' as it is officially known, on O'Connell Street, has been shelved for the foreseeable future. The legality of the monument was challenged in the High Court by the artist, Michael O'Nuallain, on the grounds that Dublin Corporation had not commissioned an environmental impact study. A judgement against the monument stated that the height of the spike prevented it from conforming to the scale of O'Connell Street. It means that it will certainly not be built before 2000.

■ There was a preponderance of summer group shows during this month. The *Kerlin Gallery* had an impressive exhibition, featuring photographic work, works on paper, and sculptural work by a wide range of well-known gallery artists. Among those showing new or recent work were **Barrie Cooke, Dorothy Cross, Richard Gorman, Brian Maguire, Kathy Prendergast, Sean Scully, Stephen McKenna** and **Willie Doherty**. The members show, with works selected by Ted Hickey, was held at *Temple Bar Gallery and Studios*. The *Hallward Gallery* also had a summer exhibition with paintings and sculpture by both Gallery and invited artists. Works by artists such as **Mildred Anne Butler, Nathaniel Hone, Samuel Taylor, Camille Souter** and many others featured at the *Frederick Gallery's* summer show.

■ The winner of the *Glen Dimplex Award* was English photographic artist, **Catherine Yass.** She is best known for her vividly-coloured photographic transparencies displayed on lightboxes which she uses to explore the architecture and life of public spaces and buildings. Yass received £15,000 as the award. A non-monetary award for sustained contribution to the visual arts in Ireland was made to distinguished Irish painter, **Tony O'Malley.**

■ IndustriaArt's Second Bi-Annual Exhibition of Contemporary Art took place at the *Bank of Ireland Arts Centre.* It consisted of over fifty contemporary works by emerging Irish and international artists. Works included oils, photographs, mixed media, works on paper and etchings. Some of the artists include **Anne Stahl, Jo Scanlon, Joanna Kidney, Lindsay Namara,** and **Carmel Cleary.**

■ In **Nigel Rolfe's** 'Dead Flowers' at the *Green on Red Gallery*, the visitor entered a darkened space where screen-sized images of dead flowers were projected on to the wall accompanied by a haunting soundtrack. The video piece, entitled, 'Life without Life' referred to the Nazi description of those with physical deformities or mental handicaps as 'life unworthy of life'. The entire piece made for compelling viewing.

■ **Patrick Conyngham** also used sound as a background for his paintings and poems in 'Deep Currents' at the *Origin Gallery.* **Francis Tansey** showed hard-edged geometric works at the *Grosvenor Gallery.* **Francis Carty's** new work, 'There's no place like it', was on show at the *Kevin Kavanagh Gallery.* This show featured a multiplicity of views combined in one image. At the *Paul Kane Gallery*, a fine show of works by **Cathy Addis** and **Jane Byrne** took place.

■ The *Galway Arts Festival* had a busy visual arts programme this year. An exhibition of works on paper from the personal collection of renowned West Coast realist painter, **Wayne Thiebaud,** went on show at the *UCG Gallery.* The show was organised with the assistance of Los Angeles-based art dealer, Jack Rutberg, who has been involved in the festival exhibitions for a number of years. Thiebaud is most famous for his paintings of confectionery which he first exhibited in New York in 1961. While the artist is seen as being one of the pioneers of pop art, he sees things quite differently. He states, 'I see myself as a traditional painter...interested in the concept of realism and the notion of inquiring into what the tradition of realism is all about.' A number of other exhibitions took place during the festival. Works by **Barrie Cooke** were on show at the *Galway Arts Centre.* **Paul Mosse's** elaborate paintings were on show at the *Logan Gallery.* Another painting exhibition of note was that of the late **Joe Quilty** who was a productive outsider artist. A retrospective of his paintings was shown at the *Kenny Gallery.*

Top: Francis Tansey at the Grosvenor Room Gallery

Above: John Duncan at the Triskel Gallery

Frank McKelvey at the Frederick Gallery (detail)

■ At the *Ulster Museum* in Belfast, 'Exploring Modern Art: Towards Abstraction' opened.

■ **Tori Wood's** 'All Zones Off Peak', a record of a 15-year photographic odyssey around Liverpool, was on show at the *Gallery of Photography* in Temple Bar. The paintings in **Simon English's** 'Archive' at the *Temple Bar Gallery* depicted display cabinets and other items of furniture, and sideways views of landscape details.

■ The works in *Iontas,* the Tenth National Small Works Art Exhibition, organised annually by *Sligo Art Gallery* were generally of a high standard. The selectors this year were painter, Campbell Bruce, sculptor, Jackie McKenna, and Alexander Moffat from the Glasgow School of Art. Among the artists whose work was exhibited were **Deirdre Morgan, Gerald Cox, Kirsten Doyle, Helena Gorey, James McCreary, Ann Mulrooney, Caroline Stapleton, Mary Hurley** and **Siobhán O'Leary,** to name but a few.

■ Highlights of 'Just a Glance', an exhibition of contemporary Mexican ceramic sculpture at the *American College*, included **Jorge Marin's** figures and **Miriam Medrez's** allegorical figure studies. The show moved to the *Garter Lane Arts Centre* in Waterford.

Art Diary - July-August

■ The *Boyle Arts Festival's* main exhibition at the Convent of Mercy Complex featured an eclectic mix of works by established academicians, recent art school graduates and local artists. Works by **Sean Fingleton, Mike Fitzharris** and **Veronica Bolay**, were among the most striking. There was also a high standard of sculptural representation with works by **Catherine McCormack Greene, Jim Flavin, Robin Buick** and **Brid Ni Rinn**.

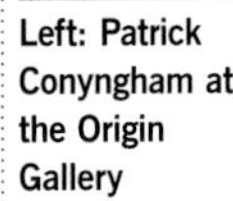

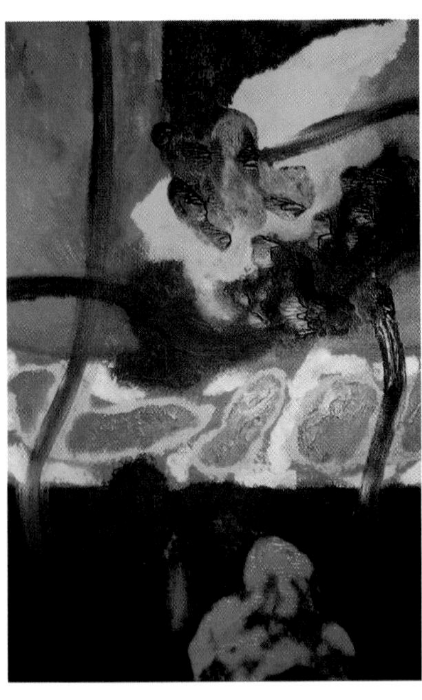

Left: Patrick Conyngham at the Origin Gallery

■ At the *Triskel Arts Centre*, 'Be prepared', an exhibition of the Belfast-based photographer, **John Duncan** took place. The images in this solo exhibition formed part of an ongoing project and all the photographs record journeys made by foot around Beltast. The reading of the Belfast landscape was related to the political atmosphere in Northern Ireland and Duncan's own personal physical sense of unease. This was followed by **Mark Clare's** 'Still Life', an exhibition which reflected Clare's innovative approach to the Irish landscape using the traditional backdrop of sky, sea and mountains with the more contemporary markers of new technologies such as satellites and telecommunications networks.

Right: Pauline Bewick at the Taylor Galleries

August

■ '75 years of giving', the Friends of the National Collections 75th anniversary exhibition of the FNCI, was held to celebrate the major contribution that this organisation has made to Irish Museums and Galleries since its establishment by Sarah Purser in 1924, at a time when there was no state support for developing art collections throughout the country. This exhibition of many of Ireland's valuable treasures was assembled from more than 700 works of artistic importance and historical interest donated to the nation by this organisation to the collections of the *National Gallery of Ireland, Chester Beatty Library, Hugh Lane Gallery, Limerick Museum, Irish Museum of Modern Art* and the *Ulster Museum*. 150 works ranging from paintings, sculpture, carvings, stained glass, silver, furniture, costumes and other artefacts dating from the 16th century up to the present day were on display at the *RHA Gallagher Gallery* and the *Hugh Lane Municipal Gallery of Modern Art*. The exhibition included key works by artists such as **André Lhote, Joseph Albers, Pierre Bonnard, Alphonse Legros, George Roualt, Nathaniel Hone, Sir William Orpen, Walter Osborne, Sean Keating, Augustus John, William Leech, and Jack B Yeats.**

■ Perspective 99, the *Ormeau Baths Gallery* Annual Open Exhibition, went into its second year of existence. The aim of this show was to highlight the diversity and quality of contemporary visual art practice across a wide range of disciplines, embracing photography, painting, sound installation, video, sculpture and performance art. The selector for this show was Philip Dodd, Director of the Institute for Contemporary Arts, London. The exhibition featured the work of **Mark Dale, Kevin Francis Gray, Lizzie Hughes, Ronnie Hughes, Aileen Kelly, Mary Kelly/Abigail O'Brien, Colin McGookin, Shauna McMullan, Carol Murphy, Clive Murphy, Stuart Purdy, Peter Richards, Paul Rooney, David Sheery** and **Theo Sims.**

■ At the beginning of the year, the *Douglas Hyde Gallery* asked for submissions from artists resident in Ireland for an exhibition on the theme of 'utopias'. One hundred and sixty proposals were received, from which seventeen artists were chosen to participate in the show which took place during this month. 'Utopias', curated by John Hutchinson, included sculpture, painting, installation, video, photography, drawing and sound-work. The show brought together a selection of some of the most interesting new work being made by upcoming Irish artists. Artists participating in the 'Utopias' were **Enda Bowe, Gerard Byrne, Blaise Drummond, Brendan Grant, Katie Holten, Paddy Jolley, Alan Lambert, Clare Langan, Peter Maybury, Ronan McCrea, Maurice O'Connell, Marie-Pierre Richard, Eva Rothschild, Orla Ryan, Andrew Vickery, Walker & Walker** and **Grace Weir**. A new venue in Freshford, Co Kilkenny hosted an exhibition by major Irish artists including works by **Brian Bourke, Camille Souter, Paddy Graham** and **Brian Maguire.**

■ At the *Graphic Studio Gallery*, the summer group show took place and included original prints by both Gallery and visiting artists, **Carmel Benson, Felim Egan, Michael Farrell, Alice Hanratty, Taffina Flood, Pauline Macey, Jane O'Malley, Tony O'Malley** and many others. The 'Summer Exhibition' at *Hillsboro Fine Art*, featured a selection of paintings and sculpture by some of Ireland's most important 20th-century artists, including **Arthur Armstrong, Gerard Dillon, Neil Shawcross** and **Camille Souter.** Elsewhere in Dublin, colourful abstract paintings by **Paul Doran** filled the spaces at the *Hallward Gallery* and contemporary works on paper by a wide range of artists including **Damien Hirst, Bridget Riley** and many others were on show at the *Green on Red Gallery*. *Jorgensen Fine Art's* 'Summer Exhibition' included works by **Walter Osborne, Maurice MacGonigal, Colin Middleton, James Cahill, Anna Kostenko, Elizabeth le Jeune** and many others. At the *Temple Bar Gallery & Studios*, 80 small works with an emphasis on colour by Japanese artist, **Toru Kamiya**, went on show. Kamiya has shown extensively in Japan and this series of new paintings were produced while on a residency at the Temple Bar Studios.

■ At the *West Cork Arts Centre*, sculpture by artists including **Vivienne Roche, Alice Maher, Eilis O'Connell and Maud Cotter** featured. Participating artists at the Group exhibition at the *Sligo Art Gallery* included **Brian Bourke, Sean Fingleton, Bernadette Kiely, Mary Lohan, Paki Smith** and **Nancy Wynne Jones.**

■ A busy and varied exhibitions programme formed a significant part of this year's Kilkenny Arts Festival. Brazilian artist, **Ana Maria Pacheco**, who is currently Associate Artist with the National Gallery, London, showed both paintings and sculptures during the festival. Renowned locally-based painters **Bernadette Kiely and George Vaughan** exhibited landscape paintings in the *Grennan Mill*, Thomastown, together with the acclaimed English painter, **Michael Porter**. The work of all three artists for this show was firmly rooted in their experience of the natural world. Exhibiting in the Lower Gallery at the *Mill*, were **Gus Mabelson**, ceramic artist, and **Lorna Donlon**, weaver. The work of **Ruth Rogers**, a recent graduate in painting from the National College of Art and Design, and recipient of an award from the Cap Foundation, was on show at the train station in Kilkenny town. The breathtaking Kells Priory was the venue for a major exhibition of works by emerging and established Irish-based sculptors, centred around the work of a major international sculptor. This year the major artist was **Barry Flanagan,** world renowned and acclaimed for his large scale sculptors of hares. Among the other twenty artists exhibiting were **Martina Galvin, Michael Quane, Christine Mackey, Saturio Alonso** and **Dick Joynt**. The *Upper Stableyard*, a new venue in Freshford, hosted a group exhibition of works by major Irish artists including **Brian Bourke, Camille Souter, Paddy Graham** and **Brian Maguire**. At the *Rudolf Heltzel Gallery*, the work of **Paula Bastiaansen** featured and American artist **Petah Coyne**'s intricately woven horsehair sculptures were exhibited at the *Butler Gallery* in Kilkenny Castle. The Kilkenny Archaeological Society presented a major exhibition of the art of the Irish miniaturist from 1650 to 1830, with particular emphasis placed on the work of **John Comerford,** who was born in Kilkenny c.1770.

Henry Moore from the Hugh Lane Municipal Gallery of Modern Art

■ At the Taylor Galleries Pauline Bewick was preparing for the September opening of an exhibition of her recent work.

Dogs and Celtic Deities
Pre-Christian Stone Carvings in Armagh

Helen Lanigan Wood

suggests that the subjects of a group of idols are drawn from Irish mythology

A collection of stone carvings in Armagh Cathedral includes five which are generally accepted as pre-Christian. Two of these are of animals and the other three are human representations. One of the latter is exhibited in the nave of the cathedral; the rest are kept in the cathedral chapter room alongside carved stones of medieval and post-medieval date, some of which may have belonged to the cathedral before it was restored in the 19th century. It is not known how or why the supposedly pre-Christian carvings came to be stored in the cathedral.

Formerly, there were three animals (Fig 6) in Armagh Cathedral, each a different size,[1] but the smallest one was stolen some years ago. Generally described as bears and probably carved by the same hand, their bear-like characteristics are at best ambiguous and the animals appear to have as much in common with dogs as with bears. While the stance of the small missing animal has been compared with that of a stone bear from Limoges in France,[2] its general appearance and well-preserved ears and snout are as much suggestive of a dog as a bear. Similarly, the other two animals (Figs 1 and 2) with their long forelegs, narrow hind legs and badly-damaged ears and snouts, could as convincingly represent dogs as bears. A noteworthy feature on the largest animal (Fig 1) is an unmistakable canine head with recognisable ears and snout, carved in relief on both sides of a panel set between the big animal's front and back legs.[3]

Whether as dogs or bears, the stones can be linked with religious beliefs and rituals relating to animals which were prevalent throughout the Celtic world. Bears were revered among the Continental Celts, probably for their strength and potency. One of the divinities associated with them was the goddess Artio, whose name means bear, and who may have acted both as guardian of bears and protector of humans against them.[4] The latter role, however, was probably not relevant in Armagh, there being no evidence that bears were still extant in Ireland at the time these carvings were made. Dogs, on the other hand, featured prominently in Irish mythology and were strongly associated with the mythical hero, Cú Chulainn (Cú meaning hound), who in turn is identified with the Celtic god, Lugh.[5] Dogs had an important function throughout the Celtic world for hunting, guarding and fighting and there is also some evidence from Britain and the Continent that they were sacrificed and buried

1. Large Carved Animal. Pre-Christian. Probably sandstone. 50 x 60 cm. (Armagh Cathedral). One of two stylistically-similar animal carvings in Armagh Cathedral, the precise origin of the sculptures is unknown. A noteworthy feature is the canine head carved, on both sides, underneath its body.

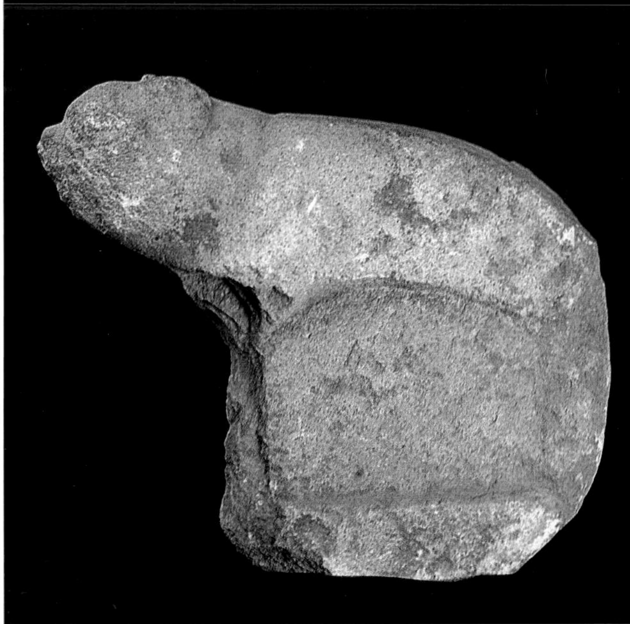

2. Smaller Carved Animal. Pre-Christian. Probably sandstone. 46 x 54 cm. (Armagh Cathedral).Traditionally described as bears, the author argues that the sculptures, with long forelegs, narrow hind legs, ears, and snouts, are much more likely to be dogs.

(Opposite) **3.** Carved Figure with Horse's Ear. Medieval or post-Medieval. Probably sandstone. 71 x 51 cm. (Armagh Cathedral). The figure is crudely carved on two stones. The face is particularly grotesque and the body is naked except for a curved loin cloth in the form of a raised band with parallel hatching. This figure probably represents an Irish version of the King Midas story.

4. Carved Figure. Uncertain Date. Unidentified Stone. 50 x 25 cm. (Private Collection). The symbolism of this figure is similar to that of the *Tanderagee Idol* (Fig 6). The object which the figure grasps in his right hand may be intended as an elbow socket. The small tubular object held in the left hand compares with a similar feature in the *Tanderagee Idol*.

(Opposite) **5.** Carved Idol. Pre-Christian. Probably sandstone. 54 x 38 cm. (Armagh Cathedral). This powerful carving is one of the most remarkable pagan idols in Ireland. It is known as the *Tanderagee Idol* because in 1912 it was brought from Armagh Cathedral to Tanderagee and kept there for a time.

for ritual purposes.[6] Sometimes only their skulls were deposited and sometimes dog meat was part of ritual food offerings. Dogs were also the subject of sculptures[7] and at Lydney Park beside the river Severn in Gloucestershire numerous dogs were found among the votive objects at the Romano-Celtic temple dedicated to the god Nodons.[8] The Armagh animals may have had a similar cult function.

The most remarkable of the Armagh carvings is known as the *Tanderagee Idol* (Fig 5) because it was brought from Armagh Cathedral to Tanderagee in 1912 and kept there for a time at the rectory.[9] It is a carving of considerable strength, the work of a skilled and original artist, comparable in quality with a few other early stone masterpieces such as the three-faced Corleck head from county Cavan and the well-known two-faced idol from Boa Island in Fermanagh.

A clue to the meaning of the *Tanderagee Idol* may be found in the way the right arm is shown stretched over a small tube-like protuberance on the upper left arm. It could represent the god Nuadhu, the Irish equivalent of the god Nodons in Romano-Celtic Britain, who was associated with healing, hunting and the sun. Early Irish legend relates how Nuadhu, king of the Tuatha Dé Danann had his arm severed by the Fir Bolg warrior, Sreang, at the first battle of Moytirra.[10] Because a king had to be without blemish, Nuadhu was then deposed. However, seven years later the physician, Dian Céacht, made him a silver arm, enabling him to make a successful return to power. This may be the moment of triumph captured in the *Tanderagee* sculpture, the mythical god/king clad in his horned helmet, his eyes set in a dignified stare and displaying the new arm for all to see.

An alternative interpretation holds that the figure represents the mythical Ulster hero, Conall Cearnach.[11] In the Ulster Cycle, there are two stories about Conall fighting in single combat against warriors with only one arm; to make the fight more fair Conall ties one of his hands to his side.[12] In one of the stories, a text written down in the 10th-llth centuries, Conall kills the one-handed Leinster king, Meas Geaghra, and has his brains cut out, mixed with lime and made into a brain-ball. Conall then brings the brain-ball to the court of King Conchobhar Mac Nessa at Eamhain Macha (Navan Fort in county Armagh) but later it is stolen and used as a missile to inflict a serious wound on the king, one which eventually killed him. The protuberance shown in the right hand of this figure could represent a brain-ball and this would strengthen the case for identifying this carving as a representation of Conall Cearnach.

There is a third possible interpretation of the hand placed on the shoulder. An account in the *Táin Bó Cualnge*, that great epic tale of the Ulster cycle, describes how Conall Cearnach suffered a dislocated shoulder.[13] Conall was guarding Ulster when the young Cú Chulainn arrived, eager to win fame, and offered to take his place. Conall not only scorned his impudence but also insisted on accompanying Cú Chulainn southwards to protect him. To prevent this, Cú Chulainn cast a stone, which broke Conall's chariot in two and caused him to fall out and dislocate his shoulder.

57-1935

Another stone figure (Fig 4) which was at one time in Armagh is now in private hands. Its symbolism seems identical to that of the *Tanderagee Idol* although it is a much inferior sculpture.[14]

A plausible reason for the different identifications of these carvings has been provided by the archaeologist, Richard Warner,[15] who has suggested that the mythological tales, originally part of an oral tradition, were changed to suit the locality in which they were recounted. Carvings such as the *Tandaragee Idol* would have been known to the storytellers in the Armagh area although their original symbolism might have become forgotten. Each storyteller would provide his own explanation of the idols; in one region it might refer to the god Nuadhu, in another to the ancestor god, Conall Cearnach.

The two remaining idols in the chapter room of Armagh Cathedral, one a carved head (Fig 8), the other a small figure (Fig 7), may represent sun-gods, although damage to the carved head makes its identification uncertain. Both have what look like sun rays emanating from their faces.[16] The rays on the small figure are particularly convincing and suggest that this figure could represent Lugh, the great Celtic deity and mythological hero. One of Lugh's epithets was 'leathshuanach' (side-mantled) and the explanation given for this, that 'a red colour used to be on him from sunset till morning', has been convincingly interpreted as a reference to the sun at dawn and evening.[17] There is also a reference in one narrative to the brilliance of Lugh's face being like that of the sun.[18] Lugh is linked with both Nuadhu and Cú Chulainn and may even have been coupled with the god Apollo, whose attributes included healing and hunting and who was also a sun god.[19]

Another stone carving (Fig 3) in Armagh Cathedral,[20] probably of later date, also draws its inspiration from a legendary source, this time from an Irish version of the King Midas story, a legend which occurs not only in Greek and Roman culture but also in many folktales throughout the world. Two Irish versions are known, the earliest one, about the semi-historical king, Labhraidh Loingseach, surviving in a text which may be as early as the 8th century.[21] In this tale King Labhraidh Loingseach, in order to conceal the blemish of having horse's ears, used to kill his barbers after they discovered his secret. When the turn came for a widow's only son to cut the king's hair, she sought the king's mercy and he promised to spare her son provided he did

6. CARVED ANIMALS. Pre-Christian. Probably sandstone. (Armagh Cathedral). The smallest carving was stolen some years ago. It has been suggested that the animals as well as the pre-Christian human figures (Figs 4, 6 & 8) are all from the same school of sculpture if not by the same sculptor.

(Opposite) **7.** CARVED SUN GOD IDOL. Pre-Christian. Probably Sandstone. 66 x 34 cm. (Armagh Cathedral). This may represent the great Celtic deity, Lugh, whose affinity with the sun is suggested on this figure by clearly-defined rays emanating from the face.

8. CARVED HEAD IDOL. Pre-Christian. Possibly limestone rather than sandstone. 31 x 23 cm. (Armagh Cathedral). The head, although badly damaged, may possibly be identified as a sun god on account of what looks like rays emanating from the face. In this respect the head may be compared to Fig 8.

not reveal what he saw. Later the burden of the secret made the son ill and to obtain a cure he was advised to tell the secret to a particular willow tree. The wood from this tree was later used to make a harp and when the harp was played it told everyone about the king's blemish. The Armagh carving may depict the final part of the story when the king displays his ears for all to see.

In the other Irish version of the story, which survives in a 10th-century text, the king is called Eochaid and the unfortunate youth selected to cut his hair is called MacDichoim. Sapling trees eventually reveal the king's deformity and he removes his golden crown to reveal the horse's ears.

In the collections of Armagh County Museum there is a stone head with horse's ears which is almost certainly another version of King Labhraidh or King Eochaid.[22] Both versions are likely to be medieval or post-medieval in date, and perhaps illustrate the enduring influence of Irish mythology in the Armagh area.

The presence of these pre-Christian idols in Armagh has prompted suggestions that there was a pagan sanctuary on the site of the present cathedral. However, the evidence to support this theory, drawn mainly from place-names and the archaeological remains of a hill-top enclosure on the site,[23] is weak and the carvings themselves, being transportable, are by no means securely associated with the site of the cathedral. However there is some stylistic evidence that the idols belong together as a group,[24] and further geological research, if it establishes that the rock for the carvings came from the same source, could lend support to the case.[25] If, as it is here suggested, the animals depict dogs, they could be symbolic of the same gods represented by the other three idols, that is the apparently interchangeable gods such as Lugh, Nuadhu, and their equivalent god/heroes in Irish mythology, Cú Chulainn and Conall Cernach.

Did these idols belong to a shrine or temple which incorporated healing and other cults comparable with those surrounding the god Nodons in Romano-Celtic Britain? Did they come from a place of worship on either the cathedral hill or on another site in the vicinity of Armagh? It is tempting to look towards Emain Macha (Navan Fort) where there may have been a sanctuary, shrine or temple,[26] perhaps even a temple of Apollo,[27] but there is no evidence that the stone carvings ever came from there.

Helen Lanigan Wood is the Curator of Fermanagh County Museum and author of Images of Stone: Figure Sculpture of the Lough Erne Basin *(1976, 1985).*

Acknowledgements: I am very grateful to the photographer, Anne Cassidy, for taking all but two of the photographs;I would like to thank Dr Patrick J McKeever for all the geological information; and Richard Warner for reading this article in draft and for his helpful comments.and suggestions.

1 The maximum height of the largest animal is 53 cm maximum length 60 cm. The maximum height of the middle-sized animal is 46 cm, maximum length 54 cm.
2 A Ross, *Pagan Celtic Britain* (London and New York 1967), pp. 349, 380-81, pls 84a, 84b and 85b.
3 It could be a dog's or a wolf's head.
4 M Green, *Animals in Celtic Life and Myth* (London 1992), pp. 217-18
5 D Ó hÓgáin, *Myth, Legend and Romance: An Encyclopaedia of the Irish Folk Tradition*, (London 1991), p. 131.
6 Green (as note 4), pp. 24, 66.
7 Green (as note 4), p. 111.
8 Ross (as note 2), pp. 176-78, fig 120.
9 There is conflicting and inconclusive evidence about its history. One suggestion is that it was found in a bog near Newry. See A Kingsley Porter, 'A Sculpture at Tanderagee', *Burlington Magazine* (Nov 1934), p. 228. Another suggestion is that it came originally from Armagh. See T G F Paterson and O Davies, 'The Churches of Armagh', *Ulster Journal of Archaeology* (1940), p. 90.
10 Ó hÓgáin (as note 5), pp. 326-27.
11 Ó hÓgáin (as note 5), pp. 101-3. Conall Cearnach is identified as an ancestor-hero of the Conailli who occupied north Louth in Early-Christian times and also had branches in parts of counties Armagh and Down.
12 Ó hÓgáin (as note 4), pp. 101-2.
13 C O'Rahilly (ed), *Táin Bó Cualnge* (Dublin 1970), pp. 165-6.
14 Paterson and Davies (as note 9) p. 91, pl x. This figure is slightly smaller (50 cm high) than the *Tanderagee Idol*. Its right hand is stretched across to the upper left arm where it grasps a small circular joint with a central hole which may represent an elbow socket. The left hand is holding a small tubular object similar to that held by the right hand of the Tanderagee figure.
15 Personal communication.
16 The 'rays' on the carved head are incomplete because of damage to the left side, and it is possible that what is represented here is hair rather than sun rays.
17 M MacNeill, *The Festival of Lughnasa* (Dublin 1982), p. 6.
18 M MacNeill (as note 17), p. 5.
19 R Warner, 'Navan and Apollo', *Emania*, vol. 14 (1996), pp. 77-81.
20 The Labraidh or Eochaid figure is 71 cm high and is crudely carved on two stones, the upper one wider and thicker than the lower. The face is particularly grotesque, breasts are prominently shown and the body is naked except for a curved loin cloth in the form of a raised band with parallel hatching. There is a crude rope moulding along the bottom edge of the stone.
21 A Kingsley Porter, 'A Relief of Labhraidh Loingseach at Armagh', *Journal of Royal Society of Antiquaries Ireland* (1931), pp. 142-50.
22 Carved on a rough block of stone, this stone was set into a gable wall at 15 Dawson Street in Armagh, not far from the cathedral. Museum registration no 1966.130. I would like to thank Roger Weatherup for helping me to locate this stone.
23 C Gaskell Brown and A E T Harper, 'Excavations on Cathedral Hill, Armagh 1968', *Ulster Journal of Archaeology* (1984), pp. 109-61.
24 E Rynne, 'Celtic Stone Idols in Ireland', *The Iron Age in the Irish Sea Province: C.B.A. Research Report* 9 (1972), pp. 79-98. Rynne's belief that the idols in Armagh Cathedral are from the same school of sculpture, if not by the same sculptor, is justified by some of the comparative evidence he presents, in particular the remarkable similarity between the fingers/claws of the *Tanderagee Idol*, the 'sun-god' figure and the two remaining animals.
25 According to Dr Patrick J Mc Keever of the Geological Survey of Northern Ireland who examined the Armagh Carvings, a precise identification of the rock used in these idols will not be possible until layers of grime and some protective coatings are removed. However, the animals and the sun-god figure appear to be made of the same kind of fine to medium-grained buff coloured sandstone. The *Tanderagee Idol* also appears to be made of similarly grained sandstone but it was not possible to determine its original colour. It is also difficult to determine the rock of the carved head idol (Fig 4) and it may be made of limestone rather than sandstone. Armagh city is built on a small area of sandstone although much of the surrounding countryside is made of limestone.
26 C J Lynn, 'Comparisons and interpretations', *Excavations at Navan Fort 1961-71* (Belfast 1997), pp. 220-21, 228-30.
27 Warner (as note 19).

An Ulster Sculptor
Sophia Rosamond Praeger (1867-1954)

Catherine Gaynor

describes the life and work of a long-lived artist

1. *Sophia Rosamond Praeger in her studio.* Praeger bought her studio, which she called St Brigid's, in Holywood, Co Down in 1913 with the proceeds of sales from her sculpture, *The Philosopher* (Fig 5). The plaster in the background (right) is *Two's Company* (cat no 63).

Sophia Rosamond Praeger, named after her paternal grandmother, Sophia, was born on 17 April 1867 in Holywood, county Down, the only daughter of Maria Ferrar Patterson and Willem Emil Praeger and the third of their six children.[1] Her life was to span nine productive decades before she would find a final resting place in an Ulster glen on 16 April 1954.

Creativity was in the family and it was the driving force behind Praeger's preferred passion for sculpture.[2] Many of the details of her early childhood (her father died when she was fourteen) are obscure but valuable minutiae are contained in a memoir by her uncle, W H Patterson, *Some Family Notes*,[3] and also in the pages of her brother's writings on Irish natural history. It can be inferred from her uncle's writings that the Praeger family was comfortable financially, living at various addresses in or near Holywood on the 'gold coast' of county Down. She probably attended a small private school, similar to the one attended by her brothers,[4] before moving in 1879 to Sullivan School, also in Holywood, where she remained until 1882. Robert Lloyd Praeger (1865-1953), the author of '*The Way That I Went*', was undoubtedly Sophia Rosamond's favourite brother. She would immortalise him in bronze and other media several times during their lifetimes (Fig 4). Like Robert, Rosamond demonstrated a fierce sense of independence and a tenacity that was to endure throughout her lifetime.[5]

Early drawings in charcoal attest to a precocious ability and innate competence and demonstrate that her family's mutely-declared confidence in her artistic ability (in that they allowed her to attend art schools) was well placed. These drawings, one of James Dunlop Barbour, the other of his daughter, Gail Hilda May Barbour, c.1885 (Figs 2 & 3), show a discerning and sympathetic penetration of the sitters' character.[6]

After leaving Sullivan School, Praeger attended the Government School of Art in Belfast from 1883-88 where she studied under George Trobridge, ARCA (1851-1909) and on 4 October 1888, when she was twenty-one, she enrolled at the Slade School in London. Teaching at the Slade was always by artists for artists, and their training was founded on the maxim that constant study from the 'Life model' was essential. Draughtsmanship was a pivotal concern.[7] Alphonse Legros (1837-1911), who was Slade Professor during Praeger's formative years,[8] was an authoritative force in the revival of cast bronze as a medium in England, particularly in the execution of bas-relief and it was his influence which governed Praeger's preferred style and medium.

It is apparent from the records of the Slade that Praeger was a diligent and resolute student and that her application resulted in many college awards, the principal ones being in drawing and sculpture. She gained as many as five prizes in her first year and thereafter won at least a second-class prize for sketching from life annually. Her capacity for expression through line revealed itself later in the more plastic form of sculpture. Praeger's artistic legacy from the Slade and, in particular, from Alphonse Legros who encouraged and nurtured a facility of hand and an acute visual memory for detail, remains evident throughout her career. On leaving the Slade in 1892, Praeger probably went to study in Paris,[9] then considered the hub of artistic developments in Europe, and where sculpture, in particular, was experiencing a dynamic revival in the work of Rodin (1840-1917).

Following her time abroad, Praeger returned to live in Holywood, establishing her studio initially at Donegall Place in Belfast and then at Hibernia Street, Holywood, calling it 'St Brigid's' after a specific work of hers. She divided her time between sculpture, her real passion, and illustration, a more remunerative pursuit. Between 1896 and 1921, she conceived, wrote, and illustrated with line drawings twelve children's story books. The titles and themes were varied and discerning, commencing appropriately with *A Visit to Babyland* (1896), *Adventures of the Three Bold Babes* (1897), *How They Went to School* (1903), and concluding with *Billy's Garden Plot* (1918) and *The Fearful Land of Forgets* (1922). *Billy's Garden Plot*, subtitled *How He Helped the Food Supply in Wartime*, was a moral tale, a soulful reminder of the hardship incurred during the Great War and of the duty of each individual, including the young, to assist the war effort. A manuscript, *The Young Stamp Collectors*, written in the 1940s, but rejected by her publisher, was finally accepted for publication as recently as 1985.[10] The two books upon which she collaborated with her brother, Robert, *Open Air Studies in Botany* (1897) and *Weeds; Simple Lessons for Children* (1913) are not merely indicative of an adeptness in rendering pure line but also demonstrate her acute visual recall and understanding of nature as experienced in the field.

Praeger's sculpture, the less remunerative but more essential aspect of her creative *oeuvre*, began to receive public recognition shortly before the outbreak of the First World War. She worked in a variety of media, modelling in clay and plaster, casting in bronze, and carving in stone. With regard to stone, she used marble, sandstone, limestone, granite, Caen, and Portland stone. Occasionally she employed mixed media, such as lead over concrete, seen in the group study entitled *Two Seated Children*. Only

(Top, right). **2.** Sophia Rosamond PRAEGER: *Portrait of James Dunlop Barber*. c.1885. Charcoal on paper. (Holywood Public Library).This early drawing by the artist was done when she was about eighteen and is evidence of her precocious talent.

(Bottom, right). **3.** Sophia Rosamond PRAEGER: *Portrait of Gail Hilda May Barber*. c.1885. Charcoal on paper. (Holywood Public Library). The sitter was the daughter of James Barber who was a friend of Praeger's uncle, William Hugh Patterson, and fellow patron of the Belfast Art Society.

rarely did she combine form with colour in the shape of her coloured plaster reliefs.

'Sculpture itself is not a paying line', she is quoted as saying, 'for though it receives much appreciation it is too expensive to prove popular' but, she added, 'it is such delightful work, I ... (had) to take it up ...'[11] At this time, her perceptive depiction of a young toddler seated deep in thought captured international attention. *The Philosopher* (Fig 5) exhibited for the first time in plaster at the Liverpool *Autumn Exhibitions* in 1912 and in marble at the RA in 1913, was, in effect, her *magnum opus*, a creation which liberated her from the more lucrative occupation of author and illustrator and encouraged her to spend more time exploring the possibilities of expressing herself in three dimensional form. The financial rewards she reaped[12] permitted her to purchase a premises in Holywood in December 1913. The property, which she named St Brigid's, consisted of two working studios, one large with a shed to the rear and the other a smaller space, adjoined by a 'little walled garden.'[13] Aesthetically pleasing, the studio was also practical as it could accomodate life-size figures, moulded archways for public buildings, plaster casts of fountains, and a host of individual plaster or stone objects, depending on current commissions or demand.

In her professional and public life, Praeger exhibited the qualities of independence, self-reliance, and competitiveness that are more normally attributed to a male artist but, at the same time, she choose to remain narrowly within the 'Woman's sphere'[14] which is most clearly demonstrated in her abundant representations of children. In her private life, Praeger steered a course diametrically opposed to most other women of her time in that she remained unmarried. This was, however, common among women artists.[15]

Aspects of Praeger's personality can be deduced from surviving newspaper reviews and articles, from memories of those who sat for her, and from letters which have survived.[16] She was, at once, 'friendly, shy, blunt, outspoken, sympathetic, and kindly.'[17] She was remembered as an outstanding woman, as much for her personal qualities as for her artistic achievement. John Hewitt, author of *Art in Ulster*, and sometimes a fellow committee-member with Praeger,[18] recalls that 'Miss Praeger was altogether different...with a distinguished air...assured but not pompous or absurd, she carried the dignity of a good breed with her...' He describes two incidents where his own credibility as an art critic was called into question by her. He had, on the first occasion, 'with the rashness of youth', referred in print to her small plaster-children as 'confections'. To this, she rejoined with a withering reproach in the form of a satirical caricature of him.[19] The second occasion was in 1951 after he published his book, *Art in Ulster I*, in which he failed to include Wilhelmina Geddes. Praeger was of the opinion that he had managed to omit Ulster's most important artist.[20]

4. Sophia Rosamond PRAEGER: *Bust of Robert Lloyd Praeger* (1865-1953). Bronze miniature, 30 x 20 x 10 cm. Cat no 5b. (National Gallery of Ireland). The sitter was the sculptor's brother. Author of *The Way That I Went*, he was an eminent botanist and President of the Royal Irish Academy. His book, *Open Air Studies in Botany* (1897), was illustrated by his sister.

5. Sophia Rosamond PRAEGER: *The Philosopher*. c. 1920-22. Marble, 43.2 x 16.3 x 22.5 cm, Cat no 55E (Ulster Museum, Belfast). Donated by the sculptor to the Museum in 1929, this was her second marble version of the enormously popular statuette which she first modelled in 1908 and which was subsequently reproduced very extensively.

Praeger was a lifelong friend and intimate ally of Wilhelmina Geddes whom she referred to as 'Daisy' in her correspondence. She was quick to see the potential in Geddes's vigorous, powerful, drawings[21] and she brought them to the attention of Sarah Purser (1848-1943). It was through Purser, founder of *An Tur Gloinne* (a studio factory for the manufacture of stained glass) that Geddes came to take up stained glass. Praeger, more closely associated with the artistic community in Belfast, ultimately achieved a respect there similar to that which Purser attracted in Dublin.

As regards her sculpture, Praeger appears to have found a niche in the market and the means to fill that niche with her small genre works. She refers frequently in her correspondence to the 'doll factory' which was the workshop where multiple copies of *The Philosopher* and other images of children were reproduced in different sizes and materials. It is not known where exactly the 'doll factory' was located but it was probably in Belfast: Wilhelmina Geddes wrote to Sarah Purser in 1916, '...Miss Praeger is here (Belfast) often, that is

6. Sophia Rosamond PRAEGER: *Riddel Hall Memorial.* 1915. Bronze bas-relief, 57 x 152.5 cm. Cat no 26 (Arts Council of Northern Ireland). The sculpture was commissioned by the Queen's University, Belfast as a memorial to Eliza and Isabella Riddel who bequeathed their home to Queen's University as a residence for women. It was subsequently purchased by The Arts Council of Northern Ireland.

considering she lives so far away (Holywood). She is not idle, her *doll factory* seems to be getting on well and she has found a very good forewoman ...'[22]

A significant number of Praeger's sculptures which were executed in plaster have survived. For the most part, whether bas-relief or in the round, they are finished in white, either heightened with a wash or glazed, but several have a bronze paint finish and some of her bas-reliefs have been polychromed. A work entitled *St Brigid of Kildare*,[23] a version of which hung inside the door of her studio,[24] was exhibited by Praeger at the Belfast Art Society in 1904. The catalogue included the information, 'Della Robbia Pottery, Very Durable', thereby linking Praeger to the Della Robbia pottery which had been established in Birkenhead in 1893 and was centred around many of the leading exponents of the Arts and Crafts Movement including William Morris, William Holman Hunt, Ford Maddox Brown, and Robert Anning Bell.[25] The pottery based its tin-glazed earthenware relief plaques and hollowware on the established techniques and practices of the *Quattrocento* artists, Lucca and Andrea Della Robbia, whose palette of white on a blue ground with some passages of yellow and green they also imitated. Two of Praeger's works, now located in her local church in Holywood (cat nos 24A and 47), are executed, like the *St Brigid*, in the Della Robbia style. Two artists in particular amongst the Della Robbia group, both designers for the pottery, influenced Praeger: Robert Anning Bell (1863-1933), director of the Liverpool School of Art and Architecture and Ellen Mary Rope (1855-1934), modeller and sculptor. Praeger called one of her sculptures *Harvest* (Fig 15) and it seems to have been directly inspired by a work of Bell's.[26] The proximity of Birkenhead to Liverpool is noteworthy as Praeger took part in the *Autumn Exhibitions* at the Walker Gallery in Liverpool during the years 1901, 1903, 1905, and 1906, a period which coincided with the existence of the Della Robbia Pottery in Birkenhead and it seems likely that Praeger and Rope were acquainted. In a letter from Geddes to Purser in 1926, Geddes – who was then living permanently in London and working in a stained glass studio – comments that '...I wonder why glass people in adjoining studio keep to themselves so? I should never have known the Ropes were it not for the Praeger connection.'[27]

Rope, who also trained at the Slade, had exhibited with the Liverpool *Autumn Exhibitions* from 1886 to 1915, showing approximately thirty-seven works during this period. Her work was invariably executed in bas-relief and a close examination of her sculpture would indicate that Praeger was greatly influenced by the older woman's work.[28] Several of Rope's titles reappear as titles of works by Praeger at a later date. These include *Boy on Dolphin*, *Child Angel*, *The Guardian Angel*, *A Dream of the Sea*, *A Rush through the Surf*, *Children Piping*, and *Mother and Child* relief.

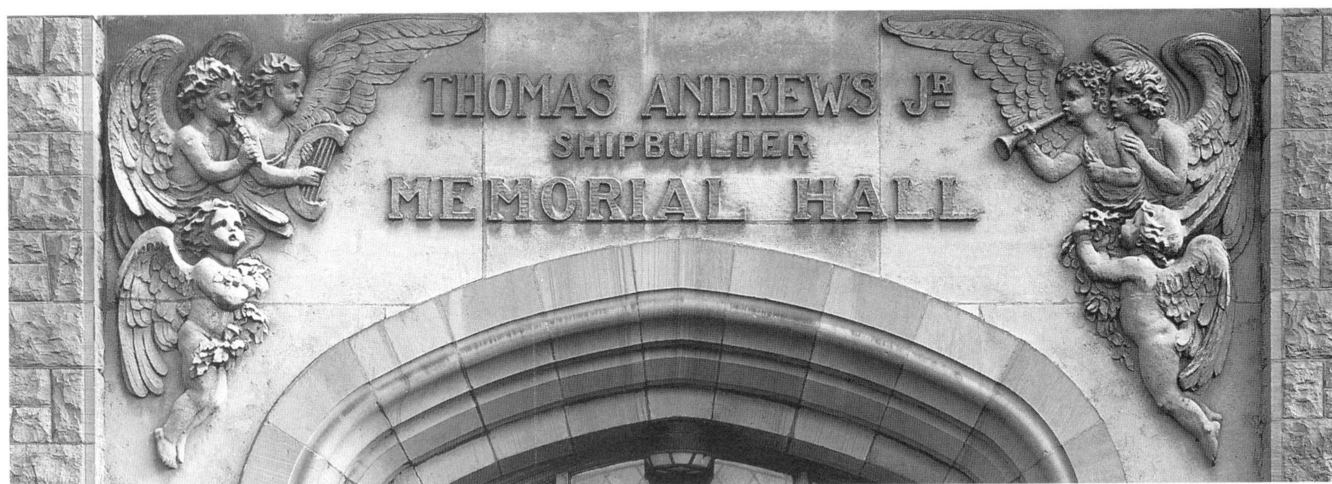

7. Sophia Rosamond PRAEGER: *Andrews Memorial Hall.* 1928. Portland Stone, Cat no 16 (Comber, Co Down). The spandrels of trumpeting angels on either side of the inscription are the work of Praeger. The hall was built in honour of those who died in the Great War and commemorates Thomas Andrews who, as the Managing Director of Harland and Wolff, drowned on the Titanic.

8. Sophia Rosamond PRAEGER: *Angel Lunette.* Plaster polychromed, 30 x 14 cm. Cat no 47. (Holywood Non-Subscribing Church, Co Down). The sculpture, which has the form of a lunette, is finished in the Della Robbia style which Praeger first used about 1904.

9. Sophia Rosamond PRAEGER: *Carnegie Library Spandrels.* Sandstone. Cat no 32. (Carnegie Library, Falls Road, Belfast). The three figures represent (from left to right) Art, Literature, and Science. Modelled by Praeger, they were carved under her supervision by a Mr Winter.

10. Sophia Rosamond PRAEGER: *The Shawls.* 1930. Limestone. 109 x 51 x 9 cm. Cat no 36. (Bangor Heritage Centre, Co Down). By the time she carved this relief, Praeger was very well established in Ulster art circles and her work was both popular and well-known.

11. Sophia Rosamond PRAEGER: *The Fairy Fountain.* 1901. Marble, 66 x 77 x 15 cm. Cat no 45B. (Ulster Museum, Belfast). The sculpture was intended by Praeger as a fountain and she drew her inspiration from one of her poems, 'The Gully'. The group of two elves to the left was repeated by the artist in her sculpture, *The First Aeroplane.*

12. Sophia Rosamond PRAEGER: *Finola and the Children of Lir.* c.1915. Plaster. (Ulster Museum, Belfast). Existing in several versions, the sculpture was commissioned by two sisters, Helen and Beatrice McNaughten, for the Community School, Bushmills.

13. Sophia Rosamond PRAEGER: *Looking West.* 1910. Plaster bas-relief, 31.5 x 24 cm, Cat no 39 (Ulster Folk and Transport Museum, Cultra, Co Down). The work is no doubt intended to refer to the theme of emigration. The figure of the child is similar to one of the elves in *The Fairy Fountain* (Fig 11).

14. Sophia Rosamond PRAEGER: *Working model for the Maitland-Beath Memorial* . 1932. Plaster polychromed, 79 x 32cm. Cat no 24 (Holywood Non-subscribing Church, Co Down). This is the plaster working model for the stone Maitland-Beath Memorial (Fig 16).

15. Sophia Rosamond PRAEGER: *Harvest.* Plaster polychromed. 107 x 68 x 7 cm. Cat. no 41 (Ulster Folk and Transport Museum, Cultra, Co Down). Coloured in ochre and brown, this may be the sculpture entitled *The Sheaves* which the artist exhibited at Mill Hall in 1930.

Throughout this period Praeger was alternating her commissioned public works with imaginative subjects and remarkable portrait studies which were sincere attempts at rendering character. If Praeger was devoted to her creative output as a sculptor, she did not neglect the importance of administration involved in the arts. The steady progress she experienced in her creative life was recognised in a complementary manner by leading members of the artistic community. In 1920, John Lavery nominated her as a member of the Belfast Art Society, an exhibiting body with which she had enjoyed a long association since she had first exhibited there in 1888. She exhibited regularly, seldom missing a year, and she also contributed on an administrative level over her lifetime. She was elected as vice-president in 1902, a year in which her uncle, William Hugh Patterson, served as President, and again in 1903, 1906, and 1907. Her organisational and administrative skills found their penultimate expression in 1930 when the Belfast Art Society became the Ulster Academy of Arts and Praeger was included among the twelve nominated Founder-Academicians. In the following year, Queen's University conferred an Honorary MA degree on her, recommending in the Senate Minutes that 'the degree of *Honoris Causa* be conferred on Miss Rosamond Praeger. She is one of the senior members of the artistic community in Ulster. Her studies of child life are remarkable not only for their artistic merit but for their fidelity.'[29]

Acclaim on the academic front was to resonate in the public sphere when, early in 1939, Praeger, was awarded an MBE. Perhaps the supreme artistic accolade for a Northern artist was when, in 1940, Praeger was elected as President of the Ulster Academy of Arts, a role she fulfilled for two consecutive years. Praeger was also a constant exhibitor at the Royal Hibernian Academy and a less frequent participant in the Royal Academy. In 1927, the RHA elected her an Honorary Member in recognition of her continued and committed contribution to the Arts. Another exhibiting body, not formerly associated with Praeger, is the Liverpool *Autumn Exhibitions*. It is of interest that her most popular work, *The Philosopher*, was shown for the first time at this venue before any of her more usual exhibiting venues and was not purchased.[30]

16. Sophia Rosamond PRAEGER: *Maitland-Beath Memorial*, 1932. Caen Stone, 122.5 x 47.5 x 10 cm. Cat no 24B (The Royal Maternity Hospital, Belfast). The work was commissioned by the Maitland-Beath family.

17. Sophia Rosamond PRAEGER: *Drinking Fountain*. c.1912-14. Bronze, 90 x 40 x 20 cm. Cat no 50 (Bangor Heritage Centre, Co Down). This early sculpture is in a pronounced Art Nouveau style with sinuous stems on either side rising to tulip flowers and a cherub sitting on the top.

Praeger held several joint exhibitions, the first with her close friend, Wilhelmina Geddes, in Belfast in 1924, and another with Hans Iten in Mills Hall, Merrion Row in 1930. She also exhibited that year at the *Exposition d'Art Irlandais* in Brussels, showing two works along with fellow artists, John Hughes, Albert Power, Oliver Sheppard, and Rose Brigid O'Brien. Praeger held an 'At Home' exhibition jointly with Morris Harding in her studios in Holywood in July 1937.[31] Public recognition continued to manifest itself. In 1943, Praeger was invited to sit in on an advisory committee for the Council for the Encouragement of Music and the Arts in Northern Ireland, CEMA. Praeger thought very highly of this body, about which she commented in 1950 that *it has taken us a long time to accept art in Ulster as part of the life of the people, but I think I have seen a gradual awakening…There are several young people doing good work in Northern Ireland and although I know they consider me old-fashioned and although I do not like some of the trends today, it is a good thing to see a lively interest being taken in the Arts, CEMA, I think, is doing a fine job…*[32]

The year 1953 saw Praeger, now in her eighty-sixth year, with her indomitable will and determination unaltered, still maintaining an interest in art. The studio she had so diligently acquired had become physically inaccessible and she relinquished it[33] with sadness. She died peacefully at her home in Craigavan on April 16 1954 in her eighty-seventh year.

Praeger's contribution to Irish sculpture was significant. It would appear to be easy to dismiss her work as 'confections' or 'trivial', even 'ephemeral', or to classify it along with other women's work as 'sentimental' and therefore unworthy of a fair appraisal. However, by establishing a niche as a woman sculptor and identifying a market for amiable domestic-type imagery alongside her large commissioned work, Praeger was able to maintain her autonomy in the art world.

Sculpture was essential to Praeger, she maintained that 'it's part of my life, I couldn't stop it.'[34]

CATHERINE GAYNOR MA *is a graduate of the Department of the History of Art, University College Dublin. She practices as a fine art consultant.*

1 Her eldest brother, William Emilius Praeger (1864-1936) was to distinguish himself in the field of biology. Emigrating to the USA c.1884, he graduated from Illinois University in 1900 with a degree in science. He was appointed Professor of Biology and Geology at Kalamazoo College in Michigan in 1905. His early education was in Holywood and then at The Royal Belfast Academical Institute, a pattern followed by all of her brothers. A bas-relief portrait of William was executed by Sophia Rosamond, its exact location is unknown. Robert Lloyd began his distinguished career as a civil engineer, moving in 1893 to Dublin and the post of Assistant Librarian in the National Library of Ireland. He had a profound interest in the study of nature from an early age, particularly in the fields of botany, zoology, geology, and archaeology. He published widely on all these subjects, acquiring an international reputation, and ultimately he was elected President of the Royal Irish Academy in 1931. Henry John, or Harry, as he was affectionately known, followed directly after Sophia in the family line. He was closely followed by Egmont Apjohn (1873-1919) and Owen Maurice (1874-1905), of whom very little historical data is known. Harry emigrated to California, USA, married Bessie Huiskamp and they had one son Donal. Egmont (1873-1919), like his sister, Sophia, lived in Holywood with his mother and was 'devoted to yachting.' He served as Sub-Lieutenant in the Navy during the First World War (1914-1918), being honourably discharged with diabetes towards the end of the war. She immortalised him and several of his comrades in a bronze bas relief, located in the entrance portico of their Non-Subscribing church in Holywood. Her youngest brother Owen, a medical doctor of whom very little else is known, died at a young age in Belfast in 1905. T Collins, *Floreat Hibernia* (Dublin 1985), p.14.

2 Her uncle, William Hugh Patterson (1835-1918), showed annually with the Belfast Art Society from 1888-c.1915, serving several terms on the committee, as vice-president in 1899 and 1900 and as President in 1901. He was one of the original members of the Board of Governors in the Belfast School of Art founded in 1870, a seat he occupied for thirty years.

3 W H Patterson, *Some Family Notes* (Belfast 1911).

4 R L Praeger refers to Rev Dr Macalister's school in Holywood in *A Populous Solitude* (Dublin 1941), p. 36.

5 He recalls in *A Populous Solitude* (1941) that 'sometimes we wandered far off into the unknown ...we left Holywood and crossed over the hills by way of Craigauntlet to Dundonald, four miles distant, where we feasted sitting on top of the grassy Norman motte by the church. Thence towards Belfast and through by-roads to Strandtown, where dwelt a hospitable aunt, with whom we were fain to tarry. Finally, northward three miles toward Holywood and super-bodily sustenance was of high importance in those days – and half a mile from home, footsore though not famished, we were met by my mother and an aunt, on their way to the police station to sound a general alarm.' The book is dedicated 'To my sister.' In their adult lives, Rosamond executed all of the line drawing in Robert's other volumes concerning the natural sciences, including *The Irish Naturalist* (1892) and *Open Air Studies in Botany* (1897).

6 James Barbour was an old schoolfriend of Praeger's uncle, William Hugh Patterson.

7 J Fothergill, 'The Principles of Teaching Drawing at the Slade,' *The Slade School. A Collection of Drawings and Some Pictures done by Past and Present Students of the London Slade School of Art, 1893-1907* (London 1907). Also quoted, 'Some Women Art Students At The Slade: 1895-9', *Art History*, vol 9, no 2 (June 1986).

8 Praeger owned *Etude de Tête*, a sanguine drawing by Legros which she lent to the BAS for exhibition in 1899. She bequested it to Belfast Corporation and it is now in the collection of the Ulster Museum.

9 The earliest reference is in her uncle's publication, *Some Family Notes* (as note 3), p. 80. He notes the schools she attended and the fact that she went to Paris to study. If Praeger studied in Paris during the 1890s, she may well have attended the Academie Julian, the extant women's registers are in private hands, however, and it has not been possible to gain access to them.

10 Subsequently, Praeger gave the book in manuscript form to Gordon, the son of her friend, John Vinnycomb. This work was finally published in 1985 and a small percentage of the profit of each book sold was donated appropriately to the Save the Children Fund. *The Young Stamp Collectors* (1985).

11 G Duns. 'An Irish Lady Sculptor's Studio', *The Lady of the House* (1914), p. 7.

12 Praeger herself estimated in 1943 that approximately 20,000 cast copies of *The Philosopher* were sold.

13 J Hewitt, 'James Stoupe to Rosamond Praeger,' *Saturday Miscellany* (1956).

14 For further information on the 'Women's Sphere', see W Chadwick, *Women, Art and Society* (London 1990), pp. 210-35.

15 Harriet Hosmer, America's most powerful neo-classical sculptor, held very strong views on the role of female artists: 'Even if so inclined, an artist has no business to marry. For a man, it may be well enough, but for a woman, on whom matrimonial duties and cares weigh more heavily, it is a moral wrong, I think, for she must either neglect her profession or her family...so I wage eternal feud with the consolidating knot ...' C Streifer Rubinstein, *American Women Sculptors* (Boston 1990), p. 36.

16 Approximately one hundred letters from W Geddes to S H Purser, dated 1915-1940, MS 10201, S Purser Papers, NLI. Two Letters from S R Praeger to S H Purser, MS 10201, S Purser Papers, NLI. One further letter from Praeger to Purser not accounted for in the Praeger-Purser file but in the Geddes Purser file, MS 10201, NLI.

17 *Irish News and Belfast Morning News* (3 Jany 1939).

18 Praeger sat on an advisory committee with John Hewitt and others on the Council for the Encouragement of Music and Arts in Northern Ireland, CEMA.

19 J Hewitt (as note 13). The drawing is not extant, Hewitt himself misplaced it.

20 J Hewitt (as note 13). Praeger is recorded by Hewitt as having written to him about this omission. For further information on W Geddes see N Gordon-Bowe, 'Wilhelmina Geddes, *Irish Arts Review*, vol 4, no 3 (1987), pp. 53-59.

21 W Geddes exhibited with BAS between 1907 and 1910 and again between 1925 and 1928. Praeger exhibited with this body yearly from 1888 on and Purser exhibited occasionally with the BAS exhibiting *Le Petit Dejeuner* by special invitation in 1910. Praeger's attention had been drawn by Beatrice Elvery to Geddes's drawing.

22 Letter from W Geddes to S Purser, MS 10201, S Purser Papers, NLI.

23 The Ulster Museum has a version of this work (Cat 4720). It has not been possible to view this or other Praeger works in the collection as they were in storage and unavailable.

24 Interview with author and local historian, C Auld, Holywood, Co Down (Nov 1995).

25 For further information on the Della Robbia Pottery, see B Tattersall, 'The Birkenhead Della Robbia Pottery,' in *Apollo*, no 97 (Feb 1973), pp. 164-8.

26 The First Issue of *The Studio* (1893), p. 44 and p. 53 includes an anonymous article, 'A New Treatment of Bas Reliefs in coloured plaster.' The article features two bas-relief reproductions by Bell, *Honeysuckle*, and *Harvest* in which the quotation by Praeger is discernible.

27 Letter from Geddes to Purser dated 1926, Purser Papers, MS 10201, NLI. The address 404C, Fulham Road, London, SW is registered to Rope in RA and LAE records after 1914.

28 The Williamson Gallery in Birkenhead, Liverpool houses a large collection of Rope's work, executed for the Della Robbia Pottery, in which it is possible to discern Praeger's source.

29 Recorded in the Senate Minutes, The Queens University, Belfast (1 Apr 1938).

30 *The Philosopher* (original marble) had initially been offered by Praeger to her local corporation, but was rejected by them. It was subsequently purchased by an American who saw it at the RA in 1913.

31 A copy of the invitation is among the Praeger Papers in the Ulster Museum.

32 *Belfast Newsletter* (15 May 1950).

33 Praeger bequeathed her smaller studio to her friend and fellow sculptor, Morris Harding and his daughter Rita – who had assisted Praeger with casts – for the duration of their lifetime. She bequested the larger studio to the children of Holywood. Originally, it was her wish that it would be used as a solarium, where children would benefit from the use of UV ray treatment, for physiotherapy, for art classes, and also as a hall for various children's functions. The terms of the will rendered this option inoperative, and the studio reverted into her residuary estate.

34 *Belfast Newsletter* (15 May 1950).

ABBREVIATIONS: BAS: *Belfast Art Society*. LAE: *Liverpool Autumn Exhibition*. MH: *Mills Merrion Row, Dublin. Exhibition of works by Rosamond Praeger (and Hans Iten), 1930*. PEH: *Praeger Exhibition, Holywood, 1975*.

PORTRAIT BUSTS

1 MONA ALEXANDER ALYMER. 1941. Plaster 40.5 x 22.5 x 16 cm. *Family descent to present owner. Private Collection.*

2 MISS E. M. MCCORMICK. 1947. Bronze. 49.5 x 26.5 x 12 cm. *Ulster Folk and Transport Museum, Cultra, Co. Down.*

3 ROBERT LLOYD PATTERSON, 1907. Inscr: *R. Ll. P.* and *S.R.Praeger*. Bronze 27 x 18 x 10 cm. Exh: BAS 1897 no 175; RHA 1909 no 386; PEH 1975 no 59. *Donated by the Artist to the South Eastern Education and Library Board Holywood Public Library.*

4 WILLIAM HUGH PATTERSON, MRIA. 1896. Medium unknown. Exh: BAS 1896 no B (under Sculpture).. *Location unknown.*

5a ROBERT LLOYD PRAEGER. 1907. Plaster 30 x 22.5 x 10 cm. Exh: BAS 1907 no 174A; RHA 1909 no 387. *By decent from the artist to the RIA. The Royal Irish Academy, Dublin.*

5b ROBERT LLOYD PRAEGER. 1907-1909. Inscr: *R. LL. P.* Bronze 30 x 22 x 10 cm. Exh: RHA 1909 no 387. *Purchased Belfast, Mrs E. Carrothers, 1963. National Gallery of Ireland.*

5C ROBERT LLOYD PRAEGER 1928-29. Inscr: *S.R.Praeger*, and *S.R.* verso. Plaster (bronzed) 70.5 x 40.5 x 27 cm. Exh: RHA 1929 no 447. *By descent from the artist to the RIA. Royal Irish Academy, Dublin.*

6 A NEAPOLITAN. Medium unknown. Exh: RA 1891 no 1950; BAS 1892 no 410. *Location unknown.*

7 BUST OF A FEMALE. Plaster (bronzed) 36 x 12 x 14 cm. *Presented by the artist to the South Eastern Education and Library Board. Holywood Public Library, Co. Down.*

8 ITALIAN BOY. Plaster 46 x 20 x 17.5 cm. Exh: PEH 1975 no 60. *Presented by the artist to the South Eastern Education and Library Board. Holywood Public Library, Co Down.*

BAS-RELIEF PORTRAIT BUSTS.

9 SIR EDWARD CARSON. c.1920. Bronze. *Commissioned by the Northern Ireland Government. St Anne's Cathedral, Belfast.*

10 EDWIN LAWRENCE GODKIN. Bronze 61 x 48.5 x 2.5 cm, inset 24 x 9 cm. *Entrance Hall, Lanyon Building, Queens University Belfast.*

11 LORD EDWARD MACNAGHTEN. 1913-15. Plaster 18 in diam. *Commissioned by the MacNaghten Family. Causeway School Museum, Co. Antrim.*

12 PETER. 1944. Inscr: *Peter* and signed *S.R.Praeger*. Plaster 30 x 22 x 2 cm. Exh: PEH 1975 no 23. *Commissioned by the Family. Private collection.*

13 RT. HON. SIR ANDREW MARSHALL PORTER, BT. 1948. Limestone 45 x 44 x 5 cm. *Commissioned by Queens University, Belfast. Entrance hall, Lanyon Building, Queens University, Belfast.*

14 ELLISON ANNESLEY VOYSEY. 1938. Inscr: *Ellison Annesley Voysey*, signed *S.R. Praeger. 1938*. Plaster 32.4 x 20 cm. *Purchased at auction, by present owner. Private Collection.*

15 MRS DOROTHY WEAVING. c.1930-40. Inscr: *S.R.Praeger*. Plaster 28.5 x 21 x 3 cm. Exh: PE H 1975 no 22. *By family descent to the current owner. Private collection.*

MEMORIALS

16 ANDREWS MEMORIAL. 1920. Portland Stone. Exh: PEH 1975 no 120. *Commissioned by Comber memorial committee. Thomas Andrews Jr, Memorial Hall, Comber, Co. Down.*

17 CAMPBELL COLLEGE BELFAST, WAR MEMORIAL. 1922. Sandstone. Exh: PEH 1975 no 126. (photograph) *Commissioned by the Board of Governors, Campbell College, Belfast.*

18 JOHN DOWNEY MEMORIAL. c. 1936-37. Plaster (bronzed) 70 x 96 x 2.5 cm. Signed:. *S.R.Praeger*. Exh: PEH 1975 no 112. *Commissioned by the Governors of Methodist College. Entrance Hall, Downey House Prepatory School, Belfast.*

19 JAMES EWART MEMORIAL. Limestone 91 x 125 x 12 cm. *Commissioned by Sir William and Isabella Lady Ewart. St. Annes Cathedral, Belfast.*

20 MARY GARDINER MEMORIAL. 1928-30. Plaster 40 x 25 x 21 cm. Exh: RHA 1928 no 128 (as *Study for an Angel, plaster*); Mills Hall 1930 no 20 (as *Kneeling Angel*); PEH 1975 no 69. *Presented by the artist, in memory of her cousin. Downey House Preparatory School, Pirrie Park, Belfast.*

21 THOMAS CRAIG GORDON MEMORIAL. Portland stone 99 x 71 cm. Exh: PEH 1975 no 108. *Commissioned by John and Agnes Gordon. Stormont Presbyterian Church, Co. Down.*

22 HAMILTON HARTY MEMORIAL. 1945. Granite 183 x 66.5 x 66.5 cm. Exh: PEH 1975 no 107. *St. Malachi's Parish Church, Hillsborough, Co. Down.*

23 HOLYWOOD NON-SUBSCRIBING PRESBYTERIAN CHURCH, WAR MEMORIAL. c1920. Bronze 49 x 92.5 x 2.5 cm. *Commissioned by members of Holywood Non-Subscribing church. Holywood, Co. Down.*

24 A MOTHER AND CHILDREN (MAITLAND-BEATH MEMORIAL). 1932. Inscr: *S.R.Praeger*. Plaster (polychromed) 79 x 32 cm. Exh: RHA 1933 no 336. *Presented by the Artist. Non-Subscribing Presbyterian Church, Holywood, Co. Down.*

24B MAITLAND-BEATH MEMORIAL. 1932. Inscr: *S.R.Praeger*. Caen Stone 122.5 x 47.5 x 10 cm. *Donated by Mrs R. Maitland Beath. The Royal Maternity Hospital, Belfast.*

25 PRAEGER FAMILY MEMORIAL. Sandstone 164 x 153 (archive); 136 x 153cms (inset). Inscr: *In Memoriam Patris Mei, S.R. Praeger fecit*. Exh: PEH 1975 no 130. *Erected by the Artist. Priory Graveyard, Holywood, Co. Down.*

26 RIDDEL HALL MEMORIAL. 1915. Bronze 57 (65.5 inset) x 152.5 x 5 cm. Exh: Mills Hall 1930 nos. 32 and 33; PEH 1975 no 100. *Commissioned by Governors of Queens University, Belfast. Entrance Hall, Arts Council of Northern Ireland, Riddel Hall, Stranmillis Rd, Belfast.*

27 JOHN ROGERS MEMORIAL. c.1934. Plaster 18.5 x 72.5 cm. Exh: PEH 1975 no 29. *Presented by the artist. Sullivan Upper School, Holywood, Co. Down.*

28 WORKMAN MEMORIAL. Plaster (coloured) 40 x 32 x 6 cm. *Presented to Folk and Transport Museum in 1967. The Folk and Transport Museum, Cultra, Co. Down.*

PUBLIC WORKS

29 CHERUBS. Portland stone approx 29 x 22 cm each. Exh: PEH 1975 no 114. *Commissioned by St. Anne's Cathedral. St. Anne's Cathedral, Belfast.*

30 WOMANHOOD CAPITAL. Portland Stone. *Commissioned by St Anne's Cathedral. St. Anne's Cathedral, Belfast.*

31 WISDOM CAPITAL. 1928. Portland stone. *Commissioned by St. Anne's Cathedral. St. Anne's Cathedral, Belfast.*

32 ARCHITECTURAL SPANDRELS. Sandstone approx 88 x 60 cm. *Commissioned by the Carnegie Library. Carnegie Library, Falls Road, Belfast.*

33 INSETS FOR DOOR. Lead 47.5 x 38.5 cm. *Commissioned by the Carnegie Library. Central Library, Belfast.*

34 MOTHER AND CHILD MEDALLIONS. Portland stone. 59.5 cm diam. Inscr: *Praeger*. Exh: RHA 1932 no 377. *Commissioned by The Royal Victoria Maternity Hospital, Belfast. Royal Maternity Hospital, Belfast.*

35A THE NEW BABY. Plaster 167 x 90 x 20 cm. *Presented by the Artist. Children's Wards Ulster Hospital, Dundonald, Belfast.*

35B THE NEW BABY. Stone approx 167 x 90x 20 cm. *Commissioned by the Jessop Hospital, Sheffield. The Jessop Hospital Sheffield, England.*

35C THE NEW BABY. Bronze 167 x 90 x 20 cm. Exh: PEH 1975 no 111 (photograph). *Presented by Miss Edith Tate. Entrance Hall Ulster Hospital, Dundonald, Belfast.*

IDEAL WORKS

36 THE SHAWLS. 1930. Limestone 109 x 51 x 9 cm; 90 x 34 cm (inset). Exh: Mills Hall 1930 no 30; PEH 1975 no 105. *Donated by the Artist. Bangor Heritage Centre, Bangor, Co. Down.*

37 SADIE. 1907. Bronze 73 x 61 cm. Exh: PEH 1975 no 117. *Presented by the Artist to the School. Causeway School Museum, Bushmills, Co. Antrim.*

38A FINOLA AND THE CHILDREN OF LIR. c.1915. Limestone 89 x 132 x 9 cm; 83 x 120 x (inset). Signed: *S.R.Praeger*. Exh: BAS 1915 no 139; PEH 1975 no 118. *Commissioned by Hon. Helen & Beatrice MacNaghten. Causeway School, Bushmills, Co Antrim.*

38B FINOLA AND THE CHILDREN OF LIR. 1915. Plaster (polychromed) 80.5 x 94 x 7 cm. Inscr: *S.R.Praeger*. *Donated to the Folk Museum by person unknown. Cultra, Folk and Transport Museum, Co. Down.*

38C FINOLA AND THE CHILDREN OF LIR. 1913-15. Plaster (bronzed) 49 x 32 x 3 cm. Exh: RHA 1921 no 345; Mills Hall 1930 no 37. *Donated by the Artist in 1926. Vice-Chancellors office, Queens University, Belfast.*

39 LOOKING WEST. Plaster 31.5 x 24 cm. Inscr: *Looking West*, signed *S.R.Praeger*. Exh: BAS 1910 no 243. *Donated by the McCormick Family in 1967. Cultra, Folk and Transport Museum, Co. Down.*

40 PATRIC ON SLEMISH. Plaster 44.5 x 21 cm. Inscr: *S.R.Praeger, Patric on Slemish. Purchased at Auction 1994. Cultra Transport and Folk Museum.*

41 HARVEST. Plaster (polychromed) 107 x 68 x 7 cm. *Donated by Holywood Social Club, 1980. Ulster Folk and Transport Museum, Cultra, Co Down.*

42 FAITH HEALING. Plaster 33 x 41cm. Inscr: *S.R.Praeger*. Exh: BAS 1900 no 92; RHA 1901 no 377; BAS 1915 no 140; PEH 1975 no 24. *Presented by the Artist to Downey House. Downey House Preparatory School, Methodist College, Belfast.*

43 BOYS BATHING. Plaster 28 x 17 cm. Inscr: *S.R.Praeger*. Exh: RHA 1927 no 331; PEH 1975 no 26. *Donated by the Artist to Downey House. Downey House Preparatory School, Methodist College, Belfast.*

44 FEEDING THE BIRDS. Plaster 2.5 x 17.5 cm. Inscr: *S.R.Praeger*. Exh: PEH 1975 no 4. Downey House Prep School, MCB.

45A THE FAIRY FOUNTAIN. c.1900-01. Plaster 66 x 77 x 15 cm. Inscr: *S.R.Praeger*. Exh: RA 1901 no 1773: LAE 1901 no 1627 (relief plaster); BAS 1901 no 178, 1923 no 280; RHA 1902 no 349; PEH 1975 no 11 (marble). *Donated by the Artist to Downey House. Downey House Prep. School, Methodist College Belfast.*

45B THE FAIRY FOUNTAIN. c.1900-01. Marble 64.8 x 76.5 x 16.5 cm. Inscr: *S.R.Praeger*. *Purchased from the Artist in 1926. Ulster Museum, Belfast.*

46 DOWN THE HILL. Plaster 30 x 19.5 cm. Inscr: *S.R.Praeger. Purchased by the present owner at auction, c1980s. Private collection, Belfast.*

47 ANGEL LUNETTE. Plaster (polychromed)approx 30 x 14 cms. Inscr: *S.R.Praeger. Presented by the Artist to her Practicing Church. Non-Subscribing Presbyterian Church, Holywood, Co. Down.*

48 A RAPSCALLION. Medium and size unknown. Exh: UA 1936. *Unlocated.*

49 THESE LITTLE ONES. Plaster. Exh: RA 1922 no 1307 (marble); LAE 1922 no 1551 (green marble). *Unlocated.*

DRINKING FOUNTAINS

50 WALL FOUNTAIN. 1912-14. Bronze 90 x 40 x 20 cm. Exh: BAS 1912 no 108; Mills Hall 1930 no 31; PEH 1975 no 32. *Donated by the Artist to her local council. Bangor Heritage Centre, Bangor, Co. Down.*

STATUES

51A JOHNNY THE JIG. Plaster 91 x 44 cm, overall height 208 cm. *Donated by Paul and Elizabeth Morton. Bangor Castle Heritage Centre, Bangor, Co. Down.*

51B JOHNNY THE JIG. Bronze on granite plinth 91 x 44 cm, overall height 208 cm. *Funded and Realised by the S. Rosamond Praeger Memorial committee. (Exterior to) Children's Playground, Holywood, Co Down.*

52A A WAIF. 1905. Bronze 71 x 27 x 26 cm. Inscr: *S.R.Praeger, 1905.* Exh: RA 1905 no 1796; LAE 1905 no 1712 (plaster version); RHA 1906 no 307 (bronze); BAS 1908 no 336. *Presented by the Artist in 1926. Hugh Lane Municipal Gallery of Modern Art, Dublin.*

52B A WAIF. Bronze 72 x 727 x 25cm. Exh: PEH 1975 no 53. *Presented by the Artist to Holywood Urban Council. Holywood Library, Holywood, Co. Down.*

53 SHEILA. Bronze. Exh: BAS 1916 no 188. *Location unknown*

54A SAFETY FIRST. 1931. Plaster 17.5 x 9.5 x 6 cm. Inscr: *S.R.Praeger, 1931.* Exh: RHA 1932 no 388; PEH 1975 no 44. *Purchased by the present owner. Private Collection.*

54B SAFETY FIRST. 1932. Ballycullen stone 44 x 23 x 21 cm. Exh: RHA 1932 no 388; RHA 1936 no 406. *Commissioned by Mrs Nancie Heyn-Darling. Private Collection.*

55 THE PHILOSOPHER. Exh: BAS 1912 no 107, 1913 no 298, 1920 no 300; LAE 1912 no 2154 (plaster), 1922 no 1558 (marble); RA 1913 no 1999 (marble); RHA 1913 no 555; Mills Hall 1930 no 7 plaster bronzed); Exposition D'Art Irlandais 1930 no 275 (marble); CEMA 1953 no 60; CAS 1967 (no numbers); PEH 1975 no 52 (bronze).

55A THE PHILOSOPHER. Plaster (bronzed) 48 x 16.5 x 22.5 cm. Inscr: *S.R.Praeger. 'The Philosopher'. Presented by the Artist to her local borough Council. Public Library, Holywood, Co. Down.*

55B THE PHILOSOPHER. Plaster 27.5 x 15 x 11 cm. Inscr: *S.R.Praeger. The Philosopher. Presented by the artist to Downey House. Downey House Preparatory School, Methodist College, Belfast.*

55C THE PHILOSOPHER. Plaster 13 x 7 cm. *By Family descent. Private collection.*

55D THE PHILOSOPHER. Marble. *Purchased by an American collector in 1913. Museum and Art Gallery, Colorado Springs, USA.*

55E THE PHILOSOPHER. Marble 43.2 x 16.3 x 22.5 cm. Inscr: *S.R.Praeger. The Philosopher. Presented by the Artist in 1929. Ulster Museum, Belfast.*

SMALL STATUES

56 THE FIRST AEROPLANE. Plaster 17.5 x 16.5 x 12 cm. Inscr: *S.R.Praeger. 'The First Aeroplane'.* Exh: RH.A 1927 no 302; Mills Hall 1930 no 19; PEH 1975 no 45. *By descent to present owner. Private Collection.*

57A BABY. Plaster 42 x 23 x 16 cm. Exh: BAS 1909 no 23; Mills Hall 1930 no 35; PEH 1975 no 111 (Photograph, bronze version). *Presented by the Artist to Sullivan Upper Preparatory Dept. Entrance Hall, SUllivan Upper Prep Dept, Holywood, Co. Down.*

57B BABY. Plaster 21 x 9 x 6 cm. *By family descent to the present owner. Private Collection*

58 BOOKEND: BOY AND GIRL (a pair). Plaster 18 x 11 x 10 cm (each). Inscr: *S.R.Praeger.* (each). Exh: PEH 1975 no 42. *Presented by the Artist to her school. Headmaster's office, Sullivan Upper School, Holywood, Co. Down.*

59 DAPHNE. 1932. Plaster 25 x 16 x 10 cm. Inscr: *S.R.Praeger, 1932.* Exh: PEH no 64. *Commissioned by Mrs Helen Heyn. Private Collection.*

60 MY FIRST HAT. Plaster 13 x 9.5 cm. Inscr. *S.R.Praeger.* Exh: Mills Hall 1930 no 18; PEH 1975 no 41. *Presented by the artist to Sullivan Upper School, Preparatory Dept. Sullivan Upper Preparatory School, Holywood, Co. Down.*

61 PATRICIA. 1932. Plaster 24 x 9.5 x 7 cm. Inscr: *Patricia Helen.* Exh: Mills Hall 1930 no 28; RHA 1944 no 337; PEH 1975 no 65. *By Family Descent. Private Collection.*

62 RONALD. 1932. Plaster 27.5 x 18.12 cm. Inscr: *S.R.Praeger 1932.* Exh: Mills Hall 1930 no 29; PEH 1975 no 63. *Commissioned by Mrs. Helen Heyn. Private Collection.*

63 TWO'S COMPANY. Plaster 22 x 14 x 9.5 cm. Inscr: *S.R.Praeger. Two's Company.* Exh: PEH 1975 no 49. *By descent to present owner. Private collection.*

64 UP THE STEPS TO HAPPINESS. c.1953. Clay. Terracotta. *Unlocated.*

UNTRACED WORKS

The following works, exhibited at the BAS, the RHA or the LAE, are not included in the catalogue as they are either untraced or unavailable.

1 1892 BAS 40 *The Ancient Mariner*, Medium unknown. **2** 1893 BAS 550 *Silence*, Plaster. 1899 RHA 374 **3** 1894 BAS 439 *Leonie.* (Bas-relief), Medium unknown. **4** 1894 BAS 404 *Study of a Head.* Medium unknown 1895 BAS C 1904 RA 335 **5** 1896 BAS *D L'allegra.* Medium unknown **6** 1896 BAS C *A Penerosa.* (head). Terra cotta. 1896 RA 1860 **7** 1896 BAS A *An Elf.* Medium unknown. **8** 1898 BAS 180 *Bubbles.* Plaster. (relief) 1898 RA 1908 1899 RHA 375 **9** 1898 BAS 194 *Fortune Telling.* Plaster. (relief). 1898 RA 1902 1899 RHA 376 **10** 1899 BAS 232 *Treasure Trove. Plaster.* (relief). **11** 1901 BAS 178 *The Snail Race.* Medium unknown. **12** 1901 RHA 376 *Nora Criona.* (Bush). Plaster bronzed. **13** 1903 BAS 170 *St Brigid of Kildare.* Plaster. (relief). 1903 L.A.E. 1469 1904 BAS 379 (Della Robbia Pottery, Very Durable). 1930 MH 15. **14** 1906 RHA 384 *The Breadwinner.* **15** 1906 L.A.E. 1906 *A Dream Child.* Plaster. **16** 1908 BAS 242 *Scandal.* **17** 1908 BAS 325 *'Craig.'* **18** 1908 BAS 326 *'Kathleen.'* **19** 1910 BAS 245 *By Donegal Bay.* **20** 1910 BAS 246 *The Daughters of J Mc. C. Lowenthal.* **21** 1911 BAS 135 *The Woodcutting.* **22** 1911 BAS 134 *The Woodburning.* **23** 1911 BAS 138 *The Ould Plaid Shawl.* 1911 RHA 507 **24** 1913 BAS 299 *Dick, Son of J. Bagnell.* 1914 RHA 533 **25** 1916 BAS 186 *'Jeffrey.'* **26** 1916 BAS 187 *'Sheila.'* **27** 1916 BAS 189 *Study for a Child's Head* **28** 1917 BAS 232 *Portrait of a Child* **29** 1917 BAS 233 *The West Wind.* Terra cotta. **30** 1917 BAS 234 *The East Wind.* Terra cotta **31** 1920 RHA 338 *'Barbara.'* **32** 1920 RHA 343 *'Jean.'* **33** 1922 RA 1307 *These Little Ones.* Green Marble. 1922 L.A.E. 1551 Marble Group. **34** 1927 RHA 301 *'Pat.'* Plaster Statue. **35** 1927 RHA 303 *Reverse of Campbell Memorial Medal.* Bronze. **36** 1927 RHA 307 *'Anne'.* Plaster Bust. **37** 1928 RHA *Study of a Boys Head.* **38** 1929 RHA 4 **39** *The Fairy Fiddler.* Plaster relief (Copyright reserved.) **40** 1929 RHA 443 *In Galilee.* (Study for group in Marble.) Plaster. (Copyright reserved). **41** 1930 RHA 343 *The Right Hon. C C Craig.* **42** 1930 RHA 354 *Study of a Small Boy.* **43** 1930 MH 1 *The Judge.* (working model for marble) **44** 1930 MH 2 *The Island Man.* Plaster. **45** 1930 MH 4 *Study of a Small Girl.* **46** 1930 MH 8 *The Prayer.* Bronze. 1930 E.d'A.I. 274 *The Prayer.* **47** 1930 MH 9 *Three Little Ones.* **48** 1930 MH 12 *Who's That.* **49** 1930 MH 13 *The Leprechaun* **50** 1930 MH 14 *The Wee Baa.* **51** 1930 MH 16 *Sirocco.* **52** 1930 MH 17 *On The Sea Wall.* **53** 1930 MH 21 *Bedtime.* **54** 1930 MH 22 *Tiny Wee.* **55** 1930 MH 23 *Schemer.* **56** 1930 MH 26 *'Niall'.* (Statuette). **57** 1930 MH 27 *'Stanley'.* **58** 1930 MH 40 *Offerings.* (Small Relief). **59** 1930 MH 42 *St. John.* **60** 1930 MH 43 *Logs.* (Panel in Silver.) **61** 1932 RHA 376 Plaster Figures for Headstone carried out in Bronze. **62** 1935 RHA 415 *The Youngest One.* Plaster. (Copyright reserved.) **63** 1937 RHA 405 *Lead Inset* (for Headstone). **64** 1937 RHA 432 *One of Set of Insets.* **65** 1937 RHA 433 *One of Set of Insets.* **66** 1937 RHA 440 *One of Set of Insets.* **67** 1938 RHA 378 *The Dolphin Race.* Plaster Painted. **68** 1938 RHA 395 *St Fiachre of Ireland,* Garden Saint of France. 1939 RHA 388 *St Fiachre of Ireland,* Garden Saint. **69** 1939 RHA 389 *The Standing Stone.* (Suggested decoration for the Children's Park) **70** 1939 RHA 392 *On the Seashore.* (Coloured plaster relief). **71** 1940 RHA 327 *Mr Justin McNaghten.* (Study for Marble Bust). **72** 1943 RHA 351 *'There are Fairies at the Bottom of the Garden.'* **73** 1944 R.HA. 324 *The Rough Road.* **74** 1975 PEH 1 *Child with Daffodils.* (Plaster relief). **75** 1975 PEH 2 *The Pet Lamb.* (Plaster relief). **76** 1975 PEH 3 *Ring-a-Rosie.* (Plaster relief). **77** 1975 PEH 7 *Apple Orchard.* (Plaster relief). **78** 1975 PEH 14 *Patric at Armagh.* (Plaster relief). **79** 1975 PEH 19 *'Kelsie'.* (Plaster relief). **80** 1975 PEH 20 *Marian McCready.* (Plaster relief). **81** 1975 PEH 21 *'Anne'.* (Plaster relief). **82** 1975 PEH 25 *Boar's Head.* (Plaster relief). **83** 1975 PEH 30 *'They shall return again with rejoicing bearing their sheaves with them.'* (Plaster relief). **84** 1975 PEH 31 *Saint.* (Plaster relief). **85** 1975 PEH 33 *Going to School.* (Plaster relief). **86** 1975 PEH 35 *St. Francis.* (Plaster relief). **87** 1975 PEH 54 *Newel Post.* (Plaster relief). **88** 1975 PEH 58 *Shakespeare.* (Small status). **89** 1975 PEH 61 *Little Mother.* (Small status). **90** 1975 PEH 62 *Christopher.* (Small status). **91** 1975 PEH 66 *Ann.* (Small status). **92** 1975 PEH 67 *Moya.* (Small status). **93** 1975 PEH 68 *John.* (Small status). **94** 1975 PEH 103 *Sullivan.* Stone. **95** 1975 PEH 104 *Mourning Women.* Lead. **96** 1975 PEH 121 *Thomas Andrews Jr. Memorial.* Bronze. **97** 1975 PEH 128 *The Seven Ages of Man.* Stone.

WORKS BY PRAEGER IN THE ULSTER MUSEUM

The number preceding the title is the Museum's catalogue number.

1176 *The Philosopher.* 1908. Bronze (statue). **1177** *The Philosopher.* c.1920 Marble. **1167** *The Fairy Fountain.* c.1900-01. Marble. **2217** *Tug-of-war in Hopton Wood.* c.1934 Limestone. (relief). **2218** *Spring.c.*1934. Limestone. (relief). **2221** *Old Hannah.* C.1900-20. Plaster (bust). **2224** *Child feeding Birds.* c.1900-30. Plaster. (relief). **2226** *Fionnuala.* The Daughter of Lir. C.1910-11. Plaster (relief). **2227** *Fionnuala,* The Daughter of Lir. c.1910-11. Plaster. (relief). **2228** *By Donegal Bay.* C.1910. Plaster. **2229** *Three Figures with Baskets.* 1900-30. Plaster. **2230** *Two Shawls.* c.1930. Plaster. **2478** *Two Seated Children.* 1928-29. Lead over Concrete. **4721** *Two Children.* Plaster. **4713** *Girl with a Baby.* Plaster. **4714** *Pulman Statuette.* Plaster. **4715** *Safety First.* Plaster. **4716** *St. Fiachra.* Plaster. **4717** *Sleeping Boy.* Plaster. **4718** *The First Aeroplane.* c.1927. Plaster. **4719** *The Philosopher.* Plaster. **4720** *St. Brigid of Kildare.* Plaster.

'A Wonderfully-Pretty Rurality' Drawings by Mrs Delany

Ruth Hayden

has discovered a pocket sketchbook by a noted chronicler of 18th-century Ireland

'The poverty of the people makes my heart ache, I never saw greater appearance of misery; they live in great extremes, either profusely or wretchedly.' These observations were made by Mrs Pendarves, later renowned as Mrs Delany (1700-88), when making her first visit to Ireland in 1732. Then a widow, Mary Pendarves was the guest of the Bishop of Clogher and his wife, Mrs Clayton, as they travelled from Dublin to Killala on the west coast of Ireland.

With her observant eye, quick to appreciate all she saw from the carriage window, Mary Pendarves noticed a great deal and she recounted in letters to her sister, Anne, at home in Gloucester, descriptions of the people and the landscapes of Ireland where, a decade later, she was to make her home and to settle so happily. For it was through the Claytons that Mary met Dean Jonathan Swift and his friend, Dr Delany, whom she would marry as his second wife (Fig 12).

1. Mrs Delany's Pocket-book: Red leather, tooled in gold. 13 x 8 cm. (Private collection).The small size of the pocket book allowed Mrs Delany to keep it in her pocket or pouch. It would have been tied with tapes to her waist under her overskirt, through which there was a slit for her hand to pass.

It was with considerable excitement that I was shown, in the spring of 1998, a pocket-sized sketchbook of Mrs Delany's travels when, in 1744 as Dr Delany's bride, she moved from London to take up residence at Delville near Dublin and, in the summer months, near Downpatrick in the north of Ireland.

The little album of drawings (Fig 1), bound in red leather and tooled in gold, has two metal clasps and measures thirteen by eight centimetres; its small size would have enabled Mrs Delany to have kept it conveniently in her pocket or in the pouch which would have been tied with tapes to her waist under her over-skirt through which there was a slit for her hand to pass.

Amongst the fifty-three drawings there is a rich diversity of subjects, from ladies dressed in fine clothes, servants in workaday attire, to desperately poor and barefooted country people. Landscapes include views of Delville, Glasnevin near Dublin, and Hollymount, Downpatrick. Made 'on the spot', the drawings were later used by Mrs Delany as *aides memoires* when she came to prepare the eighty or so detailed landscape drawings that are now in the National Gallery of Ireland. As Mrs Delany dated several of her sketches and as she was writing prolifically to her sister, Anne (who was now Mrs Dewes of Wellesbourne in Warwickshire), at the same time, some can be linked to her letters and made to illustrate her written words.

After their marriage in England in 1743, the Delanys set out for Ireland the following year, staying at inns and at Calwich Abbey, Staffordshire, the country house of Mary's elder brother, Bernard Granville. Not all the overnight accommodation is recorded but halts were made in Barnet and in Leicester where the inn-keeper's wife (Fig 13) is shown dressed in simple cotton or linen attire. Mrs Delany retained a skill in needlework all her life and an interest in fashion; her eye for detail is shown in the three sketches of ladies grandly dressed. Each lady is shown wearing an indoor cap with, in the centre, either the tuck, pinch or ornament which was popular from 1730-60; and each has laceing on her stomacher. *A Modern Lady 1744* (Fig 14), with lace-edged apron over her large skirt, wears a choker at her neck above a gauze handkerchief and has high-heeled buckled shoes: holding a snuff box, her fingers are poised as if having just taken a pinch.

Another lady (Fig 15) wearing evening dress, annotated 'NB head tuckers and ruffles edge with silver lace', is bejeweled with necklaces and earrings and has a wide skirt which would have had a support, possibly of whale-bone, under the dress; she holds a fan. A more mature figure (Fig 4) is dressed formally in a cloak for outdoors with a hood over her cap, a tippet possibly of swansdown, and a rococo border to the skirt.

On arrival at Calwich Abbey the Delanys were joined by Mary's mother, Mrs Granville, and her sister, Anne. Five sketches were made of the beautiful Dovedale district while the Calwich garden features among the more finished drawings now in the National Gallery of Ireland.

By early June the travellers were on their way again, fond farewells having been made, particularly between the two sisters who were devoted to each other. The Delanys set out for a lodging near Chester, stopping overnight at Trentham and Nantwich, in preparation for their embarkation across the Irish Sea. An indication of the hazards of travel in the 18th century is gathered from Mary's comments to Anne: *The roads were very good for we had no occasion to get out of the coach the whole way, the road to Nantwych was rocky ... our inn was a poor one but your excellent chicken furnished us with an admirable repast.*

Unfortunately, Dr Delany fell ill and their embarkation was delayed by two weeks. Jottings at the end of the sketch-book indicate £3.3.0d was paid to the doctor, £1.10.0d to the apothecary and £14.13.3d to the lodging-keeper, 15/-d to the maids (presumably tips), and 5/-d- 'to the horses'.

Once on board, Mrs Delany, with favourable weather at the start of the voyage, 'sat on deck the whole day and ate a very good dinner and an egg for my supper and worked and drew two or three sketches.' *The Master, Mr Cuthbeard* (Fig 3), is drawn with fashionable beaver hat on his bob wig, with a cravat and a full-skinned coat with pleats at the side seams headed by a button. He has a waist-coat, knee-breeches and buckles on his leather shoes. The wind got up and *the ship began to roll, and we were very ill all night, and the next day till about 5 ... they came to the cabin and said we were just entering the bay of Dublin; upon which we got up, and were soon cured by the good weather and fair prospect of landing.*

On arrival at Delville, Dr Delany's small estate of twelve acres, Mary was charmed by all she saw: 'I have traversed the house and garden and never saw a more delightful and agreeable place.' The garden was of particular interest as it was designed on informal lines, influenced by the ideas of Dr Delany's friends, Dean Swift and, more particularly, Alexander Pope, whose garden at Twickenham on the Thames had such appeal with its new natural style of informality.

James Potter, the gardener at Delville, is shown at work in one of Mrs Delany's sketches (Fig 9) with a wide-brimmed hat and flowing hair and wearing an overcoat; other drawings made in the garden show several of the features which she mentions in a letter that describes the garden in detail: *a bowling green, a little brook with hanging woods of evergreen trees, a border of flowers, a wall covered with fruit trees and the greatest quantity of roses and sweet briars I ever saw; towards the bottom is placed our hayrick* (Fig 5), *which is at present making, and from our parlour window and bed chamber I can see the men work on it ... [there] is a terrace walk that takes in a sort of parterre, that will make the prettiest orangery in the world for it is an oval of green, planted round in double rows of elm trees and flowering shrubs with little grass walks between them, which will give good shelter to exotics ... there is a door that leads to another ... handsome terrace ... and the walk well gravelled so that we may walk securely in all weathers ... a pretty portico* (Fig 6), *painted within and neatly finished without.* This idyllic scene ends with a description of fields where the deer and cows are kept, 'and the rurality of it is wonderfully pretty.' A favourite resting place for the couple as they walked round the garden was *'the beggar's hut* (Fig 7) *which is a seat in a rock ... placed at the end of a cunning wild path ... the little robins are as fond of the seat as we are, it just holds the Dean and myself, and I hope in God to have a tete-a-tete there with my own dear sister.*

Earlier in 1744, Dr Delany had been appointed to the deanery of Down so in August the Delanys, wishing to acquaint themselves with the district, set out for a visit of two weeks to stay with friends near Downpatrick. The journey of about seventy miles was of mixed comforts, as notes on the first page of the book indicate: *Thursday dined at Drogheda, Friday at Mrs Hamilton's at Dunleer, pleasant; at Dundalk. So, so – 2 sketches* (Figs 10 & 11); *I lay at Newry, ye dirty inn; dined at Rathfoyland, smoaky house.*

2. Mary DELANY: *A Northern Cabbin.* Pencil on Paper, 13 x 8 cm. (Private collection). Dated 1745. Mrs Delany was not inclined to ignore the poverty around her so she 'made shifts and shirts for the poor naked wretches of the neighbourhood.'

3. Mary DELANY: *Mr Cuthbeard, Master of ye Yacht.* Pencil on Paper, 13 x 8 cm. (Private collection). Dated 26 June 1744. Mr Cuthbeard was Master of the 'Pretty Betty' which was the private vessel of the Viceroy and aboard which the Delanys sometimes travelled.

4. Mary Delany**:** *Lady in a Cloak***.** Pencil on Paper, 13 x 8 cm. (Private collection)**.** She is wearing an outdoor cloak with the serpentine or rococo border which was fashionable in the mid-18th century.

5. Mary Delany**:** *Building a Hayrick.* Pencil on Paper, 13 x 8 cm. (Private collection).This hayrick would have been drawn from Mrs Delany's parlour window. Pastoral scenes delighted Mrs Delany who once described the garden at Delville as 'paradisiacal'.

6. Mary Delany: *Entrance to ye Portico walk at Delville.* Pencil on Paper, 13 x 8 cm. (Private collection). This was the Delany's garden near Dublin. A touch of formality has been introduced to the garden by the arch and niches and it is possible that ivy is growing around them.

7. Mary Delany**:** *Beggars' Hut, Delville.* Pencil on Paper, 13 x 8 cm (Private collection). Dated 14 May 1745. Chaffinches and robins ate from Dr Delany's hand when he and wife sat here. The seat is incorporated into a larger drawing in an album of Mrs Delany's in the National Gallery of Ireland.

8. Mary DELANY: *A Ruin'd Church at Dundalk*. Pencil on Paper, 13 x 8 cm. (Private collection). Dated 31 August 1744. Mrs Delany's drawings of ruined castles and abbeys feature frequently in the pocket-book.

9. Mary DELANY: *James Potter, gardener to the Delanys*. Pencil on Paper, 13 x 8 cm. (Private collection). There is no record of Mrs Delany having actually planted anything herself.

10. Mary DELANY: *Ye Carpenter at Dundalk*. Pencil on Paper, 13 x 8 cm. (Private collection). Dated 31 Aug 1744. He holds an awl in his mouth. Mrs Delany would have drawn this image when she and her husband passed through Dundalk on their journey to Down.

11. Mary DELANY: *At Dundalk*. Pencil on Paper, 13 x 8 cm. (Private collection). Dated 28 May 1744. A poor pregnant mother carries her baby. These illustrations illustrate the disparity between the well-off and the poor in 18th-century Ireland.

Passing through the hills of Newry in the depth of the countryside, Mary must have been sadly disturbed by the ragged figures she saw and drew. Of five sketches from this area, all the people of whatever age appear to be wearing the Irish mantle, a simple woven woollen cloth, and they are barefoot. The following year she drew 'the northern cabbin' (Fig 2) with ropes, both horizontal and vertical, to keep the thatch in place, a ladder and up-turned stool secured to the roof, and a seated figure defined in the doorway.

Arthur Young, the 18th-century agriculturist, wrote in *A Tour of Ireland* that *the cottages of the Irish, which are called cabbins, are the most miserable-looking hovels that can be conceived...The furniture of the cabbins is as bad as the architecture; in very many consisting of a pot for boiling their potatoes, a bit of a table, and one or two broken stools; beds are not found universally, the family lying on straw.* The French traveller, Le Chevalier de la Tocnaye, who published *A Frenchman's Walk Through Ireland*, wrote: *Half a dozen children almost naked, were sleeping in straw with a pig, a dog, a cat, two chickens and a duck. The poor woman spread a mat on a chest, the only piece of furniture in the house, and invited me to lie there. The animals saluted the first rays of the sun by their cries and began to look about for something to eat. The dog came to smell me, the pig put up her snout at me and began to grunt; the chickens and duck began to eat my powder-bag, and the children began to laugh. I got up very soon for fear of being devoured, I should add that I had no small difficulty in making my hostess accept a shilling.*

Mrs Delany was not one to look passively on these signs of poverty, for she wrote to Anne in June 1745: 'After supper I make shifts and shirts for the poor naked wretches in the neighbourhood.' Another cause for anxiety was the prohibition of imports of Irish cloth into England. In November of the same year Mary wrote that 'The poor weavers are starving – all trade has met with a great check this year.'

Realising that she could, in her own modest way, help the weavers, she and 'Mrs Chenevix, the Bp of Killaloe's wife, agreed to go to the Birthday in Irish stuffs.' This had the desired effect, for later she wrote: *On the Princess of Wales' birthday there appeared at Court a great number of Irish stuff, Lady Chesterfield, the Vicereign, was dressed in one, and I had the satisfaction of knowing myself to have been the cause but dare not say so here, but I say 'I am so glad to find my Lady Chesterfield's example has had so good an influence.'*

In the deanery of Down, the Delanys settled in Hollymount (Fig 16) and later moved to another more convenient and larger house, Mount Panther. Generally about three months were spent in the north, varying from May to October. In June 1745,

(Left, top) **12.** Mary DELANY (1700-88)**:** *Dr Patrick Delany, Dean of Down*. Pencil on paper, 13 x 8 cm. (Private collection). Dr Delany was a tutor at Trinity College, Dublin and was made Dean of Down in 1744. He was a friend of Swift and Pope and he introduced the natural style of gardening into Ireland.

(Left, bottom) **13.** Mary DELANY: *Hostess at Leicester*. Pencil on Paper, 13 x 8 cm. (Private collection). Dated 25 May 1744. This is a drawing of an Inn keeper's wife. When travelling the Delanys stayed with relatives and friends or lodged at inns.

Mary describes Hollymount: *This really is a sweet place, the house ordinary, but it is well enough for a summer house ... on the side of one of the hills is a gentleman's house with a pigeon-house...half a mile off is a pretty wood with the finest carpeting, primroses and meadow-sweets...it is called Wood Island* (Fig 17)...*the ruins of an old cathedral are on an eminence just opposite Wood Island from whence I have taken a drawing.*

Picnics and excursions were a favourite pastime when Dr Delany's duties permitted and so there are sketches of 'cats castle near Clogh' and an untitled drawing of what appears to be Ardglass Castle. Mary was increasingly aware of her obligation to get to know the local people around Downpatrick so she entertained enthusiastically: 'On Tuesday sixteen people here at dinner, on Wednesday ten, on Thursday twenty-two.' The younger generation were entertained to small 'drums' at which local musicians would play for the dances.

Enjoyable though Mary found her visits to the north, she was always glad to return to Delville and, taking advantage of any character or building that caught her attention, she continued to fill her book with sketches. A country girl is shown wearing a cotton cap and simple gown in Glasnevin church and an undated view covering two pages (Fig 18) is of the Old Mens' Hospital near Dublin (now the Royal Hospital, Kilmainham).

In June 1747, Dr and Mrs Delany enjoyed a day by the river a few miles from Dublin: *We spent a very pleasant day in the country with Mr and Mrs Lowe at their bleechyard, 9 miles off, near the famous salmon leap of Leixlip. They have a pretty cabin there, and gave us some fine trout.* A call was then made at Mr Conolly's house, now Leixlip Castle, where they walked in the gardens: *They are on the top of a hill, that winds round the river Liffey... wandering paths and steps by degrees carry you down to a winding terrace by the river-side...every step there shows you some new wild beauty of wood, rocks and cascades.* Mrs Delany's illustration (Fig 19), dated 1746, shows the leap with two baskets secured to stakes, each with a salmon.

So immediate is the appeal of the sketches which the talented Mrs Delany made in her pocketbook, and so varied their subject matter, that the volume is indeed a treasure; and, when studied in conjunction with her copious and informative letters, it further brings to light a wonderfully-observant chronicler of 18th-century Ireland.

RUTH HAYDEN is a lecturer on Mrs Delany and the author of Mrs Delany: Her Life and Her Flowers *(1980) and* Mrs Delany and Her Flower Collages *(1992), both published by the British Museum Press.*

ACKNOWLEDGEMENTS:
I am most grateful to the owners of this gem of Mrs Delany's travels for their generosity in allowing me to examine and photograph the book.

14. Mary DELANY: *A Modern Lady*. Pencil on Paper, 13 x 8 cm. (Private collection). Dated 1744. The woman is depicted taking a pinch of snuff. Mrs Delany was interested in all aspects of fashion throughout her life.

15. Mary DELANY: *Lady with a Fan*. Pencil on Paper, 13 x 8 cm. (Private collection). Dated 13 May 1744. Attention to detail, as in this drawing of a lady in evening dress, was typical of Mrs Delany's observant eye. Note the head and tuckers and ruffles edged with silver lace.

16. Mary DELANY: *A View, possibly from Hollymount.* Pencil on Paper, 13 x 8 cm. (Private collection). The Delanys initially settled in Hollymount when Dr Delany was appointed to the Deanery of Down.

17. Mary DELANY: *Wood Island.* Pencil on Paper, 13 x 8 cm. (Private collection). Dated 1745. The Delanys created a wild garden here which became a favourite walk 'finding many pretty spots enamelled and perfumed with a variety of sweet flowers, particularly the woodbine and wild rose.'

18. Mary DELANY: *Old Mens' Hospital near Dublin.* Pencil on Paper, 13 x 8 cm. (Private collection). This is now the Royal Kilmainham Hospital. In 1680 the Duke of Ormonde laid the first stone of the hospital for old soldiers.

19. Mary DELANY: *Leixlip Water Fall and Salmon Leap.* Pencil on Paper, 13 x 8 cm. (Private collection). Dated 1745. Rivers and cascades were a natural source of inspiration in Ireland and England for Mrs Delany's pen.

Academician Supreme
The Paintings of David Hone

Julian Campbell
writes about a former President of the Royal Hibernian Academy

David Hone has been one of Ireland's most prominent portrait painters. Many eminent figures from Irish academic or public life, from scientists and politicians, to bishops and cardinals, have sat for portraits in his studio. He is also highly regarded for his brilliant and sympathetic portraits of children. He has exhibited at the Royal Hibernian Academy nearly every year since 1948, increasing his involvement with the Academy until he served as its President for five years, 1977-1982. Having worked as a painter for fifty years, his work is much more varied in range than might be supposed from his public profile as a portraitist. During his schooldays, for instance he had greatly admired the artists of the Living Art generation and began his career as a landscapist, painting scenes mainly in Connemara, but also in county Wicklow and on the Continent. He is also a still-life painter. In Hone's portraits, the sitter often looks at the viewer directly, with a level gaze. Moreover, although painted in the studio, these portraits are often featured in an open air setting, against a blue or cloudy sky, so that Realism is combined with a heightened dream-like mood.

1. John F KELLY (b. 1921): *Portrait of David Hone*. 1953. Oil on canvas, 45.75 x 35.5 cm. (Collection David Hone). John F Kelly, one of Hone's teachers at the School of Art in the late 1940s, captures the young artist in his mid-twenties in profile. The figure is outlined in thin oil paint, the tonality is monochrome but the planes of the face are sensitively modelled. Hone admires Kelly both as a teacher and a portraitist.

Nevertheless, having been such a central figure within the academic tradition in Ireland, Hone remains something of a shadowy figure within the overall context of Irish art. His work has been little written about by critics and he has not been afforded a retrospective exhibition of his work to date. He was briefly mentioned as an academic artist in Bruce Arnold's *Concise History of Irish Art*, published in 1969, but has received no mention in recent books, such as Theo Snoddy's excellent *Dictionary of Irish Artists, Twentieth Century*; John Turpin's scholarly history, *A School of Art in Dublin since the Eighteenth Century*; or Brian Fallon's provocative book, *An Age of Innocence, Irish Culture 1930-1960*.[1]

This obscurity may be due in part to Hone's own reserved and retiring personality. But it is equally due to the fact that he may be regarded as an academic, a 'traditionalist', and not a 'modernist', which would bear out Dr Philip McEvansoneya's assertion in the 1997 *Irish Arts Review* that many Irish artists of his generation have been marginalised by the new art 'establishment': *Little or no effort has been made to evaluate those artists who have perpetuated established artistic ideas and worked continuously outside avant-garde contexts. Not even artists with the stature of Sean Keating or Charles Lamb... have been given the same detailed appraisal as comparatively minor modern artists.*[2]

The Hone family has played an enormous role in the artistic and cultural life of Ireland over the past two hundred and fifty years. David Hone was born into a literary and artistic milieu in Dublin in 1928. His family is related to the landscape painter, Nathaniel Hone (1831-1917). His father was writer and critic, Joseph Hone (1882-1959), biographer of George Moore and W B Yeats, who had known artists such as Augustus John and Henry Tonks in London in his younger days. David's mother, Vera (née Brewster), was a beautiful woman, who had inspired William Orpen to paint some of his most haunting portraits in the years before the First World War.[3]

Joe Hone's first cousin was painter and stained glass artist, Evie Hone. He knew Jack B Yeats and Beatrice Glenary and other artists would call to the house. David's uncle was the distinguished Ireland cricketer, Patrick Hone.

At about the age of eight David Hone had his first art lessons when Lillian Davidson would visit his preparatory school. He also attended classes at Mainie Jellett's studio. On the walls of his school were reproductions of Paul Henry's West of Ireland landscapes which helped to arouse the young Hone's own interest in landscape. During his school holidays he would visit Henry quite often in his studio in county Wicklow. At secondary school, Hone's art teacher was sculptor, Oisín Kelly, and he was a fellow-pupil of writer, William Trevor.

In this artistic environment, it was natural perhaps that Hone himself should become a painter. Neither feeling the burden of an artistic heritage, nor taking it for granted, Hone seems accepting of his vocation as a painter.

In c.1943 during his teenage years, he sat for a portrait to Frances Kelly. This large canvas, showing the young Hone

2. David HONE (b. 1928): *A Summer's Day in Connemara*. 1947. Oil on board, 32 x 40 cm. (Crawford Municipal Art Gallery, Cork). One of Hone's first landscapes, this picture, which was bequeathed to Cork by the playwright, Dr Lennox Robinson, was painted during his first visit to Charles Lamb in Connemara in 1947.

3. David HONE: *View of College Green Dublin*. c.1948. Oil on canvas, 35.5 x 40.75 cm. (Private Collection). Exhibited at the RHA in 1949. This is an early outdoor study by Hone, painted during his student days. The picture was painted from a rooftop, showing the Bank of Ireland on the left and a tram passing in front of Trinity College on a bright sunny day.

seated with flowers beside him, was exhibited at the *Living Art* but, in retrospect, Hone believes that Kelly's handling of paint and use of colour are sketchy and stylised.

At his secondary school, St Columba's College in Rathfarnham, his art teacher was sculptor, Oisín Kelly, whose significance as a teacher should not be underestimated. Amongst the other occupants of the art room were Patrick Pye; Michael Biggs, later to become a sculptor and letterer; Trevor Cox, who first practised as a sculptor, then, changing his name to 'William Trevor', became the celebrated novelist and short story writer.

Two or three times a year, Hone would cycle from his home in Enniskerry over to Kilmacanogue to visit Paul Henry and his wife, Mabel. Hone believed that in his early days Henry had done some paintings from nature, but later made pencil notes from which he worked in the studio. He would give pragmatic advice to his young visitor, remarking that 'there's no point in painting out of doors because the weather changes all the time.' Hone recognised that Henry was a brilliant technician but that his paintings seemed to be composite pictures taken from different parts of the landscape, rather than views of particular scenes.[4]

Hone started to exhibit early and when he was only seventeen, he exhibited at the *Irish Exhibition of Living Art* in 1945. After leaving school a year or two after the end of the War, Hone directly entered the School of Art in Kildare Street where he studied in the Diploma course in painting. Fees were only £5 a year for full-time students and Michael Burke was Director of the School at that time. According to Hone, the painting staff, which comprised Sean Keating, Maurice MacGonigal, and John F Kelly, was excellent. MacGonigal, he remembers, as being 'up in the clouds', while Keating was 'down to earth', pragmatic, and a consistent teacher. He would assert that 'if you couldn't draw, you couldn't be an artist.' The present writer's mother recalls David Hone's good looks as a young man and he was admired by the girls in the School of Art; some of them referred to him as Shelley because of his romantic appearance.

Library facilities in the School were almost non-existent although, of course, the National

Library was right next door. The School of Art followed the academic system, but this was partly because there was a lack of funds to provide for additional staff. In retrospect, Hone regrets that there were not more gifted young painters, such as Patrick Hennessy, teaching there. Some students came and went, and 'the casualty rate' was high. Amongst 'the regulars' in the life class, along with Hone, were Thomas Ryan, John Coyle, and Michael Morrow. Morrow, whose talents lay in illustration and who became an expert on the history of Early Music, aroused the ire of Keating for his tendency to paint the model green rather than pink. Hone himself worked away steadily, producing numerous life drawings and painting figure studies. His cousin, Evie, was encouraging. At the same time, he sensed that she resented the fact of his being at the School of Art and a student of Keating's, rather than being in Paris studying under Lhote or the painters of the Ecole de Paris.

When asked who he admires, Hone replies immediately: 'Augustus John'. A formative experience during his student days was a visit to England to meet this leading portraitist. Hone's father had known John in his young days and had been painted by him in 1932. The portrait was, Hone recalls, executed in a 'broken' manner, with a 'dream-like quality' about it. Regrettably, Joe Hone could not afford to buy it at the time and the painting is now in the collection of the Tate Gallery. He did, however, gain an introduction for his son and in 1947, at the age of nineteen, David Hone visited John in Salisbury in England and stayed overnight. The elderly artist collected the Irish student at the station and brought him to his house.

John had a purpose-built studio, and was working on a large composition. Offering his visitor a large glass of brandy, he enquired: 'What's the tradition of the painting school in Ireland?'

'The Orpen tradition', Hone replied.

'That's a lousy tradition!' John exclaimed, and turned away.

Fifty years earlier, John and Orpen had both been brilliant students of Henry Tonks at the Slade School and had formed a close friendship, but John had come to resent Orpen. In retrospect, Hone feels that he was too young to visit the studio of a celebrated,

4. David HONE: *Sandymount Strand, Looking Towards Killiney Hill*, c.1978. Oil on canvas board, 63.5 x 76.25 cm. (Private Collection). Hone skillfully captures the impression of clouds on a gusty day as they are reflected in the shadows of Sandymount Strand. With the small flight of seabirds and rippling waves, there are echoes here of the Malahide seascapes by the artist's relative, Nathaniel Hone.

5. David HONE: *Sandymount Strand Looking South*. c. 1978. Oil on canvas, 46 x 61 cm. (Private Collection). The clouds are treated with great subtlety and the figures are larger than is usual in Hone's Sandymount series.

6. David HONE: *Landscape near Carraroe, Co Galway*. 1950. Oil on canvas board, 31 x 41 cm. (Private Collection). This picture was painted on Hone's second visit to Charles Lamb in Carraroe in 1950 and shows Hone's precocious brilliance as a landscapist when still a student. Painted with bold, direct brushstrokes and using bright colours, he conveys a sense of the Connemara landscape on a summer's day.

7. David HONE: *Ringsend Docks, Dublin*. c.1980. Oil on canvas, 30.5 x 35.5 cm. (Collection of the Artist). Hone vividly conveys the image of the tall industrial buildings at Ringsend in shadow and the radiant light reflected off the surface of the docks. As with American artist, Edward Hopper, the view is one glimpsed from a passing train.

(Opposite) **8.** David HONE: *Moeunna Dennis*. c.1980. Oil on canvas, 61 x 51 cm. (Private Collection). In one of his most brilliant studies of children, Hone vividly captures the pretty girl in a yellow dress who is seated upon a grassy bluff in an original pose. The setting of the figure upon a grassy cliff, against sea and cloudy sky, pays homage to William Orpen's figure studies painted on Howth Head in the years before the First World War.

if controversial, artist but the meeting obviously made an impact upon his own later career as a portraitist and he continues to admire John's draughtsmanship, use of colour, and his development from an early academic manner to a more 'painterly style'.

A second important experience during Hone's student days, as for Barbara Warren and other young artists, was his contact with Charles Lamb in Connemara. Lamb ran a summer school at his home near Carraroe. A small group of students, only four or five, would attend each summer. Hone visited twice: once in 1947 and again in 1950, just after leaving college. Most of the students lodged in Carraroe but Hone stayed in Lamb's house and got to know the family well. The traditional life of the Connemara Gaeltacht made a deep impression upon the young Dublin student: picturesque thatched cottages, donkeys and carts hauling seaweed, and women in red petticoats working in the landscape. Lamb and his students went out each day and painted landscapes directly from nature. With Lamb standing at his own easel nearby, it would have been possible to look over his shoulder and copy what he was doing but this would not have been acceptable. However, the influence of Lamb – and indeed that of MacGonigal – painting landscape directly with bold brushstrokes and bright colours, can be seen in Hone's own Connemara landscapes. They have a striking freshness. Several of these were exhibited at the RHA and at the Oireachtas in the late 1940s and early 1950s;[5] Hone also showed the occasional county Wicklow landscape. It was thus as a landscapist, rather than a portrait painter, that he first established himself.

He received his Diploma in painting from the School of Art in 1950. For students and young artists alike, the annual exhibitions of the RHA and *Living Art* were eagerly awaited. Hone found both events stimulating. Although attracted more to the academic tradition, he felt that the Living Art had a distinctive role in this period. It helped to show an Irish audience what was going on in Paris. Sales, however, were poor in both venues and there was a lack of jobs for artists. Earlier, Paul Henry had remarked to Hone that 'you don't have to worry about whether you become an artist; you either are

D. HONE '63

9. David HONE: *Sandymount Strand, Looking Towards Howth*. c.1994. Oil on canvas, 35.5 x 46 cm. (Private Collection). Hone's Sandymount paintings show a sensitivity towards the painting of clouds. He was aware that the treatment here of blue sky and clouds had a close affinity with the atmospheric paintings of his relative, Nathaniel Hone.

10. David HONE: *The Grand Canal, Venice*. 1998. Oil on canvas board, 20.25 x 25.5 cm. (Collection of the Artist). A small oil study painted directly from the motif, Hone captures the bright Venetian light falling upon the palaces and reflecting off the waters of the canal. The artist's relative, Nathaniel Hone, had represented similar views in Venice one hundred years earlier.

(Opposite) **11.** David HONE: *Portrait of Christopher Hone*. c.1957. Oil on canvas, 61 x 51 cm. (Private Collection). Exhibited RHA 1958. An early portrait by Hone of his nephew, Christopher. It is unusual in its profile pose but sets a pattern for Hone's later studies of children in an outdoor setting. Christopher Hone, who was at primary school with the author, is now a government specialist in radiation safety.

one or you are not.' Evie Hone had advised her cousin not to 'be a full-time painter', meaning that one was not able to make a living out of painting. In spite of his own position as a painter and teacher, Sean Keating had also been pessimistic, remarking that 'of course, Hone, you'll never make a living from this. Painting is dead.'

Hone's father did not discourage him in his career but his mother was more cautious. Originally the Hones had been well off but Joe Hone, working as a writer, was not able to earn much of a living. His means were not sufficient to maintain the lifestyle of his youth and early married life. Many writers and artists were to feel the pinch in the 1950s which were David Hone's twenties. What might have been a happy, optimistic period turned out to be melancholy. In the early fifties, during a fit of depression and frustration, Hone destroyed all the life drawings and figure paintings from his art school days. He bundled two or three years work into a fire and burnt them, an action which he now deeply regrets. He laments the time wasted in this period; not doing more drawing, not making contact with other artists or not going to London. He admired, for example, the work of Peter Greenham who taught at the Royal Academy Schools in London. Greenham was a sensitive portraitist who brought a different vision to his figures than, for example, Orpen would have done.

Hone was persuaded to study architecture and he 'hung around' UCD for a while but he was unhappy there and detested 'the International Style' in architecture. Hone's looks, as a young man at this time (1953) are captured in a profile portrait by John F Kelly (Fig 1).

In the meantime, he continued to paint. He held his first one-man exhibition at the Dublin Painter's Gallery in St Stephen's Green in 1955. His work included landscapes, both of Connemara and of the Costa Brava near Barcelona. Hone recalls Jack B Yeats, then in his eighties, visiting the exhibition and expressing admiration for his Spanish paintings. Hone also enrolled for the Purser-Griffiths Diploma in Art History at UCD which was run by Dr Françoise Henry. About 1957, he won an Italian Government Grant, which enabled him to travel to Italy. In Florence, he visited the art galleries and

D. HONE 1957

12. David HONE: *Portrait of Robin*, c.1976. Oil on canvas board, 56 x 51 cm. (Collection of the Artist). Exhibited RHA 1977. Hone's portraits are painted from life, generally over about eight sittings, in his Dublin studio.

13. David HONE: *Portrait of Professor Cornelius Lanczos*, c.1965. Oil on canvas, 45.75 35.5 cm. (Collection of the Artist). Hungarian-born Cornelius Lanczos was a mathematician and Professor in the Institute of Advanced Studies.

met Pietro Annigoni casually in a restaurant. This celebrated portraitist recommended Hone to study in Mme Simi's academy in Florence which emphasised the academic tradition. Hone spent six months there but he felt older than the other students at Mme Simi's, most of whom were 'well-heeled' girls. Whilst in Italy, he also visited Venice.

Hone returned to Dublin. He took a garret studio in Parliament Street; Edward McGuire and Patrick Pye had studios in the same building. Hone moved to a studio in Merrion Row, formerly occupied by Leo Whelan, and in 1961 settled in a studio in Lower Baggot Street. He considered becoming a portrait painter. At that time, there were four or five portraitists in Ireland but he believes that if all their incomes had been combined, there might have been just enough to support one family. As Hone reached thirty, sadness befell his family. His elder brother, Nathaniel ('Nat'), died in his mid-forties. His death hit their mother, Vera, hard and brought despondency on to his family.

Hone married Rosemary d'Arcy in 1962. The couple had two sons and a daughter. In 1963 he painted his first official portrait, that of James Dillon, leader of the Fine Gael party. Thenceforth, most of his career was to be devoted to portrait painting. His sitters included many eminent public figures: the physicist, Professor P J Nolan, the geographer, Frank Mitchell, Eoin 'Pope' O' Mahony from Cork (National Gallery of Ireland), Terence de Vere White, Cardinal Cathal Daly, former primate of all Ireland (Fig 17), Donald Caird, former Archbishop of Dublin (Fig 19), and the late Erskine Childers. His most recent 'official' commission was that of Professor Dervilla Donnelly for the RDS. Amongst his early portraits on which he places most value are those of the Hungarian mathematician, Cornelius Lanczos (Fig 13), and the publican, James Toner (Fig 16). Toner, from the North of Ireland, ran the traditional pub on Merrion Row and his old-fashioned appearance with high collar prompted Hone to paint his portrait in 1966. The picture marked a decisive moment in his career and his decision to become a portraitist.

Hone has also painted members of his own family and many children, including his daughter Juliet, with great sympathy. Sometimes his children are set in the open-air against a cloudy sky, echoing Orpen's outdoor portraits. He takes the sitters, whether an ordinary member of the public, a child, or an eminent public figure, as they come, without any special privilege. Cardinal Cathal Daly, for instance, he remembers as relaxed, easy to get on with, and an interesting conversationalist.

14. David HONE: *Portrait of Peter Somerville-Large*. 1993. Oil on canvas, 61 x 51 cm. (Private Collection). Peter Somerville-Large is a writer and explorer, who has produced many novels and books on Irish travel and social history and on travel in Tibet, Nepal, and the Middle East.

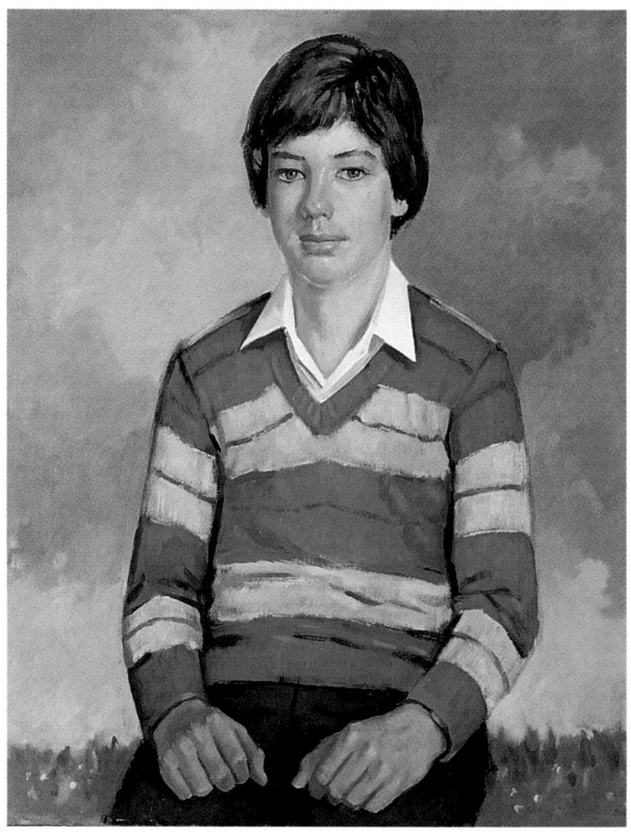

15. David HONE; *Portrait of a Boy*. Late 1970s. Oil on canvas, 61 x 51 cm. (Private Collection). Although painted in the studio, Hone places the figure in an outdoor setting against a cloudy sky.

Children are the most relaxing models to paint. Most difficult, he finds, are middle-aged women.

Hone's portraits are painted from life in his studio in Lower Baggot Street, within a stone's throw of the National Gallery and the School of Art. Baggot Street and Merrion Row have long had artistic resonances; painters such as Nathaniel Hone, Paul Henry, and Leo Whelan had studios there in the early years of the century. David Hone's studio is an old-fashioned, high-ceilinged room, with large windows facing north. Old canvases and books fill a couple of shelves. The model is seated on a chair, placed upon a small wooden platform close to the windows. The easel is placed not in front of but to one side of the sitter, allowing the artist room to walk backward and forward. Hone prefers to work in the middle of the day when the light is at its brightest. Using large canvases, measuring 91.5 x 60.9 cm, his official commissions take about eight sittings. Although painted from life, Hone may concede to using photographs as an aid in articles of clothing.

Hone's portraits have an alertness and intensity; his sharpness of observation capturing the likeness of the subject. The face is firmly modelled, the eyes in particular having an intent, vital quality to them. Yet there is also a sense of calmness and repose, conveying the living quality of the sitter. There is evidence of his careful training and discipline, following the academic tradition of the Slade School, of Orpen, and of Keating. The early portraits have a 'Flemish' clarity and sobriety but recent paintings, especially his informal studies, have a liveliness and rich colour sense, showing his continued admiration for Augustus John. Significantly, when he is referring to portraits by other artists, he is concerned less with academic drawing than that they convey a 'mood' or atmosphere.

Hone has exhibited at the Royal Academy, London, and the Royal Society of Portrait Painters. He has been deeply involved with the RHA in Dublin for all of his professional life. From his first exhibits in the late 1940s, he has continued to show with the Academy for over fifty years. He became an associate member in 1969 and an academician in 1972. Following the death of Raymond McGrath, Hone was elected President of the RHA in 1977. He held this post for five years until 1982. He also served on the Board of the National Gallery of Ireland from 1977 to 1982. He regards himself as having been a loyal member of the Academy but he is diffident about his skills as an administrator or fund-raiser and does not feel he was significantly gregarious.

Hone works slowly and is not a prolific artist. If he is unsatis-

16. David HONE: *Portrait of James Toner*. 1966. Oil on canvas, 91.5 x 76.25 cm. (Private Collection). Escaping the Troubles in Belfast in the early years of the century, James Toner had moved south to Dublin. He became proprietor of Toner's well-known public house on Merrion Row. Hone was fascinated by his old-fashioned appearance with starched collar and upright pose and, painted on a larger canvas than usual, this picture marked a decisive moment in Hone's career as a portraitist.

17. David HONE: *Portrait of Cathal Daly*. 1997. Oil on canvas, 91.5 x 76.25 cm. (Courtesy, Cahal Daly). Cardinal Cahal Daly served as Primate of all Ireland from 1991 to 1996. Hone remembers him as a sympathetic sitter and a good conversationalist. Hone's portrait is used on the cover of the recently-published book of the Cardinal's memoirs and reflections, *Step on my Pilgrim Journey* (1998).

fied with a picture, he 'wipes it out'. He recognises that he has sold fairly well but he does not want to paint any more 'boardroom portraits'. As he grows older, he would like to have some of his pictures around him. He has become increasingly interested in landscape and still life; he sketches landscapes from the motif on small boards and then works these up in the studio. Figures may then be added from notebooks. A recent series shows Sandymount Strand with children playing on a sunny day. Although his early Connemara landscapes were painted *en plein air*, Hone now regards himself as a studio painter. He admires the still lifes of English artist, William Nicholson, for their painterly skill and simplicity of composition.

18. David HONE: *Still Life with Fish*. 1998. Oil on canvas, 30.5 x 35.5 cm. (Private Collection). In recent years Hone has become increasingly interested in the subject of still life. He admires the still lifes of William Nicholson for their simplicity of composition and painterly qualities.

Hone regards himself as a representative, 'objective' painter and not as a modernist. He follows the honourable vocation of the artist to paint what is before his eyes as truthfully as possible. He remains true to his own academic training and has a strong belief in tradition. The Slade School artists, such as John and Nicholson, remain the strongest influences upon him but he also admires Irish artist, John F Kelly, one of the finest academic artists of his generation, and Barbara Warren, whose figurative subjects also evoke a sense of mood.

For Hone, the old debates, such as the 'RHA versus Living Art' or the 'Orpen tradition versus School of Paris', still remain alive. He has observed with some scepticism developments in art over the past fifty years and is critical of 'all this dribble stuff,' and what he would regard as the gimmickry of contemporary art. Referring presumably to the work of Abstract Expressionists or Neo-Expressionists, it is ironic that far from representing a new movement, the former group of artists were gaining attention after the War when Hone himself was a student:

The Cubists appear to have been those most affected by the mechani-

cal world around them...sometimes in the composition it was difficult to find any sign of life. Pieces of firewood were fastened on the canvas as part of the design (I found a piece at an exhibition which had fallen on to the floor)... A visit to almost any modern exhibition will reveal to the visitor how far deformation has gone and how little respect there is for the proportion and construction of the human body...This tendency of the artist to paint his ideas derived from within himself, rather than actually relate ideas to something visual is an important difference between the present time and the past.[6]

These are not Hone's words, but were written over sixty years ago by Henry Tonks in an essay entitled 'The Vicissitudes of Art' but Hone reflects upon them much and finds them as appropriate today as they might have been in 1932.

If he is still suspicious of French influences and 'Modernism', it may be his loss. While it is a mercy that he was not affected by the stale Cubism and lifeless abstraction of Mainie Jellett, perhaps he has missed out on the qualities of 'painterly' lyricism and colour as represented by his cousin, Evie Hone. This is only partially true, however, as David Hone is not just a draughtsman as he has a strong sense of colour and his own early landscapes were direct and impressionistic. Henry Tonks continues: *...at present there is a fairly hard line between those who call themselves, and are called by the critics, 'advanced', and the smaller body who may be called...the old fashioned. In the end all good art can..hang together, and all good artists should be able to recognise one another. But today, if we are not advanced we are old-fashioned, as if of necessity art must go on improving, which it certainly does not.*[7]

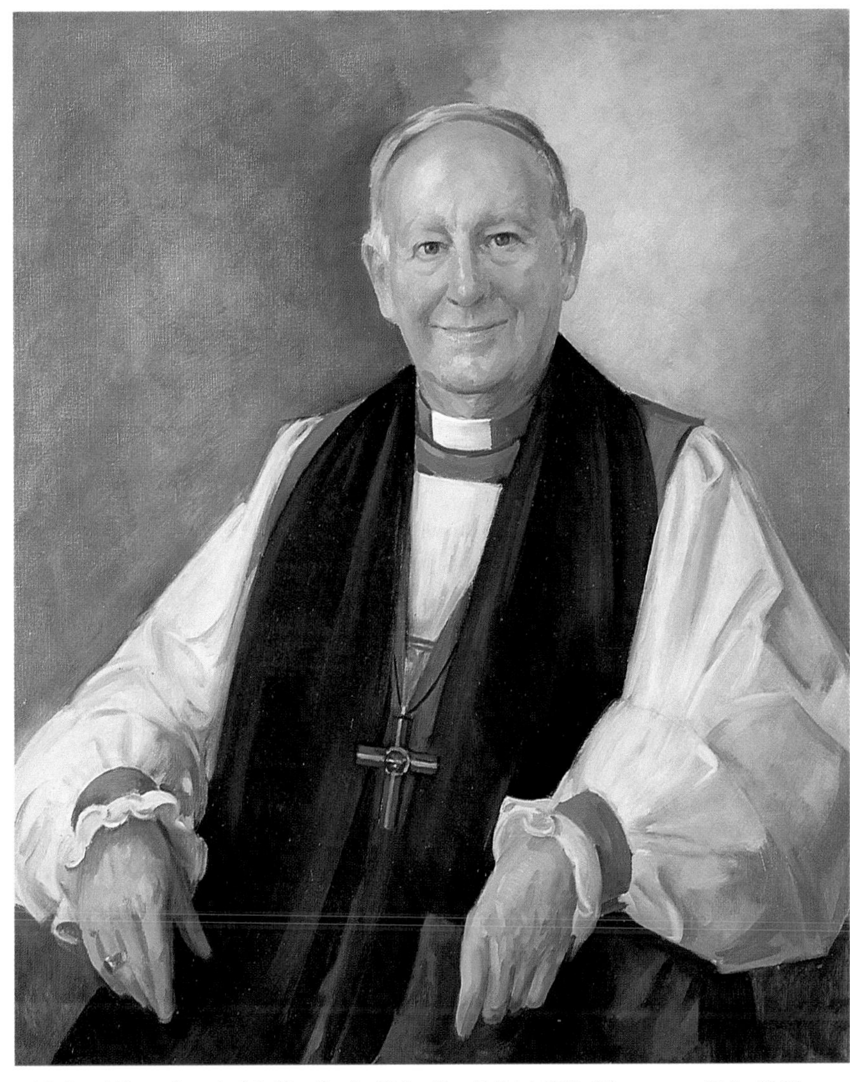

19. David HONE: *Portrait of the Very Rev Archbishop Donald Caird.* 1997. Oil on canvas, 91.5 x 76.25 cm. (Church of Ireland House). Donald Caird, who is an Irish scholar, served as Bishop of Meath and Kildare before being appointed Archbishop of Dublin.

A portrait painter who is also a landscapist, a reserved man who holds strong opinions on art, there are many more aspects to David Hone's career and work than simply the public portraitist. Memories of his own life as well as the texture and ideas of several generations of Irish cultural life are evoked vividly in conversation with him: from the days of Orpen, Henry and Yeats, to memories of his father's artistic friends, to the differences between the RHA and the Living Art generation, to the debates of the present day. It is of regret that the views of David Hone and others of his generation who shun the limelight are not heard more often.

JULIAN CAMPBELL is a tutor in the History of Art at the Crawford College of Art, Cork and is the author of many books and catalogues on Irish artists in Brittany.

ACKNOWLEDGEMENTS: I am very grateful to the artist, David Hone, for conversing with me in November 1998 and March 1999 and to Gillian Buckley for all the photography.

1 Regrettably, T Snoddy's book does not list living artists.
2 P Mc Evensoneya, 'Insider on the Outside: Thomas Ryan PPRHA', *Irish Arts Review Yearbook*, vol 13 (1997), p. 169
3 See B Arnold, *Orpen, Mirror to an Age* (London 1981).
4 I am very grateful to David Hone for conversing with me. Unless otherwise stated, all quotations are made by Hone.
5 See A Stewart, *Royal Hibernian Academy of Arts. Index of Exhibitions, 1862-1929* (Dublin 1985).
6 H Tonks, 'The Vicissitudes of Art', from *Fifty Years, Memories and Contrast. A Composite Picture of the Period 1882-1932* (London 1932), p. 58-60.
7 H Tonks (as note 6), p. 62.

A Kiln Fired by Turf
Grattan Freyer and the Terrybaun Pottery

Peter Lamb

describes an unusual and remarkable enterprise

The Terrybaun Pottery fired its first kiln in August 1950 at a remote lakeside location in county Mayo, halfway between Castlebar and Ballina.[1] The site had been chosen by Grattan Freyer and his French-born wife, Madeleine Giraudeau, because of the proximity of pottery clay deposits. Both Madeleine and Grattan had previous careers: he had been an academic and she a nurse and, following an apprenticeship with Bernard Leach, they came to Ireland to start an Irish country pottery which ran for thirty-three years under their direction. They produced a red earthenware with characteristic coloured-slip and *sgraffito* decoration created by themselves and their apprentices. Visiting friends, however, were also allowed to decorate and collaborations with the artists Oisín Kelly and Pauline Bewick in the late-1950s and early '60s produced some very interesting results.

Coming to Terrybaun for Grattan was also a return to his roots. Born in Cambridge in 1915, he had grown up in England[2] but his father, the writer and art collector, Dermot Freyer, belonged to a west of Ireland family of Huguenot descent which had been connected with the sea and the coastguard service. His grandfather, the surgeon Sir Peter Freyer (1851-1921), although born in county Galway, had lived in India and London and become rich and famous on account of the prostate gland operation he developed. Sir Peter was famously rewarded by one of his patients, the Nawab of Rampur, with a lakh of rupees said at the time to be worth £6,600.[3] Although much of the money was gone by the time Grattan came back to Ireland, there was still enough to enable him to set up the Terrybaun Pottery.

Grattan was a lithe, 'extremely handsome', man with dark hair and a beard. All his life he swam and exercised; he had a great capacity for physical work and loved horses. He was also clever and scholarly but he was moody and had a dry sense of humour. At Cambridge, he had flirted with communism and Spanish republicanism but rejected these ideas in later life and converted to Catholicism. He had taken Natural Sciences and English in his Cambridge Tripos in 1936, studying under F R Leavis and writing his thesis on the Development of Irish Drama.

Following Cambridge, he took a PhD (awarded in 1940) at Trinity College, Dublin[4] and during his research on Machiavelli spent part of the time living in Florence with Madeleine (whom he had met on a bus from Cork to Achill in 1935 and married in 1939) and part in Dublin where he made many friends in artistic and literary circles. Madeleine was 'tiny' and 'adorable'; the daughter of a Breton doctor,[5] she was also talented, good company, and interested in food and wine. She loved pictures, collecting them whenever she had any money and she spent a lot of her youth travelling to places such as Norway and Turkey. Grattan had also travelled extensively in France, Poland, and Russia and, even after they had settled in Mayo, they continued to move around. Madeleine had the use of a small flat in Paris, they went on foreign holidays together, and in later life Grattan travelled widely in America and Europe on lecture tours.

After Grattan's very lengthy and expensive education, the couple moved to London and he took up teaching as a career. It was while working for the 'People's Education Association' that he encountered Bernard Leach, the great English studio potter, and a friendship developed. In 1946, Grattan conceived the idea of starting a pottery in Ireland and Leach wrote to him encouraging the idea, envisioning 'a small factory humanised and with discretion, and total control of form, material, and decor.'[6] Shortly afterwards, in 1946-47, Grattan undertook an apprenticeship at the Leach pottery at St Ives. Madeleine, who also learned to 'throw' and decorate there, became the pottery's salesperson and Leach's private secretary. Grattan progressed swiftly, acquiring potting skills and learning the secrets of glazing, particularly the old English techniques of slip-decoration which were rediscovered by Leach and Hamada in the 1920s.[7] In April and May of 1947, he made a tour of sixteen English potteries and seven museums, visiting Sam Haile and Bernard Forrester at Dartington, Fishley Holland at Clevedon, and Ray Finch at Winchcombe where he arranged

1. Grattan (1915-1983) and Madeleine (1909-1999) FREYER. This photograph was probably taken about the time of the couple's marriage in 1939. They both trained as potters with Bernard Leach and then founded the Terrybaun Pottery in Co Mayo in 1950.

(Opposite) **2.** TERRYBAUN POTTERY: *Adam and Eve Dish. c.* 1960. Earthenware with scraffito decoration by Oisín Kelly, 24.6 cm high. (Private collection). The sculptor, Oisín Kelly, (1915-81) bought a holiday home near the Terrybaun Pottery in 1956 and from time to time collaborated with the Freyers in decorating their wares.

3. Terrybaun Pottery: *Dishes.* Early 1950s. Earthenware with scraffito decoration. 11.5 cm diam. (Private collection). The dish on the left has an Irish motto which was supplied and inscribed by the historian, Margaret Griffith. Translated it reads: 'Listen to the sound of the river and you will catch a fish'; the centre dish, which is dated 1953, shows a Terrybaun apprentice (probably John Kenny) using a kick wheel; the dish on the right shows Soizick (or Zic), the Freyer's first cat, with his date of birth, drawn in scraffito by Madeleine Freyer.

4. Terrybaun Pottery: *Dish. c.*1960. Earthenware with coloured slip decoration, 53.5 cm long. (Private collection). This characteristic 'marbled' effect was part of the standard production of the pottery and was executed by all members of the studio. The slip was composed of ball clay mixed with the same local clay as the body ensuring a good fit.

5. Terrybaun Pottery: *Dishes.* Early 1950s. Slipware with 'marbled' and 'feathered' decoration by Madeleine Freyer, each c.14 cm diam. (Private collection). The techniques for making this traditional country pottery decoration were rediscovered in the early 1920s by Bernard Leach and Shoji Hamada and have been copied by many people since. The Freyers were the first to use the style in Ireland, having previously practised it at the Wenford Bridge Pottery in Cornwall.

to continue his apprenticeship for the last two and a half months of the year.[8] By 1948, he was experienced enough to undertake the management of the Wenford Bridge Pottery in Cornwall during the absence in Ghana of its owner, Michael Cardew (Leach's first apprentice). The year he spent there proved to be an invaluable work experience and an ideal preparation for Terrybaun.[9]

Grattan's dream of having his own pottery progressed during the year as he carried out research into Irish pottery-clays. Leach had pointed out to him that Ireland was geologically a 'potter's paradise' and with the help of Fairlie's *Notes on Pottery Clays*[10] he got clay samples from Cork and Mayo which he tested at Wenford Bridge. He also researched the use of turf as a fuel for firing kilns. 'The heating effect,' he discovered 'is generally less than firewood, about 2,600 to 3,600 calories per kilogram compared to 4,600 to 5,000 for wood, 7,000 to 7,600 for coal, and 9,000 for oil.' Turf had been successfully used in Switzerland in 1809 by a M Fourmy who fired a kiln packed with porcelain for twenty-eight hours, using twenty-three 'bannes' of turf.[11] When Grattan finally acquired Terrybaun the following year, it came with turbery rights and turf from his own bog was used to fuel the first kiln which continued to be in use until 1958 when an electric kiln was installed.

6. Grattan FREYER: At work in the pottery in the 1960s. He is seated at one of the kick-wheels which he built in 1950, based on prototypes at Michael Cardew's pottery at Wenford Bridge in Cornwall.

It took time to find Terrybaun. The original idea had been to set up in Dublin but life in English country potteries had changed all that and Grattan, whose great uncle had been a successful jockey, wanted to keep horses. Deciding against Youghal in county Cork, they finally chose the area near Ballina in county Mayo where crocks and bricks had been made within living memory and where pottery-clay was easily available. There was also a family consideration: they wanted to be near Grattan's father, Dermot, who after a life spent in London and Cambridge, had retired to Achill where he maintained a famously-eccentric establishment at his home, Corrymore House, behind which he had built a Greek theatre where he held folk-dancing displays.

Grattan and Madeleine purchased Terrybaun in 1949 from Martin Harte. It was a smallholding of about twelve acres just north of Pontoon on the west shore of Lough Conn and it had beautiful views of farmland, bog, and lake in a landscape dominated by Nephin, one of Mayo's most spectacular mountains. It took a year to transform the place, renovating the cottage and clearing the site for the new pottery which they built themselves: both Grattan and Madeleine became expert bricklayers in the process. With help from two local men, Owen Holmes and John Conroy, they cleaned the orchard, made a vegetable garden, planted trees, and made a drive, entrance, and courtyard. Grattan fitted up the house and it soon filled with his books and Madeleine's pictures (including works by Matisse, Marie Laurencin – a friend of Madeleine's – and Alfred Wallis, the St Ives' painter). The house acquired a warm, civilised atmosphere. Colour was added with rugs by the Mayo weaver, Patrick Madden. Printed linens with abstract designs by contemporary Irish artists hung on the windows, adding interest to the rooms. Their first cat, 'Zic', arrived in 1950 and their first pony, 'Maeve', the same year. During this period of preparation, they were visited by Muriel Gahan (of The Country Shop in Dublin), the chief promoter of country crafts in Ireland, who became one of their first customers.[12]

7. TERRYBAUN POTTERY: The original cottage at Terrybaun bought by the Freyers with a 12 acre smallholding in 1949.

8. TERRYBAUN POTTERY: This photograph, taken in the 1960s, shows the pottery building to the left and the house, now much enlarged, on the right.

9. TERRYBAUN POTTERY: *Dish.* 1964. Earthenware with scraffito decoration by Pauline Bewick, 36 cm long. (Private collection). The design shows a reclining nude and a sailing ship. Bewick (b.1935) lived at the pottery for several months in 1964 and decorated 150 to 200 pieces during her stay.

10. TERRYBAUN POTTERY: *Jugs.* c.1960. Earthenware thrown by Grattan Freyer, the tallest, 34 cm high. (Private collection). The influence of the domestic ware products made at the Bernard Leach Pottery in St Ives where Grattan trained is apparent in these jugs.

11. TERRYBAUN POTTERY: *Dish with the Last Supper.* c.1960. Earthenware with scraffito decoration by Oisín Kelly. 36.5 cm long. (Private collection).This is one of a series of individual art pieces using biblical imagery produced at the pottery following Grattan Freyer's conversion to Catholicism in 1958.

Having carried out further clay tests, Grattan eventually chose to use clay from the Clarke farm near Ballina which he was able to buy, dug and delivered, for one shilling a hundredweight. He then built a kick wheel (based on examples at St Ives and Winchcombe) and made his first pots of 'Terryduff Clay' on 4 July 1950. Building the kiln took about three weeks and the first biscuit firing (using three hundredweights of hand-hewn turf) took place on 28 August and the first glost firing (using about seven hundredweights of mixed hard wood) on the 31st. The kiln was unpacked the following day with excellent results and a telegram was dispatched to Bernard Leach. Within days samples were taken to potential customers but it was November before a real consignment of pots was ready for sale and Grattan drove with it to Dublin. He made sales to The Country Shop, to Pilkington's (an interior decorator) and to Miss Granger. He took orders from Whyte's (the china and glass shop in George's Street), the Dublin Art Shop (run by Gertie Grew and Margaret O'Keefe), and various friends and relations including his brother, Michael, Françoise Henry, the Boydells, and Mrs Hanrahan.[13] After this first trip goods were normally dispatched by train from Ballina or by post from Lahardane. It also became the custom to hold an annual pre-Christmas Exhibition at the Painter's Gallery in Stephen's Green, Dublin and occasional exhibitions at The Country Shop. At the beginning it took five firings to produce £100 worth of goods at wholesale prices.

The pottery settled down to a routine of hard physical work and an apprentice was soon taken on. He was Brian Kiernan from Castlebar and he was joined in 1953 by Michael Quinn, a farmer's son, who cycled in ten miles to work every day. Brian and Michael stayed ten and fourteen years respectively. (Michael now pots at Cree in county Clare.)[14]

The price list of 1956 lists fifty-three different items 'for table and kitchen' as well as offering to produce 'presentation wares' to order, with prices ranging from 1/6 for an egg cup to 63/- for a large fruit bowl. The list includes Terracotta Ware and Traditional Slipware. Initially the Slipware was virtually identical to that produced at the time at Wenford Bridge but it soon became a distinctively Terrybaun variation. Madeleine and Grattan both became adept at this marbelising effect and Madeleine achieved some very striking results; one of her pieces won a prize at an exhibition in Munich. Another form of slip decoration which they used was 'slip trailing', a technique by which a line of 'slip' is used to create a drawing. Madeleine was particularly skillful at this, being capable of very free and lively expression and she specialised particularly in horses and fish. The other main kind of decoration used was *sgraffito* in which lines are drawn through a coating of slip to reveal the underlying red-clay body. This was also Madeleine's department and she drew marine life, 'celtic' patterns (copied from Françoise Henry's *La Sculpture Irlandaise*), customised ashtrays for hotels and restaurants, and a variety of items for tourists. When lettering was required, as for instance when wine beakers were decorated with mottoes or a commemorative plate or tea-set was ordered, it was Grattan who did the inscription.

Terrybaun became a great meeting place; people visited from across the world, many of whom were invited to help with decorating the pottery. For example, Thurloe Conolly, the painter, spent a day in November 1950 decorating tiles and vases; Françoise Henry, the art historian would come and draw 'celtic' patterns in person; and Margaret Griffith (Director of the Public Record Office in Dublin) helped by supplying and inscribing mottoes in Irish. Bernard Forrester of the Dartington Pottery and Alec Sharpe, a fellow Leach apprentice from Scotland, visited and decorated in the early years. A local friend, Desmond MacAvock, from Ballina, made slip pictures based on woodcuts by Henri Laurens. Liam de Paor, the archaeologist, visited Mayo in the mid-1950s and

12. TERRYBAUN POTTERY. *Plate. c.*1960. Earthenware with scraffito decoration by Oisín Kelly, 18.5 cm diam. (Private collection). The design, showing men in currachs, is one of a series produced by Kelly illustrating life in the West of Ireland.

13.TERRYBAUN POTTERY: *Commemorative Plate. c.*1972. Earthenware with scraffito decoration by Madeline Freyer, 28 cm diam. (Private collection). Commissioned by Alec Wallace of the Old Head Hotel near Louisburgh, Co Mayo as a present for his fellow Mayoman, Sir Terence Garvey, the British Ambassador in Belgrade.

12. TERRYBAUN POTTERY. *Dish.* Early 1960s. Earthenware with slip-trailed decoration by Madeleine Freyer, 26.2 cm diam. (Private collection).

made a location map for the pottery and the Japanese professor Kuni Imaeda[15] visited in 1959 and decorated plates with Japanese texts. The arrival of Oisín Kelly, the Dublin-based sculptor,[16] in the area sometime in 1956 (when he bought a holiday cottage at Massbrook) led to a fruitful collaboration which lasted for six or seven years. His marvellous drawings on Terrybaun ware perfectly captured scenes of life in the west of Ireland: musicians, dancers, fishermen in curraghs, and men working the fields. He also illustrated Irish myths and created a biblical series depicting such scenes as *The Last Supper, Adam and Eve, Noah's Ark,* and the struggle between good and evil as represented by angels and demons. In 1964, the young Pauline Bewick lived in Terrybaun for several months decorating plates with her distinctive drawings of clothed and unclothed females and other subjects, completing between one hundred and fifty and two hundred pieces during her time at the pottery.[17] In the 1960s and '70s, many others came and went whose names have not been recorded. In 1974, there was another Japanese visitor, the artist, Tadao Ono, who was in Ireland to study ancient rock-scribings[18] and he drew birds and figures on Terrybaun ware.

The pottery was favourably noticed by the Swedish report, *Design in Ireland,*[19] in 1961 and Telefís Eireann made a short documentary about Terrybaun in 1963.[20] Throughout the '50s and '60s a series of apprentices came and went, many of them learning the 'knack' of throwing from Madeleine who was a good teacher. The apprentices were all locals and included Bobby Butler (for a short time in the early-'50s), John Kenny (*c.*1958-65), Anthony Roche (two to three years), Kathleen Ford (about six years), Noreen Quinn (about four years), Lilia Foley (1965-68), and, 'the best potter they ever had', Eileen Cawley (mid-'60s to mid-'70s). Sadly, none of these, with the exception of Lilia Foley and Michael Quinn, ever made pottery their life career, probably because they were poorly paid and Grattan was slow to praise and extremely secretive about glaze recipes. The atmosphere in the pottery could appear rather serious as Grattan was a solemn person and expected everyone to work as hard as he did. However, 'the children' – as the Freyers referred to them – had a great deal of fun behind his back and Madeleine herself often participated. Grattan's fun was his involvement with horses which he kept and bred and he went trekking in the hills. He was also a good step-dancer and a keen swimmer who swam in the lake every day, summer and winter, once famously swimming naked on horseback. The neighbours were not used to seeing swimmers and on one occasion a local farmer, thinking Grattan was an otter, got his gun and took a shot at him.

Grattan was also a considerable book-collector and in the late-1960s and throughout the '70s he turned more and more from pottery to academic work in the field of Anglo-Irish Literature. He published books on Peadar O' Donnell and W B Yeats,[21] established the Irish Humanities Centre – which published books – and administered study courses for foreign students. He frequently travelled abroad on lecture tours and would leave the pottery in the care of Madeleine and various

16. TERRYBAUN POTTERY. *Dishes.* Late 1950s. Earthenware with scraffito decoration by Oisín Kelly, 10.6 to 13.7 cm diam. (Private collection). Kelly's work at Terrybaun illustrated many themes from Irish Mythology to Bible stories and life in the West of Ireland.

17. TERRYBAUN POTTERY: *Plates.* Late 1950s, early 1960s. Earthenware with brushwork decoration by Oisín Kelly, 12.4 and 17.8 cm diam (Private collection). Cats and horses, as on these plates, were the favourite animals of the Freyers. Grattan bred horses but a plan to import Lippizaners as breeding stock from Slovenia came to nothing.

(Opposite) **15.** TERRYBAUN POTTERY. *Plate* . Early 1960s. Earthenware with sliptrailed decoration by Madeleine Freyer, 26.7cm. (Private collection). Both Freyers used this technique, but Madeleine generally decorated on the flat whereas Grattan worked on curved surfaces.

18. Terrybaun Pottery. *Plate. c.*1960. Earthenware with scraffito decoration by Oisín Kelly of fishermen in currachs 18.5 cm diam. (Private collection).

19. Terrybaun Pottery: *Dish.* Early 1960s. Earthenware with slip-trailed decoration by Madeleine Freyer, 26.2 cm high. (Private collection).

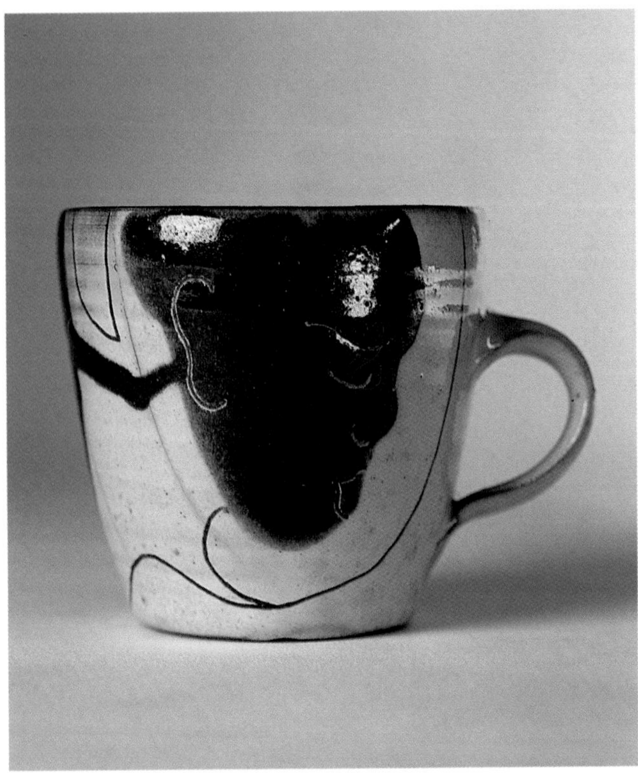

20. Terrybaun Pottery: *Cup*. Probably mid 1950s. Earthenware with scraffito decoration, 7 cm high. (Private collection). A blob of liquid slip has been transformed into a human face in this interesting example.

21. Wenford Bridge Pottery: *Jar and Cover*. 1948. 21 cm high. (Private collection). This jar was made by Grattan at the time he ran the Wenford Bridge Pottery in Cornwall in 1948 during Michael Cardew's absence in Ghana. This piece bears the simple incised mark 'GF'.

22. TERRYBAUN POTTERY: *Dishes*. c.1960. Earthenware with scraffito decoration by Oisín Kelly, 10 to 10.5 cm diam. (Private collection). The decoration consists of scenes from the west of Ireland.

23. TERRYBAUN POTTERY. *Tile*. 1950. Earthenware with scraffito decoration by Thurloe Conolly (b. 1918), 8.2 x 8 cm. (Private collection). Conolly was a member of the White Stag Group in Dublin in the 1940s.

24. TERRYBAUN POTTERY: *Lampbase*. 1950s. Earthenware with coloured slip decoration, 21 cm high. (Private collection). This lampbase is in the form of a 'bottle' with dimpled sides.

25. TERRYBAUN POTTERY: *Three Circular Dishes*. Earthenware with scraffito decoration by Kuni Imaeda, 7 cm diam. *Oval Dish*. 1974. Earthenware with scraffito decoration by Tadao Ono, 2.27 cm long. (Private collection). Imaeda was a Japanese professor at the Dublin Institute of Advanced Studies; Ono visited Ireland to study Ancient Irish rock scribings.

employees and students, including her nephew, Henri Hedou, the American, Kathy Kershner, the Danish potter, Jens Carlsen, the Swiss potter, Monica Neracher, and Jackie Brett, an award-winning potter from Clonmel. It was difficult for Madeleine to carry on in this way and when Grattan got cancer and died in 1983, it was the end of their Terrybaun.[22] He was buried in the local graveyard at Addergoole. A year or two after his death, Madeleine retired to Dublin and sold the pottery to her nephew, Henri Hedou, under whose direction it began a second incarnation. It continues to flourish to this day.

The achievements of the Freyers at Terrybaun are now largely forgotten; there has never been a retrospective exhibition and the history of the pottery has hitherto been unrecorded. Consequently, their work has probably not commanded any influence in Irish pottery with one notable exception in the work of Cormac Boydell, a leading contemporary Irish ceramic artist who works in earthenware. His parents, Brian and Mary Boydell, took him to visit Terrybaun when he was only five years old, an event he would regard as one of the seminal experiences of his life. He also grew up in a house where Terrybaun ware was in daily use as his parents were among the first patrons of the pottery and the fact that they gave 'equal status to ceramics, glass, and contemporary painting'[23] undoubtedly played a part in forming his artistic make-up. It is to be hoped that when more examples of Terrybaun Pottery come to light, an exhibition will be held which will give the Freyers the recognition they deserve and bring their pioneering work at Terrybaun in the 1950s to the attention of a new generation.

Peter Lamb *is a collector of 20th-century Irish decorative arts.*

Acknowledgements

For information used in preparing this article, I warmly acknowledge the help received from many individuals. I would like particularly to thank the late Madeleine Freyer and Margaret Griffith; Patrick Freyer, Marie Devanney, Michael Quinn, Lilia Foley, Jens Carlsen, and William Carron.

Note on the pottery marks:

The pottery used at least eight marks, either stamped, impressed or inscribed. Five of them included a triskel device with different combinations of the words Terrybaun, Irish Handmade, or Ireland. Of the others, one used the initials G.F. (for Grattan Freyer) another the initial F. (for Freyer) and the last was simply the hand-written word 'Terrybaun'.

1. Terrybaun was the first Irish country-pottery (1950), preceeding by three years the Shanagarry Pottery of Phillip Pearce and Gerald Pringle, which opened in Co Cork in 1953. Strictly speaking, however, Peter Brennan was the first post-war studio potter in Ireland. He began potting in Kilkenny in the early 1940s at his 'Ring Ceramic Studio' and had his earliest training with Louis Keeling at the Carrigaline Pottery in Co Cork. In the early 1950s he was joined by John ffrench who had trained in Italy and who produced his beautiful hand built vessels in Kilkenny for several years.

2 G D Freyer was born on 25 July 1915 at Cambridge and died 20 June 1983 at Ballina, buried Addergoole, Co Mayo; second of three sons of Major Dermot Freyer (1883-1970) and his New Zealand born wife, Lorna Doone McLean (1889-1919).

3 See J B Lyons, *Brief Lives of Irish Doctors*, (Dublin 1978), pp. 122-23.

4 His PhD thesis was entitled *The Fortunes of Machiavelli* and was later turned into a book under the title *Aspects of Machiavelli: An Enquiry into the Role of Machiavelli in the Intellectual Life of the West*. However, the book was never published.

5 M G A Giraudeau was born in France at La Boissière du Doré (Loire Atlantique) on 22 Aug 1909, the daughter of Breton parents, Dr E Giraudeau (died 1927), a doctor and pharmacist, and his wife, G Creton (1884-1954). She grew up partly in St Nazaire and partly in the old pottery village of St Amand-en-Puisaye. She studied nursing in the Nursing School of the French Red Cross, qualifying in 1934. Her Professor at 'La Charité', the Paris Hospital described her as 'the best nurse...gentle, wise, intelligent, devoted.' She married G Freyer at the Dublin Registry Office on 16 Aug 1939, and they were married again on 10 July 1958 with full nuptial Mass in Ballina, the day after Grattan was received into the Church. (There were no children.) She died on 6 Aug 1999 and was buried at Addergoole, Co Mayo.

6 Letter from Leach to Freyer, The Leach Pottery, St Ives, Cornwall (10 July 1946).

7 G Freyer Notebook No 1.

8 G Freyer Notebook No 2.

9 G Freyer, 'Pottery Diary for Wenford Bridge', Notebook No 3.

10 J Fairlie, *Notes on Pottery Clays* (London 1901). Grattan also consulted R Kane's *Industrial Resources of Ireland* (Dublin 1845); J R Kilroe's *A Description of the Soil Geology of Ireland* (Dublin 1907); and G H Kinaham 'Slates and Clays of Ireland' in *Scientific Proceedings of RDS*, vol 6, part 3, pp. 143-68 (1888).

11 G Jako, *Keramische Materialkunde* (Dresden and Liepzig 1928); M Fourmy, 'Rapport fait a la societé d' Agriculture, Arts et Commerce du Department de Doubs du succés des tentatives executées à la manufacture de Migette pour fair servir la tourbe à la cuisson de la porcelaine' (1809).

12 Terrybaun Work Journal (1949). G Mitchell, *Words not Deeds: The Life and Work of Muriel Gahan* (Dublin 1997).

13 G Freyer, Diary 13 (Mar 1950-28 Dec 1950).

14 For photographs of the pottery apprentices see D MacAvock 'A Pottery in the West', *Irish Housewife Annual* (1961).

15 K Imaeda was a professor of Theoretical Physics at the Dublin Institute of Advanced Studies from 1959 until 1981.

16 Oisín Kelly was also involved with ceramics at St Columba's College, Dublin, where he taught art; at the Kilkenny Design Workshops; and he fired some of his work at Flemmings Fireclay Works at the Swan in Co Laois.

17 P Bewick, although primarily a painter, has had other encounters with ceramics, notably in her 'Yellow Man' series of Majolica ware made at the Rampini Studios in Tuscany in 1996.

18 *Rubbings from Ancient Irish Monuments*. Collected by T Ono in 1974 (Japan 1975).

19 K Franck, E Herlow etc., *Design in Ireland: Report of the Scandinavian Design Group in Ireland* (Dublin 1962).

20 The documentary on Terrybaun which ran for 3 minutes, 54 seconds, was an insert in the 'Broadsheet' series and was broadcast on 30 Jan 1963 (Ref: P2/63.)

21 Freyer's publications include: 'Ireland's Contribution' in *The Pelican Guide to English Literature*, vol 7 (1973); *Peadar O'Donnell* (1973). (He also republished O'Donnell's novel *The Knife*.); *Modern Irish Writing*, a prose and verse anthology, edited by Freyer (1979); *Yeats and the Anti-Democratic Tradition* (1981); *Integrating Tradition: The Achievement of Sean O' Riada*, edited by G Freyer and B Harris (1981); 'Montale and Other Friends' in *Sagatrieb*.(1982). (Eugenio Montale, the nobel prize-winning Italian writer was a friend and Grattan Freyer was the first to translate his work into English); *Bishop Stock's Narrative of the Year of the French* (1982). This was a republication of an eyewitness account of the French Invasion at Killala in 1798. When he died, he was working on his latest book, with Sheila Molloy, *Eyewitnesses of 1798*.

22 An obituary entitled 'Grattan Freyer Dies' appeared in the *Irish Times* shortly after his death on 22 June 1983. It mentions his frequent contributions to the *Irish Times* 'Book Page' and lists his publications.

An Edo Masterwork Restored
The Chogonka Scrolls in The Chester Beatty Library, Dublin

Kate Robinson

introduces a treasure of Japanese art from the 17th century

For many reasons, the *Chogonka Scrolls* are among the most important treasures of the Chester Beatty Library in Dublin. Japanese in origin, they were painted by Kano Sansetsu during the Edo period in the 17th century and are based on a 9th-century Chinese epic poem by Bai Juyi, *The Song of Everlasting Sorrow*. Painted on silk lined with dyed mulberry-paper, the scrolls had become very fragile, damaged, and stained and as a result were sent to Japan for conservation and restoration in recent years. They are now on display at the Chester Beatty Library in its new home in Dublin Castle.

Bai Juyi, writing in 807 AD, fifty years after the events he describes, commemorates the tragic story of the 'Brilliant Emperor', Xuanzong of the Tang Dynasty, and his beloved concubine, Yang Guifei.

The Tang dynasty, which lasted for almost three centuries from 618 to 907 AD, ruled China at a time known as the 'Golden Age' when its empire was the largest ever known, its poets the most prolific, and Buddhism was at its height. From the highly-educated ranks of the administrators rose the painters, poets, and calligraphers who defined the cultural splendour of the Tang: they came from all classes of society, requiring only ambition and the courage to face years of unrelenting study to gain their goal. Though poets had greater prestige, the art of the painters was also greatly esteemed. There were two styles, one in which colour predominated and another wherein the colour was held firm in the line, whether faint or strong. Tang painting retained its reputation for centuries.

Kano Sansetsu was a member of a family of artists of Kyoto who worked in the traditional Chinese style, specifically the landscape art of Hangzhou. The school was founded in the 15th century by Kano Masanobu whose relatives had won notice as courtiers of literary culture. The Kano School had brought to all its paintings, on screens, murals, *emakimono* (horizontal handscrolls), *kakemono* (vertical handscrolls), the luxury of gold, silver, and exquisite balances of colour based on the finest Chinese models. But when Sansetsu painted the Chester Beatty scrolls in 1646-47, the taste for authentic Chinese painting was already ebbing. The convention, over more than two centuries, had been a court style for the ruling Shogunate but this art was now less popular and less practised. The School of Sotatsu and Korin, which followed almost immediately, turned to the portrayal of Japanese sensibility in both style and subject-matter.

1. Kano SANSETSU (1590-1651): *Chogonka Scroll.* 1646-47. (The Chester Beatty Library, Dublin). The scrolls are painted on silk lined with dyed mulberry-paper. They had become fragile, damaged, and stained and thus were sent to Japan for conservation and restoration. They are now on display in the Chester Beatty Library in Dublin Castle.

Sansetsu's *Chogonka Scrolls* differ in some respects from the principles of traditional Chinese painting. The line throughout is strong, as is the colour. There is no text: the artist has interpreted the poem, act by act, and none is needed. Unrolling the scrolls and entering into the events through the various incidents to the final tragedy is enough. The second scroll is Sansetsu's interpretation of the legend of the lovers after the execution of Yang Guifei. The architecture framing the episodes is authentic; the minute figures, the hair and clothing in true Tang idiom, are spread over the surface of the scroll.

Bai Juyi's poem immortalises the story of Emperor Xuanzong,

(Overleaf). **2.** Kano SANSETSU (1590-1651): *Yang Guifei is chosen for the Emperor. Chogonka Scroll.* 1646-47. (The Chester Beatty Library, Dublin). Yang Guifei, accompanied by some of her Emperor's concubines, is presented at court.

3. Kano SANSETSU (1590-1651): *A Messenger from Emperor Xuanzong visits the house of the Yang family. Chogonka Scroll.* 1646-47. (The Chester Beatty Library, Dublin). Yang Guifei is in the inner chamber (to the right) while the master of the family receives the messenger of the Imperial court (centre). Her mother (left) listens at the entrance to the house.

4. Kano SANSETSU (1590-1651): *Yang Guifei at her bath. Chogonka Scroll.* 1646-47. (The Chester Beatty Library, Dublin). On a cold day in spring, according to the poem, the Emperor (standing on the left), is at the Winter Palace where he sees Yang Guifei who has just bathed in the hot spring in the background.

5. Kano SANSETSU (1590-1651): *A blossom viewing party at the garden of the tree peonies. Chogonka Scroll.* 1646-47. (The Chester Beatty Library, Dublin). By the light of many candles, the Emperor and Yang Guifei prolong their enjoyment of the blossoms. The Emperor raises his cup and a maid pours wine for Yang Guifei.

who at the age of sixty was living a life of seclusion, lacking any interest in his three thousand concubines or the pomp of court life. Yet he wished for companionship. When the courtiers heard of *a young girl grown to womanhood, reared in the inner apartments and scarcely known...she was taken and presented to the Emperor...In a warm bed netted with hibiscus she passed the spring nights: O spring nights too short, O sun too early on high...the King never summoned his morning levees* but was led into the gentle arts of sensuous gratification.

Bai Juyi was not the only Chinese poet to write of the tragic story of the Emperor and his concubine. Du Fu, considered the greatest of Chinese poets, also lauded the splendour of the court and the gaiety and beauty of Yang Guifei. But, in his poem, he condemned the abuses of power of her brother, Yang Guozhang, made prime minister by the besotted Emperor, and nor did the excesses and cruelties of officials escape him. He wrote:

Behind the red-painted doors wine and meat are stinking,
On the wild roads lie corpses of people frozen to death.
A hairsbreadth divides wealth and utter poverty.
This strange contrast fills me with unappeasable anguish.

Ruin came to Xuanzong when An Lushan, a regional Governor, revolted. Chang'an, meaning 'Eternal Peace', home of a million inhabitants and great trading city at the end of the Silk Road, was sacked and destroyed. The Emperor fled to Shu (Sichuan) together with his beloved and an army of three-quarters of a million men (the normal apportionment for an emperor). At Ma Wei the army mutinied and refused to proceed until Yang Guifei was executed. Before the Emperor's stricken eyes, she was strangled and the long march over the mountains moved on.

In his depiction of these scenes of inhospitable territory, Sansetsu demonstrates the supreme grandeur of Chinese painting, reinterpreting the wonders of nature true to the art of almost a thousand years before: the rocky ravines, the crashing waterfalls, and the surging peaks are contrasted with the lush river valley in which life and love were destroyed.

The first scroll is a record of a tumultuous event in Chinese history. In the second, Sansetsu illustrated what had over the centuries become a legend. Reaching a retreat in Xianshan, the Emperor Xuanzong became aware of the spirit of Yang Guifei in the Halls of Heaven. He sent his astrologer to seek her, sending a pathetic message: to ask for one of her golden hairpins, her characteristic adornment. With this relic the Emperor took his own life, so as to rejoin his lover and fulfil their vows: 'In heaven, we shall become birds flying ever wing to wing; on earth we shall become trees with branches entwined...' These paintings through ranges of cloud and ethereal mountain peaks emphasise how paltry man is in the immensity of space, a constant in Chinese art.

The *Chogonka Scrolls* were purchased by Sir Alfred Chester Beatty in 1926 from the estate of the well-known French collector of Japanese art, Louis Gonse, but they were in very poor condition when they were 'discovered' by the then Japanese Curator at the Chester Beatty Library, Mrs Yoshiko Ushioda, in the 1980s. With the support of the Japanese Ambassador to Ireland, Mr Hatano, and assistance from the Japan Foundation, Tatsuji Handa, conservationist at the Tokyo National Museum and his nephew, Tatsumi Sasaki, came to Ireland and stabilised the scrolls prior to their being sent for conservation to the Handa Kyuseido laboratories in the National Museum, Tokyo in 1994-95. As such scrolls, by their very nature, must be rolled and unrolled for viewing, it is inevitable that many areas of the silk on which they are painted will become separated from the lining and crease while, in other areas, tension between the silk and the lining-paper will lead to a distortion of the former. This is what had happened with the *Chogonka Scrolls*. Previous repairs had led to further damages and the painted surfaces were stained and fly-spotted in places while discolouration of the lining-papers added further to the scrolls' unsightliness.

In Tokyo, the scrolls were thoroughly examined and their condition documented. Next the old linings were removed, the paintings washed, and any loose pigments were affixed. Where patches of the silk were missing, new infills were inserted. New lining-papers of thin *mino* paper, dyed to match the old ones with a mixture of *yasha* dye and *sumi* (Indian ink), were applied and new outer covers were added. These are of a gold-threaded brocade with a geometric (*shokko*) pattern that was often used in Tang China.

Ireland has benefited greatly as a result of the generosity of the Japanese and their conservators and, as a result, the Chester Beatty Library now has two scrolls that have been preserved and made safe for future generations. A CD-Rom with a history of the scrolls and the story depicted on them has been published by the Trustees, designed and developed by X Communications. It is available in the Library. Bai Juyi's entire poem is read by Ms Xiao Hong of Trinity College, Dublin in Mandarin: it is an aural delight.

KATE ROBINSON *is an art historian, critic, and curator. She is a guide at the Chester Beatty Library, Dublin.*

ACKNOWLEDGMENTS: *Information about the restoration processes were taken from the book,* Restoration of Japanese Art in European and American Collections *(1995). It is intended as an introduction to the Japanese arts of conservation by the group, First Aid for the World's Cultural Heritage.*

I am deeply indebted to Mrs Yoshiko Ushioda, until recently Curator of the Japanese Collections at the Chester Beatty Library, also to the present Curator of East Asian Collections at the Library, Dr Clare Pollard, both of whom gave generously of their time and knowledge. I should also like to thank Mr Don Bagley and Miss Sheila Kulkarni, both of the Chester Beatty Library, for their consideration and assistance.

(Opposite) **6.** Kano SANSETSU (1590-1651): *Yang Guifei ready to receive the favour of the emperor. Chogonka Scroll.* 1646-47. (The Chester Beatty Library, Dublin). The Emperor and Yang Guifei are seen on a raised stage, their bed chamber, with curtains of hibiscus and lotus flower design draped around the room.

(Overleaf) **7.** Kano SANSETSU (1590-1651): *The execution of Yang Guifei. Chogonka Scroll.* 1646-47. (The Chester Beatty Library, Dublin). Kneeling beside a stream, Yang Guifei is to be executed. An officer, holding a white silk cord, prepares to do the deed. Her hair ornaments are strewn on the ground beside her.

8. Kano SANSETSU (1590-1651): *The rebel army breaches the palace gate. Chogonka Scroll.* 1646-47. (The Chester Beatty Library, Dublin). An Lushan, his lieutenant on horseback, and several foot soldiers armed with lances burst through the gate of the palace.

9. Kano SANSETSU (1590-1651): *Xuanzong escapes from Chang'an. Chogonka Scroll.* 1646-47. (The Chester Beatty Library, Dublin). In the middle distance, the Emperor's party, escaping from the burning of Chang'an Palace, is passing through mountains and clouds.

10. Kano SANSETSU (1590-1651): *The Emperor looks at the lotus blossoms at the pool of Taiyi. Chogonka Scroll.* 1646-47. (The Chester Beatty Library, Dublin). The Emperor, pining the loss of Yang Guifei, is reminded of her beauty by the lotus petals and weeps in grief.

(Overleaf) **11.** Kano SANSETSU (1590-1651): *The lonely Emperor in his night chamber. Chogonka Scroll.* 1646-47. (The Chester Beatty Library, Dublin). A year has passed and the Emperor, unable to sleep, still thinks of Yang Guifei.

Double Identity
Aloysius O'Kelly and Arthur Oakley

Julian Campbell

has discovered that an Irish artist had an American alter ego

In 1893, the Irish artist, Aloysius O'Kelly (1851-1928), exhibited a watercolour entitled *A Game of Draughts* at the Royal Hibernian Academy. The following year, 1894, he again showed the picture (which is probably identical with a painting of the same title that he exhibited at the London Royal Academy in 1889) at the Liverpool Autumn Exhibition.[1] In the catalogues of both these exhibitions, O'Kelly gave his address as '86 Bolsover Street, London'. By coincidence, a painting with an identical title was exhibited at the Royal Society of British Artists the same year, 1893-94. It too was painted by an artist who lived at 86 Bolsover Street, London; but that artist was called 'Oakley', Arthur Oakley[2]

Arthur Oakley, who is said to have been born in New York, is mentioned in various editions of *American Art Annual* and *Who's Who in American Art* as a former pupil in Paris of Bonnat and Bouguereau.[3] He showed in occasional exhibitions in America. Becoming a student at the Académie Julian in Paris in 1901 where he was a pupil of Bouguereau and Gabriel Ferrier,[4] he is listed in Catherine Fehrer's *Index of Students at the Académie Julian*[5] but not, surprisingly, in Mantle Fielding's comprehensive *Dictionary of American Artists*. Nor, for that matter, is he included in either of the standard encyclopedias of artists' biographies, Benézit or Thieme-Becker. His address in Paris was at 13 rue St Sulpice[6] but by 1904 he had moved to Brittany where, from an address at the Hôtel de France, Concarneau, he sent paintings to the Paris Salon in 1904 (*Conté de Grand-père)* and again in 1905 (*La Bonne Aventure* and *Interieur Breton)*.[7] In the Salon catalogue of 1904, Oakley listed Bouguereau and Ferrier as his teachers; in the catalogue for 1905, he added Bonnat to the list.

Oakley's painting, *La Bonne Aventure* (Fig 4) was reproduced as a small black and white postcard. One of these cards, on which the artist has written a brief message in a flowing hand – 'à Mademoiselle Delobbe avec les compliments du peintre Oakley' (Fig 4)[8] – is in the archives of the Musée de Pont-Aven. The picture is of an interior with five young girls in Breton costume consulting an old fortune-teller. The painting was also exhibited under its English title, *Fortune Telling*, at the Chicago Art Institute in 1905. Another of Oakley's paintings, dating from 1906 and probably painted at Pont-Aven once hung in the Pension Gloanac there.[9] It shows a seated Breton girl and is painted in a broad, simple style with touches of pure colour, such as blue and red (Fig 1).

Aloysius O'Kelly, who was born in Dublin, had also studied in Paris; but that was in the 1870s as a pupil of Gérôme at the Ecole des Beaux Arts, some thirty years before Oakley joined the Académie Julian in 1901. Coincidentally, O'Kelly had lodged at 4 Rue St Sulpice,[10] just across the road from where Oakley was later to live. O'Kelly's presence in Brittany by 1877 is documented in a rare portrait drawing which is inscribed *Al. O'Kelly Pont-Aven Dec. 19/77*. The drawing could be a self-portrait by O'Kelly but it may be of O'Kelly by his compatriot, Thomas Hovenden: an alternative hypothesis is that it is a portrait of Hovenden by O'Kelly.[11]

After France, O'Kelly lived variously in the West of Ireland, Egypt, England, and America and then, in the early years of the 20th century, he returned to Brittany, staying at Pont-Aven where, like Oakley, some of his portraits of Breton villagers entered the collection of the Pension Gloanec. By 1905, O'Kelly was at Concarneau and for the next four years he painted Breton interiors, harbour scenes, and landscapes. Some of these he sent to the Paris Salon: in 1908, *La Sortie* and *Devant le Feu* and, in 1909, *Ave Maria, Procession Religieuse en Bretagne* and *L'auberge, Bretagne*. Like Oakley (in the years 1904 and 1905),

Arthur Oakley
Aloysius O'Kelly.

(Overleaf). **1.** Arthur OAKLEY: *Young girl of Pont-Aven*. 1906. Oil on canvas, 60 x 50 cm. Signed and dated Oakley '06 (Private Collection, Brittany). Although signed 'Oakley', this study of a Breton girl may be by O'Kelly. In contrast to the 'Dutch' tonality of some of O'Kelly's interiors of the early-20th century, the picture has an unusual simplicity and sweetness of colouring in the touches of pink and blue in the child's doll-like face and bonnet.

O'Kelly's address in the Salon catalogue was given as the Hôtel de France, Concarneau and, again like Oakley, none of O'Kelly's paintings was for sale.[12] Even more striking is the similarity between the catalogue descriptions of the two artists. In 1905, for example, Oakley lists himself as *Oakley, Arthur, né à New York (Etats Unis d'Amerique) – elève de M.M.Bonnat, Bouguereau et Gabriel Ferrier. – A Concarneau, (Finistère), Hôtel de France* while, in 1908, O'Kelly is *O'Kelly, Aloysius, né a New York, (Etats-Unis d'Amerique) elève de M.M.Bonnat, et Gabriel Ferrier. – A Concarneau, (Finistère), Hôtel de France.*[13]

It seems to me that O'Kelly and Oakley are one and the same and that to the many confusions already surrounding Aloysius O'Kelly – his age, his place of birth, his date of death, his travels, his training, the varieties of styles in which he worked, his signature – must now be added his actual name, even his nationality. In actual fact, he is recorded, in an unpublished biography of the New Zealand artist, Sydney L Thompson, who also worked at Concarneau, as having referred to himself on occasion as 'Oakelly'.[14]

The identity of the two artists as one and the same goes some way to explaining several of the mysteries surrounding O'Kelly. In the Salon catalogues of 1908-09, O'Kelly lists his teachers as Bonnat and Ferrier while in the *American Art Annual* for the years 1907-10, he gives Gérôme, Bouguereau, and Bonnat.[15] Oakley, on the other hand, states (in the Salon catalogue, 1904-05) that his masters were Bonnat, Bouguereau, and Ferrier. This suggests that O'Kelly had studied with Gérôme and Bonnat in the 1870s but had later, in 1901-03, been a pupil of Bouguereau and Ferrier at the Académie Julian. It also explains why O'Kelly had not, as previously thought, studied at the Académie Julian where many of the artists who later moved to Brittany had trained. He did study there, but as an artist in his fifties calling himself Oakley and as an American. In this latter respect

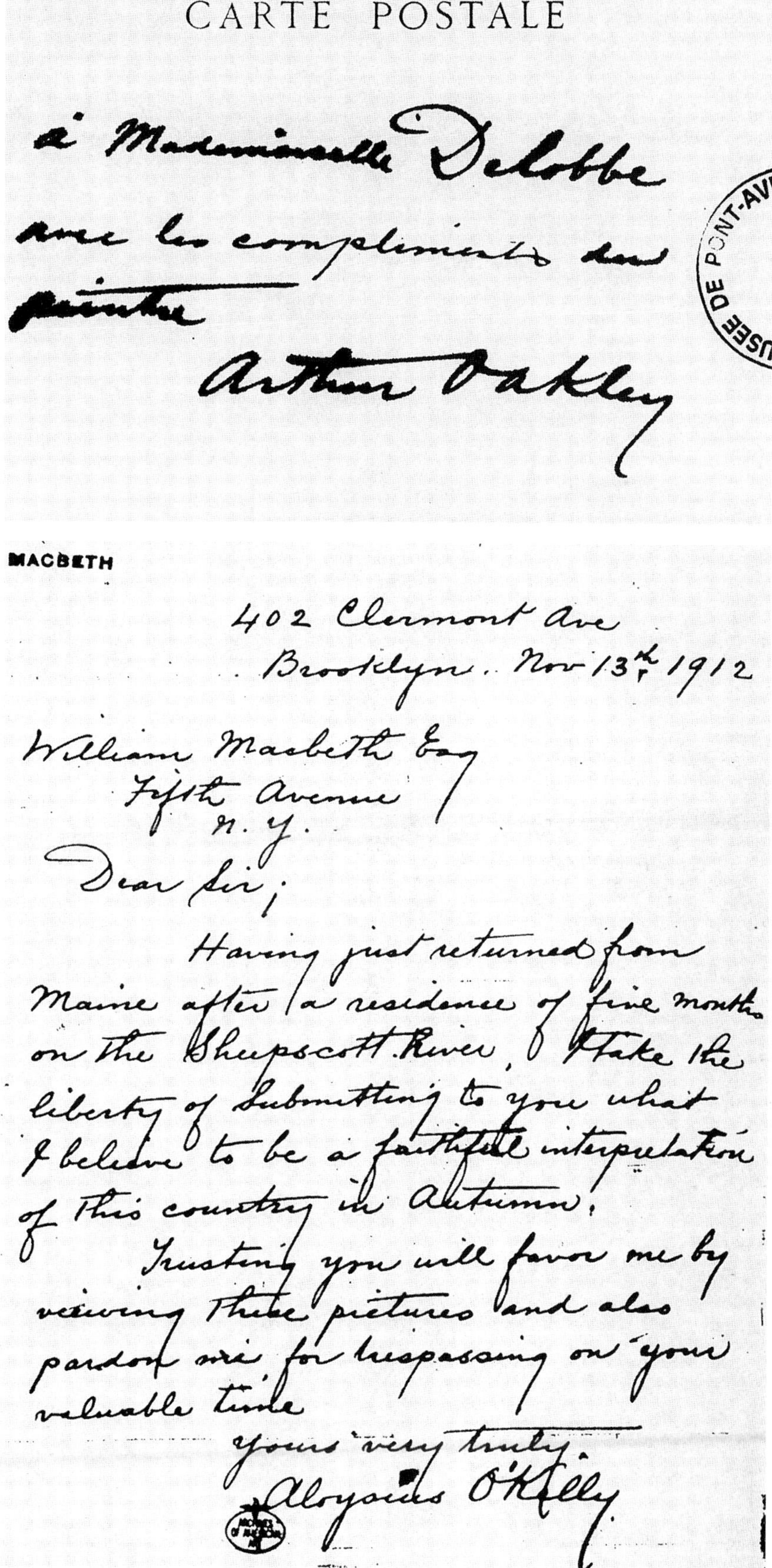

CARTE POSTALE

à Mademoiselle Delobbe
avec les compliments du
peintre
Arthur Oakley

MACBETH

402 Clermont Ave
Brooklyn. Nov 13th 1912

William Macbeth Esq
Fifth Avenue
N.Y.

Dear Sir;

Having just returned from Maine after a residence of five months on the Sheepscott River, I take the liberty of submitting to you what I believe to be a faithful interpretation of this country in Autumn.

Trusting you will favor me by viewing these pictures and also pardon me, for trespassing on your valuable time

Yours very truly
Aloysius O'Kelly

2. Arthur OAKLEY and Aloysius O'KELLY: *Their Handwriting Compared.* The postcard (above) was sent by Oakley to Mademoiselle Delobbe about 1906; the letter (below) was written by O'Kelly in 1912. The writing in the two documents is remarkably similar.

3. Thomas HOVENDEN or Aloysius O'Kelly: *Portrait of Aloysius O'Kelly.* 1877. Ink on paper, 9.5 x 7.5 cm. Inscribed: *Al. O'Kelly Pont-Aven Dec. 19/77.* (Kennedy Galleries, New York). This tiny ink drawing, made at Pont-Aven in December 1877 is a rare portrait of O'Kelly in Brittany in his mid twenties. It is believed to be a portrait of O'Kelly by his compatriot Thomas Hovenden from Co Cork, but it may be a portrait of Hovenden by O'Kelly. The handwriting appears to be that of O'Kelly, so it may actually be a self-portrait. The inscription *Pont-Aven, Dec.19 '77* is of significance in that it confirms that O'Kelly remained in Brittany into winter.

O'Kelly/Oakley was not misrepresenting himself as he had been admitted an American citizen on 1 May 1901.[16]

The most compelling identification between O'Kelly and Oakley, however, is their handwriting. The confident message written by Oakley, in his postcard to Mlle Delobbe (Fig 2), has close similarities with O'Kelly's early signatures and with the writing in his letters written to William Macbeth in New York, 1909-1912 (Fig. 2).[17]

Valuable new biographical details may now be proposed for O'Kelly: that he first adopted the name Oakley as early as 1893; that, after a few years in America *c.*1895-1901, he returned to France in *c.*1901; that, around the age of fifty, he became an art student in Paris for the second time, studying in the Académie Julian, 1901-1903, and lodging in the same street where he had lived thirty years earlier; that in the atelier of Bouguereau and Ferrier, he was a fellow-pupil of his compatriate, W J Leech, of Sydney Thompson, and of the Austrian Carl Moser; that he may have influenced the plans of these younger artists to visit Brittany and may have lived between Pont-Aven and Concarneau from *c.*1903-1909, longer than is previously thought (which would confirm Homan Potterton's speculation that some of the time that O'Kelly was believed to be in America, he was in France);[18] and that between 1904 and 1909, he signed some of his pictures *O'Kelly* and some *Oakley;* and that he exhibited at the Paris Salon in 1904-05 as well as in 1908-09 (under the pseudonym of 'Oakley'). He may have known the French artist, Alfred Delobbe.[19]

But why did O'Kelly, who was born in Dublin, state (in the Salon catalogues and in registering at the Académie Julian) that he was an American and born in New York? Had he forgotten his Irish heritage? There is no reason why he should have wished to lose his historic Irish name. Perhaps what started out as a punning joke amongst friends led him to adopt a pseudonym. Perhaps, after spending too much time in the bazaars of Cairo or the mountains of Morocco, O'Kelly had become forgetful. Or perhaps the political unrest which he had witnessed in Ireland in his younger days, the fact that his brother James O'Kelly had been a member of the IRB,[20] and later had become friends with Charles Stuart Parnell,[21] made him (Aloysius) wish to put his Irish background behind him for a while, and take on another 'American' identity. The long-awaited Aloysius O'Kelly retrospective exhibition at the Hugh Lane Gallery of Modern Art this year, selected by Niamh O'Sullivan, will help to provide answers to some of these questions.[22]

JULIAN CAMPBELL is a tutor in the Crawford College of Art, Cork and is the author of many books and catalogues on Irish artists in Brittany.

ACKNOWLEDGEMENTS: I am very grateful to the following people in my research for this article: Mme Catherine Puget, Conservateur of the Musée at Pont-Aven; Dr David Sellin: Dr Catherine Fehrer; and Dr Margarita Cappock.

4. Arthur OAKLEY: *La Bonne Aventure*. 1905. Postcard, 8.5 x 13.5 cm. (Archives, Musée de Pont-Aven). The hearth appeared in many paintings of Breton interiors from the 1860s onwards. O'Kelly had represented a hearth in *The Evening Pipe*, c.1877, and this painting by 'Oakley' has affinities with O'Kelly's *Before the Fire*, 1908. The seated woman on the left is telling the five younger girls their fortunes. Such was the popularity of Breton subjects in the early-20th century that some artists made postcards of their paintings. Oakley's picture was exhibited at the Paris Salon in 1905, but its present whereabouts is not known.

1 RA, 1889, no 1003; RHA, 1893, no 169, £20; Liverpool *Autumn Exhibition* (1894), no 919, £15-15. The painting, included amongst several Cairo pictures, was no doubt also an Egyptian subject. See O'Kelly's oil painting *Game of Draughts*, 1889, no 31 in *The Irish Impressionists* (1984).

2 Listed in J Johnson, *Works exhibited at the Royal Society of British Artists, 1824-1893* (London 1975). The watercolour was priced at £20 which, as an added coincidence, was the same price as O'Kelly's RHA picture.

3 I am very grateful to Dr D Sellin in Washington for sending me this information. Dr Sellin, the authority on the subject of American artists in Brittany, had found little information on Oakley.

4 Registers of Académie Julian, Archives Nationales de France.

5 C Fehrer, *The Julian Academy Paris 1868-1939* (New York 1989).

6 Registers of Académie Julian.

7 Catalogues of Paris Salon, Société des Artistes Français, 1904-05.

8 Mlle Delobbe may have been the daughter of the French academic painter, Alfred Delobbe, who was a regular visitor to Brittany.

9 Information supplied by Mme Catherine Puget, conservateur of Musée de Pont-Aven.

10 Registers of Ecole des Beaux Arts (Gerome's atelier), Archives National de France.

11 The exact identity of this ink drawing (Kennedy Galleries, New York) has not yet been established. It was listed in an exhibition of Hovenden's work (*Thomas Hovenden, 1840-1895*, Woodmere Art Museum, Philadelphia, 1995, no 12) as a drawing of O'Kelly by Hovenden. David Sellin speculates that it may be a portrait of Hovenden by O'Kelly (Letter to the author, 15 May 1998). A third possibility is that it is a self-portrait, perhaps given to Hovenden by O'Kelly at Pont-Aven.

12 Catalogues of Paris Salon, 1908-09. Both Oakley's three Salon entries, 1904-05, and O'Kelly's four entries, 1908-09, are marked with an asterix. This indicates that all the pictures belonged to the artist, i.e. were not for sale.

13 Catalogues of Paris Salon, 1904-05 and 1908-09.

14 Cited by D Ferran in *William John Leech. An Irish Painter Abroad*, National Gallery of Ireland (1996), p. 29, 32; p. 303, note 41. My curiosity as to the uncertainty over the names O'Kelly and Oakley was aroused in 1993 when Mme Catherine Puget showed me photographs of Breton portraits and figures by O'Kelly. In subsequent correspondence, Mme Puget informed me that the present painting, *Young Girl of Pont-Aven* was signed 'Oakley' and not O'Kelly.

15 H Potterton, 'Aloysius O'Kelly in America,' *Irish Arts Review Yearbook*, vol 12 (1996), p. 91.

16 Potterton (as note 15), p. 92.

17 Letters from O'Kelly to W Macbeth, Archives of American Art.

18 Potterton (as note 15), pp. 91-95.

19 François Alfred Delobbe (1835-1915) was in the Pont-Aven and Concarneau region in 1904-05, exactly the same time as O'Kelly or Oakley.

20 N O'Sullivan, 'Through Irish Eyes, the work of Aloysius O'Kelly in the *Illustrated London News*, *History Ireland*, vol 3, no 3 (Autumn 1995), p. 10-16.

21 See M Cappock, 'Aloysius O'Kelly and *The Illustrated London News*', *Irish Arts Review Yearbook* (1996).

22 N O'Sullivan, *Re-Orientations. Aloysius O'Kelly: Painting, Politics and Popular Culture*, Hugh Lane Municipal Gallery of Modern Art (Dublin 1999).

Pageantry or Propaganda? The Illustrated London News and Royal Visitors in Ireland

Margarita Cappock

examines some revealing images of 19th-century Ireland

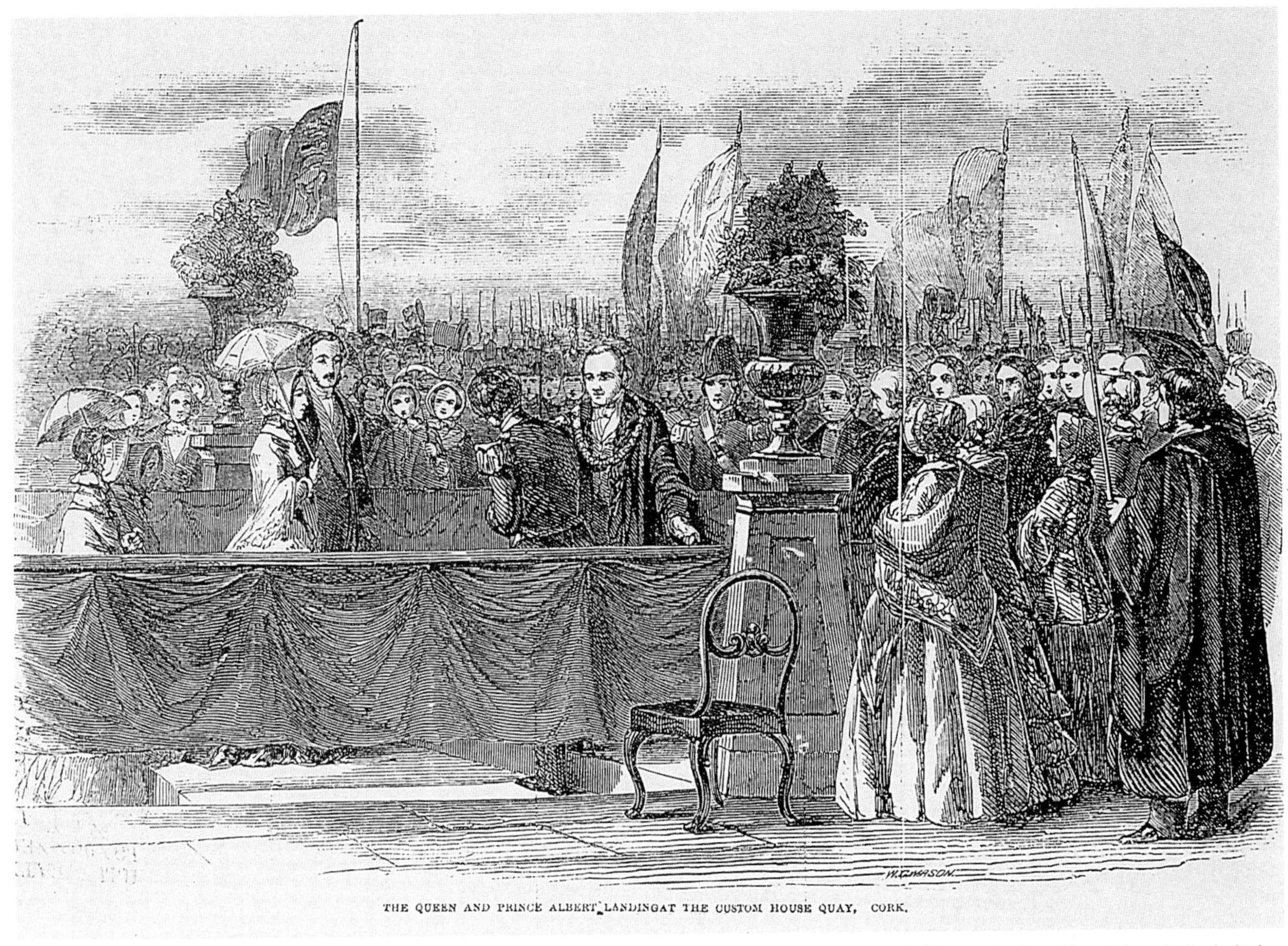
THE QUEEN AND PRINCE ALBERT LANDING AT THE CUSTOM HOUSE QUAY, CORK.

1. The Illustrated London News: *The Queen and Prince Albert landing at the Custom House Quay, Cork.* 11 Aug 1849. This was the first of four visits to Ireland which Queen Victoria made during her long reign. She is dressed in simple attire and holding her own parasol; she is greeted by the Mayor of Cork.

The publication of the first issue of the *Illustrated London News* on 14 May 1842 marked a revolution in the gathering and presentation of news through its pioneering use of pictorial reportage. From its inception, this weekly magazine gave a considerable amount of coverage to Irish events, with political, social, and industrial activities featured extensively. A fascinating aspect of these reports is the depiction of tours in Ireland by members of the British royal family and a total of one hundred and sixty-seven illustrations of royalty in Ireland were published between the years 1842 and 1900. Queen Victoria (1819-1901) went to Ireland on four occasions – in 1849, 1853, 1861, and 1900 – and several of her children, her eldest son, the Prince of Wales, most frequently of all, also ventured across the Irish sea. Popular destinations for the royal visitors were Dublin, Belfast, and the south of Ireland.

All the royal visits were politically motivated, well-orchestrated, and their timing was carefully calculated. The intention was that all sections of the populace should be brought together to celebrate and, more importantly, to feel a sense of unity with their British neighbours. However, in assessing the visual and written coverage of these events, a number of issues must be considered: the accuracy of the illustrations in their provision of a contemporary record of the royal visits; the ceremonial aspect and ephemeral architectural constructions erected during a royal visit; the Irish reaction to the aura of pageantry surrounding the monarchy and whether this reaction can be interpreted as a sign of allegiance to the throne or merely as a non-political enjoyment of the grandeur, symbolism, and theatricality of the monarchy.

Numerous sources note that Queen Victoria had little time for the Irish and visited Ireland more out of a sense of duty rather than with any great feeling of pleasure.[1] Rumours of Fenian assassination plots, the prevalence of Irish secret societies, and the general air of unrest and revolt in Ireland did little to cultivate any sense of fondness for the Irish in the Queen, who possessed a strong fear of rebellion in any guise.[2] Although the issue of acquiring an Irish residence was raised with her, she turned down the suggestion and reserved her favours for her Scottish home, Balmoral, where she passed many years of her reign in contrast to the relatively few weeks in total that she spent in Ireland. Successive Prime Ministers, most notably William Gladstone, attempted to change the Queen's negative attitude towards Ireland but their attempts were frequently thwarted by the Queen's personal prejudices. Indeed her relationship with Gladstone became fraught with tension over two issues, both of which she opposed – the disestablishment of the Church of Ireland and the campaign for Home Rule in Ireland.[3] The Prime Minister also proposed the abolition of the Lord Lieutenancy of Ireland and its replacement with the residence of the Prince of Wales in Dublin for four or five months every year but that suggestion was also firmly rejected by the Queen who already disapproved of the hedonistic lifestyle of the Prince of Wales.[4] It is not surprising that, on resigning office in August 1886, Gladstone allegedly said of Queen Victoria, 'Poor Ireland. It holds but a small place in her heart.'[5]

Queen Victoria's first visit to Ireland in 1849 was significant because it took place towards the end of the Famine. Lord Clarendon, the Lord Lieutenant, had indicated to Lord John Russell, the Prime Minister, in June 1849 that the country and its people were no longer in an agitated state and that a visit by the Queen would be propitious.[6] It had been twenty-eight years since a British monarch had visited Ireland, the preceding royal visit being that of King George IV in 1821. The Queen, Prince Albert, and their four children arrived in Cork in the month of August 1849 and travelled onwards to Dublin and Belfast. The visit was immediately perceived as an event of national importance. *The Illustrated London News* printed an extra number supplementary to its issue of 11 August while the panoramic view of London, which was the standard masthead of the paper, was substituted by a harp and shamrocks to mark the Irish theme.

2. THE ILLUSTRATED LONDON NEWS: *The Procession passing through the Mardyke, Cork.* 11 Aug 1849. The temporary structures erected for the royal visit to Cork were decorated with Blackpool gingham which was subsequently donated to the poor.

3. THE ILLUSTRATED LONDON NEWS: *The Procession passing through the Grand Quadruple Arch at Anglesey-Bridge, Cork.* 11 Aug 1849. Triumphal arches such as this one were a standard feature of the royal visits in both Victorian England and Ireland but they were of a temporary nature.

The Queen travelled to Cork from the Isle of Wight by boat and her reception at Cork is the subject of a number of illustrations. *The Queen and Prince Albert landing at the Custom House Quay, Cork* (Fig 1) is interesting in that the Queen is depicted in quite simple attire wearing a bonnet and holding her own parasol. Indeed, the Mayor is more elaborately dressed than the monarch. The reason for the lack of embellishment in the Queen's dress was probably due to the fact that she realised that it would not be prudent to arrive in famine-stricken Ireland in any finery. The image is typical of the early illustrations appearing in the publication in that it is quite small in scale and sketchily executed with little evidence of detailed portraiture. The accompanying article noted that the Queen was anxious that no expensive arrangements should be made for her reception in Cork. The triumphal arches there were decorated with Blackpool gingham which was subsequently donated to the Ladies Clothing Society for the benefit of the poor. *The Procession passing through the Mardyke, Cork* (Fig 2) and *The Procession passing through the Grand Quadruple Arch at Anglesey Bridge, Cork* (Fig 3) show the type of temporary structures erected.

The tone of the editorial was optimistic and paternalistic noting that '...the landing of Queen Victoria in Ireland – like a beneficent messenger of peace and good-will – will be celebrated throughout the country with manifestations of popular love and rejoicing, to which the previous history of Ireland can offer no parallel.' But despite the professed sympathy of the Queen with Irish suffering, she was spared having to witness any of the unpalatable horrors of a country barely recovering from a devastating famine: 'The Queen, it has been alleged, will not see the dark side of Ireland. She will not behold with her own eyes the wretchedness of the peasantry – the fertile acres lying uncultivated for want of capital and of skill – the roofless cabins of myriads of homeless people, and the vast tracts of land that have

4. THE ILLUSTRATED LONDON NEWS: *Dance of the Peasantry on the Lawn at Carton*. 18 Aug 1849. Scenes such as this one indicate that the Queen was spared having to witness any harrowing scenes of the hardships of peasant life in post-famine Ireland.

5. THE ILLUSTRATED LONDON NEWS: *Illuminations in Sackville-Street, Dublin*. 11 Aug 1849. Illuminations were an important aspect of the celebrations. Professor Gluckman of Trinity College pioneered this interesting use of electric light which was directed from the top of Nelson's column.

6. THE ILLUSTRATED LONDON NEWS: *The Procession at the Grand Triumphal Arch in Upper Baggot-Street, at the entrance to the City of Dublin*. 11 Aug 1849. This is a particularly fine example of a triumphal arch; many of the Dublin arches were funded by committees or by private individuals.

7. THE ILLUSTRATED LONDON NEWS: *The Royal Arch High-Street, Belfast*. 18 Aug 1849. A considerable amount of effort went in to the Queen's visit to Belfast in 1849 and many elaborate arches were constructed especially for the visit.

8. THE ILLUSTRATED LONDON NEWS: *Arch at Turner's Hammersmith Iron-Works, Dublin*. 11 Aug 1849. An early illustration of a privately-funded arch in Ballsbridge, a strongly Unionist area of Dublin. Made from metal, it was paid for by Thomas Turner, who owned an ironworks in the area.

9. The Illustrated London News: *Reception of the Prince and Princess of Wales at Belfast: Festive Arches and Decorations.* 2 May 1885. As well as being symbols of welcome, many of the arches were thematic. These particular arches celebrate technology and industry.

10. The Illustrated London News: *Opening of the Dublin Great Industrial Exhibition.* 4 June 1853. The Queen made no less than four visits to the Great Exhibition of 1853 where she purchased Irish products on display.

never been turned by spade or plough, nor yielded food for human kind.' On her way from Cork to Dublin, the royal couple visited Carton House in county Kildare and images such as *Dance of the Peasantry on the Lawn at Carton* (Fig 4), with sturdy-looking peasant couples dancing before them, demonstrate the happy and idealised version of Ireland that was offered rather than any evidence of famine, poverty or disease.

In Dublin, the total transformation of the city with the erection of triumphal arches, the encrustation of buildings with lights, and the huge influx of people was visually documented. The contemporaneous quality of this coverage makes it fascinating and it is notable that the Dublin authorities took a less frugal approach to the visit than those in Cork. Visitors from England, Scotland, and Wales meant that hotel prices in Dublin reached exorbitant rates although the presence of an unsavoury element in the form of pickpockets was also reported. The less well-off bivoucacked on Killiney Hill in order to catch a glimpse of the arrival of the Queen's vessel. Illuminations were an important feature of the pageantry of royal visits and would also appear to have been a contentious issue as many people considered these to be a waste of tallow and gas but light was obviously a symbol of welcome and its function was to enliven the general appearance of the city during a royal visit. Various Dublin buildings were illuminated as is evident in the illustration entitled *Illuminations in Sackville-street, Dublin. The Electric Light on Nelson's Pillar* (Fig 5). One notes that the facade of Francis Johnston's General Post Office is illuminated by two beams of electric light which shine from the top of Nelson's Pillar. This interesting use of electric light was due to the efforts of a Professor Gluckman of Trinity College. The royal visit generated employment as well: 'Architects, builders, gas-fitters, carpenters, painters, decorators, and others, found abundant occupation in making preparations for the forthcoming ceremonial and its after festivities.' Shopkeepers also welcomed the opportunity to sell native Irish manufactures such as Killarney arbutus, poplin, and tabinets and these products were apparently placed in prominent positions in order to attract the attention of wealthy English visitors. This theme of commercial exploitation was extended with the commodification of the royal visit by the mass production of celebratory souvenirs.

11. THE ILLUSTRATED LONDON NEWS: *Her Majesty's visit to Mr and Mrs Dargan at Mount-Anville, Dublin*. 10 Sep 1853. While in Ireland in 1853, the Queen took the unprecedented step of visiting William Dargan and his family at home. Ironically, they were out observing the preparations for the royal celebrations when she called.

12. THE ILLUSTRATED LONDON NEWS: *Her Majesty reviewing the troops on the Curragh of Kildare*. 7 Sep 1861. The presence of the Queen and the displays of troops generated a considerable amount of excitement, with spectators travelling from far and wide to catch a glimpse of the activities.

13. THE ILLUSTRATED LONDON NEWS: *Review by her Majesty on the Curragh of Kildare – Charge of Cavalry*. 7 Sep 1861. The power of the military presence in Ireland is strongly conveyed by this image. The emphasis on the military offered comfort to Unionists but nationalists would only have seen it as an expression of power by an oppressor.

In Dublin, a number of triumphal arches were erected, for example, at Nassau Street and Eccles Street. The arch at Baggot Street was particularly fine, as evidenced by the illustration of *The Procession at the Grand Triumphal Arch in Upper Baggot-Street, at the entrance to the city of Dublin* (Fig 6). Some of these arches were paid for by a committee, whereas others were funded by private individuals. The Eccles Street triumphal arch was built and paid for by Messrs Williams[7] of Talbot Street. Williams also presented Her Majesty with a fawn-coloured dove with a white ribbon around its neck, as a symbol of peace. This dove was lowered down to the royal carriage as the royal party passed under the triumphal arch. One of the early illustrations of a privately-funded triumphal arch is the illustration entitled *Arch at Turner's Hammersmith Iron-Works, Dublin* (Fig 8). Turner's Ironworks was located in Ballsbridge, a strongly Unionist area of Dublin. Thomas Turner was the architect of the Palm Houses at Kew Gardens in London and this is alluded to in the illustration as the word 'Kew' appears under the triumphal arch. The image shows large crowds gathered to witness the passage of the horse-drawn royal carriage and procession which seems to be travelling at great speed. It is not entirely successful in that it does not accurately convey the scale or detail of the arch which is vividly described in the accompanying article.

Within the visual coverage of the Irish royal visits one notes a difference between the type of arches erected in Dublin and those in Belfast. This difference is already apparent in the coverage of the earliest visit in 1849. *The Royal Arch High-Street Belfast* (Fig 7) and *The Royal Procession in the High-Street, Belfast* show sturdy-looking structures and platforms of a more elaborate nature than the Dublin arches (many of which were constructed from metal and decorated with foliage) while for a later visit, that of The Prince and Princess of Wales to Belfast in May 1885, the arches were even more elaborate. The difference could be interpreted as a reflection of the comparative wealth of Belfast and the popularity of the monarchy in loyalist Ulster. In addition to being symbols of celebration, some of the arches were thematic. In the illustration entitled *Reception of the Prince and Princess of Wales at Belfast: Festive Arches and Decoration (Fig 9)*, the bicycle club's arch, with the inscription, 'Welcome Patrons of the Wheel', highlights the intrinsic link between the royal visits and the celebration of modern technology. The royal visitors were seen as champions of industry and new technology. Part of the reason for their visits to Ireland was to promote it as a possible location for British industries.

The royal endorsement of Irish industry and manufacturing also extended to Irish products. When visiting Ireland, the female members of the royal party, including the Queen, wore Irish-made materials such as poplin and Irish lace; they frequently purchased Irish items, in particular Irish-made furniture.[8] The Queen made no less than four visits to the Great Exhibition of 1853 in Dublin and purchased Irish products on display. One of the better illustrations of this exhibition is *The Opening of the Dublin Great Industrial Exhibition* which was published on 4 June 1853 (Fig 10). The royal couple did not visit the exhibition until September 1853 when they also took the unprecedented step of visiting William Dargan (1799-1867), the Irish railway entrepreneur, who was responsible for the Exhibition. *Her Majesty's visit to Mr and Mrs Dargan at Mount-Anville, Dublin* (Fig 11) depicts this unusual event. Ironically, Dargan and his family were not at home when the royal party first arrived – they were out observing the preparations being made for the illuminations to celebrate the royal visit!

On surveying the illustrations in *The Illustrated London News*, it is difficult to gauge how popular Queen Victoria actually was in Ireland or what the genuine reaction of the populace was to her presence or that of her family.[9] To an extent, the coverage is a propagandist exercise on the part of the publication with the intent of creating a positive image of the monarchy's relationship with Ireland. As a result, there is no visual coverage of any negative incidents which took place during the visits although they are referred to briefly in the written coverage, nor is it possible to ascertain the degree of ill-feeling which may have been occasioned. It would appear that the Irish populace became involved in the pageantry surrounding the visits although whether that can be taken as a sign of allegiance to the Crown is questionable. It is most likely that the crowd of people depicted in many of the images was responding to a normal human impulse of interest in spectacle and that its presence was merely a reflection of this.

Vehement counter-demonstrations took place during the visit of the Prince and Princess of Wales in 1885, particularly when they visited the south of Ireland. The Fenians in the United States had offered $10,000 for the body of the Prince, alive or dead, something the London publication neglected to mention.[10] A demonstration took place on Parnell Bridge in Cork when the royal party were crossing, yet the illustration entitled *The Royal party passing over 'Parnell Bridge', Cork* (Fig 14) belies the fact that there was any animosity. An immense crowd has gathered to see the royal party and the social mix of this crowd is clear with the battered hat of the Irishman and the top-hats of the gentry much in evidence. Similarly, *The Visit of the Prince and Princess of Wales to Ireland: The Royal Procession passing College-street, Dublin* (Fig 15) conveys a sense of a warm reception in Dublin. Large crowds, of mainly well-dressed spectators, are shown waving their top hats at the horsedrawn procession. The Prince of Wales lifts his top hat to acknowledge this reception. A small group of children have clambered onto the pedestal of the statue of William III to gain a better vantage point. The illustration is well-drawn with reasonably accurate depictions of the architecture of the Bank of Ireland and Trinity College.

The illustration of *The Prince and Princess of Wales at the Lakes of Killarney* (Fig 17) creates a very positive and, most likely, distorted impression. The royal party are seen travelling by horse and carriage up the mountainous terrain surrounding the Killarney Lakes. Killarney was, of course, *the* Victorian tourist resort in Ireland and the Queen, who had visited the Lakes in 1861, played an important role in inducing wealthy British tourists to visit Ireland. The absence of any vegetation and the

14. THE ILLUSTRATED LONDON NEWS: *The Royal Party passing over 'Parnell Bridge', Cork.* 25 Apr 1885. Signed bottom left, *T. Robinson*. In spite of the welcoming crowd represented here, there was a protest demonstration on the bridge during the visit of the Prince and Princess of Wales.

15. THE ILLUSTRATED LONDON NEWS: *Visit of the Prince and Princess of Wales to Ireland: The Royal Procession passing College-street, Dublin.* 25 Apr 1868. A sense of a warm reception in Dublin is conveyed by this image. Large crowds of well-dressed spectators are shown waving their top hats at the horsedrawn procession.

THE ROYAL PARTY ON THE LAKE AT KILLARNEY.

16. THE ILLUSTRATED LONDON NEWS: *The Royal Party on the Lakes of Killarney.* 2 May 1885. Signed bottom right, *WHO*. The Prince and Princess of Wales took a boat trip on the Lakes of Killarney which was one of the most popular tourist destination for Victorian travellers.

17. THE ILLUSTRATED LONDON NEWS: *The Prince and Princess of Wales at the Lakes of Killarney*. 2 May 1885. Signed bottom left, *E C Dalton*, bottom right, *W H Overend*. This image of a dutiful, subservient, and sympathetic peasantry supplying members of the British royal family with refreshments has a strongly propagandist flavour.

18. THE ILLUSTRATED LONDON NEWS: *Children's Day in Phoenix Park*. 14 April 1900. Signed bottom left, *S. Begg*. The queen accepts a bunch of flowers from a child on her final visit to Ireland. Children from all over the country gathered in the Phoenix Park to greet the Queen.

presence of three goats in the later image indicate the barren nature of the landscape. The Prince of Wales is seen accepting two glasses of milk from a barefoot peasant girl. This image of the dutiful, subservient, and sympathetic peasantry supplying members of the British royal family with refreshment has strongly propagandist undertones. It gives the impression of allegiance in the face of adversity which was not the case, particularly in the south-western portion of Ireland where land agitation was extensive in the 1880s. During this trip, the Prince and Princess of Wales went on a boat trip on the lakes which is visually documented in the illustration entitled *The Royal Party on the Lakes of Killarney* (Fig 16).

There was also a concerted attempt throughout the reportage of *The Illustrated London News* to portray the Queen as someone who identified with her people and also to demystify her. The device of humour was used to show the human face of the monarch and to endear her to her subjects. In written coverage of one of the Queen's early visits to Dublin, the journalist for *The Illustrated London News* writes that 'An accredited correspondent states that as the Queen's carriage approached the Circular-road a countryman roared out at the top of his voice, "Arrah! Victoria, will you stand up and let us have a look at you?" Her Majesty immediately rose, when the countryman again cried out, "God bless you for that, my darling." The Queen resumed her seat, and, with Prince Albert, laughed heartily at the incident.'

Aside from ingratiating herself with her Irish subjects, the purpose of the royal presence was also to highlight the power of the British empire both in military and naval terms. In 1861, at the instigation of Prince Albert, it was decided that the nineteen-year old Prince of Wales should spend ten weeks at the Curragh camp for infantry training.[11] The Queen and Prince Albert visited the Prince and, while there, the royal couple reviewed the troops. The visit was well-documented visually and a large topographical oil painting of the encampment was executed by Dr Jones Lamprey, Army Staff-Surgeon.[12] The Curragh illustrations were based on photographs taken by Captain E D Fenton, 86th Regiment.[13] The excitement generated by both the presence of the Queen and the display of the troops is evident in illustrations such as *Her Majesty Reviewing the Troops on the Curragh of Kildare* (Fig 12) and *Review by Her Majesty on the Curragh of Kildare – Charge of Cavalry* (Fig 13). The emphasis on the military offered comfort to Unionists while nationalists, on the other hand, saw it only as an expression of power by an oppressor.[14] The entire coverage by *The Illustrated London News* creates an impression of a successful sojourn in Ireland for the

Prince of Wales but the reality was quite different. The Prince's progress on the field was quite poor[15] and he had been given a bad report prior to the arrival of his parents.[16]

The coverage, with a combination of photographs and lithographs, of the Queen's final visit to Ireland in 1900 is quite detached in tone and *The Illustrated London News* is less fervent in its promotion of this visit. That the Queen would appear to have received immense support at places such as Trinity College is evidenced from the illustration entitled *The Queen's Visit to Ireland. Trinity College students singing 'God save the Queen' after the passing of the Royal Procession* (Fig 19). The illustration, *Children's Day in Phoenix Park* (Fig 18), shows the Queen accepting a bunch of flowers from a child. The Queen wears shamrock in her headdress, the only feature of the illustration that has a specifically Irish flavour. Most of these late images of the Queen show her seated in a carriage. At this stage, she was over eighty years of age and obviously in quite a feeble state.

When analysing this body of images of the royal visits to Ireland, one must be fully aware of the British-centred, imperial outlook of the Victorian journal in question. This ideological stance is reflected in the visual output and the result is, to some extent, a distorted and propagandist account of these events. Aimed at a predominantly British middle-class readership, the publication was fully aware of the power of these images in creating an exaggerated impression of Ireland's allegiance to the Crown. Nevertheless, in the absence of an equivalent publication in Ireland in the 19th century, the value of the visual documentation provided increases significantly because it assists in the reconstruction and interpretation of the past.

DR MARGARITA CAPPOCK has written a doctoral thesis on the depiction of Ireland in the Illustrated London News *from 1842 to 1900. She is Project Manager of the Francis Bacon Studio at the Hugh Lane Municipal Gallery of Modern Art.*

ACKNOWLEDGEMENTS: I would like to thank Professor John Turpin for his helpful comments during the preparation of this article; and the staff of the Picture Library at the offices of the Illustrated London News *for their kind assistance.*

19. THE ILLUSTRATED LONDON NEWS: *The Queen's Visit to Ireland. Trinity College students singing 'God save the Queen' after the passing of the Royal Procession.* 14 Apr 1900. Inscription: *By Special Artist, Mr. S. Begg.* Signed bottom left, *S. Forestier*. Throngs of students wave their mortar boards as the Queen passes by Trinity College.

1 C Ford and B Harrison, *A Hundred Years Ago. Britain in the 1880s in Words and Photographs*, p. 319.
2 N Grant, *Victoria, Queen and Empress* (London & New York 1970), p. 137.
3 Grant (as note 2), pp. 134-35.
4 F Hardie, *The Political Influence of the British Monarchy, 1868-1952* (London 1970), p. 12.
5 Hardie (as note 4), p. 18, quoting Gladstone, p. 340.
6 Lord Clarendon to Lord John Russell, 7 June 1849, as quoted in H Bolitho, *The Reign of Queen Victoria* (New York 1948), pp. 110-11.
7 One can deduce that the Messrs Williams referred to in the accompanying article corresponds to an entry on p. 810 of the 1849 edition of *Thom's Directory* which reads as follows: Williams, Arth. & Sons, builders and contractors, 41 and 42 Talbot Street.
8 P Larmour, *The Arts & Crafts Movement in Ireland* (Belfast 1992), p. 22, p. 104. Larmour notes that throughout her reign, the Queen regularly commissioned Irish items such as curtains for Windsor Castle and embroidered coverlets for Buckingham Palace.
9 G M Young, *Portrait of an Age, Victorian England* (London 1936). Annotated Edition by George Kitson Clark (London, New York, Toronto 1977), pp. 308-9. Young states that Queen Victoria was initially well-received in political circles with O'Connell crediting her with liberal views. On the other hand, younger politicians who followed O'Connell tended to be more republican.
10 Sir S Lee, *King Edward VII*, vol 1, p. 418, as quoted in Bolitho (as note 6), p. 316.
11 G St Aubyn, *Edward VII. Prince and King* (London 1979), p. 50, as quoted in C Costello, *A Most Delightful Station: The British Army on the Curragh of Kildare, Ireland, 1855-1922* (Cork 1996), p. 98.
12 This painting was exhibited at the Gorry Gallery and featured in their exhibition catalogue of 18th-, 19th- and 20th-Century Painters in April 1989.
13 Costello (as note 11), p. 104, notes that these photographs are now in the Royal Archive at Windsor Castle in an album entitled *Souvenirs of Soldiering at Camp Curragh* which was compiled either for Queen Victoria and Prince Albert or for the Prince of Wales. He also remarks that they provide a unique record of the royal visit and of training on the plain and a valuable record of the encampment and surrounding places in 1861.
14 Costello (as note 11), p. 106.
15 Costello (as note 11), p. 100.
16 G St Aubyn (as note 11), pp. 52-55 as quoted in Costello (as note 11), p. 103. During his stay, the Prince became involved with a young actress named Nellie Clifden who was smuggled into the Prince's quarters at night by the other officers. Prince Albert was disgusted by his son's conduct on the Curragh and felt strongly that the liaison between the Prince and the actress had caused irreparable damage to his reputation. When Prince Albert died of typhoid fever before Christmas of the same year, the Queen held the Prince of Wales responsible for upsetting his father and causing him to become ill.

New Irish Architecture
The Architectural Year Reviewed

Colm Tóibín

casts a critical eye over some new and interesting buildings

1. James O'Donoghue: *Studio for the painter, Hughie O'Donoghue, Thomastown, Co Kilkenny.* '...a brutal space, a cross between a barn and a Norman keep, yet inside it has an intimate, mysterious and almost warm feeling...'

The painter, Hughie O'Donoghue, has his studio beside a Georgian house in the Nore valley outside Thomastown in county Kilkenny. He paints on a large scale and was always going to need an enormous studio, having used factory spaces before he moved to Kilkenny. His new studio of almost three thousand square feet was designed by James O'Donoghue in Kilkenny (Fig 1). It is a brutal space, a cross between a barn and a Norman keep, and yet, once you go inside, it has an intimate, mysterious, and almost warm feel to it.

O'Donoghue wanted a simple light-box with a screen at one end which would allow him access to the outside world. The huge glass doors, framed in wood, look south on to an old walled, formal garden with trees beyond, and this vista works against the volume of empty space in the studio. The colours inside are neutral, there is none of the customary white of many painters' studios; instead, the walls are plastered with extra lime and are what O'Donoghue describes as 'a warm stony colour.' There are bow trusses across the openings in the curved roof and these are painted white and they soften and spread whatever light comes from the roof. The floor is concrete.

The studio is not an architectural statement but a functional space. Hughie O'Donoghue can work in daylight here even in the winter and he can work on a number of huge paintings at the same time. There is good storage space in an old barn attached to the new studio. The new building is notable for its modesty and clarity and subdued tones. And yet it has a considerable and understated power. The apparent modesty is only in the use of dulled colours and clear space, almost factory space, and the lack of frills or funny angles or any distractions. Perhaps it has something to do with the raked light of the south east, the lack of sharpness in the light, and how easily it seems to gather in this space, distilled and softened even further. However it works, and obviously the walled garden in front has something to do with it; the space where Hughie O'Donoghue works has managed, almost despite itself, to exude the same hard-won, masculine, deeply spiritual aura as his paintings, nothing showy or obvious, but seriously considered and seriously affecting.

De Blacam and Meagher have designed a library in the School of Art housed in the old Redemptorist seminary outside Galway (Fig 2). The original building itself is undistinguished, except for some fine oak floors, and this makes the library even more startling when you walk into it from an ordinary corridor. It is an elaborate game of hide and seek played with wood and light over five floors. The old building has been gutted, but the windows, which look over Galway Bay, have been left in place. The central stairs is like the stairs to a pulpit, and there is a constant feeling as you wander around the maze of floors and strange spaces that you are in a new sort of church.

Light flows in from the windows and from the roof; the benches and chairs and balustrades and partitions and stairs and shelves are all made of oak, and they centre around an atrium, like branches of a tree around a central trunk. Although each floor is low, there is a sense of space and light and sheer excitement in the opulence of the wood and the angles. The tables for reading in the higher floors jut out into the atrium and get natural light from the atrium and the windows. The higher you go, the more exciting the view below, not just of wood and books but other students. The library has all the atmosphere of a medieval whispering gallery, a massive theatrical space, or an installation. It is one of the most original new public spaces in recent years.

2. DE BLACAM & MEAGHER: *Library in the School of Art, Redemptorist Seminary, Galway*. '...it is an elaborate game of hide and seek played with wood and light over five floors. Although each floor is low, there is a sense of sheer excitement in the opulence of the wood and the angles...'

The Morrison Hotel, designed by John Rocha, on Ormonde Quay in Dublin (Fig 3) shows what could have happened on Dublin's quays had the planners insisted that every new building be a showcase for good architecture and design. The hotel has all the hallmarks of John Rocha's work in fashion: it is stylish without being stuffy, spare without being cold, and playful without losing a sense of precision and purpose. There is a bravery in putting huge plate glass windows at the front of the hotel looking on to the quays themselves. This is where the bar is, but there is a separate entrance from the side of the building to the lobby which can remain cool and empty even when the bar is full of barristers. The walls and pillars here are finished with marble dust plastered on and waxed; there is throughout the hotel an Asian flavour mixed with a sort of minimalist luxury. Every single object from the carpet to the light fittings to the paintings to the hand-painted design on the cushions to the stain on the wood to the Portuguese limestone on the floor has been carefully thought out and placed.

Besides the bright bar which looks on to the quays, there is another darker bar which has a serious speak-easy atmosphere and a restaurant at the back of the hotel which seats eighty-five and rises to a vast, impressive height. Downstairs in the basement, using a separate entrance, is a club with table service. The upstairs part of the hotel has all the atmosphere of one of those massively trendy New York hotels such as the Paramount or the Mercer. The corridors, for example, widen as they move away from the lift, and the rooms, which are small, are informal, each one has a curved wall; they use black and white in the clever and playful way that John Rocha has made his own.

The work which Sister Concepta Lynch performed at the Sacred Heart Oratory in Dún Laoghaire between 1920 and 1936

3. John ROCHA: *The bar of the Morrison Hotel, Ormonde Quay, Dublin:* '...stylish without being stuffy, spare without being cold, and playful without losing a sense of precision and purpose, the building shows what could have happened on Dublin's quays had the planners insisted that every new building be a showcase for good architecture and design.

could not be further away from John Rocha's minimalist style. She came from a family of Celtic illuminators and worked in a time when Celtic illustration in places like the Cuala Press was much in vogue. She was an art and music teacher and worked out an elaborate system of stencils and overlays for use in illumination. She was, as is clear from this magnificent oratory, a very talented colourist. She simply could not leave blank space alone and every inch of the small oratory is covered with Celtic and Byzantine motifs and designs, birds and beasts, including a number of contented-looking devils. She spent a whole year just doing dots. There is nothing like this anywhere. The nuns sold the convent to become The Bloomfield Shopping Centre, leaving the oratory alone in the grounds. Conor Moran in the Office of Public Works had a brief to create a building which would surround and preserve the oratory (Fig 8).

His building is bright and interesting and goes much further than merely fulfilling its function. However, it does not attempt to compete with the oratory. Its presence off Library Road, essentially in the corner of a shopping centre, is sane and calm, almost classic. It could be a modern church. It is painted an ochre and plays with various semi-circular shapes, including the entrance lobby which puts a semi-circular desk opposite a semi-circular wall and a round piece of coloured ceramics in the centre. All this is tactful and cleanly done. The roof is stainless steel and there is a tiny alcove in wood attached to the building. In a sense the building has no purpose other than to protect Sister Concepta Lynch's work, but its elaborate structure and sense of its own value and weight and size and overall design pay homage to the extraordinary jewel which is inside.

As space become more and more valuable in Dublin and elsewhere, the design of mews houses becomes more important. Recently, four new buildings have appeared in Dublin which use a tiny site, and come up with novel ideas, and are each in their own way gems of contemporary Irish architecture. Perhaps the most spectacular – if you can use that word about mews sites – is by Grafton Architects, Shelley McNamara and Yvonne Farrell, at Denzille Lane behind Merrion Square and the Davenport Hotel (Fig 5). On three floors, it consists of a car park, a reception area for a film company, a small cinema and two apartments. It is an ambitious building in its use of stone and cobble and steel and glass and glazed screens; it manages a difficult site with considerable flair.

Nothing here is uniform and the use of the glazed screen on the front of the building is fascinating. Of all the buildings mentioned here, this is the one you could happiest stand outside and watch the play of textures and feel much as you would standing in front of a new Sean Scully or Felim Egan painting. Inside, some of the detail is extremely interesting such as the doors that look like lift doors or the floor of the kitchen which is polished screed with marble chips made by Pat Ryan in Kildare.

The other three are single mews houses and the most beautiful of these is by McCullough Mulvin at Louis Lane in Dublin 6 for Peter Sweeney and Helen Roycroft (Fig 4). This is about two thousand square feet, on two floors, the front looking on to a narrow lane and the back onto a garden and the back of houses on Leinster Road. Downstairs, there is a study, a bedroom which looks on to the garden, a bathroom, a tiny Japanese garden and a space for an organ which also looks on to the garden. All of this is functional and cleanly designed.

But it is the upstairs which takes your breath away. It is a room the length of the house, the floor in lightly-varnished wood, the cupboards in the kitchen part are hidden and barely noticeable, the radiators are similarly hidden. The room is painted white and there are no paintings. A stairwell protected by glass comes up into the middle of the room, but manages not to break the sense of a dreamy white space with hardly any furniture, all cool and soft and minimalist. This effect is greatly helped by the use of glass at the back of the house, half of which is glazed, to give light and avoid glare and, one presumes, to stop the neighbours looking in without having to draw curtains.

The other two mews houses are on Bessborough Parade at the side of Corrigan's pub off Mountpleasant Avenue in Ranelagh in Dublin. The first, at seventeen hundred square feet, on the corner, is designed by Grafton Architects for Frank and Pauline Hall (Fig 6). Outside, it has the stark, almost brutal look of an office, but it is clear, once you go inside, that the brick and raw concrete and aluminium and plate glass have been brilliantly used to create intricate and intimate living quarters. This is helped by books and paintings, but it is mainly achieved by taking in as much light as possible and building the house around a deck. All windows on the first floor open on to this deck, as on to an internal courtyard. And against this sense of intimate space, the use of raw concrete, plywood and aluminium is brave and unapologetic.

The roof garden has a full view of the dome of the church in Rathmines, but is also has a little cockpit, with glass on three sides and room for just a sofa.

At the other end of the terrace – there is a group of small modern houses in between – is the mews house, eighteen hundred square feet, that De Blacam & Meagher have designed for Barry Meagher (Fig 7), and this, like the Hall house, has elements of humour and clever pastiche. However, it goes much further, resembling in its huge upstairs room a ship turned upside down, with the timber rafters exposed and a port-hole window in the roof. The floor is Portuguese limestone, the roof is copper and thickly insulated. Behind the big ship of a living-cum-dining -cum kitchen (the kitchen is cleverly out of sight), there is a bedroom, cut off from the main room by a sliding door. Downstairs, there are two bedrooms and a study. Again, like the

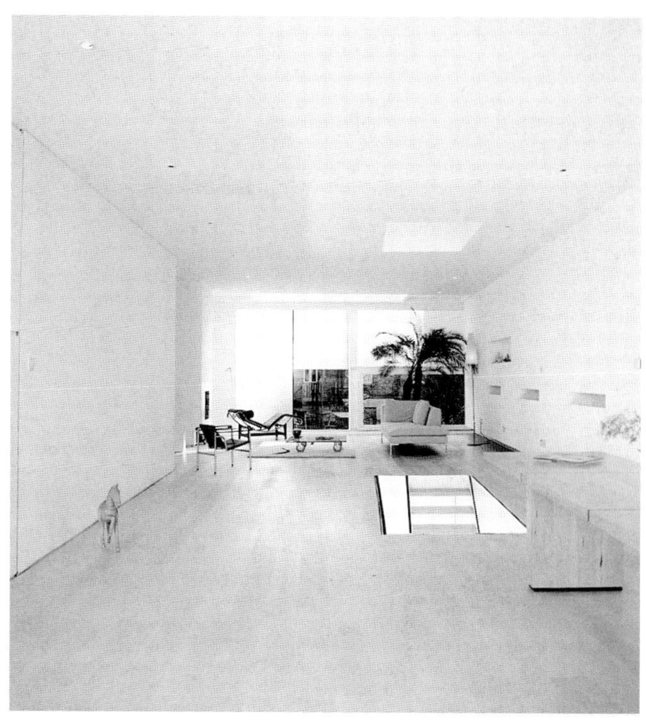

4. McCULLOUGH MULVIN: *Mews House, Louis Lane, Dublin 6*. 'It is the upstairs which takes your breath away. It is a room the length of the house... all cool and minimalist...'

5. GRAFTON ARCHITECTS: *Office and Apartments, Denzille Lane, Merrion Square, Dublin*. By Shelley McNamara and Yvonne Farrell, 'it is an ambitious building in its use of stone and cobble and steel and glass and it manages a difficult site with flair.'

6. GRAFTON ARCHITECTS: *Mews House, Bessborough Parade, Ranelagh.* '...it has the stark, almost brutal look of an office, but it is clear, once you go inside, that the brick and raw concrete and aluminium have been brilliantly used to create intricate and intimate living quarters...'

7. DE BLACAM & MEAGHER: *Mews House, Bessborough Parade, Ranelagh.* It has elements of '...humour and clever pastiche, ...and a sense of bravery and theatricality...'

8. Conor MORAN/OPW: *Sacred Heart Oratory, Dun Laoghaire.* The brief was to create a building which would surround and preserve the original Oratory which contains the paintings with which Sister Concepta Lynch covered the walls between 1920 and 1936.

9. RICHARD MURPHY ARCHITECTS: *House at Killeenaran, Co Galway.* '...looking like a boat and also a wonderful barn, it uses, to brilliant effect, a dry stone wall front which everyone designing a house in the west of Ireland should be asked to look at...'

Hall house, the Meagher house centres around a deck, has a full view of the dome of Rathmines church and has a sense of bravery and theatricality, especially in the light-filled stage set, the party-giver's dream which is the room upstairs.

In the west of Ireland at Killeenaran, south of Galway city, right on the sea, Richard Murphy Architects, based in Scotland, have designed a house for Rod Stoneman and his wife (Fig 9). This too looks like a boat, but it also looks like a wonderful barn and it uses, to brilliant effect, a dry stone wall front which everyone designing a house in the west of Ireland should be asked to look at. This cladding covers the bottom floor, with two small windows, like a ship's windows. The upstairs looks more like a sail built in timber and glass and galvanise.

You enter the house from the side. To the right are the front bedrooms, to the left an entrance to a dining room and kitchen. Above this is a high curved timber roof and an open corridor, like a ship's bridge. This leads from a magnificent room which spans the front of the house on the first floor to a bedroom and bathroom. Both the bathroom and the front room have wooden panels which can be pulled back to allow communication to the dining room below. Thus you can lie in the bath and pull back the panel and discuss the state of the Irish film industry with those dining below.

Every room in the house has a view of the sea, but the front upstairs room of the Stoneman house has the best view, a corner window framing a narrow road, a stony beach, the Hills of Clare and the Atlantic Ocean. Since so many new holidays homes all over the country have a dreary suburban sameness and sadness to them, this house in Killeenaran stands out as a serious example of what can be done using local materials and a lot of imagination.

COLM TOIBIN'S latest novel The Blackwater Lightship was nominated for the Booker Prize 1999.

Object in a Landscape
Robin Walker's Weekend House, Kinsale

Alexander Kearney

assesses the design of an unusual architectural commission

1. Robin WALKER (1924-91): *Weekend House, Kinsale*. 1963-65. Photographed by Norman McGrath, summer 1966. The 36 x 36 ft house is perched on eight stilts. The services are carried within an external concrete core.

The Weekend House, Summercove, Kinsale was designed and built between 1963 and 1965. The achievement of its architect, Robin Walker (1924-1991), was recognised by the Royal Institute of Architects of Ireland who awarded it the triennial Housing Gold Medal for the period 1965-67.[1] The Weekend House is one of only four significant domestic commissions Walker realised after his return from America in 1958.[2] Unexecuted projects of great ambition and considerable originality exist on paper and on microfilm.[3] The professional context for Walker's handful of houses was a thriving practice headed by Michael Scott which was focused on large scale public commissions. The attraction of working on a private dwelling was the comparative simplicity of its requirements. The smaller scale tested the architect's ingenuity in planning and prompted him to devise more personal solutions. The Weekend House (36 x 36ft) gave Walker the chance to clarify his principles in miniature form.

Walker's house designs divide sharply between those which share the stark language of concrete, glass and steel and those which represent his attempt at a specifically rural idiom. The Weekend house belongs to the first group. Also belonging to this group is a mews house the architect built for himself and his family in Ballsbridge, Dublin (1963-64) and another which he built for clients (1974-76) in the same area.[4] In the second, 'rustic' group is Walker's family holiday home at Kilcatherine (Bothar Buí), county Cork (1970-72) and an unrealised project for Louis Le Brocquy in Pulleen, county Cork (1973-74).[5]

In this article I will explore the themes of the Weekend House in relation to the other houses (built and unbuilt) of that first group. These themes concern handling of site, structural expression, internal planning, and the choice of materials and furnishings. I will compare the Weekend House with Walker's alternative project for the site and assess the dominant influences in his work. This last point is pertinent as Walker's two chosen mentors were Le Corbusier and Mies van der Rohe.

Walker worked in the office of Le Corbusier between 1947 and 1948 under a French government scholarship. At this time Le Corbusier's office was devoting much of its energy to the *Unité d'Habitation* housing scheme in Marseilles.[6] Walker himself produced drawings for the project. The immediate influence of this period upon the young architect was an interest in the expressive possibilities of reinforced concrete[7] and the proportional system of the *Modulor*. The lasting significance of Le

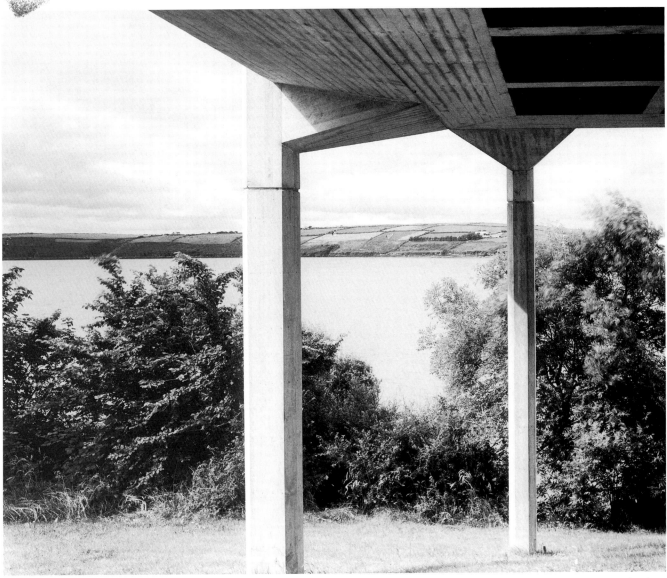

2. Robin Walker: *Weekend House, Kinsale. View underneath the House*. Photographed by Henk Snoek, 1966. The bevelled edges of the stilts are echoed in the broad chamfer of the underside. The direction of the concrete shuttering traces the building's every turn and change of angle.

Corbusier for Walker's architecture is more difficult to assess. Walker's use of reinforced concrete, post 1958, differs from that of Le Corbusier in its rejection of wilful forms. His refined concrete finishes are quite unlike the rough textured surfaces of the Swiss master's late work. Walker's devotion to systems of order was certainly lasting, but there is no evidence of his use of the *Modulor* in any of his surviving house designs.[8] The Weekend House is the most dramatic of Walker's built houses. Yet even here the plastic exuberance of Le Corbusier has been subjected to the severity of Mies van der Rohe.

The two years (1956-58) which Walker spent studying under Mies van der Rohe at the Illinois Institute of Technology[9] had the most profound effect on his subsequent work. The late Miesian themes of large expanses of glass, slender structural members, and the isolation of service cores now came to characterise Walker's designs. The teachings of Ludwig Hilberseimer, another Bauhaus *émigré*, informed his handling of orientation.[10] On his return to Dublin, Walker was not alone in his preoccupation with Mies. Ronald Tallon, a rising star in Michael Scott's practice, shared his high esteem for the architect.[11] Together the two, with the approval of Scott, forged a Miesian identity for the practice. It was in this stimulating environment of high ideals that Walker received an unusual commission from Mr Michael O'Flaherty.

The bachelor client was the thirty-year-old managing director of Volkswagen Distributors Ltd.[12] He was friendly with Michael Scott and the artist, Patrick Scott (no relation), who had been an architect in the practice until 1960. It is very likely that they recommended Walker to O'Flaherty, who wanted a thoroughly modern house for a remarkable site.

The property is located on the northern stretch of the natural inlet into Kinsale harbour. The site is of roughly one and a half

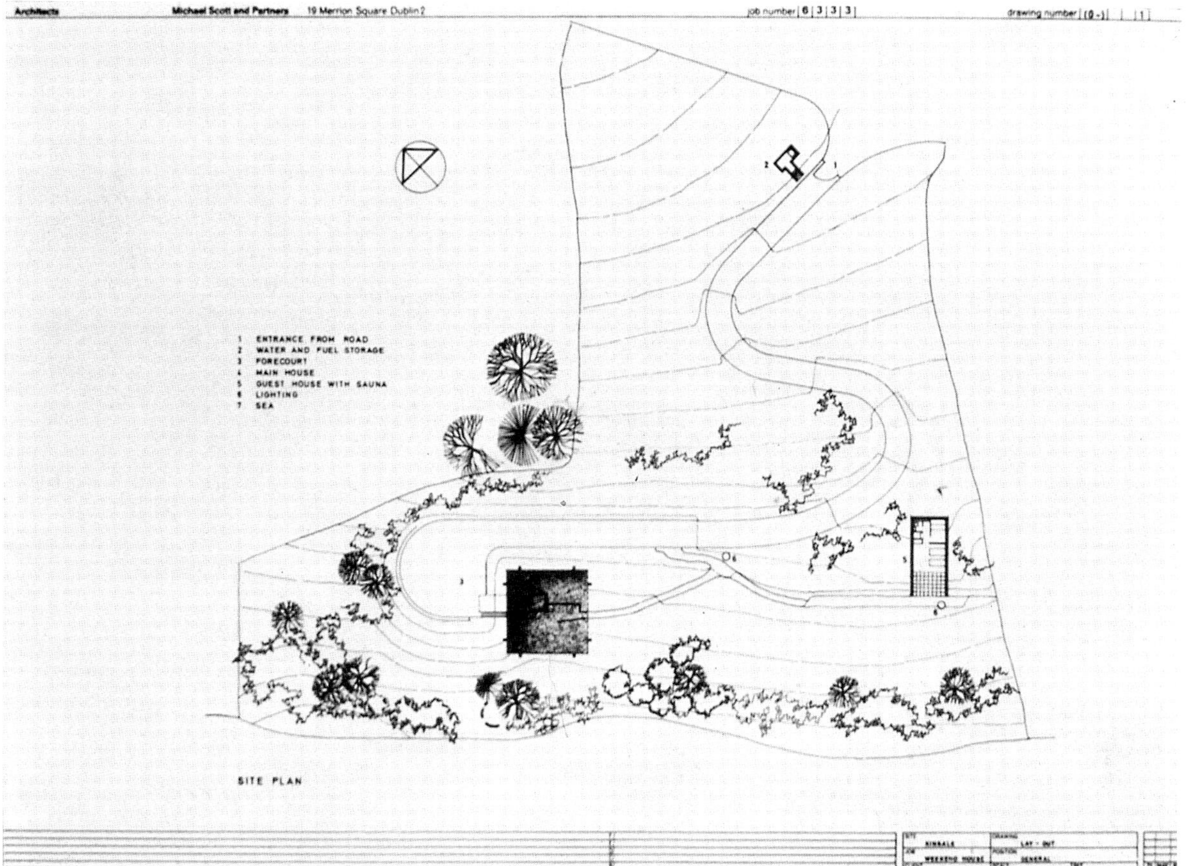

3. Robin WALKER: *Weekend House, Kinsale. Site plan*, 9/4/64 & 21/5/65 (Scott Tallon Walker Archive). The sinuous driveway was a response to the steep slope of the site. It also provided the visitor with an intriguing approach to the house. The buried guest house is on the extreme right of the plan.

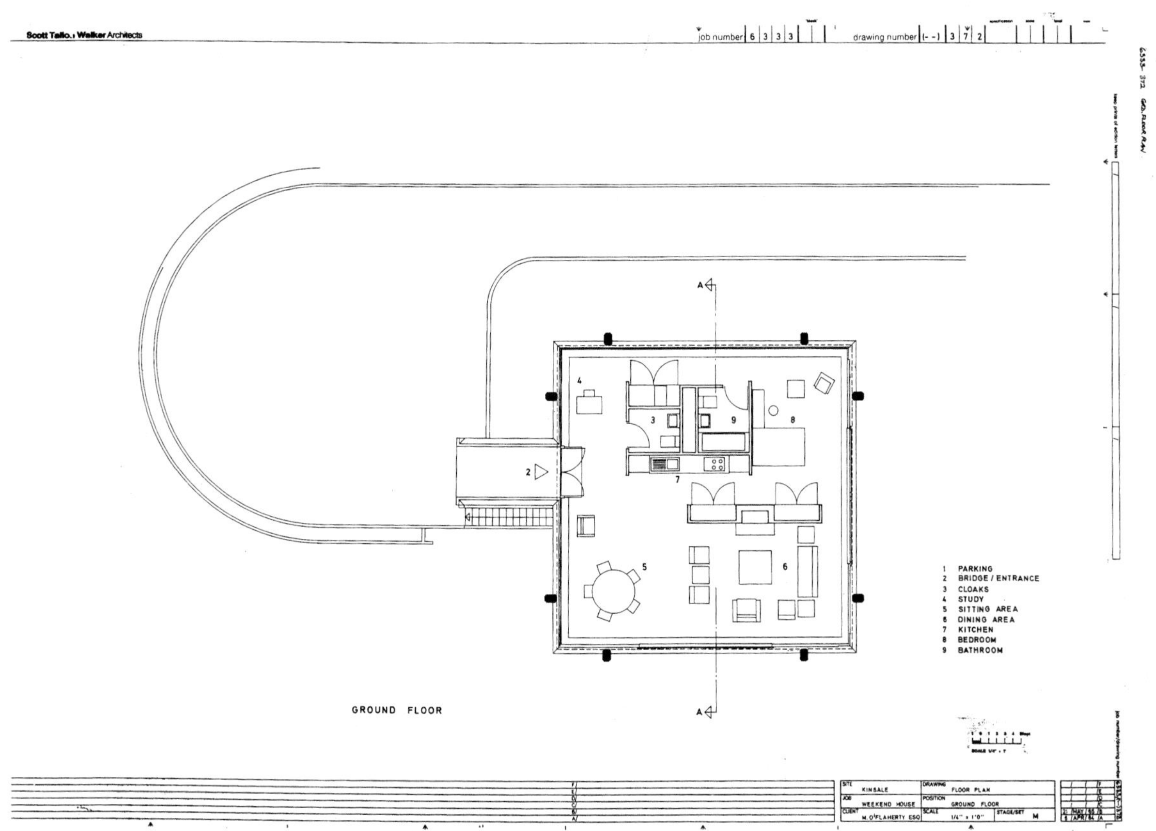

4. Robin WALKER: *Weekend House, Kinsale. Floor plan of Main House*, 9/4/64 & 21/5/65 (Scott Tallon Walker Archive). The design is open plan with no doors between the bedroom and other interior areas. Toilets and bathroom are contained within an independent core.

acres, steeply sloping to the water's edge. It occupies a position between the sheltered harbour and the mouth of the inlet to the Atlantic ocean. The views from this spot encompass a number of ruined fortifications and the picturesque town itself. The prospect from the threshold of the ocean to the low hills of the bay is one of the most panoramic and beautiful in the area.

The architect devised two projects for the site. The essential brief for a weekend retreat remained the same, but Walker's two interpretations of it, however, differed greatly. The unrealised project was for a timber-framed, three bedroom house erected on battered concrete brick piers (Fig 5). Its planning was elegant but relatively conventional while the executed scheme represents, unusually, a more daring approach. The main house has been conceived as a perfect single-room pavilion, with one guest house as an entirely separate entity (Fig 3). The method of construction is reinforced concrete, but what prompted the change from timber-frame is not known. When recently shown plans for the unrealised scheme the client could not recall it,[13] though Walker had worked on this proposal from March to October 1963. Nor is the chronology of the two schemes straightforward.

tel. These piers hold up the roof but tell us little about the task. The reinforced concrete columns of Walker's Restaurant Building in UCD (1967-70) aspire to the thinness of steel I-beams.[17] They emulate the Miesian vision of *beinahe nichts* ('almost nothing'). It is only in the Weekend house that Walker allows structure to resemble sculpture.

This, however, is a sculpture of reason and restraint in which form and detailing are fused to produce a disciplined result. The bevelled edges of the stilts are echoed in the broad chamfer of the underside (Fig 2) and the louvred chimney stack and services vent are juxtaposed in a right-angled composition. All the concrete surfaces are shuttered except for the roof. The direction of the shuttering traces the building's every turn and change of angle. The result is a carefully-crafted object whose form is enhanced by its texture.

The volume of the house can be appreciated from a variety of positions. For example, the floor slab with its coffered centre is intended to be seen from beneath and the gridded concrete roof is designed to be seen from the descending slope. A sinuous approach continues past the landward face of the house and

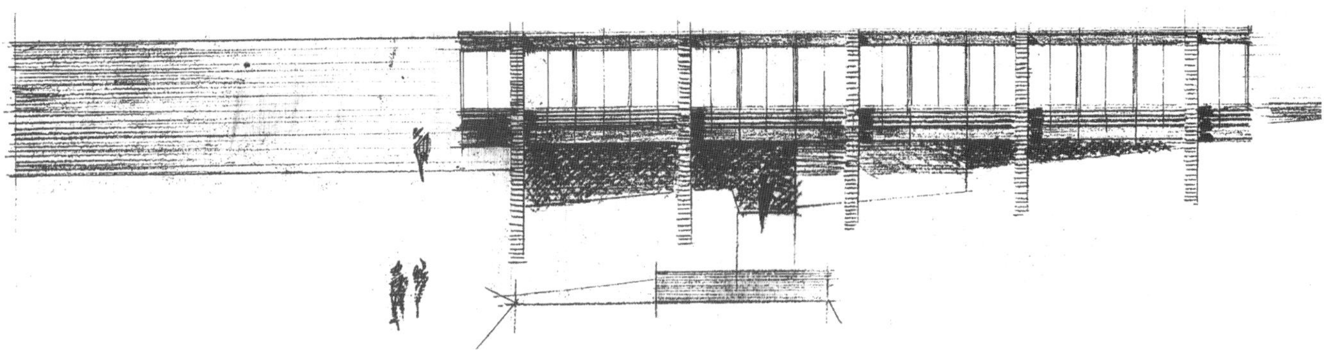

5. Robin WALKER: *Unrealised Project for the Weekend House, Kinsale, Elevation.* 18/3/63 (Scott Tallon Walker Archive). Walker made more detailed plans for this proposal in October 1963. While the unrealised project was larger than the executed house, it was also less daring.

It appears from the dated drawing that Walker conceived the essentials of the executed project (first dated drawing 3 Jan 1963) before the unrealised project (first dated drawing 12 Mar 1963).[14] It is possible that Walker persuaded O'Flaherty to return to a design once rejected as too expensive or extreme. Walker's powers of persuasion were considerable.[15]

The completed house is held aloft on stilts on all four sides (Fig 10). These stilts represent a solution specific to the medium of reinforced concrete[16] (steel might have corroded in the sea air). The inward branching roof capitals and the lower spreading floor brackets lean in and under to support the body of the house. The knuckle-like heads of the capitals concentrate the roof load down the slender stilts. The lower brackets flare out to gather all the weight channelled between the coffers of the underside. The stilts rise outside the plan of the house and so do not interrupt the continuous glazing.

The clear expression of structure is a near constant theme in Walker's architecture, yet nowhere in his mature work is it expressed quite like this. The internal piers of his second mews house (1976) are simple posts run through by a continuous lin-

curves round into a forecourt beside the north west entrance. Before even entering the house we are led to witness it from above and from three of its four sides. The visual isolation of the structure is confirmed by the bridge between forecourt and entrance.

The manipulation of our route and the object status of the house may be contrasted with the unrealised project (Fig 5); here a long screen wall shields the house form the drive. This acts as a barrier between views of the house and views from the house. The landscape can only be savoured once past the thresholds of screen wall and sitting room door. In the final work there is no wall between the house and its approach. The edifice is something unified and distinct within the landscape. Indeed, the house is part of the view.

The one-bedroom guest house is designed as the complementary opposite to the main house (Fig 3). Whereas the main house is raised on stilts, the guest house is buried into the side of the slope. Whereas the main house has views on every side, the guest house has a single view framed by embankments. One house is very visible, the other is hidden. A contrast of a differ-

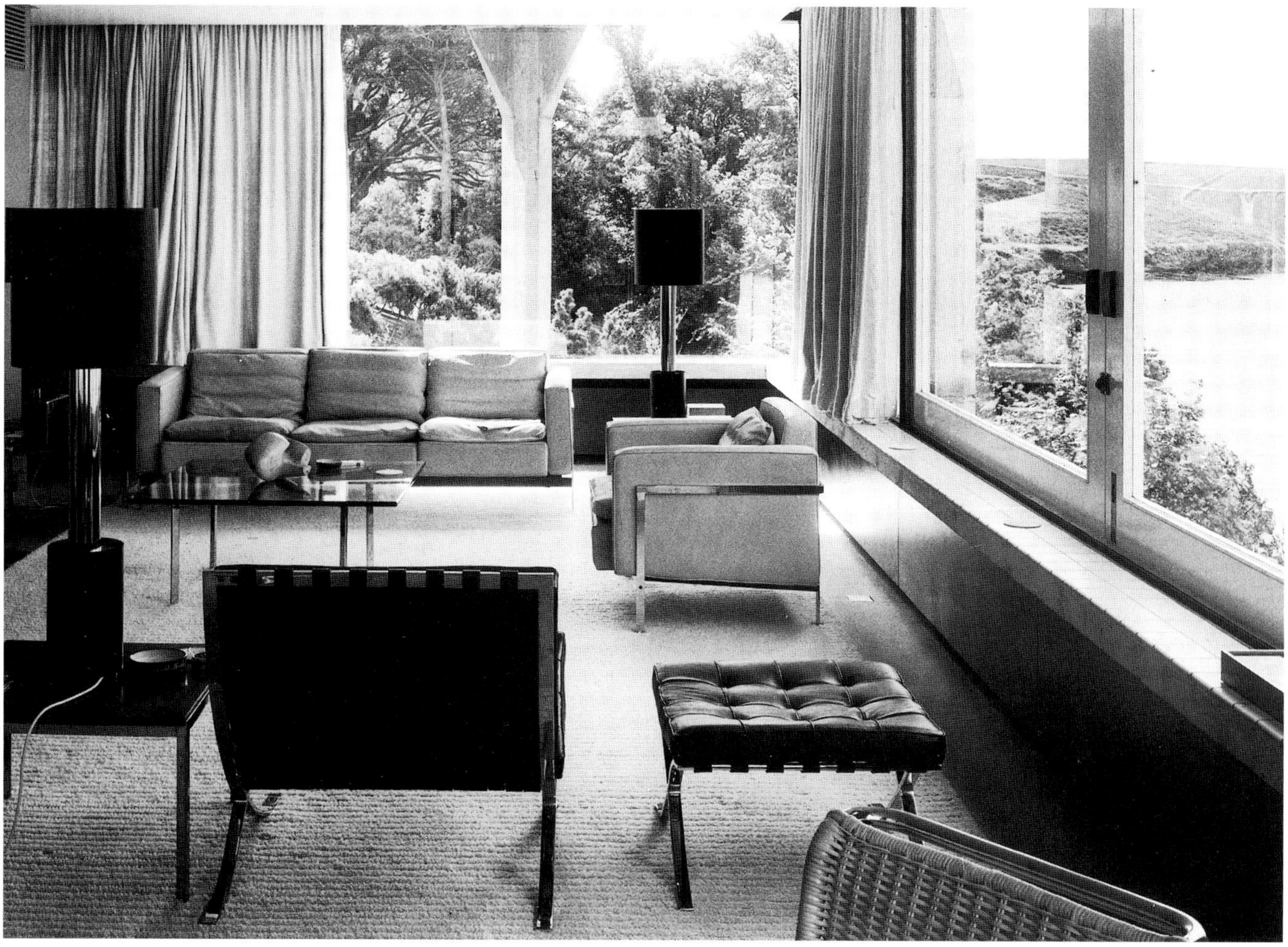

6. Robin WALKER: *Weekend House, Kinsale; the sitting area.* Photographed by Henk Snoek, 1966. The imposing table lamps were designed especially for the house by artist Patrick Scott. Scott also selected the other furnishings.

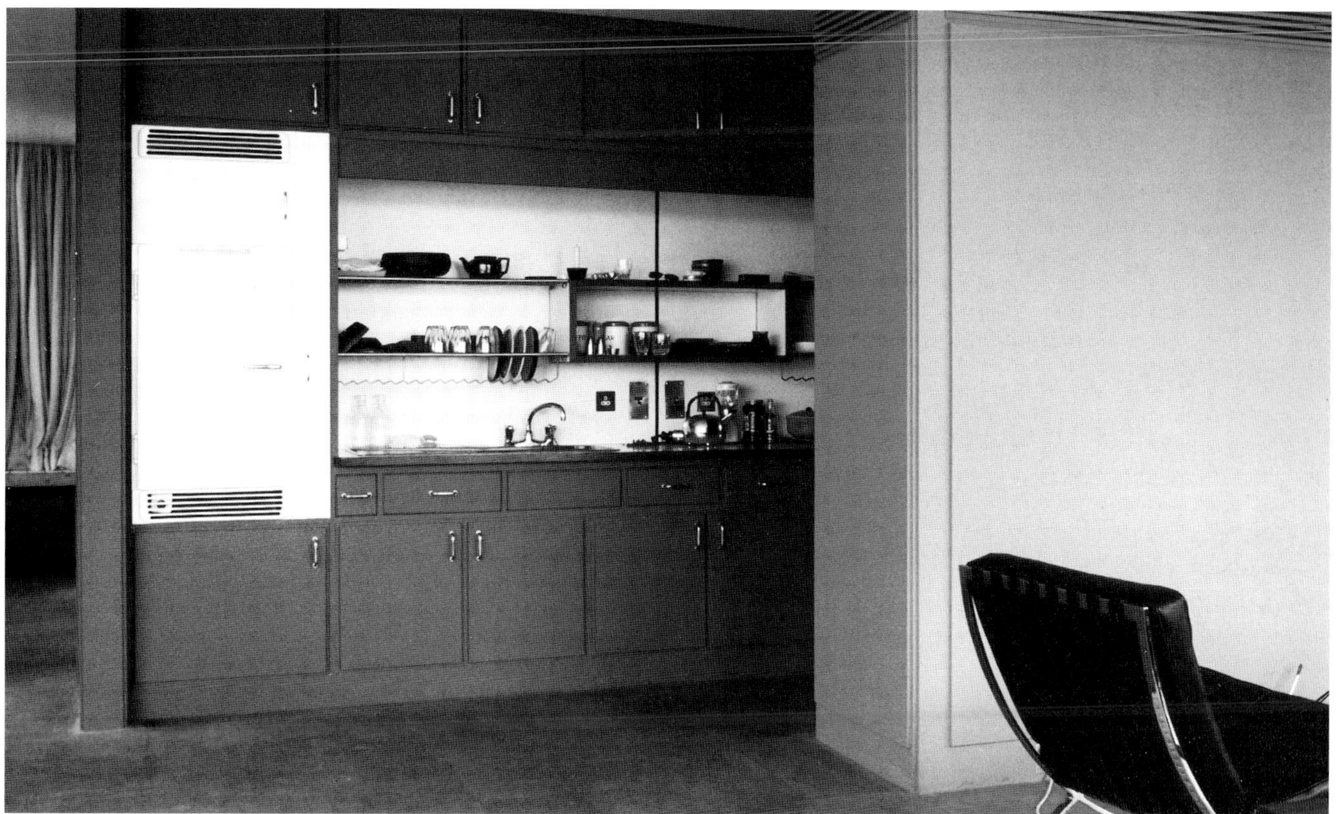

7. Robin WALKER: *Weekend House, Kinsale; detail of kitchen/bathroom core and hearth/storage partition.* Photographed by Norman McGrath, Summer 1965. The overlapping planes of core and partition add a dynamic accent to an otherwise static space. This effect is accentuated through an unusual use of colour.

8. Robin WALKER: *Weekend House, Kinsale; view from sitting area to the Atlantic Ocean.* Photographed by Norman McGrath, summer 1965. While the dining/sitting area enjoys the broad sweep of the inlet, much of its own land remains out of sight.

(Opposite). **9.** Robin WALKER: *Weekend House, Kinsale; view along window of sitting area.* Photographed by Norman McGrath, summer 1965. The stilts rise outside the plan of the house and so do not interrupt the continuous glazing.

ent kind is suggested in the first dated drawing for the realised project (3 Jan 1963). In this site-plan the guest house is a two-bedroom structure whose walls are disposed in pinwheel fashion. The closed envelope of the main house finds its antithesis in the radiant configuration of the guest house. A possible inspiration for the guest house is Mies van der Rohe's famous plan for a Brick Country House (1923).[18] It is clear that Walker did not confine his interest to Mies's later work but on occasion sought inspiration in his early studies.

The square plan for the main house reflects the reductive basis of the executed scheme (Fig 4). Walker frequently resorted to the square as a compositional component in the absence of other limitations. Its characteristics of order, symmetry and self-containment lend the Weekend House its forceful unity. Elsewhere, it inspired Walker's gift for complex abstract planning.[19] This appears most noticeably in his unrealised house for Michael O'Flaherty in Ballybrack, Killiney, county Dublin (1968) and his first house project for Louis Le Brocquy in Pulleen, county Cork (*c.*1972-73). The principal elements of the Ballybrack plan are semi-complete squares which slide underneath a large, single span square roof and the central motif is the diagonal overlap of roof and swimming pool terrace (Fig 11).

In the Pulleen project a steel structure is set within a grass mound in the shape of a truncated pyramid. Its square roof and regular supports set the order against which the free composition of the interior can be read. They establish the datum for internal arrangements.

A further theme on the square is the grid. The Weekend House is regulated by not one but two grids. The external dimensions of the house are 36 x 36 ft and both grids share the same module of 4 x 4 ft. One grid fits precisely within the perimeter of the building. The only visible expression of this grid is the 1:4:1 placement of the stilts. Each stilt is aligned with the centre of an invisible four by four feet module and each floor bracket expands to fill that module.[20] The other grid is more boldly stated. It manifests itself in the 4 x 4 ft divisions of the concrete screed roof finish and is embodied in the 4 x 4 ft coffers of the floor (Fig 10) and roof slabs (exposed and concealed

10. Robin WALKER: *Weekend House, Kinsale*; Photographed by Norman McGrath, summer 1966. The main house can be appreciated from beneath as well as from above. The exposed coffering of the underside is the boldest expression of the grid throughout the structure.

respectively). This grid does not fit precisely within the perimeter of the building but projects beyond it by 2 ft. The two grids are thus out of step with one another. The corner of a square from one grid corresponds to the middle of a square from the other. The 1 x 1 ft cork floor tiles conform to both. The apparent simplicity of the Weekend House is underpinned by a mesh of seen and unseen lines. The result is a house whose measured area can be read from above, below, and within.

Walker's use of modules was entirely compatible with the idiom of Mies van der Rohe's late works (notably his Berlin Art Gallery). On occasion it went beyond it. The insistent modular expression of the Weekend House is not to be found in Mies's built houses. The only equivalent is his unexecuted 50/50 project house (1950/51), where the grid is translated into the structural form of the ceiling. Mies, though, is more concerned with the reduction of the house to a glass-sheathed skeleton. The Weekend House is, instead, a concrete monument to the grid.

The interior of the Kinsale house is open plan (Fig 4). The main house was designed for only one resident, reducing the need for privacy between different areas. The choice of this plan once more invokes the example of Mies, in particular his Farnsworth House, Illinois (1945-50) and the 50/50 project house. In both cases freestanding elements (kitchen, services, wardrobes) imply different zones within a single space free of internal supports. The two most famous examples of this planning, the Farnsworth House and Philip Johnson's Glass House, New Canaan, Connecticut (1949), were both designed as single-person country retreats. The open plan in the Weekend House was thus typologically appropriate.

The internal space is divided according to view, orientation, and relative privacy. The dining and sitting areas enjoy views across three sides of the house, from the town to the ocean. The bedroom is oriented toward the east, sacrificing external privacy to the driveway; it is the most contained free area in the house and is invisible from most other internal points.

The defining elements of the interior are the kitchen/bathroom core and the hearth/cupboard partition, both of which are panelled in painted plywood (Fig 7). Their staggered positions subtly direct progress from the front door towards the dining and sitting areas. The independent core is a recurrent theme in Walker's domestic and public architecture.[21] It derives from the Miesian procedure of concentrating services (including toilets, lifts and stairs) into a central unit or units in an office plan. Mies, himself, adapted the approach for his Farnsworth House (where it becomes a utility spine). Walker's first project for a house in Pulleen goes one further and places entire bedrooms within cores. In the Weekend House the overlapping planes of core and partition add a dynamic accent to an otherwise static space.

The original colour scheme boldly emphasised this effect. This has long since been painted over but interior colour photographs by Norman McGrath reveal it as it was in June/July 1965.[22] These give an imprecise record of the true colours but show them to have been used in an unusual way. The kitchen/bathroom core was painted a mid brown whereas the hearth/storage partition was painted in a creamy beige. Colour was used to play one element off against another. The colour scheme did not emulate the natural tones of Mies's Farnsworth House. Rather, its earth colours were an attempt to relate these masses to their landward setting.

The richness of this colour scheme is certainly not typical of Walker. His usual preference was for numerous shades of white.[23] The artist, Patrick Scott, who chose the furniture, does not recollect being responsible for the colours. It is probable, nonetheless, that this unique solution owed more to Patrick Scott than to Walker.[24]

Scott's choice of furniture fully agreed with Walker's taste.[25] He selected classic designs by Mies, Le Corbusier, and Charles Eames. The artist also designed four cylindrical table lamps specially for the house (Fig 6). These are physically imposing objects which help punctuate the unitary space. A tapestry (1966/67) by Scott once hung above the bed where its colours soon faded in the harsh maritime light. This was the first of Scott's Aubusson tapestries, another of which hangs in the second Ballsbridge mews house (1976). Neither work was commissioned by Walker. The clients, themselves, sought a Scott tapestry as the natural complement to a Walker interior.

The interior of the Weekend House is, above all things, devoted to the view (Fig 8). Its continuous glazing stretches to the very corners of the building. The stilts rise beyond the featureless suspended ceiling as if the room had slipped its moorings and begun to float. The sensation of looking out to sea pleased Walker greatly: 'When you look out from the house you have no immediate land foreground, it's almost like being on a ship.'[26] The illusion succeeds through the steepness of the slope, the elevation of the house and the proximity of the water's edge. While the dining/sitting area enjoys the broad sweep of the inlet, much of its own land remains out of sight. The viewer is left to contemplate the scenery without knowing precisely where he stands.

The Weekend House is the closest Walker came to turning a domestic commission into a work of art.[27] The price for such daring was a large cost overrun and subsequent technical problems.[28] Financial limitations may explain why the frames of the sliding windows were of timber rather than bronze.[29] The result was a false note in an otherwise harmonious structure.

An example of what Walker might have achieved with far greater resources can be seen in his Ballybrack house design for the same client (1968). The house is an extraordinary synthesis of Mies's domestic projects over a thirty year period. These range from the Brick Country House (1923), which is recalled in the low entrance elevation, to the steel and glass grammar of the 50/50 house, employed in the garden facade. An outdoor swimming pool would have passed into the main living space and the grounds were to have contained a sculpture garden. Initial enthusiasm quickly gave way to considerations of commitment and cost. The plans were shelved and the site eventually sold.[30]

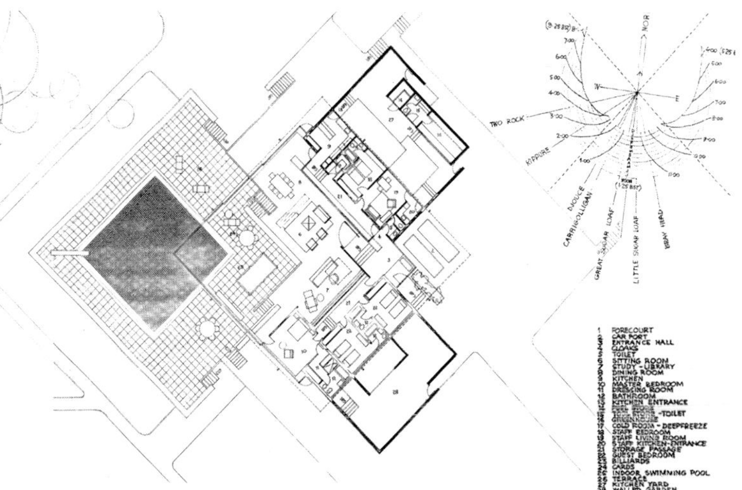

11. Robin WALKER: *Ballybrack house project (unrealised); ground floor plan.* Microfilm copy from original pencil on tracing paper (Scott Tallon Walker Archive). This is the most ambitious of Walker's house designs and an extravagant homage to Mies van der Rohe. Its principal elements are semi-complete squares which slide underneath a large single span square roof.

From the diminutive size of the Weekend House to the grand scale of the Ballybrack scheme, Walker's domestic architecture is clever and assured. His projects for O'Flaherty were designed for leisure but conceived with rigour. They embody a vision shared by Mies and Le Corbusier, that of domestic living as an aesthetic pursuit. A comment Walker made in 1972 suggests that the ideal was still potent. 'Someday I'll build a palace for somebody.'[31] It was an ambition he never fulfilled.

ALEXANDER KEARNEY is currently working in the Hugh Lane Municipal Gallery of Modern Art on the Francis Bacon Studio Database.

ACKNOWLEDGEMENTS: I would like to thank Dr Edward McParland for his guidance and advice during the preparation of both dissertation and article. I wish to thank the following for their kind help and co-operation: Dorothy Walker; Patrick Scott; Michael O'Flaherty; Mary and Michael Minihan; Dr Ronald Tallon; Louis Le Brocquy; and the owners of the second Ballsbridge mews house. I am particularly indebted to Simon Walker Architects, Gráinne McCabe of the Scott Tallon Walker archive, the staff of the Irish Architectural Archive, and the studio of Norman McGrath for their assistance. I would also like to thank Nicholas Simms and Joseph Kearney.

1 The architect was also awarded the 1970 RIAI Gold Medal for his Restaurant Building, UCD.
2 A house in Howth which Walker built for his parents before he went to America has been comprehensively altered.
3 Few of Walker's early designs survive. Numerous drawings, models and other documents relating to built and unbuilt projects were lost/destroyed before the development of a practice archive. Much of the material from the 1960s exists solely on microfilm. This reproduces poorly. The drawings that do survive testify to Walker's considerable skills as a draughtsman.
4 Name and address withheld at clients' request.
5 This was the second of two projects for the site. A portfolio of six presentation drawings was made for each project. The present whereabouts of these portfolios is unknown. The only reproductions the author has found are in a small exhibition catalogue of architectural drawings and paintings for European Architectural Heritage Year 1975 (Dublin 1975).
6 'I've never seen the building but did a few drawings towards its construction.' Plan Profile: R Walker, 'To Explore Architecture's own Logic', *Plan Magazine*, vol 4, no 2 (Nov 1972), p. 16.
7 Photographs taken of Walker's models for two unrealised schemes for a church at Lettermore, Co Galway (1955) strongly suggest the influence of post-war Le Corbusier. Walker's first scheme is particularly reminiscent of Le Corbusier's church at Ronchamp (1950-55). Scott Tallon Walker Archive.
8 Patrick Scott recounts that a house design for AH Masser (1954) was based specifically on Modulor proportions. The plans for this house are listed in the practice archive but no longer exist. Interview with P Scott, 17 Nov 1997. STW Archive.
9 A list of all graduate students and their course choices is given in R Achilles, K Harrington, C Myhrum (eds), *Mies van der Rohe: Architect as Educator* (Chicago 1986). This contains the names of other Irish students of Mies, a subject which is beyond the scope of this article.
10 This is most evident in Walker's own house in Ballsbridge (1963-64), where the planning perfectly fulfils Hilberseimer's criteria. L Hilberseimer, *The Nature of Cities* (Chicago 1955), pp. 203ff.
11 Though Ronald Tallon never studied under Mies, his work up until the 1980s records a persistent interest in the Miesian language of steel and glass. Like Walker, he built a small number of private houses. The most spectacular of these is the Goulding House (1975), a small steel cantilever structure erected over a steep, wooded river bank at Dargle Glen, Co Wicklow.
12 His father, Stephen O'Flaherty, obtained the Volkswagen assembly concession in the immediate post-war years. Around this time O'Flaherty commissioned the office of Michael Scott to design a car showroom in Ballsbridge, (since demolished). Second interview with M O'Flaherty, (21 Dec 98).
13 Second interview with M O'Flaherty (21 Dec 98).
14 The title 'Weekend House II' appears on the first extant drawings for the executed project (3 Jan 1963). These drawings were made two months before the earliest sketch plan and elevation for the alternative scheme (12 Mar 1963). This scheme was given the title 'Weekend House'. Walker later returned to his first concept in a drawing dated 30 Jan 1964. This and subsequent drawings for the built project were titled 'Weekend House II'. It is likely that Walker used this title to distinguish the executed project from the alternative scheme. He may then have post-titled the drawings dated 3 Jan 1963 to link them with drawings made after 30 Jan 1964. To confuse the matter further, the publication plans for the final house are simply titled 'Weekend House'. Microfilm, STW Archive.
15 Walker was both eloquent and highly determined. The clients of the second Ballsbridge mews house (1976) recount how Walker talked them out of having a chimney in the house. He reassured them that an indoor garden (a glazed court) would be a far superior focal point for the living room. Walker's fireplaces had a habit of filling with smoke and he may have wished to circumvent the problem altogether. Interview with the clients (26 Oct 1997).
16 This structure and the second Ballsbridge mews house (1976) were engineered by the Dublin office of Ove Arup and Partners.
17 On this occasion Walker took his love of slender supports to a risky extreme. Such was their thinness the four corner columns (struts)began to buckle during tensioning of the roof beams. These struts did not, in fact, support the roof but anchored its corners to the ground. Engineers from Ove Arup, with Walker's consent, reinforced the struts with narrow steel angles. The slender profiles of the structure were preserved. Conversation with S Walker (18 Dec 1998).
18 There are no elevations for this design nor evidence of Walker developing the concept further. The guest house was to have been reached by a terrace which swept underneath the stilts of the main house. Microfilm, STW Archive.
19 This gift is also demonstrated by the plan of the Restaurant Building UCD with its ingeniously handled mezzanine. The vast roof (144 x 144ft) is carried on only five load bearing columns.
20 These measurements are taken from the more detailed plans on microfilm dating from 1964, STW Archive. I am indebted to Dr McParland for his analysis of the relationship between the two grids.
21 Among Walker's public buildings independent cores appear in the Tourist Board Headquarters, Baggot Street Bridge, Dublin (1959-61) and the National Bank of Ireland, Suffolk Street, Dublin (1962-66). In his private house designs they appear in the Weekend House, the two Ballsbridge mews houses, and the first Pulleen house project. The core plan of the Tourist Board Headquarters is the first instance of its use in Ireland (and possibly the British Isles) according to the Michael Scott and Partners brochure for the building (undated but pre-1972).
22 Norman McGrath's photographs are the only formal record of the original colour scheme known to the author.
23 Walker specified over seven shades of white in certain commissions. For the second Ballsbridge mews house he directed that the in-built cupboards be painted a very pale green to match the colour of the clerestory vitrolite windows. Interview with D Walker (16 Sept 1997). Interview with the clients of the second Ballsbridge mews house (5 Oct 1997).
24 M O'Flaherty recalls that Scott did devise the colour scheme. The Michael Scott and Partners brochure (pre-1972) for the Weekend House refers only to P Scott's choice of furniture. There is no mention of the colour scheme though a reference is made to the owner's private painting collection. There is no photographic evidence for this collection and the client recollects that he did not hang paintings in the house. Second interview with M O'Flaherty (21 Dec 1998).
25 Walker designed the furniture in his own Ballsbridge mews house. His sofa and two types of chair are particularly graceful. All three are of tubular steel and were executed in a workshop behind the practice office in Merrion Square. Walker also designed the simple circular dining table in the Weekend House. The designer of the buckskin sofa and armchair has not been established. Second interview with D Walker (5 Feb 1998). Interview with P Scott (17 Nov 1997).
26 *Plan Magazine*, vol 4, no 2 (Nov 1972), p. 17.
27 Walker devoted considerable care to the design of interior and exterior fixtures. He made a couple of drawings for concrete garden lamps of an 'expressionist' crystalline form (3 May 1965). These lamps were not executed. Microfilm, STW Archive.
28 The initial cost estimate of the house was £18,000 approx. The final figure was closer to £24,000. The problems with the house included the concrete roof coping which shifted in the heat, land subsidence of the embankment beneath the forecourt, and a fireplace which filled with smoke. The difficulties were overcome but the appearance of the house has suffered from neglect since first being sold in 1986. First interview with M O'Flaherty (20 Dec 1997).
29 M O'Flaherty recounts that the door frame and sliding window frames were originally to have been of bronze. There is no indication from the plans that Walker considered the more expensive option. The weight of the plate glass necessitated the extra thickness of the timber frames. First interview with M O'Flaherty (20 Dec 1997). STW Archive.
30 The microfilm hard copies of the elevations are too unclear to publish. STW Archive. First interview with M O' Flaherty (20 Dec 1997).
31 *Plan Magazine* (Nov 1972), p. 17.

The Mink and Diamonds of Irish Fashion Sybil Connolly

Robert O'Byrne

recalls one of the most remarkable Irish women of the 20th century

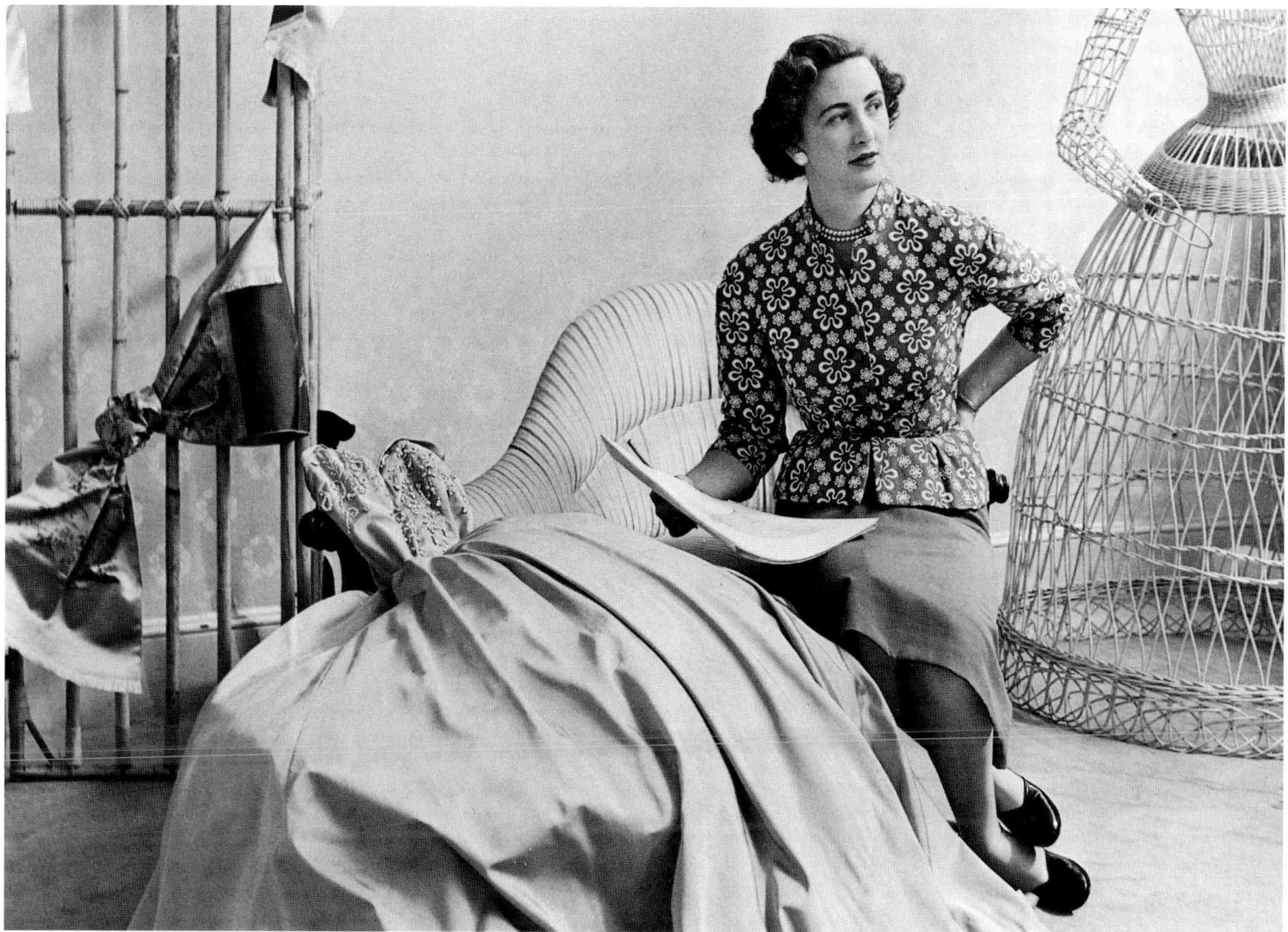

1. Sybil Connolly at Work: 1953. Probably photographed in her salon at 71 Merrion Square, Dublin. 'The House that Linen Built' as she called it.

'Ireland', wrote former *American Vogue* editor, Bettina Ballard, in her 1960 book of memoirs, *In my Fashion*, 'was a completely unexpected centre for fashion for everyone but Carmel Snow. We were drawn en-masse to Dublin by the personable, milk-skinned Irish charmer named Sybil Connolly who showed a small collection made of Irish tweeds and linens in Dunsany Castle and bewitched us all into buying models or filling our editorial pages with them.'

Forty-five years after performing this extraordinary and unexpected feat, Sybil Connolly died in May 1998. She had been ill and largely unseen in public for the previous two years but her career as a fashion designer had begun its retreat decades earlier. Indeed, given her relatively low profile during the 1980s and 1990s, the notion of Sybil Connolly as a global celebrity was hard to imagine for anyone not familiar with the history of Irish fashion. But this had really once been the case: during the 1950s, she had been the most famous, most admired, most industrious, and most travelled Irishwoman in the world. For a few years, she had appeared to represent modern Ireland, then a young country aware (and proud) of its past but prepared to take on the future with confidence. Then, in the 1960s, she gradually lost the high position attained, the attention dwindled, the press cuttings diminished. By 1970, although she still had twenty-eight years to live, Sybil Connolly appeared to belong to a vanished era.

Because her ascent was so rapid and her acceptance of acclaim so confident it would be understandably easy to imagine that Sybil Connolly's career as a fashion designer had been carefully planned. Perhaps this was the case, but the available evidence suggests otherwise. Born in Wales on 24 January 1921, the daughter of an Irish father (originally from county Waterford, he worked for an insurance company) and a Welsh mother, she only moved to Ireland after the death of the former when she was fifteen. Always keenly interested in clothes, at the age of seventeen she was apprenticed to a London dressmaking firm run by two

Irish brothers, Jim and Comerford Bradley. In later years, she liked to tell how, as a junior, she had held pins at fittings for Queen Mary in Bradley's where, she said, there were no less than ninety-eight fitting rooms due to the large number of English debutantes who bought their clothes from the company.

With the outbreak of the Second World War, Sybil Connolly returned to Ireland in 1940 and found a job in Dublin at Richard Alan, a business which both manufactured and sold women's clothes. Owned by the redoubtable Jack Clarke, Richard Alan was to provide Sybil Connolly with her launching pad as a designer, but not before she had worked there for more than ten years. Since so much attention was paid to her after she had become successful, little is recorded of this long period in waiting. But she was obviously learning her trade and preparing herself for the opportunity which eventually came her way. In a profile of the designer written in 1960, the novelist Kate O'Brien remembered seeing Sybil Connolly at a party in Dublin's Gresham Hotel in 1946 long before she had received any recognition for her work. Asking about a striking, dark-haired woman, O'Brien learnt that her name was Sybil Connolly and that she worked at Richard Alan where she designed clothes. '"If she does," I thought," she can wear them too; and she must be her own best model." For the girl in the severe gold vesture, sitting alone with her dark head bent in the harsh light of that banqueting hall was a figure to impress imagination and memory.'

If, as Kate O'Brien suggests, Sybil Connolly was already designing at Richard Alan in the immediate post-war period, she was receiving no public recognition for her efforts. During this period, Jack Clarke hired a French designer, Gaston Mallet, formerly with the house of Balmain to work for him in Dublin. According to an interview with the *Irish Times* in January 1982, Sybil Connolly was upset that Mallet during his five seasons with Richard Alan never used any Irish fabrics. 'I felt like a voice in the wilderness', she said of her first efforts to promote domestic materials.

Eventually, she was given an opportunity to do so. In early 1952, Gaston Mallet left Richard Alan seemingly at short notice and Sybil Connolly was placed in charge of the workrooms with official responsibility to produce the next season's collection. Here, after a very long period in the wings, was a chance to take centre-stage and she seized it with all the eagerness of an actress given her moment in a Hollywood musical. Rather than simply continue in the French vein established by Mallet, she decided to give her clothes a distinctively Irish flavour. When I decided to do a collection of my own, she rather grandly told the *Detroit Times* in May 1959, *I thought it certainly should have a theme, and why not an Irish one? But what? One twilight evening in Donegal, I stopped to talk with some little ones playing in front of a white-washed cottage. Their mother came to call them and as she stood framed in the door of her cottage wearing the traditional plaid skirt and black shawl, I knew that was what I would design.* A later telling of this story moved the location from Donegal to Connemmara, but that scarcely matters; this is a perfect example of Connolly's romantic approach to fashion: the twilight evening, the remote rural spot, the white-washed cottage, the 'little ones' and their mother in her traditional costume, and the designer's ability to come up with a good story when she needed one.

Sybil Connolly made her public debut as a designer in 1952, the same year that John Ford's *The Quiet Man* was released and this film shares certain characteristics with her clothes, in particular a sophisticated but understated deployment of apparently timeless motifs. Maureen O'Hara's costumes in *The Quiet Man* would not have looked out of place in an early Connolly collection, with the designer's emphasis on traditional materials and forms.

It is not known exactly how Sybil Connolly came to the attention of Carmel Snow, the Dalkey-born editor, from 1932-57, of American *Harper's Bazaar* but, within months of Connolly designing her first collection for Richard Alan, Snow brought a group of American fashion press and buyers to Ireland. This was in July 1953. With the encouragement of Lady Dunsany, herself a client of the designer, a Sybil Connolly collection – followed by a candlelit dinner – was shown to the visitors in the elegant surroundings of Dunsany Castle. The occasion, which was a triumph for the designer, launched her American career and, by the time Connolly set out on her first trip to the States in the autumn of that year, she had already been featured on the August cover of *Life* magazine with a romantic photograph of the well-known model, Ann Gunning, in a full-length red Kinsale cape and white crochet evening dress and the headline, 'Irish invade Fashion World.' Inside, there were further photographs of Gunning at Dunsany Castle where she was also shot by Richard Avedon for a spread in the October 1953 edition of *Harper's Bazaar* while Virginia Pope in the *New York Times* wrote: 'Fashion was interwoven with the lore and customs of Ireland in a fascinating manner in the Sybil Connolly collection.'

During that first trip in 1953, Connolly – in a routine that she was to continue on her two annual visits to America throughout the fifties – covered some twenty thousand miles over five weeks visiting every major city where she provided commentary for showings of her clothes as well as giving countless interviews and attending a large number of social engagements; but it was an introduction to New York's foremost fashion publicist, Eleanor Lambert, on this visit which was to prove most propitious. Lambert, who was to become a lifelong friend, was captivated. '(Sybil) was a smash hit in America as soon as she arrived', she told the *Irish Times* in November 1997. 'Her charm seemed to diffuse throughout the country. Everything about her was so glamourous and wonderful. She was almost alone in Irish fashion; she brought over a feeling of it as an entity in itself.' Thereafter, like Carmel Snow, Lambert – who had a widely-syndicated newspaper column – promoted Connolly at every turn.

Not that the designer was difficult to promote because she was not. 'American women are more remarkable than American skyscrapers', she announced on her first visit. It was a comment that was picked up by newspapers across the United States and

(Opposite). **2.** Sybil CONNOLLY: *Ballgowns, modelled by Ladies Melissa and Caroline Wyndham-Quinn at Petworth, Sussex.* Photographed by Norman Parkinson for *Vogue*, July 1954.

it can have done little harm in promoting sales of her clothes which, by the end of the debut visit, were carried by nine American and three Canadian department stores. 'No woman can be really elegant until she's over forty', was another of Connolly's 'soundbites' and one that must have gratified her clients as few of them would have been younger. She featured regularly in gossip columns like that in the *Hollywood Reporter* of March 1955: 'Sybil Connolly emerged from Louella Parsons's house after a late night soirée and exclaimed, "It's like Ireland – there's dew on the grass!" "What did you expect?" Mike O'Shea said, "Chanel No 5?"' She knew how to keep her name in the news and, at one time or another during the 'fifties, it was reported that she had been offered a job designing costumes for Hollywood; that she was about to produce a line of clothes for men; that an American company would make a film of her life; and that she had been commissioned to write her autobiography. Other stories, while seeming even more improbable, were actually true: she redesigned the habits of no fewer than three orders of nuns and a Sybil Connolly perfume was created for her by the monks of Caldy Island in Wales.

In a *Saturday Evening Post* profile of the designer in November 1957, it was noted that three-quarters of her gross earnings (then estimated at $500,000 per annum) originated in the United States, 'a tribute of American womanhood to Sybil's stylesmanship.' In the same feature, she commented, 'America made me. America will always have first claim to my production.' Notwithstanding this renown across the Atlantic, Connolly twice travelled to Australia – in October 1954 and in August 1957 – where a similar success attended her.

During the 1950s, an Irish woman travelling around the world in this manner and running her own successful business was a highly unusual phenomenon. 'I am a freak in Ireland', she told the *Saturday Evening Post* in November 1957. By the end of the 'fifties she employed around one hundred women, half of them working from their own homes where they wove tweed or hand-crocheted lace. While her character was unquestionably tough, she also had great charm and this was what most people who dealt with her professionally were shown. In the *Saturday Evening Post* profile, it was reported, 'American department store executives find themselves charmed by Sybil's smiling hazel eyes and, at the end of a delightful conversation, discover that they have been face to face with an astute saleswoman. Sybil has proved herself repeatedly an expert at the Invisible Sell.' The same feature remarked that 'her charm is thought worth mentioning even in Ireland' and indeed charm – along with references to the beauty of her pale skin, her large hazel eyes, and soft, seductive voice – is a word repeatedly used in all press interviews with Sybil Connolly. 'Her charm was faultless and alarming', wrote Gabrielle Williams in a posthumous notice published in the Adam's catalogue for the sale of Sybil Connolly's possessions in November 1998. 'She was not only a great designer', wrote Williams, 'she was also a great opportunist, seizing the moment unhesitatingly.'

But was Sybil Connolly as great a designer as she was an opportunist? Her cut and sense of proportion were never especially original, but she knew how to interpret current trends for her own clientèle. Her drawing skills were not strong, but this is by no means unusual among designers and she preferred to drape fabric over a model when deciding how it should be used. She constantly mentioned her great love of material and how this was the starting point for her ideas. When the chance to design a collection for Richard Alan arrived, she wisely used the fabrics of her own country, in particular linen at its lightest. She used to say that she first discovered this featherweight weave in a Northern Irish factory where it had been manufactured many years earlier to be made into fine linen handkerchiefs for the monarchs of Europe, but that after the First World War 'there weren't enough of them left around.' Famously, she took this linen and had it closely pleated to produce lengths which might then be used for dresses and skirts. Nine yards of linen were needed to create one yard of finished material. The first piece made in this way to be shown in the United States, a white evening dress called *First Love*, using three hundred linen handkerchiefs and containing more than five thousand pleats caused a huge stir and helped to make her name among Americans. The greatest merit of her pleated linen was that it was uncrushable as a fabric. *Harper's Bazaar* noted in June 1958 that a Connolly pleated linen skirt 'will pack into a small duffel bag and emerge unscathed.' Sybil Connolly's pleated linen is as remarkable a contribution to fashion history as Mario Fortuny's Delphos pleated silk dresses made at the beginning of the 20th century and like them will forever be associated with the name of one designer.

Pleated linen was by no means the only instance of Sybil Connolly taking old forms and giving them a fresh twist for the non-Irish market. She bought large bales of red flannel traditionally used for petticoats in Connemara and had this made into quilted skirts which were then shown, in the time-honoured manner, with white cambric blouses and black shawls. By reinterpreting peasant dress, the designer was anticipating bohemian fashion created by designers such as Yves Saint Laurent and Bill Gibb in the 1970s. She also recognised the demand for fabrics that had none of the stiff heaviness of their predecessors, as customers demanded greater freedom and ease of movement from their clothes. Therefore, although she loved to use tweed in her collections, this was specially woven for her in unusually light weights and rich colours. And she was not above deploying the most mundane of fabrics when so inspired; a dress called *Kitchen Fugue* for summer 1954 had a full billowing skirt made from lengths of striped linen tea towelling. Examples of Carrickmacross lace and hand-made crochet were other regular features of her collections. Much of this material was produced for her by outworkers in their own homes. Production was, therefore, relatively slow; it would take five weeks to make a pleated linen dress and up to nine months for one in Carrickmacross lace. Exclusivity was one advantage of this long production process. In March 1955, she told the *Los Angeles Examiner* that her work was rarely copied 'because of the individual handwork that is done on them.

The fabrics are all handmade in our cottage industries.' In its cover story on the designer, *Life* magazine observed that 'because of inexpensive labor costs in Ireland, US stores can import the styles ready-made and, even after duty, sell them at prices relatively low for a top European label.' A strapless pleated linen evening dress by Sybil Connolly was shown in the *New York Times* in April 1954 selling for $300 and prices remained largely unchanged over the next few years. In November 1957, the *Saturday Evening Post* gave $130 as the price for a day dress, $180 for a custom-tailored suit in Donegal tweed and $350 'or thereabouts' for an elaborate ballgown. This meant that Sybil Connolly's clothes were usually much cheaper, not only than those of other European designers, but also those of the top American names at the time, and it is this fact which may go some way towards explaining her popularity in the United States.

3. *Sybil Connolly preparing for one of her shows c.1970.*

Another lure – as far as her American clients were concerned – was the inherent romanticism of her work and she played on American perceptions of Ireland as a simple, unspoilt country. '"The trouble with the world," Miss Connolly feels,' announced the *American Holiday* magazine in February 1962, '"is that people have forgotten about romance" and her fashions, with their generous sweep of gossamer linen and silk, are an eloquent plea for a return to bygone fancies.' Her inspiration almost invariably came from the past. 18th-century Irish plasterwork designs were reproduced in embroidery on her dresses for spring/summer 1954 and late-19th-century ladies' riding costumes were obviously the basis for her collection a year later. Then there were the touches of Irish peasant style that consistently cropped up in her designs, not just through items such as red flannel skirts but also in woven straw caps for her summer 1954 collection inspired by the thatch on Connemara cottages. She often gave her clothes Irish names: a 1954 evening ensemble was called *Man of Aran* and a flecked tweed suit from the same period *Lough Corrib*. In January that year, Betty Spurling, head of fashion television at the BBC, remarked on 'the Connolly flair for taking the simple, age-old weaves worn by Irish peasants and introducing them to the world of haute couture.' But not everyone, and least of all the Irish, was enchanted with her vision of Irish peasantry. Myles na Gopaleen satirised her in his *Cruiskeen Lawn* column in the *Irish Times* and, in a June 1953 profile of her in the same paper, she responded to criticisms that her work was at times too 'stage-Irish' with the observation, 'This is a terribly competitive business. Unless Ireland can produce something distinctive, she will get nowhere.' Abroad, she promoted Ireland and boasted of the influence the country had on her: 'I couldn't design a button anywhere but in Ireland' she told *Time* magazine in March 1953 and in July 1954 explained to the *Evening News*, 'You see, I think I'd be a flop anywhere else. I just couldn't design unless I lived here.' 'It's a shame to have such beautiful fabrics, such resources for fine handwork and not use them in fashion' she is quoted as saying in the *Dallas Morning Post* in October 1953.

When Sybil Connolly had eventually departed from Richard Alan in March 1957, she had indulged her fondness for the romantic past by moving into a large house at 71 Merrion Square, Dublin. 'The house that linen built', as she called it, reflected Sybil Connolly's outlook and was furnished predominantly with antiques from the 18th century or copies of such pieces. Here she lived alone for more than forty years. She never married, even though her name was associated with a number of men during the 1950s. 'For the moment, I like to buy my mink and diamonds myself', she told the *Daily Mail* in January 1957. She was keenly religious all her life, claiming that her Roman Catholic faith meant 'everything to me. It is the whole centre of my life.' She would have each new collection blessed by a priest prior to its presentation and gave pride of place in her Merrion Square private sitting room to a very large French carved fruitwood statue of the Virgin Mary while a French ivory figure of the crucified Christ hung over her bed. These instances of a personal faith contrast with the press cuttings of her public life which suggest a constant round of social and professional engagements.

During the latter part of the 1950s, Sybil Connolly had become one of the foremost figures in Ireland. In January 1956 *Punch* had noted that while there were indisputably other Irish fashion designers, 'it is the Connolly collection which has become a bi-annual social event attended by the Irish gentry, men as well as women.' The gentry were among Connolly's best customers. In addition to Lady Dunsany, there were the Earl of Dunraven's two daughters, Ladies Melissa and Caroline Wyndham-Quin, photographed by Norman Parkinson for the July 1954 edition of *Vogue* wearing Sybil Connolly ballgowns. In the *Irish Times* in November 1997, Melissa Wyndham-Quin, now Lady Brooke (her 1959 wedding dress had also come from Sybil Connolly) remembered meeting the designer in 1953. 'She wasn't really known then, and we used to get fitted in a tiny room behind Richard Alan's shop. I remember one beautiful dress–it was strapless and made of white men's linen handkerchiefs banded in white satin. Cecil Beaton photographed me in it but unfortunately I don't have the dress anymore; I gave my boyfriends all the handkerchiefs.'

So established had Sybil Connolly become by this time that she was able to ask her clientèle to model for her. The late Aileen Plunket was photographed in 1954 wearing a Connolly ballgown in the grounds of Luttrellstown Castle while for the *Holiday* magazine spread of February 1962, models included Mariga Guinness in Leixlip Castle, the Marchioness of Waterford (formerly Caroline Wyndham-Quin) at Curraghmore, the Countess of Donoughmore at Knocklofty House, and Wendy Slazenger in Powerscourt House. Her list of American clients was just as impressive, numbering members of the Rockefeller, Mellon, and Dupont families. Film actresses who bought her clothes included Merle Oberon, Rosalind Russell (for whom Sybil Connolly designed the costumes of a 1965 film called *Mother Superior*), Elizabeth Taylor, Dana Wynter, and Julie Andrews. A feature on Adele Astaire in *Women's Wear Daily* in October 1968 noted that 'Sybil Connolly makes many of her clothes.' Jacqueline Kennedy was painted for her official White House portrait wearing one of the designer's pleated linen dresses and when the presidential widow visited Dublin in July 1967, she lunched with Sybil Connolly in Merrion Square.

By that date, however, Sybil Connolly's career as a fashion designer was already on the wane and her scrapbooks show a steady diminution in press attention through the 1960s, with the last entries dating from 1970. Tastes in fashion changed but Sybil Connolly remained the same and so, gradually, she found herself left behind. Even at the height of her success, there had been signs that this decline would happen sooner or later. The *Irish Times* review of her autumn/winter 1954 range observed that the Connolly day suits were 'basically much the same as those in her previous collections.' Two years later, the London *Times* reported that neither Sybil Connolly nor Irene Gilbert, her only major competitor as a designer in Dublin, 'offer any startling ideas likely to revolutionise the fashion world, but both continue their pioneer work in the development to couture level, and presentation, of their native fabrics.' By February 1959, the *New York Times* could comment of a Sybil Connolly collection that she 'showed tweeds, as she always has and always will.' In October that same year, she told the *Washington Post* that all women designers 'know that good fashion does not need to change.'

Regretfully, her judgement was wrong and, as a result, Sybil Connolly found herself overlooked once trends moved on from the style of her heyday. Although not yet aged fifty, she managed to sound like an old woman when she told the *Irish Times* in December 1970, 'I never liked the mini styles and I always remember what Dior once said to me in Paris. He said, "A woman should show her curves, not her joints" and this was so true.' In September 1972 she told the *Irish Press*: 'I cannot understand why young people today set out so deliberately to make themselves look so awful. As for trousers, I hate them too and only ever showed two as a concession in my collection ... My clients did not approve as they said they had always associated me with such feminine clothes.'

In 1992, the designer's clothes looked little different to those she had produced some forty years earlier. She still offered ballooning pleated linen skirts, Carrickmacross lace blouses, tweed day suits, and coats. But her clientele was greatly reduced and by this time Connolly was focussing her attention on other areas of design. Her own house in Merrion Square had always been a showcase of her excellent if conservative taste in interior decoration – among the earliest features on the property was one in *House Beautiful* in 1967 – and this preoccupation came to take up more of her time. She was responsible for the internal refurbishment of the late 18th-century Swiss Cottage in Cahir, county Tipperary; wrote or co-authored several books on Irish homes, gardens, and crafts; and helped to revive interest in the flower pictures of Mrs Delany, the 18th-century friend of Dean Swift and Fanny Burney. In the 1980s, Sybil Connolly began to work as a designer of tableware for Tiffany & Co of New York, of glassware for Tipperary Crystal, and of linens for Brunschwig & Fils and Schumacher, as well as becoming associated with the Kilkenny potter, Nicholas Mosse.

She kept herself busy and, as much as possible, in the public eye even if the latter was no longer especially interested in her fashion designs. Sybil Connolly's abiding fame in Ireland was shown six months after her death when the contents of 71 Merrion Square were auctioned in November 1998. A record of visitors came to the four-day pre-sale viewing – more than two thousand on one day alone – and the James Adam salerooms were completely filled for the auction itself of 600-plus lots. The preponderance of women private bidders reflected the nature of Sybil Connolly's appeal, as did the prices paid for certain items. While many furniture lots fetched figures comfortably within the estimates, individual pieces of personal significance to the designer tended to surpass all expectations. A set of eight cushions, for example, carrying an estimate of no more than £300, went for £1,300; a box of the designer's sketches (estimate £100-£200) made £1,600; and £440 was paid for a bale of her pleated linen in black, although its estimate was only £150-£250. Sybil Connolly might no longer be as famous as she had once been, but her name had not slipped out of the spotlight.

In February 1954, the *Daily Telegraph* fashion correspondent, Winefride Jackson, writing about whether women could ever truly succeed as fashion designers, noted that a year or two earlier American buyers and press had been 'looking for a new idea, a new person to write about, and there was Sybil Connolly with all the romanticism behind her, plus her own skill.' Presciently, Jackson added 'it remains to be seen, after the fuss and the furore has died down, just what place she will eventually occupy in fashion.' That place is not as great as might once have seemed to be the case but Sybil Connolly deserves to be remembered in Irish history for more than just her designs. She was the country's first fashion designer to attract international attention, the first woman in Ireland to set up her own successful business selling overseas, and one of the first people to promote Irish products and skills in the global market. If she was not a designer of the first rank, she was nonetheless one of the most remarkable women in Ireland in the 20th century.

ROBERT O' BYRNE *is a Fashion Writer*

ACKNOWLEDGEMENTS: *The author and editor are most grateful to John Connolly for permitting Sybil Connolly's scrapbooks to be consulted and photographed.*

4. Sybil CONNOLLY: *Ballgown and Cape*. 1955. Published in the German magazine, *Ihre Freundin*. The cape, inspired by the traditional Irish peasant dress, was, like her pleated linen, one of Connolly's signature designs.

In the Shops: a Coat, a Dress from Dublin

• Opposite: characteristic coat from Sybil Connolly—wrapping over, hooded for outings after five, made of wonderful Irish tweed. Under it, a creamy worsted dress, tabbed at the waist. In London, at Jacqmar.
• Below: misty beige worsted dress with a high scarf collar. On its own, an excellent street dress; equally good under a coat, especially one that is collarless. Sybil Connolly, at Jacqmar.

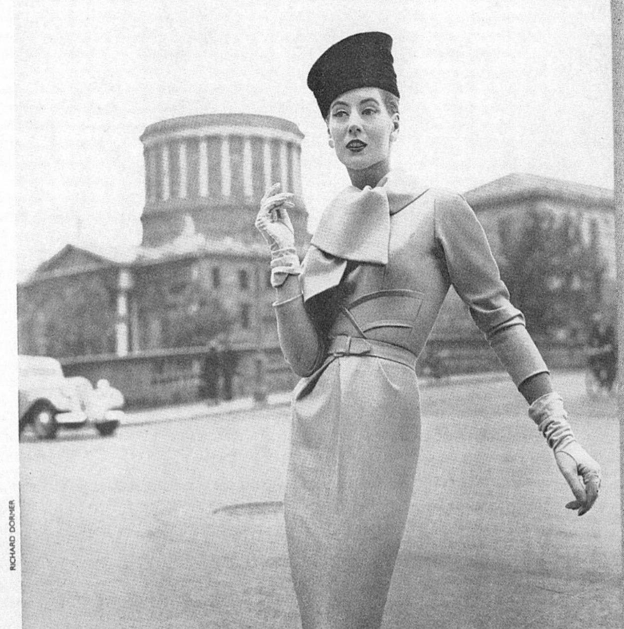

(Above) Worsted street dress with high scarf. From Harper's Bazaar, October 1956.

The TATLER and Bystander, May 16, 1956

(Above) Woollen dress, inspired by a monk's habit, and made from a single piece of fabric. From The Tatler and Bystander, May 1956.

MRS. ANTHONY NUTTING, THE FORMER ANNE GUNNING, WHOSE LOOKS ARE AS INDELIBLY IRISH AS THE DRESS SHE WEARS HERE: PLEATED IRISH LINEN, BY SYBIL CONNOLLY.

(Above) Anne Gunning (Mrs Anthony Nutting) models a pleated Irish linen ballgown for Vogue, March 1962.

The QUEEN

(Left) Organza short evening dress with applique of Irish hand-crochet threaded with matching velvet ribbon. From The Queen, September 1955.

(Below) Sybil Connolly models her ballgown, First Love. It was made in 1954 from linen handkerchiefs.

JULES SCHICK

Sybil Connolly, talented designer from Dublin, poses in her handkerchief-linen ball dress, "First Love," at Gimbels in Philadelphia

(Above.) 'For dinner at home: mohair made-for-motion hostess gown.' The skirt of Donegal mohair tweed, the bodice of pleated black handkerchief linen. Modelled by Hilary Frayne (later Weston) at Powerscourt, 1963.

(Above) Donegal tweed suit with semi-fitted jacket and wide sailing collar. 1954.

(Above) The Rose Look'. Gossamer pleated Irish linen. From Harper's Bazaar, 1957.

All-Irish sporting entry

An Irish background for two Irish stories. The first concerns the suit—in Irish tweed, black, blue and peat-brown, by Irish designer Sybil Connolly. The long top, easy as a sweater, goes over a narrow skirt and under a knee-length coat with shoulder-wide collar. Jacqmar have an adaptation of this suit in London . . . The second Irish story concerns the horse: a bay hunter gelding, since sold to Italy to be trained as a show jumper, photographed at Blackwater House, Kells, County Meath, home of Mr. John Brady, who holds him

157

(Above) Irish tweed suit. From Vogue, October 1955.

(Right) Irish linen dress, full skirted black crisped with the white of a linen jerkin cardigan. From Harper's Bazaar, 1955.

(Above) Pleated linen skirt. From Harper's Bazaar, October 1955.

(Above) Evening dress in handwoven pleated linen. From Ihre Freundin, June 1958.

(Below) Wedding dress in white, Irish lawn, swagged and ruched. From Connolly's 1953 collection for Richard Alan.

(Above) On the left, a short dance dress: 'for control, the smooth-fitting strapless bodice is boned and interlined.' On the right, 'An afternoon dress with back interest.' From McCall's, April 1957.

Ein großes Abendkleid aus gelbem Irish Poplin, das Oberteil aus geflochtenen Seidenpopeline-Bändern in mehreren Farben. Modell Sybil O'Connolly. Foto Richard Dormer

(Below) Evening dress. 1956.

(Left) Irish poplin evening skirt and blouse. 1965.

For the guest room, too—IRISH LINEN

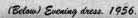

Here is a guest being pampered to the nth. Nothing but the best. Tempting tray, springy pillows, and above all, the smooth-threaded luxury (*certainly* it's a luxury) of Irish linen bedding. An unbeatable elegance this, and one that makes the most sophisticated guest say, "Oh! *Linen!*"

and now, news: SYBIL CONNOLLY, Dublin couturier, is designing never-before beauties for the bedroom in the finest Irish linen. Bedspreads of permanently-pleated gossamer linen, blanket covers of uncrushable pleats and crochet, laced with satin; sheets, perhaps a foot deep in embroidery (done by the nuns in Ireland) or traditionally hemstitched. All, of course, in top-tradition Irish linen, all soon-to-be available in the very best stores.

(Above) Connolly bedlinen. 1957. Bedspreads of permanently pleated gossamer linen and sheets, perhaps a foot deep in embroidery (done by nuns in Ireland).

Fashions by Sybil Connolly

Who needs Paris? Deep in the land of the bogtrotter, this talented dressmaker creates high fashions for the best-dressed women in New York.

By ERNEST O. HAUSER

(Above) Cocktail sheath with a fish-tail bustle. From Saturday Evening Post, November 1957.

SHELAGH WILSON'S FASHION

A moment to remember. In her "waterfall" dress of soft Irish lawn, she waits for her wedding. She can later take off the shoulder band and have a strapless ball dress — Sybil Connolly £120

(Above) Waterfall wedding dress of Irish lawn. From She, April 1957.

Guest Collector
Contemporary Irish Art

John McBratney

makes some suggestions for starting a collection of work by Irish artists of today

1. Elizabeth MAGILL: *Scenic Route (three)*. 1997. Oil on canvas, 152 x 183 cm. (The Kerlin Gallery). Magill's prices range between £1,100 and £10,000. If one wanted to purchase a landscape to start a collection, then Elizabeth Magill's work would be an excellent choice.

When you reach a stage in your life when you may have some money to spend that is not destined automatically for mortgage repayments, a new washing machine, or reducing the Visa account, it is time to spend it on yourself. In our commercially-aggressive world, there will be many siren voices imploring you – a new luxury car, holidays to obscure places – and many of the goods and services on offer will give you instant gratification, although it is only rarely that they will provide any lasting pleasure. Contemporary art is not such a voice. Its exponents work calmly away and the art they produce continues to provoke, entertain, and fascinate for many years after the siren voice has fallen silent. Because contemporary art is not promoted with the commercial raucousness of the advertising and marketing world, because it is not 'packaged', it has one serious disadvantage: many people think it is 'beyond them' or 'not for me'. But this is a deception. Everyone who has the imagination to use their eyes and stretch their vision can enjoy the world of contemporary art and, for those who want a little adventure, one or two purchases along the way can be guaranteed to add a bit of 'zing' to life as one contemplates, admires, or puzzles over the purchased work while it gradually insinuates itself into one's everyday life.

Setting out on such an adventure, the first step is to find your local public gallery. When you find it, start looking at what you see there. In Dublin, you can begin by visits to IMMA, the

Douglas Hyde Gallery, the RHA Gallery, and the Hugh Lane Municipal Gallery. Go to any of these – or to your local gallery if you live in the country – with an open mind. Accept that the work on display has integrity. You may not like it but that is not any reason to sneer and a good idea is to look again – and again – at the pieces which you find most difficult. If the work is contemporary, it is quite likely that it may seem strange in the first instance, but give it – and yourself – time. In IMMA ask the attendants for guidance: many are young artists and are more than willing to impart their knowledge. If, following a visit, you find that some image, which you may not even have liked when you saw it in the gallery, haunts your inner vision, then you will know that the adventure is starting to create its own life and force within you. You are beginning to see with a new insight. The fun is beginning.

When you feel the time is approaching when you want to spend some money, to make a purchase, start going to the commercial galleries. These are as various in their character as are their respective owners and, as a consequence, they illustrate perfectly the kaleidoscopic variety of human vices and virtues. The galleries with which I am concerned are those which act as artists' agents and the vast majority of the work which they show is the most recent work by artists for whom they act. I have a preference for abstract and figurative art and, in recent years, a fascination with photographic work. Landscapes, in the main, with one or two exceptions, for some reason do not seem capable of arresting my soul or even my attention for any substantial period of time. I, therefore, would be slow to recommend anyone to start with the purchase of a landscape however soothing or comforting it may appear to be. However, as all prejudices must have an exception, Elizabeth Magill's paintings (Fig 1) would make an excellent one.

I favour the Kerlin, the Green on Red, the Rubicon, the Taylor and the Hallward galleries. Between them, these will provide a solid core of artists with which you can gradually become familiar but two more recent galleries, the Paul Kane and Kevin Kavanagh, which have not yet had the time to develop a track record, might also be visited. Enter any of them without fear or trepi-

2. Dorothy CROSS: *Bulls Eye*. 1994. Dart board and cow's teat. (The Kerlin Gallery). Cross's prices range from £1,000 for a photograph to £20,000 for a sculpture with a video projection. Cross uses photographs among the many different media which she employs so dextrously but she is possibly best known for her series of sculptures using Freiesian cow hides.

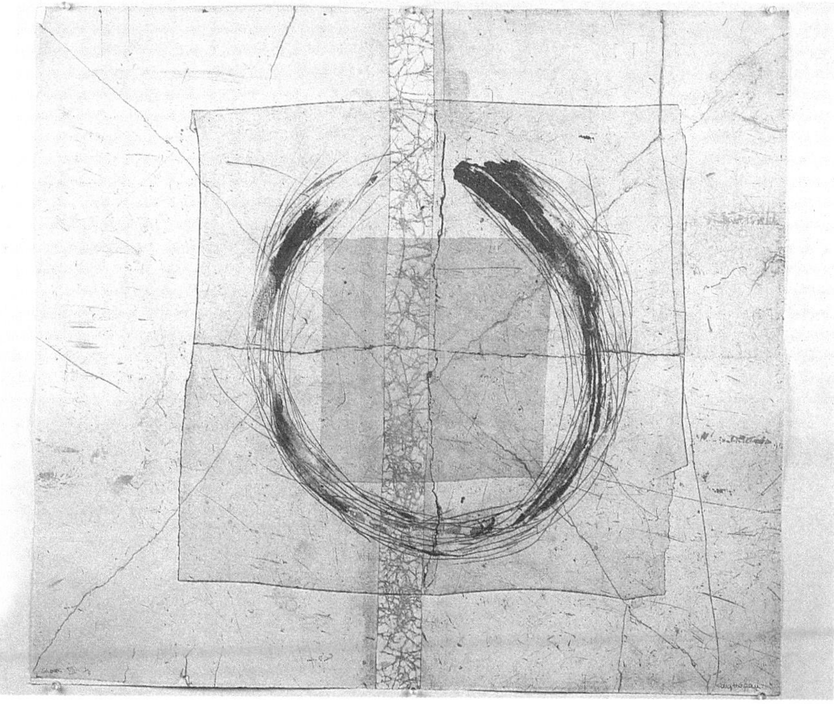

3. Sarah HORGAN: *Ghosts VII*. Edition of three, lamination and lino etched, 70 x 80 cm. (Original Print Gallery). Horgan's prints cost around £300. A print makes a very good first purchase and Sarah Horgan makes the most subtle work in very small editions.

4. Paul NUGENT, *Cardinal No 4.* 1998. Acrylic and oil on board, 85 x 56 cm. One of a series of seven paintings. (Kevin Kavanagh Gallery). At his second one-man exhibition at the Kavanagh Gallery in September 1999, prices ranged upwards from £1,000.

5. Michael COLEMAN: *Oil on Twelve Canvasses.* 1998. Oil on canvas, 150 x 150 cm. (Green on Red Gallery). Coleman's works range in price between £475 and £10,000. He creates paintings and works on paper which are apparently only in one colour but in fact have many grades of the colour.

dation. Do not be disturbed by the fact that you may be the only person there. Ask for information. You will find the vast majority of the owners and their staff helpful especially if you make it clear that you want to understand what may seem inexplicable. Once you show interest, it will not be long before you find yourself on invitation lists to openings but do not feel any necessity to buy at an opening. If you are thinking of buying, do not be rushed. If you are undecided, it is likely the gallery owner may reserve a work until the following day or longer. Do not be afraid to sleep on an idea overnight. Can you remember the image in the morning when you wake up? Maybe it is a different work that emerges in your brain as you awake. Go back and look again. The decision-making process is part of the joy so do not lose that pleasure in a snap decision. You will undoubtedly lose some works by such forbearance but you will make fewer errors. Such errors stay in your possession once you have bought them and will serve as reminders that collecting contemporary art is nothing to do with making money.

I would recommend that serious consideration be given to buying a print as a first purchase. Two artists who work almost exclusively in this medium are Sarah Horgan and John Graham. Sarah Horgan (Fig 3) makes the most subtle work in very small editions, sometimes as few as four. Her work has a layered quality of veils which accentuates a certain mystery which is all pervasive. In contrast John Graham (Fig 6) works in black on a white ground and the images he creates are of form with strength and substance which yet float in the space in which he places them. In fact the purchase of a print by each of these artists would give any collection a very sound base from which to proceed.

Photography is an art form which is very largely ignored in Ireland although Willie Doherty, who has an international reputation, has been a pioneer in the use of the camera and video for the last decade. His works (Fig 7) usually appear in editions of three. He places words in block capitals on the photographic image, thereby transforming the words used and the image seen and the results are memorable with images that haunt the brain.

Dorothy Cross and Kathy Prendergast both use photographs amongst the many different media which each employs so dextrously. Cross (Fig 2) is possibly best known for the series of sculptures she made using Friesian cow hides but there is an earlier beautiful sculpture by her in the Hugh Lane Gallery called *Shark Lady in a Balldress* which is well worth viewing. Prendergast (Fig 13) won the junior section of the Venice Biennale in 1997 and has had a solo exhibition in the Tate Gallery, London. She has worked on a substantial scale as is evidenced by the piece entitled *Stack* at IMMA. However, her smaller works are more relevant to a private collector and she creates an intimacy between the work and the viewer which is enduring. Prendergast is not prolific and it may take some time before work becomes available of a suitable scale for a private collector: instant gratification is not always possible when collecting but having to wait very often increases the pride and pleasure in a purchase when it is eventually made.

Michael Coleman (Fig 5) has been a favoured artist of mine for a long time. He creates paintings and works on paper which are apparently in only one colour but, when looked at reflectively, are seen to have many grades of the colour as well as a great panache and strength in the application of the paint. Coleman moves paint with passion and his passion is there for the viewer to experience. There is a splendid blue painting of his, very poorly hung, in the John Field Room of the National Concert Hall. Fergus Martin (Fig 10) also allows a single colour to predominate but his surface is invariably smooth and the gradations in the colour are minute. He uses borders of white and there is always a perfect balance and harmony. His work is far from obvious and it may not have immediate appeal but the more you are prepared to relax into one of his paintings the more satisfying it becomes. Do not be disappointed if you do not 'get it' initially: persevere.

If you want an alcoholic beverage and at the same time extend your knowledge of art go to the bar in the Fitzwilliam hotel on Stephen's Green where there are a series of yellow and black paintings by John Cronin. His initial predilection was towards blue and black paintings but in his recent work (Fig 8) he is using both paint and photostat images to create a visually layered surface which is in fact smooth. Sean Hillen (Fig 12) has made wonderful collages incorporating John Hinde images of Ireland with new and somewhat unlikely additions such as a view of Carlingford Lough with the pyramids in the middle ground; at the moment he is in the process of making greater use of the computer in creating his images. I am not sure if his work is in any public collection but keep an eye out for him as the more of his work you see, the more you like the 'zany' brain that produces it. He is in the course of producing a book of his images. Paul Nugent (Fig 4)is a young artist who produced a remarkable one-man show of paintings about two years ago with a stern, seated figure in clerical garb which was shrouded in various degrees of overpainting in brown which concealed to a greater or lesser extent the image of the figure. Consequently, the visibility of the underlying figure was substantially altered by the light or the lack of it. As he is at the start of his career, it was an accolade that two of those paintings were bought by

6. John Graham: Three prints: *Untitled*. 1998. Carborundum. (Green on Red Gallery). Graham's prints range in price from £200-£850. He works in black on a white ground and the images he creates are of form with strength and substance.

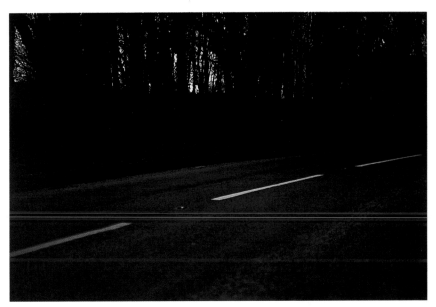

7. Willie Doherty, *The Side of the Road*. 1999. Cibachrome on aluminium. (The Kerlin Gallery). Edition of three. Doherty's photographs range in price from £3,346 to £10,410. Doherty, who has an international reputation, has been a pioneer in the use of the camera and video for the last decade.

8. John Cronin: *[Sic]*. 1998. Oil and pigment on steel. 120 x 240 x 10 cm.(Green on Red Gallery). Cronin's prices for oils on paper, aluminium or steel range between £350 and £5,000. His initial predilection was towards blue and black paintings but in his most recent work he uses both paint and photostat images.

9. Pat Scott: *Gold Painting*. Gold Leaf and Tempera on canvas, 116.8 x 127 cm (Taylor Galleries). Scott's work ranges in price from £2,000 to £15,000 for a gold leaf painting. In many aspects of Irish life over the last fifty years, Scott has fought for good design and simplicity of form.

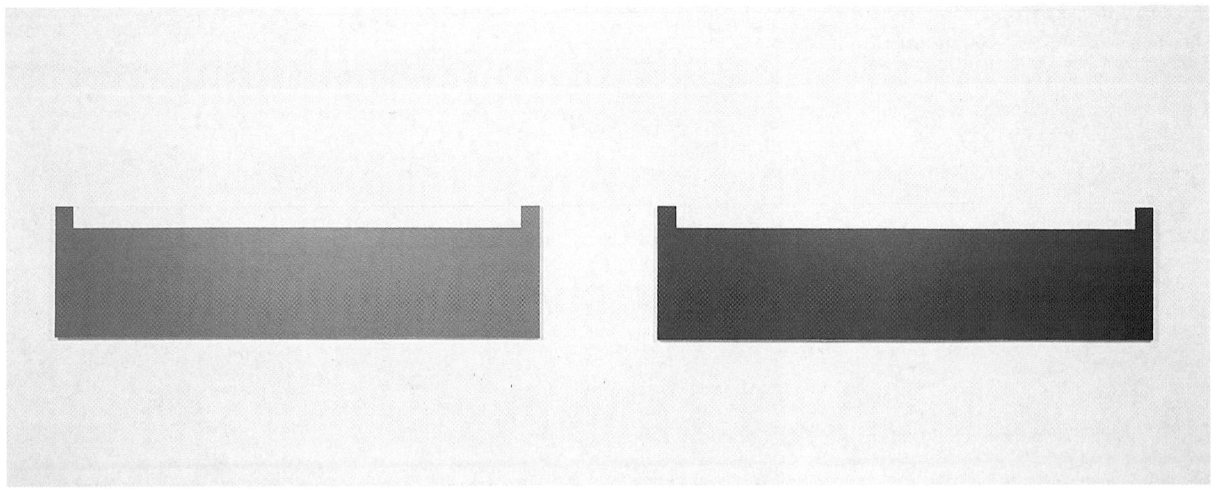

10. Fergus Martin, *Untitled*. 1999. Acrylic on canvas 238 x 61.5 cm. (Green on Red Gallery). Prints, drawings, and paintings by Martin range in price between £400 and £5,000. Martin's work is far from obvious and it may not have immediate appeal but the more you are prepared to relax into one of his paintings, the more satisfying it becomes.

11. Brian MAGUIRE, *Memorial*. 1998. Mixed media on linen 269 x 424 cm. (The Kerlin Gallery). Maguire's prices range from £1,400 for a mixed media on board painting to £17,000 for the work illustrated. Maguire's message may not be very comfortable or comforting to the viewer but his work beats a drum for those in our society who are outsiders for whatever reason.

12. Sean HILLEN: *Great Pyramids of Carlingford*. 1994. Collage. (Anya von Gosseln Gallery). Hillen's work ranges in price from about £45 for a digital print in an unlimited edition to £2,800 for a collage. Hillen has made wonderful collages incorporating John Hinde images of Ireland and the more you see his work, the more you like the 'zany' brain that produces it.

IMMA. Brian Maguire (Fig 11) is a painter who often chooses hard political subject matter as the inspiration for his work. The fate of prisoners in the Maze and similar institutions is the stuff which stirs the humanitarian principles within his soul. His message may not be very comfortable or comforting to the viewer but he has stuck to his last and his work beats a drum for those in our society who are outsiders for whatever reason. The viewer's conscience as well as his vision are the targets of Maguire's work.

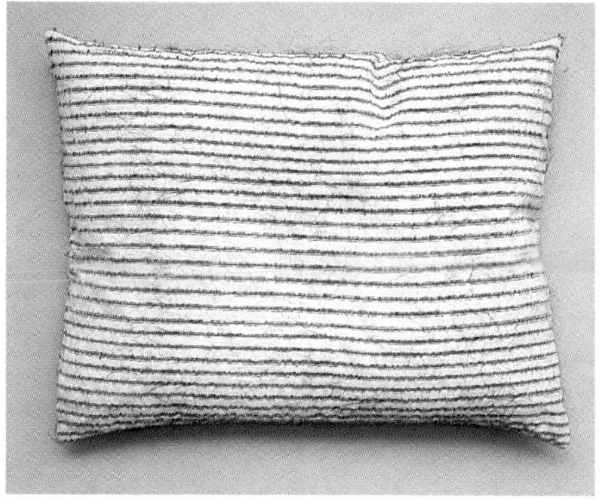

13. Kathy PRENDERGAST: *After*. 1999. Woven cotton and human hair. (The Kerlin Gallery). Works by Prendergast range in price between £1,400 and £7,000. Prendergast is not prolific and it may take time before work becomes available but having to wait increases the pride and pleasure when an eventual purchase is made.

Finally, I come to Patrick Scott (Fig 9) who, in many aspects of Irish life over the last fifty years, has fought for good design and simplicity of form in all things. Decoration for its own sake is no part of his world. His most distinctive work employs gold leaf applied to the canvas usually in geometric forms which complement other lightly applied geometric marks made on the canvas. For a long time I did not 'get' these works but when, by chance, I saw a large number of them in twilight, the penny dropped and the radiance of the gold in the half light gave these strange and beautiful pieces a sense of perpetuity and reassurance. Recently I stayed in a bedroom where I had the privilege of seeing one of them in the half light of early morning. I cannot imagine why it took me so long to see their strength but it was my loss.

This is my selection of artists but there are many others. I am aware that, Dublin being the small place that it is, my list will undoubtedly offend some artists whose work I admire and whom I like personally but whose names I have omitted. My defence is that I had to produce a list which had to be relatively brief in order to be of any use to a person at the start of an adventure. And it cannot be an adventure if everything is signposted at the start.

JOHN MCBRATNEY is a Barrister and a sometime collector of contemporary art.

Elizabeth Magill, Dorothy Cross, Kathy Prendergast, Willie Doherty, and *Brian Maguire* are all represented by the **Kerlin Gallery**, Anne's Lane, South Anne Street, Dublin 2.
Sarah Horgan is represented by the **Original Print Gallery**, 4 Temple Bar, Dublin 2.

John Graham, Michael Coleman, Fergus Martin, and *John Cronin* are represented by the **Green on Red Gallery**, 26-28 Lombard Street East, Dublin 2.
Sean Hillen is represented by the **Anya von Gösseln Gallery**, The Gate Lodge, Huntington Castle, Clonegal, Co Carlow.

Paul Nugent is represented by the **Kevin Kavanagh Gallery**, 66 Great Strand Street, Dublin 1.
Pat Scott is represented by the **Taylor Galleries**, 34 Kildare Street, Dublin 2.
The **Paul Kane Gallery** is at 53 South William Street, Dublin 2.

Time, Process, Memory
Installation Art by Andrew Kearney

Aisling Molloy-Badrawi

in conversation with a contemporary Irish artist

It was probably his one person show, *Temporal Change* (Figs 3, 4 & 5), at The Douglas Hyde Gallery in 1994, in which themes of growth, death, and rebirth were explored that first brought Andrew Kearney to the notice of the Dublin public. The following year he was nominated to take part in the Glen Dimplex Awards at IMMA (Fig 1). In both these exhibitions as well as in his one-person show at The Camden Arts Centre, London in 1995 (Figs 8 & 9), the combination of sensory effects extended the installation form beyond the visual to a manipulation of energy in the artist's use of sound, image, and lights. More recently, Kearney's work was included as Mebh Ruane's *Critic's Choice* at the RHA Banquet Exhibition (October-November 1997) and in an exhibition of three Irish artists commissioned by BAA which was installed at Heathrow Airport in 1997-98 (Fig 7). These two most recent works explored the subject of time and drew attention to the dominance of time-keeping in contemporary culture.

1. Andrew KEARNEY: Installation (detail). 1995. (Irish Museum of Modern Art: Glen Dimplex Awards Exhibition). One of five 16 cm video monitors on aluminium brackets. The video played images of thunder and storm. The tape ran on a 30 minute loop relayed from a central computer terminal.

The piece exhibited at the RHA, *Last Seduction*, gave the viewer a taste of themes explored in the more extensive installation shown at Heathrow and offered a preview of current work in progress to be exhibited in The Crawford Gallery, Cork, in the year 2000. *Last Seduction* consisted of a digital clock set into a huge tree stump placed inside the wooden crate, lid ajar, in which it had been delivered. The viewer's curiosity was awakened, questions arose, one walked around the work, and became involved in the process. According to Kearney,[1] the viewer's responses are necessary for the completion of the work and s/he becomes more of a 'participator' in the process. Some might have been inclined to read the piece as a comment on the environment but for

2. Andrew KEARNEY: Installation. 1992. (Serpentine Gallery, London: Barclays Young Artist Award). This installation was composed of corrugated galvanised steel, with wooden and steel supports. The steel tracks on the wheels enabled rotation by motor.

Kearney, 'the point is its fragility and loss, a reclaiming of its pride and memory. By becoming part of the work it begins another life-cycle.' The tree-stump is one of several which the artist rescued from a derelict site near his studio in London. Kearney describes it as 'torn and damaged' and for him it represents the various life experiences of pain, suffering, and isolation which often trigger his creative process. The piece was a celebration of the growth and potential which occurs in the cycle of time.

The installation at Heathrow's Terminal 1 Pier 4a, entitled *A Long Thin Thread,* was situated in the link bridge along which passengers walk from Irish flights to reach the main airport. This work used imagery taken from contemporary culture and illustrated the reliance upon time-keeping in our world. Kearney says that 'it's something we're seeing every day, we're clocking up numbers, the years we live or the days in the week, everything is numbered, the minutes in the hour, how many hours we work in the day.' Together with Frances Hegarty and Philip Napier, Kearney was one of three Irish artists chosen to exhibit there. Because it is different to the usual gallery space, the airport tunnel presented both challenges and opportunities to the artists who were chosen by BAA who set out, in commissioning art for the airport, to challenge people's perception of what constitutes art. Kearney responded by creating forms which blended into the architectural space and also reflected the functional nature of the airport.

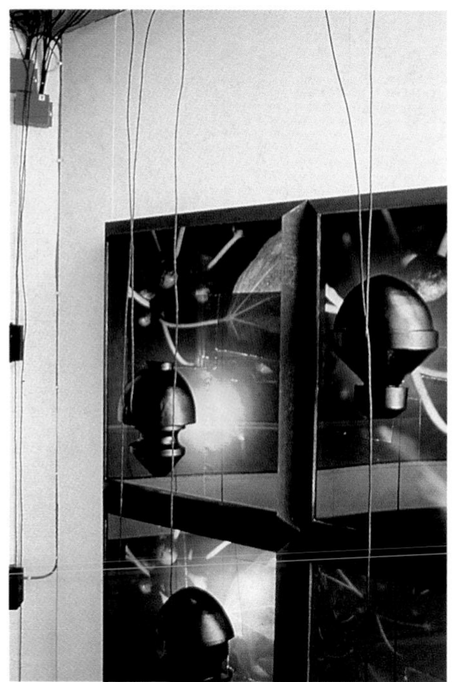

3. Andrew KEARNEY: Installation: *Temporal Change.* 1994. Nine black wall cases, 122 x 100 x 26 cm. (Douglas Hyde Gallery, Dublin). Inside each case was a photographic image of a fig tree. The nine cases were pieced together and a black vacuum-formed shape was placed in front of each box which was lit from within. Three speakers on each side emitted a sound track of thunder and rain falling on foliage. These tracks were on a 2 minute loop stored on a digital track housed in a central computer terminal.

The design of the link bridge is based on the inside of an airplane wing. Kearney placed uniform sculptural forms containing digital screens (LEDS) at random heights along the curved sides of the tunnel. The sculptures' organic shapes contrasted with the screens which recorded on digital clocks the passengers arriving and leaving. The screens (Fig 9) were coloured red on the out-going side and green on the in-coming side. Kearney said he chose the colours partly because of their associations with 'stop' and 'go' and partly as a reference to the difference between green letter boxes in Ireland and red ones in England. The artist's use of technology to record the unpredictability of human life is very advanced and, in this respect, the work bears some visual similarity to that by Japanese artist, Mijayama. However, Mijayama uses LEDS or digital screens to record rather than count time whereas Kearney's use of the LEDS is more functional than decorative and involves the viewer in an interactive experience.

The nature of the airport space, where the contrast between a highly-efficient technological organisation on the one hand and the possibility of human error, accident, or emergency on the other, suggested the notion of chaos to the artist: 'In the order there was a sense of chaos as well....that sense of tension (that) anything can happen.' The screens were made with slightly different chips which take up the command differently so that if two people come into the space at the same time one monitor might receive both of them whereas another will register only one and vice-versa. Kearney placed the monitors at random heights to reflect the fractional differences in the figures which each one records to offset the regimented design of a functional space. Kearney felt that it was important to achieve a sense of natural growth in the space so that the forms would reflect the nature of chaos. To achieve this he cast the corrugated shape of the wall and then cast the domes on them so they fitted exactly onto the wall. By way of contrast to the 'vulnerability' of the organic forms, heavy conduits made of strong industrial material carried the wiring and they formed an 'outer hard shell to protect the core'.

In this work Kearney revealed an intuitive awareness of the principles of chance and chaos currently being explored by scientists and his work may be interpreted as revealing a new consciousness of our reality. Since the 1980s, when Benoit Mandelbrot[2] introduced a new system of geometry called fractal geometry, scientists from various quarters have been discussing the existence and effects of chaos in their research projects. Perhaps the clearest scientific analogy for Kearney's work at Heathrow is that of the pin-ball machine referred to by Iain Percival in an essay *Chaos: A Science for the Real World.*[3] Percival explains how this simple, time honoured, machine confounds the long-accepted basis of Newtonian dynamics which is a cornerstone of western scientific thinking. When the ball is dropped in from the top and as it moves down it has an equal chance of hitting the pins on either side on the next level, and so on, down to the lowest level. He has plotted one thousand and twenty-four possible different paths from the top to the bottom. In short, 'the motion of the pinball is chaotic' just as the reality of human activity is shown to be by Kearney's sculptures which record the people entering the space at random. At any given time the digital screens were showing slightly different numbers.

The site at Heathrow gave the artist the opportunity to engage the viewer to an even greater extent than in previous

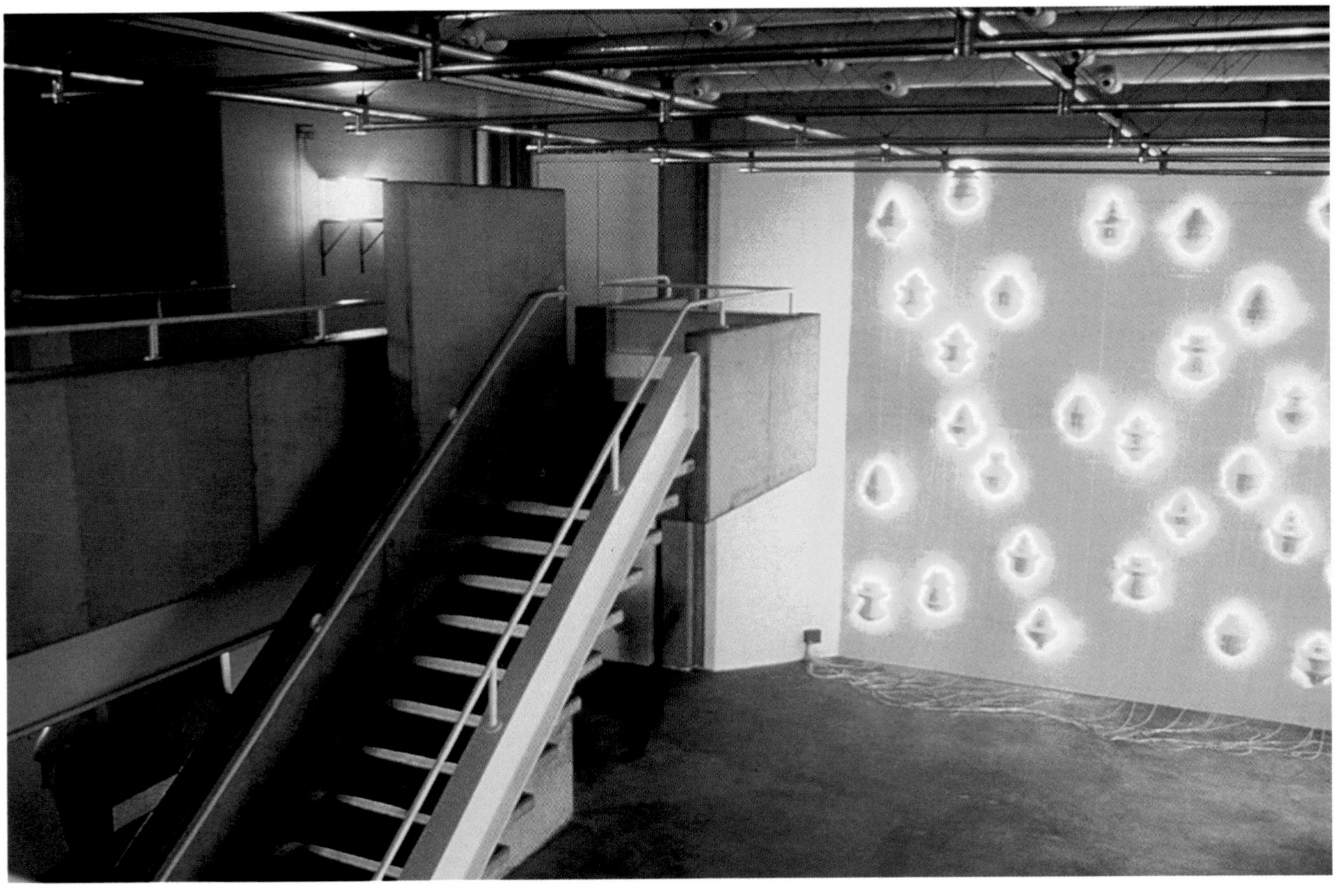

4. Andrew KEARNEY: Installation: *Temporal Change*. 1994. 60 plaster casts in 9 different shapes. (Douglas Hyde Gallery, Dublin). A warm interior light source connected to a light sensor on a window mimicked the daylight outside.

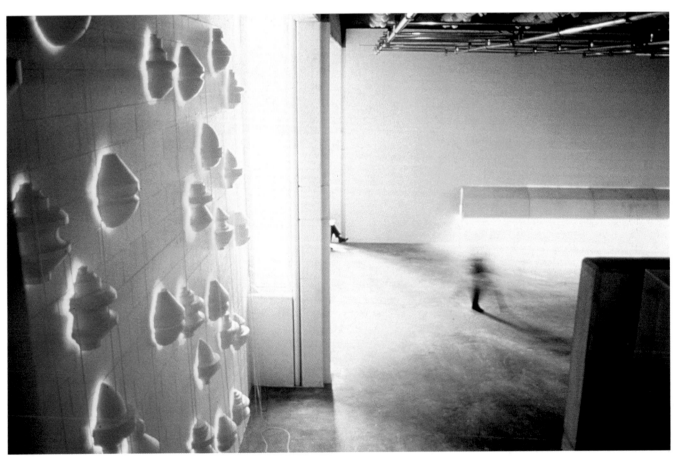

5. Andrew KEARNEY**:** Installation: *Temporal Change*. 1994. (Douglas Hyde Gallery, Dublin). Themes of growth, death, and rebirth were explored using five metre long plaster casts on a black wall housing fluorescent strip lights.

6. Andrew KEARNEY: Installation: *Sense of Time.* 1993. (Institute of Contemporary Art: PS1 Gallery, New York). The installation consisted of cast plaster containers with light bulbs sandwiched between them and a huge photograph made up of forty-eight sheets of fibre-based paper.

7. Andrew KEARNEY: Installation: *A Long Thin Thread.* 1996-97. (Heathrow Airport, Pier 4A, London). Using imagery taken from contemporary culture, the installation was in the link bridge along which passengers walk from Irish flights to reach the main airport.

8. Andrew KEARNEY: *Policing of Pleasure.* 1995. Cast plaster hemispheres, 76 x 102cm. Neon rods, 90 cm. (Camden Arts Centre, London). This view of the installation space, taken from the entrance, shows the screened window and plaster cast hemispheres.

9. Andrew KEARNEY: *Policing of Pleasure.* 1995. (Camden Arts Centre, London). A double infra-red beam monitored viewers to the space and recorded them on a digital clock.

installations although there were restrictions on the use of sound. The forms created indicated the way in which a sculptural installation using technology can work alongside design to humanise a space and make it more welcoming.

In the 1970s, a series of essays entitled *Inside the White Cube* by artist/critic Brian O'Doherty drew attention to the rarefied anaesthetic atmosphere of the modernist gallery space. O'Doherty described the gallery as an 'unshadowed, white, clean, artificial-space' which 'is devoted to the technology of aesthetics.'[4] Within this space the viewer was often vulnerable and alienated. However, more recent developments in installation sculpture, as shown by Kearney's use of the public space offered by the commission at Heathrow, open up new possibilities for artist-viewer communication.

Such spaces are different from the usual gallery in that people encounter the artist's work unexpectedly rather than coming in specifically to view it. Kearney says that 'it maybe works even more intensely than a gallery space because you're not going in with any expectations of what you're going to see.' Another factor which differentiates this type of space from a gallery is the fact that greater numbers of people see the work and many of these may not seek out art in the normal course of their lives. Kearney is aware that some may only glance at the work, some may not even notice it, while others may find the number counting interesting and be prompted to question the meaning of the piece. But at whatever level people perceive and receive the work, they are taking part in it as they enter the space and are recorded by the monitors.

In October 1997, Kearney worked on an installation piece to be included in a group show of Irish artists living in London entitled *0044*. This exhibition was held at the PS 1 Studios in New York in the summer of 1999 and will be shown at The Crawford Gallery, Cork in spring 2000. Kearney's contribution will be a development of *The Last Seduction* and if his Heathrow installation — an admirable combination of art, design, and technology — was anything to go by, we may look forward to even further developments from him in the future for communication in art based upon viewer involvement.

AISLING MOLLOY-BADRAWI is a Lecturer in the Limerick School of Art and Design.

ACKNOWLEDGEMENTS I would like to thank Helen Cadwallader, the Art Programme Manager of BAA, for all of her help and assistance.

1 In conversation with the author (October 1997). All other quotations from the artist are from the same conversation.
2 B Mandelbrot, *The Fractal Geometry of Nature* (San Francisco 1983).
3 I Percival, 'Chaos: A Science for the Real World', *The New Scientist Guide to Chaos*, N Hall (ed), (London 1992).
4 B O'Doherty, *Inside the White Cube* (San Francisco 1986), p. 15.

Evocative and Symbolic Memorials and Trophies by Percy Oswald Reeves

Nicola Gordon Bowe

examines some Irish Arts & Crafts metalwork

Percy Oswald Reeves does not warrant the public oblivion which shrouds his memory and his work. He was singly responsible for designing and making an impressive amount of highly-original and beautifully-crafted metalwork for a wide variety of purposes and for many distinguished clients in Ireland and abroad between 1903 and 1937. He also played a key role in reinstating the contemporary relevance of an ancient Irish artistic legacy in this medium while instilling a receptive generation of craftsmen and women in Ireland with the tenets of the English Arts and Crafts ideology in which he himself was trained.[1] During the first twelve years or so of this century, he set up metalwork and enamelling workshops at the Dublin Metropolitan School of Art, collaborated closely with the Dublin Goldsmiths' Corporation and the progressive Architectural Association of Ireland, established the Guild of Irish Art Workers, and subtly restructured the Arts and Crafts Society of Ireland as an active design force. He responded practically and articulately to a growing national belief at the time that 'if art as a whole is ever to come into everyday touch with the community, it will inevitably be by way of craftsmanship, not painting.'[2] He recognised the vital need for inspired native development maintaining that the art and design of any country should express individual character while manifesting 'the strongest tendency in the current of feeling of the race.' Thus a lively, progressive Irish style should be derived 'from the impetus and nature of modern life and thought'[3] rather than from a 'slavish reversion to ancient forms, however beautiful.'[4]

1. P Oswald Reeves (1870–1967): Cover design for the first volume of the weekly journal, *The Irish Architect and Craftsman* (January 28-July 22 1911), printed in green on buff, 25.5 x 17.8 cm, signed 'POR' monogram (National Library of Ireland).

In the summer of 1911, Reeves contributed a series of articles accompanied by strongly graphic cover designs and half-title line drawings to the weekly journal, *The Irish Architect and Craftsman,* in the name of The Arts and Crafts Society of Ireland and Guild of Irish Art-Workers (Fig 1).[5] Here he began to articulate aspects of the philosophy he had been developing through his teaching at the Dublin Art School:

To acquire the mastery of tools needed for the practice of an applied art is to develop a power of the highest order. It must, therefore, call for an endeavour of the most earnest kind: patience unlimited, and self-criticism most exacting... The artist never emulates the parrot. He works with a clear conviction, original and creative, arrived at by himself – a certain inward harmony. He selects by careful study and experiment, a precise means of revealing this conviction in every stroke of the hand ...[so that] his work becomes the embodiment of a certain spirit of deep harmony and beauty, of a high and vital truth.[6]

He firmly believed that art should not be the 'the portrayal of *things*' or a static, merely photographic, representative form of expression but rather the dynamic outward expression of 'the inward universe'. His belief that art should 'represent mental purpose, animation, ecstasy...the nature of force...and the whole a complex of contending purposes'[7] was to become increasingly apparent during the course of his long working life. For him, courage, 'a modern ideal of human dignity'[8] and the individual effort involved in interdependent artistry and workmanship, placed within a consciously-created, productive environment should underpin the national style to which he aspired in his adopted country.

While Reeves's life and work have received some scholarly attention within the last few years,[9] the present article focuses on a small selection of the many memorials and trophies which he made after 1915 when his reputation was firmly established both nationally and internationally. All of the pieces featured are accessible to the public, but are little heeded today. They exemplify Reeves's lifelong commitment to the fundamental principles of vigorous, fitting design realised through skilled craftsmanship.

Reeves's training in Birmingham and in London led him to set strong store by the distinctive lettering he incorporated into his

(Opposite and above) **2.** P Oswald REEVES: (overall design and enamelled panel), James Hicks (cabinet), George Atkinson (illuminated lettering), James Wallace and John Hunter (metalwork), *War Memorial*, ebonised cabinet 74.9 x 45.7 cm with two doors, each 45.7 x 15.9 cm, two glazed gilt copper-framed inscribed panels, each 42.5 x 11.4 cm, central *basse-taille* enamelled panel 38.4 x 26.7 cm, *repoussé* copper inscription panel 9.5 x 34.9 cm. (All Saints' Church, Grangegorman, Dublin).

designs.[10] This is particularly notable in the War Memorial he designed in 1920 as a small, wall-mounted triptych for All Saints Church, Grangegorman, Dublin (Fig 2). In an ideal Arts and Crafts collaborative venture, Reeves's richly-coloured, enamelled *Allegory of Peace* is enclosed by James Hicks's ebonised cabinet casing, with metal and silverwork made by Reeves's two assistants, J F Hunter and James Wallace, and the names of those commemorated in the wing panels are inscribed in a black and gold uncial font by George Atkinson.[11]

Lengthy inscriptions also play a major role in the stall plates he designed and executed in 1921 for two of the last Knights of the Order of St Patrick, the Earl of Bessborough (Fig 3) and Viscount French (Fig 4), created in 1915 and 1917 respectively. With their strong, contemporary design and fine craftsmanship, Bessborough's red and white *champlevé* enamel shield and spirited rampant lions on *repoussé* copper and French's boldly-delineated rifle-bearing servicemen in khaki and cobalt enamel *champlevé* on copper still hang in St Patrick's Hall in Dublin Castle where they are outstanding among their neighbouring thirty-two conventional plates.[12] Incorporating the Order's chain device, they were mounted there beneath the respective banner, crest, helmet and sword of each Knight.

Lettering is the main component of a modest, but elegantly-composed, stone tablet in the small church of St John, Kill, county Kildare, recorded by Reeves as being designed in 1920.[13] The memorial stone records another Knight of St Patrick, Dermot Robert Wyndham Bourke, 7th Earl of Mayo (1851-1927), founder and, for many years, President of the Arts and Crafts Society of Ireland. Reeves unqualifiedly acknowledged Mayo's 'continuous untiring personal effort' in sustaining and guiding 'the work of the Society, taking the large share of the most arduous and difficult tasks, and securing that the cause should not suffer avoidably through lack of funds.'[14] The Earl's wife, Geraldine, daughter of a son of the 4th Earl of Bessborough, also played a crucial role in the Irish Arts and Crafts Movement in her enlightened revival of the Royal School of Irish Needlework, in the establishment of the Kildare Carpet Industry, and in the furnishing of their house, Palmerstown, county Kildare.[15]

A monumentally-treated figurative wall panel (c.1932) in the church of St Bride, Mount Nugent, county Cavan (Fig 8), poignantly commemorates Oliver St George Percy Nugent of nearby Farren Connell. It is incised, low-relief, and in coloured plaster. An inscription from the *Book of Psalms* refers to a contaminated cup which led to Nugent's death in 1929, aged only thirty; it also purportedly reflects his interest in the Holy Grail and, as the cup of suffering, the bereavement of his mother. The focus of the composition is an idealised figure, dramatically gesturing in grim determination. Although recalling Mantegna's tunic-clad soldiers, it was conceived as 'a romanticized traveller from an unspecified past.'[16] Symbolic use is made of leaves, of the robin which comforted his last weeks in a New Forest sanatorium, of the snipe he loved on the wild Irish bogs, and of a seagull, emblematic of his Middle and Far Eastern

THEIR GLORY SHALL NOT BE BLOTTED OUT
INRI
BUT THEIR NAME LIVETH FOR EVERMORE

Dublin Horse Show
Perpetual Challenge Trophy.
Presented by
The Tattoo Committee, Saorstat Army.
For award to the Exhibitor
whose horses obtain the greatest number
and value of prizes in the Hunter Classes.
1963 N. Galway-Greer
1964 N. Galway-Greer
1965 N. Galway-Greer
1966 N. Galway Greer
1967
1969 N. Galway Greer
1970 N. Galway-Greer

3. P Oswald Reeves: *Stall Plate for The Most Noble and Puissant Lord Edward, Earl of Bessborough*, invested Knight of St Patrick May 1915. Made March 1921. *Champlevé* enamels, *repoussé* copper and oxidized copper, mounted on wood, 36.9 x 26.6 cm (St Patrick's Hall, Dublin Castle). Adapted from the design of Sir Nevile Wilkinson.

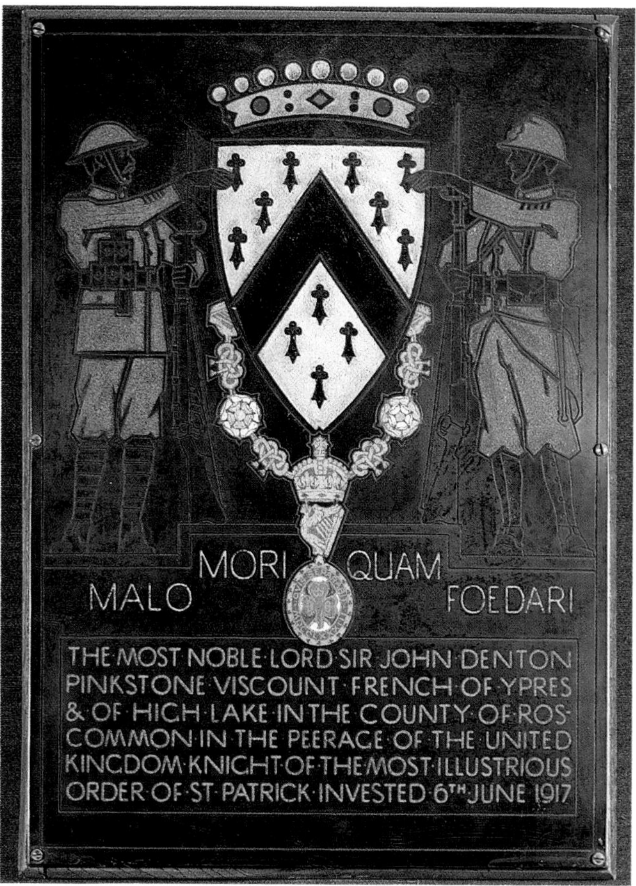

4. P Oswald Reeves: *Stall Plate for The Most Noble Lord Sir John Denton Pinkstone, Viscount French of Ypres*, invested Knight of St Patrick June 1917. Made April 1921. *Champlevé* enamels on oxidized copper, mounted on wood, 35.6 x 25.5 cm. (St Patrick's Hall, Dublin Castle). Adapted from the design of Sir Nevile Wilkinson.

Army travels. Like the ensuing four pieces, it is clearly signed with Reeves's monogram.

Three years later, leaves recur as a motif in a beautiful table-piece, commissioned in 1934 by the Saorstát Army Tattoo Committee for presentation to the Royal Dublin Society as a Perpetual Challenge Trophy to the highest-scoring exhibitor at the Dublin Horse Show in the hunter classes (Fig 5). In metalwork relief, they appear to grow out of a silver mat which bears the gracefully-kneeling, bowed figure of a damsel. Inlaid in silver on the rounded rectangular hood of a shining copper trophy, she intently plays a golden harp with silver strings to a listening horse engraved behind her. Stylised symbols, representing the original aims of the RDS to improve 'Husbandry, Manufactures, and other Useful Arts and Sciences', appear on the two narrow side panels of the trophy.

In that same year, 1934, he made the Mullingar Town Trophy which was commissioned by local traders for presentation to county Westmeath Gaelic Athletic Association for inter-county hurling and football tournaments (Fig 6). It also commemorated the Golden Jubilee of the foundation of the national GAA. Conceived as a symbolic 'tower of strength', it is a more sober, rectangular, figural trophy in copper and is geometrically streamlined, four-sided, and sparingly enamelled in warm scarlet, turquoise, yellow, black, and white. Amongst its restrained emblematic devices are two outstanding panels: one of engaged hurling sticks and ball, the other of a hooded, athletic and

(Opposite) **5.** P Oswald Reeves: *Perpetual Challenge Trophy*, presented by the Saorstát Eireann Military Tattoo Committee to the Royal Dublin Society for award to the exhibitor whose horses obtain the greatest number and value of prizes in the hunter classes 1935. Copper inlaid with silver and gold, signed 'POR' monogram, 38.8 x 21 x 5.1 cm deep, 10.2 cm at base (Royal Dublin Society).

(Overleaf left with detail) **6.** P Oswald Reeves: *Mullingar Town Trophy*, presented to the Westmeath Gaelic Athletic Association to commemorate the GAA's Golden Jubilee year, 1934. Oxidised copper, chiselled and chased with gold, silver and enamelled enrichments, 59.7 x 11.4 cm on 4.4 cm black marble plinth (Westmeath Gaelic Athletic Association).

(Overleaf right) **7.** P Oswald Reeves: *President's Trophy for the Irish Red Cross Society*, presented annually to senior county teams competing in First Aid. 1943. Copper with silver, gold and brass enrichments, enamelled cross on lid of upper hexagonal vessel, containing a wooden box, signed 'POR' on central vertical panel in copper relief, 10.2 x 3.8 cm, four horizontal framed and riveted illustrative copper panels, each 10.2 x 2.9 cm; total height 68.6 x 34.3 cm (Irish Red Cross Society).

1977
Co. na Gaillime
1979
Co. Corcaige
1980
Cill Mhantáin
1981
Co. Cill Mhantáin
1984
Co. Áta Cliat (1)
1985
Co. Áta Cliat (1)
1986
Co. Corcaige
1987
Co. Corcaige

naked male, heroically poised with a handball[17] above two charging horses' heads which are set with gold and silver bridles.

Heroic figures recur in two low-relief panels set into Reeves's Irish Red Cross Trophy of 1943 (Fig 7). Made for annual presentation by the President of Ireland to county teams competing in first aid skills, they depict wounded warriors being tended at the Battle of Clontarf by women bearing bandages and healing leaves. The trophy is in the unusual form of an octagonal silver casket on a hexagonal column shaft above a wooden podium bearing winners' names. The casket is set with copper low-relief panels: those referred to above and two others where a dove tends a broken-winged bird in the nest and scrolled bandages enclose sheaves of bound leaves. Reeves's working design shows that only the vertically-proportioned panel, depicting a traveller bathing his wounds in a wooded stream, is intended to face the viewer. The octagonal lid is emblazoned with a scarlet-enamelled cross and opens to reveal a simple pearwood box inside. Reminiscent of a miniature baptismal font in polished copper, the trophy is decorated with neo-Byzantine chevrons on its shaft and set with small symbolic lozenges in silver, brass and gold. Douglas Hyde's signature is engraved on the base of the trophy.

8. P Oswald REEVES: *Memorial Wall Tablet to Oliver St George Percy Nugent* (1899-1929), c. 1932, coloured plaster, carved and incised, signed 'POR' monogram, 119.4 x 62.2 cm (St Bride's Church of Ireland, Mount Nugent, Co Cavan).

Besides many other trophies and memorials, Oswald Reeves made free-standing figurative plaques, boxes, crosses, badges, pendants, shop signs, candlesticks, book covers, jewellery, costume and stamp designs, tabernacle doors, bookplates, posters, graphics. His unstinting technical skill was rare and his restrained but innovative designs, which are both evocative and symbolic, deserve reappraisal.

NICOLA GORDON BOWE'S *latest publication (with Elizabeth Cumming) is* The Arts and Crafts Movements in Dublin and Edinburgh 1885-1925 *(1997). She is a Lecturer in Art and Design History, National College of Art and Design, Dublin.*

ACKNOWLEDGMENTS: *Henry McDowell, Mary Kelleher, Thomas R Wallace, Seámus Whelan, Myles and Susan Stoney, Mrs Alison Hirschberger, the late Mrs Doreen Allen Reeves, Dr Raymond Refaussé, Archdeacon Raymond G F Jenkins, Commandant Victor Laing, The Irish Red Cross Society, James Hickie, Patricia Woods, The Rev Michael Wooderson, Peter Lamb, Tommy Sheeran, Elaine Sisson and Patrick Bowe.*

1 Reeves was raised and educated in Birmingham, one of the most important centres of the English Arts and Crafts Movement and of British metalsmithing. He attended and taught at the Birmingham School of Art, which pioneered the development of Arts and Crafts theory into educational practice, before he proceeded to Southport and then London, where he attended the Royal College of Art. In 1900, he entered the Kensington studio of Alexander Fisher, the leading figure in the Arts and Crafts revival of figurative enamels, before taking up his appointment to the recently restructured Metropolitan School of Art in Dublin in 1903.

2 Editorial, *The Irish Architect and Craftsman: A Journal of Architecture, Allied Arts and Crafts, and The Official Organ of the Arts and Crafts Society of Ireland* (22 July 1911). The editorial is unsigned, but was probably written by the editor, H T O' Rourke.

3 P O Reeves, *Foreword to the Catalogue of the 7th Exhibition of the Arts and Crafts Society of Ireland* (1925), p. 19.

4 P O Reeves, 'Irish Arts and Crafts', *The Studio*, vol 72 (15 Oct 1917), p. 17.

5 Reeves was Honorary Secretary of the Society from 1906 until his retirement from the Dublin School of Art in 1937, aged 67, and was instrumental in the organisation of its periodical exhibitions and exemplary catalogues, in whose design and content he played a key role from 1910. He was a founder member of the Guild of Irish Art-Workers in 1909.

6 Unsigned article, 'The Mastery of Tools', *The Irish Architect and Craftsman* (12 Aug 1911), p. 400.

7 'Art and Nature', *The Irish Architect and Craftsman* (26 Aug 1911), p. 428 and 'Art and the Inward World', *The Irish Architect and Craftsman* (9 Sept 1911), p. 456.

8 Reeves (as note 2), pp. 18-20.

9 See N G Bowe, *The Dublin Arts and Crafts Movement 1885-1930* (Edinburgh 1985), exhibition catalogue entries under Reeves and his school; P Larmour, *The Arts and Crafts Movement in Ireland* (Belfast 1992), pp. 172-182; N Gordon Bowe, 'Percy Oswald Reeves (1870-1967), Metalworker and Enamellist, Forgotten Master of the Irish Arts and Crafts Movement', *Journal no 18* of The Decorative Arts Society, 1850 to the present (Brighton 1994), pp. 61-8; N Gordon Bowe and E S Cumming, *The Arts and Crafts Movements in Dublin and Edinburgh 1885-1925* (Dublin 1997), pp. 173-178; P Larmour, 'The works of Oswald Reeves (1870-1967), Artist and Craftsman: An Interim Catalogue', *Irish Architectural and Decorative Studies, The Journal of the Irish Georgian Society*, vol. 1, 1998, pp. 34-59.

10 He was strongly influenced by the revived focus on handwriting and calligraphy set in motion by the master Arts and Crafts calligrapher, Edward Johnston (1872-1946), author of *Writing and Illuminating and Lettering*, c. 1906.

11 Gordon Bowe and Cumming (as note 9), cat. no 163.

12 The stall-plates of those Knights created before the disestablishment of the Church of Ireland are in the Chancel of St Patrick's Cathedral, their original home. After his appointment as Registrar of the Order in 1908, Sir N Wilkinson, Ulster King-at-Arms, a trained artist, and creator of Titania's Palace (1907-22), designed four plates for St Patrick's Hall, two of which he signed – although these were made by trade engravers. In 1921, Wilkinson invited Reeves to 'adapt' two subsequent, if mediocre, designs and execute these. See P Galloway, *The Most Illustrious Order of St Patrick* (Chichester 1983).

13 His design for the inscription is recorded in his *Workbook* (private collection) for 1920, although it was not executed until after Mayo's death on 31 Dec 1927.

14 Reeves (as note 4), p. 16.

15 Located just outside Naas, it was burned in the Civil War. See Gordon Bowe and Cumming (as note 9), pp. 183-4, 206.

16 Letter from St George Nugent's sister, Mrs A Hirschberg (20 Nov 1997). Lady Nugent was probably referred to Reeves by her late husband's fellow Commanding Officer in the War, Major-General Sir W B Hickie of Slevyre, Co Tipperary, for whom Reeves had made various memorials since 1920.

17 See W F Mandle, *The Gaelic Athletic Association and Irish Nationalist Politics 1884-1924* (Dublin 1987), p. 17 and p. 98; and M de Búrca, *The GAA: A History* (Dublin 1980).

A Freedom Box for 'a Hot Whiffling Puppy' Tighe Family Silver from Kilkenny

Thomas Sinsteden

publishes a rare Irish treasure in the Museum of Fine Arts, Boston

Ordered that Richard Tighe Esq. be presented with his Freedom of this City in a Gold Box of the Value of twenty Guineas for his Singular Service in the Chair of the Committee of the House of Commons upon the Bill for regulating this Corporation & that Robert Hacket do take care to Get the same Done.

So it was entered on 2 August 1718 on page sixty-three of the Kilkenny Corporation Minute Book No. 5.[1] In Kilkenny by the early years of the 18th century as in other cites in Ireland such as Cork, Waterford, Limerick, and Dublin there was an established tradition of awarding the Freedom of the City.[2] A certificate (called, in the case of Kilkenny, a cocket) would be presented to the person so honoured inside a small gold or silver box. The Freedom of the City conferred certain privileges such as the partial or complete exemption from taxes or tolls.[3] Gold boxes were given to persons of distinction such as the Lord Lieutenant, the Lord Chancellor, an archbishop or to someone who had performed a significant service for the community. The first Dublin Freedom Box was given by Dublin Corporation on 29 September 1674 to Edward, Lord Viscount Conway and Killulta and, in the following decade, Waterford Corporation awarded a gold box (on 4 September 1686) to Henry Hyde, 1st Earl of Clarendon. It was made by William Smith, goldsmith and council member of the Waterford Corporation.[4] The earliest Irish gold box that has survived was made by Thomas Bolton in June 1707 and is now in the National Museum of Ireland at Collins Barracks.[5] It was awarded on 24 June 1707 to Richard Freeman, Lord High

1. Tighe Freedom Box. 1718. 22 carat gold, 7.7 cm diam, 1.8 cm high and 148 grams. (Museum of Fine Arts, Boston). The top of the box is engraved with the arms of Kilkenny and struck with an unidentified maker's mark *HA* with no surround (incuse). The magnificently-executed engraving of the arms is in the style of the Kilkenny seal with the surround banner *Insignia Armorium Civitatis Kilkenniesis*. The engraving would have been contracted out to an engraver after the box was made. The maker of the box is probably not the same as the engraver.

Chancellor. The freedom box presented to Richard Tighe was the fourth gold box presented by Kilkenny Corporation.[6]

Richard Tighe (1678-1736), a man of short stature, was known as 'Little Dick Tighe'. His grandfather was twice mayor of Dublin in the 1650s and he had a distinguished career, being elected MP for Balturbet in 1703, for Newtown in 1715, for Augher in 1727, and was then made Irish Privy Councillor under George I, gaining the title of 'The Right Honorable'. He married Barbara Bor (co-heiress) of Drinagh, county Wexford in 1708. Two years later, while in London, Dean Swift overheard an altercation between the newlyweds in the neighbouring house. In his *Journal to Stella* he described Richard Tighe as 'a hot whiffling puppy, very apt to resent.'[7]

This superb beautifully engraved, 22 carat gold, Tighe freedom box is now in the collection of the Museum of Fine Arts, Boston. Its engraving is of the most extraordinary quality with the arms of Tighe with Bor in an escutcheon of pretence on the base, those of Kilkenny on the lid, and the dedication, inscribed verbatim from the corporation minute book, on the inside of the lid. The shallow box measures 7.7 cm in diameter, 1.8 cm in height, and weighs 4.8 oz. It is constructed of flat circular sheets of gold for the lid and base with an applied moulding on the base and on the rim of the lid. The maker's mark of capital letters *HA* incuse (i.e. without surround) is struck on the side of the base. There are no hallmarks and as yet no attribution to a specific maker has been made. Incuse marks on gold or silver in Dublin of this period are rare. They were used by Abraham Voisin, Arthur Weldon, John Garrett, James Walker, and Thomas Wheeler, a Dublin gold watchcase-maker.[8] In London, incuse marks were used by watchcase-makers[9] but not by goldsmiths in general.

Robert Hackett, the person assigned to 'get the same done', was the Kilkenny Corporation Clerk who, as legal advisor, was an important official and, as he would have travelled to Dublin and even to England in this capacity, he would have had ample opportunity to order a box to be made and engraved in either place. In spite of the similarity between the maker's initials and Robert Hackett's name, it is unlikely that he himself was the maker as there is no evidence that he was a goldsmith. The style of the box is very similar to an unmarked silver box presented to Sir John Stanley on 15 October 1714 by Dublin Corporation[10] and this may indicate that the Tighe Box is also of Dublin origin. It is much finer in quality than the silver box made by Jonathan Buck which was awarded to Richard Tighe by the city of Limerick in 1726.[11]

In its quality, the engraving on the box compares to that of Blaise Gentot, the master of George Vertue,[12] and it clearly shows the hand of a master engraver who was possibly brought to Ireland by an enlightened Irish patron. There is little documentation about engravers working on precious metals in Dublin and England at this time and only rarely is such engraving signed by the engraver.[13] It was looked down upon for an engraver to sign his work, presumably because all he was doing was copying the painter's picture. To quote George Vertue: *Joseph Simpson was very low in his profession, cutting arms on pewter plates, till having studied in the academy, he was employed by Tillemans on a plate of Newmarket, to which he was permitted to put his name, and which, though it did not please the painter, served to make Simpson known.*[14] The only Dublin piece of silver of this period with a firm attribution to an engraver is the Racing Punch Bowl of 1751 by William Williamson.[15] It was won by *Black & All Black* at the Curragh on 5 September 1751 for Sir Ralph Gore. The engraving of the race on the bowl appeared in reverse in the Noble and Keenan map of Kildare in 1752 and was signed by

2. Tighe Freedom Box: *The Base.* The base of the box is engraved with the arms of the Tighe family with Bor in an escutcheon of pretence. The inscription reads: 'For the Rt. Hon. Richard Tighe who married Barbara Bor and co-heiress of Christian Bor, Esq. of Drinagh, Co Wexford.' These magnificently-engraved arms of the finest quality are unsigned, as are most other fine engravings on precious metal. The engraver remains unidentified.

Daniel Pomarede of Dublin. Engravers working in Dublin, who were probably brothers of the Painters', Stainers' and Stationers' Company of Dublin, the Guild of St Luke, were mostly employed as copperplate engravers for the printing trade[16] although some may also have been seal cutters, precious metal engravers, watch case and clock engravers, clock face and back plate engravers as well as heraldic artists. As most pieces of silver of this period have at least the family arms or crest engraved on them, engravers would have been employed in that way as well. In the early 1700s about 50,000 ounces of silver were produced annually in Dublin. The demand to engrave that quantity of silver would have sustained several engravers and encouraged a high standard of engraving. A few names of engravers associated with the Goldsmith Hall have come to light. Mr Phillip Simms was admitted to the Goldsmiths' Guild on 2 February 1735 and sworn a free brother on 2 August 1735 for having engraved a copper plate for the Summons Card of the Goldsmiths' Hall;[17] on 1 November 1715 Mr William Owen (Oven) was paid £2-15-6 by the Goldsmiths' Hall for engraving a copper plate for the apprenticeship indenture;[18] a Mr Hartwell (probably Thomas Hartwell) was paid 6s-6d on 25 November 1715 for engraving a cup awarded to Sheriff David King, goldsmith, and a salver given to the Lord Mayor, Thomas Bolton, goldsmith;[19] Thomas Brown, engraver, also a free brother of the Goldsmiths, was a seal and punch cutter responsible for cutting the date letters and harp crowned hallmarks for the Goldsmiths' Hall.

Awarding freedom boxes was a particularly Irish phenomenon. The majority of freedom boxes are Irish. It is thus likely that the Tighe Gold Box was made and engraved in Dublin. Mr Richard Tighe may have been 'a hot whiffling puppy, apt to resent' but it is doubtful that he resented this award. The gold box is not only one of the finest freedom boxes extant but it also represents one of the finest examples of precious metal engraving. It is hoped that recognition of this magnificent piece will encourage further research into the traditions of engraving and heraldry in Ireland.

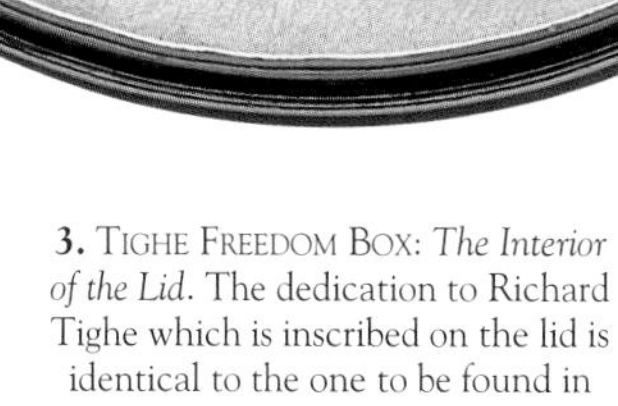

3. TIGHE FREEDOM BOX: *The Interior of the Lid.* The dedication to Richard Tighe which is inscribed on the lid is identical to the one to be found in Kilkenny Corporation's minute book.

THOMAS SINSTEDEN *is a graduate of Trinity College, Dublin and a silver collector with a particular interest in the Irish Goldsmiths.*

ACKNOWLEDGMENTS : *I am indebted to the Museum of Fine Arts, Boston for permission to view and publish photographs of the box and in particular to Ellenor Alcorn, Assistant Curator, European Decorative Arts, for her enlightened support and many hours of discussion. I would like to thank the Goldsmiths' Company of Dublin, M. Ronald Le Bas and Susanne Le Bas for allowing me to examine the company records in detail. I acknowledge my debt to Ida Delamer, Christopher Hartop and Arthur Grimwade, from whose publications I have taken great guidance. I thank Harry Williams-Bulkeley and Mr John Lumley of Christies for their help and Mr Tony Sweeney for sharing his vast knowledge of the Irish Print Trade and his love of Irish Silver.*

1 Kilkenny City Minute Books. Book no 5, p. 63.
2 I Delamer, 'Irish Freedom Boxes', *Proceedings of the Silver Society*, vol 4/2 (1983), pp. 18-23; I Pickford, 'Freedom Boxes', *The Antique Dealer & Collector's Guide* (Oct 1978), pp. 75-80.
3 J Dollard, *Calendar of Ancient Records of Dublin* (Dublin 1895), vol 5, p. 54.
4 S Pender (ed), *Council Books of the Corporation of Waterford*. IMC Stationary Office (1964), p. 267.
5 J Teehan, The Company of Goldsmiths of Dublin, 350th Anniversary Exhibition, National Museum of Ireland (1987), p. 33.
6 E J Law, 'The Presentation Plate of the Corporation of the City of Kilkenny 1684 - 1834', *Old Kilkenny Review* (1994), no 46 (1994) p. 57.
7 J Swift, *A Journal to Stella*, H Williams (ed), (Oxford 1948), p. 343
8 Sir C Jackson, *Goldsmiths and their Marks*, I Pickford (ed), 3rd ed (London 1989).
9 P Priestly, 'Early Watchcase Makers and their Marks 1671-1720', *The Silver Society Journal*, vol 10 (1998).
10 I Cameron, *Das Grosse Antiquitaten Lexicon* (Freiburg 1983), p. 129.
11 'Irish Silver', ROSC Exhibition (1971), no 243.
12 A Grimwade, 'The Master of George Vertue', *Apollo* (Feb 1988), pp. 83-9.
13 C Oman, *English Engraved Silver 1150-1900* (London 1978).
14 H Walpole, *A Catalogue of Engravers of England* (London 1782), p. 218.
15 M Holland, 'Racing Trophies', *Silver* (July/Aug 1978), p. 30.
16 R Munter, *A Dictionary of The Print Trade In Ireland 1550- 1775* (New York 1988).
17 Goldsmiths' Hall Dublin Record; Enrolment Book of Freemen and Officers.
18 Goldsmiths Hall Dublin Records; Account Book; Hamilton Accounts.
19 J Webb, 'The Guilds of Dublin', *The Sign of the Three Candles* (Dublin 1929). p. 289.

Iames Duke of Ormond

The Ormonde Picture Collection

Jane Fenlon
sifts through some Irish inventories of the 17th century

When Thomas Dinely visited Ireland in the later years of the 17th century, he noted in his diary 'The Castle of Kilkenny ... famous for spacious Roomes, Galleries, Halls, adorn'd with paintings of great Masters.'[1] The painting collection of the 1st Duke and Duchess of Ormonde at Kilkenny was certainly the largest, and probably the finest, formed by Irish patrons during the 17th century. Overall, the collection numbered some five hundred paintings housed in various residences in both Ireland and England. The collection was formed mainly during the period 1660-84 and consisted of a series of grand portraits, some large historical and religious pictures, and great quantities of decorative landscapes, still-lifes, and flower pieces. More paintings were added by the 2nd Duke at a later date, but he does not seem to have been a collector in any serious way. The collection was broken up in the early-18th century, following the Duke's support for the Jacobite cause in 1715 and the consequent bill of attainder for treason. The Forfeited Estates Commissioners seized Ormonde properties, the paintings were sold off in London, and a sale was also advertised at Kilkenny Castle in 1718.[2] What remained of the collection thereafter has proved difficult to trace as no family inventories or lists of paintings have been found but an account of Kilkenny Castle written towards the middle of the 18th century[3] describes only sixty-three paintings as hanging there, not including those in the Duchess's closet. The Kilcash branch of the Butler family had inherited the Ormonde estates and titles and before 1820 the picture collection had been augmented by a group of portraits from that house. During the 19th century, efforts were made, particularly by John Butler, 2nd Marquess of Ormonde, to rebuild the collection. By 1875, the number of pictures at the castle had risen to two hundred and seventy-six with one hundred and eighty-four of these hanging in the new Long Gallery. Some of these had come through a family bequest that included many 17th-century works[4] but, from the late-18th century, many works were again dispersed, particularly among family members. Recently the Office of Public Works (Heritage Section) secured what remained of the collection on behalf of the Irish State by purchasing most of the paintings and tapestries at Kilkenny Castle from the Ormonde Estates. Many of the paintings acquired and all of the tapestries date from the 17th century. These works are now on display there.[5]

Prior to the time of the 1st Duke, earlier generations of the Ormonde family had been important patrons of the arts. For instance, the Duchess's grandfather, Thomas Butler, 10th Earl of Ormond (c.1532-1614), is known to have had forty-four paintings hanging in the splendid long gallery of his house at Carrick-on-Suir.[6] Thomas's father, James Butler, 9th Earl was drawn by Hans Holbein the Younger, the outstanding artist at the court of Henry VIII. A century later, another James Butler, then Marquis and later Duke of Ormonde, sat for his portrait to the Flemish artist, Peter van der Faes (known as Peter Lely), in 1647, soon after that artist came to England. This sitting marked the beginning of a long association between Lely, who became Principal Painter at the court of Charles II, and the Ormonde family. It was Lely who painted the finest surviving portrait of the Duke in 1662. The splendid image of Ormonde in garter robes, holding the long white wand of office, mirrors the rise in the fortunes of the Ormonde family, following the restoration in 1660 of Charles II to the throne of England.

1. Unknown artist, after Michael DAHL (1659-1743): *James Butler, 2nd Duke of Ormonde* (1666-1745). Oil on canvas, 125 x 102 cm. (Kilkenny Castle). This portrait by an unknown artist would appear to have been executed in the 1690s. The pose is similar to that used by both Sir Godfrey Kneller and Michael Dahl. An original portrait by Dahl that is very similar is in the Devonshire collection at Hardwick Hall.

(Opposite) **2.** Sir Peter LELY (1618-80): *James Butler, 1st Duke of Ormonde* (1610- 88). *c.*1662-3. Oil on canvas, 224 x 131 cm. This is the finest extant portrait of the duke. The pose is striking and seems to be unique to Ormonde. He is depicted in Garter Robes, holding the wand of office of Lord Steward of the Royal Household in his right hand.

3. Studio of Willem WISSING (1656-87): *Anne Hyde, Countess of Ossory* (1669-85), 1st wife of James, 2nd Duke of Ormonde. Oil on canvas, 122 x 89 cm. (Kilkenny Castle). The pose and costume used in this portrait are almost identical to those used in the portrait of *The Countess of Derby* (Fig 4). The only difference is a variation in the position of the left arm and the inclusion of a dog.

4. Willem WISSING (1656-87): *Elizabeth Butler, Countess of Derby* (d. 1717). Oil on canvas, 127 x 101 cm. (Kilkenny Castle). The painting in this portrait is of a higher quality than that of the studio piece (Fig 3). The sitter was identified from a contemporary engraving by R Williams.

Information about the Ormonde picture collection is to be found in inventories, account books, and family correspondence. Prior to the Restoration, there is just one brief reference which informs us about a number of paintings. It occurs in an inventory of goods taken when the royalist Ormondes found themselves in very difficult circumstances, having fled with their young family from war-torn Ireland, via London, to exile in France. The reference to 'forty fine paintings and their frames', probably denotes pictures brought from Ireland in their baggage.[7] When Lady Ormonde returned some years later to her house at Dunmore, county Kilkenny, it is likely that most of the items listed on the inventory were installed there.

The 1st Duke of Ormonde made a triumphant return to Ireland in 1662. He had been elevated to a dukedom and a grateful King rewarded him with many honours. Following the dramatic changes in their circumstances, the Ormondes, particularly the Duchess, set about refurbishing and rebuilding their properties in Ireland and renting or acquiring new houses in England.[8] Vast quantities of rich new furnishings were poured into these houses, such as elaborate beds, carpets, cabinets, mirrors, hangings, porcelain, and hundreds of paintings. When it came to forming a picture collection, aristocrats, such as the Ormondes, acquired their paintings in various ways. The most direct method was by commission when they sat for portraits to fashionable artists. Sometimes works of art were acquired through marriages; otherwise agents were used to purchase paintings on their behalf. For instance, the marriage of Ormonde's second son, Richard, Earl of Arran to Lady Mary Stuart was the likely source for a pair of portraits of her parents, the Duke and Duchess of Richmond, painted by Sir Anthony van Dyck. In the enormous archive of Ormonde papers and documents, a comment by Thomas Butler, Earl of Ossory, Ormonde's eldest son, seems to be the only artistic evaluation made by a family member. He writes to the Duke: 'I have bought a painting from Mr Van Hill, *The History of King Solomon*, 50 guineas I gave him, they say it is touched by van Dyck.'[9] Another even more intriguing and tantalising piece of information, which may prove to be a key piece of evidence for the formation of the collection, is that the Duchess engaged a Dutchman, Abraham van Uylenborgh, as her painter.[10] It is likely that this man was expected also to act as her agent in acquiring suitable works of art to hang on the walls of the newly -refurbished houses, notably Kilkenny Castle and Dunmore House. The Uylenborghs were a well-known, well-connected family of painters and art dealers in Amsterdam. Rembrandt's first wife, Saskia, was a cousin. It is said that Abraham died shortly after his arrival in Dublin in 1668.

Information about this painter has been difficult to find – the only reference in the Ormonde papers is to a 'winding sheet' for his corpse[11] – but here again Sir Peter Lely provides a link. He was known to the Uylenborgh family and may have played some part in Abraham's appointment. In a document apparently drawn up when the Uylenborghs were endeavouring to recover money from the Duchess of Ormonde, Lely is described as 'attorney and procurator' to Abraham's brother and sisters.[12] The career of Abraham's brother, Gerrit, also provides some interesting evidence. He had worked in Lely's studio painting landscapes and later served as Purveyor and Keeper of the King's pictures for some years during the 1670s. The Royal post entailed choosing appropriate paintings and moving and arranging the King's pictures at Windsor Castle. There Uylenborgh was required to *take particular measure of a roome wherein His Ma[jes]ty intends to eate which is to be furnished with pictures; And therefore you are to design what pictures will be most proper and Ornamental there to furnish ye room round, as many as may with good Order & decency be place there.*[13] This may have been the intended role for Abraham as the Duchess's painter. No evidence has been found, as yet, that Abraham ever reached Kilkenny, but the picture-hanging arrangements described in inventories taken there point to a professional hand.[14] After a brief interval the Duchess hired another painter, Robert Trotter, again probably of Dutch origin, who was to work for her throughout the 1670s.[15] Trotter may have been employed to act in a similar capacity to Ulyenborgh; however, the Duchess's

5. Jan de [van] HERDT: Incorrectly called *The Pearl Stringers*. (Its correct title is possibly *A Jeweller and his Family, an Allegory of Romance*). Signed and dated 1673. Oil on canvas. 158 x 193 cm. (Kilkenny Castle). Only two other paintings by this artist, both in the Staatliche Kunsthalle, Karlsruhe, have been identified. The picture is one of the most important subject pictures to have survived in the Ormonde Collection.

description of him as 'having some knowledge in matters of building' which 'consequently may prove useful to the comptroller in assisting towards those repairs in both houses' suggests a broader role.[16]

Apart from numbers of paintings, information is somewhat limited as to the exact content of the Ormonde collection. Between 1675 and 1678, there were about three hundred and twenty paintings hanging in various Ormonde residences in Ireland. Of these, forty-seven were portraits, the rest were subject pictures, including landscapes and flower pieces which were mainly of Dutch or Flemish origin. When the next inventory was taken in 1684, the numbers had increased to three hundred and sixty-nine, of which eighty were portraits. In Ireland, the paintings were housed at Kilkenny Castle, Dunmore House, Clonmel, and at the Viceregal apartments at Dublin Castle and Chapelizod. Another one hundred and thirty or so paintings were in their houses in England.[17]

A survey of available inventories of the period demonstrates that no other Irish collection came near in terms of numbers.[18] When considering English collections, comparison may be made between the Ormonde's English properties and those of the Duke and Duchess of Lauderdale because of that couple's similar social and political standing. In matters of taste and setting, the collections were very similar. Subject pictures predominated in both collections. Landscapes set in panelling and used as over doors and over mantles were popular at both houses, as were copies after works in the Royal Collections.[19] At Ormond House in St James' Square, there were paintings by several artists whose work featured at Ham and some also at Whitehall Palace. Both collections seem to fit the description of 'Dutch style', a term used to describe collections consisting mainly of Dutch paintings of a kind that were briefly fashionable in the years immediately following the Restoration. In a collection of this nature, 'perspectives' of the type painted by Samuel van Hoogstraten and peasant interiors by van Heemskerck would have been prized.[20] These Dutch pieces were interspersed with paintings by English artists such as Francis Barlow and William Gouw Ferguson with a sprinkling of Italian works or copies after Italian masters.

Several artists' names appear in the Ormonde inventories; Dutch painters such as Jan Victors, Abraham Hondius, Hendrick Danckerts, Gerbrand van Eeckhout, Jan Wyck, Rembrandt van Rijn, and others are listed; the Flemings, Sir Peter Paul Rubens and Jacob Jordaens also feature. A handful of paintings are attributed to Italian artists and are described mainly as copies, as in *A Piece of Venetian Senators a Copy after Titian*, although a *Virgin Mary and our Saviour and Others by Old Palmer*, seems to have been accepted as a work by Palma Vecchio. Bassano and possibly Tintoretto are also mentioned.[21]

None of these attributions can be verified as the paintings have not been traced. There are, however, three subject paintings that may have survived from the Ducal Collection. The most important of these is a large canvas, now entitled *The Pearl Stringers* (Fig 5), which is signed J de Herdt. This is not a correct title as the only other works known by this artist have both been interpreted as genre pieces. In fact, the figure of the old woman portrayed in the Kilkenny work is identical to that in a painting entitled *Die Gelzäherlin* (The Miser).[22] A large, unattributed Dutch landscape with a dramatic waterfall (Fig 6) may be also from the original collection. The third picture is a Dutch subject painting, entitled *The Stirrup Cup*, now attributed to Dirck Maes (Fig 7). Because of the very brief descriptions given in the inventories, such as 'a Dutch Droll,' 'A Large Rockpiece', and 'A Perspective of a Church', it has not been possible to ascertain which subject pictures from the original Ducal Collection might have survived at Kilkenny Castle.

Many more portraits, as opposed to subject pictures or landscapes, from the Ducal Collection have survived. The tracing and attribution of these has been somewhat easier because sitters can be identified and in some cases related to inventory listings. Members of the family had been painted by most of the fashionable portrait painters of their generation. The 1st Duke was painted by Lely (Fig 2), Willem Wissing, Henri Gascars, John Michael Wright, the miniaturist Samuel Cooper, and others. His grandson, the 2nd Duke, favoured Sir Godfrey Kneller and Michael Dahl (Fig 1). Minor artists were also patronised: figures such as James and William Gandy, Edmund Ashfield, Bishop Simon Digby, and a painter called van Treat are all known to have painted portraits of the family. There were eleven portraits either attributed to or after Sir Anthony van Dyck in the collection and portraits of the Duke and Duchess of Richmond by that artist were valued at £150 in 1717, then the most expensive items in Kilkenny Castle. The fine Lely portrait of the first Duke (Fig 2), now returned to Kilkenny Castle, had been with the Cowper family at Panshanger for some time. It had passed to that family through a sister of the 2nd Duke.[23] The earliest portrait of the Duchess, still hanging at Kilkenny, is a double portrait with her son, Lord Ossory, attributed to David des Granges. There are also several portraits of daughters, a son, daughters-in-law, grand-daughters, and grandsons of the Ducal couple. A large, though damaged, version of Van Dyck's portrait of the *Five Eldest Children of Charles I* has survived at the castle which may be the painting that was originally hanging in Ormond House in London. Two important portraits, not family members, were sold in 1719 at the sale at Ormond House. Painted by John Michael Wright, these were the then famous portraits of *Sir Neil O'Neil as the Irish Chief* and *Lord Mungo*

(Opposite, top) **6.** CIRCLE OF NICHOLAS BERCHEM (1620-83): *Landscape with Waterfall*. Oil on canvas, 139 x 181 cm. (Kilkenny Castle). Of the three hundred or more paintings hanging in various Ormonde residences in the 1670s, the vast majority were subject pictures, landscapes, and flowerpieces of Dutch and Flemish origin.

(Opposite, bottom) **7.** Attributed to Dirck MAES (1656-1717): *The Stirrup Cup*. Oil on canvas, 90 x 122 cm. (Kilkenny Castle). The names of several well-known Dutch painters appear in the Ormonde inventories but, because of the very general manner in which the subject matter is described, it is not always easy to identify the pictures referred to with certainty.

9. John Michael WRIGHT (1617-94): *Elizabeth Poyntz, Lady Thurles* (1588-1673). Oil on canvas, 127 x 102 cm. Mother of the first Duke, this is another of the portraits painted by Wright during his visit here. This portrait was painted posthumously, the face being copied from an earlier portrait now in a private collection in Ireland.

Murray as the Highland Chief. Another version of the *Highland Chief*, described by John Dunton and listed in the inventories, had been hanging in the Gallery at Kilkenny Castle when he visited there.[24] Wright, who visited Ireland during the period 1679-83, also painted the Duke as well as posthumous portraits of his mother, Lady Thurles (Fig 6) and his sister, Lady Clancarty. A splendid portrait of the 1st Duke by Willem Wissing, now in the National Portrait Gallery in London, was sold out of the collection a few years ago. An unusual double portrait of the 1st Duke and his valet, Mezendier, painted by Henri Gascars, recorded in the inventories at Kilkenny Castle, is now in the collection of the National Gallery of Ireland.[25]

During the 2nd Duke's stewardship of the collection, few paintings of note were added. Several sea-pieces and battle scenes painted by members of the Dutch Van de Velde family were bought for him between 1686 and 1687 before he succeeded to the title.[26] Other additions included a dozen or so oval portraits of female family members and other ladies. During the later part of the 1690s payments were made on his behalf to the artists, Edward Polehampton, Thomas Highmore, Henry Cook, and Sir Godfrey Kneller.[27] By the end of the 17th century fashions had changed and prints had become more popular. Forty-nine prints were purchased in Dublin to hang in his drawing room at Dublin Castle. Several of these were engravings after originals by French and Italian artists, such as Charles Le Brun, Simon Vouet, and Annibale Carracci.[28] An inventory taken in 1716 at the Duke's villa at Richmond demonstrates that prints were predominant in the collection there.[29]

The setting for the picture collection in the Long Gallery at Kilkenny Castle was particularly splendid. The rascally bookseller and author, John Dunton, described that room when he visited there in 1696-97 as '[the] noble gallery, which for length, variety of gilded chairs, and the curious pictures that adorn it, has no equal in the three Kingdoms, and perhaps not in Europe.'[30] Although given to exaggeration, Dunton's description of the gallery was in fact closer to the truth than many of his other extravagant statements about Ireland. Some idea of the impressive setting for the picture collection in this room can be gained from an inventory taken there in 1684. At that time, the Long Gallery measured over one hundred feet in length and was about thirty feet wide.[31] All of the paintings in the room are described as having elaborate gilded frames. Artificial lighting was provided by three crystal chandeliers, suspended by chains and twelve carved and gilt sconces. Over three dozen chairs with gilded frames covered with crimson and yellow figured-velvet lined the length of the room. Mirrors with richly-carved gilt frames were hung over matching carved tables. The paintings were arranged to impress the viewer with a dozen or so of the most important full-length portraits in their elaborate frames ranged to either side of the great window on the approach from the great stairs. Sixty-five pictures were hanging there in 1684, almost half that number were portraits, the rest were subject pictures and landscapes. The selection of pictures coincides with that of contemporary English collections, where family portraits and portraits of friends and political associates predominate.[32] Apart from family, other portraits hanging there were *The Earl and Countess of Pembroke*,

Ormonde's friend and mentor, *Thomas Wentworth, Earl of Stafford after van Dyck*, plus several portraits of various Stuart monarchs and their consorts. The remaining pictures in the gallery consisted of religious paintings, 'History' paintings, 'Italian' pictures, and the inevitable landscapes and flower pieces.

Within thirty-five years the gallery was no longer as impressive as it had been. The room was dilapidated, furniture was worn, chandeliers were described as broken and the contents, including pictures, were put up for sale. Members of the Ducal family were never to live in Kilkenny again. When Chetwood visited the castle in 1748, he described a depleted gallery, commenting how 'this stately home was once hung with fine paintings.' Sadly most of the Dutch, Flemish and Italian paintings were gone forever, ending the brief existence of this once great picture collection.

JANE FENLON has published extensively on Irish art and architecture and is a consultant to Dúchas, the Heritage Service.

ACKNOWLEDGEMENTS: I am grateful to Anne Crookshank for reading and commenting on this article. I would also like to thank Edward McParland for giving me the references to the valuable Ormonde inventories in the Public Record Office at Kew, London; and Jane Cunningham and her staff at the Photographic Survey, Courtauld Institute of Art, University of London for their help with the illustrations.

1 E P Shirley and Rev J Graves, 'Extracts from the Journal of Thomas Dineley, Esq., giving some account of his visit to Ireland in the reign of Charles II', *Journal of the Kilkenny and S. E. of Ireland Archaeological Society*, New Series, vol 4 (1862-3), pp. 104-5.
2 A sale of 'the Goods and Furniture of the late Duke of Ormond in the Castle of Kilkenny and the house of Dunmore', was advertised in *The Dublin Gazette* (Aug-Sep 1718). Several paintings from Kilkenny Castle have found their way into private collections and to the National Gallery of Ireland. Some of these are known to have been passed down through family connections while others may have gone through salesrooms.
3 E Ledwich, *Antiquities of Ireland* (Dublin 1804). In an account of Kilkenny Castle and its contents, written after a visit there towards the middle of the 18th century, only 63 paintings are described.
4 This bequest came from Mrs Staples and the paintings were to be added to the collection at Kilkenny Castle in 1871.
5 See J Fenlon, *The Ormonde Picture Collection* (Dublin 1999).
6 *Calender of State Papers Ireland* (1647-60), p. 78. Although this reference is dated 1626 and the 10th Earl died in 1614, it is probable that these paintings had belonged to him rather than to Richard Preston, Earl of Desmond, his daughter's second husband. For further information on the Ormondes as patrons, see J Fenlon, 'Episodes of Magnificence', in T Barnard and J Fenlon (eds), *The Dukes of Ormonde* (Woodbridge 1999).
7 National Library of Ireland, MS 2552, ff.21-23v.
8 These included the purchase of Moor Park, Hertfordshire and later in 1682, Ormond House in St James's Square, London. The 2nd Duke leased a villa on the Thames, Richmond Park in 1704.
9 HMC Ormonde MSS, new series, 5, p. 94.
10 For Uylenberg or Uylenburgh see 'Drie Weinig Bekende Kunstenaars', *Oud-Holland* (1884), pp. 219-20. I am grateful to Mr Richard Everard for this reference.
11 NLI MS 2528.
12 As note 10.
13 Public Record Office, Kew, LC3/24. List of the Royal Household drawn up between 1681-84. I am grateful to Katharine Gibson for this reference. See also O Millar, *The Queen Pictures* (London 1984), pp. 81-2.
14 J Fenlon, 'Her Grace's Closet', Paintings in the Duchess of Ormond's Closet at Kilkenny Castle', *Bulletin of the Irish Georgian Society*, vol 36 (1994) , pp. 30-47.
15 NLI MS 2503, Letter (1 July 1671). He may be the 'Dutch painter' referred to by the Duchess in her letter of this date.
16 NLI MS 2503, Letter (10 Feb 1672).
17 NLI MSS 2527, 2554. It is not possible to be absolutely accurate as paintings were moved about between houses.
18 A survey of available inventories of the period has been carried out and these do not usually include pictures with house contents. It may be that lists of paintings were taken separately, as sometimes happened at Kilkenny Castle and Dunmore House and that these documents have been lost. The Percival and Southwell families had in their Co Cork houses, respectively, 15 paintings in Burton House and 11 at Kinsale.
19 For instance, portraits by Holbien of Erasmus and Johannes Frobenius (Froben), that were in the Royal Collection of Charles I; and panels after the Roman artist Polidoro de Caldara.
20 See C Brown, 'Patrons and Collectors of Dutch Painting in Britain during the reign of William and Mary', in D Howarth (ed), *Art and Patronage in the Caroline Courts* (Cambridge 1993), pp. 12-31. Perspectives are listed among the paintings at Kilkenny Castle.
21 A large painting of *King Ahasuerus and Queen Esther* by 'Teatress', may mean it was by or after Tinteretto.
22 It was in the collection at Staatlichekunsthalle, Karlsruhe, no 19. For a discussion on the subject of Dutch portrait/genre, see D R Smith, 'Irony and Civility: Notes on the Convergence of Genre and Portraiture in Seventeenth-Century Dutch Painting', *The Art Bulletin* (1987), vol 39, no 3, p. 407-30.
23 It has not been possible to locate exactly which portraits of the 1st Duke were situated in which houses. When the sale took place of the contents of Ormond House in St James's Square, it is apparent from the catalogue that most of the family portraits had been removed which would suggest that these were probably distributed among the extended family. The Cowper family at Panshanger were descendants of Henrietta, Countess of Grantham, sister of the 2nd Duke of Ormonde. Thomas, Earl Cowper had succeeded as heir general to the Butler Baronies of Lord Dingwall and Lord Butler of Moore Park in 1871.
24 J Fenlon, 'John Michael Wright's 'Highland laird Identified', *Burlington Magazine* (October 1988), vol 130, no 1027, pp. 767-69.
25 *Illustrated Summary Catalogue of Paintings*, (Dublin 1981), National Gallery of Ireland, no 4198, English School 'Double Portrait of Two Gentlemen'. There is another version of this painting in a private collection in England, my thanks to Sir O Millar for this information.
26 Rev J Graves. 'Extracts from the Household Accounts of James Earl of Ossory', *Journal of the Kilkenny and S E of Ireland Archaeological Society*, vol 1 (1849-51), p. 410.
27 NLI MS 2547, f. 10-11. Thomas Highmore (1660-1720), uncle of Joseph, the more famous 18th-century painter.
28 NLI MS 2524, 'An Account of Prints bought in Dublin for ye Drawing Room in his Graces Appartment.'
29 In 1714 out of a total of 118 pictures at Richmond, there were 23 oil paintings, 38 prints, and 57 'Indian pictures'.
30 J Dunton, *The Life & Errors of John Dunton* (London 1818), p. 594.
31 J N Brewer, *The Beauties of Ireland* (London 1825), p. 417. Brewer visited Kilkenny Castle before the extensive building alterations of the 1820s and '30s took place, and describes the long gallery as measuring 180 feet in length at that time. It would seem that space from at least one of the circular towers was incorporated into the length of the original gallery on the second floor of the castle.
32 O Millar, *Portraiture and the Country House, The Treasure Houses of Britain* (New Haven and London 1986), pp. 28-29.

From Rome to Dublin in 1848
A Madonna for St Audoen's

Eileen Kane

has found letters which throw light on a rare sculpture commission

We are occupied in building a large new chapel in a fine situation. Thus, on 27 August 1841, the Revd James Corr wrote from Chapel House, Bridge Street, Dublin, to the Very Revd Dr Paul Cullen, Rector of the Irish College in Rome, opening a correspondence which, one hundred and fifty years later, provides a social and art-historical context for a statue of the *Madonna and Child* (Fig 1) which may still be seen in the place for which it was created.[1]

The Roman Catholic chapel of St Audoen's, from the residence of which Fr Corr wrote to Dr Cullen, was, in 1841, a small, run-down building dating from Penal Days situated in an alley off Bridge Street which leads uphill from the Liffey to the high ground of Corn Market and High Street. To provide more appropriately, in the new era following Catholic Emancipation, for the large numbers of Mass-goers in this densely-populated district of the old city, the foundations of a new church were laid on 2 July 1841 in High Street on a site adjoining the remains of the medieval church of St Audoen's. That 'large new Chapel' is the fine neo-classical church on the north side of High Street, a stone's throw away from Christ Church.

2. Raphael (1483-1520): *Madonna del Granduca.* 1504. Oil on panel, 84 x 55 cm. (Pitti Palace, Florence). Bonanni's statue was erroneously stated to have been inspired by a *Virgin and Child* by Guido Reni but its design owes more to this famous painting by Raphael.

(Opposite). 1. Pietro Bonanni (b. 1810): *Madonna and Child.* 1847. Marble, 210 cm high (St Audoen's, High Street, Dublin). The statue, in Carrara marble, was commissioned by a contract dated 8 September 1844 from the sculptor by Dr Paul Cullen, Rector of the Irish College in Rome, on behalf of the parish priest of the new church of St Audoen's.

The priests who, in 1841, were 'occupied in building' the new church were the Parish Priest, the Very Revd James Monks, and five curates of whom James Corr was the most recently-arrived. Fr Corr was appointed to St Audoen's in 1838. It was his second appointment in the diocese after his return from Rome where he had been a student at the Irish College. He was well acquainted with Paul Cullen, Rector of the Irish College since 1832.

From the next extant letter from Fr Corr to Dr Cullen, it becomes clear that negotiations for the purchase of a statue were already started – indeed, they had already reached an impasse – by September 1842. This letter suggests that the first artist to be approached in the matter was the Irish sculptor, John Hogan. Fr Corr wrote, *We are very anxious to hear from you about the statue, its state of completion and who it is who is making it. You mentioned in your last letter that it was likely that Hogan would come on terms about it. If so I hope that he is going according to the model sent to you. He had a design of his own which we do not approve of. Please write to me as soon as you conveniently can.*[2]

John Hogan would indeed have been an obvious first choice for the Parish Priest of St Audoen's in the early 1840s.[3] Born in Cork, he had gone to Rome as a young artist in 1824 and soon began to make his way there. On his first return visit to Ireland, in 1829, he brought with him a full-size figure, in marble, of the *Dead Christ*. This was exhibited in Dublin and bought for the Carmelite church in Clarendon Street where it was installed beneath the high altar. More recently, in 1837, he had completed in plaster a large *Pietà* group which won much praise in Rome before being shipped to Dublin to be set above the high altar of the church of St Nicholas of Myra in Francis Street, only a few minutes' walk away from the site of the new St Audoen's.[4]

Two factors seem to have caused negotiations with John Hogan to come to nothing – the design he was offering and the price he was asking. Fr Corr refers again to Hogan in his next letter to Cullen on 10 March 1843: *Our parish priest gave you a commission on your last departure from Ireland about a statue of the Blessed Virgin,* he wrote. *He sent the design and dimensions after you to Liverpool...Hogan requiring too much we have accordingly differed with him...We are willing to give two hundred and fifty pounds for it. It must be life size or larger and of the best workmanship.*[5]

Unless it be that he was trying to negotiate with John Hogan, Dr Cullen appears not to have moved in the matter of the statue for many months. Nor did he reply to Fr Corr's letters. Just before Christmas 1843, Fr Corr wrote: *I beg of you to favour me by an immediate answer about the statue of the Madonna. I wish most particularly to know did you receive the drawing and the proportions of it sent after you to Liverpool...We are most anxious to have it executed at once and in the best manner, we have the price at present so I beg of you for*

3. John HOGAN (1800-58): *The Immaculate Conception.* 1843. Plaster, 132 cm high. (Sacred Heart Convent, Villa Lante, Rome). Initially, the Irish sculptor, Hogan, who was then working in Rome, was approached to execute the statue for St Audoen's but negotiations with him fell through.

4. Pietro TENERANI (1798-1869): *Allegorical Figure.* 1844. Gesso bozzetto, 44 cm high. (Museo di Roma, Rome). This statue, designed as part of a funerary monument to Princess Torlonia, shows the figure in a standard neo-classical pose which was also adopted by Bonanni for his *Madonna and Child.*

5. Pietro TENERANI: *Madonna and Child.* Undated. Gesso bozzetto, 32.5 cm high. (Museo di Roma, Rome). While the design of this group by Bonanni's master differs considerably from the St Audoen's statue, the positioning of the feet in both groups is similar.

Her sake to have it commenced immediately by the best artist in Rome...We require it six feet and a half in height not including the pedestal. Our Chapel or rather our New Church promises to be a very fine one. On you devolves the procuring of one of its chief ornaments. I again beg of you execute our commission at once.[6]

The note of urgency which had crept into that letter is evident again some three months later, written by Fr Corr on 18 March 1844, *I have written to you several months ago about the Statue of the Blessed Virgin, and have received no ac[knowledge]m[ent]. Did you ever receive the drawing sent after you to Liverpool?...In case of it having escaped your memory I shall again repeat it. We wish you to get a statue of the B. Virgin by the best artist in Rome, of the finest marble and workmanship to stand six feet and half high excluding the pedestal which will I suppose be about two feet more with the Divine Infant in her arms. We are willing to give two hundred and fifty pounds for it...But it must be finshed in the very finest manner and the sooner the better...I beg of you to have it executed as soon as possible. We are roofing the New Chapel and this causes me to urge you so much.'*[7]

Faced with the necessity of deciding who was the 'best artist in Rome' in 1844, Paul Cullen had an interesting scene to survey. The prevailing neo-classical style had been decisively established there by the Venetian sculptor, Antonio Canova (1770-1822), and affirmed, with a predominantly Greek inspiration, by the Dane, Bertel Thorwaldsen (1770-1844). Thorwaldsen had returned to settle in Copenhagen in 1838, but his influence remained immense in Rome, not only through his own work in the city but also through the artists who had been his students and studio assistants. Outstanding among these, and now at the peak of his own career, was Pietro Tenerani (1798-1869) from Carrara. But Rome, in the first half of the 19th century was also still attracting artists from abroad. Among these, the Englishman, John Gibson (1760-1866), was enjoying a very successful career, particularly among English patrons, and John Hogan was not only attracting favourable notice from the critics but had received the signal honour for a non-Italian in being elected a member of the Virtuosi del Pantheon in 1839. If Dr Cullen had to exclude John Hogan the obvious artist to turn to as the 'best artist in Rome' would be Pietro Tenerani.[8]

Like his own master, Thorwaldsen, Pietro Tenerani ran a busy and well-organised studio in which teams of men carried out clearly-defined tasks: making full-scale models in clay of the master's designs, roughing out the marble blocks, bringing the roughed-out blocks to a close enough degree of finish to enable

Tenerani to impart the subtleties of expression and detail which depended on his master's hand. As was the practice in his time, he depended heavily on his assistants and would also entrust the running of the studio to one or other of them whenever he was absent from Rome.[9]

The year 1844 was one of the busiest and one of the most difficult in Tenerani's career. When the year opened, he had on hands a commission for a funerary monument for the late Princess Torlonia. He was also finishing a statue in marble of St Benedict for the basilica of St Paul's Outside the Walls. He was, however, in indifferent health and in early July, on the recommendation of his doctors, he left Rome on a journey which would take him to Munich and Berlin, and then on to Vienna, before returning to Rome via Trieste and Florence. He arrived back in his studio on 31 October.

On 8 September 1844, while Tenerani was still absent abroad, Cullen signed the contract for the statue for St Audoen's.[10] The artist who signed with him was Pietro Bonanni, one of Tenerani's then closest assistants and one to whom, to quote Tenerani's biographer, the master 'happily entrusted his own marbles.'[11] Like Tenerani, Pietro Bonanni (b. 1810) was born in Carrara, the heart of the marble-quarrying area of the Apuan Alps. He studied sculpture at the Carrara Academy, won the Academy's Rome Prize in 1834, and set out for Rome the following year. Instead, however, of enrolling in the Roman Academy, he entered the studio of Tenerani. The brief note on Bonanni which is included by Oreste Raggi in his exhaustive study of Tenerani and his 'School' makes mention of only three works by Bonanni. The first two were pieces which, as a student funded by a scholarship from Carrara, he sent back to his own Academy to give proof of his progress in his first and second years. 'The third is a Virgin with the Child in her arms...which he modelled himself and carried out in marble in 1847, on commission from the Archbishop of Dublin', in other words, the statue now in St Audoen's. 'But afterwards', continues Raggi, 'he continued to work for Tenerani, nor, as far as I know, has he left us any other work of his own.'[12]

The contract signed by Bonanni and Cullen stipulates that Bonanni shall 'execute and finish...a statue representing Our Lady with her divine Son in her arms, 6 feet 9 inches in height, with its pedestal 2 feet 8 inches high.' The work is to be completed within about two and a half years; the statue is to be executed in 'marble called statuary marble from Carrara', and the pedestal in 'ordinary marble, likewise from Carrara'; the price for the work is to be 1150 Roman scudi, payable in four-monthly installments. Under these conditions, Bonanni 'binds himself to execute with the greatest diligence possible to him, the above-mentioned commission' and the contract is to be 'ratified by the Rev Mr Corr, of Dublin, by 15th October following.' The first payment, of 50 scudi, was received by Bonanni on 7 November 1844, and the payment is noted and receipted by his signature on the verso of the contract itself.

Early in the new year of 1845, obviously delighted that the statue was at last in hand but otherwise gravely preoccupied by the grim conditions at home in those days when the country was poised on the brink of the Great Famine, Fr Corr wrote to Dr Cullen one of the most moving letters in this long correspondence. *Your long expected letter has arrived at last,* he wrote, *and I hasten to send you an immediate answer with a draft for Fifty pounds for the Statue of Our Blessed Lady. O how truly have you said that we require her powerful intercession now more than ever...Ireland from end to end is filled with the extremity of sorrow and affliction...The fifty pounds I now enclose you was collected from the poorest of the poor. And it is a fact worthy of being recorded that within the space of two years we collected the sum of two hundred and fifty pounds in farthings from mendicants, from creatures living on a single meal during the day; given by them for the purpose of erecting an altar in honor of the Blessed Virgin in our New Church. Behold an example of the Faith and Religion of our Beloved Flock.*[13]

In Rome, Pietro Bonanni seems to have begun at once the long process of making the statue. As he was not an independent artist with a studio of his own but worked as an assistant to Tenerani, we may be sure that the procedures of making a full-scale model in plaster and roughing out the marble block were carried out by his own hand.[14] In spite of the fact that Tenerani's studio was now as busy as it had ever been, Bonanni pressed ahead. By May 1846, Dr Cullen was able to write to Fr Corr: *My dear Father Corr, I am happy to inform you that the Statue of the B. Virgin is progressing rapidly. It is already very far advanced in the marble, and to an unskilful eye, it would appear nearly finished. However the sculptor says he will still require a considerable time to bring it to perfection, and it wd not be creditable to him to let it out of his hands until it should have received the last touch. I have paid him all I rec[eive]d from you and Rev Mr Monks and £20 more. As the work advances, he will be calling for cash, so it [will] be well to forward at least £80 more...Be so kind as to speak to Mr Monks, and get the money forwarded, otherwise new delays will arise. I am sure the Statue will be greatly admired in Dublin.*[15]

In reply to this, in June 1846, Dr Cullen heard from both Fr Corr and the Revd John Hamilton, Archdeacon of Dublin and Administrator of the Pro-Cathedral. Archdeacon Hamilton was sending an order for one hundred and twenty-five pounds *on the part of poor Rev Mr Monks. He is at present I am sorry to say in a very precarious state of health, and begs you will have the kindness to repay yourself whatever you may have advanced for the statue.*[16] Fr Corr was letting Dr Cullen know he could expect to receive from Archdeacon Hamilton 'the entire remaining sum for the Madonna', adding: 'Urge the artist to complete the work, we are most anxious to have it home when finished', and confirming the news about Fr Monks: 'Our parish priest is on his death bed.'[17]

It may well have been the strain of trying to complete the building of the new St Audoen's that accounted for Fr Monks' ill-health[18] but the project was kept moving and Fr Corr's next letter to Rome, dated 14 October 1846, was sent, no longer from Chapel House, Bridge Street, but from a new address: 21 High Street. *I hope you are encouraging the artist about our Madonna,* he wrote to Dr Cullen, *The New Church was dedicated on the feast of il Nome di Maria, it has its beauties, among others, an extremely lofty ceiling...and is in such an elevation as to situation that I term it the Ara Coeli of Dublin...I remain your much obliged servant, James Corr.*

He affixed his new address a second time at the end: 'New R. C. Church of St Audoen High Street Dublin.'[19]

The appalling conditions of hardship, famine, and disease leading to the death or emigration of so many people in those months are brought home to us by Fr Corr in February 1847. Writing once more to Dr Cullen, his principal message in this letter is not about the statue but about the tragic death of the mother of one of the students of the Irish College on a ship taking her and her family to a hoped-for new life in America. Then, turning to other matters, he writes: *We are in the New Church for the last six months; it is not yet ceiled and the cold of it is intense. The general poverty affects us very severely...How is the Statue progressing? Take care to have it ensured for the voyage homeward.*[20]

If, in February 1847, Fr Corr was already thinking of the statue's homeward voyage, he was running somewhat ahead of the course of events. On 3 September, Bonanni receipted the final payment but six months later Fr Corr was still anxiously waiting. On 3 March 1848 he wrote *Revd. and dear Sir we are all feeling considerable anxiety in getting no account of the Statue. I beg of you to let me know at your earliest convenience the name of the vessel which conveys it, also the time she left Leghorn and the time we may expect her to arrive in this port, or that of Liverpool. Any further particulars concerning it, you will also mention.* [21]

Happily, the longed-for statue arrived safely in Dublin and, on Monday 14 August, *The Freeman's Journal* carried an article headed: 'Dedication of a statue of the Madonna in St Audeon's (*sic*) Church, High-Street.' The writer, who remained anonymous, used superlatives to describe the emotion he felt during the private view conceded to him the previous day *through the kindness of one of the rev. gentlemen attached to the church, (Fr Corr?) of the exceedingly beautiful work of art, executed to order in Rome, a statue, semi-colossal, of the Madonna with the infant Saviour...carved out of one block of the purest and whitest Carrara marble...We have never felt more sensibly, he wrote, the dearth and inadequacy of language to describe...the heavenly calm, and unearthly beauty of the Madonna's countenance.*

'With more than usual magnificence', the ceremony of the dedication of the statue was performed on the following Sunday, 20 August, which was the 'Sunday within the Octave of the Assumption'. Decorated 'as for the greater festivals', three altars 'blazed with innumerable waxen tapers.' 'Eleven o'clock was the hour named for the commencement of the ceremonies; but long previous to that time every part of the noble building was densely crowded.' High Mass was celebrated 'with every splendor' and a sermon was preached by the Revd Moses Furlong. [22]

One hundred and fifty years later, the statue is still in place in St Audoen's. It stands in the right transept in a niche above the altar of Our Lady. It measures two hundred and ten centimetres high, including a base of nine centimetres high, which is carved in one piece with the figure. On the side of the base, beneath the Virgin's right foot, are inscribed the signature and the date: 'PETRUS. BONANNI. / FECIT. ROMAE. 1847 ~' (Fig 6). The Virgin is a solemn figure. She holds the child on her left arm in such a way that he is actually sitting on her hand. With her right hand, she steadies him as he turns around to look at the people imagined as gathered below. His right elbow is resting on her shoulder in a relaxed, familiar manner, leaving his hand free beside his face. His left hand rests on his mother's chest.

The grouping of the two figures sends us back to the earliest letters in the correspondence in which the design of the statue is mentioned several times. First, Fr Corr wrote that if Hogan had come to an agreement about the price, he hoped that he was 'going according to the model sent to [Dr Cullen]', adding that 'he had a design of his own which we do not approve of.' Later, we learn that Fr Monks had 'sent the design and dimensions after [Dr Cullen] to Liverpool.' Later again, the design is referred to as a drawing: 'did you receive the drawing and the proportions of it?' and the commission is repeated in such a way as to suggest that the four important factors in it were that it be: 'by the best artist in Rome, of the finest marble and workmanship, to stand six and a half feet high...with the Divine Infant in her arms.'

If the 'design of his own' which John Hogan had proposed did not meet with approval, and if the 'best artist in Rome' had to follow the design sent to him from Dublin, then who designed the statue? A clue to the answer to this is provided by the reporter for *The Freeman's Journal* describing the statue on the occasion of its dedication and blessing on 20 August. 'The mother of the Redeemer', he wrote, 'is represented as in Guido's famed picture, holding the infant Saviour enfolded in her arms.' The name Guido must surely indicate Guido Reni (1575-1642), much in favour in the age of neo-classicism, but there is not, nor was there so far as can be ascertained, in the accepted or ascribed *oeuvre* of Reni a *Madonna and Child* which could have been a model for the statue in St Audoen's. There is, on the other hand, in the work of Raphael (1483-1520), who was equally admired and copied in the 19th century, a *Madonna and Child* which is very close indeed to it in design and could certainly be described as 'famed', the *Madonna del Granduca* (Fig 2), now in the Pitti Palace in Florence. The pose of the child and the way his mother holds him are, in almost every detail, the same in the sculpture as in the painting. Perhaps, then, it was a drawing or, more likely, an engraving of Raphael's *Madonna del Granduca* that was the design sent after Dr Cullen to serve as the model for the new statue.[23]

It would be interesting to know what it was about the design by John Hogan that did not meet with approval at St Audoen's. There is no finished *Madonna and Child* in Hogan's *oeuvre* which might serve as an indication of what he was proposing. There is (or was), however, a plaster model of the Madonna with the Child as a young boy standing on a globe by her side.[24] There would, perhaps, be less emphasis on the motherhood of Mary in such a design than when she is shown holding the child in her arms. It would also, as a statue, be more blocky and less appropriate for its intended place above an altar. There is also a statue of the *Immaculate Conception* (Fig 3) in plaster in Rome which Hogan made on commission from a Miss Hynes for the chapel of the Sacred Heart convent at the Villa Lante in 1843 soon after the negotiations for St Audoen's fell through. A curious detail links this statue with Bonanni's – in the draperies of both figures of the Madonna, the corners of her veil are decorated with a little bobbin.[25]

In fact, the image of the Virgin with the child in her arms is not one which occurs frequently in the work of neo-classical artists. In the work of Pietro Tenerani, whose output was enormous and very diverse as to subject-matter, there is, again, no finished statue on that theme, nor is a commission for such a piece recorded by his biographer. There is, however, among the plaster sketch-models which came from the Tenerani museum established after the sculptor's death by his son, Carlo Tenerani, a small *bozzetto* or sketch-model of the Madonna holding the child in her arms (Fig 5).[26] This differs considerably from Bonanni's marble version as to the grouping of the two figures. However, in view of the fact that the *Madonna del Granduca* is not a full-length figure and that the arrangement of the lower half of the figure and the draperies down to the feet in the statue would be left to Bonanni's own invention, comparison of the two pieces is instructive. Bonanni gave the characteristically neo-classical pose to the figure with the weight of her body taken by her left leg leaving the right knee bent. That pose is the same in the little *bozzetto* but what is interesting is that the Madonna's feet are identically placed in the two pieces. In each statue the right foot juts out diagonally to fill the corner of the base and the left is placed just past the centre point of the base leaving room for a large swathe of draperies to fall beyond and above it. It is also interesting to note that a similar arrangement was adopted by Tenerani in a *bozzetto* for a female allegorical figure intended for the Torlonia monument (Fig 4). There is, then, a certain resemblance between Bonanni's statue and the two *bozzetti* which makes one wonder whether Tenerani had a hand in the design of Bonanni's statue. It would be much less likely that Bonanni had made the two *bozzetti* as such sketch-models were normally the artist's first ideas for a project and would therefore be personal work, and not the work of an assistant.

The requirement that the statue for St Audoen's be 'of the finest workmanship' was well fulfilled. In particular, the figure of the child is admirably carried out and Bonanni has imparted to it a most attractive vitality. Details of texture, in the child's hair and the draperies, are well crafted and there is a little touch of bravura in the detail of the upturned hem of the Madonna's mantle above the left foot. The discrepancy between the required dimensions, especially of the pedestal, and the actual piece are perhaps to be explained by suggesting that the artist knew better than Fr Corr or Fr Monks what proportions between statue and pedestal would look well in the proposed position above an altar. That Bonanni would probably have ascertained where in the church the statue would be placed and what the principal view-point would be is indicated by the fact that the child is so placed in his mother's arms as to look best when viewed, as it is, from the left, and this is also the spectator's view-point in the *Madonna del Granduca*.

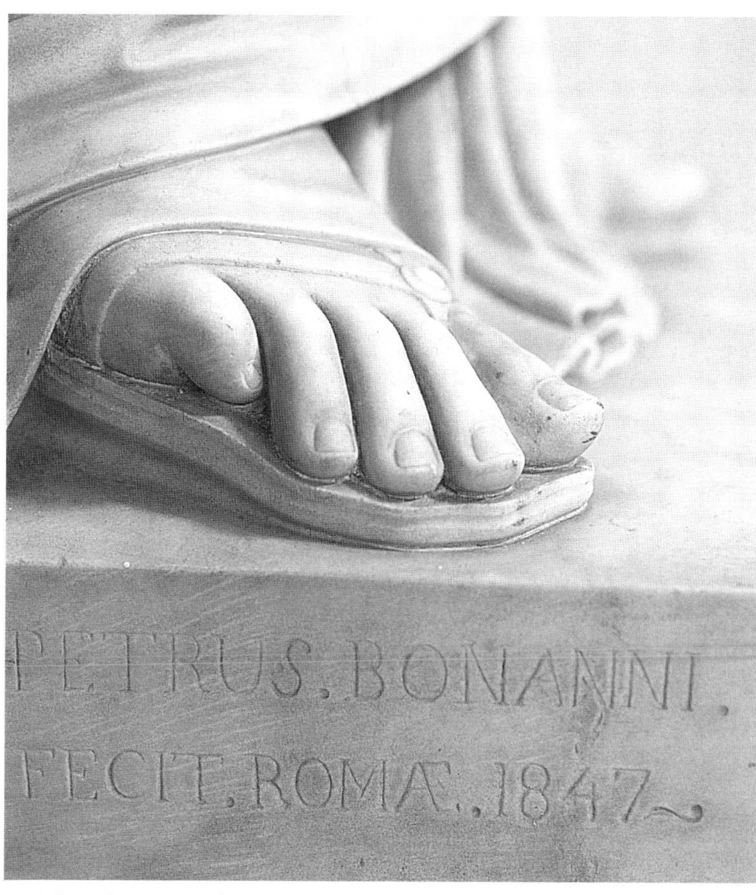

6. Pietro BONANNI: *Madonna and Child*. Detail of the signature. (St Audoen's, High Street, Dublin). The sculptor's signature is carved into the side of the base of the statue beneath the Virgin's foot.

In spite of the fact that the statue is clearly signed and dated and that at the time of its inauguration the identity of the artist – and his being a 'gifted and already distinguished pupil of the great Zenerani [*sic*]'[27] – was loudly proclaimed, Bonanni's name was soon either forgotten or mis-remembered as 'Benzoni, of Rome'.[28] The mention of Benzoni is, of course, interesting as he was a friend of John Hogan and also to some extent a rival for commissions in Irish churches in the 1850s when Hogan had returned to Ireland and was experiencing difficulties in making a living.

Fr Corr's last reference to the statue in the correspondence is dated 16 March 1850, as he concludes in a long letter to Cullen's successor as Rector of the Irish College in Rome, Dr Tobias Kirby: *We have our Roman Madonna long since installed in due pomp. The Archbishop officiated. Our parish church is crowded always with faithful and persevering clients of the Refuge of Sinners, the Comforter of the afflicted. Believe me your affectionate and sincere friend James Corr, S. Audoen's, Dublin.* [29]

Pietro Bonanni's statue of the *Madonna and Child* is a Roman neo-classical statue in a Dublin neo-classical church. Visually, it fits perfectly in its architectural setting but there is more to it than that. As the letters of Fr Corr reveal, its presence in St Audoen's symbolises the faith and generosity of the people and the energy of their pastors at a time of extraordinary hardship in Ireland.

EILEEN KANE *is a lecturer in the Department of the History of Art in University College, Dublin.*

1 The correspondence on which this article is based is preserved in the archives of the Pontifical Irish College, Rome. I am greatly indebted to the Right Revd Monsignor John Fleming, Rector of the College, for so readily facilitating and encouraging my research in the archives, and for permission to publish the material contained in this article. The letter dated 27 Aug 1841 is referenced: I.C.R.A. Cullen 672. I am also most grateful to the Revd Martin Tierney, Rector, St Audoen's, for his interest in and encouragement of my work there.

2 I.C.R.A. New Cullen v, folder 1, item 42

3 On John Hogan, see: J Turpin, *John Hogan, Irish Neoclassical Sculptor in Rome 1800-1858* (Dublin 1982).

4 Count Hawkes Le Grice wrote of Hogan's *Pietà* that 'the style is truly grand, and the execution is worthy of the style. This group is in truth a masterpiece, and reflects the highest honour on the artist.' See *Walks Through the Studii of the Sculptors at Rome* (Rome 1841), p. 68,

5 I.C.R.A. New Cullen v, folder 2, item 1. The date on this letter is unclear, but is probably to be read as Mar 10. Paul Cullen was in Dublin in the summer of 1842. It was his usual practice to travel to and from Rome via Liverpool where he had relatives.

6 I.C.R.A. New Cullen v, folder 2, item 59: 20 Dec 1843. The statue of the Madonna and Child was intended to be much more than an 'ornament' in St Audoen's. In line with the intention of the Archbishop, Dr D Murray, to foster devotion to Our Lady in Dublin while the parish was still centred in Bridge Street chapel in 1840, a branch of the Association of the Sacred Heart of Mary, recently formed in Paris, was set up there by Fr Monks and Fr Corr conducted an intensive programme of devotions in the Marian month of May. On this point see especially Revd Dr M Ronan, *An Apostle of Catholic Dublin* (Fr H Young) (Dublin 1944) pp. 236 foll; and also *The Catholic Directory* (Dublin 1841), p. 278.

7 I.C.R.A. New Cullen v, folder 3, item 16.

8 For Pietro Tenerani's status see Count Hawkes Le Grice (as note 4) who mentions the studios of Thorwaldsen, Crawford, Hogan, Tenerani, Rinaldi, Bienaimé, and Laboureur as worthy of a visit. *Murray's Handbook for Central Italy and Rome* (London 1843) lists 13 sculptors working in Rome, beginning with Thorwaldsen and including Gibson, Tenerani and Hogan.

9 On Tenerani, see O Raggi, *Della Vita e Delle Opere di Pietro Tenerani, del suo Tempo e Della sua Scuola Nella Scultura* (Florence 1880).

10 I.C.R.A. New Cullen vi, folder 3, item 9

11 Raggi (as note 9), pp. 409-410, under the heading 'The principal pupils of Tenerani' (*Gli Scolari Principali del Tenerani*) gives a note on Pietro Bonanni. This seems to have been the source for the notice on Bonanni in V Vicario, *Gli Scultori Italiani dal Neo-classicismo al Liberty* (Lodi 1994).

12 It is curious that Raggi was not aware of another work by Bonanni, a marble bust of Pope Gregory XVI made for the Irish College in Rome during the time that Paul Cullen was Rector. V Rev J Donovan records the bust as it was to be seen in the Sant'Agata dei Goti location of the College: *Opposite the landing on the first floor is the marble bust of the reigning Pontiff, executed by Bonani [sic], in the studio of Tenerani, beneath which is a marble slab with the following inscription recording the donation of the college to the Irish Church by his Holiness Gregory XVI.* The bust and the inscription can be seen in the left-hand corridor of the ground floor of the Irish College in its present location, Via dei Santi Quattro 1. The work does not appear to be signed, so Donovan must have received his information orally, quite possibly from Cullen. See Donovan's *Rome Ancient and Modern and its Environs*, vol iii (Rome 1842-1844), p. 972

13 I.C.R.A. To Cullen 1844-1845: 1009. The underlinings are Fr Corr's own.

14 Making the full-scale model in plaster was usually the work of a specialist, and the heavy preliminary work of reducing the marble block to roughly the size and shape required was seldom done by the master himself. Raggi's note on Bonanni (as note 11) explicitly states that 'he himself modelled' (*modellò del suo*) 'and carried out in marble' (*e condusse in marmo*) the statue of the Virgin and Child.

15 28 May 1846: Dublin Diocesan Archives: AB3/34/9

16 I.C.R.A. To Cullen 1209 (22 June 1846).

17 I.C.R.A. To Cullen 1210 (24 June 1846).

18 Most Revd N Donnelly DD writes that 'The heavy work of collecting for and building the Church completely shattered the health of Fr. Monks, who was seldom seen after the opening ceremony (13 Sept 1846), and in 1847 he was assisted by an Administrator.' Fr Monks died in 1850. See Donnelly's *A Short History of Some Dublin Parishes, pt.* 8 (Dublin 1911), p. 178

19 I.C.R.A. New Cullen VI folder 2, item 25. In the Roman missal, the normal date for the Feast of the Most Holy Name of Mary was Sept 12.

20 I.C.R.A. To Cullen 1323.

21 I.C.R.A. To Cullen 1554.

22 *The Freeman's Journal* (23 Aug 1848). The Revd Moses Furlong is an interesting figure, as is his connection with St Audoen's. With the Roman Fr L Gentili, he was one of the first members of the new Institute of Charity [Rosminians]. In the early summer of 1848, Frs Gentili and Furlong accepted the invitation of Fr J Corr, who had been a friend of Gentili's during his student days in Rome and remembered his special devotion to Our Lady, to come to Dublin to preach the devotions for the month of May at St Audoen's. The two preachers preached for a second month in Rathmines and in Sept were in St John's Augustinian church, near St Audoen's. There Fr Gentili fell ill on Sept 16, just a few days after the dedication of the statue in St Audoen's, and died of cholera, 'the famine fever', on 28 Sept 1848. See D Gwynn, *Fr Luigi Gentili and his Mission, 1801-1848* (Dublin 1951), pp. 250-251.

23 It was not unusual for sculptors to use designs by painters. For sculptors' practices in the 17th century, including the translation into sculpture of painters' designs, see J Montagu, *Roman Baroque Sculpture:The Industry of Art* (New Haven and London 1989), particularly p. 77 foll.

24 Illustrated in J Clarke [pseud Benmore], *Memorials of John Hogan: The Great Irish Sculptor, 1800-1858* (Omagh 1927), p. 15. C P Curran, 'Concerning John Hogan' in *The Capuchin Annual* (1946-1947), pp. 172-203, lists among Hogan's religious work 'a Madonna in the possession of his family in which classical grace and Christian tenderness are characteristically blended.' J Turpin (as note 3), p. 170, records the piece as 'untraced'.

25 This statue is c.52 inches high, therefore smaller than Bonanni's. I am most grateful to Mother Giuseppina Polimeni for her gracious welcome and assistance on the occasion of my visit to the Villa Lante in May 1997, to see Hogan's work.

26 Now in the Museo di Roma, Rome. I am greatly indebted to Dottoressa Emiliana Ricci, Dirigente del Museo di Roma, for arranging for me to examine these *bozzetti* and for sharing her knowledge of them with me. They are numbered: A.M. 3982, Raggi 112 (the Madonna and Child), and A.M. 3983 (Figura femminile mon. Torlonia).

27 *The Freeman's Journal* (14 Aug 1848).

28 In 1907, Cosgrave and Strangways, *Dictionary of Dublin*, p. 15, noted in St Audoen's 'a fine and beautiful statue of the Madonna and Child by an Italian sculptor'; in 1911, Donnelly (as note 18), p. 179, refers to 'the blessing by Dr Murray in 1849 [sic] of the imposing marble statue of Our Lady, by Benzoni, of Rome.' The attribution to Benzoni is repeated by F P Carey, *Catholic Dublin: An Ecclesiastical Guide*, (Dublin 1832), p.53: *a statue in marble of Our Lady – a work of imposing dimensions – particularly arrests attention. This is actually one of the creations of the Roman sculptor, Benzoni.'* Finally, in 1946, C P Curran (as note 24), referring to the neglect which Hogan suffered in Ireland after his return from Rome, wrote that *'to their common astonishment, another commission – the Madonna and Child in St Audoen's Dublin – was given to his friend Benzoni.* The Benzoni in question is Giovanni Maria Benzoni, born 1809 near Bergamo, died Rome 1873. There is an Immaculate Conception by him in the Cathedral of St John, Limerick.

29 I.C.R.A. To Kirby 688.

Book Reviews

The latest books on Irish art and culture

Nature in Ireland

EDITED BY JOHN WILSON FOSTER AND HELENA C G CHESNEY

Lilliput Press 1998 h/b £40
658 pp. 46 b/w ills 1-874675-29-5

Joep Leerssen

A CHAR CAUGHT IN LOUGH NEAGH: From *Nature in Ireland: A Scientific and Cultural History*. 'Many essays in this book and, indeed, the tone of the book as a whole do much to develop a fresh look at the interplay between nature, history and natural history in this country...'

People nowadays are inclined to smile at Standish O'Grady's *History of Ireland* of 1880 which opened with a chapter on geological and geographical developments since the Pleistocene. But there was more than mere whimsy at issue: O'Grady's *History*, approaching native antiquity from a staunchly Unionist perspective, attempted to show that Ireland had for centuries, indeed millenia, been continually overrun by new strata of nature and of human settlement, and that, therefore, the Protestant Ascendancy had, despite its more recent arrival, as good a title to hold sway as any earlier denizen from Elk to Gael.

Seeing Ireland in terms of its natural history appears to be an Anglocentric stance, not only in the individual case of O'Grady but almost structurally. As a result, the congenial framework for natural history has been 'The British Isles' and Ireland's natural history has rarely been considered in the country's own specific context. However, 'natural history' is not just the location of certain layers of carboniferous sandstone or the presence or absence of snakes or guillemots, holly or butterwort; it is also our way of looking at rock, animals, and plants. Nature, in and of itself, may be the very opposite of culture and of history; but our way of looking at nature and of coming to terms with it is a culturally and historically-rooted praxis which may indeed profit from being studied with due regard for the specificity of the Irish situation. Dorinda Outram made this case in 1986 in a powerful essay published in the *Irish Review* and her call has been taken up by John Wilson Foster in the present volume. Professor Foster is, of course, one of the most insightful critics on Irish literary history and he has always shown a penchant to apply his sources not just in literary criticism but rather to 'mentality' history. This collection is obviously a topic close to his heart for not only did he edit the volume but he also contributed substantial portions to it. His introductory essay 'Encountering Traditions' (somewhat misleadingly placed in second position) is a wide-ranging survey of the human interaction with the Irish natural environment, from Celtic times to modern environmentalism, using a variety of sources to striking effect; his 'Nature and Nation in the Nineteenth century' is a less surprising synopsis of existing research and insights from the fields of literary and intellectual history; the concluding 'The Culture of Nature' links nature and natural history back to literary treatment; Seamus Heaney, needless to say, looms large here.

Foster has assembled a wide array of scholars and specialities around him. Dorinda Outram herself is there, with a brief but trenchant theoretical *mise a point*; Brendan McWilliams confirms the high standard of the *Irish Times* 'Weather Eye' columns by giving a learned and well-researched survey of reactions to that most egregious of natural phenomena, the Irish weather. Another *Irish Times* columnist, Michael Viney, has a contribution on hunting, that prime meeting ground between nature and culture, which is likewise full of interest. One could mention more essays, full of interest in their own right; without wanting to take from the high standards of all the other contributions, I particularly like Eoin Neeson on woods and woodland, Christopher Moriarty on fish and fisheries, and Sean Lysaght on the nomenclature of flora and fauna in this language-ridden country.

There is a reason for preferring precisely those articles. They derive their particular interest from drawing on, and comparing, both Gaelic and Anglo-Irish sources, and as such they embody the possibility of conducting the history of nature in the specifically Irish aspect of this country's biculturalism. In Ireland we confront the presence of two different cultural traditions: Gaelic pastoralism and Englishimported agriculturalism and urbanity, each looking at nature and at natural features from its own standpoint and background, both interacting, one doomed to dwindle before the other. For if this collection is situated between the poles of 'scientific and cultural history', as the subtitle puts it, it is by the same token also facing a dilemma vis-a-vis Ireland's specific biculturalism: for, while there is plenty of Gaelic cultural history, there is (barring some medieval theology and philosophy) no Gaelic scientific history. Accordingly, a fair portion of *Nature in Ireland* (the portion dealing with scientific history) is therefore dealing with an imperial, Victorian country. (The section on 'Irish naturalists abroad', while intrinsically full of interest and insights, had a particularly strong J G Farrell flavour). On the whole, an enterprise like this is in a difficult position, for the native attitude to landscape, environment, and natural resources must be reconstructed from scanty written materials of medieval and early-modern vintage, or else from its oral survival in folklore; while the anglophone part of the country's traditions is so much better preserved, so much more alive and accessible, so much closer to us ourselves.

John Andrews, author of *A Paper Landscape* (that classic book on the 1835 Ordnance Survey which was so disastrously misinterpreted in Brian Friel's *Translations*), puts it squarely at the outset of his article: 'Ireland is too small to have developed a native map-making tradition. The first maps to show any close knowledge of the interior were those commissioned by the English government (....).'

Well, yes, But that does beg a few questions. Too 'small' – was the failure of Gaelic Ireland to latch onto the post-1500 European burst of cartography a question of mere size? Or should we believe, *pace* Andrews, that it is yet another example of arrested development, much as in the case of the failure of post-1500 Gaelic literature to reach into the medium of print, and to be explained from political circumstances quite other than 'smallness'? And, while I am at it, does the very absence of native cartography not raise intriguing questions as to the nature and social importance of geographical knowledge in Gaelic culture, which after all, was particularly rich in topographical writing and which in its cultural lore laid great emphasis on the relation between tribes and territories?

Thus, *Nature in Ireland* still leaves things to be desired for future research: a similarly-oriented project focusing on Gaelic Ireland, and employing the methods of historical anthology, maybe. But then again, it is the hallmark of good scholarship that it whets rather than sates our appetite, and many essays in this book and, indeed, the tone of the book as a whole do much to develop a fresh look at the interplay between nature, history, and natural history in this country and to situate it between its two cultures. The diversity between the various essays, in topic and approach, never becomes annoying; thanks in good part to the careful editing (although one is sometimes puzzled as to the order of the various contributions) and to the useful index, as well as to Foster's conceptual pieces drawing the issues in the various contributions together. This handsomely-produced volume will be a gratefully-used point of reference for scholars for years to come.

Joep Leerssen is the author of Remembrance and Imagination: Patterns in the Historical and Literary Representation of Ireland in the Nineteenth Century (1996).

Ancient Ireland: Life Before the Celts

By Laurence Flanagan

Gill & Macmillan 1998 h/b £16.99

264 pp. 143 b/w ills. 0-7171-2434-7

Etienne Rynne

This book, copiously illustrated with generally relevant maps and other illustrations, and with a most attractively coloured dustjacket showing Pouluabrone Dolmen to great advantage, is like the proverbial curate's egg. Though clearly not aimed at the specialist, nor even at those already *au fait* with Irish prehistory, it nonetheless contains much of interest for such readers, though the more general reader might find some of it a little confusing.

The book, particularly in Part 2, has many thought-provoking, often almost throw-away statements or questions, as for instance on p. 39-40 where Flanagan tells us that the outside of Neolithic pottery vessels was often polished or burnished, 'which would have had the effect, in the absence of glazes, of making the pot more watertight', or on p. 154 where he asks if the inclusion of the highly decorated flint mace-head in the mound at Knowth, 'which could be interpreted as a symbol of power, [might] imply not merely the death of a priest-king but the end of a dynasty?' or, in other words, was the mace-head a personal or a communal status-symbol? He does, however, occasionally fly a kite too high, as, for instance, when on p. 161 he offers a glib (his term) but just about possible explanation for three Earlier Bronze Age burials at Sonnagh Demesne, county Westmeath: two of the burials were of adults, both in pits, both headless, one extended, the other crouched, and buried with them was a cremated child in a cist; the headless adults, Flanagan speculates, may have been 'put to death as pederasts, the child - of whatever sex – their victim.' An interesting, if not very nice, thought, though it smacks of modern-day tabloid journalism.

Speculation, though of a more thought-provoking and justifiable kind, occurs elsewhere in the book too, as for instance when the manufacture of the Tievebulliagh axeheads is discussed on pp. 185-6, or ten pages later when he discusses the 'cost' of producing a typical axehead of the Earlier Bronze Age, the 'cost' being the time, food and up-keep of all those involved in supplying ore, wood, etc., for about twenty days' labour. Indeed, the chapters on 'Manufacturing' and 'The Food Industry' are among the most interesting in the book; how many are aware, for instance, that during the Earlier Bronze Age pigs were slaughtered lying down and opened up from the rear? And that between smoking the bacon and making sausages, the killing of one pig would involve at least two people for between seven and twelve days?

One finds much to question in the book and much to comment upon, but regrettably one also finds much to fault. There are some minor sins of commission and some major sins of omission such as the anthropomorphic carving popularly known as 'The Clown' or 'King Tut' in the passage tomb at Fourknocks, Pygmy Cups, an important type of funerary vessel, and the extraordinary richness of the Later Bronze Age in North Munster. There is no mention anywhere of the outstanding and relatively numerous gold gorgets, biconical hair ornaments, etc., from the area, and the 'Great Clare Find', the largest prehistoric gold hoard ever found north of the Alps, only receives cursory mention, while neither it nor the Gorteenreagh Hoard are even mentioned on p. 165 when the author briefly discusses gold hoards of the Later Bronze Age. All-in-all, Ireland's marvellous and important collection of prehistoric gold gets very short shrift in this book.

Perhaps most annoying, however, are many of the illustrations. They are almost all taken from previously-published sources and are all so acknowledged, but most of the references as to where they were originally published are not given in the bibliographies on pp. 240-251, but maybe the less said about these bibliographies, the better...they look impressive anyway!

Ah well, the curate's egg, after all, was 'good in parts'.

ETIENNE RYNNE is Professor Emeritus in Archaeology at the National University of Ireland, Galway.

The Irish Round Tower. Origins and Architecture Explored

BY BRIAN LALOR

The Collins Press, 1999 h/b £20

247 pp. 20 b/w ills 1-898256-64-0

Roger Stalley

Over the course of the last two centuries round towers have been the focus of more speculation and eccentric theorising than almost any other class of Irish monument. While notions of fire temples, astronomical observatories and centres of phallus worship, have long been despatched to the lunatic fringe, the subject is still capable of stimulating unorthodox views. In 1984 a professor of entomology from Kansas argued that the location of the towers was related to the position of the stars at the winter solstice and that they were 'magnetic antennae used for concentrating paramagnetic energy' for agricultural purposes.

TIMAHOE, CO LAOIS: From *The Irish Round Tower: Origins and Architecture Explored* by Brian Lawlor. With its raised Romanesque doorway, this 12th century tower embodies the underlying structural principles practised by the monastic master masons with little modification for three hundred years.

Brian Lalor's fresh study has a series of introductory chapters (eighty-three pages) followed by an inventory of the towers (one hundred and thirty-eight pages). The text, however, is altogether more balanced and level-headed and it provides a good synopsis of current thinking. Lalor accepts the evidence of the annals which indicate that round towers were constructed between c.950 and 1238 AD and that they were designed as bellfries. The oft-stated myth that they were built for defence against the Vikings deservedly comes in for ridicule and the author points out that they were not much good as lookouts either.

The most original aspects of the book relate to the physical fabric of the towers: there are interesting comments about how they were built and an excellent comparative study of doorways and he stresses the variations that exist, something that has tended to be overlooked in the past. Although there are worthwhile comparisons with Carolingian architecture (the gatehouse at Lorsch) and Ottonian building (St Pantaleon in Cologne), the chapter devoted to the origins of the Irish towers in early-medieval Europe is less convincing. These are murky waters and the author is at a disadvantage through his lack of familiarity with recent literature. The five round towers in the neighbourhood of Ravenna, for example, are now generally assigned to the early 11th, rather than the 7th century, and there was a 'domus clocarum' (bell house) at York in 801, a word which sounds suspiciously like 'cloicteach', the Latin equivalent of the Irish word for round towers. But a more fundamental weakness is the failure to cite sources. While the absence of footnotes makes the volume more accessible to general readers, it will limit its value as a source of reference. The lack of citations also masks the extent to which the author is dependent on previous studies.

It is worth asking what type of bells were rung from the towers and why Irish bellringers failed to use bellropes like their counterparts in Europe (it meant that Irish bell ringers had to climb almost five thousand feet per week). What religious and historical circumstances led to the introduction of the towers in the 10th century? Presumably the towers had something to do with improving religious discipline at a time when monastic settlements were becoming larger and noisier places. Which monastery built the first tower? In this context a good case can be made for Armagh, which is more convincing in historical terms than Mr Lalor's candidate on Scattery island. And why were the towers so high? Here the anachronistic use of metric measurements disguises a rather interesting fact. The height of a fair number of the towers hovers around 29.5

metres, which happens to be 97 (English) feet. While the values of the medieval foot varied from place to place, it is at least worth asking whether some symbolic value was attached to the notion of a 100 foot high tower. Glendalough incidentally has a height of 30.48 metres, in other words 100 (English) feet, and its circumference is 15.30 metres, which is 50 feet 2 inches. It is difficult to believe that the 2:1 ratio is a coincidence. Finally there is the question of access. Instead of flimsy ladders stretching up to the doorways, it seems far more likely that there was some form of fixed (wooden) stair; apparently evidence for this was discovered at Iniscealtra by the late Liam de Paor.

Thanks to the arrival of Mr Lalor's beautifully-presented book, there is a good chance that these and other questions will be more actively debated in the future. The author is a man of many parts – architect, archaeologist, travel writer, printmaker and photographer – and his lucid and entertaining commentary provides a landmark in the study of this most enigmatic group of monuments. Moreover, he is not completely free from the spell of eccentricity which the subject has habitually cast over authors. A number of factual errors should be noted, the most curious of which is the statement that the tower at Ferrycarrig was built to commemorate those who died in the Boer War (unlikely in a monument erected in the 1850s).

ROGER STALLEY is Professor of the History of Art at Trinity College. His own study of Irish round towers will be published in the near future by Princeton University Press and by Town House and Country House.

Medieval Ring Brooches in Ireland, a study of Jewellery, Dress and Society

BY MARY B. DEEVEY

Wordwell Monograph Series No. 1, 1998 h/b £29.95

142 pp. 34 col ills 25 figs 1-869857-24-0

Roger Stalley

One of the most spectacular finds made during the course of excavations in the city of Waterford some years ago was an ornate gold brooch of 13th-century date. The brooch, which is circular in form, is decorated with gold filigree and furnished with four green and blue glass 'stones'. While not as large or elaborate as the penannular brooches of the early Christian era, the Waterford brooch is nonetheless an attractive example of a type encountered over much of northern Europe during the middle ages. One hundred and forty such 'ring brooches', as they are called, have been found in Ireland, and these have now been studied as a group by Mary Deevy.

Ring brooches were essentially a practical device, used to fasten the slit or vent below the neck in lieu of buttons. They could also be used like a modern safety pin to fasten purses, keys, paternoster beads, and even aprons on to any garment that was being worn. Most of the examples depicted in sculpture are worn by women which raises an interesting gender question: did men in the middle ages wear brooches? Kings and noblemen most certainly did and Mary Deevy produces evidence to show that ring brooches were worn by men, women and children, and by all sections of society.

Some of the brooches are little more than simple rings of bronze or even iron, but many are far more ornate. One group contains side plates decorated with animal designs or human faces and another is decorated with a pair of hands projecting out from the lower edge, a design signifying love or betrothal. Most of the types can be paralleled elsewhere in Europe, a point which reflects the extent to which Ireland became part of the European world following the Anglo-Norman invasion. The author uses taxonomy as a basis for dating the brooches, but with objects that were made for both practical and artistic purposes this approach runs into some trouble. In fact it is clear that the various designs were manufactured over long periods and that 'antique' brooches continued to be worn for decades, and perhaps centuries, after they were first made. The book includes chapters devoted to the distribution of the brooches, their methods of manufacture, and the way in which they were worn and it concludes with a catalogue describing each brooch in detail. There is also an appendix listing depictions of ring brooches in Irish stone carving.

Medieval Ring Brooches is a well-written and informative volume, attractively produced with excellent drawings and colour illustrations. The one blemish in the publication is the use of bracketed references instead of footnotes at the bottom of the page, a habit for which there are no excuses in the modern era of word-processing. When will the (archaeological) fraternity learn that brackets are anathema to (good) prose?

ROGER STALLEY is Professor of the History of Art at Trinity College, Dublin.

Ireland and Scandinavia in the Early Viking Age

EDITED BY HOWARD B CLARK, MAIRE NI MHAONAIGH AND RAGHNALL Ó FLOINN

Four Courts Press 1998 h/b £25

468 pp. 46 b/w ills 1-85182-235-6

The Archaeology of Medieval Rural Settlement in Ireland

BY KIERAN DENIS O' CONNOR

Royal Irish Academy 1998 h/b £20

144 pp. 34 col ills 1-874045-61-5

Lynda Mulvin

In October 1995 a major conference was held in Dublin Castle to commemorate the 1200th anniversary of the arrival of Vikings to these shores. The conference spanned the archaeology, history, literature, and art history of the relations between Ireland and Scandinavia in the Viking Age and the papers given at the conference have now been collated in a superb and important publication. With a distinctive and accessible approach, the subjects are divided into two principal sections: archaeology in Scandinavia, Scotland, and Ireland and the literature and history of the Viking Age. The result is a challenging series of new interpretations of the Viking Age in these islands.

The history and literature section contains three Scandinavian accounts of the Vikings in Norway, a wonderful account of the Irish in the Icelandic tradition, and a comparison of Norwegian legends and Irish voyage tales. Other papers include a thought-provoking historiography pre-

RATHGALL, CO WICKLOW. From *The Archaeology of Medieval Rural Settlement in Ireland* by Kieran Denis O'Connor. The innermost stone-walled circle seems to have been a purpose-built medieval castle or fortified enclosure.

sented by Charlie Doherty, a rigorous and closely-argued account exploring the urbanisation of Ireland and Britain by Howard Clarke, and, finally, a profile of the Vikings as perceived by the Irish in literature.

The archaeology papers begin on a high note with contributions from scholars, Myhre and Wamers, reviewing the origins of the Early Viking Age in Norway. These are followed by two essays on the Viking presence in Scotland and the Irish Sea Area, including a lively discussion on raiders and traders. Four substantial papers on the Vikings in Ireland include an account of the recent findings at the Viking burial sites of Kilmainham and Islandbridge while Raghnall Ó Floinn's overview of the subject makes essential reading.

The invaluable index conjures up wonderful images: place names include Annagassan (Linn Duachaill), Hafrsfjord, Hesket-in-the-Forest and Thingmote, Dublin; listed people include the aptly-named Eric Bloodaxe, Harald the Hard-Ruler, and Helgi the Lean; literary references are also made to the *Annals of Inisfallen* and the *Eddic Verses*. Information on artefacts, on beach-markets, religious houses, and the Icelandic sagas is all readily accessible. Throughout, the text is complemented with distribution maps, graphs, clearly-captioned photographs, and some fine line drawings. This collection of papers sets a benchmark for future publications on the subject.

The placing of an illustration of the most-exciting discovery in Irish late-medieval wall painting – that at St Bridget's Church, Clare Island, county Mayo – on the cover of *The Archaeology of Medieval Rural Settlement in Ireland* simply hints at the quality and sparkling nature of the book. In a carefully-written and absorbing analysis of the development of settlement in rural Ireland, the author sets out to consider 'all settlements, regardless of status or function, that lay outside true towns during the period from *c.*1100 AD until the late-seventeenth century.' With such a far-reaching objective, the author begins with a literature review and moves quickly to the evidence of extant remains of castles, country houses, and the manor house. He clearly distinguishes settlement patterns in the Anglo-Norman dominated parts of medieval Ireland from those of the Gaelic dominated parts and places a welcome emphasis on the importance of regional styles. All in all, this is a most impressive monograph. One small gripe for this reader was the lack of survey drawings and architectural plans to illustrate the meticulously-researched and enticing findings.

DR LYNDA MULVIN lectures in Classical and Medieval Art in the Department of the History of Art, University College Dublin.

Drawings of the Principal Antique Buildings of Ireland

BY GABRIEL BERANGER. EDITED BY PETER HARBISON

Four Courts Press/National Library of Ireland 1998 (p/b) £14.95
228 pp. 105 col ills 1-85182-427-8.

The A to Z of Georgian Dublin: John Rocque's Maps of the City in 1756 and the County in 1760

EDITED AND INDEXED BY PAUL FERGUSON, WITH AN INTRODUCTION BY J H ANDREWS

Harry Margary/Trinity College Library 1998 (h/b)
77 pp. 9 b/w ills 64 pp. maps 0-903541-48-3.

Philip McEvansoneya

In 1991 the Royal Irish Academy published a selection of forty-seven of the ninety-one water-colours by Beranger in an album in the RIA. Now the entire contents of a companion volume in the National Library have been published, again under the editorship of Peter Harbison. Following the format of the earlier publication, *Drawings of the Principal Antique Buildings of Ireland* contains clear, colour reproductions, one to a page, with a short commentary opposite each of the ninety-eight surviving drawings and a few other images. In the introduction, which puts the drawings and Beranger into context, Harbison speculates that the albums may have originated in the unrealised plans of the short-lived Hibernian Antiquarian Society to produce an illustrated publication on important Irish sites, a plan partly fulfilled when Francis Grose's *Antiquities of Ireland* appeared in 1794-6.

A number of constituencies will greet this well-produced publication with enthusiasm. Beranger has a place in the history of art in Ireland, not least because his entire working life was spent here as print-seller, framer, drawing master, flower and bird painter, topographical draughtsman, and civil servant. Given that the buildings illustrated date from as early as the 10th century, it serves as something of a primer in the history of lost Irish castles and churches which are the main types of building included.

Those with an interest in the historiography of Irish antiquarianism will also benefit from the accessibility of Beranger's

Gabriel BERANGER: *Rathfarnham Castle*. From *Drawings of the Principal Antique Buildings of Ireland* by Gabriel Beranger, edited by Peter Harbison. '...all readers will be intrigued to see how Beranger's watercolours compare with the present appearance and surroundings of surviving buildings such as Rathfarnham...'

drawings in published form and all readers will be interested to see how the water-colours compare with the present appearance and surroundings of surviving buildings such as Rathfarnham Castle or Leighlin Bridge and Castle. Dramatic changes have occurred to buildings and to the landscape: most of the tower houses which once dominated the county Dublin skyline have now disappeared, except from the pages of Beranger's album.

Although the water-colours have a charm and interest of their own, the question of the reliability of Beranger's images as historical evidence remains unanswerable. His are unique records of many structures which, already in ruins when they were 'Designed on ye spot' – as Beranger puts it – have since been demolished. This makes it hard to judge the balance between observation and imagination which the water-colours contain. A contemporary certainly thought Beranger exercised some licence which is hardly surprising given that almost half of the water-colours in the album, especially those of sites outside Leinster, are based on drawings supplied by others, including the landscape artists William Ashford, Thomas Roberts, and George Barrett.

John Rocque's maps of Dublin continue to be studied as a fairly reliable primary source of information about urban development and expansion, not least since they record the city street plan before the improvements of the Wide Streets Commissioners which did so much to give the inner city its present layout. The great value of this new edition of the maps is Paul Ferguson's comprehensive indices of City and County which allow the maps to be used exactly as described in the title. These two books are valuable reminders of 18th-century interests in recording – both utilitarian and antiquarian – and of a lost landscape.

PHILIP MCEVANSONEYA is a Lecturer in the Department of the History of Art, Trinity College, Dublin.

The Irish Châteaux: In Search of the Descendants of the Wild Geese

BY RENAGH HOLOHAN WITH ILLUSTRATIONS BY JEREMY WILLIAMS

Lilliput Press 1999 p/b £9.99
188 pp. 52 b/w ills 1-901866-34-3

Toby Barnard

The deserved reputation of the Lilliput Press under its founder, Anthony Farrell, for care over the appearance of its books is amply confirmed by this attractive reprint. Originally published in 1989, the new edition recalls the Puffin classics issued during the 1940s and 1950s. The wispy and wistful drawings by Jeremy Williams of moated and spired castles remind of the deftness with which Lynton Lamb and Edward Ardizzone ornamented even commonplace works. In this case, the text needs considerable embellishment and it is for Williams's delicious decorations that this production will be treasured.

It is unclear at whom the writing is aimed. Renagh Holohan's tour of the present representatives in France of these exiled Irish and Anglo-Irish families uncovers a gallimaufry of the aggrieved and aggressive. Some have adapted with consummate ease to the values of modern society but others groan under what they regard as the unjust burden – imposed inevitably by socialists – of taxes and partible inheritance. Not the least of the confusions with which the author bespatters the book is the belief, voiced by several of the malcontents visited on the journey through France, that things were different (and better) in the Ireland from which their forbears departed. In practice, descent based on primogeniture was a gift from the hated English invaders of Ireland. The contemporary quarrelsomeness of members of these houses, at which

Jeremy WILLIAMS: The *Chateau de Sully*. From *The Irish Châteaux: In Search of the Descendants of the Wild Geese* by Renagh Holohon with illustrations by Jeremy Williams. '...it is for Williams's delicious decorations that this production will be treasured...'

Holohan hints, conjures up irresistibly the succession disputes of old Ireland. Piquant, too, is the obsession of these wild goslings with genealogies. In their sequestered havens, if they no longer cherish thoughts of revenge and a return to ancestral acres, they pore over pedigrees which – at the very least – link them with Charlemagne, Pepin and Brian Boru, if not with Adam or Noah.

From a journalist like Renagh Holohan one might have hoped for memorable vignettes but it is perhaps politeness towards erstwhile hosts and hostesses which inhibits her from expanding on what clearly could have been a notable gallery of eccentrics and rogues. Only occasionally is her bland tone interrupted by tartness. The Duc de Magenta, prone on his sun-lounger, alongside his 'girl friend', his sumptuous château of Sully closed against the hoi-polloi, raging against socialist iniquities, might have merited a longer passage. More sympathetic, and again crying out for expansive treatment, is the current head of the O'Byrnes. Sensibly enough, Edward O'Byrne has not encumbered himself with the title of Marquis de St Géry because he lacks the resources to support the empty dignity. Unlike some of the subjects here he has not called the world of commerce to his rescue.

The author draws no general conclusions about the wild geese as a breed. Probably unintentionally, the book reveals the varied reasons why the migrants took wing from Ireland. Not all were driven away by persecution; nor did all come of Catholic and Old Irish families. Ironically, a number who have adjusted best to their new habitats, like the Butlers, Burkes or de Warrens, belong to dynasties which had followed the Normans to England and then took part in the Cambro-Norman settlement of Ireland. More like spawning salmon than birds, the strongest have struggled back to the land of their origin. Surprising, too, is the presence among the exiles of apparently successful Irish Protestant families such as the Bartons and Exshaws.

However, this is not a study on which a great weight of scholarly interpretation should be loaded and anyone seeking a reliable history of these families must look elsewhere. Often it is unclear who is to blame for the many inaccuracies: the subjects who have fashioned an imagined past or the author. But, with an avowed intention of entertaining, as the scenes and their occupants rush past, there is much to divert, although it is a shame that the author allows so little time to linger. However, the breathless itinerary completed, we can at least return to savour the many evocative illustrations.

Toby Barnard is Keeper of Hertford College, Oxford.

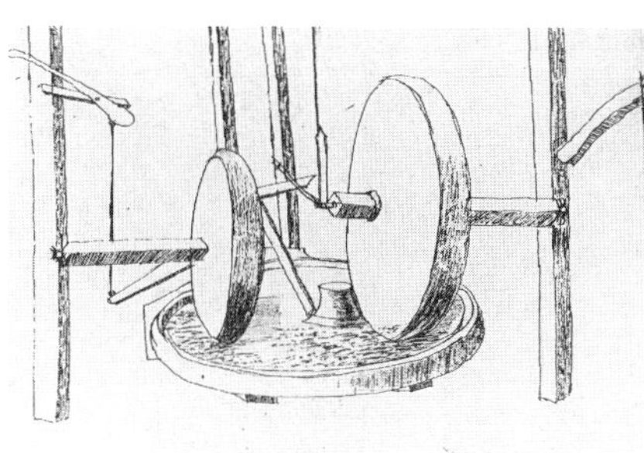

James Cavanah Murphy: *Plan of the Upper and Lower Part of the Mortar Machine at Worsley*, 1790. From *Building the Georgian City* by James Ayers. 'References to Ireland are rare and an early reference is embarrassingly ignorant in describing our distinguished scholar, author, and engineer, James Cavanah Murphy, as 'an Irish bricklayer.'

Building the Georgian City

By James Ayers

Yale University Press 1998 (h/b) £45

280 pp. 51 col i1lls 311 b/w ills 0-300-07548-0

Michael McCarthy.

This is a book so beautifully designed and illustrated that it is a joy to hold and to have. It is no small compliment to the author to say that it is also a delight to read. It is so full of detail as to materials and methods and costs that it provides a reference work for various aspects of the building trade in the 18th century. At the same time it is that rare thing, a technical book that is readable throughout.

Its nine chapters are supplemented by four Appendices of such particular content that their relevance to the text is oblique at best. These are followed by the most useful Glossary and an Index with figure references in bold type. The illustrations are rare and new to the literature for the most part, though always to the point and of the highest quality of reproduction in colour and in black and white.

The text is marshalled in successive chapters following the sequence normally to be found in the building of the Georgian city or the Georgian house of whatever dimensions: from the architects and builders, through sites and supplies in stone, brick and timber, to hardware, plumbers, glaziers, plasterers, and painters. The author is Director of the John Judkyn Memorial near Bath and his research findings are centred on Bath and Bristol principally, with reference to comparable museums in New England. But he keeps his eye on the London scene, mainly by reference to the holdings of Sir John Soane's incomparably rich Museum. He also has comprehensive knowledge of relevant patternbooks and ephemeral trade tracts.

Some generalisations are too broad to be acceptable; such is the assertion that 'In the mid century the 'bow window' was understood to be a bow on elevation not on plan. It was synonymous with the 'Venetian window' and even this was described as having been 'uncommon' at this time'. This is untenable historically in Ireland as well as in England. A reference on p.208 to the late Dorothy Stroud's monograph on Henry Holland is cited to suggest that Holland employed Bartoli in the oval hall of the south front of Stowe in 1775. But the text of Stroud quite rightly offers no support for such a reading. On the same page a reference to Geoffrey Beard's work is also misleading in respect of Joseph Alcott. He is described here as 'by trade a carpenter', though Beard quotes the man himself in his subscription to George Richardson's *Vitruvius Britannicus* of 1802, as 'Scagliola column-maker' and it is in that capacity that he is known to architectural history

References to Ireland are rare and an early reference is embarrassingly ignorant in describing our distinguished scholar, author, and engineer, James Cavanah Murphy as 'an Irish bricklayer' (p. 62). There is a more knowledgeable acquaintanceship shown when it comes to the research of Joseph McDonnell in a discussion of Rococo Irish plasterwork. At that point the author shows (Figs 305 and 307) ceilings from a two-roomed 'cabin' in Freshford, county Kilkenny, one Baroque in style and the other Neo-classical. These are designated as 'simply a rehearsal for work in the neighbouring big house.' That was Upper Court Manor in Freshford. The ceilings are lost now but an account of them, not noted by the author, was published by Desmond Guinness in *Ireland of the Welcomes* (Oct 1977).

MICHAEL MCCARTHY is Professor of the History of Art at University College Dublin.

The Pleasing Hours: The Grand Tour of James Caulfield, First Earl of Charlemont (1728-1799), Traveller, Connoisseur and Patron of the Arts

BY CYNTHIA O'CONNOR

The Collins Press, 1999 (h/b) £20

294 pp. 13 b/w ills 1-898256-66-7

Toby Barnard

It was in 1948 that Maurice Craig published his first book: a life of Charlemont. As with everything from that master, the biography can still be read with profit and pleasure. Its title, *The Volunteer Earl*, contrasts with Mrs O'Connor's, *The Pleasing Hours*, and, in part, this reflects the discoveries and altered perspectives of the intervening half century. Mrs O'Connor taps the large store of knowledge about grand tourism, to which she herself added signally. She lingers longer over Charlemont's exhilarating and innovative endeavours in Italy, Turkey and the Greek Islands. When the future earl disembarked in the Netherlands in 1747, he was taking a route well known for more than a century to those Irish seeking education or recreation. Indeed, Charlemont's own ancestors are to be encountered on the continent in the 1680s.

Charlemont, as Mrs O'Connor tantalisingly notes, although journeying in a predominantly Irish party, regarded himself as English. Moreover, his hosts generally took him at his own estimation. Indeed, even his servant in Rome, Barney, surely a Teige, was recorded as *inglese*. At the same time, Irish friars sprang to the defence of their fellow countryman despite their confessional differences. Mrs O'Connor suggests that Charlemont's stance of Englishness was intended to distance him in Rome from the embarrassing parvenus from Protestant Ireland, such as Joseph Leeson, Joseph Henry and Ralph Howard. But, since similar examples of such ethnic confusions and elisions occur among the Irish when abroad, it may tell of other attitudes.

After Richard LIVESAY: Lord Charlemont. From *The Pleasing Hours: The Grand Tour of James Caulfield, First Earl of Charlemont, Traveller, Connoisseur and Patron of the Arts* by Cynthia O'Connor. 'Charlemont', as Ms O'Connor tantalisingly notes, although journeying in a predominantly Irish party, regarded himself as English...'

Aided by the Levantine travel journals published in 1984 by W B Stanford and E J Finoploulos, we follow the young nobleman on his heroic expedition. Ardour in measuring and recording the hitherto unknown, notably Halicarnassus, was repeated in the bagnios and brothels to which the members of the group repaired. Charlemont's boon companion was Frank Burton, portly heir of Buncraggy in county Clare. Burton, written off by his always disapproving great-aunt, the widow of Castletown, Katherine Conolly, put his bulk to more unexpected uses. Among the amusements of Malta was a character with the 'talent of venting wind backwards ad liberium'. The man from Clare sought in vain to imitate the *pétomane*. Burton's presence also hints at an interesting Clare connection. Subsequently the county supplied Charlemont with expert medical advice through the demagogic apothecary, Charles Lucas, and then, belatedly, a fecund wife, Mary Hickman.

The biographer fully explores how Charlemont, once back in Ireland, applied what he had seen. He invested classicism with an ethical value. His buildings, centred on the Marino Casino and Charlemont House in Dublin, together with the collections which they housed, had exemplary functions. Although constrained by an income less ample than he needed, the earl nevertheless attended dutifully to his public responsibilities. A regular at the House of Lords; commander of the Volunteers; president of the new Academy: all are sketched in. Only the fad of sea-bathing, urged by Lucas and safely undertaken solely in Dublin Bay, kept the peer from his ancestral acres in Ulster. However, politics are not the author's prime concern. Rather she offers the most thorough summary of the connoisseurship displayed in his two Dublin houses. Here she is helped by the fortunate rediscovery of the medal cabinet which Chambers designed for Charlemont. Identified among the fixtures of Elveden in Suffolk, Mrs O'Connor first wrote about it in this journal in 1984. Thanks to her assured touch and measured judgement, Charlemont emerges as both more amiable and more sympathetic than Lord Burlington, to whom he is appropriately likened. Not only did both aspire to polite taste, but they spent heavily from their Irish rents to do so. In contrast to the habitually absent Burlington, Charlemont embellished Ireland. This charming life persuades of his virtues without hiding his vices.

TOBY BARNARD is Keeper of Hertford College, Oxford.

Mausolea Hibernica

BY MAURICE CRAIG AND MICHAEL CRAIG

Lilliput Press 1999 h/b £15.95

128 pp. 33 b/w ills 1-901866-30-0

Nicholas Robinson

Mausolea Hibernica, an elegant addition to many distinguished and eclectic titles from the Lilliput Press, is divided into two parts: Maurice Craig's introductory essay, bestrewn with vignettes, covers the whole field of Irish mausoleums, historically, sociologically, and architecturally. Thirty-three plates by Michael Craig, accompanied by short descriptions illustrate some of the finest and most interesting specimens. A picture book, they call it modestly in the preface and what a treat it is, with Michael's exquisite plates – suitably Lilliputian – and vintage Maurice text: erudite, laced with digressions, asides, quotations. ('Personally', says Samuel Beckett, 'I have no bone to pick with graveyards, I take the air there perhaps more willingly than elsewhere, when take the air I must. My sandwich, my banana, taste sweeter when I'm sitting on a tomb.')

And, of course, a definition: 'Some years ago I attempted one which the most distinguished of my contemporaries has done me the honour to adopt: "a funerary structure having the character of a roofed building, and large enough to stand up in, or at least having that appearance."'

If Irish mausolea tend to be more humble in scale of the Craig definition, they, too, contain much that is fascinating. One at Mainham, on the doorstep of Clongowes Wood College, is commended for 'some agreeably macabre touches.' And the Stephenson mausoleum at Kilbride, county Antrim is, after all, a miniature Taj Mahal built of cut stone, while reproduced on the jacket is Richard Malone's mausoleum at Kilbixy, county Westmeath, its design, pyramid on a cube, a nod to Queen Artemisia's original at Halicarnassus.

The book contains some splendid inscriptions and epitaphs. One commemorates, in 1821, 'a nobleman distinguished for the possession of those many eminent virtues which adorn life whether we consider him in the character of a husband, father, landlord or friend...' The subject of this encomium was the Rt Hon Charles Bingham, Lord Baron Clanmorris of Newbrook, county Mayo, the monument being erected by 'his affectionate and sorrowful widow, Baroness Clanmorris, as a memorial of conjugal affection.' I wonder if he is the same Lord Clanmorris described by Sir Jonah Barrington as a 'very savage nobleman' when he 'horse-whipped most severely in the public street' a 'very brave King's Counsel', John Philpot Curran? A caricature of that incident, published in London in 1791, is entitled *An Amorous Irish Barrister performing a Principal Character in a new Afterpiece called the Disagreeable Surprise!*

I have often thought that Michael Craig's work has something in common with that of a precision instrument-maker: what he draws has beauty as well as precision, while his eagle eye reflects an acute understanding of how it is built, how it works. Whether it is an architectural arrangement of fiendish complexity or (as in his previous book, *Fish Out of Water*) the subtly differing textures of various fish – be they gudgeon or stickleback or common carp – this technical virtuosity is put at the service of a wider artistic creativity, with results that are often dazzling.

Above all, *Mausolea Hibernica* is the collaboration of two very distinctive personalities, each a maestro, a collaboration enriched by the extraordinarily close bond between father and son. Let us salute them and their work (for as George Crabbe reminds us) 'monuments themselves memorials need.'

Michael CRAIG: *The Stephenson Mausoleum, Kilbride Co Antrim*. From *Mausolea Hibernica* by Maurice Craig and Michael Craig. 'The book is the collaboration of two very distinctive personalities, each a maestro, a collaboration enriched by the extraordinarily close bond between father and son.'

NICHOLAS ROBINSON *is the author of* Edmund Burke: A Life in Caricature *(1996).*

Dublin's Victorian Houses

MARY DALY, MONA HEARN, PETER PEARSON

A & A Farmar in Association with Sherry Fitzgerald 1998 h/b £20

170 pp. 17 col 69 b/w ills 1-899047-42-5

Jeremy Williams

Mary Daly contributes an introductory general history to this book and she is followed by Mona Hearn and Peter Pearson. Mona Hearn's contribution is the most explorative, even if it makes painful reading. It illuminates the world of Joyce's *Dubliners* and explains the emigration of so many intellectuals to London and Paris. Only the affluent paterfamilias had a comfortable, but hardly enviable, existence (though their clubs are barely mentioned). Indeed the entrepreneurs who created the city, its waterworks, its docks, and railways remain shadowy figures. The references to house builders are tantalisingly brief. Many of them were English fortune seekers on the run from a failed speculation in their birthplace, such as the architect, Daniel Robertson, who may have been responsible for Harcourt Terrace.

Coppinger Ashlin, not Askin, was the most prolific church architect in Ireland. There is a photograph of a lofty drawing room with Puginesque wallpaper but no location is given. Above all, the craftsmen still remain almost as anonymous as their medieval predecessors. Victorian Dublin still awaits a study like Paul Larmour's *Belfast* which revealed so many who helped to create that city, but Belfast City Hall preserves the names of all the engineers and architects who applied for connections to the city's water supply. Dublin – due to its more momentous history – has lost its files.

The final section is by Peter Pearson, whose architectural study of Dún Laoghaire and Rathdown, *Between the*

CLARINDA PARK, DUN LAOGHAIRE: From *Dublin's Victorian Houses* by Mary Daly, Mona Hearn & Peter Pearson. 'Victorian Dublin still awaits a study like Paul Larmour's Belfast....'

Mountains and the Sea (reviewed in this volume, below), has just been published. While that is crammed with information on architects, artists, craftsmen, and their patrons, his contribution here is a concise manual on restoration which is informed by a lifetime of experience. He performs a valuable service for would-be restorers who have so often been the helpless victims of experts and builders untrained in conservation. Even house-selling blurbs are more historical and informative. William Orpen is no longer confused with his half-brother and credited with every partly-tiled villa in Carrickmines. The support of the auctioneers, Sherry and Fitzgerald, for books like this will – one hopes – start a new trend.

JEREMY WILLIAMS is the author of A Companion Guide to Architecture in Ireland 1837-1921 *(1994).*

Between the Mountains and the Sea: Dún Laoghaire/Rathdown County

BY PETER PEARSON

O'Brien Press 1998 h/b £25

381 pp. 610 b/w ills. 0862785820

Peter Murray

In 1890 a series of articles written by Weston St John Joyce for the *Evening Telegraph* was reprinted under the title *Rambles Around Dublin*. Joyce noted that Dublin 'is one of the most picturesquely situated cities in Europe, yet comparatively few of its inhabitants appear to either know or believe this to be the case.' A century later, Peter Pearson believing that it is still the case, has provided a substantial reminder in *Between the Mountain and the Sea*, a cross between an architectural gazetteer and a social history. In the course of 380 pages, illustrated with 700 photographs, engravings and maps, Pearson takes the reader on a series of rambles through environs of what some years ago would have been called South County Dublin but which is now correctly termed Dun Laoghaire-Rathdown County.

A hundred years ago, Joyce recommended that the cyclist or walker should purchase the 'distinct and correct' one inch Ordnance Survey map of Dublin, costing one shilling, cut it into squares and paste it onto calico. For the area covered by Pearson, this map would have remained substantially correct up to fifty years ago.

A century ago, trains left every hour from Harcourt Street to Dundrum. From Dundrum, it was a brisk walk to Two Rock Mountain, from where there is a panoramic view of Pearson's domain. Standing on its peak, St John Joyce was moved to exclaim 'One cannot fail to be struck by the matchless beauty of the district, which excited in turn the cupidity of every race that visited it, from the Firbolgs, De Danaans, and Milesians down to the Danes and the Anglo-Normans.' Joyce failed to mention those other tribes who so successfully invaded the area in more recent times, the lawyers, bankers and merchants of Dublin, to whom cupidity was not an unknown virtue. It is their houses and villas, extinct, extant, and defunct, which form the substance of Pearson's book. By the 1970s, the maps had changed dramatically, as substantial housing estates were built at Stillorgan, Galloping Green, and Glenageary. The spread of the city is further recorded in the 1987 OS map, the area between Sandyford and Galloping Green being transformed from light brown into the slate grey of suburbia. To the east, new housing engulfed Ballybrack in the same period, and like a brush fire leaped ahead to transform both Shankill and Bray into substantial satellites. This process continues apace today.

A century ago, descending from Two

MARLAY HOUSE, RATHFARNHAM: From *Between the Mountains and the Sea: Dun Laoghaire/Rathdown County* by Peter Pearson. The house is currently being restored by Dun Laoghaire-Rathdown County Council. Pearson's book is 'a cross between an architectural gazetteer and a social history...'

Rock mountain, St John Joyce passed 'the straggling, poverty-stricken village of Bornaculla, the inhabitants of which eke out a scanty subsistence by stone-cutting and quarrying.' This village is not marked on my Ordnance Survey map, but, emulating Tim Robinson, Pearson has it located on his map 17. There was considerable employment for labourers in quarrying stone for the new villas and castellated houses that dotted the bare hills of Killiney and Dalkey. More congenial employment could be found in the gardens and greenhouses, but perhaps the least congenial employment for labourers was to be found at the lead mines of Ballycorus, where a large stone-built flue ran the best part of a mile up the mountain, to a tall chimney, cleverly designed to carry off the poisonous fumes to someone else's land. This landmark chimney, with its external cantilevered spiral stone staircase, survives today. At Ballycorus, Pearson records, the flue was regularly cleaned and 'valuable arsenic was collected by men who scraped the walls', but in true Victorian spirit he makes no mention of any adverse effects on their health. He includes in his excellent gazetteer some houses of manual workers, such as a traditional quarryman's cottage at Ticknock, or Larkins' Forge and cottage at Baker's Corner. Pearson himself is no stranger to hazardous occupations. He has spent much of his life clambering through derelict ruins, retrieving sections of decorative plasterwork, woodwork and cast iron. The book is illustrated with some of these treasures which form a museum of architectural decoration in themselves.

While not making any claims to being a definitive work (inevitably, many interesting houses have been omitted) *Between the Mountains and the Sea* is marvellous both for the detail of the text and for the wealth of photographs and engravings which illustrate Pearson's peregrinations. Fine little maps abound, the houses listed in the gazetteer indicated by little symbols; those destroyed marked by a diagonal line. If nothing else, the book shows how, at one easy stroke, as in a game of *Monopoly*, two centuries and more of architectural heritage can disappear. The book is also embellished with photographs taken by the author, as well as photographs from the 'sprightly nonagenarian', Daniel Gillman, of Bray, and commissioned photographs by Robert Vance. It is beautifully printed and bound, by O'Brien Press, which the title page tells us, 'receives assistance from the Arts Council'. But evidently not with their spelling. Such minor quibbles apart, *Between the Mountains and the Sea* is a magnificent achievement.

Peter Murray is Director of the Crawford Municipal Gallery, Cork.

Irish Houses and Gardens from the Archives of Country Life

By Sean O'Reilly

Aurum Press 1998 h/b £35

192 pp. *200 b/w ills* 1 85410 580 9

John Coleman

For over one hundred years *Country Life* has been publishing articles on British and Irish country houses illustrated with specially-commissioned photographs. The quality of the photographs and the number of houses covered have ensured that the magazine has accumulated a unique photographic archive which, together with *The Georgian Society Records* published in five volumes in the years following 1913, provides the most comprehensive early record of Irish architecture. From this archive, Sean O'Reilly has selected two hundred photographs, most of which are from glass plate negatives and many of which are published for the first time as they were not used in the original *Country Life* articles for which they were commissioned. There are chapters on twenty houses.

Although Irish interiors had featured in *Country Life* in a series of articles by Lord Powerscourt in 1899, it was not until 1910 that a growing interest in Georgian architecture led to an exploration of the Irish contribution to the genre. At the same time, some recently-completed houses such as those by Lutyens at Heywood, Howth and Lambay were included.

Sean O'Reilly's introduction provides a thought-provoking analysis of *Country Life's* coverage of these Irish houses. Rightly, he pays tribute to the authors Christopher Hussey and, later, Mark Girouard and John Cornforth, who considered these houses in such depth; and he acknowledges the role the magazine has played in providing a forum for the work of Irish scholars such as Maurice Craig, the Knight of Glin, Edward McParland, and Alastair Rowan. The text which accompanies the photographs of each house combines information from the original articles with a critique of the original text and photographic material as well as incorporating new scholarship about the houses and up-to-date information on their current state.

W E Hensen was principal photographer at *Country Life* from 1916-57 and, understandably, many of the photographs are his. O'Reilly remarks in relation to Hensen that, in his anxiety to produce aestheticised interiors, he required the household 'to be on hand to pull blinds as required and move quantities of furniture; lawns had to be re-mowed if the lines ran the wrong way, and branches – and even once a tree – had to be felled if they were in the way of a composition.' This means that one must regard the evidence provided by the photographs with regard to the arrangement of contents with some caution. O'Reilly wonderfully illustrates this by comparing a photograph by Henson of the hall at Castletown Cox with a photograph of the same room in *The Georgian Society Record*. In photographing the interiors of the vacant Charleville Forest, the magazine went so far as to install furniture temporarily from another family property, Belvedere, county Westmeath.

There is interesting information to be gleaned from the photographs of picture collections. The full-length portrait of King George III at Caledon is from the studio of Sir Joshua Reynolds and not by Sir Thomas Lawrence as suggested by O'Reilly; in the drawing room at Heywood there is a very fine full-length portrait of a gentleman that looks as if it might be by George Romney and could represent Michael Frederick Trench, cousin of the Earl of Clancarty and builder of the house; the saloon at Carton features Reynolds's

CHARLEVILLE FOREST, CO OFFALY: From *Irish Houses and Gardens from the Archives of Country Life* by Sean O'Reilly. 'In photographing the interiors of the vacant Charleville Forest, the magazine went so far as to install furniture temporarily from Belvedere, Co Westmeath.'

superb seated portrait of the 2nd Duke of Leinster over the mantle (now in a private collection in the US) and it is flanked by William Ashford's large-scale landscapes of the Carton estate, acquired by the current owner of the house from the present Duke of Leinster some years ago. The feature on Russborough includes an important photograph of the new Dining Room (formerly the Library) including the series of landscapes by the late- 18th-century Irish painter, George Barrett (now in the National Gallery of Ireland). The Earl of Milltown must have commissioned the Barretts for the house, considering the peculiar dimensions of the one over the mantle and the specially-made cartouches that have decorative features in common with the niches in the hall. As the house was photographed in 1935, when occupied by a member of the Daly family of Dunsandle, county Galway, it is interesting to note Reynolds's portrait of Denis Daly MP over the chimneypiece in the hall. (Incidentally, O'Reilly elevates the late Sir Alfred Beit, who was a baronet, to the peerage as Lord Beit on two occasions.)

On glancing through the book, it is remarkable to find that so many of the houses featured have survived, some in the hands of their original owners while others have found new life, ready to be photographed and written about all over again.

JOHN COLEMAN is an art historian and Operations Manager of the Chester Beatty Library in Dublin Castle.

Mary Carbery's West Cork Journal 1898-1901, or 'From the Back of Beyond'

EDITED BY JEREMY SANDFORD

Lilliput Press 1998 h/b £14.95

158 pp. 10 b/w ills 1-874675-36-8

Homan Potterton

Reading the reviews of Juanita Carberry's recently-published, *Child of Happy Valley*, I was tempted to pick up again James Fox's *White Mischief* which details life in Kenya's Happy Valley around the time that Lord Erroll was found on the floor of his Buick with a bullet through his head. That was in 1941 and there followed a celebrated murder trial with Jock Delves Broughton – the husband of Erroll's lover, Diana – in the dock and Juanita's stepmother, June Carberry, as a principal witness for the defence. June Carberry was the third wife of John Evans-Freke who at the age of six had become the 10th Baron Carbery of Castle Freke, county Cork. Having dazzled the citizenry of his native county with his daring as an aviator (he landed in Blackrock), Lord Carbery had, by the time of Happy Valley, lost one wife through divorce (on the grounds that he was in the habit of taking a cattle-whip to her) and another in a flying accident; he had dropped the use of his title (adding an 'r' to his surname in the process); had adopted the pretence of being an American; and had purchased an estate in Kenya where he had settled very comfortably into the atmosphere of adultery, alcohol, and altitude that characterised life in the foothills of the Aberdares: the Happy Valley. Lord Carbery was given to thrashing: apart from his wife, he thrashed the servants, he thrashed his daughter, and he encouraged her stepmother (and her governess) to do the same. As light relief, he compelled Juanita to swim in the harbour at Mombassa where the local slaughterhouse was known to attract sharks: an indignity which, if anything, was more pleasant than most of the other ordeals to which he subjected her. Not for nothing had Lord Carbery been born the heir to Castle Freke although it was some time after it had been burned down (in 1910) that he completely assumed the nature which the designation of his inheritance implied. In short, the 10th Lord Carbery was a fiend.

Believing, as one may do, that parents must be allowed to take some of the credit for the way their offspring develop, it was with some interest that I took up the diary of Lord Carbery's mother written in the years 1898-1901 when Lord Carberry (as he already was) was aged between six and nine.

So, what was Mother Carbery actually like? An Englishwoman, she met her future husband at a May Ball in Cambridge and married him the following November. She was twenty-three at the time. Her husband, already a consumptive, was to die eight years later leaving her, as mistress of Castle Freke, with two young sons.

Now, there are Englishwomen who have married into Ireland and have loved everything that they found there; and there are Englishwomen who have married into Ireland and have lived out a life of hell. It was all to do with the rain. Mary Carbery loved rain – 'The rain is coming down, not in drops, but in rods infinitely fine' – and as a consequence, she loved Ireland as well. She also loved her tenants, the peasantry in their cabins, lunatics, beggars, tinkers, stories of fairies, superstitions, Gaelic, Irish history, the dying, and she loved nature. 'I am obsessed by nature she wrote' and she was. Flowers, bees, birds, the bracken, and the bell-heather were as humans to her. She was fey and disliked 'society' but had a sense of duty when it came to carrying out good works. She writes in a lyrical way and in her attempts to capture the language of the natives, the obvious comparison is with Somerville and Ross; but it is not a comparison that stands up to scrutiny and she does not have their sense of humour.

But what did she do to her eldest son (Jacky, she calls him in her journal) to turn him into a monster? We can blame the Inquisition in Cork. When she was pregnant with him and living in a villa above Algiers (for her husband's health), she had a nightmare that the Inquisition had come to Rosscarbery. 'I would rather be burnt,' Lady Carbery told them, 'than join the Church of Rome.' The Inquisitors handed her a slip of paper. 'We should have been obliged to burn you at the stake,' it read. 'However, as you are expecting a child, you are reprieved.'

LORD CARBERY: From *Mary Carbery's West Cork Journal, 1898-1901*. Edited by Jeremy Sandford. Inheriting the title at the age of six, the 10th Baron Carbery of Castle Freke, Co Cork was to become one of the most-notorious members of Kenya's Happy Valley set in the 1930s and '40s.

HOMAN POTTERTON *is Editor of* Irish Arts Review.

Irish Conservation Directory

EDITED BY NIAMH MCGUINNE

Archaeology Ireland 1998 p/b £7.95

170 pp. 0-9512807-1-6

Traditional Building and Conservation Skills: Register of Practitioners 1998

Irish Georgian Society 1998 h/b £20

Judith Hill

The effect of reading a conservation directory from cover to cover is to become aware of oneself as an agent of destruction: your elbows ready to push precariously-placed ceramics, your fingers prepared to deposit moist or inky stains on a clear stretch of paper, your watch liable to snag fine cottons or silks, not to mention your inveterate negligence which fails to record cracking, iridescence, flaking, rising damp, discolouration, warping, or your general clumsiness which means that you grasp chairs by their back rails and pile porcelain in the sink ready for washing. The world of conservation is the material world seen through a microscope. Yet, while the *Irish Conservation Directory* alarms, it also placates and mollifies. It tells you how to clean, how to handle, when to call in the expert, and who that might be. It is gentle and encouraging with its advice. There is no room for jargon here. It is quietly authoritative in tone. It is, though, palpably incomplete.

In many ways this directory is expressive of the contemporary conservation/restoration scene in Ireland. In other words, as a relatively new activity on a significant scale, conservation expertise is evolving and the client base is growing. More people now have the money, the interest, and the desire to consider that their heirlooms and purchases might warrant conservation and they must consider the distinctions between preventive or passive conservation (the steps taken to prevent further decay or reduce its rate), restoration (in most contexts referring to repairs and additions), and conservation (intervention to redress damage) which this directory repeatedly defines in the different sections. This brings one to the beguiling dilemma of the conservator: whether to aim for the perfect fit, the immaculate join, the deceptively-identical look, or to announce the impossibility of exactly matching a particular piece of aged walnut with a modern infill and let the difference show. The summaries of 'gilding' or 'glassware' or 'horology' or 'musical instruments' (the categories are interestingly inconsistent), take the reader from material composition, the likely processes of decay, and advice about cleaning and handling, to the lists of further reading and useful addresses; the salvation of the expert. Here, unfortunately, the directory can disappoint, for the lists are often small.

This is where the Irish Georgian Society's Register of Skills comes in. For, in the area of building technology, which in fact overlaps many of the areas covered by the Irish Conservation Directory down to 'clock repairers' and 'organ restorers', it manages much longer lists of practitioners. Cheaply produced, it invites its readers to contribute to its updating. As is appropriate for an activity where skill and experience are essential, it attempts to indicate levels of these for each entry. Unfortunately it is anything but ubiquitous, available only at the Irish Georgian Society book shop in its Merrion Square basement. It is notably terse in its introductory remarks. In many ways the two directories, with their different strengths and weaknesses, complement each other nicely. Together they announce the coming of age of conservation in Ireland.

JUDITH HILL *is the author of* Irish Public Sculpture: A History *(1998).*

BALBRIGGAN LIBRARY: From *Irish Carnegie Libraries: A Catalogue and Architectural History* by Brendan Grimes. 'One of sixty-two public libraries which were, to a large extent, the gift of Andrew Carnegie to the people of Ireland...'

Irish Carnegie Libraries: A Catalogue and Architectural History

BY BRENDAN GRIMES

Irish Academic Press 1998 h/b £39.50

278 pp. 50 b/w ills 0-7165-2618-2

Peter Pearson

Many libraries in Ireland are of a great age and some, such as Marsh's Library in Dublin, possess a unique sense of antiquity. A considerable amount has been written about these important libraries but Ireland also possesses a remarkable legacy of some sixty-two public libraries which were, to a large extent, the gift of Andrew Carnegie to the people of Ireland. These were endowed between the years 1897 and 1913, and the buildings date mainly from the early years of the 20th century.

The arrival of a new publication which is devoted exclusively to the study of a particular aspect of the history of Irish architecture is always to be welcomed, but especially so when the subject is one which has never been thoroughly examined before.

With its subtitle 'a catalogue and architectural history', Grimes's book is a revealing and exhaustive study. It puts together a most useful catalogue of all sixty-eight Carnegie Libraries in Ireland, and includes architectural sketches, ground plans, and photographs. It is attractively presented and has an appropriately-restrained dust jacket featuring a watercolour of Skerries Library.

The first half of the book describes the life of Andrew Carnegie and discusses the origin of the public library as we know it. An interesting map shows the uneven distribution of the libraries which were curiously concentrated in counties Dublin, Down, Antrim, Cork, Kerry, and Limerick. By far the greatest concentration of Carnegie Libraries lay in Dublin, Limerick, and Kerry. Grimes explains how Carnegie would only assist a community which was prepared to help itself and had already taken the initiative by acquiring a site on which to build a library.

The library buildings were in some towns often the most distinguished architectural feature to be seen. The Carnegie Libraries at Rathmines, Skerries, and Clondalkin are among the more grandiose but there were many delightful small examples too, such as the stone-fronted library at Glencullen.

The book is especially timely and useful as the comprehensive listing of buildings throughout the State will soon become a mandatory function for all local authorities, who are, of course, the owners of most Carnegie Libraries. If I have any quibble, it is with the publishers and more particularly with the printers. The reproduction of such an interesting photographic record is in many cases rather grey and lacks sharpness. This criticism could also be made of another important book by the same publishers, *Irish Stone Bridges* by O'Keefe and Simington (1991). However, it would be unfair to single out just one Irish publisher as being guilty in this respect, for nearly all of them appear to accept less than the best when it comes to black and white reproduction! Contrast the quality of pictures in Thames and Hudson's *Irish Art and Architecture* or Yale's *Irish Follies and Garden Buildings*.

It is also remarkable that with all the boasting and bragging about how computers have revolutionised publishing, the end product is no better looking than it was a hundred years ago! Having made my plea, I must say that Brendan Grimes's book is nonetheless beautiful and the pictures are of a decent size.

Irish Carnegie Libraries is a scholarly and accurate account of the subject and should serve as a good model for similar books on subjects such as Irish Workhouses or Courthouses.

PETER PEARSON *is the author of* Between the Mountains and the Sea: Dún Laoghaire-Rathdown County *(1998)*.

An Age of Innocence: Irish Culture 1930-1960

BY BRIAN FALLON

Gill and Macmillan 1998 h/b £19.99

295 pp. 0-7171-2461-4

Terence Brown

It is Brian Fallon's contention in this maturely-reflective, thought-provoking essay that the period covered in its pages has been too harshly judged both by historians and by current popular opinion. What can usefully be termed de Valera's Ireland, the place Benedict Kiely named the 'Grocer's Republic', has, he insists, been too easily identified by historians and commentators as an era of isolationism, censorship, Catholic bigotry, and cultural stagnation, which make it seem a terrible betrayal of the ideals of pre-revolutionary Ireland.

At various points in his argument Fallon wisely grants that there is indisputably a case to answer – the book censorship was often an absurdity; the Church was frequently philistine, its clergy lacking in general culture; aggressive nativism had a strident voice. As he admits: 'The oddity, the crankery and the ingrown quality which are an essential aspect of the decades this book is about must seem virtually incomprehensible to young people today'. Yet this is far from the full story, he insists, given the several terrible disadvantages with which the country had to contend in the period. The record of cultural achievement in those thirty years when de Valera set the tone of public life and ruled in cunningly authoritarian fashion, is far from discreditable. For the new nation possessed limited economic resources without quite being impoverished; there was the trauma of linguistic loss to recover from (and Fallon reckons the loss of Irish a desperate national blow) which 'many commentators prefer to ignore, or at least to discount'), in their assessments of the period; and the country possessed no substantial upper-middle class, with considerable traditions of liberal thought, to act as a steadying hand on the tiller of national life. Once these things are properly appreciated, Fallon implies, the wonder is not that Ireland in those years achieved so little but that it achieved so much.

One of the reasons the de Valera years in Ireland have had such a bad press, Fallon suggests, is because they were preceded by the era of Yeats and Joyce. Many critics, especially those from abroad, have accordingly read the period in question as a disappointing Yeatsian aftermath or have seen modern Ireland as the place Joyce was forced to flee. To counter these simplifications Fallon offers astute accounts of Joyce and Yeats in their Irish and European contexts and complicates our sense of the Irish Literary Revival with sympathetic portraits of George Moore and George Russell (Russell is saluted as 'a great European liberal'). The effect is to allow subsequent literary achievement in Ireland to seem continuous with the complex reality of the Irish Literary Revival and not a decline from former glories.

This forensic strategy permits Fallon to explore the literary, intellectual, religious, artistic and journalistic life of three decades with a nice critical tact. It is good to be reminded in his pages of the generation of writers and poets who made real contributions to letters in the era before Arts Council Grants and the media hype of current cultural self-congratulation. Fallon's is a well-stocked mind and he makes an agreeable companion in his several forays into the cultural detail of pre-60s Ireland (a well-judged chapter on music and the English composers who adopted the Celtic mode made me keen for more).

Yet it is Fallon's very balance and wide-ranging good sense that make his argument read at times as a sustained plea in mitigation. He can so readily set the Ireland of de Valera, censorship, and a public rhetoric of moral crusade in broadly comparativist contexts – in the contexts of Catholic and Latin Europe, of other parts of the English-speaking world, of European history as ongoing process, in which forces akin to those that affected Irish life also held sway – that almost anything can be understood and therefore made to seem, if not acceptable, then pardonable. For all his wide reading and assured knowledge of 20th-century art and literature, he does not seem willing to acknowledge that the definitive European realities of this grim century have been discontinuity, crisis and rampant disorder, to which Irish social and cultural developments over three decades were one troubling set of responses. In this awful century, now ending, no-one has enjoyed 'an age of innocence'.

Terence Brown is the author of Ireland: A Social and Cultural History 1922-1985 *(1981).*

Irish Country: A Personal Look at Decorating with Pottery, Fabrics and Furniture in the Irish Style

By Nicholas Mosse

London Ebury Press, 1998 h/b £19.99

144pp. 140 col ills 1 3579 10 8642

Irish Country Style: A Celebration of Ireland's Enduring Charms

By Bill Laws

Aurum Press 1999 h/b £16.99

138pp. 129 col 5 b/w ills 1 85410 523

Claudia Kinmonth

Both of these volumes compete to provide striking colour photography and an easy, accessible prose (without footnotes) and both share similarly generous formats with red and gold spines. But from there the similarities fade. Nicholas Mosse must be one of Ireland's best known and most successful potters and his traditional spongeware features frequently amongst Debbie Patterson's photographs; as such it is a brilliant showcase for his work. Each chapter on pottery, fabrics, and furniture includes a project for the reader to try with step by step instructions, photographs, and templates closely allied to Mosse's own pottery designs, right down to instructions on how to make a cup rack.

Nicholas Mosse: *Irish Cups and Pots,* From *Irish Country: A Personal Look at Decorating with Pottery, Fabrics, and Furniture in the Irish Style* by Nicholas Mosse. 'Mosse must be one of Ireland's best known potters and ...the book is a brilliant showcase for his work...'

For me the best chapter is where Mosse is on home ground, discussing pottery and particularly describing some of the history and evolution of Irish potteries but it left me hungry for more detailed information about his sources (there is neither a bibliography, nor references to illustrations from the text). Mosse mentions only one of Ireland's increasingly impressive museums and folkparks, many of which display Irish material culture in its context with complete explanations. Instead, readers are provided with a list of 'useful addresses', including those of over two dozen antique dealers, and a section devoted to 'buying furniture' which will inevitably encourage further export of this increasingly rare resource.

He admits that 'Our ancestors would have been horrified to allow cheap wood to be seen naked in their homes, and stripped pine would have caused total apoplexy.' Yet nearly half his illustrations of furniture lack paintwork. As a furniture historian, I cannot ignore his careless use of terminology, especially when he alludes to the settle bed as 'a box bed' and then fails to provide an illustration of one to explain its ingenious design.

Bill Laws's book provides a contrast by incorporating a far broader range of inspiration for his (equally subjective) interpretation of the same subject. Unlike Mosse, Laws is the author of a variety of other books such as *Old English Farmhouses*, *Traditional Houses of Rural Spain*, *Traditional Houses of Rural France*, and *The Perfect Country Cottage*. One might expect a book on style to focus on interiors but his most fascinating and authoritative chapter is on 'Irish Gardens'. Although much of the text draws on other familiar histories, aptly matched by illustrations from museums, folkparks, and photographic archives, his descriptions of furniture almost inevitably gloss over the unpalatable context of hardship, famine, and poverty which gave rise to such an ingenious range of vernacular designs. His text is wide ranging, including a chapter on 'The Irish Province', another on 'Irish Country Life', and one on 'Irish Bathrooms and Bedrooms', although the latter necessarily moves up the social scale and draws on contemporary rather than traditional arrangements. He incorporates quotes from Yeats, Shaw, Allingham, and other early Irish writers decoratively amongst the illustrations but usually the quotes (like all the text) lack any dates or footnotes. One wonders, moreover, if the following statement is an apt advertisement for Irish country style: '...our mad colour schemes. There is not an ounce of good taste about them...but they all add up to good fun.' A better commentator might have been Synge, who observed in 1905 that a fireside quilted bed 'lacked the ordered neatness of an English Peasant's cottage, but [was] picturesque to a degree, with dancing flame and Rembrandtesque masses of shadow, and highlights on occasional spots of colour.'

CLAUDIA KINMONTH is author of the award winning book, Irish Country Furniture 1700-1950, *and is Senior Research Fellow at Buckinghamshire University College.*

ALFRED COCHRANE'S BEDROOM: From *Irish Houses: Eclectic and Unique Interiors* by Ianthe Ruthven. 'As for the master bedroom, it would surely have appealed hugely to Oscar Wilde and he might not have felt that either he or the wallpaper would have to go...'

Irish Houses: Eclectic and Unique Interiors

BY IANTHE RUTHVEN

Gill and Macmillan 1998 (h/b) £19.99

176 pp. 195 col. ills 0-7171-2754-0

Ann Cremin

This is a most attractive book and is all set to join the weighty tomes produced in their times by Desmond Guinness and the late Brian de Breffny. The author, lanthe Ruthven, who is also the photographer, has hand picked a few examples in differing styles to illustrate her point about what she calls 'absent presences', by which she means that the home in the mind can be so much more durable than bricks or stones. She has done some serious research and has managed to encompass what might seem a bewildering array of styles and appearances in well chosen pictures.

The book is divided into five main chapters, going from 'Militant Grandeur' to 'Restoration and Revival' and taking in other genres along the way. Each theme is meticulously presented with a quick sketch of the history of the house and its owners as well as an account of what motivated the inclusion of each particular gem. It starts inevitably with Castletown and Castlecoole and proceeds to show us three Dublin Georgian houses in the throes of loving and careful restorations.

The book proceeds apace, with good examples in the 'Romantic Elegance' chapter of houses which are actually lived in and utilised as dwellings and are not just museums and showcases. It becomes very intriguing with the 'Sweet Disorder' chapter, where Tender Loving Care often replaces expensive restoration and refurbishments. The houses in this and the next chapter, 'Versions of the Pastoral', are appealing in the manner by which their various owners 'fell in love' with some place and made it comfortable and original. The most astonishing, to my mind, is the dwelling of the Birdmen of Mullett. The Coyle brothers have remained in their mother's old cottage together for over forty years. Passionate about wild-life and birds, they have created a miniature folk and nature museum, while breeding birds as well as drawing them, and turning out *papier maché* versions. It is reminiscent of other 'originals', such as the Facteur Cheval in France, which are now accorded the status of 'artworks'.

My personal favourite house in the book is Corke Lodge in Bray where Alfred Cochrane has made a witty dwelling, mixing with great panache and elegance many variegated forms of culture. The Mediterranean feel of the conservatory, alongside the post-modernist idiom of solid plate glass tables and elaborate contemporary furniture, provide the house with a delightful cosmopolitan ambience. As for the master bedroom, it would surely have appealed hugely to Oscar Wilde and he might not have felt that either he or the wallpaper would have to go.

The photographs are well thought out and chosen, enhancing the text and providing a clear idea of scale, both inside the houses and in their surrounding landscapes. This is altogether a delightful book and certainly good value for money. It will grace many a guest room in the coming months and should do well in a European market with the current craze for all things Irish.

ANN CREMIN *is an international art critic.*

Into the Light: An Illustrated Guide to the Photographic Collections in the National Library of Ireland.

BY SARAH ROUSE

National Library of Ireland, 1998 p/b £9.95

120 pp., 12 col 74 b/w ills 0-907328-29-6

Highlights of the Print Collection National Gallery of Ireland.

BY JANE MACAVOCK

National Gallery of Ireland 1998 p/b £5

48 pp. 11 col 40 b/w ills 0-903-16291-1

Margarita Cappock

Into the Light by Sarah Rouse was published to coincide with the opening of the National Library's new Photographic archive in Meeting House Square, Temple Bar. Located in a purpose-built building, this new archive houses the Library's extensive collection of 300,000 photographs. Rouse's guide describes, indexes and selectively illustrates approximately ninety different collections. Photographs of Irish people, places and events, from the mid-1840s to 1996 are the main focus of this guide. The format of the individual entries makes it easy to consult and includes information on the provenance of the images, the timespan covered and how to gain access to the collections. A short description of the contents of each collection is accompanied by a representative image. Whereas the Lawrence collection is probably the best-known and most popular source for photographic reproductions, this guide highlights other lesser-known and equally fascinating collections. The range of collections include examples of early photography, topographical views, portraits, amateur snapshots, the arts, family photographs, industry and transport, regional collections, and modern photographs. Experimental photography is also represented in the collections with John Joly colour slides, 19th-century stereoscopic views, wide-angle and three-dimensional formats. A helpful glossary of photographic terms, chronological analysis and collection size is listed at the back of the book. On the whole, it is another beautifully-produced publication from the National Library and will no doubt prove to be an excellent guide for researchers.

Published to accompany an exhibition of prints from the National Gallery of Ireland's permanent collection, *Highlights from the Print Collection* is a catalogue of a selection of prints dating from the 1630s to the 1970s. The format consists of fifty-one individual entries which feature a short biographical note on the artist/printmaker, a description of the work, and an accompanying image. Some of the more notable prints include those by Giovanni Battista Piranesi, William Hogarth, John Smith, James McArdell, Thomas Rowlandson, James Malton, James Barry, Joseph Malachy Kavanagh, Henri Matisse, Albert Gleizes, and Stanley William Hayter. The text is by Jane MacAvock and a glossary of terms is provided by Niamh McGuinne. Overall, this publication is somewhat disappointing. It is poorly served by a weak, unstructured introduction which fails to explain the criteria of selection for the images and provides little contextual or historical information on printmaking. The exclusion of information relating to the circulation of prints, the leading countries involved and the developments in the art of printmaking throughout the centuries is a serious omission. A strictly chronological approach was taken whereas a thematic one might have been more interesting. As it is, the text does not read easily and would have benefited from more rigorous editing. The catalogue is nicely produced and of a manageable size with an emphasis firmly on the 18th rather than the 19th and 20th centuries. In conclusion, this publication does not maintain the standards of previous Gallery publications.

DR MARGARITA CAPPOCK *completed her doctoral thesis on the depiction of Ireland in the* Illustrated London News *from 1842 to 1900. She is Project Manager of the Francis Bacon Studio at the Hugh Lane Municipal Gallery of Modern Art.*

KISSING THE BLARNEY STONE IN THE 19TH CENTURY. From *Into the Light: An Illustrated Guide to the Photographic Collections in the National Library of Ireland* by Sarah Rouse. One of over 300,000 photographs in the National Library which the Guide describes, indexes and selectively illustrates.

Art in Transition: Guidelines for Transition Year Students

BY MARIE BOURKE

National Gallery of Ireland 1998 p/b £9.95
66 pp. 12 b/w ills 0-90316-2814

Antoinette Murphy

The intended audience for *Art in Transition* is primarily transition year teachers who may wish to visit the National Gallery of Ireland with their students. The book, which has an attractive cover featuring a reproduction in colour of A *Bouquet of Flowers* by Jan Van Huysum (1682-1749) and *Fiery Leaves* by Jack P Hanlon (1913-68) on the back, draws attention to the services provided by the Education Department of the National Gallery of Ireland for visiting teachers and students. Initially the book sets out guidelines for a successful gallery visit, with a strong emphasis on forward planning. The bulk of the book, however, consists of a series of ten themed worksheets, running to almost forty pages. Each worksheet deals with four masterpieces chosen from the National Collection and contains line drawings of the selected works of art, a few facts about each one, and a number of questions to engage the interest of the students. The danger of this approach is that the students may concentrate on the worksheets instead of on the overall aesthetic impact of the paintings and sculptures themselves. It seems a pity that at least some of the chosen masterpieces from the Collection could not have been reproduced in colour or in black and white instead of these line drawings. Some good advice is given about follow-up work in the classroom towards the end of the book, such as making worksheets, setting up a classroom museum, and organising an exhibition. It concludes with a summary of some current facts about the National Gallery of Ireland. A more expanded version of this summary at the beginning of the book giving a short history of the Gallery and its most prestigious acquisitions, such as benefactions from the George Bernard Shaw endowment and details of the Milltown and Beit bequests, might engender more enthusiasm and excitement in the teachers and students rather than the drier analytical approach of the worksheets.

ANTOINETTE MURPHY has written young persons' guides to the ROSC exhibitions in 1984 and 1988.

Roderic O'CONOR: *Nature Morte*. From *Roderic O'Conor: Vision and Expression* by Roy Johnston. Published on the occasion of the opening of the O'Conor room in the Hugh Lane Municipal Gallery in which the gallery's two paintings were joined by a number of others from private collections.

Roderic O'Conor. Vision and Expression

BY ROY JOHNSTON

Hugh Lane Municipal Gallery of Modern Art 1996 p/b £60 pp. 70 col 5 b/w ills 09514246 7X

Roderic O'Conor 1860-1940. Catalogue de l'oeuvre gravé: The Prints of Roderic O'Conor

Museé de Pont-Aven 1999 p/b.
112pp 45 b/w ills 2-910128-16-4

Julian Campbell

Roderic O'Conor now rivals Jack B Yeats in the amount of critical attention which he receives from a variety of writers in exhibition catalogues, books, articles, and research papers. Both of these catalogues are by Roy Johnston, one of the foremost of O'Conor scholars.

Roderic O'Conor: Vision and Expression was published on the occasion of the opening of the superb O'Conor room in the Hugh Lane Gallery in 1996, for which the two gallery pictures were joined by O'Conor paintings loaned from private collections. Johnston's introductory essay 'Exhibitions and Critics' provides an invaluable chronicle of how O'Conor's work was praised in France from the 1880s onwards by leading contemporary critics, as well as by fellow artists and collectors. Such praise confirms O'Conor's status as a leading figure in contemporary French art.

Johnston naturally deals with the French context but it is also worth noting that O'Conor's 'bold' style had earlier been praised by an Irish critic at the RHA in 1883 who stated that 'Mr. R.A. O'Conor's 'Sylvan Quest'... has much pleasing fancy. Its suggestion is of woodland softness, and there are bold touches in the trees.' (*Irish Times*, 8 Mar 1883). This may have been the earliest critical reaction to O'Conor's work.

In his 1992 monograph on O'Conor, Jonathan Benington gave credit to Johnston 'for discovering the full extent of O'Conor's work as a print maker.' The second publication, *The Prints of Roderick O'Conor*, compiled for an exhibition held at the Museum at Pont-Aven in 1999, is a *catalogue raisonné* of O'Conor's graphic work.

Forty-three prints are listed, including a couple previously believed to be by Séguin. The majority of O'Conor's prints were made at Le Pouldu in Finistère in 1893 where he was taught to etch by Séguin. Apparently, the two artists used 'roofing quality' zinc plates and O'Conor 'drew' directly on to these in the landscape.

While the majority of O'Conor's prints are of landscapes, his ten portraits and figurative studies are of significance. (It is ironic that while he was representing peasants in Brittany, O'Conor, as an absentee landlord, was having problems with his own tenants in county Roscommon.) *The Gleaners* (no 34 in Johnston's catalogue) is surprisingly Gauguin-like, while *Nude Standing* (no 43) has affinities with Gauguin's monotype *Nave Nave Fenua* (1894). Number 35, formerly identified as Séguin, is now thought to be a local peasant, although to me the heavy features of the sitter have some similarity to fellow painter, Maxine Maufra.

The cataloguing is scrupulous in both publications with only a couple of omissions. The painting *Landscape with Farm Buildings* was also exhibited in *Onlookers in France* in Cork in 1993, while etching no 9 was illustrated in Antoine Terrasse's book on the Pont-Aven School (1992). Surprisingly, O'Conor's date of birth is given on the cover of the print catalogue as 1870, not 1860.

Johnston makes no mention here (or in any of his recent publications) of this reviewer's researches on O'Conor. There is no reference to the catalogue, *Irish Impressionists* (1984) which offered the first detailed study of O'Conor published in Ireland; there is no mention of my thesis (1980) which provided the first list of O'Conor's exhibits at the Paris Salons; there is no acknowledgement that it was I who first discovered the impressionist painting, *Group of Poplars* (now in the Hugh Lane Gallery), and a companion landscape, *Snow Scene,* in a private collection in Grez-sur-Loing, and that I passed my discoveries on to Johnston.

JULIAN CAMPBELL is the author of numerous catalogues and books on Irish artists in Brittany.

Art in State Buildings 1970-1985

GOVERNMENT STATIONARY OFFICE 1998 *p/b £15*
120 pp. 76 col 4 b/w ills 0-7076506-74 .

Ted Hickey

The Office of Public Works manages the largest property portfolio in the State which includes Leinster House, Consular Offices, Ambassadorial residences, departmental buildings, Garda stations, office blocks, and prisons. The present Art Management Group, set up in 1991 and fuelled by the Per Cent for Art Scheme, has received proper praise and a high profile for their imaginative and sensitive commissioning and purchasing of works of art, particularly for the State Buildings in Dublin. Important aspects of their commitment to good curatorial practice are both their annual exhibition of part of the collection and its documentation.

In 1997, they published a handsome catalogue of Acquisitions from 1985 to 1995 (reviewed *Irish Arts Review,* vol 14). This equally handsome new publication is a summary catalogue of over 700 acquisitions in the previous decade and a half from 1970 to the end of 1984. The final volume will focus on art works acquired by the OPW on behalf of the state from 1922 to 1970. The reverse chronology of their publication programme, however, does make for difficulties for the reviewer.

Patrick J Murphy in an enthusiastic introductory essay surveys the art of the period and reminds us of the vital role of the first two Rosc exhibitions in 1967 and 1971 in shaping public responses to contemporary art. He rightly stresses the strengths of the collection and draws attention to the many fine works by artists such as Patrick Collins, Nano Reid, Tony O'Malley, Louis le Brocquy, Colin Middleton, T P Flanagan, Mary Swanzey, and Sean McSweeney and notes the absence of support for the new expressionism of Paddy Graham and Brian Maguire. Prints are well represented with several artists purchased in depth such as Le Brocquy and Mary Farl Powers, although fifty-nine Patrick Hickeys, good as they are, against one beautiful William Scott screenprint does seem an imbalance Although OPW patronage must have been a boon to both artists and galleries I regret that they seem to have very rarely strayed beyond walking distance of St Stephen's Green and thus neglected the

Vivienne ROCHE: *Abstract Stairwell.* From *Art in State Buildings 1970-1985*. This handsome publication is a summary catalogue of over seven hundred acquisitions for the State's collection.

opportunity of major works by Sean Scully, Michael Craig Martin, and F E McWilliam, all of whom work so well on a grand scale. Photography, too, is barely recognised; there is only a set of six black and white photographs of 'Rural Life' by Bill Doyle. The collection is not exclusively confined to contemporary art as on two rare excursions outside the capital in 1972, which I would guess were 'rescue' ventures, they purchased ten decorative oil paintings by Peter de Gree (d. 1798) from the Mount Kennedy sale and in London the set of four Italianate landscapes by George Mullins (given here as 'Mullens') which, according to Crookshank and Glin, were commissioned for the Earl of Charlemont's house at Marino in 1768 even though they are dated here as 1760. The commissioned work during this period with few exceptions, like Patrick Scott's large tapestry, was not inspired, but this is something the present Management Group have gone a long way to rectify.

TED HICKEY was formerly Keeper of Art in the Ulster Museum, Belfast.

The Irish Museum of Modern Art. Catalogue of the Collection May 1991-1998

COMPILED BY CATHERINE MARSHALL & RONAN MCCREA

Irish Museum of Modern Art 1998 p/b £12
90 pp. 6 col 656 b/w ills 1-873654-69-3

Rosemarie Mulcahy

In 1991, when the Irish Museum of Modern Art opened and a collection had to be formed from scratch, the decision was taken to purchase only current work by living artists and to buy from primary rather than secondary markets (from gallery exhibitions and studios rather than from private collections and auctions). At the same time, loans and donations of works from as early as the 1940s were encouraged. The decision to concentrate on the art of today was a practical one given the Museum's slim purchasing budget of about £100, 000 a year – (recently, this has been increased).

Eight years on the first catalogue of the collection is greatly welcome. This is an illustrated summary catalogue arranged alphabetically by artist and listing five hundred and eighty-three works – since publication this number has already increased. Leafing through its pages one is immediately struck by the extent to which the collection is comprised of donations by the Gordon Lambert Trust: they account for well over half the collection. This important gift (see *IAR*, vol 15, 1999), generously made without conditions relating to permanence of display, comprises over three hundred works by leading artists from the United States, Latin America, Europe, Britain, and Ireland, ranging from the 1950s to the 1990s. IMMA has been enriched by other important donations, notably by Vincent and Noeleen Ferguson (thirty-two paintings by Irish artists), by Sidney Nolan (six Wild Geese paintings), and by the Friends of the National Collections. Long-term loans have also been an important resource for the Museum's display.

Pablo PICASSO Etching from the *Vollard Suite*. From *The Irish Museum of Modern Art. Catalogue of the Collection, May 1991-1998*. From the Gordon Lambert Donation which accounts for well over half the museum's holdings.

What about the purchases during the last eight years? Sculpture has fared well with good pieces by Janine Antoni, Dorothy Cross, Kathy Prendergast, Alice Maher, Janet Mullarney, Vivienne Roche, and Kiki Smith. There are also interesting works by Antony Gormley, Richard Long, Stephan Balkenhol, John Kindness, Michael Warren, and Vong Phaophanit. Although the print collection at IMMA has not been particularly developed, the increasing acceptance of photography as an art form is reflected in purchases which include a powerful and disturbing series of photos documenting a performance by the Yugoslav artist, Marina Abramovic, in which she mutilates her own body. Willie Doherty and Paul Seawright, with grim photographs based on the 'troubles' in Northern Ireland are also included; indeed, Northern artists are strongly represented throughout. Conceptual and Installation art is reflected both in the Museum's exhibition programme and in its purchases, with notable pieces by James Coleman, Maurice O'Connell, Joseph Kosuth, and Lawrence Weiner. Among the paintings there is a strong showing of non-figurative work by Ciaran Lennon, Mark Francis, Richard Gorman, Fionnuala Ni Chiosáin, Sean Scully, and Sean Shanahan.

Inevitably there will be gaps in any collection, particularly such a young one as IMMA's, but there are some that should be filled without delay. Nano Reid, one of Ireland's most original early modern painters, is unrepresented, there is only one painting by Tony O'Malley, now in his eighty-sixth year, and none by Charlie Brady. There is only one portrait by Edward McGuire, although the contents of McGuire's studio have been donated by the artist's widow and it is to be installed in a dedicated space. It is to be hoped that serious consideration will be given to acquiring other examples of his work.

This catalogue of a collection in the making shows that some excellent work has been done; it will undoubtedly help to make IMMA better known. Inevitably, it raises the question of the Collection's display and here the situation is less satisfactory. Visitors to the Museum are given little sense of the development of modernism in Ireland or abroad. There is no display dedicated to the major artists working in Ireland since the 1940s, visitors are provided with little general context within which to view modern art, and little opportunity to get to know the work of important Irish artists. Artists of the stature of Nano Reid, Camille Souter, and Tony O'Malley have yet to be given shows at IMMA (both Reid and Souter have had retrospectives in the Droichead Arts Centre in Drogheda) and Basil Blackshaw's retrospective was held at the RHA. From the Museum's own holdings, supplemented by loans from other sources, it should be possible to mount a series of small exhibitions that would introduce the public to modern Irish art. There seems to be no policy of showing new art by young artists on any regular basis. Most of the new Irish art is provided by the community groups who participate in the Museum's community programme and to which generous exhibition space is dedicated. IMMA's policy as stated by its director, Declan McGonagle, in the foreword to the catalogue of the collection shows a strongly anti-historical bias, although the language in which it is expressed is sometimes not easy to penetrate, phrases such as 'renegotiate the matrix' are not particularly helpful. This approach may be valid for a *kunsthalle* or exhibition space without a collection, but IMMA is a national museum and it has a duty to educate and inform.

ROSEMARIE MULCAHY is Honorary Senior Fellow in the Department of the History of Art, University College, Dublin.

Flora of County Dublin

COMPILED AND EDITED BY DECLAN DOOGUE, DAVID NASH, JOHN PARNELL, SYLVIA REYNOLDS & PETER WYSE JACKSON

The Dublin Naturalists' Field Club 1998 h/b £150. 558 pp. 19 col 6 b/w ills 0-9530037-0-1

E Charles Nelson

Handsome books are a special pleasure and the limited edition of *Flora of County Dublin* is one of which the The Dublin Naturalists' Field Club, the editors, designer, printer, and binder can be proud. The Club's badge is embossed in gold on the slip-case and the book is quarter-bound in leather with marbled boards. It has a frontispiece, not included in the ordinary edition, reproducing a watercolour by Mrs Wendy Walsh, which depicts the first plant scientifically recorded from the county, the diminutive spring squill that the Revd Richard Heaton, Rector of Birr, found at Ringsend before 1650. Mrs Walsh also contributes a series of four of her distinctive monochrome Chinese ink illustrations of some of Dublin's rarer plants. Thus, *Flora of County Dublin* is another essential purchase for collectors of Wendy Walsh's work; the four 'Chinese inks' have not been reproduced before, whereas the frontispiece first appeared in *An Irish Florilegium II* (1988), a fact not acknowledged anywhere in the present book.

Flora of County Dublin is in one sense the culmination of a project started in 1986 when the Club celebrated its centenary, yet it is also the culmination of almost three and a half centuries of botanical observations by a very diverse group of individuals ranging from Heaton who was a native of Yorkshire, through the Wiltshire-born Quaker physician, Dr John Rutty, and the Scottish horticulturist, James Townsend Mackay, to the current members of the DNFC. The book chronicles the native and naturalised flora of County Dublin, both present and past, recording, for example, the extinction of oysterplant (last seen in Dublin in 1858) and the arrival as garden escapes of such exotica as red-hot pokers from South Africa and giant buglosses from the Canary Islands. It is an historical flora which is designed primarily with botanists in mind but is at the same time a fascinating document that will enthral anyone interested in the history and natural history of the Dublin area. Maps show the distribution within the county of about 200 plants. There are chapters on geology, soils, climate, and habitats as well as a summary of the history of the recording of the county's plants. While modern records of the species take precedence, one novel aspect of this book is the inclusion of extensive quotations from Nathaniel Colgan's *Flora of the County Dublin* (1904).

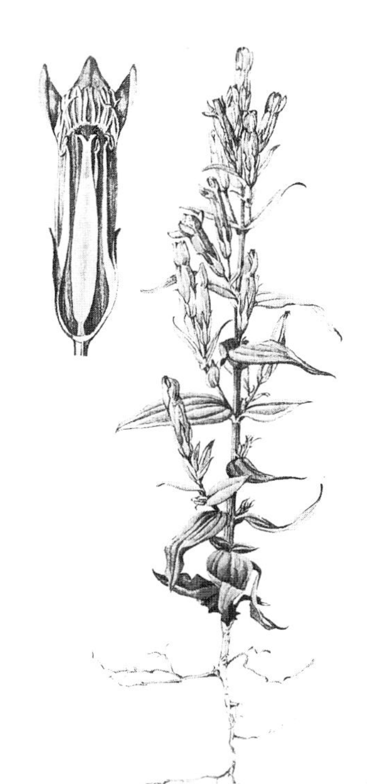

Wendy WALSHE: *Autumn Gentian*. From *Flora of County Dublin*. Compiled and edited by Declan Doogue and others. 'The book is the culmination of almost three and half centuries of botanical observations by a very diverse group of individuals...'

Plant records come in many forms: from printed books, manuscripts and preserved specimens. Illustrating the antiquity of the last are photographs of two specimens, probably once in the possession of the Revd Dr Caleb Threlkeld (1676-1728) and recently unearthed in Trinity College, Dublin. They are burnet rose which once grew 'very plentifully upon the sandy Brows below the black rock near the sea', and common restharrow which, as the label states, 'The Fingallian Irish call Strong-bow' (i.e. sreang bogha). Dr Threlkeld's book *Synopsis Stirpium Hibernicarum*, published on 27 October 1726, one day before *Gulliver's Travels*, was the first flora of County Dublin and thus the specimens, if authentic (which I believe they are), must be more than two hundred and seventy years old. This new flora, albeit bulkier and heavier and hardly something one would carry out into the field, is a worthy – indeed essential – companion for that antique tome. No collection of books about Dublin can be complete without it.

E CHARLES NELSON (formerly Taxonomist in the National Botanic Gardens, Dublin) is the editor of The First Irish Flora, Synopsis Stripium Hibernicarum [by] Caleb Threlkeld *(1988).*

EV+A reduced: Exhibition of Visual+Art 1999

EDITED BY JEANNE GREENBERG
Gandon Editions 1999 p/b £10
164 pp. 89 col 3 b/w ills 0946846-26x

Peter Murray

One of the most refreshing things about EV+A is its unpredictability. This exhibition of contemporary Irish visual art, held in Limerick every year, never sits still, or remains quite the same. EV+A has grown in size and in reputation to be one of the most important visual arts events in Ireland. Yet each year it demonstrates quite a different balance and feel, reflecting the way in which art has developed but reflecting also the viewpoint of the curator. At the outset, EV+A was selected by a group of artists from within Ireland, but after two years the decision was taken to invite one solo curator from outside the country to undertake the task of selecting and inviting artists. This year's EV+A revealed how contemporary Irish art is seen through the eyes of a young but highly experienced curator and art historian from New York, Jeanne Greenberg Rohatyn, currently adjunct professor at the Fashion Institute of Technology.

As it was her first visit to these shores, Greenberg took the time to read the two books that literate New Yorkers have adopted as their introduction to Irish life and culture; *Angela's Ashes* by Frank McCourt and Thomas Cahill's *How the Irish Saved Civilisation*. As the latter work demonstrates convincingly that the Irish did just that, it is to be hoped that when her plane touched down at Shannon she was in a positive frame of mind. It is also to be hoped that she did not attempt to take the airport bus from Shannon to Limerick, a service so miserable it could provide Frank McCourt with material for a mini-series.

The exhibition had a New York flavour, but this is a flavour which travels easily in the modern world. Alienation, paranoia and the urban environment were here aplenty – in the quietly frantic circuit diagrams of Katie Holten, in the videos of Maeve Connolly and Sean Taylor, in the Frida Kahlo-like paintings of Rita Duffy which highlight the hidden perils of domesticity, and in Carissa Farrell's underground car-park drawings. Photography, the quintessential medium of the urban artist, dominated. Carmel Cleary photographed iron bridges, Dara McGrath followed small ads from newspapers and photographed the people who placed them. A black and white football scarf appeared in each of Amanda Coogan's photographs of young men and women. Martin Healy provided unsettling glimpses of living rooms that could be anywhere, while Eamon O'Kane printed directly from colour negatives giving an hallucinatory quality to his city scenes. Paul O'Neill's *Petrol Station: Prelude to an Incident*, an installation of 88 photographs of the same filling station from the same angle at different times of day and night, while not exactly original, was a work realised with intensity and presence.

Brian KENNEDY: *Monad*. From *EV+A reduced*. The experience of visiting EV+A was enhanced by the simplicity and beauty of the renovated old Carnegie Library on Pery Square which houses the Limerick City Art Gallery.

There was an interest in consumerism and packaging. Deirdre O'Mahony's paintings of wrapped rocks, Jeanette Doyle's witty still-lifes of groceries from Tesco's with the cash register receipts etched onto brass plates, or Joyce Duffy's equally witty video of sales patter being used to sell old master paintings. (This last was sited in a nearby shop, the check-out girl wonderfully unaware of its existence). Another welcome touch of humour came in the form of Peter Morgan's video *Balance (5 Easy Pieces)* where word and image nudged each other in the search for a definition of the concept of balance.

There were many works in EV+A 99 representing qualities of transience, of moving. These were among the most beautiful and poetic in the show, and they also teased out our sense of reality. Oliver Comerford's paintings brought to mind snapshots of a snow covered landscape taken from a speeding car, while Jim Savage's gentle landscape drawings had a Chinese quality where the landscape seemed on the point of disappearing. Sandra Meehan's evocative short texts dominated the hallway and stairs in the City Art Gallery but also appeared on the city streets, in the windows of shops, restaurants, and pubs. Less dogmatic than Barbara Kruger, less didactic than Jenny Holtzer, they hovered between thinking and understanding. Robert Janz, accomplished as an artist, grows more accomplished as a poet and is not afraid of using computers (www.vers.com/janz)

There were three main schools of painting in EV+A 99. The first, represented by Stephen Loughman, Margaret Corcoran, and Rita Duffy, was figurative and inspired by Surrealism. The second, represented by Austin McQuinn, Geraldine Behan, Maureen O'Connor, Ronnie Hughes, and Sarah Durcan, showed paintings which by and large are abstract, harmonious and were 'about' painting and representation.

The third major school of painting in EV+A belonged to the monochrome surface brigade, a broad church which extended from hard-line minimalist Fergus Martin, through the more modulated monochromes of Helena Gorey and Seamus O'Rourke, to the architectural tiled colour patterns of Terry McAllister and the linear architectural renderings on perspex of Aine Nic Giolla Coda.

Coming from New York, a city where being Irish is often defined in ways surprising to visitors from Ireland, Greenberg perhaps responded to traditional Irish (and Catholic) signifiers and stereotypes in the works submitted. In Michael Canning's elegant paintings, statues of the Blessed Virgin Mary and the Infant of Prague were reduced to abstract silhouettes beneath layers of Limerick lace and scraped paint. Flag-draped coffins and grim housing estates were used yet again to define Northern Ireland, in Eoin McCarthy's *Land* photograph, while Brendan Earley's colour photograph provided an apt metaphor for contemporary Ireland, showing an anonymous housing estate embellished with a fake dolmen.

Ultimately the vision presented by Greenberg, whether it was of Ireland, contemporary art, or her own viewpoint, was fairly depressing. What little there was in the way of humour, a quintessential part of Irish life, was subsumed beneath a bleak narrative; but in the way that reviews can tell us more about the reviewer than the work, so seeing EV+A may perhaps tell us more about Jeanne Greenberg than about the state of contemporary art in Ireland.

This year's EV+A contained too few surprises. Greenberg eschewed risk and worked hard to bring together a show that behaved itself. Rather than an artists' brawl in the Cedar Tavern, she gave us a party in a beautifully renovated SoHo loft, where half the guests were in recovery and the rest were baking their own bread. The loft in this case was the Limerick City Art Gallery, with its distinguished and elegant new skylit galleries, designed by the Clare-based architect, John O'Reilly. The experience of visiting EV+A was enhanced by the simplicity and beauty of his interventions and renovations in the old Carnegie Library on Pery Square which houses the Limerick City Gallery. It is no coincidence perhaps that O'Reilly worked on the conversion of the Guggenheim in SoHo before returning to Ireland some years ago. He brings a metropolitan flavour to Limerick's architecture and it is to be hoped that his full plans for the renovation and extension of the City Art Gallery may be realised in the not-too-distant future.

PETER MURRAY is Director of the Crawford Municipal Gallery, Cork.

Michael Farrell
EDITED BY JOHN O'REGAN
Gandon 1998 p/b £7.50
47 pp. 24 col 6 b/w ills 0-946846-13-8

Carmel Mooney
EDITED BY JOHN O'REGAN
Gandon 1999 p/b £7.50
47 pp. 17 col 6 b/w ills 0-96846-22-7

Paul Spellman

These two books continue the series of medium-format books on contemporary Irish art published by Gandon Editions. The first book under consideration profiles the career of an artist 'widely regarded as the enfant savage of Irish painting.' Michael Farrell, born in Kells, county Meath, studied commercial art at St Martin's School in London. During the 1960s he befriended some of the most renowned British artists of the time such as Francis Bacon, David Hockney, and R B Kitaj. A sojourn in New York in 1966 broadened his horizons further where he came into contact with *avant-garde* artists Robert Rauschenberg, Roy Lichtenstein and Frank Stella. Farrell returned to Dublin the following year and set up a drawing school at Lincoln Lane. In subsequent years Farrell moved to the artist's quarter of La Ruche in Paris and eventually to Cardet in the south of France where he continues to work today.

Gerry Walker contributes a concise introduction to the book alongside an interview with the artist. To his credit, he takes a back seat in the interview and allows the artist to do most of the talking. While this works well, some of Farrell's answers begged for more probing by Walker. For example, on leaving Dublin for Paris in 1969, Farrell explains 'I was becoming uneasy with the favourable attention I was receiving at home.' Another unexplored comment is when Farrell says 'the politics in my life become the politics of living with somebody else.'

Michael FARRELL: *Self-portrait*. From *Michael Farrell* edited by John O'Regan. 'Farrell was widely regarded as the enfant savage of Irish painting...'

The main essay by Aidan Dunne is a well-written piece which provides an excellent overview of the artist's work. Dunne details the phases of Farrell's work such as his hard-edged celticism, the Pressé series, the Pressé Politique, the Miss O'Murphy series, and the Café Triste series. The only criticism of the book as a whole is that it is slightly repetitious with all three sections listing the phases of his career and referring to his well-known nationalist and anti-clerical opinions. Despite this mild irritation, the real value of this book is the excellent colour reproductions of twenty four of Farrell's key paintings with the *Madonna Irlanda* (now in the Hugh Lane collection) making for a brilliant, eye-catching front cover.

The second publication is a catalogue of recent work by the Kilkenny-born artist and former Artistic Director of Daon Scoil, An Daingean, Carmel Mooney. The book coincided with two exhibitions by Mooney, at Gallery 27, London and the Hallward Gallery, Dublin respectively. Included are seventeen illustrations of paintings inspired by volcanic landscapes. The book opens with a short introduction by Patrick J Murphy who writes knowledgeably about vulcanology and of Mooney's familiarity with two sites in particular; Timanfaya in Lanzarote and Mount Etna in Sicily. In a separate essay the composer John Buckley, who collaborated with Mooney on two pieces in the exhibition, highlights the similarities between music and visual art.

The final section includes an interview between Frances Ruane and the artist. The artist's answers are informative but the content of the interview suffers as a result of Ruane's discussion of Mooney's work within the context of the semi-abstract school of Irish landscape painting. However, elsewhere the interviewer does allow the artist to give real insight into her painterly concerns and working methods. All in all, both publications serve their purpose which is to give a taste of the artists' work in attractive, accessible and affordable publications.

PAUL SPELLMAN MA completed his thesis on Peter Collis at UCD and has also published on Roderic O'Conor in a previous edition of Irish Arts Review.

Treasures of the Royal Dublin Society: A Summary Catalogue of the Works of Art in the Collection of the Royal Dublin Society

COMPILED BY JAMES WHITE AND KEVIN BRIGHT

Royal Dublin Society 1998 p/b £9.50

98pp. 19 col 6 b/w ills 0-86027-043-2

Homan Potterton

Anyone who feels, with a sense of regret, that in recent years the Royal Dublin Society – by jettisoning many of its traditional roles particularly in the fields of arts and learning – has lost its way will have reason to be grateful to James White and Kevin Bright for this timely reminder of the Society's extremely distinguished record as a patron of 'husbandry, manufactures, and other useful arts and sciences' over more than two and a half centuries. There have been earlier histories of the Society, notably by Henry Berry, Terence de Vere White, and the 1981 volume edited by James Meenan and Desmond Clarke, but this is the first time that a catalogue of the not-inconsiderable collection of artworks belonging to the Society has been attempted. There are abundant references in the Society's Minutes and Proceedings to works of art coming into its care by commission, gift, or bequest but, although lists were prepared from time to time, no systematic record of these works of art was ever maintained. The task of preparing this attractively-presented and accessible catalogue was not, therefore, an easy one.

The better furniture – ranging from the magnificent President's chair designed by James Mannin and made by Thomas Cranfield in 1767 to late-19th-century pieces by the Dublin furniture makers, Arthur Jones & Co, have been assessed by Brian Coyle and are included in the catalogue as is the Dun Emer carpet designed by Lucius O' Callaghan in 1928 for the Ballsbridge building (of which he was the architect); but the bulk of the catalogue reflects James White's own expertise and experience in that it describes the paintings and sculptures. There are highpoints: superb 18th-century busts by Van Nost, James Barry's *Cymbeline*, Lavery's *Dublin Horse Show* of 1926, choice (and large) landscapes by Barret and Ashford, what remains of John Henry Foley's collection of plaster models (bequeathed to the Society by the artist in 1874), and a random and interesting selection of minor old master paintings which were bequeathed to the Society by the philanthropist, Thomas Pleasants in 1818. Of these, attributed to such artists as Benjamin Cuyp, van Balen, Egbert van Heemskerk, Pier Francesco Mola, the finest is undoubtedly a *Narcissus* given to Boucher which Dr White considers of sufficiently-high quality as to be perhaps autograph. One familiar picture, a portrait of the actress Peg Woffington, traditionally given to John Lewis as a version of his painting in the National Gallery of Ireland, is reattributed convincingly to James Latham on the basis of the floral-pattern background.

The catalogue, containing many such nuggets of research and detective work, is a credit to the diligence of the authors. Let us hope it will lead the Council and members to value more highly the collections in their care, not least their library, which (although, of course, outside the scope of Dr White's remit) has been sorely underfunded in recent years.

HOMAN POTTERTON is Editor of Irish Arts Review.

When Time Began to Rant and Rage: Figurative Painting from Twentieth Century Ireland

EDITED BY JAMES STEWARD

Merrell Holberton 1998 £29.95

288 pp. 75 col 84 b/w ills 75 col. ills. 1-85894-059-1

Alistair Smith

This ambitious and interesting publication accompanied an exhibition which was shown throughout 1999 in Liverpool, Berkeley, New York, and London. Despite the fact that both the Department of Education for Northern Ireland and the Department of Foreign Affairs in Dublin are credited with providing funds for the exhibition, no showing in Ireland resulted. The exhibition comprised seventy-five paintings, dating from 1902 (Walter Osborne's *Tea in the Garden*) to 1997 (James Hanley's unsubtle and unsubtly-entitled *Weight of his Story*). The principal selector of the exhibits was John Christen Steward of the Berkeley Art Museum. In his foreword to the catalogue, he tells how he first visited Belfast in 1993 and goes on to describe the aims of the exhibition. These are diverse, one being 'the presentation of a balanced and unbiased selection of what we can consider to be the best Irish painting in the representational, figurative idiom.' He justifies this focus 'as this seemed the most compelling area in which cultural issues and subject-matter could be explored' and where the exhibition could examine 'the intersection of Irish painting, culture and politics', bringing 'a new awareness of Irish painting to audiences in England and the United States.'

The varied aims of the exhibition inevitably resulted in its having a rather schizoid character, with paintings which could certainly claim to be among the best produced by Irish artists during the period (although Bruce Arnold's essay cites 'paintings falsely raised above the second-rate'), and others which could only be included because of their relationship with the intersection quoted above. I do not want to grumble overmuch on the selection/omission issue, but it results in the writers of the catalogue displaying great ingenuity in introducing political content into their commentaries on paintings which are devoid of it. Lavery's idyllic scenes of boating on the Thames, for example, are said to 'transcend the existence of any savage conflict in Europe.' Surely the verb should be ignore? Equally, Leo Whelan's sensitively understated portrait of his sister, Lily, at the piano inspires the following desperate ploy: '...the ambience of repose...contrasts with the volatile conditions existing in Dublin in 1920.'

In short, it is difficult to escape the feeling that, while the selection was made to represent the diversity of the century, the 'voice' of the catalogue is more narrowly arraigned towards sociological commentary. This lack of co-ordination between the exhibition and catalogue has the effect of authors dwelling time and again on artists and works which are not exhibited. Colm Tóibín's essay on 'Public, Private and National Spirit', for example, constructs an interesting proposition around

Eileen MURRAY: *This or Emigration* from *When Time Began to Rant and Rage: Figurative Painting from Twentieth-century Ireland*. '...founding an argument about the significance of Irish 20th-century painting based on a selection which supposedly reflects the political history of the country is a deeply flawed procedure.'

Tony O'Malley's Wexford landscapes: 'Somehow the pure act of art done in a place where art was unknown and unheard of had immense implications.' Yet there is no work by O'Malley exhibited. Kenneth McConkey's recasting of his earlier paper on Orpen's *Homage to Manet* follows, asserting, if anything, that truth is stranger than fiction, in that George Moore 'had, in the front of his mind, the bizarre connection between the Irish cultural renaissance and the fight to convert everyone to French art.' Sadly, the important Orpen, which gave rise to McConkey's argument was not exhibited. I could cite more examples of this lack of 'fit' between exhibition and essay, particularly in those by Aidan Dunne, Peter Murray, and Sighle Breathnach-Lynch. However, I wonder if this constitutes evidence of a larger issue. I think that what we are witnessing here is the application of a doctrine to works of art which do not support it. The theory being applied is that every object in the exhibition can be decoded to offer a reflection of its historical context and that the core of that context is 'Irishness'. The theory peters out in many cases where artists have become more closely allied to an international movement (as is often pointed out). To me the least interesting paintings are the most obviously political, those which bear the deadly touch of the propagandist. These would include works like *Eire* (by Lady Glenavy) and their more modern equivalents.

Although painting is far from dead (despite what many would have us to believe), political painting is as dead as the dodo, video and photography (those spinoffs of the documentary mindset) having created a whole new spectrum more appropriate to visual political commentary. Founding an argument about the significance of Irish 20th-century painting based on a selection which supposedly reflects the political history of the country is a deeply flawed procedure. A simplistic view results and artists who do not conform to the stereotype are omitted. How can you have an exhibition of Irish painting without Camille Souter? (Incidentally, the illustration of her work which Peter Murray includes, and which was very welcome, is reversed which might be dangerous on a *Turn to Base Leg*.)

A final thought. Caoimhin Mac Giolla Leith's interesting essay focuses on exhibitions of Irish art mounted in the 1990s. He dwells on the work of Kathy Prendergast. Any Irish exhibition which can justify omitting her work, as this one does, really has a problem.

ALISTAIR SMITH is Director of the Whitworth Art Gallery, University of Manchester.

Re/Dressing Cathleen: Contemporary Works from Irish Women Artists

EDITED BY JENNIFER GRINNELL AND ALSTON CONLEY

McMullen Museum of Art, Boston College p/b 1997 144pp. 18 col 54 b/w ills 0-9640153-8-2

Gerry Dukes

This substantial large-format book is the supporting documentation and catalogue for an exhibition of Irish artists held at the McMullen Museum of art in late

1997. The stated aim of both the exhibition and the book, as articulated by Nancy Netzer in her Director's Preface, was to 'celebrate the contributions of women to Irish culture and contemporary society as a fitting tribute to the particular burden borne by them during the Great Famine.' In order to achieve this aim the book features illustrations of the work of the thirteen participating artists, interviews with most of the artists and essays on the works and cognate topics by a variety of critics and commentators.

The keynote essay, titled 'Re/Dressing Cathleen: A Local Perspective' is by Medb Ruane. The essay is stimulating and provocative, as is to be expected from Ruane. While the essay's heart is in the right place, its head is occasionally astray. Ruane identifies what she calls the 'Cathleen principle', that construct of nationalist ideology which programmatically 'required women to offer up their lives and their bodies in the service of higher ideals.' Just what these ideals were is not specified, nor is there a discernible trace of irony in the use of the word 'higher'. In other words, Ruane's 'Cathleen principle' is a retrospective and generalising rationalisation, a surgical amputation of a social form from a body politic subject to the press of history. The currently fashionable orthodoxy that presents the colonisers oppressing the colonised and they in turn oppressing women is attractive but surely wrong, because far too simple. Back in December 1904 the young Joyce wrote in *The Irish Homstead* that the inhabitants of Inchicore and environs constituted 'the gratefully oppressed'. The full force of that oxymoron has yet to be adequately investigated and assessed. Nevertheless, Ruane's account of the decay of modernism and the liberating consequences of that decay on the production of art and art practices in provincial or marginal centres is compelling.

The same cannot be said for the second keynote essay, 'Visual and Ideological Pluralism in Practice: Contemporary Irish Women Artists in Context' by Claude Cernuschi of Boston College. Writing about Rita Duffy's painting, *Becoming*, featuring a woman bent over a receptacle containing a baby, Cenuschi has this to say: 'The use of a strainer to contain the baby is blatantly incompatible with its traditional function as a cooking utensil: its womb-like spherical shape may (at first sight) denote the protectiveness of a baby basin, but its very function to prepare food (when that food is a human child) violently alters its shape to suggest a coffin.' Duffy's painting is very much more richly ironic than this extraordinarily tentative commentary suggests. He makes no reference to the profusion of shamrocks pouring from the woman's mouth as she bends over the child posed in the strainer rendered as a leaky chalice or baptismal font. Cernuschi's categorisation of Duffy as a neo-expressionist who incorporates narrative dimensions into her paintings is reasonable but one would expect that a critic making such categorisation would be able to read the narratives.

There are some seven other contributions of varying quality to the book and a suite of interviews with most of the artists participating in the exhibition. An interesting appendix of emigrant 'American letters' is also included. The proofing, here and there, is shaky.

Gerry Dukes is an academic and critic.

Nearly Ninety: Reminiscences

Chalmers (Terry) Trench

The Hannon Press 1996. pb £8.99

184pp. 30b/w ills 0-9516472-4-5

Homan Potterton

The tall and gentle figure of Terry (CEF to me and others who do not presume to know him well) Trench has been a familiar presence (with his wife, the artist Bea Orpen, until her death in 1980) at art functions in Dublin and throughout Ireland for as long as most people can remember. The title of his unaffected and unassuming volume of reminiscences, *Nearly Ninety*, explains why: he was born in 1909 so that the life which he outlines spans the century. Educated in England (at Repton) and with a degree in Modern Languages from Cambridge, Trench has pursued throughout his life the most difficult and select profession of being an 'amateur'. He has many achievements to his credit (among them the founding of An Oige and the Drogheda Municipal Art Gallery, not to mention a role at the Abbey with Orson Welles) but he describes these as though they were happy accidents. Ambition is a stranger to Terry Trench; good citizenship his credo.

His father was successor to Dowden in the Chair of English Literature at Trinity, his mother (dogged throughout her life by asthma and arthritis) was a professional invalid; and Trench himself, the youngest of four children, comes across as a lonely child who scorned sports, liked music, art (even knitting) and, at later stages, languages and travel. The family were Protestant but Trench, who would understand the niceties which differentiate middle-class Protestants from the true Anglo Irish, makes no claim to being Anglo Irish. The Trenchs would never have thought of themselves as other than Irish and there is a lesson in this for those who, even today, are under the impression that being really Irish and being Protestant are incompatible.

Although politics were not discussed at home, CEF became a Nationalist while still at Prep school and posted pictures of Michael Collins inside his locker door; his brother Paddy, while a student at Trinity, carried despatches between Republican forces following the Treaty and later became what Trench calls 'an Irish Trotskyist'; CEF sought (in vain) to study the Irish language as part of his Cambridge Tripos but later learned it in Dublin where he also took up Irish dancing; his first job (which lasted ten years) was with Colm O Lochlainn at the Three Candles Press where he immersed himself in Irish culture.

Photographs in the book show Trench with Mary Robinson, with Queen Beatrix, with Garret FitzGerald, and of course with Bea and his family. His has been a life on the periphery but, as the photos show, a life upon which he has always smiled.

Homan Potterton is Editor of Irish Arts Review.

Auction Records, 1998-99

A Table of New Record Prices for Irish Painters

Mildred Anne BUTLER *Green Eyed Jealousy.*
IR£28,000

James Humbert CRAIG *Children on the Beach.*
IR£25,300.

William Percy FRENCH *Extensive Bogland Landscape.*
IR£13,000

William CONOR *The Picture House Queue*
IR£89,500

Mildred Anne BUTLER
IR£28,000
Green Eyed Jealousy
Watercolour 38 x 26 ins. S
James Adams, 31 March 1999, Lot 45.

William CONOR
IR£89,500
The Picture House Queue
Drawing 30 x 24 ins.
Sotheby's, 21 May 1999, The Irish Sale, Lot 379.

James Humbert CRAIG
IR£25,300
Children on the Beach
Oil 15 x 22 ins. S
Sotheby's, 21 May 1999, The Irish Sale, Lot 373.

William Percy FRENCH
IR£13,000
Extensive Bogland Landscape
Watercolour 20 x 30 ins. S
James Adam & Bonhams, 9 December 1998, Lot 64.

Eva Henrietta Hamilton *A Summers Day in the West* IR£12,000

Paul Henry *The Bog Workers* IR£210,500.

Mainie Jellett *Composition* IR£40,000

Evie Hone *Four Elements* IR£16,000 .

John Luke *The Bridge* IR£441,500 .

Daniel Maclise *King Cophetua and the Beggar Maid* IR£353,500.

Eva Henrietta HAMILTON
IR£12,000
A Summers Day in the West
Oil 19 x 23.5 ins. S
Hamilton Osborne King,
The RDS Sale, 31 May 1999, Lot 190

Paul HENRY
IR£210,500
The Bog Workers
Oil 24.5 x 31 ins. S, I,
Sotheby's, The Irish Sale, 21 May 1999,
Lot 310.

Evie HONE
IR£16,000
Four Elements
Oil 29 x 24 ins, S
de Veres, 22 June 1999, Lot 34

Mainie JELLETT
IR£40,000
Composition
Oil 24 x 36 ins.
Sotheby's, The Irish Sale, 21 May 1999,
Lot 310

Sir John LAVERY
IR£1,321,500
The Bridge at Grez
Oil 30 x 72.5 ins.
Christie's, 8 December 1998, Lot 17

John LUKE
IR£441,500
The Bridge
Tempera 25.5 x 31 ins. S, D, I.
Christie's, The Irish Sale,
20 May 1999, Lot 217

Daniel MACLISE
IR£353,500
King Cophetua and the Beggar Maid
Oil 47 x 71.5 ins
Christie's
10 June 1999, Lot 19

Norah McGUINNESS
IR£19,000
The Customs House, Dublin - From the South Quays
Oil 27 x 36 ins. S, D.
James Adam & Bonhams,
26 May 1999, Lot 36

Frank McKELVEY
IR£54,300
Summer Days
Oil 18 x 27 ins. S, I.
Sotheby's, The Irish Sale, 21 May 1999, Lot 384

Sir John LAVERY *The Bridge at Grez*. IR£1,321,500.

Norah McGUINNESS *The Customs House, Dublin - From the South Quays* IR£19,000.

Frank McKELVEY *Summer Days*. IR£54,300.

Colin MIDDLETON *Requiem for Dan O'Neill* IR£40,000.

Roderic O'CONOR *Nature Morte aux Pommes* IR£276,500.

Maurice Canning WILKS *Above Letterfrack, Co. Galway* IR£9,775.

Daniel O'NEILL *Divorce and Departure* IR£62,000.

Jack B. YEATS *The Wild Ones* IR£1,233,500.

Colin Middleton
IR£40,000
Requiem for Dan O'Neill
Oil 26 x 30 ins. D, I.
Christie's, The Irish Sale,
20 May 1999, Lot 70

Roderic O'Conor
IR£276,500
Nature Morte aux Pommes
Oil 22 x 15 ins.
Sotheby's
December 1998, Lot 1

Daniel O'Neill
IR£62,000
Divorce and Departure
Oil 27 x 38 ins. S, I.
Sotheby's, The Irish Sale,
21 May 1999, Lot 363

Maurice Canning Wilks
IR£9,775
Above Letterfrack, Co. Galway
30 x 40 ins. S
Christie's, The Irish Sale,
20 May 1999, Lot 36

Jack B Yeats
IR£1,233,500
The Wild Ones
Oil 14 x 21 ins. S.
Sotheby's, The Irish Sale, 21 May 1999,
Lot 331.

Price Guide to Irish Art

An Index of Prices paid for Irish Pictures at Auctions between July 1998 and July 1999

Compiled by Eve McAulay

John LEWIS, *Portrait of Bridget Vaughan of Derllys, Mrs Bevan (1698-1779)*, sold at Sotheby's Derwydd Mansion, 15 September 1998 for £18,400

The artist's name and date is followed by the painting's title. Next is the medium, referred to by a single letter symbol (as indicated below) followed by the measurements of the work. The letters 'S', 'D', or 'I' indicate where the painting is signed, dated, or inscribed. The letter in parentheses refers to the sale and is followed by the lot number.

Prices are quoted in local currencies.
In the case of James Adam, de Veres and other Irish salerooms, the prices are hammer prices and do not include the buyer's premium (on average, 15%). Prices at sales in British auction houses include the buyer's premium. Unsold pictures, and pictures which fetched less than £200, are not included.

The medium is indicated by the following letters:
A: Acrylic; C: Collage; D: Drawing; O: Oil; M: Mixed media; P: Pastel; Pr: Print; T: Tempera; W: Watercolour/Gouache/Wash. Stained-glass, sculpture, tapestries, etc. are not included in the *Price Guide* although, for example, in the case of Harry Clarke his auction record is for a work in stained-glass.

THE FOLLOWING SALE CATALOGUES, REFERRED TO IN THE *GUIDE* BY A SINGLE LETTER SYMBOL, HAVE BEEN INDEXED

A: Sotheby's, Derwydd Mansion, Llandeilo, Carmarthenshire - 15 September 1998
B: Christie's South Ken., Twentieth Century British Art - 16 September 1998
C: de Veres, Alicia Boyle Studio Sale - 22 September 1998
D: James Adam, Important Irish Art - 30 September 1998
E: Sotheby's, Modern British and Irish Paintings, Drawings and Sculpture - 30 September 1998
F: Phillips, Modern British & Irish Paintings, Drawings and Sculpture - 6 October 1998
G: de Veres, Art for Omagh - 14 October 1998
H: Christie's South Ken., British and Continental Watercolours and Drawings - 14 October 1998
I: Christie's London, Twentieth Century Art - 23 October 1998
J: Christies London, Twentieth Century British Art - 6 November 1998
K: Sotheby's, Victorian Pictures - 11 November 1998
L: Christie's South Ken., Portraits and British Pictures - 12 November 1998
M: Sotheby's, Realms of the Mind: Fantasy Art and Illustration - 12 November 1998
N: Phillips, Modern British & Irish Paintings, Drawings and Sculpture - 17 November 1998
O: de Veres, Sale of Art - 17 November 1998
P: Christie's South Ken., British and Continental Watercolours and Drawings - 19 November 1998
Q: James Adam & Bonhams, The Sybil Connolly Collection - 25 November 1998
R: Christie's South Ken., British and Continental Pictures - 26 November 1998
S: Sotheby's, Modern British and Irish Paintings and Drawings - 3 December 1998
T: Sotheby's, 20th Century British Works of Art from the Hiscox Collection - 3 December 1998
U: Christie's London, Impressionist & Nineteenth Century Art - 8 December 1998
V: James Adam & Bonhams, Important Irish Art - 9 December 1998
W: James Adam, Christmas Art Auction - 16 December 1998
X: Christie's South Ken., British and Continental Watercolours and Drawings - 21 January 1999
Y: Christie's South Ken., Twentieth Century British Art - 27 January 1999
Z: Phillips, Twentieth Century British & Irish Art - 2 March 1999
AI: Christie's South Ken., British and Continental Watercolours and Drawings - 3 March 1999
BI: Sotheby's, Modern British and Irish Paintings, Drawings and Sculpture - 3 March 1999
CI: Christie's South Ken., Twentieth Century British Art - 4 March 1999
DI: Christie's London, 20th Century British Art - 5 March 1999
EI: de Veres, Sale of Art - 9 March 1999
FI: Christie's South Ken., British and Victorian Pictures - 11 March 1999
GI: Sotheby's, Victorian Pictures - 17 March 1999
HI: James Adam, Important Irish Art - 31 March 1999
II: Phillips, British and European Watercolours and Portrait Miniatures - 19 April 1999
JI: Christie's South Ken., Twentieth Century British Art - 28 April 1999
KI: Sotheby's, The Marine Sale - 28 April 1999
LI: James Adam, Contemporary and Traditional Art - 12 May 1999
MI: Christie's South Ken., British and Continental Watercolours and Drawings - 20 May 1999
NI: Christie's London, The Irish Sale - 20 May 1999
OI: Sotheby's, The Irish Sale - 21 May 1999
PI: James Adam & Bonhams, Important Irish Art - 26 May 1999
QI: Christie's South Ken., Twentieth Century British Art - 3 June 1999
RI: Christie's London, 20th Century British Art - 4 June 1999
SI: Phillips, Twentieth Century British & Irish Art - 8 June 1999
TI: Sotheby's, Important British Paintings and Watercolours - 8 June 1999
UI: Christie's London, Important British Art - 10 June 1999
VI: de Veres, Sale of Art - 22 June 1999
WI: Sotheby's, Modern British and Irish Paintings, Drawings and Sculpture - 23 June 1999
XI: Christie's South Ken., British and Continental Watercolours and Drawings - 23 June 1999
YI: Christie's South Ken., Twentieth Century British Art - 14 July 1999
ZI: Thomas Adams, Blackrock, Irish and Continental Paintings - 12 October 1998
AII: Thomas Adams, Blackrock - 8 December 1998
BII: Thomas Adams, Blackrock - 23 February 1999
CII: Thomas Adams, Blackrock - 12 April 1999
DII: Thomas Adams, Blackrock - 26 April 1999
EII: Hamilton Osborne King, The RDS Sale - 27 November 1998
FII: Hamilton Osborne King, The RDS Sale - 31 May 1999
GII: Mealy's, Castlecomer - 6 & 7 October 1998
HII: Mealy's, Raford House, Co. Galway - 20 October 1998
III: Mealy's, Castlecomer - 9 & 10 March 1999
JII: Mealy's, The Hermitage, Cobh, Co. Cork - 18 May 1999
KII: Mealy's, Castlecomer - 13 July 1999
LII: Christie's South Ken., Twentieth Century Prints - 16 June 1999
MII: Christie's South Ken., British and Continental Watercolours, Drawings and Pictures - 22 July 1999

ADDEY, Joseph Poole (1852-1922)
Hillside Cottage
W 10 x 14", S, D, (EI: 8) £650
AITKEN, James Alfred (1846-1897)
The Glow of the Morning
W 20 x 30", S, (PI: 130) £2,100
ALEXANDER, Douglas (1871-1945)
On the Kenmare River, Co.Kerry
W 15 x 21", S, (D: 76) £1,000
Lake and Mountain Landscape
O 10 x 12", S, (D: 92) £900
Lake and Mountain Landscapes
W (2) 10 x 14", S, (D: 132) £500
Ballinahinch
W 10 x 14.5", S, (HI: 1) £300
Mount Errigal, Donegal and
Near Leenane, Connemara
W (2) 10 x 10", S, (HI: 97) £950
Near Ballisrabe;
Mountains and Moors
W (2) 10 x 14", S, (PI: 5) £520
Lough, Cottages and Mountains
W (2) 10 x 14", S, (PI: 114) £1,000
Peat Stacks
W (2) 10 x 14", S, (PI: 160) £1,700
Dunluce Castle, Co. Antrim
W 8 x 11", S, (ZI: 23) £280
Evening sun on peatland
O 15 x 17", S, (CII) £1,250
Gathering Turf, Connemara
W 14.5 x 20.5", S, (DII: 30) £800
Mountain and Lake Landscape
O 19.5 x 23.5", S, (FII: 188) £1,700
A Mountain Lake
O 19 x 23", S, (FII: 189) £1,400
Near Louisburg Connemara
W 10.5 x 15", S, (GII: 1436) £570
Among the Twelve Pins, Connemara
W 9 x 11", S, (GII: 1474) £320
On the Wicklow Coast
W 11 x 15.5", S, (III: 1172) £550
Near Sneem, Co. Kerry
W 11 x 15.5", S, I, (III: 1173) £600
Near Leehane, Connemara
W 15.5 x 22", S, (JII: 231) £850
Among the Twelve Pins, Connemara
W 11 x 15", S, (JII: 479) £520
Landscape, Co. Donegal
O 21 x 25", S, (JII: 482) £2,500
Near Recess, Connemara
W 10.5 x 15", S, (JII: 483) £900
ALLEN, Harry Epworth (1894-1958)
Village Street
D 6.5 x 8.5", S, (B: 118) £403
The Little Orchard
O 15 x 22", S, (V: 102) £2,500
The Red House
P 12.5 x 14", S, (CI: 30) £322
The Farmyard
W 9 x 12", S, (CI: 88) £748
Mending the Nets
O 14 x 19.5", S, (EI: 50) £3,200
Crowlink, Sussex
T 14.5 x 21.5", S, I, (NI: 44) £4,370
Ballindooley, County Galway
O 8.5 x 10", S, (PI: 8A) £2,600
ARMSTRONG, Arthur (1924-1996)
Auction Record: IR£7,700
Two Men in a Spanish Interior
Oil 22 x 26 ins.
The Studio Sale, deVeres, 3 February 1998, Lot 26
Access to the Garden
O 16.5 x 23", (EI: 14) £1,800
Old Harbour, Roundstone
O 13 x 20", S, I, (EI: 54) £2,200
Figure in a Blue Landscape
O 43 x 35", S, I, (EI: 72) £5,200
Surf and Rocks
C 15 x 20", S, (PI: 102) £500
Evening Landscape (1971)
O 11.5 x 9", I, (PI: 123) £620

Rose BARTON, *The Physic Garden, Chelsea*, sold at Christies South Kensington, 3 March 1999 for £1,495

Shoreline
O 16 x 20", S, (VI: 10) £2,400
Field, Connemara
O 13 x 16", S, (VI: 17) £2,100
Near Bertraghboy
O 20 x 23", S, I, (VI: 113) £1,400
Connemara Coast
O 12 x 16", S, I, (VI: 124) £1,500
Connemara Landscape
O 8 x 10", S, (AII) £820
A Beach Scene in Connemara
O 24 x 30", S, (DII: 26) £1,100
ASHFORD, William (1746-1824)
Auction Record: £120,000
Punt on the River Clodiagh, Charleville
39 x 50 ins. S & D 1801
Christie's, 12 July 1991, Lot 67
A Mill near Bantry
W 9.5 x 14.5", I, (V: 54) £1,200
Ruins near Bandon, Co. Cork
D 4.5 x 7", S, I, (V: 157) £380
Eagle's Nest, Lower lake Killarney
O 16 x 25", S, D, (NI: 142) £6,900
BALLARD, Brian (b.1943)
Rocks at Howth
O 18 x 24" (G: 3) £1,900
Girl at Window
O 23 x 30", S, D, (EI: 118) £3,600
Pewter Pot & Vase
O 10 x 14", S, D, (EI: 119) £2,600
White Lady and Teapot
O 16 x 20", S, D, (HI: 92A) £1,500
Irises and Iron
O 18 x 24", S, D, I, (PI: 53) £1,900
White Jug
O 24 x 30", S, D, (PI: 122) £2,400
Rose & Apple
O 8 x 6", S, (VI: 72) £970
Still Life
O 9 x 13", S, D, (VI: 73) £1,100
Two Lilies
O 14 x 10", S, (VI: 74) £1,400
Still Life - Flowers
O 13.5 x 9.5", S, D, (VI: 118) £1,600
Hot Hill
O 29 x 37", I, (ZI: 45) £200

Still Life, vase of summer flowers
O 14 x 10", S, (DII: 75) £1,050
BARRET, George (Senior) (1728-1784)
Auction Record: £154,362
The Dukes of Cumberland & York driving a Landau in Windsor Great Park
41 x 54 ins. S in monogram
Sotheby's (New York), 14 January 1994, Lot 85
Cattle in a clearing, a church beyond
P 16 x 23", (NI: 143) £3,450
River Landscape with three Fawns
P 14 x 21.5", (VI: 92) £2,700
BARRY, Moyra (1886-1960)
Still Life Study of Flowers
O 18 x 14", S, (D: 25) £1,300
Study Flowers
W 12 x 17.5", (G: 5) £280
Roses in Bloom
O 19.5 x 15.5", S, (O: 132) £820
Summer Blossom
O 12 x 16", S, (V: 79) £1,100
Still Life, Roses
O 9.5 x 13.5", S, (EI: 55) £870
Self Portrait
O 15.5 x 11.5", S, D, (HI: 48) £650
BARTON, Mary (1861-1949)
A Galway Bog
W 13.5 x 20.5", S, I, (NI: 188) £920
BARTON, Rose Maynard (1856-1929)
Auction Record: IR£25,000
The Custom House, Dublin, before the Rebellion
Watercolour 10 x 14 ins. S
Mealy's (Brooke Sale, Knoctoran), 30 June 1987, Lot 301
Jack and Tom
W (2) 4 x 6", S, D, (D: 146) £3,000
Figures in a Punt on the Thames
W 6.5 x 9", S, D, (H: 76) £1,495
The Physic Garden, Chelsea
W 21 x 14", S, D, (AI: 25) £1,495
The Young Artist
W 13 x 10", S, D, (OI: 272) £19,550
Feeding the Chicks
W 10 x 13.5", S, D, (ZI: 14) £600
The Tenters House
W 5 x 4.5", S, I, (JII: 127) £1,400
BEHAN, John (b.1938)
Two Figures
D 20 x 16", (D: 5) £240
BELTON, Liam (20th Century)
Sicilian Garden
P 21.5 x 20", (G: 10) £320
The Palette Irish Landscape
O 50 x 38", S, D, (V: 117) £5,400
BERGER, Alice Hammerschlag (1917-1969)
Death of Cuchulain - Image
O 6 x 10", S, I, (EI: 142) £260
Crystalline Light Structure
M 31 x 23", S, D, I, (EI: 143) £480
BEWICK, Pauline (b.1935)
A Hungarian Violinist
W 32 x 23", S, (O: 95F) £2,600
Nettles and Bluebells, Killarney
W 32 x 23", S, (O: 95G) £2,800
Still life study
M 32 x 22", S, D, (Q: 106) £3,800
Still Life with Honeysuckle and Dove-painted Jug
W 22.5 x 30", S, D, (OI: 390) £4,025
Asleep with Moon and Fruit
W 22 x 29", S, D, (PI: 112) £3,700
BLACKHAM, Dorothy (1896-1975)
West of Ireland landscape with cottages
P 11.5 x 17", S, (W: 34) £260
West of Ireland - woman on a hill
O 9.5 x 13", S, (JII: 476) £1,200
BLACKSHAW, Basil (b.1932)
The Studio Field
O 16 x 19.5", (G: 13) £4,200
A Man and his Dog
O (2) 3 x 3", S, (EI: 120) £750

Girl Reading
O 30 x 25", S, (**NI**: 81) £6,900
Exercising
O 19 x 23.5", S, D, (**OI**: 405) £21,850
BOLAY, Veronica (20th Century)
Blues, Broken
O 23.5 x 27.5", (**G**: 14) £800
BOURKE, Brian (b.1936)
Mother & Child
Pr 12 x 11.5", (**G**: 237A) £320
Switzerland
M 18 x 14", S, D, (**W**: 62) £900
Triptych
O (3) 14 x 14", S, (**HI**: 98) £1,300
Mother Feeding her Baby
D 17.5 x 13", S, D, (**VI**: 174) £820
BOWEN, Greta (1880-1981)
Four Courts, Dublin
O 20 x 24", S, I, (**HI**: 25) £800
Party Time along the River
O 17.5 x 23", (**VI**: 117) £950
BOYLE, Alicia (1908-1997)
The Galway Hooker
W 11 x 14", S, (**C**: 1) £300
Hockey's House
W 19 x 14", S, (**C**: 3) £200
First Light, Mykonos
O 7 x 9", S, (**C**: 4) £360
Sin's Landscape, Pendoylan
O 14 x 18", S, (**C**: 6) £380
Plates & Saucers
W 10 x 12", S, (**C**: 7) £240
The Rehearsal, Bantry House
W 10 x 13", S, (**C**: 11) £200
Waggon
O 10 x 14", S, D, (**C**: 13) £380
Temple, North Africa
W 8 x 10", S, (**C**: 14) £340
Burren Landscape
O 14 x 18", S, (**C**: 15) £400
Limavady Landscape, Co. Derry
W 14 x 19", S, (**C**: 16) £380
David
O 18 x 14", S, (**C**: 17) £420
Ponies at Delphi
W 14 x 19", S, D, (**C**: 18) £820
Paisley, Bible Truth not Roman Error
O 30 x 20", S, D, (**C**: 20) £540
Fledgling Hawk
O 10 x 14", S, (**C**: 22) £360
Boat and Castle by Shore, Mykonos
O 13 x 16", D, I, (**C**: 24) £380
Juan at Supper
O 17 x 13", S, (**C**: 26) £1,600
Blue Lough near Carna
W 14 x 19", S, (**C**: 28) £260
Ruined House in Bishop Street, Derry
W 10 x 12", S, D, (**C**: 33) £320
Donegal Tweed, Ardara
O 15 x 12", S, (**C**: 34) £1,100
Sotillo Yellow
W 14 x 19", S, D, (**C**: 26) £400
Monkstown Hospital
W 14 x 19", S, (**C**: 38) £300
Clickers at Work
O 19 x 15", S, D, (**C**: 40) £2,400
Clontarf
O 12 x 20", S, D, (**C**: 42) £500
Birney Boyle
O 14 x 10", S, D, (**C**: 43) £200
Crochet and Kittens
O 18 x 14", S, (**C**: 45) £1,300
Curragh and Lobster Pots
W 10 x 14", S, D, (**C**: 46) £400
The Severn near Worcester
O 10 x 14", I, (**C**: 49) £290
Sofa in Interior
W 10 x 14", I, (**C**: 50) £360
Over the Range
O 20 x 30", S, (**C**: 51) £950

Alicia BOYLE, *Sotillo Yellow*, sold at de Veres, Alicia Boyle Studio Sale, 22 September 1998 for £400

Sun Stone, Nerja
O 30 x 40", S, D, (**C**: 53) £770
Working Mill
W 6 x 15", S, D, (**C**: 54) £210
Mallow and Pear Orchard
O 18 x 14", S, D, (**C**: 55) £400
The Towpath
W 6 x 15", (**C**: 57) £320
Blue Cow, Shanveagh
O 10 x 14", S, D, (**C**: 59) £220
Karin at Shanveagh
O 18 x 14", S, D, (**C**: 60) £920
Duston Mill
W 14 x 19", S, (**C**: 62) £360
Three Storks
W 8 x 6", S, D, (**C**: 64) £360
Landscape
O 10 x 14", S, (**C**: 67) £200
Ardara Weaver, Donegal
O 18 x 22", S, (**C**: 70) £760
The Lobster Boat
W 4 x 9", (**C**: 72) £260
Men in Fishing Boat
W 5 x 7", (**C**: 75) £240
Naxos
O 16 x 12", D, I, (**C**: 77) £280
Fishing Boat, Galway
W 14 x 19", S, D, (**C**: 78) £360
Triumph of Learning
W 9 x 12", S, (**C**: 79) £480
Docken Orchard
O 14 x 18", S, (**C**: 83) £380
Cucumber and Company
W 10 x 13", S, (**C**: 84) £320
Blue and Green Figure
O 14 x 10", S, D, (**C**: 87) £2,200
Siobhan, Attic Nude
O 14 x 18", S, D, (**C**: 89) £390
Crescent Red
O 28 x 36", S, (**C**: 90) £1,700
The Last Drop
O 14 x 18", S, (**C**: 91) £1,700
Paris, 1951
O 14 x 10", S, (**C**: 98) £900
Mykonos, 1939
W 8 x 11", S, (**C**: 99) £220
Girl with Goat, Shanveagh
O 36 x 28", S, (**C**: 100) £3,400
Bus Stop, Monkstown
O 10 x 14", S, (**C**: 102) £540
Battersea Evening
O 10 x 14", S, D, (**C**: 103) £280
Derry Street
W 18 x 13", I, (**C**: 104) £280
Charlotte
O 18 x 14", S, D, (**C**: 105) £2,200
Pink Orchard in Flower
O 18 x 14", S, (**C**: 106) £380
Oileanacusha from Reenacappul
W 14 x 19", S, (**C**: 108) £460
Waterwheel, Mykonos
O 10 x 14", S, (**C**: 110) £280

Portrait in Interior
O 10 x 14", S, (**C**: 111) £480
Henfold
O 13 x 16", S, (**C**: 112) £380
Mallorcan Pathway
W 14 x 10", S, D, (**C**: 113) £320
Flood Victim
O 24 x 18", S, D, (**C**: 115) £1,700
Pendoylan Garden
O 18 x 14", S, I, (**C**: 116) £560
La Trilla Siguenza
W 14 x 19", S, D, (**C**: 118) £260
Arezzo
O 8 x 11", I, (**C**: 119) £340
The Blue Curragh
W 10 x 14", I, (**C**: 120) £400
The Fisherman
W 8 x 6", (**C**: 121) £260
Tower Through the Maize
W 19 x 14", S, (**C**: 124) £360
Hurdle Makers' Tent
O 16 x 20", S, D, (**C**: 125) £560
Sherkin Abbey
O 18 x 30", S, (**C**: 127) £770
Glassworker
O 20 x 30", S, (**C**: 128) £1,100
Home Farm, Hampton Court
O 14 x 18", S, D, (**C**: 129) £620
Monastery Quay, Roundstone
W 14 x 19", S, D, (**C**: 130) £500
Settignano
O 13 x 16", D, I, (**C**: 131) £460
The Coach
O 18 x 14", S, (**C**: 132) £560
Low Tide, Battersea
O 14 x 18", S, D, (**C**: 133) £650
Dunmanus Donkey
O 12 x 16", S, (**C**: 135) £970
Rabbit Hutches, Henfold Cottages
W 14 x 19", S, I, (**C**: 136) £520
Sweeny Dreaming
O 10 x 14", S, (**C**: 138) £580
The Artist's Friend
W 18 x 13", S, (**C**: 139) £260
The Gate, Newtownards, Co. Down
O 30 x 20", S, (**C**: 140) £580
Los Dos Naranjas
W 7 x 10", S, (**C**: 142) £480
Alan
O 16 x 20", S, (**C**: 146) £380
The Convent Door
W 19 x 14", S, (**C**: 147) £280
Higham
O 14 x 18", S, (**C**: 148) £280
Gang of Workers
D 9 x 13", (**C**: 149) £200Z
Zinnias
O 22 x 18", S, (**C**: 151) £1,100
Bread on the Waters
O 10 x 14", S, (**C**: 153) £520
Delphi
O 10 x 14", D, I, (**C**: 154) £3,100
Stacking Hay, County Donegal
W 10 x 15", S, D, (**C**: 156) £260
Harleston Fancy
O 14 x 18", S, D, (**C**: 158) £650
Saving the Hay
W 12 x 10", S, D, (**C**: 168) £380
O'Brien's House
W 14 x 19", S, D, (**C**: 171) £350
Balcony, Reenacappul
O 20 x 24", S, (**C**: 172) £580
Park Bench
O 6 x 10", S, (**C**: 173) £460
Barge
O 10 x 14", S, (**C**: 174) £280
El Azotea, Sevilla
W 10 x 13", S, (**C**: 175) £220
Dance of the Duck
O 23 x 20", S, (**C**: 176) £1,800

The Pad, Shanveagh, Betsy's Gate
O 14 x 10", S, (**C**: 177) £400
The Sandhopper
O 16 x 12", S, D, (**C**: 178) £950
Seaweed and Sow Thistle, Dunmanus Bay
W 14 x 19", S, (**C**: 180) £280
Farm Landscape, Mykonos
O 13 x 16", S, (**C**: 182) £360
Flood Victim, 1954
W 6 x 4", (**C**: 183) £200
SS Uganda, Vigo Bay
O 8 x 10", S, (**C**: 185) £570
Well, Mykonos
O 16 x 13", S, D, (**C**: 186) £360
Three Yellows, Four Shadows
O 27 x 35", S, D, (**C**: 188) £2,600
Roofspace, Reenacappul
O 20 x 30", S, (**C**: 189) £580
Naxos
O 16 x 19", I, (**C**: 191) £400
Putney High School, London
W 14 x 19", (**C**: 192) £280
North Derry Dry Stone Wall
O 10 x 14", S, (**C**: 193) £340
Settignano
O 10 x 14", D, I, (**C**: 194) £340
Peasant in a Doorway
W 14 x 10", S, D, (**C**: 195) £380
Orchard
O 13 x 17", S, (**C**: 196) £360
Boy Climbing Fence
O 30 x 20", S, (**C**: 200) £3,800
Seville Oranges
O 14 x 18", S, (**C**: 201) £950
Pylons
O 30 x 20", S, (**C**: 202) £360
Orchard in Flower
O 18 x 14", S, (**C**: 206) £360
Tree Form by the Cam
O 20 x 14", S, D, (**C**: 209) £570
Otra Naranja
W 7 x 11", S, (**C**: 212) £460
The Machines of Learning 1938
W 7 x 9", (**C**: 214) £240
Lighters at Battersea
O 30 x 20", S, (**C**: 215) £4,700
Boat
O 10 x 14", (**C**: 216) £380
Mallorcan Sunday
W 6 x 8", (**C**: 218) £260
The Spell
W 6 x 6", I, (**C**: 219) £400
Bar, Dun Laoghaire
O 14 x 10", S, D, (**C**: 221) £540
Landscape in Spain
W 8 x 10", S, D, (**C**: 222) £260
The Fall 1986
O 30 x 20", (**G**: 15) £470
Shadows in a Courtyard
O 14 x 18", S, I, (**O**: 33) £820

BRADY, Charles (1926-1997)
Watering Can
O 18 x 24", S, (**O**: 97) £12,500
Farm Buildings
O 11.5 x 18", S, (**O**: 107) £3,600
Letter from Amsterdam
O 11 x 14", S, (**EI**: 109) £2,500
Artists Tissue Roll
O 9 x 10.5", S, (**EI**: 110) £2,300
Standing Books
O 16 x 12", S, D, (**EI**: 121) £1,700
Envelope
O 13 x 9", S, D, (**EI**: 122) £1,600
Standing Pencils
O 13 x 15.5", S, (**VI**: 50) £2,600
In the Knockmealdowns
O 8 x 14", S, (**VI**: 51) £2,200
Pink Envelope
O 9.5 x 13.5", S, D, (**VI**: 52) £2,200
Thatched Cottage
O 9 x 11", S, (**VI**: 81) £1,500

BRANDT, Muriel (1909-1981)
Portrait of Ban de Valera
D 9.5 x 7.5", S, (**LI**: 145) £380

BRANDT, Ruth (1936-1989)
Ranelagh
Pr 6.5 x 5", S, D, I, (**W**: 60) £200

BRENAN, James Butler (1825-1889)
Portrait of Robert William Cary Reeves of Burrane and his Wife
O (2) 14 x 12", S, D, (**L**: 90) £690

BROPHY, Elizabeth (20th Century)
Gathering Wild Flowers
O 11 x 16", S, (**GII**: 1416) £550
Wicklow Mountains
O 12.5 x 16", S, I, (**JII**: 243) £480
The Flower Market
O 12 x 16", S, (**JII**: 245) £525
Pink Cloud - children on a beach
O 13.5 x 17.5", S, (**JII**: 451) £475
Beach Games
O 12 x 16", S, (**JII**: 503) £1,000
Two Boys and a Boat
O 12 x 16", (**KII**: 651) £420
Children picking wild flowers in a wood
O 12 x 16", (**KII**: 659) £500

BROWN, Henry J. of Kingstown (19th Century)
The Paddle Steamer RMS 'Leinster' entering Kingstown Harbour
O 17 x 29", S, D, (**FII**: 175) £900

BROWNE, Nassau Blair (fl.1867-1940)
A Nice Day Maam, we might go to see the Cowes Regatta I Think?
O 9 x 15.5", (**O**: 74) £400

BRUEN, Gerald (20th Century)
Flower Study
O 18 x 29.5", (**G**: 21) £520

BURCH, Lawson (20th Century)
End of Summer
A 18 x 18", (**G**: 23) £470

BURKE, Augustus (c.1838-1891)
Cattle on the Road
O 24 x 36", (**OI**: 284) £4,025
Portrait of a Boy
O 17 x 15.5", S, I, (**FII**: 169) £1,100

BURKE, Mary (20th Century)
Pearl Street Studio
O 11.5 x 8", (**G**: 24) £350

BUTLER, Mildred Anne (1858-1941)
New Auction Record: £28,000
Green Eyed Jealousy
Watercolour 38 x 26 ins. S
James Adam, 31 March 1999, Lot 45

Young Jackdaws
W 9.5 x 13.5", (**O**: 55) £2,400
Pigeons at the Pump, Kilmurry
O 22 x 16", (**O**: 62) £8,500
A Girl at a Cottage Door
W 5 x 7", S, (**V**: 74) £2,100
Doves at the Water Trough, Kilmurry
W 10.5 x 14.5", (**V**: 86) £6,700
Cattle grazing in Mountain Landscape
W 10.5 x 14.5", S, (**V**: 88) £4,000
Crows
D 18 x 23", (**V**: 109A) £1,600
The Black Pony
W 14.5 x 10", S, D, I, (**V**: 130) £5,800
Crows resting in a snow covered Landscape
W 7 x 10", S, D, (**X**: 180) £1,495
Aix les Bains
W 6 x 9", S, I, (**AI**: 45) £1,035
Green Eyed Jealousy
W 38 x 26", S, (**HI**: 45) £28,000
Peacocks in a Field
W 9.5 x 13.5", S, (**HI**: 59) £8,000
Crows in the snow
W 5 x 7", S, (**OI**: 267) £1,840
Sheep grazing in the pasture
W 5 x 7", S, D, (**OI**: 269) £2,070
Madonna Lilies
W 14.x 10", S, (**OI**: 273) £8,050
Trees by a Meadow
W 11.5 x 7.5", S, (**OI**: 275) £1,840
The back of the house, Kilmurry
W 10 x 14", (**PI**: 81) £9,000
Peace
W 10 x 14", S, (**PI**: 82) £3,000
Grazing Time
W 10 x 14", S, (**PI**: 83) £2,000
Snowdrops
W 7 x 10", S, (**PI**: 85) £1,700
Peacocks
W 5.5 x 6", S, (**PI**: 95) £2,100
Flaming Torches
W 10 x 7", S, (**PI**: 110) £5,200
Cattle in a Woodland Stream
W 7 x 10", S, (**PI**: 168) £1,900
A Happy Family
W 10.5 x 14", S, (**PI**: 170) £7,200
Study of Young Jackdaws
D 17.5 x 22.5", (**VI**: 131) £1,000
Gardens at Kilmurry
W 10 x 14", S, (**ZI**: 52) £4,100
Two Figures on a Garden Path; Woman in Flower Garden; Herbaceous Border
O (3) 7 x 5", S, (**GII**: 1479) £2,000

BYRNE, Gerard (20th Century)
The Grand Canal
O 19 x 28.5", S, (**LI**: 77) £200

BYRNE, Peter (20th Century)
The Orchard
O 20 x 16", (**G**: 27) £700

CAMPBELL, Arthur (20th Century)
At Keel, Achill
O 8.5 x 10", (**VI**: 116) £460

CAMPBELL, Christopher (1908-1972)
A Stately Garden
O 12 x 15", S, (**O**: 9) £770
A Young Minstrel with his Horse
D 18 x 28", S, (**O**: 10) £380

CAMPBELL, George (1917-1979)
Auction Record: IR£17,000
Mozart Quartet
30 x 36 ins. S
James Adam, 14 December 1989, Lot 69

Abstract Composition
M 22 x 28", S, D, (**D**: 62) £900
Two Waiting Men
O 40 x 28", S, I, (**O**: 56) £8,000
Play of Shapes, Azticiana
O 50 x 17", S, (**O**: 78) £5,200
Mountain Village, Andalucia
O 19 x 14", S, (**O**: 95C) £3,000
Western Landscape
O 12 x 16", (**V**: 34) £1,700
Clown
O 15 x 11.5", S, (**V**: 92) £900
Andalucia, Mountain Town
O 36 x 30", S, D, (**V**: 140) £6,400
Don Quixote and Sancho Panza
O 30 x 21", S, (**V**: 158) £3,700
Western Landscape
O 18 x 24", S, (**W**: 150) £1,700
View over Clifden
W 7 x 9", S, (**W**: 151) £520
The back road to Clifden
W 4 x 6", (**W**: 153) £300
Extensive Landscape
W 6 x 8", (**W**: 154) £320
Landscape, Co. Clare
M 4 x 6", (**W**: 155) £200
Donegal
O 5.5 x 7.5", (**W**: 159) £400
Mother & Child
W 17 x 11", S, D, (**EI**: 27) £770
Fishing, Errisbeg, Connemara
O 13 x 17", S, I, (**EI**: 34) £3,200
Blitz Playground, Belfast
O 24 x 16.5", S, I, (**EI**: 61) £3,000
Two Clowns
W 19.5 x 14", S, (**HI**: 24) £800

Boxer
O 24 x 20", S, I, (**HI**: 33) £3,800
Female Nude
Pr 10 x 15", (**LI**: 65) £320
Street Scene, Malaga
O 20 x 23.5", S, (**VI**: 7) £10,500
Rain
W 8 x 5", S, (**VI**: 14) £770
West of Ireland Landscape with Figure at Work
O 18 x 24", S, (**VI**: 22) £4,200
The Tramp
O 20 x 15.5", S, (**VI**: 26) £2,800
Coastal Landscape
O 6 x 8", S, (**VI**: 115) £970
Grey Day Connemara
W 8 x 14.5", S, I, (**ZI**: 24) £400
Female Nude
O 17 x 7", S, (**DII**: 40) £4,300
In Circus Mood
O S, (**DII**: 71) £2,100
Paddy Moloney, 'The Chieftains'
O 29.5 x 19.5", S, (**DII**: 72) £4,600
CARACCIOLO, Niccolo d'Ardia (1941-1989)
Early Morning on the Ponte Vecchio, Florence
O 13 x 17", (**O**: 80) £4,400
Female Nude Study
W 10 x 15", S, (**O**: 81) £1,000
Still Life
O 20.5 x 30", S, (**EI**: 15) £6,400
Summer in the Park
W 7 x 11", S, (**EI**: 157) £1,600
O'Connell Bridge, Dublin, Spring 1989
O 24 x 36", S, (**PI**: 44) £34,000
The Shelbourne Hotel, Dublin - Spring 1989
O 18 x 26", S, (**PI**: 127) £5,000
14-17 St. Stephen's Green - Spring 1989
O 18 x 26", S, (**PI**: 129) £13,000
Francis Street, Dublin
O 10 x 14.5", S, (**VI**: 150) £4,400
CAREY, Joseph William (1859-1937)
Kate Kearney
W 10 x 7.5", S, (**EI**: 40) £270
Carrickfergus Castle, Co. Antrim
W 8 x 13.5", (**NI**: 161) £2,760
CARR, Tom (b.1909)
Near Dromara, Co. Down
W 11 x 14", S, (**HI**: 52) £2,700
Silk Cut
W 29 x 22", S, (**NI**: 196) £9,200
The Front, Newcastle, Co. Down
O 18 x 22", (**OI**: 398) £12,650
Washing Day
W 11.5 x 8", S, (**PI**: 163) £1,600
Still Life - Daffodils & Flowers in a Vase
M 11 x 17.5", S, (**ZI**: 73) £2,450
CARRICK, Desmond (b.1928)
National Yacht Club, Dun Laoghaire
O 20 x 16", S, (**V**: 126) £650
The Village of La Chapelle, Reanville
O 19 x 24", S, (**W**: 12) £1,100
Cattle in pasture
O 12 x 16", S, (**W**: 93) £320
At the Beach
O 18 x 24", S, (**EI**: 203) £920
House by a River
O 18 x 24", S, (**HI**: 113) £460
Sunday Afternoon on Punta Lara Beach, Nerja (Malaga)
O 18 x 24", S, (**PI**: 28) £900
CARROLL, Marie (20th Century)
Lake Garda, Italy
O 24 x 36", S, (**LI**: 103) £460
Sailing Scenes
O (2) 9.5 x 11.5", S, (**LI**: 104) £320
CARRON, William (20th Century)
Clouds over Slievemore
A 13.5 x 8.5", (**G**: 31) £300
CARSON, Robert Taylor (b.1919)
Two Figures with Donkey and Cart
O 17 x 24", S, (**V**: 72) £850

Itinerant Family
O 15.5 x 19.5", S, (**DII**: 29) £1,650
CARVER, Robert (fl.1750-1791)
Auction Record: £15,972
Pastoral Landscape
47 x 61 ins. S & D 1754
Goteborg's (Goteborg, Sweden), 11 May 1993 Lot 135
CASHEN, A.J (20th Century)
Kilmainham
O 16 x 20", S, (**W**: 110) £550
CLARKE, Brid (20th Century)
Howth Harbour
W 27.5 x 35.5", (**G**: 34) £400
CLARKE, Carey (b.1936)
Still life with some fresh figs
O 20 x 25", (**G**: 35) £2,600
Promise of Summer
O 32 x 36.5", S, (**V**: 125) £4,100
CLARKE, David (b.1920)
Cruinniu Na mbad, Connemara
P 21 x 27", S, (**EI**: 161) £500
CLARKE, Harry (1889-1931)
Auction Record: £331,500
Queens (Nine stained glass panels)
Each panel 12 x 7 ins. S
Christie's, 21 May 1997, Lot 65
The Fairy Tales of Perault
D 11 x 9.5", (**D**: 33) £1,400
Dearest and Best, with my whole heart I love thee
W 12 x 9", S, (**M**: 157) £10,925
Fantasy
W 4 x 5", S, D, I, (**NI**: 77) £2,300
The Playboy of the Western World
W 17 x 10", (**OI**: 308) £12,650
St. George
W 15 x 8", (**VI**: 39) £560
The Two Princesses - Saints Fidelma & Eithne & St. Gobnait
W 15.5 x 6", I, (**VI**: 54) £1,800
Saints Doulough & Columba
W 15.5 x 6", S, D, I, (**VI**: 55) £1,800
Design for Stained Glass - Virgin & Two Angels
W 12 x 6", (**VI**: 86) £560
The Annunciation - Design for Stained Glass
D 9.5 x 4", (**VI**: 87) £560
CLARKE, Margaret (1888-1961)
Pastoral Landscape
P 14 x 21", S, (**D**: 115) £460
CLARKE, Maria (20th Century)
Angel of incidence
O 22 x 12", (**LI**: 37) £300
Chronicles: "Next Month"
O 10 x 10", (**LI**: 38) £240
CLARKE, Nuala (20th Century)
Journey
M 20 x 23.5", (**G**: 37) £300
COLEMAN, Michael (20th Century)
Untitled, 1978
M 18 x 22", S, (**LI**: 78) £480
Black Emerging
D 31 x 22", (**LI**: 84) £480
COLEMAN, Simon (b.1916)
West Meath Pastures
O 10.5 x 12.5", S, D, (**O**: 90) £470
In the Phoenix Park
O 24 x 20", S, (**HI**: 28) £500
Ploughing
O 29 x 39.5", S, (**HI**: 115) £300
Trees in Phoenix Park
O 11.5 x 15.5", S, D, (**LI**: 111) £200
Glendalough, Co. Wicklow
W 10.5 x 14.5", S, (**ZI**: 42) £300
COLLIE, Clifford (20th Century)
From a Spanish Table
A 28.5 x 33.5", (**G**: 40) £600
COLLIE, George (1904-1975)
Portrait of a Young Woman Wearing a Shawl
O 19.5 x 15", S, I, (**EII**: 309) £850

COLLINS, Patrick (1911-1994)
Auction Record: IR£40,000
The Liffey Quays
Oil 27 x 31 ins. S, D
James Adam & Bonhams 27 May 1998, Lot 85
Weed and Stone Head
O 12 x 16", S, D, I, (**O**: 95D) £4,000
Night Raider
O 21 x 19", (**W**: 173) £800
Predatory Fish
O 11 x 16", S, (**EI**: 224A) £7,500
Swans at Erval Lough
O 24 x 30", S, I, (**HI**: 62) £22,000
Blue Landscape
O 15.5 x 19.5", S, (**VI**: 20) £14,000
Sheltering Cows
O 9.5 x 10", S, (**VI**: 23) £4,700
Sun in the Woods
O 11.5 x 16", S, (**VI**: 145) £4,800
COLLIS, Peter (b.1929)
Mountain Near Laragh
O 5 x 7", (**G**: 41) £460
Mountain Path
O 8 x 9", (**G**: 42) £600
Rough Seas
O 10 x 10.5", S, (**O**: 104) £620
Wicklow Landscape
O 11.5 x 10.5", (**O**: 127) £700
The Railway Line Near Monkstown
O 9 x 11", S, (**EI**: 112) £500
Mountain Road
O 15 x 18", S, (**EI**: 130) £600
Still Life
O 30 x 36", S, (**EI**: 135) £2,400
Still Life
O 12 x 14", S, (**EI**: 136) £1,300
Coastal Landscape - Possibly Killiney
O 16 x 17", S, (**EI**: 146) £670
Snow at Glencree
O 14 x 16", S, (**EI**: 217) £660
Woodland Path
O 5 x 7", S, (**LI**: 107) £400
Kanturk Mountain
O 9 x 11", S, (**PI**: 16) £800
Dalkey Island
O 15 x 17", S, (**PI**: 100) £1,200
Strawberry Beds Road
O 12 x 14", S, (**PI**: 126) £1,200
Powerscourt Mountain
O 12 x 14", S, (**VI**: 135) £660
Landscape at Roundwood
O 14 x 16", S, (**GII**: 1447) £525
Mountains near Laragh
O 12 x 13", S, (**GII**: 1451) £440
Farm at Glanasmole with closed Gate
O 30 x 34", (**GII**: 1462) £1,200
Old Farm
O 30 x 34", S, I, (**GII**: 1465) £950
COLLIS, Sylvia Cooke (1899-1973)
Unloading the catch, Ballycotton pier
O 15 x 21", (**JII**: 252) £800
Baltimore
W 10.5 x 13", (**JII**: 492) £1,000
Standing stone near Baltimore
W 9 x 12.5", (**JII**: 493) £1,050
COMERFORD, Oliver (20th Century)
Visitor's Reading
M 16 x 12", S, D, I, (**W**: 77) £240
CONOR, William (1881-1968)
New Auction Record £89,500
The Picture House Queue
Drawing 30 x 24 ins.
Sotheby's, 19221 May 1999, Lot 379
The Dockyard
D 15 x 12", S, (**V**: 101) £1,400
The Bog Road
O 15.5. x 12.5", S, (**HI**: 82) £7,200
The Kelp Gathering
D 13 x 16", S, I, (**NI**: 67) £9,775
The Twelfth
D 20 x 15", S, (**NI**: 205) £19,550

The Picture House Queue
D 30 x 24", (**OI**: 379) £89,500
Remnants
W 14 x 10.5", S, (**PI**: 40) £6,500
The Boxing Match
W 8 x 6.5", S, D, (**PI**: 41) £1,300
Orangemen
P 13 x 9", S, (**SI**: 99) £3,795
COOKE, Barrie (b.1931)
Punishment, Study for Heaney's Bog Poem 1974
D 14.5 x 14.5", (**G**: 45) £670
Feale River Bank
M 18 x 18.5", S, D, (**W**: 83) £650
Banana Tree Grove from Genting
W 7 x 9", S, I, (**EI**: 175) £660
Dusk Kuala Perkhi
O 57 x 49", S, I, (**LI**: 80) £3,800
COOKE-COLLIS, Sylvia (b.1900)
Children catching Tadpoles
O 9.5 x 11.5", S, (**VI**: 46) £1,100
COOPER, William F. (20th Century)
Autumn in Donegal
W 7 x 10", S, (**DII**: 33) £300
COPE, Elizabeth (20th Century)
Playtime
O 30 x 24", S, (**D**: 10) £650
Still Life
O 24 x 32", S, (**EI**: 137) £970
Still life with vase
O 24 x 14", S, (**LI**: 94) £700
Reuben
O 29.5 x 21.5", S, I, (**VI**: 156) £580
COSTELLO, Malachy (20th Century)
Near Castlerea
O 19 x 24.5", (**G**: 49) £400
COYLE, John (20th Century)
Still life with palette
O 11.5 x 11", S, (**W**: 90) £400
COYLE, Rosemary (20th Century)
Barge on the River
O 13 x 17", S, (**ZI**: 13) £370
CRAIG, Henry Robertson (1916-1984)
Coastal Scene with Nude Youth
O 6 x 4", S, (**D**: 169) £320
Low Tide, Algarve
O 10 x 14", S, (**V**: 91) £1,200
CRAIG, James Humbert (1878-1944)
New Auction Record £25,300
Children on the Beach
Oil 15 x 22 ins. S
Sotheby's, 21 May 1999, Lot 373
Moored Boat on a River
P 12 x 9", S, D, (**B**: 74) £920
Gypsies
O 15 x 20", S, I, (**D**: 84) £4,000
Gweebarra River
O 11.5 x 15.5", S, (**D**: 97) £1,500
The Old Layde Road to Cushendun
O 11 x 16.5", S, I, (**V**: 86A) £3,400
Children along the Riverbank
O 16 x 20", S, (**EI**: 16) £6,500
Ratray Islanders, County Antrim
O 9 x 12", S, I, (**EI**: 29) £2,800
Coastal Landscape
O 8 x 11", S, (**EI**: 30) £1,300
Storm Over Rosses Point
O 11 x 13", S, (**HI**: 7) £1,500
Evening Sea
O 22 x 30", S, D, (**NI**: 43) £14,950
Coastal Landscape with Sheep
O 12 x 17", S, D, I, (**NI**: 48) £6,900
Cattle Returning
O 11.5 x 15", S, (**NI**: 49) £4,140
Homeward Bound
O 10 x 14", S, (**NI**: 105) £3,105
Muckish, Co. Donegal
O 8 x 11", S, I, (**NI**: 106) £4,025
Knocknacarry, Cushendun, Co. Antrim
O 10 x 14", S, (**NI**: 107) £2,070
Children on the Beach
O 15 x 22", S, (**OI**: 373) £25,300
Children playing by the River
O 20 x 16", S, (**OI**: 376) £8,625
God's Country - Landscape near Letterkenny, Co. Donegal
O 20 x 24", S, (**OI**: 381) £14,950
Lough Inagh, Connemara, Ireland
O 20 x 24", S, I, (**OI**: 385) £4,370
Cloud Shadows in the Rosses, Co. Donegal
O 20 x 24", S, I, (**OI**: 386) £9,200
Lough Finn, County Donegal
O 15 x 20", S, I, (**OI**: 388) £7,475
Cattle near the water's edge
O 14 x 19", S, (**SI**: 94) £3,450
Coastal scene with houses
O 9.5 x 13", S, (**SI**: 96) £3,680
Alton Lake, Donegal
O 11 x 14.5", S, (**VI**: 63) £2,200
Gathering the Peat, Co. Donegal
O 20 x 24", S, (**DII**: 52) £3,800
Showery weather in the Rosses, Co. Donegal
O 12 x 17", S, (**JII**: 249) £5,200
CRAMPTON-WALKER, John (20th Century)
On the Achill Coast
O 10 x 13.5", S, I, (**D**: 4) £800
CREAN, Emma (20th Century)
Melody III
M 33 x 29.5", (**G**: 50) £350
CRONE, David (b.1937)
Seated Woman
W 25.5 x 21.5", S, D, (**VI**: 183A) £560
Abstract - Forest, Mountain River
O 39.5 x 29.5", (**EII**: 367) £200
CROZIER, William (b.1930)
Irish Garden
O 20 x 16", (**G**: 237C) £2,400
Landscape
O 10 x 14", S, (**O**: 114) £1,700
Garden View
W 10 x 12", S, (**EI**: 133) £380
Abstract
O 30 x 35", S, (**VI**: 82) £3,800
Abstract
O 20 x 16", S, D, (**YI**: 258) £437
CRYAN, Clare (20th Century)
Tulips
O 20 x 24", S, D, (**W**: 40) £270
CUDWORTH, Jack (20th Century)
Belturbet
O 23.5 x 26.5", (**G**: 52) £600
Girl in a red hat
O 15 x 13.5", (**G**: 53) £380
CULLEN, Charles (20th Century)
Warrior
O 19 x 12", S, D, (**W**: 106) £200
CULLEN, Michael (b.1946)
Based on 'The Song of Wandering Aengus' by W.B. Yeats
O 64 x 79", (**HI**: 92K) £1,800
Study for Deposition with Zebra
M 22 x 29.5", S, D, I, (**VI**: 183E) £650
CULLEN, Stephen (20th Century)
Shoppers in a City Street
O 31 x 39", S, (**LI**: 132A) £1,300
Figures swimming at Seapoint
O 16 x 24", S, (**AII**) £500
CULLEN, Tom (20th Century)
Dublin Views
O (3) 14 x 10", S, D, (**W**: 89) £200
CURLING, Peter (b.1955)
Riding Out
P 12 x 16", (**W**: 181) £650
Striding Out
P 18 x 17", S, (**W**: 182) £650
The Last Furlong
W 14 x 20", S, (**HI**: 85) £700
Classic performers at the Park
Pr S, (**LI**: 147) £400
Riding Out in Autumn
O 22 x 30", S, (**OI**: 403) £7,475
Riding Out
O 15 x 19", S, (**PI**: 89) £4,000
DANBY, Francis (1793-1861)
Auction Record: £35,000
Winter Sunset
27 x 41 ins. S & D 1850
Sotheby's, 14 July 1993, Lot 93
DANBY, Thomas (c.1817-1886)
Mending Nets; At the End of the Day
O (2) 8 x 10", S, (**KI**: 27) £2,530
DAVEY, Rosaleen (20th Century)
After Rembrandt
P 19.5 x 16.5", (**G**: 56) £300
DAVIDSON, Lillian Lucy (1893-1954)
Auction Record: £20,700
Gathering Kelp
Oil 25 x 29 ins. S
Sotheby's Irish Sale, 21 May 1998, Lot 358
Riverside Cottages
W 8.5 x 12", S, (**D**: 8) £260
Continental Riverside
W 16 x 13", S, (**D**: 142) £1,740
A Boy and his Donkey
O 14 x 17", S, (**VI**: 33) £5,200
DAVIS, Gerald (20th Century)
Evening Rider
O 8 x 10", (**D**: 172) £320
Somewhere before
O 20.5 x 30.5", (**G**: 57) £700
Another summit
O 19.5 x 15.5", S, D, (**W**: 101) £250
Landscape form in Red
O 24 x 30", S, (**LI**: 83) £550
Separation
O 16 x 20", S, D, I, (**LI**: 141) £380
Night Scenes
O (2) S, (**DII**: 62) £300
Forms in an Interior
O 8.5 x 11.5", S, D, (**DII**: 63) £280
DAVIS, Philip Y. (20th Century)
Barn at Glenbeigh Co. Kerry
O 16 x 20", (**G**: 58) £260
DAVISON, Sarah (20th Century)
Donegal Landscape
A 13.5 x 17.5", (**G**: 59) £350
DeBURCA, Michael (1913-1985)
Achill Landscape
O 14 x 20", I, (**HI**: 32) £800
Bog Workers
O 17.5 x 22", (**HI**: 90) £1,500
Achill View
O 14 x 16", S, I, (**HI**: 107) £850
DeGENNARO, Gaetano (1890-1959)
Sybill Point, Kerry
O 18 x 24", S, (**HI**: 35) £1,800
DELANEY, Edward (b.1930)
For a still life Animal
O 36 x 29", S, I, (**LI**: 108) £650
Project 16 - Figures and Animals
O 29.5 x 38.5", S, (**LI**: 109) £650
Figures and Animals
O 30 x 38.5", (**LI**: 110) £650
DELARGY, Diarmuid (20th Century)
The stone in the field
Pr (**G**: 61) £280
DENARO, Melita (20th Century)
Slanu (The Saving)
O (**G**: 62) £380
DENNIS, Jill (20th Century)
Red Shadow (1998)
O (**G**: 63) £600
DILLON, Gerard (1916-1971)
Auction Record: £89,500
Girl in a bedsitter with a cat
Oil 18 x 24 ins. S
Sotheby's Irish Sale, 21 May 1998, Lot 403
Horses and Carriages
W 9.5 x 13.5", S, (**D**: 13) £1,100
Blue Moon
C 8 x 10", S, (**D**: 82) £2,200
The Jockey
O 25 x 30", S, I, (**O**: 28) £52,000

Mid-day Rest, Innislacken
O 17 x 22.5", S, (**O**: 31) £17,500
A Resting Place
O 24 x 30", S, (**O**: 48) £11,000
Study of a Young Man in Blue
O 19.5 x 8.5", S, (**O**: 79) £4,200
Abstract Composition
M 7 x 9.5", S, (**O**: 93) £1,400
Abstract Composition
M 20 x 24", S, (**V**: 118) £1,500
Study of a woman
W 4.5 x 6.5", S, (**W**: 148) £900
Lovers by the Shore
O 13.5 x 17", S, (**EI**: 26) £9,200
Abstract
M 17 x 11", (**EI**: 47) £750
"When I was Young"
W 10 x 7.5", S, I, (**EI**: 224L) £750
Boy and Girl
O 14 x 11", S, I, (**HI**: 36) £10,000
Aran Horses
O 15 x 19.5", S, I, (**HI**: 55) £15,500
Blushing Corn
O 14 x 18", S, (**HI**: 63) £11,500
The Lobster Pots, Roundstone
O 20 x 24", S, (**NI**: 21) £79,600
The Road by the Tide
O 15.5 x 20", S, I, (**OI**: 356) £67,500
Aran Horse Man
O 15 x 19", S, D, (**OI**: 359) £11,500
Farmyard Scene, Aran Islands
O 14 x 18", S, (**OI**: 369) £12,650
Weeds From the Deep
O 36 x 48", S, I, (**OI**: 370) £2,070
Small Birds
M 7 x 18", I, (**VI**: 11) £1,800
The Envelope
M 11 x 14", S, (**VI**: 24) £1,100
Evening Light
Pr 7 x 7.5", S, I, (**VI**: 27) £400
Interior Decorators
O 14 x 18", S, (**VI**: 32) £28,500
The Luton Girls' Choir
O 17 x 21", S, (**VI**: 49) £20,500
Seated Female Nude
D 16 x 16.5", S, (**VI**: 147) £520
DINAN, John (20th Century)
Study of Botanic Gardens
O 21 x 25", S, (**ZI**: 57) £440
DIXON, James (1887-1970)
S.S. Queen Mary passing Tory Island
O 22 x 30", S, D, I, (**NI**: 72) £1,840
Ringnet Fishing
O 21.5 x 29", S, D, I, (**NI**: 73) £4,600
German Mine stuck in Fishermen's Nets
O 19 x 29", S, D, I, (**NI**: 74) £3,450
Ave Marie, The Oldest Motor Boat on Tory Island
O 22 x 30", S, D, I, (**OI**: 391) £2,875
H.M.S. Wasp
O 20.5 x 30", S, D, I, (**OI**: 393) £2,875
The First Life Saving Rocket that was Fired on Tory Island
O 22 x 29.5", S, I, (**OI**: 394) £1,725
DOBBIN, Kate, Lady (1868-1948)
Still Life - Flowers in a jug
W 12 x 16", S, (**JII**: 484) £775
Patricks Bridge and Shandon, Cork
W 17.5 x 14", S, (**JII**: 487) £4,600
Still Life - Flowers in a jug
W 14.5 x 12.5", S, (**JII**: 496) £420
Still Life - Roses on a Ledge
W 5.5 x 9.5", S, (**KII**: 642) £320
DONNELLY, Anne (20th Century)
Canal Locks
O (**G**: 64) £550
DONNELLY, Mary (20th Century)
Sheep in Landscape
A (**G**: 65) £370
DOUGLAS, Jessie Oyston (fl.1892-1925)
Seated girl with rabbits in an orchard
W 19 x 26", S, D, (**OI**: 285) £3,220

Gerard DILLON, *Mid-day Rest, Innislacken*, sold at de Veres, 17 November 1998 for £17,500

DOWLING, William J. (1907-1980)
Near Caherdaniel, Co. Kerry
O 12 x 16", S, (**EI**: 58) £370
The Twelve Pins, Connemara
O 14 x 18", S, (**HI**: 42) £320
DOYLE, Marie (20th Century)
Iris with Lilies
O (**G**: 67) £320
DUFFY, Patrick Vincent (1836-1900)
Sunset
O 8 x 11.5", S, (**EI**: 71) £500
River Landscape at Sunset on Innisfallen
O 6 x 13", S, (**DII**: 19) £340
DUNCAN, Mary (1885-1964)
Breton Woman peeling vegetables
O 12.5 x 9.5", (**JII**: 488) £1,700
DUNIN-MARKIEVICZ, Count Kasimir
An Avenue of Hollyhocks
O 22 x 33", S, (**PI**: 117) £2,600
DUNLOP, Ronald Ossory (1894-1973)
Portrait of Norah
O 16 x 10", S, I, (**B**: 7) £863
Ferry crossing on a shiny Day, Wexford
O 10 x 14", S, (**B**: 126) £575
Shepperton-on-Thames
O 14 x 18", S, (**E**: 29) £1,725
A Paris Street
O 16 x 12", S, (**E**: 316) £1,725
The Girl from the Village
O 20 x 16", S, (**F**: 10) £644
The Riverside
O 16 x 20", S, (**F**: 12) £690
Boats at Anchor
O 14 x 18", S, (**F**: 18) £748
Seated Female Nude
O 25 x 30", S, (**V**: 149) £850
Wintry Day
O 13.5 x 11", S, (**Y**: 43) £862
Boats at Anchor
O 14 x 18", S, (**BI**: 105) £2,185
The Thames near Shepperton
O 18 x 26", S, (**BI**: 139) £2,070
In the Harbour
O 25 x 30", S, (**CI**: 100) £2,530
The Bridge, Littlehampton
O 25 x 30", S, (**CI**: 104) £1,495
Still Life with Daisies and Milk Bottle
O 30 x 25", S, (**CI**: 120) £978
The Ferry at Weybridge
O 20 x 24", S, (**DI**: 129) £3,220
Harbour at Tangiers
O 17 x 14", S, (**QI**: 39) £632
Punting
O 10.5 x 14.5", S, (**QI**: 76) £2,530
Figures by a Bridge
O 8 x 14", S, (**QI**: 77) £402
The Locks at Malding
O 18 x 24", S, (**QI**: 78) £2,185
Cottages in the Trees
O 14 x 18", S, (**QI**: 79) £805
The riverside, Oxford
O 16 x 20", S, (**RI**: 35) £2,300

View of a coastal town
O 20 x 24", S, (**RI**: 250) £1,955
Portrait of a Woman in a green Dress
O 24 x 20", S, (**YI**: 13) £575
Bridge at Sunrise
O 25 x 30", S, (**YI**: 47) £575
EARLEY, Leo (20th Century)
Entering Dublin Port
O 13.5 x 19", S, (**D**: 162) £300
EGAN, Felim (b.1952)
Strand Study
W (**G**: 68) £920
Untitled 1992
M 24 x 24", (**HI**: 92C) £1,300
Hercules & Antaeus
A (2) 55 x 63", S, D, I, (**NI**: 84) £4,830
Hercules & Antaeus
A (2) 55 x 63", S, D, I, (**NI**: 85) £5,175
Perseus (Preparing for Battle)
A 55 x 63", S, D, I, (**NI**: 86) £5,520
EGAN, Orla (20th Century)
Kilronan, Aran
O 12 x 14", (**G**: 69) £1,600
Awaiting the Steamer from Galway on Aran
O 14 x 12", S, (**EI**: 160) £360
Bringing home the Lobster Pots
O 11.5 x 13.5", S, (**VI**: 162) £620
EGGINTON, Frank (1908-1990)
Reenooe Strand, Waterville, Co. Kerry
W 14.5 x 20.5", S, (**D**: 11) £1,200
A Summers Day, Connemara
W 14.5 x 21", S, (**D**: 24) £1,200
Near Creeslough, Co. Donegal
W 14.5 x 21", S, D, (**D**: 77) £3,000
A Bend in the River
W 21 x 31", S, (**V**: 78) £4,200
Kylemore Lough, Connemara
W 21 x 30", S, (**HI**: 50) £2,800
Pony and Trap in a Connemara Landscape
W 21 x 30", S, D, (**HI**: 95) £6,500
Building a Turf Reek, Connemara
W 21 x 30", S, (**HI**: 104) £4,300
The Maamturk Mountains, Connemara
W 21 x 29.5", S, I, (**II**: 137) £8,050
Near Connemara
W 8 x 12", S, (**MI**: 178) £322
Blacksod Bay, Co. Mayo
W 14 x 20.5", S, (**NI**: 163) £1,265
Low Tide, Cashel, Connemara
W 14.5 x 20.5", S, I, (**NI**: 164) £977
A Lake, Connemara
W 20 x 29.5", S, (**NI**: 169) £3,450
Divis from the Castlereagh Hill, Co. Antrim
W 14.5 x 20.5", S, I, (**NI**: 183) £1,610
Cottage in a west of Ireland landscape
W 14.5 x 20.5", S, (**PI**: 20) £1,500
Connemara Valley
W 21 x 30", S, (**PI**: 39) £1,800
The Maam Valley, Connemara
O 24 x 36", S, I, (**PI**: 97) £3,200
The Inagh Valley, Connemara
W 21 x 30", S, D, (**PI**: 135) £2,800
Thatched Cottages with Church beyond
W 9.5 x 13.5", S, D, (**PI**: 145) £850
Kylemore Lough, Connemara
W 21 x 30", S, D, (**PI**: 151) £3,200
Dunlevy, County Donegal
W 14 x 20.5", S, (**PI**: 156) £1,400
An Estuary View
W 14 x 20.5", S, (**PI**: 164) £1,300
Gathering Seaweed, Strangford Lough, Co. Down
W 15 x 20.5", S, I, (**FII**: 191) £1,900
West of Ireland Landscape
W 14.5 x 20.5", S, D, (**HII**: 213) £900
Off the Donegal Coast
W 15.5 x 22", S, (**III**: 1171) £1,500
Scariff Island, Co. Kerry
W 22 x 31", S, D, (**JII**: 477) £2,900
Lough Coppal, Co. Kerry
W 22 x 31", S, D, (**JII**: 481) £3,800

A Cart Shed in Co. Kerry
W 22 x 31", S, D, (**JII**: 485) £4,000

EGGINTON, Wycliffe (1875-1951)
...the road to Postbridge (late autumn)
W 10.5 x 15", S, (**V**: 84) £400
Two Figures on a Country Road
W 7 x 10", S, (**V**: 98A) £850
A harbour scene with rowing boats
W 15 x 22.5", S, (**V**: 110) £1,100
Horses grazing by a Rivers Edge and Sheep in a Field
W (2) 7 x 10", S, (**V**: 156) £2,600
In the Ledr Valley
W 10 x 14", S, (**MI**: 157) £632
The Drinking Pool; Highland River; Cattle Grazing
W (3) 10 x 14", S, D, (**OI**: 268) £3,220
A Moorland View
W 14 x 20", S, (**PI**: 113A) £1,100
The Blue Boat
W 12 x 16", S, (**JII**: 219) £950
Low Water Polzeath
W 10.5 x 15.5", S, I, (**JII**: 236) £1,300

EMERSON, Edward (20th Century)
Sea mist Achill and Fisherfolk, Irish coast
W (2) 14 x 20", S, (**LI**: 36) £420

ENGLISH, James (b.1946)
Rock Stallion (1981)
M 16 x 19", S, (**D**: 171) £200

EVANS, Lorna (20th Century)
The Red Umbrella
O 17.5 x 24", S, (**LI**: 35) £200

FAHY, Owen (19th Century)
A Project for a Monument to the Duke of Wellington
W 27 x 19", S, I, (**EII**: 363) £1,600

FARRELL, Michael (1893-1948)
James Joyce
Pr 25.5 x 18.5", S, I, (**D**: 158) £370
Presidents Letter
Pr 22.5 x 30", (**G**: 71) £320

FAULKNER, John (c.1830-1888)
Auction Record: £20,125
A Woodland Retreat
Oil 84 x 108.5 ins. S
Sotheby's Irish Sale 21 May 1998, Lot 290
Near the Village of Ashmor, Warick
W 16 x 27", S, I, (**D**: 120) £2,200
Figures on a Country Road
O 30 x 40", S, D, (**V**: 44) £3,200
Under Way to Port
W 17 x 28", S, (**V**: 67) £2,500
The Day's Catch
W 17 x 28", S, D, (**X**: 135) £1,035
At Glendalough
W 24 x 18.5", S, I, (**EI**: 96) £2,200
On the Beacanbrack River, Loch Corrib, Connemara
W 16.5 x 29", S, D, (**OI**: 279) £2,070
Gull Island, Achill, County Mayo
W 27 x 47", S, (**PI**: 153) £2,300
At Beyflut [?] Surrey
W 18 x 29", S, I, (**III**: 1170) £900

FERGUSON, Mary (20th Century)
The Drawing Room at 27 Upper Pembroke Street
W 18 x 14", (**JII**: 125) £1,100

FERRAN, Brian (20th Century)
Tain Theme 21
A 12 x 12", (**G**: 74) £670

FERRAN, Denise (20th Century)
Donegal Waves
A 12 x 12", (**G**: 75) £460

FEWER, Angela (20th Century)
Drift
O 50 x 35", (**G**: 76) £620

FINGLETON, Sean (20th Century)
Daffodils in a Vase
O 21.5 x 26", (**O**: 101) £750
Primavera
O 28 x 41", S, D, I, (**HI**: 65) £520

FISH, George Drummond (1876-1938)
O'Connell Bridge, Dublin
W 12.5 x 9", S, (**CI**: 10) £322
A View in Kerry
W 9.5 x 14.5", S, (**EI**: 7) £280
A County Mayo River & Mountain Landscape
W 10 x 13", S, (**ZI**: 7) £300

FITZHARRIS, Mike (20th Century)
Rural Dwellings
O 12 x 11.5", (**G**: 78) £500

FLACK, James H. (20th Century)
Evening Light on the Burren
W 23 x 30.5", (**G**: 79) £570

FLANAGAN, Catherine (20th Century)
In Glencarr
W 15 x 17", (**G**: 80) £240

FLANAGAN, Terence P. (b.1929)
Lough Hume, Ely Island, Co. Fermanagh
W 15 x 18", (**G**: 81) £2,800
After Rain
O 20 x 27", S, (**W**: 56) £550
Roughra Hearth I
W 31 x 23", S, (**W**: 57) £550
Rosslea - Autumn
O 24 x 24", S, (**EI**: 114) £1,500
Near Cushendall
W 13.5 x 19", S, I, (**EI**: 173) £400
Summer Moonlight 3
O 11.5 x 12", S, (**OI**: 392) £1,150
Winter Orchards
O 28 x 36", S, D, I, (**OI**: 402) £2,875
Winter Landscape
O 13.5 x 17.5", S, D, (**VI**: 142) £920

FLYNN, Pauline (20th Century)
Abstract
C 16 x 10.5", S, D, (**LI**: 19) £200

FORBES, Stanhope Alexander (1857-1947)
Auction Record: £96,000
Entrance to Mousehole Harbour, Cornwall
Oil James Thompson, England, May 1990
The Old Courtyard, Cahors
O 24 x 20", S, (**J**: 107) £8,625
The Archway, Chateaudun
O 19.5 x 13", S, I, (**N**: 1) £5,060
The Village Street, Newlyn
O 20 x 25", S, (**DI**: 74) £20,700
The Blue River
O 24 x 30", S, D, I, (**DI**: 76) £19,550
Rural Landscape
O 12 x 15", S, D, (**EI**: 23) £3,500

FORRESTER, James (1730-1776)
An Italianate wooded river Landscape, with figures in the foreground beside a tomb
O 27 x 44", D, (**NI**: 141) £5,980

FOX, Kathleen (1880-1963)
The Road that He went
M 11 x 15", S, D, I, (**O**: 95K) £750
Still life study of a yellow rose
O 7 x 12", S, (**Q**: 120) £2,000
Summer Flowers
O 16 x 12", S, (**PI**: 78) £400

FRENCH, William Percy (1854-1920)
New Auction Record: £13,000
Extensive Bogland Landscape
Watercolour 20 x 30 ins. S
James Adam & Bonhams, 9 December 1998, Lot 64
Bogland River Landscape
W 7.5 x 11", S, (**D**: 12) £4,000
Sunshine Over Lake
W 6 x 10", S, D, (**D**: 44) £4,300
In the Kingdom of Kerry
W 7 x 10", S, D, (**D**: 93) £5,600
A Coastal Inlet
W 9.5 x 13.5", S, (**V**: 4) £4,800
River Estuary
W 6 x 9", S, D, (**V**: 16) £2,800
Bog Road and Landscape
W (2) 6.5 x 8", S, D, (**V**: 29) £5,200
Sun breaking through Clouds over a Mountain Landscape
W 7 x 10", S, (**V**: 42) £4,800
Extensive Bogland Landscape
W 20 x 30", S, (**V**: 64) £13,000
A Lakeside Ruin and A Heather Path
W (2) 6.5 x 9.5", S, D, (**V**: 87) £6,200
A Coastal Road
W 7 x 10", S, (**V**: 124) £3,100
Bundoran
W 6.5 x 9.5", S, D, (**V**: 135) £3,500
Bogland River Landscape
W 6 x 9", S, (**V**: 139) £2,700
A sunlit shoreline
W 7 x 9.5", S, D, (**V**: 163) £1,900
A sunlit lough with mountains beyond
W 8.5 x 13", S, D, (**V**: 165) £3,100
The Alpine Glow
W 8 x 10.5", S, (**HI**: 37) £2,000
Moorland Landscape
W 7 x 10", S, D, (**NI**: 170) £5,750
Nassau Street, Dublin
W 15.5. x 11", S, (**NI**: 181) £7,475
On the Road to Falcarragh
W 9.5 x 13", S, (**OI**: 280) £6,325
Sun breaking over a Coastline
W 5 x 7", S, (**PI**: 4) £2,800
Falcarragh, County Donegal
W 7 x 10", S, D, I, (**PI**: 77) £2,200
A Mountain Road
W 5 x 7", S, (**PI**: 115) £3,400
Landscape, Co. Cavan
W 5 x 7", S, (**ZI**: 87A) £1,600
Peat Stacks in Connemara
W 7 x 10", S, (**DII**: 31) £2,400
Dawn & Sunset
W (2) 6.5 x 14.5", S, (**DII**: 32) £4,600
A River and Mountain Landscape
W 6.5 x 12", S, (**DII**: 34) £2,100
West of Ireland Cottage in a Landscape
W (2) 7 x 11", S, (**III**: 1180) £1,500

GAGE, Sir Thomas, Bt. (c.1780-1820)
Views in Killarney: Lord Kenmare's house; and three other watercolours.
W (4) 9.5 x 13", I, (**NI**: 144) £32,200

GALBALLY, Cecil (d.1995)
Soft Day Aran
O 13.5 x 17.5", S, (**ZI**: 12) £520

GALE, Martin (b.1949)
Ghost Road
O 24 x 24", (**G**: 88) £1,600

GARSTIN, Norman (1847-1926)
Auction Record: £11,500
What's New?
14 x 20 ins. S
Phillips, 4 May 1990, Lot 81
By the River & The Waters Edge
O (2) 8 x 8" oval, (**O**: 36) £600

GEOGHEGAN, Trevor (b.1946)
Canal Lagoon, Birr
A 14 x 24", (**G**: 94) £800

GILLESPIE, George (1924-1996)
Preparing to Cast
O 23 x 35", S, (**O**: 95L) £2,600
Joyce's Country, Connemara
O 15 x 20", S, I, (**EI**: 2) £2,200
Connemara Landscape
O 30 x 40", S, (**HI**: 99) £3,000
Trout stream, Ardra, County Donegal
O 32 x 42", S, (**PI**: 154) £3,900
Estuary at Gortahork
O 20 x 30", S, (**VI**: 1) £1,900
Cushendun, Co. Antrim
O 13.5 x 17", S, I, (**VI**: 64) £2,000
Near Churchill, Co. Donegal
O 11.5 x 16", S, (**ZI**: 75) £1,550
On the Road to Achill Island
O 22.5 x 30.5", S, (**DII**: 45) £1,900
On the Bundorragha River, Co. Mayo
O 19 x 24", S, (**DII**: 48) £1,700
At Cushendun, Co. Antrim
O 16 x 30", S, (**GII**: 1408) £1,600

At Ards Forest Park, Co. Donegal
O 30 x 40", S, (**GII**: 1460) £2,700
Awenmore River - near Killarney
O 20 x 30", S, (**GII**: 1461) £1,550
Irish River Landscape
O 29 x 39", S, (**GII**: 1446) £2,400
Rough Seas near Ballintay, Co. Antrim
O 21 x 31", S, (**JII**: 117) £1,300
Bundorragh River, Co. Galway
O 24 x 36", S, (**JII**: 254) £2,200
At Ards Forest Park, Donegal
O 30 x 40", S, (**JII**: 260) £4,700

GLENAVY, Beatrice, Lady (1883-1968)
Auction Record: £27,600
The Intruder
28 x 38 ins. S, I
Christie's, London, 16 May 1996, Lot 84
White Hand
O 16 x 12", S, (**GII**: 1449) £3,500

GLYNN, Judy (20th Century)
Lilacs
O 13 x 17", (**G**: 92) £340
Summertime
O 12 x 16", (**G**: 93) £320

GOODING, Maria Simmonds (20th Century)
Gathering in the Nets
M 14 x 21", S, (**O**: 109) £2,200
Irish coastal scene
M 15 x 22", S, (**JII**: 445) £360

GORE, William Crampton (1877-1946)
Interior with the artist's wife, Yvonne and young daughter, Elizabeth, at Montreuil-sur-Mer
O 22.5 x 18", S, (**V**: 48) £21,000
Church Interior
O 24 x 20", (**OI**: 306) £4,600

GOREY, Helena (20th Century)
Untitled
O 17.5 x 21.5", (**G**: 96) £250

GOULDING, Tim. (b.1945)
Night Fires XXIX
O 20 x 16", S, D, (**W**: 13) £450
Seam
O 10 x 8", S, D, I, (**W**: 81) £200

GRAHAM, Carol (20th Century)
Track to the sea
O 14 x 20", (**G**: 100) £750

GRAHAM, Patrick (20th Century)
Study of Joe
D 15 x 22", S, D, (**O**: 98) £2,600
Figure Study
M 29.5 x 21", S, D, (**O**: 115) £600
Young Man in a Chair
M 21.5 x 16", S, D, (**O**: 116) £850
Conversation with my Mother
M 33 x 23", S, D, I, (**VI**: 71) £2,000

GREEN, Alan (20th Century)
White Painting
O 36 x 36", (**LI**: 129) £360

GREY, Alfred (1845-1926)
Going to the River
O 31 x 42", S, D, I, (**NI**: 165) £2,070
Highland Cattle and Sheep on a Mountain
O 30 x 40", S, (**JII**: 504) £2,500

GRIERSON, Charles MacIver (1864-1939)
Circus Tricks
W 23 x 30", S, D, (**PI**: 111) £3,200

GUBBINS, Beatrice (1878-1944)
McGillycuddy's Reeks
W 9.5 x 13", S, (**D**: 22) £520

GUINNESS, Grattan (20th Century)
View of West Cork; Village Scene
W (2) 7 x 12", S, (**DII**: 39) £360

GUINNESS, Lindy (20th Century)
(The Marchioness of Dufferin & Ava)
Wadl Hadramawt Yemen Say'Un
O (**G**: 101) £550

GUINNESS, May (1863-1955)
Auction Record: IR£13,000
Portrait: Two Irish Girls
51 x 40 ins.
Christie's (Dublin), 24 October 1988, Lot 87

Stanhope FORBES, *The Archway, Chateaudun*, sold at Phillips, 17 November 1998 for £5,060

Brittany Harbour
W 12 x 9", S, (**NI**: 10) £632
Seated Woman by a Balcony
P 16 x 10", (**FII**: 216) £1,600

HALL, Kenneth (1913-1946)
Portrait of Lucy Wertheim
O 30 x 20", S, D, I, (**NI**: 83) £5,520
Still Life on a Table
O 15.5 x 21.5", S, D, (**NI**: 88) £1,840
Aran Island Cottages
O 8.5 x 11.5", S, (**PI**: 136) £750
Still Life
O 24 x 20", (**PI**: 136A) £680

HAMILTON, Eva Henrietta (1876-1960)
New Auction Record: £12,000
A Summers Day in the West
Oil 19 x 23.5 ins. S
Hamilton Osborne King,
The RDS Sale - 31 May 1999
Harvesting in Mayo
O 15 x 18", S, I, (**OI**: 325) £5,290
Roundstone, Connemara
O 15 x 18", S, (**PI**: 13) £3,400
A Summers Day in the West
O 19 x 23.5", S, (**FII**: 190) £12,000

HAMILTON, Hugh (1753-1798)
Portrait of Henry Sheares, United Irishman
O 29 x 24.5", I, (**V**: 112) £4,800

HAMILTON, Hugh Douglas (1739-1808)
Portrait of Elizabeth Bridgetta Stepney, Mrs Gulston
O 58 x 45", (**A**: 82) £16,100
Portrait of Dowager Lady Cunningham
P 9 x 7.5", oval, (**NI**: 154A) £3,220
Portrait of a Gentleman of the Armstrong family of Kilsharvan
O 29 x 24", I, (**OI**: 255) £2,300
Portrait of James Colyear Dawkins of Standlynch Park, Wiltshire
P 33 x 42", (**UI**: 11) £25,300
Portrait of James Colyear Dawkins of Standlynch Park, Wiltshire
P 9 x 8", oval, (**UI**: 12) £14,950

HAMILTON, Letitia Marion (1878-1964)
Auction Record: IR£30,000
The Harbour, Roundstone
20 x 24 ins. S
James Adam, 28 September 1989, Lot 58
Upper Lough Mask, Co. Mayo
O 20 x 24", S, I, (**F**: 177) £5,520
Connemara Landscape
O 20 x 24", S, (**N**: 86) £5,750
The Reaper and the Binder
O 13 x 14", S, I, (**O**: 35) £5,000
Polo in Phoenix Park
O 7.5 x 9.5", S, I, (**O**: 75) £2,200
The Liffey with a View of the Four Courts
W 8 x 10", S, (**O**: 94) £1,100
The Meath Hunt Point to Point
O 5 x 7", S, (**V**: 9) £2,700
Continental Market Scene
O 11 x 16", S, (**Z**: 13) £3,220
Continental Market Vendors
O 12 x 16", (**Z**: 14) £3,220
Across the Rooftops
O 10 x 8", S, (**EI**: 20) £1,300
Olive Trees, Valdemosa
O 4 x 7", S, I, (**EI**: 70) £2,600
Beech Trees on the Liffey
O 20 x 24", S, I, (**NI**: 5) £2,760
Porta della Carta, Venice
O 22 x 26", S, I, (**NI**: 109) £9,200
Autumn on the Liffey
O 19.5 x 24", S, I, (**NI**: 110) £14,375
Autumn
O 20 x 24", S, (**NI**: 116) £13,800
Goff's Horse Sale
O 25 x 30", S, (**OI**: 378) £24,150
An Irish Landscape
O 12 x 16", S, (**PI**: 38) £2,000
A village street with farmers and calves
W 17 x 22", S, (**PI**: 91) £6,600
The Reaper & The Binder
O 15.5 x 17.5", S, (**VI**: 58) £9,200
Sailing Boats in a Bay
O 11.5 x 15", S, (**VI**: 69) £5,000
Headland and Trees, Co. Wicklow
O 20 x 25.5", S, (**ZI**: 59) £1,450
Mountain Farm
O 20 x 26", S, (**ZI**: 82) £4,600
A Fair Day, Clifden
O 19.5 x 23", S, (**FII**: 165) £22,000
Bantry Bay with a sailing boat
O 19.5 x 23.5", S, (**FII**: 167) £9,000
Street Scene, Market Day in Mitchelstown, Co. Cork
O 20.5 x 26", (**GII**: 1431) £6,000

HAMILTON, William Osborne (c.1750-c.1790)
A view of Lota, County Cork, the seat of Robert Rogers Esq.
D 9.5 x 15.5", S, D, I, (**NI**: 155) £22,425

HANLEY, James (b.1965)
Admirable
O 60 x 48", S, D, I, (**VI**: 151) £2,800

HANLON, Jack P. (1913-1968)
Pub Interior
W 11 x 15", S, I, (**O**: 7) £1,400
A lake through trees.
W 11 x 16", S, (**V**: 27) £850
Dried Flowers
W 22.5 x 15", S, (**V**: 37) £500
Still Life
W 15 x 11", (**W**: 74) £300
Fruit Stalls
W 13 x 17.5", S, I, (**EI**: 224D) £800
Winding Continental Road
W 11 x 15.5", (**EI**: 224E) £960
Choir Boys
W 13 x 20", (**EI**: 224F) £850
13 Steps
W 13 x 20", S, I, (**EI**: 224G) £500
Early Spanish Madonna
W 20 x 13", I, (**EI**: 224H) £360
The Apostle
W 20 x 13", (**EI**: 224I) £260

The Eviction
W 19 x 23.5", S, D, (**VI**: 16) £4,500
Gridlock
W 10 x 14", S, D, (**GII**: 1492) £575
HARPER, Charles (b.1943)
Descending Angel
W 37 x 29.5", (**G**: 102) £1,000
HARRINGTON, Aoife (20th Century)
Penumbra No. 34
O 14 x 14", (**G**: 103) £280
HARRISON, Sarah Cecilia (1861-1941)
Auction Record: £15,000
Carlos
152 x 76 cm S & D 1891
Sotheby's 14 October 1987, Lot 65
Portrait Study of Ernest
O 11 x 8", S, I, (**O**: 23) £8,000
A Rocky Outcrop and Tree Study
O (2) 10 x 9", S, (**V**: 28) £950
HARTLAND, Henry Albert (1840-1893)
A Probable View of Dollymount Strand
W 9 x 19", S, (**O**: 3) £670
Killarney
W 13 x 22.5", S, (**O**: 4) £470
Autumn Landscape
W 14 x 20", S, (**PI**: 109) £520
HARVEY, Charles (1895-1970)
Harbour in Brittany
O 20 x 23", S, I, (**EI**: 42) £1,200
Farm at Carrow-Keel
O 13 x 18", S, I, (**EI**: 43) £920
Narcissi
O 15.5 x 11.5", S, (**EI**: 44) £580
The Bridge
O 10 x 14", S, (**EI**: 45) £280
HASSELL, Edward (fl.1830-1852)
Entrance to an Ancient Spanish Mansion in Galway
O 4 x 4", I, (**O**: 13) £1,100
HAYES, Claude (1852-1922)
Figures following Horses and a Cart gathering a Crop
W 5 x 10", S, (**H**: 149) £518
In the Meadows, Fordwick
W 9.5 x 13.5", S, (**P**: 15) £299
A Pastoral Scene near Guildford
W 9 x 13.5", S, (**P**: 21) £403
Mending the Cart in an expansive wooded Landscape
W 20.5 x 27.5", S, (**P**: 120) £978
The Harvesters
W 10 x 13.5", S, (**X**: 5) £403
Watching the Hunt
W 9 x 13.5", S, D, (**X**: 113) £253
Corn Rooks
W 9.5 x 17", S, (**DII**: 68) £500
Corn Stacks in a Landscape
O 17 x 28", S, D, (**HII**: 484) £2,300
HAYES, Edward (1797-1864)
Sketch of a young gentleman
Oval, S, (**W**: 172) £300
HAYES, Edwin (1820-1904)
Auction Record: £14,000
Holy Island, Isle of Arran
15 x 54 ins. S & D 1862
Christie's (South Kensington), 13 April 1989, Lot 160
Schevening Beach
O 7 x 11", S, D, I, (**D**: 100) £3,000
On the Goodwins
O 6.5 x 11", S, D, I, (**D**: 105) £4,000
Sailing Boat Under Grey Skies
O 5 x 7.5", S, (**D**: 117) £1,200
Off Scarborough, Yorkshire
O 23.5 x 33.5", S, D, (**V**: 11) £10,000
Low Tide
O 12 x 18", S, (**V**: 45) £6,400
Sailing into Harbour
O 11.5 x 15", S, D, (**KI**: 16) £4,025
French Luggers off the Coast
W 8.5 x 19", S, (**PI**: 33) £2,100
Off Kinsale Harbour, County Cork
O 3.5 x 9", S, (**PI**: 157) £1,300
Shipping off the Coast
W 7.5 x 10.5", S, (**PI**: 159) £750

Beatrice GLENAVY, *White Hand*, sold at Mealy's, 7 October 1998 for £3,500

Letitia HAMILTON, *Continental Market Vendors*, sold at Phillips, 2 March 1999 for £3,220

Stormy weather off the Rocks, Howth
W 8.5 x 19", S, (**PI**: 166) £2,100
Ischia
W 7 x 9.5", S, I, (**PI**: 171) £620
Harbour Scene
O 7 x 11", S, (**PI**: 180) £3,400
Shipping off Dublin Port
O 9 x 12", S, (**AII**) £3,700
HAYES, Ernest (1914-1978)
Pergola
O 14 x 18", (**G**: 104) £800
HAYES, Michael Angelo (19th Century)
Portrait of General Henry James Warre, CB, seated
W 14 x 10", (**W**: 166) £280
Military charging on horseback
W 10.5 x 16", S, (**JII**: 489) £620
HAYTER, S. William (20th Century)
City
Pr 19 x 23", S, D, I, (**LI**: 88) £200
Styx
Pr 18.5 x 22.5", S, D, I, (**LI**: 127) £380
HEALEY, James (20th Century)
Dubliners
W (8) 8 x 5", S, (**OI**: 375) £3,220
HEALY, Henry (1909-1982)
Achill Island
O 19.5 x 23.5", S, (**D**: 121) £900

Huband Bridge
O 15.5 x 19.5", (**O**: 1) £450
Homeward Bound
O 14 x 18", S, (**VI**: 3) £900
Huband Bridge
O 15.5 x 19", S, I, (**VI**: 47) £750
Haymakers, Achill
O 20 x 24", S, (**VI**: 101) £1,800
HEALY, Michael Joseph (1873-1941)
Dubliner - The Butcher
W 7 x 4.5", (**D**: 57) £210
Dubliners
W (2) 7 x 4", (**D**: 136) £380
Woman in Watling Street
W 6 x 4", I, (**EI**: 24) £200
Toy Seller
W 9.5 x 5", S, (**EI**: 25) £300
HENEY, Patrick (20th Century)
The Memorial Arch, St. Stephen's Green, Dublin
W 15 x 22", S, (**W**: 42) £220
HENNELL, Thomas (1903-1945)
Loading and waiting to load, Rathcoursey, County Cork
W 9.5 x 12", S, I, (**PI**: 178) £600
HENNESSY, Patrick (1915-1980)
Auction Record: IR£15,750
Self Portrait - Through a Wardrobe Mirror with Still Life on Table
Oil 24 x 20 ins. S
Mealy's, 24 & 25 March 1998, Lot 1056
Swimming at Huband Bridge
O 12 x 17", S, (**O**: 95H) £3,800
Ben Ingan House
O 30 x 40", S, (**V**: 14) £1,700
Evening
O 24.5 x 35", S, (**V**: 82) £4,700
A Turf Mound by a Bog Pool
O 14 x 18", S, (**V**: 104) £1,700
Still life study of ruined statues
O 20 x 26", S, (**V**: 105A) £4,100
In the studio
O 18 x 14", S, (**V**: 113) £3,700
The Annabel Plate
O 25 x 35", S, I, (**V**: 134) £10,200
Still life with Conch shell, Vase and Wooden Box
O 23 x 20", S, (**V**: 160) £4,100
Portrait of Marie Knott (nee Buckley) of Cork and Greystones
D 15 x 10.5", (**W**: 175) £300
The Canal at Wilton Place
O 26 x 35", S, (**EI**: 22) £4,800
The long Road Home
O 20 x 30", S, I, (**NI**: 198) £6,670
Woman by a Window, Dublin
O 24 x 20", S, (**OI**: 374) £2,760
The Window
O 20 x 12", S, D, (**OI**: 399) £1,725
House of Cards
O 9 x 13", S, (**PI**: 24) £3,800
'Josephine Bruce' Red Rose
O 12 x 10", S, (**DII**: 41) £2,000
HENRY, Grace (1868-1953)
Auction Record: IR£19,000
Boats Chioggia
32 x 24 ins. S
James Adam, 1 June 1989, Lot 196
Sailing Boats - Chioggia
W 9.5 x 12.5", S, (**D**: 133) £460
Portrait of Evie Hone
O 26 x 23", (**D**: 138) £1,200
Achill Beach
O 16 x 24", S, (**V**: 123) £4,800
La Riviere
O 5 x 6", S, (**EI**: 52) £1,400
Flowers
O 18 x 13.5", S, (**EI**: 78) £3,000
Still Life with Marble Torso
O 23.5 x 19.5", S, (**NI**: 12) £4,600
Au Soleil - A Walk in St. Stephen's Green
O 12 x 16", S, (**OI**: 327) £4,600

The Piper
O 12 x 10", S, (**OI**: 380) £3,220

HENRY, Paul (1876-1958)
New Auction Record: £210,500
The Bog-Workers
Oil 24.5 x 31 ins. S, I,
Sotheby's, The Irish Sale, 21 May 1999, Lot 301

An Achill Bog
O 9 x 12", S, I, (**D**: 46) £22,000
Cottages before Clouds and Mountains
O 16 x 20", S, (**V**: 19) £32,000
West of Ireland Landscape with Lakeside Cottages
O 16 x 24.5", S, (**V**: 25) £19,500
Landscape and Clouds
D 18 x 14.5", S, (**V**: 33) £6,700
Cottages before a Lough and Mountains
O 12 x 14", S, (**V**: 36) £21,000
View of Connemara Hills across a lake
O 14 x 16", S, (**V**: 66) £20,000
Cottages in a Western Mountain Landscape
O 15 x 18", S, (**V**: 71) £32,000
Peat Stacks
O 14 x 16", S, (**V**: 96) £26,000
Dingle Peninsula
O 12 x 16", S, (**V**: 105) £30,000
A Kerry Bog
O 14 x 19", S, (**V**: 107) £19,000
Cottages by the Coast
O 15 x 24", S, (**V**: 142) £40,000
The Stone Walls of Galway
O 14 x 16", S, I, (**NI**: 100) £51,000
Peat Stacks, Galway
O 12 x 14", S, (**NI**: 101) £20,700
The Silver Lake
O 8.5 x 12", S, (**NI**: 102) £10,350
Turf Stacks by a Lake, Connemara
O 11.5 x 15.5", S, (**NI**: 103) £26,450
Cottages and Turf Stacks, Connemara
O 14 x 16", S, (**NI**: 212) £34,500
Coastal Cottages
O 16 x 20", S, (**NI**: 213) £14,950
The Bog-Workers
O 24.5 x 31", S, I, (**OI**: 301) £210,500
On the Path to the Mountains
O 16 x 24", S, (**OI**: 303) £40,000
Winter Trees
O 10 x 14", S, (**OI**: 326) £29,900
Altan Lough, Donegal
O 15 x 18", S, I, (**OI**: 329) £27,600
Regency Gentleman
W 18 x 14", S, (**OI**: 336) £5,520
Cottages by Water
O 14 x 16", S, (**OI**: 351) £34,500
By the Lough
O 8 x 10", S, (**OI**: 353) £17,250
Turf Stacks and Distant Mountains
O 18 x 24", S, (**OI**: 389) £40,000
Coastal Landscape, County Kerry
O 20 x 24", S, (**PI**: 52) £34,000
Cloudy Day, Connemara
O 13.5 x 15.5", S, (**FII**: 166) £22,000

HEWSTON, Jim (20th Century)
Dead Tree
O 13.5 x 18", S, (**LI**: 13) £220
Friends by Seashore
O 16 x 20", S, (**LI**: 25) £320
Tranarossan Beach
O 18 x 24", S, (**LI**: 28) £390

HICKEY, Desmond (20th Century)
Café Society
O 23 x 30", S, (**D**: 140) £2,600
Sweet Pea & Climbing Rose
O 24 x 20", (**G**: 106) £620
The Breakfast Table
O 16 x 20", S, (**PI**: 113) £1,200

HICKEY, Patrick (1927-1998)
Still life with lemons
Pr 21 x 27", S, I, (**Q**: 107) £900
Japanese Letter 6
Pr 30 x 23", S, I, (**Q**: 140) £320
Still life in blue
Pr 13 x 18", S, (**Q**: 141) £520
July Forest
O 30 x 40", S, I, (**EI**: 115) £2,200
The Start of the Waterfall
O 30 x 22", S, D, I, (**HI**: 119) £800
Glendasan, Co. Wicklow
O 42 x 60", S, D, I, (**VI**: 53) £1,300
Winter
O 30 x 40", (**VI**: 121) £700
The Months of the Year
Pr (8) 29.5 x 22", S, I, (**EII**: 332) £1,100

HICKEY, Thomas (1741-1824)
Auction Record: £89,500
Portrait of Henry Vansittart and his Family
Oil 36 x 48 ins.
Sotheby's, 8 April 1998, Lot 109

HILL, Derek (b.1916)
Tory Island Lighthouse 1958
O 8 x 13", S, (**D**: 56) £2,600
The Park at Rusborough - Evening Light
O 7.5 x 10.5", S, D, I, (**N**: 130) £1,093
Sienese Landscape
O 10.5 x 16", S, I, (**NI**: 187) £5,520

HILL, Roland (1918-1979)
Portrush
O 22 x 28", S, (**W**: 123) £500
Coastal Cottage with Figure outside
O 7 x 11", S, (**EI**: 1) £400
Ross Castle, Lower Lake, Killarney
O 20 x 30", S, (**PI**: 118) £900
Coast Road, Glenarm, County Antrim
W 8.5 x 14.5", S, D, (**PI**: 172) £250
The Strand at Port na Blagh, County Donegal
O 14 x 20", S, (**SI**: 97) £1,035
Coastal Scene with Beach in foreground
O 15 x 19", (**GII**: 1423) £450

HOARE, William (1706-1792)
Portrait of Robert Clements, 1st Earl of Leitrim 1732-1804
P 24 x 17", (**OI**: 258) £5,520

HONE, David (20th Century)
Evening, Sandymount Strand
O 25 x 30", S, (**V**: 2) £1,250
Summer, Sandymount Strand
O 20 x 24", S, D, I, (**V**: 83) £4,200

HONE, Evie (1894-1955)
New Auction Record: £16,000
Four Elements
Oil 29 x 24", S
de Veres, Sale of Art, 22 June 1999, Lot 34

Our Lady of Mercy
W 17 x 6", (**D**: 149) £1,700
Woodland Study
O 18 x 15", S, (**N**: 25) £1,840
Landscape with Hills
W 12 x 14.5", (**N**: 89) £713
The Red House
W 9 x 14", (**O**: 6) £1,300
Abstract Composition
W 24 x 15", (**O**: 60) £2,400
The Woods at Marley
W 15 x 13", (**O**: 133C) £920
St Anthony - Design for Stained Glass
W 8 x 8", I, (**Y**: 9) £299
Trees in Early Spring
O 16.5 x 11", S, I, (**EI**: 39) £2,800
Farm Landscape
W 9.5 x 14", (**EI**: 148) £1,500
Abstract
W 3.5 x 10", (**EI**: 149) £900
Tinker Family
W 14 x 10", (**HI**: 109) £800
Design for Stained Glass - Christ in front of Pontius Pilate
W 15 x 12", (**OI**: 337) £747
Landscape, County Dublin
W 10 x 14", (**PI**: 35) £2,000
Four Elements
O 29 x 24", S, (**VI**: 34) £16,000
London Interior
O 20 x 24", S, (**VI**: 35) £9,200
Irish Landscape
W 10 x 16", S, I, (**VI**: 36) £1,700
The Turn of the Road
P 9 x 13.5", S, D, (**VI**: 83) £2,200
Abstract Composition
W 5 x 3", (**VI**: 84) £1,300
Declan
W 4.5 x 9.5", S, (**VI**: 85) £750
Study for Stained Glass
W 16 x 8.5", S, (**VI**: 103) £1,000

HONE, Geraldine (20th Century)
West Wicklow Landscape
O 14 x 10", (**G**: 109) £260

HONE, Nathaniel (1718-1784)
Auction Record: £65,000
Jason, a Racehorse belonging to Sir Nathaniel Curzon, Bt.
40 x 50 ins. S & D 1755
Christie's, 14 July 1994, Lot 58

HONE, Nathaniel (19th Century)
Elegant Figures before a Chateau
W 11.5 x 14", (**MI**: 72) £437

HONE, Nathaniel (1831-1917)
Auction Record: IR£38,000
Fishing Boats in Dublin Bay
26 x 38 ins. Initialled
James Adam, 17 May 1990, Lot 81A

Houses by a Bay
W 7 x 9", (**NI**: 166) £1,380
Cows in pasture, Malahide
O 25.5 x 36.5", S, (**OI**: 287) £18,400
On the Malahide Sands
O 26 x 39", S, (**PI**: 88) £25,000
Landscape
O 8 x 10.5", (**VI**: 169) £1,000

HOURIGAN, Francis Xavier (b.1914)
All this and Yester Year
O 16 x 20", S, (**LI**: 89) £300

HUGHES, Nigel (b.1940)
Dundrum Bay from Cloughram Hill, Co. Down
O 28 x 48", S, I, (**NI**: 199) £4,600
Castleward, Co. Down
D 26 x 21", S, D, (**OI**: 395) £1,725
A Bathing Party
O 26.5 x 45", (**OI**: 404) £4,600

HULL, Frederick William (1867-1953)
The Gobbins and River Landscape
O (2) 5.5 x 8", S, (**EI**: 36) £420

HUNTER, John (1893-1951)
Stormy Headland, Co. Down
O 20 x 23", S, I, (**EI**: 170) £300
Leicester Square
O 15 x 21", S, (**OI**: 400) £2,875

HUSSEY, Phillip (1713-1783)
Portrait of Joseph Witheral
O 49 x 39", S, (**OI**: 252) £4,140

HUTCHINSON, Nicholas Hely (20th Century)
Wave Wild Coast II
W 12 x 14", (**G**: 237E) £600
Ox Mountain Road
O 10 x 12", S, (**LI**: 87) £300

HUTSON, Marshal C. (20th Century)
Woods at Rochestown, Co. Cork
W 9 x 7", S, (**D**: 23) £200
On set at Sleath Head for Ryans Daughter
O 25 x 21", (**JII**: 240) £700
Mountainous lake scene
W 15 x 22", (**JII**: 438) £360

IREMONGER, Sarah (20th Century)
Dark Blue Light No. 4
O 18 x 24", (**G**: 112) £380

ITEN, Hans (1874-1930)
Roses
O 17.5 x 24", S, I, (**O**: 38) £6,200

JACKSON, William (20th Century)
Near Tramore Bay, Co. Donegal
O 19.5 x 23", S, I, (**VI**: 95) £920
Near Rosses, Co. Donegal
O 19.5 x 23", S, I, (**VI**: 96) £600

JELLETT, Mainie (1897-1944)
New Auction Record: £40,000
Composition
Oil 24 x 36 ins.
Sotheby's, The Irish Sale, 21 May 1999, Lot 310
Wooded Landscape
W 12 x 10.5", S, D, (**W**: 48) £750
Abstract
W 9 x 4", (**EI**: 77) £1,800
Composition
O 24 x 36", (**OI**: 310) £40,000
Cotswold Scene
O 44 x 28", S, D, (**OI**: 311) £17,250
Nude in a Landscape
O 20 x 26", (**OI**: 312) £12,650
Madonna and Child
W 10 x 4", S, D, (**OI**: 313) £9,200
Three Elements
O 36 x 28", (**OI**: 315) £16,100
Studio Study - The Discus Thrower
D 13 x 10", S, D, (**OI**: 317) £632
Abstract Composition
O 72 x 36", S, D, (**OI**: 318) £27,600
Abstract Composition
W 20 x 14.5", (**OI**: 321) £5,750
Study for 'Abstract Composition', 1922
W 8 x 7.5", (**OI**: 322) £2,875
Abstract Composition (Pink and Aquamarine)
W 9 x 7", (**OI**: 323) £1,840
Pieta
O 21.5 x 22", (**OI**: 324) £4,370
Study of a Young Man
D 13 x 12", (**PI**: 131) £900
Christ
W 8 x 5", (**PI**: 161) £1,100

JERVAS, Charles (c.1675-1739)
Auction Record: £17,000
Portrait of Charles I and his page, Lord Hamilton
87 x 75 ins.
Sotheby's, 8 April 1992, Lot 18

JOHN, Augustus (1878-1961)
Galway Fisher Folk
D 10 x 14.5", S, (**OI**: 298) £2,530

JOHNSON, Benita (20th Century)
The Garden
O 16 x 20", (**G**: 114) £300
Study of Wild Flowers
O 10 x 8", (**G**: 115) £200

JOHNSON, Neville (b.1911)
Still Life - Wishbone
O 8 x 10", S, D, (**V**: 152) £2,000
Still Life - Three Apples
W 13.5 x 15", S, D, (**W**: 66) £750
Assignation
O 20 x 24", (**OI**: 357) £6,900
Composition
O 25 x 37.5", S, (**OI**: 364) £14,950

JONES, Peter (20th Century)
3 French Pears on a Purple Plate
Pr 26 x 23", (**G**: 117) £300

JORGENSEN, Patricia (20th Century)
Romneya I
W 22 x 15", (**G**: 118) £400

JOY, Arthur (c.1808-1838)
A Disagreement
W 14 x 19", (**O**: 14) £900

JOYCE, Fiona (20th Century)
Untitled
Pr 24 x 24", (**G**: 119) £200

JURY, Anne Primrose (d.1995)
The Flax Gatherers
O 10 x 14.5", S, (**O**: 50) £900
Fanad Head, Co. Donegal
O 10 x 12.5", S, (**V**: 87A) £280

KANE, Michael (b.1935)
Old Shoe
W 16 x 23", S, D, (**EI**: 223) £280

KAVANAGH, Joseph Malachy (1856-1918)
In Feltrim Meadows
O 10 x 14", S, D, I, (**D**: 67) £7,500

Sean KEATING, *Spanish Arch*, sold at James Adam, 30 September 1998, for £19,000

Priest smoking a pipe, and Priest sewing trousers
O (2) 30 x 24", S, (**ZI**: 66) £1,500

KEATING, Sean (1889-1977)
Auction Record: IR£70,000
Unloading the Catch
Oil 24 x 30 ins. S
James Adam & Bonhams, 27 May 1998, Lot 37
Spanish Arch
W 31 x 28", S, (**D**: 73) £19,000
Head of a Man of Aran
W 15 x 14", S, (**D**: 98) £3,400
Kathleen Ni Hulahan
O 33.5 x 25.5", S, D, (**F**: 175) £12,650
Sketch of a young girl
D 11.5 x 11", S, (**V**: 59) £1,300
Ireland's History - from the Bards to De Valera
W 17 x 39", S, (**V**: 138) £27,000
Head of a Woman
D 8.5 x 10", S, (**V**: 153) £1,800
Clouds over Inis Sheer
M 22 x 30", (**W**: 128) £350
Curraghs at Inis Mor
D 14.5 x 22", S, (**W**: 129) £450
Clouds over Inis Sheer
M 20 x 30", S, (**LI**: 105) £500
Launching the Curragh
O 34 x 42", S, (**NI**: 22) £41,100
Portrait of Eamon de Valera
D 18 x 14.5", S, I, (**PI**: 152) £5,200
Self Portrait (Double Sided)
D 12.5 x 15", S, (**VI**: 12) £1,150
Warrior on his Horse
O 14 x 18", S, (**DII**: 84) £2,600
Portrait of a Fireman
O 42 x 35.5", S, I, (**EII**: 364) £18,000

KELLY, Carmel (20th Century)
Galway Hooker, Carraroe
O 9 x 14", (**G**: 121) £300

KELLY, Sir Gerald Festus (1879-1972)
Mangosteens and a Casket
O 25 x 30", I, (**Y**: 167) £1,380
Jungle Girl
O 10.5 x 14", D, I, (**JI**: 34) £483
Beach Scene
O 10.5 x 8.5", S, (**PI**: 42) £3,400
A village, Burma
O 8.5 x 10.5", (**RI**: 254) £2,185

KELLY, Ita (20th Century)
Let the wind blow through me
O 48 x 36", (**G**: 122) £820

KELLY, John (20th Century)
Self Portrait
M 28 x 20", (**G**: 123) £700

KELLY, John F. (20th Century)
Still Life
O 14 x 18", S, (**VI**: 139) £760

KELLY, Paul (20th Century)
Still Life Study
O 10 x 12", S, D, (**HI**: 3) £370
Pastoral Landscape
O 15 x 18", S, D, (**VI**: 166) £650

KELLY, Robert George Talbot (1822-1910)
A Fisherman beside a rowing boat with a coastal village beyond
W 13.5 x 20", S, D, (**MI**: 126) £299

KENNY, Alan (20th Century)
Tending Peatstacks in Connemara
O 13 x 17", S, (**DII**: 21) £360

KERNOFF, Harry (1900-1974)
Auction Record: £18,000
Country Circus
48 x 60 ins. S
Sotheby's, 4 November 1992, Lot 50
A Docker
O 16 x 12", S, (**D**: 9) £2,100
Ivan Beshoff - Potemkin - 1905
D 20 x 16", S, D, I, (**D**: 99) £420
Woodcuts - published by Cahill & Co., Dublin
Pr (**D**: 153) £320
Making Hay at Renvyle, Connemara
O 14.5 x 19.5", S, D, (**N**: 90) £5,290
The Fairground
W 17 x 22", S, D, (**N**: 128) £3,105
Near Newbridge
W 9.5 x 13.5", S, D, (**N**: 131) £575
Old Houses, Westport, Co. Mayo
W 9.5 x 12.5", S, (**V**: 7) £1,900
The Twelve Bens from Renvyle
O 23.5 x 30", S, (**V**: 15) £14,000
Leeson Street Bridge, Dublin
W 13 x 9", S, (**V**: 103A) £4,400
Portrait of Eamon De Valera
D 14.5 x 11", S, (**V**: 159) £1,900
Making Hay at Renvyle, Connemara
O 14 x 19.5", S, I, (**EI**: 73) £9,000
The Lake from the Ruins of Aghadoe, Killarney
W 9 x 12", S, I, (**EI**: 189) £670
Portrait of Harry Brogan
O 8 x 6", S, (**HI**: 14) £600
Camden Place, Night
O 19.5 x 14.5", S, D, (**HI**: 81) £4,400
Portrait of a man wearing a hat
D 12 x 10", S, (**PI**: 29) £1,000
Irregular Octahedrons and Dice
O 12 x 16", S, (**QI**: 205) £2,760
On the Liffey, South Wall, Dublin
O 14 x 19", S, I, (**VI**: 18) £8,200
Study of Roger Casement in Reading Jail
P 22 x 17", S, (**VI**: 28) £1,900
Sean O'Casey - Portrait Study
O 15 x 11", S, (**VI**: 65) £1,900
Brendan Behan - Portrait Study
O 15 x 11", S, (**VI**: 66) £1,600
Courting
W 3.5 x 5", S, (**VI**: 105) £460
A Bird never flew on one Wing
Pr 4.5 x 7", S, (**VI**: 106) £340
James Joyce - Portrait Study
P 15 x 10.5", S, (**VI**: 111) £1,500
Stage Set Design
M 21 x 14.5", S, (**VI**: 132) £750
Stage Set Design
W 22 x 15", S, D, (**VI**: 133) £700
Head and Shoulder Portrait of a Young Girl
O 10 x 7", S, (**DII**: 13) £460
Jester
W 4.5 x 4", (**III**: 1206) £650

KIELY, Bernadette (20th Century)
Bannon
M 16 x 22", (**G**: 124) £260

KILLEN, R. T. (20th Century)
Locronan-Brittany
A 16 x 18", (**G**: 125) £400

KING, Cecil (1921-1986)
Composition in Brown, Orange, Green and Red
A 16 x 11", (**D**: 154) £700
Abstract
O 20 x 27", S, (**EI**: 187) £650
Baggot Street Series
P 12 x 10", S, (**EI**: 188) £400
Baggot Street Painting
O 40 x 30", (**LI**: 79) £900
KING, Leonie (20th Century)
Inequal forces in Omagh
O 12 x 16", (**G**: 126) £200
KING-HARMAN, Ann S. (1919-1979)
Louisburgh, County Mayo
W 9 x 13", S, (**D**: 147) £370
Musical Theme
O 12 x 16", S, (**D**: 148) £260
KINGSTON, Jennifer (20th Century)
Marshlands
M 20 x 17", (**G**: 127) £260
KINGSTON, Richard (20th Century)
(Memory) Achill Sound
O 30 x 48", S, D, (**D**: 50) £4,800
Lemons and a White Wall (1973)
O 16 x 12", S, (**D**: 156) £720
Apples in a dish
O 19 x 17.5", (**G**: 128) £400
A Man drinking at a bar
W 10.5 x 8.5", S, D, I, (**W**: 141) £250
A Donkey and Cart with driver
W 8.5 x 10", S, D, I, (**W**: 142) £220
Space for the Kite Flyer
O 36 x 48", S, I, (**HI**: 19) £8,000
Yellow Green Day (Donegal)
O 8.5 x 12.5", S, (**HI**: 66) £850
Autumn River
O 24 x 30", S, D, (**PI**: 17) £2,400
KIRKWOOD, Harriet (1880-1953)
A Vase of Flowers
O 30 x 24", S, (**O**: 133) £850
Along the Canal
O 25 x 32", S, (**O**: 133A) £1,300
KLITZ, Tony (20th Century)
Leinster House and Halpenny Bridge
O (2) 15 x 30", S, (**D**: 161) £400
KNUTTEL, Graham (b.1954)
Self Portrait, Night at the Opera
O 30 x 40", S, (**W**: 47) £1,800
Self-Portrait
O 23.5 x 23.5", S, (**NI**: 80) £2,530
Punch and Judy Show
O 24 x 24", S, (**DII**: 25) £2,100
A Drink
W 22 x 29", S, (**DII**: 51) £2,100
KYLE, Georgina Moutray (1865-1950)
Still Life with a Doll
O 29 x 22", S, (**NI**: 11) £2,990
Boats in Harbour
O 15.5 x 18.5", (**VI**: 183F) £1,700
LAMB, Charles Vincent (1893-1964)
Auction Record: *£24,000*
Hearing the News
James Adams, 30 March 1994
Beached Boats, Carraroe, Co. Galway
O 13 x 16", S, (**O**: 18) £5,500
Connemara Hookers
O 12.5 x 15.5", S, I, (**O**: 24) £5,000
River Landscape
O 9 x 12", S, (**O**: 49) £1,100
Boats at Carraroe, Connemara
O 11 x 14.5", S, (**NI**: 46) £3,450
Loughaneola, Connemara
O 10 x 14", S, I, (**VI**: 102) £3,400
Alone in the West of Ireland
O 10 x 13.5", S, (**JII**: 442) £3,200
LAMB, Henry (1883-1960)
Sir John Lavery in his studio at Cromwell Place, South Kensington
D 12.5 x 10", S, D, (**D**: 85) £500
A Gola Islander
D 11.5 x 8.5", S, D, (**D**: 96) £1,400
A Gola Islander
D 12.5 x 9", I, (**E**: 28) £1,092
Breton Boy
D 10.5 x 8", (**Y**: 89) £897
The Nightwatch
W 8 x 10.5", (**Y**: 90) £805
A Study of the artist John Lavery, in his Studio
W 12.5 x 10", S, I, (**EII**: 361) £1,600
LARKEN, Diarmuid (1918-1989)
In Bunowen, Connemara
O 10 x 12", S, (**DII**: 10) £420
LAVERY, Sir John (1856-1941)
New Auction Record: *£1,321,500*
The Bridge at Grez
Oil 30 x 72.5 ins. Signed & Dated
Christie's London, 8 December 1998, Lot 17
Where the Kenmare River joins the Sea
O 16 x 24", S, D, I, (**B**: 78) £29,900
Portrait of the artist's daughter Eileen
O 37 x 26", (**S**: 46) £43,300
The Bridge at Grez
O 30 x 72.5", S, D, (**U**: 17) £1,321,500
A Stranger
O 20 x 20", S, D, I, (**U**: 18) £122,500
Portrait of a young woman
O 10 x 14", S, I, (**V**: 63) £27,000
Portrait of Kathrine Juliette Felicitie Vulliamy
O 48 x 37", S, (**V**: 114) £25,000
The Rt. Hon The Lord Mayor (Sir Maurice Jenks Bt.)
O 20 x 14", S, I, (**HI**: 57) £3,000
Ariadne
O 50 x 40", S, (**NI**: 50) £342,500
Portrait of Eileen, the artist's daughter
O 14 x 10", S, D, I, (**NI**: 52) £68,600
Evening, Tangier
O 11 x 15", S, I, (**NI**: 53) £13,800
The Drawing Room, Falconwood
O 25 x 30", S, D, I, (**NI**: 54) £100,500
The Golf Links, North Berwick
O 25 x 30", S, D, I, (**NI**: 55) £309,500
Mougins, Alpes Maritimes
O 20 x 23.5", S, D, I, (**NI**: 56) £32,200
The Southern Sea
O 25 x 30.5", S, I, (**NI**: 57) £67,500
Evening on the House Top, Tangier
O 25 x 30", S, D, I, (**NI**: 58) £56,500
The Moorish Flag, Hoisted on the German Legation, Tangier
O 25 x 30", S, D, I, (**NI**: 59) £64,200
Tangier
O 10 x 14", S, I, (**NI**: 61) £14,950
Portrait of Miss Callery
O 30.5 x 25", S, D, I, (**NI**: 62) £14,950
In County Kerry
O 19.5 x 23.5", S, (**OI**: 290) £47,700
The Lady in Grey
O 14 x 10", S, I, (**OI**: 294) £19,550
The Verandah, Kingsmoor House
O 25 x 30", S, D, I, (**OI**: 295) £364,500
The Garden at Ardilea
O 25 x 30", S, D, I, (**OI**: 296) £232,500
St. Patrick's Purgatory, Lough Derg
O 24 x 20", S, I, (**OI**: 302) £45,500
Evening, Montreux
O 20 x 24", S, (**SI**: 92) £67,500
LAWLESS, Matthew James (1837-1864)
The Dinner Party
O 8.5 x 12", S, D, (**V**: 81) £25,000
LAWRENSON, Edward (1868-1940)
The Glass Bottle Makers
O 29 x 37", S, D, (**D**: 101) £2,700
LE BROCQUY, Louis (b.1916)
Auction Record: *£133,500*
Man Writing
Oil 25 x 30 ins. S
Christie's, 21 May 1997, Lot 95
Classic Theme II (September 1943) The Kiss
O 26.5 x 18.5", S, I, (**D**: 63) £30,000
Portrait of William Shakespeare
W 23.5 x 17.5", S, D, (**E**: 193) £4,830
Untitled
O 20 x 20", (**G**: 136) £21,000
Provence
M 21 x 30", S, D, (**O**: 95E) £11,000
Head Study of W.B. Yeats
O 31 x 31", S, D, (**O**: 105) £27,000
Head Study of W.B. Yeats
W 24 x 17.5", S, D, (**O**: 106) £9,000
Study of W.B. Yeats
W 8.5 x 7", S, D, (**EI**: 108) £5,200
Study towards an image of W.B. Yeats
Pr 23 x 18", S, (**LI**: 125) £770
Study towards an image of W.B. Yeats
Pr 24 x 20", S, (**LI**: 125A) £600
Study
O 14 x 10.5", S, D, I, (**NI**: 91) £9,775
Image of August Strindberg
O 31.5 x 31.5", S, D, (**NI**: 92) £20,700
Riverrun. Procession with Lilies
O 21 x 29", S, D, (**NI**: 93) £122,500
Image of Frederico Garcia Lorca
Pr 20 x 17.5", S, (**NI**: 94) £460
Fruit in the Hand
O 15 x 18", S, D, (**NI**: 95) £11,500
Life Study
O (4) 32 x 26", S, D, (**NI**: 97) £11,500
Image of W.B. Yeats
O 48 x 36", S, D, (**OI**: 347) £43,300
Image of W.B. Yeats
W 20 x 14", S, D, (**OI**: 348) £17,250
The Garlanded Goat
Tapestry 62 x 51", S, D, (**OI**: 401) £62,000
Hand
O 7 x 10", S, (**PI**: 26) £6,200
Ancestral Head
O 25.5 x 21", S, D, (**VI**: 68) £22,500
Mrs Sybil Le Brocquy (the artist's mother)
W 8.5 x 7", S, D, (**ZI**: 47) £3,100
LE JEUNE, James (1910-1983)
Auction Record: *IR£23,000*
Grafton Street
20 x 24 ins. S
Christie's (Dublin), 6 June 1990, Lot 99
Barges
O 9.5 x 13.5", (**D**: 116) £900
On the Algarve Coast
O 20 x 24", S, (**D**: 127) £4,300
Children on the Beach
O 14 x 18", S, (**O**: 95B) £4,200
St Stephen's Green, Dublin
O 16 x 20", S, (**V**: 35) £6,000
Antibes
O 14 x 18", S, (**V**: 63A) £5,200
Portrait of two Girls
O 10 x 14", S, (**NI**: 114) £3,450
Figures in a sunny Street
O 25 x 30", S, (**NI**: 115) £8,625
Fishing Village, Brittany
O 20 x 24", S, (**NI**: 201) £4,025
A Woodland Stream
O 19.5 x 23.5", S, (**PI**: 37) £1,750
Coastal Scene
O 16 x 20", S, (**DII**: 80) £2,400
Children on a Beach
O 10 x 14", S, (**GII**: 1440) £4,100
LE JEUNE, Sara (b.1955)
Still Life - Ewer and Plants
O 14.5 x 14.5", S, (**GII**: 1454) £250
Garden with Ornament
O 16 x 12", (**JII**: 88) £550
LEECH, Gladys (20th Century)
Two sides of the river
W 24 x 18", (**JII**: 437) £800
LEECH, William John (1881-1968)
Auction Record: *£265,500*
The Blue Shop, Quimper
Oil 24 x 16 ins. S, I,
Christie's Irish Sale, 22 May 1998, Lot 181
May Reading in a Chair
O 25.5 x 21", (**O**: 21) £14,500

Boats on the Stour
O 14 x 18", S, I, (**V**: 46) £26,000
Harbour Scene, near Concarneau
O 6.5 x 8", S, (**V**: 76) £7,500
Millhouse on Quay, near Concarneau
O 6.5 x 8", S, (**V**: 99) £7,200
Boats on the River Wey
O 17.5 x 14", (**HI**: 44) £14,000
Portrait of Suzanne Botterell
O 53 x 21", S, I, (**NI**: 207) £133,500
The Terrace
O 15 x 18", S, D, (**NI**: 208) £23,000
The Garden Seat
O 15 x 18", S, I, (**NI**: 209) £11,500
Harbour Scene near Concarneau
O 6.5 x 8", (**PI**: 79) £4,000

LENNON, Ciaran (20th Century)
Untitled - 1978
O 44 x 44", (**LI**: 82) £700

LEONARD, Patrick (b.1918)
North Dublin Landscape
O 14.5 x 18.5", (**O**: 100) £450
Baiting the Lines, Dungarvan, Co. Waterford
O 16 x 20", S, I, (**O**: 108) £1,400
A Garden in Cyprus
O 13.5 x 17.5", S, (**HI**: 21) £800
Beach at Rush, Ireland
O 20 x 24", S, (**QI**: 200) £1,495
Putting out the Washing
O 15 x 19.5", S, D, (**VI**: 109) £1,500
Desert
O 17 x 14", S, I, (**VI**: 130) £500
Skerries Harbour at Night
O 23 x 28", S, (**VI**: 141) £1,800
Still Life - Dresden Figure supporting Roses
O 22.5 x 17", S, (**ZI**: 33) £500
A Peaceful Read
O 19 x 17", S, (**ZI**: 43) £850
Rose, sweet pea, peaches on silver tray
O 16 x 20", S, I, (**JII**: 216) £750
Nursing Sisters - Beaumont Convalescent Home
O 17 x 21", S, (**JII**: 498) £2,900

LEWIS, Esme (20th Century)
The Clown
O 21 x 18", S, (**DII**: 36) £1,000

LEWIS, John (fl.1739-1769)
Portrait of Bridget Vaughan of Derllys, Mrs Bevan (1698-1779)
O 49 x 39", I, (**A**: 36) £18,400
Portrait of Arabella Vaughan, Mrs Thomas Williams
O 49 x 39", I, (**A**: 38) £9,200
Portrait of Elizabeth Vaughan, Mrs Lloyd
O 49 x 39", I, (**A**: 39) £10,350
Portrait of Elizabeth Eleanor Lloyd, Lady Stepney
O 49 x 39", S, (**A**: 40) £11,500
Portrait of a young girl said to be Eleanor Lloyd of Derwydd, Derllys and Danyrallt when a child
O 29 x 24", I, (**A**: 41) £23,000

LEWIS, Noel (20th Century)
From a Distance
O 22.5 x 22.5", (**G**: 133) £350

LIVESAY, Frances (19th Century)
Cottage Interior, Co. Mayo
W 14 x 20.5", S, D, (**VI**: 177) £1,200
By the Fireside, Co. Mayo
W 13.5 x 19.5", S, D, I, (**VI**: 178) £1,100

LIVESAY, John (19th Century)
Set of 4 Early 19th Century Landscapes
W (4) 9.5 x 13.5", S, (**VI**: 176) £1,900

LOHAN, Mary (b.1954)
Green Rust Plant
O 17.5 x 16", S, (**O**: 117) £750
Windy Autumn Tree
O 17.5 x 16", S, (**O**: 118) £620

LOVER, Samuel (1797-1868)
A pair of portraits of Ladies
W (2) 6.5" high , S, D, (**II**: 269) £633

William John LEECH, *May Reading in a Chair*, sold at de Veres, 17 November 1998 for £14,500

LUKE, John (1906-1975)
New Auction Record: £441,500
The Bridge
Tempera 25.5 x 31 ins. S, D, I,
Christie's London, The Irish Sale, 20 May 1999, Lot 217
On the Lagan
O 11.5 x 15", S, D, (**NI**: 216) £20,700
The Bridge
T 25.5 x 31", S, D, I, (**NI**: 217) £441,500
A Sketch for 'Shaw's Bridge'
D 13 x 18", S, D, (**NI**: 219) £1,092
Biblical Study
O 23 x 15.5", (**NI**: 220) £5,520

LYNCH, Padraig (20th Century)
Along the Dee
O 18 x 24", S, (**VI**: 138) £780

LYNDSAY, Roy (20th Century)
Morning of the Fair
O 20 x 30", (**G**: 237B) £1,500
The Cottage Door
O 15 x 13.5", S, (**HI**: 56) £400

LYONS, Alice (20th Century)
My Father's Handkerchief
O 16.5 x 14", (**G**: 139) £350

MacCABE, Gladys (b.1918)
A Day at the Races
O 15 x 20", S, (**PI**: 7) £1,300
The Tea Rooms
O 9.5 x 13", S, (**DII**: 18) £590
Before the Race
W 16 x 24", S, (**GII**: 1398) £900
On the Docks at Dun Laoghaire
O 12 x 20", (**GII**: 1400) £700
The Band in the Park
O 15.5 x 20", S, (**GII**: 1406) £1,200
The Winners Enclosure
O 24 x 48", S, (**GII**: 1413) £1,600
The Puppet Show
O 16 x 20", S, (**GII**: 1415) £950
Winter Landscape
W 14 x 18", S, (**GII**: 1417) £300
Fair Day, Co. Galway
O 9.5 x 13", S, (**GII**: 1430) £650
The Fruit Stalls
O 16 x 20", (**GII**: 1434) £800
Before the Race
O 17 x 22", S, (**III**: 1169) £700
Riverside Houses
W 16 x 24", S, (**III**: 1189) £380
The Winners Enclosure
W 16 x 30", S, (**III**: 1203) £500
The Artists Square
O 16 x 20", S, (**JII**: 91) £1,200
Kids horse-riding on a beach
O 10 x 14", S, (**JII**: 95) £460
Horse Fair
O 16 x 19.5", S, (**JII**: 244) £700
Race Day
O 15.5 x 19.5", (**KII**: 654) £825
Race Day
O 15.5 x 19.5", S, (**KII**: 662) £900

MacGONIGAL, Maurice (1900-1979)
Auction Record: IR£24,500
Gardens: a Summer's Day, Booterstown
28 x 36 ins. S
Adams Blackrock, 28 May 1990, Lot 43
Harbour Roundstone, Connemara
O 24 x 28", S, (**D**: 47) £8,045
Hikers Resting (Dingle)
O 16 x 30", S, D, (**D**: 59) £3,600
Smerick Harbour, Kerry
O 16 x 30", S, (**D**: 83) £3,600
Loading Sand, Dooagh, Achill
O 12 x 15.5", S, I, (**O**: 11) £2,600
Errisbeg, Connemara
W 8 x 13", S, D, (**O**: 17) £650
Village Square
W 11 x 14.5", S, (**O**: 66) £470
The Runners (Phoenix Park)
O 12 x 24", S, D, I, (**O**: 951) £5,700
Donkeys in the Field, Faul, Connemara
O 12 x 24", S, (**V**: 65) £3,800
Hitch Hikers resting in Dingle
O 15 x 28", S,(**EI**: 37) £4,600
Currach Racing, Roundstone, Connemara
W 9.5 x 13", (**EI**: 151) £600
Early Spring, Ballyfermot, Co. Dublin
O 12 x 16", S, I, (**HI**: 26) £4,500
Farmyard, Inverin, Connemara
O 12 x 16", S, I, (**HI**: 91) £3,700
Summer, River Landscape
O 24 x 29", S, (**HI**: 93) £7,100
Dubh Loch, on Erreloch Road from Roundstone
O 14 x 18", S, (**NI**: 195) £3,450
The Cross in the Winds - Kilmurvey Aran
O 16 x 20", S, (**PI**: 148) £4,000
Landscape, Ballyconneely, Connemara
O 24 x 28", S, I, (**VI**: 9) £6,500
The Boat Yard, Dun Laoghaire, Co. Dublin
W 10.5 x 15", S, I, (**VI**: 13) £670
Wheat Stubble
O 20 x 24", S, D, I, (**VI**: 97) £10,000
Aran Islander with Donkey & Panniers of Turf
O 10 x 21.5", S, (**DII**: 2) £2,800
Connemara Landscape
O 24 x 40", S, (**DII**: 82) £11,600
Camera Man
O 23 x 12", S, I, (**EII**: 355) £7,000
A Sunny Day
O 17.5 x 23.5", S, I, (**FII**: 206) £4,200
Salmon Run - Dingle Peninsula
O 20 x 24", (**GII**: 1412) £3,000

MacKINNON, Sine (b.1901)
Old Streets of Paris
O 20 x 24", S, (**Z**: 107) £5,060
Paris
O 18.5 x 25.5", S, D, I, (**NI**: 112) £2,300
Rocky Coast
O 15 x 18", S, (**YI**: 36) £460

MACLISE, Daniel (1806-1870)
New Auction Record: £353,500
King Cophetua and the Beggar Maid
Oil 47 x 71.5 ins.
Christie's London, Important British Art, 10 June 1999, Lot 19
Saxon Almsgiving
O 13 x 17", I, (**FI**: 263) £1,610
Robert Small, seated in black coat
W 10 x 8", S, D, (**II**: 50) £506
Miss Jane Small, standing on a balcony
W 10 x 8", S, D, (**II**: 51) £483

Mrs Robert Small, seated in black dress
W 10 x 8", S, (**II**: 52) £575
Miss Mary Small, in white dress
W 10 x 8", S, D, (**II**: 53) £460
King Cophetua and the Beggar Maid
O 47 x 71.5", (**UI**: 19) £353,500

MADDEN, Anne (20th Century)
Icarus
Pr 25 x 19", (**G**: 141) £550
Odyssey
Pr 25 x 16", (**G**: 142) £460
Study of Hill and Cloud
O 13 x 16", S, D, (**W**: 64) £200
Western Sky/ Land Sequence
O triptych 6 x 8", S, D, (**W**: 79) £450
Study of Hill & Cloud
O 13 x 15", S, D, I, (**EI**: 126) £420
Study of the flagellata in the Villa Misterii Pompeii
D 23.5 x 16.5", S, D, (**LI**: 128) £470
Aran (1957)
O 9 x 10.5", (**PI**: 124) £1,000

MADERSON, Arthur (20th Century)
The Spice Market, Luxor
O 32 x 45", (**G**: 144) £1,600
Study, Tallow Horse Fair
O 28.5 x 20", S, I, (**LI**: 102) £1,900
By the Pool
O 36 x 28", S, I, (**LI**: 115) £3,100
Winter Sunset
M 31 x 43", S, I, (**GII**: 1458) £1,750
Wet Glistering - Rosses Point
O 23 x 35", (**GII**: 1459) £2,200
Point of Sunset - Ardmore Beach
O 45 x 45", S, D, I, (**GII**: 1470) £2,200
Lismore River Pool - Midday Sun
O 45 x 44.5", S, D, I, (**GII**: 1471) £2,400
Late evening St. Patrick's Bridge, Cork
O 20 x 29", S, (**JII**: 111) £1,500
The Lower Road approaching Cork at dusk
O 20 x 32", S, (**JII**: 264) £1,400
'Pointing' - two boys looking in a river
O 31.5 x 31", (**KII**: 640) £1,400

MAGILL, Elizabeth (20th Century)
Untitled
O 6 x 8", (**G**: 158) £460

MAGUIRE, Cecil (b.1930)
Roundstone, Connemara
O 17.5 x 24", S, D, I, (**EI**: 113) £1,800
Kinnego Harbour
O 19.5 x 23", S, D, (**ZI**: 55) £840

MAGUIRE, Helena (b.1860)
Hard at Work
W 16.5 x 13", S, (**EI**: 83) £800

MAGUIRE, Katrina (20th Century)
Inside/Outside
M 47.5 x 38", (**G**: 145) £260

MAHONEY, James (1810-1879)
Violets
W 8 x 6", S, D, (**PI**: 105) £3,000
Views of Cork Harbour
W (2) 13 x 21", S, D, (**VI**: 94) £1,000

MALTON, James (1761-1803)
A picturesque and descriptive view of the City of Dublin
Pr (25) 15 x 21", (**HI**: 87) £6,000

MANLEY, Jim (20th Century)
Mackerel on a line
W 16 x 11", (**G**: 146) £360

MANN, Patricia (20th Century)
Roses in bloom
O 18 x 27.5", S, (**W**: 132) £280

MANSFIELD, Louise (20th Century)
The Beach Walk
O 7.5 x 9.5", S, (**LI**: 6) £400
Street Game
O 20 x 30", S, (**LI**: 15) £720
A Working Day
O 24 x 18", S, (**LI**: 29) £420

MARJORAM, Gerard (20th Century)
Achill Head
O 18 x 24", S, I, (**HI**: 111) £380

Maurice Mac GONIGAL, *Camera Man*, sold at Hamilton Osborne King, 27 November 1998 for £7,000

North Kerry Coast
O 10 x 14", S, (**DII**: 5) £320
Near Annamoe, Co. Wicklow
O 10 x 14", S, (**DII**: 7) £360
Sunlight in the Woods at Ballynabrick, Connemara; Bog Land with Heather and Sheep, Connemara
O (2) 10 x 14", S, (**GII**: 1419) £540
Ballinalinch, Co. Donegal
O 10 x 14", S, (**GII**: 1485) £220

MARKIEWICZ, Countess Constance (1868-1927)
In the North Dublin Union
W 11 x 9", S, D, I, (**EI**: 194) £2,800
Dorothy Macardle (portrait sketch)
D 10 x 7", S, D, (**EI**: 195) £240

MASTERSON, Bernie (20th Century)
Journey Home
O 11.5 x 14.5", (**G**: 149) £260

McALEER, Clement (20th Century)
Sea Horizon
A 19 x 23", (**G**: 161) £500
Landscape
M 33 x 37", (**G**: 162) £1,600

McALISTER, Therese (20th Century)
Stairway in Stazzena
O 13.5 x 9.5", S, (**O**: 113) £850

McAULEY, Charles (b.1910)
Donegal Landscape
O 25 x 31", S, (**SI**: 95) £3,680
The Olde Homestead
O 14 x 18", S, (**DII**: 43) £3,000
The Daly's Farm
O 17 x 22", S, (**DII**: 44) £3,000
The Gypsy Caravan
O 18.5 x 24", S, (**DII**: 46) £3,400
Returning with the Catch
O 14 x 18", S, (**DII**: 47) £2,800
Caught in a Shower
O 14 x 18", S, (**DII**: 49) £2,900

McCAIG, Norman J. (b.1929)
Port Magee, Co. Kerry
O 12 x 9.5 ", S, (**D**: 36) £760
Path to the Beach
O 20 x 16", S, (**D**: 94) £800
Lough Bawn - Donegal
O 20 x 16", S, (**D**: 95) £820
Autumn, St. Stephen's Green
O 16 x 20", S, (**V**: 128) £700
The River Moy, Foxford
O 14 x 18", S, (**V**: 131) £600
Achill Peat Bog
O 16 x 20", S, (**V**: 137) £1,000
Tying up the Boats
O 24 x 18", S, (**W**: 91) £650
Dingle Harbour
O 12 x 18", S, (**W**: 102) £450
Boats at Cleggan
O 15.5 x 11.5", (**W**: 176) £600
The Carousel
O 14 x 18", S, (**EI**: 201) £1,000
Twelve Pins, Maam Cross
O 16 x 20", S, (**HI**: 5) £850
The Liffey at Dusk
O 16 x 20", S, (**HI**: 16) £720
Fishing Boats, Old Pier, Cashel, Connemara
O 16 x 20", S, (**HI**: 40) £1,000
On the Killary at Leanane
O 16 x 20", S, (**DII**: 74) £860
A Stroll in the Park - Dublin
O 9 x 11", (**GII**: 1443) £380
Autumn Street - Stephens Green
O 9 x 11", S, (**GII**: 1444) £420
Boats in Harbour, Northern Ireland
O 15 x 19.5", S, (**GII**: 1448) £1,100
Fishermen returning
O 12 x 10", S, (**JII**: 116) £950
Guinness Barges on the Liffey
O 14 x 18", S, (**JII**: 235) £610
On Lough Ree
O 19 x 25", S, (**JII**: 242) £625
Children on the Grand Canal
O 15 x 19", S, I, (**JII**: 443) £750

McCAUGHEY, Anne Marie (20th Century)
Moorland above Pettigo
O 20 x 30", S, (**LI**: 9) £300
Western Landscape
O 20 x 30", S, (**LI**: 16) £440
The High Road past Doon Fort
A 30 x 10.5", S, (**LI**: 27) £400

McCORMICK, Arthur David (1860-1943)
Plotting the Campaign
O 36 x 24", S, D, (**FI**: 308) £3,680
The Temptation of Monmouth
O 51 x 30", S, (**GI**: 103) £10,350
Selling her charms
W 15 x 22", S, (**PI**: 2) £700

McDONNELL, Hector (b.1947)
Sawmills Arch, St.James Market
O 12 x 6.5", (**O**: 111) £2,200
Conductor at a Brendel Concert, London, 1981
D 7 x 4.5", S, D, I, (**EI**: 208) £300
Window at Seaforde
O 10 x 12", S, D, (**LI**: 139) £1,400
Fish Retailers, Monument Street
O 24 x 17", S, D, I, (**NI**: 87) £1,955
Fishmonger's Pudding Lane
O 48 x 36", S, D, I, (**NI**: 90) £12,650
Butchers Shop, Belfast 1984
O 9 x 6", S, (**VI**: 75) £1,400
Near Cromac Street, Belfast
O 13 x 10", S, D, I, (**VI**: 76) £1,800

McENTAGGART, Brett (20th Century)
Au Revoir Miranda
O 24 x 18", (**G**: 170) £1,200
Houses at Crookhaven, West Cork
O 18 x 24", S, (**W**: 125) £950
Provence
O 17 x 13", S, (**EI**: 204) £700

Andalusian Village
O 8 x 11.5", S, (**HI**: 10) £300
The Footpath, Lauzun
O 18 x 14", S, (**VI**: 136) £540
Summer Orchard
O 16 x 24", S, (**VI**: 137) £900
Straw Bales
O 13.5 x 19", S, (**FII**: 195) £700
Summer Landscape
O 11.5 x 15", S, (**FII**: 196) £400
McGEE, Kevin (20th Century)
Figure Study
M 38 x 32", (**G**: 172) £280
McGLYNN, Maura (20th Century)
Fanad Head
O 9.5 x 11", (**G**: 174) £200
McGORAN, Kieran (1932-1990)
Three Racehorses
W 12 x 11.5", S, (**D**: 157) £420
McGUINNESS, Norah (1903-1980)
New Auction Record: £19,000
The Customs House, Dublin - From the South Quays
Oil 27 x 36 ins. S, D,
James Adam & Bonhams, Important Irish Art,
26 May 1999, Lot 36
The Winding Road
W 9 x 14", S, (**F**: 178) £828
Mayo
P 11 x 12", (**G**: 175) £820
Moths Around a Lamp
O 16 x 8", (**O**: 34) £2,200
Driftwood II
O 20 x 29", S, I, (**O**: 95J) £3,000
Flowers and Sea
W 14 x 18", S, (**V**: 30) £3,200
Divided Land
W 12 x 15", S, (**V**: 166) £520
Lady outside a Country Church
D 9.5 x 12.5", S, (**EI**: 138) £970
Still life study of a jug and fruit on a table
W 10 x 12.5", S, (**HI**: 13) £1,400
A stroll in Fitzwilliam Square
W 11 x 15", S, D, (**HI**: 112) £1,700
The Last of the Shelley Banks
O 33 x 39", S, (**NI**: 20) £8,050
The Customs House, Dublin -
From the South Quays
O 27 x 36", S, D, (**PI**: 36) £19,000
Young Moon
O 16 x 22", S, (**PI**: 98) £4,200
Lawlors Grocery Shop
W 10 x 13", S, (**VI**: 2) £850
Coastal Landscape, Donegal
W 16.5 x 21", S, D, (**VI**: 57) £4,800
Cottages
W 14 x 19.5", S, (**VI**: 110) £1,900
Sussex Landscape
W 12 x 19", S, (**JII**: 215) £575
McGUINNESS, William Bingham (1849-1928)
Continental Street
W 14 x 10", S, (**D**: 35) £570
Swiss Landscape
W 11 x 18", S, D, (**V**: 12) £600
Lough Scene
W 12 x 18", S, (**V**: 29A) £720
Venice
W 9.5 x 12", S, D, I, (**HI**: 19A) £900
Cottages by a Lough, Connemara
W 29.5 x 20", S, (**NI**: 168) £1,495
A Ruined Castle with figures
W 12.5 x 18.5", S, D, (**PI**: 20A) £800
Autumn
W 20 x 29", S, D, (**PI**: 87) £1,400
Winter in Switzerland
W 9.5 x 7", S, (**PI**: 155) £650
A Venetian Doorway
W 13.5 x 9.5", S, D, (**PI**: 174) £380
River Landscape with distant Town
W 14 x 20", (**PI**: 175) £1,200
Boating Clew Bay
W 5 x 9", S, (**ZI**: 58) £200

Street Scene - Rouen
W 22.5 x 13", S, (**DII**: 17) £1,200
Sailing Boat near Castle Ruins;
French Breton Scene
W (2) 7.5 x 10", S, (**DII**: 35) £700
Near Killarney, Co. Kerry
W 10.5 x 14.5", S, (**GII**: 1407) £700
Mountainous lake scene with figures in a boat
W 19 x 29", S, D, (**JII**: 512) £1,150
Looking towards the sea
W 8 x 11", S, (**JII**: 516) £625
McGUIRE, Edward (1932-1986)
Owl
O 13 x 12", S, D, (**D**: 42) £3,500
Bird & Skull
O 13 x 9", S, I, (**NI**: 82) £2,300
McKELVEY, Frank (1895-1974)
New Auction Record: £54,300
Summer Days
Oil 18 x 27 ins. S, I,
Sotheby's, The Irish Sale - 21 May 1999, Lot 384
Children in a Park
O 14.5 x 19.5", S, (**D**: 54) £22,000
Summer 1922
O 11.5 x 16.5", S, (**D**: 75) £6,000
Cutting Turf in a West of Ireland Landscape
O 27 x 35.5", S, (**D**: 128) £21,000
Landscape, Co. Antrim
O 15 x 20", S, I, (**E**: 279) £8,050
Farmhouse, Mourne Mountains
O 20 x 26", S, I, (**O**: 20) £14,500
Picnic by the Lagan
O 14.5 x 22", S, (**V**: 32) £18,000
Summer
O 14 x 18", S, (**V**: 51) £17,000
Cows Grazing by a Sunlit River
O 12 x 17", S, (**V**: 80) £4,600
Cutting the Turf
O 16 x 20", S, (**V**: 93) £8,000
The Turf Cutters
O 18 x 24", S, (**Z**: 9) £6,900
Breaghy Head, Co. Donegal
O 15.5 x 21.5", S, (**Z**: 10) £4,370
Collecting Turf
O 14.5 x 19", S, (**EI**: 10) £7,200
River at Crolly, Co. Donegal
O 13.5 x 18", S, (**HI**: 92) £6,000
The Farmyard, Co. Antrim
O 15 x 20", S, (**NI**: 37) £19,550
Haystacks and Cottages on the Coast
O 12 x 16", S, (**NI**: 117) £5,980
Farmyard, Creeslough, Co. Donegal
W 14 x 21", S, (**NI**: 118) £4,370
Carnlough, Co. Antrim
W 8 x 10", S, (**NI**: 119) £2,875
Figures and Boats on an Estuary Beach
W 10.5 x 14", S, (**NI**: 120) £3,680
The Bathers
W 13.5 x 19.5", S, D, (**NI**: 121) £12,650
Landing the Catch
W 14 x 20.5", S, (**NI**: 122) £4,830
Picking Spring Flowers
O 11 x 16", S, (**OI**: 367) £12,075
Picking Daisies
W 11 x 14", S, (**OI**: 371) £12,650
Summer Days
O 18 x 27", S, I, (**OI**: 384) £54,300
Tory Island, Co. Donegal
O 20 x 27", S, (**OI**: 387) £31,050
Maze, County Down
W (2) 7 x 11", S, (**PI**: 6) £1,050
Chickens feeding in the snow
O 14 x 18", S, D, (**PI**: 23) £3,000
'Back of the House' - Woman feeding hens
O 20 x 27", S, (**PI**: 27) £24,000
The bend in the river
O 15 x 20", S, (**PI**: 47) £5,700
Figures by a Road, Co. Donegal
O 12.5 x 17.5", S, (**GII**: 1480) £4,250
A Village Street
O 10 x 14", (**III**: 1196) £4,600

McKENNA, Stephen (20th Century)
Studio Corner
W 17.5 x 20.5", (**G**: 176) £870
McKENZIE, William Gibbs (1857-1924)
Belfast Lough
O 14.5 x 21", S, I, (**O**: 40) £1,900
McKINSTRY, Cherith (20th Century)
Landscape
O 8 x 11.5", (**G**: 178) £520
McMAHON, Brian (20th Century)
The Artist in his Studio
O 23 x 27", S, D, (**EI**: 124) £460
McSWEENEY, Sean (b.1935)
Winter
O 23.5 x 30", S, D, (**O**: 119) £1,300
Sligo Bogland
O 9.5 x 13.5", S, D, I, (**EI**: 129) £1,000
Land and Sea, Sligo
O 17 x 23", S, D, I, (**HI**: 92D) £1,000
Bogland, Sligo
Pr 20 x 14", S, (**LI**: 67) £220
Landscape (1977)
O 20 x 25", S, I, (**PI**: 101) £1,400
Shoreline Bog, Sligo
O 24 x 32", S, D, I, (**PI**: 125) £1,200
McSWEENEY, Tadhg (20th Century)
Landscape with Magpies
O 36.5 x 39", (**G**: 182) £400
Cloud Study
O 23 x 38.5", (**G**: 183) £300
McSWINEY, M. Eugene (1866-1936)
Gypsy Encampment
O 11.5 x 19.5", S, (**W**: 11) £420
Gypsies
O 12 x 20", S, (**EI**: 32) £970
Gypsies
O 12 x 20", (**VI**: 170) £920
McWILLIAM, F. E. (1909-1992)
Woman of Belfast
W 11 x 16", S, D, (**VI**: 40) £1,000
MIDDLETON, Colin (1910-1983)
New Auction Record: £40,000
Requiem for Dan O'Neill
Oil 26 x 30 ins. D, I
Christie's London, The Irish Sale, 20 May 1999, Lot 70
Brockagh II
O 24 x 24", S, D, (**N**: 26) £2,990
October: Newcastle
O 24 x 24", S, D, (**N**: 88) £2,990
Abstract Landscape
W 5 x 5", (**O**: 51) £350
Abstract Landscape
W 5 x 5", (**O**: 52) £520
Couple in the Trees
D 6.5 x 6.5", (**O**: 53) £600
Seated Woman
D 6 x 5", S, D, (**O**: 54) £380
Fertility
O 20 x 24", S, D, I, (**O**: 61) £13,500
Flowering Meadow
O 9.5 x 15.5", S, D, I, (**O**: 95O) £2,400
Trees, Castle Park (Bangor 1954)
O 18 x 24", S, I, (**V**: 100) £3,800
Landscape
W 10 x 11", S, D, (**EI**: 19) £1,300
Willows, Dunrod
O 15 x 23", S, D, I, (**EI**: 53) £4,700
Landscape
W 4 x 4", (**EI**: 65) £360
Landscape in Evening
M 5 x 4.5", (**EI**: 66) £300
V.J. Day - American Soldier
D 8.5 x 6", I, (**EI**: 67) £300
Outhouses, Ballyhalbert
O 11 x 13", S, D, I, (**EI**: 165) £3,000
Winter Landscape
O 18.5 x 21", (**EI**: 166) £4,000
The First Communion
C 10.5 x 8.5", S, D, I, (**EI**: 167) £200
October, Newcastle
O 24 x 24", S, D, I, (**HI**: 79) £4,600

Landscape
W 5 x 7", S, D, (**HI**: 102) £300
The Cottage Garden
O 20 x 24", S, D, (**NI**: 64) £3,450
Carnmal Bridge, Co. Donegal
O 24 x 24", S, (**NI**: 65) £2,530
Surrealist Composition, 1937
O 24 x 30", S, D, (**NI**: 68) £10,120
Friday, 27 June 1943
O 24 x 30", S, D, I, (**NI**: 69) £10,120
Requiem for Dan O'Neill
O 26 x 30", D, I, (**NI**: 70) £40,000
Seven Creatures
O 48 x 48", S, D, I, (**NI**: 71) £4,600
Landscape in May, Carnmoney
O 20 x 24", S, D, (**OI**: 358) £3,220
The Morning Star
O 20 x 24", S, D, I, (**OI**: 362) £11,500
Winter - Spelga 1965
O 10 x 8.5", S, (**PI**: 90) £1,900
Wagner in Bangor
O 23.5 x 23.5", S, (**PI**: 121) £16,000
Kate's Piano
W 9 x 10", S, (**PI**: 134) £1,650
Moneycaragh
O 20 x 29", S, D, I, (**VI**: 19) £8,200
Family
D 4.5 x 6", S, D, (**VI**: 30) £460
Prisoners & Guards
O S, (**ZI**: 54) £1,600
Seated Woman
O 14 x 10", S, (**FII**: 207) £5,500

MILES, Thomas Rose (fl.1869-1888)
Moonrise, Connemara
O 24 x 36", S, (**V**: 10) £850
The Ferry Crossing
O 24 x 36", S, D, (**V**: 55) £4,400
The Breton Welk Collectors
O 13 x 17", S, (**PI**: 32) £1,000

MILLER, Marion (20th Century)
Corner
M 19.5 x 18.5", (**G**: 151) £280

MITCHELL, Flora H. (1890-1973)
The Shelbourne Hotel, Dublin
W 9 x 8", S, I, (**D**: 53) £2,700
St. Stephen's Green East
W 9 x 13", S, I, (**O**: 72) £2,100
Vances Court, Bishop Street
W 9 x 13", S, I, (**O**: 73) £720
The Four Courts, Dublin
W 10 x 8.5", S, I, (**W**: 135) £1,150
Birthplace of Jonathan Swift (1667, Holys Court)
W 12 x 9", S, I, (**EI**: 97) £1,100
The Last of Braithwaite St.
W 12 x 9", S, I, (**EI**: 98) £870
Derby Court
W 10 x 9.5", S, I, (**EI**: 99) £720
Marrowbone Lane
W 12 x 12", S, D, I, (**VI**: 104) £850

MITCHELL, Rosemary (20th Century)
Ice Cold Stream
O 16 x 20", (**G**: 154) £300

MOLONEY, Freda (fl.1904-1910)
The Blessing of the Fishing Fleet, Etaples, Brittany
O 35 x 27", S, (**V**: 89) £13,000

MOONEY, Brian (20th Century)
Looking Down
O 51 x 14", (**G**: 155) £400

MOONEY, Carmel (b.1936)
Evening Crater at Etna
O 10 x 14", (**G**: 156) £480

MOONEY, Edward (20th Century)
Bird with Red Lighthouse
O 19 x 23.5", S, (**W**: 130) £270

MOONEY, Martin (20th Century)
View of Allambra
O 18 x 24", (**G**: 157) £1,700
Head & Musical Instruments
O 56 x 110", S, D, I, (**EI**: 127) £5,000

MORGAN, Edith (20th Century)
The Flower Girl
O 15 x 11.5", (**JII**: 495) £550

MORRISON, R. Boyd (1896-1969)
Roses on a Table
O 15.5 x 13", S, (**EI**: 63) £380

MOSS, Henry William (1859-1944)
Quiet Fields, Rathfarnham
O 12 x 16", S, D, (**GII**: 1486) £500
Extensive Pastoral Landscape
O 16.5 x 21", (**GII**: 1489) £600
Oaks - oak trees in a Landscape
O 12 x 16", (**GII**: 1493A) £600

MOYNAN, Richard Thomas (1856-1906)
Auction Record: *£86,000*
Ball in the Cap
24 x 40 ins. S & D 1893
James Adam, 14 December 1994, Lot 41

MULREADY, William (1786-1863)
The Meagre Feast
W 25 x 18", S, D, (**HI**: 46) £1,800

MURPHY, Frank (1925-1979)
River Landscape with Houses
W 10.5 x 15", S, (**D**: 17) £220
Muckish Mountain, Co. Donegal
W 10 x 14.5", S, (**D**: 79) £400

MURPHY, W. (20th Century)
Snow Covered Landscape
O 28 x 24", S, (**HI**: 34) £420

MURRAY, Peter (20th Century)
Bantry House 1997
W 22 x 29.5", (**G**: 160) £200

MURRIE, Desmond (20th Century)
The Trotting Race
O 13 x 17", S, (**LI**: 17) £330
Rounding the Turn
O 25 x 27", S, (**LI**: 33) £300

NALLY, Fergal (20th Century)
Windswept Tree
O 18 x 22", S, (**LI**: 98) £350

NEILL, Henry Echelin (b.1888)
Blue Stack Mountains, County Donegal
O 16 x 20", S, (**PI**: 9) £1,400

NEWENHAM, Frederick (1807-1859)
A Lady of the Court
O 14 x 12", I, (**O**: 15) £2,200

NiCHIOSAIN, Fionnuala (20th Century)
City of Peace
M 15 x 20", (**G**: 184) £240

NICHOLL, Andrew (1804-1886)
Auction Record: *£17,000*
View of Dublin Bay with the Hill of Howth in the Distance and Sandymount Strand and Dun Laoghaire in the Foreground
Watercolour 16.5 x 25.5 ins. S
Sotheby's, 16 May 1996, Lot 408
A Bank of Poppies, Daisies & Other Summer Flowers with Killiney Bay, Bray Head and the Sugerloaf in the Distance
W 13 x 20", S, (**O**: 19) £16,500
A View across Dublin Bay from Kingstown
W 12.5 x 19", S, (**HI**: 30) £1,600
Belfast 1839
W 7 x 10", (**II**: 30) £2,070
A coastal landscape with poppies, cornflowers, daisies and grasses in the foreground
W 13 x 20", S, (**NI**: 155A) £13,225

NICHOLSON, Francis (1753-1844)
The Rock of Cashel, Tipperary
W 13 x 17", (**NI**: 148) £2,070

NICOL, Erskine (1825-1904)
Two Gentlemen of the Road
W 16 x 12", S, D, (**OI**: 282) £805
Bringing home the turf, Co. Westmeath
W 6.5 x 10", S, I, (**PI**: 1) £950
The Old Ghillie
O 14.5 x 10.5", (**PI**: 86) £3,000
The Love Letter
O 17 x 13", S, D, (**VI**: 173) £2,800

NiCUILL, N. (20th Century)
Tinkers Camp
O 35 x 45", S, (**HI**: 117) £360

NIETSCHE, Paul (1855-1950)
Portrait Study
O 14.5 x 19.5", S, D, (**O**: 2) £870
Self Portrait
D 18.5 x 15", S, (**EI**: 13) £380

NISBET, Tom (b.1909)
Dodder at Clonskeagh
W 11 x 14.5", S, (**D**: 39) £200
Autumn on the Canal
W 11.5 x 14.5", S, (**W**: 80) £270
A Walk by the Canal
W 11 x 15", S, (**HI**: 6) £350
Horse Riding in Woodland
W 11 x 15", S, (**LI**: 122) £200
Canal Walk
W 10.5 x 15", S, (**PI**: 141) £340
Mews, Dartmouth Square, Dublin
W 10.5 x 13", S, (**PI**: 144) £360
Kilbride, Co. Wicklow
W 11 x 15", S, (**VI**: 122) £220
A View of the South African War Memorial, Stephens Green
W 11.5 x 15.5", S, (**EII**: 351) £600
A View from St Stephens Green, at the Corner of Grafton St.
W 10.5 x 14.5", S, (**EII**: 353) £500
Limerick After Rain
W 11 x 14.5", (**GII**: 1435) £420
Boats at Kilmore Quay, Co. Wexford
W 15 x 11", (**JII**: 89) £320
Canal in Autumn
W 11 x 15", S, I, (**JII**: 99) £625
Canal side
W 15 x 11", S, (**JII**: 100) £320
Milltown Road, Dublin
W 12 x 15.5", S, I, (**JII**: 247) £360
Blossom Time, Leinster Lawn
W 11 x 15", S, (**JII**: 456) £320

NIXON, John (1750-1818)
The surroundings of St. Patrick's Cathedral, Dublin
W 19 x 26.5", S, (**OI**: 259) £43,300

NOLAN, James (20th Century)
Martello Tower, Portrane, Co. Dublin
O 18 x 22", S, (**D**: 2) £600
Liffey Woodland, County Kildare
O 10 x 11.5", S, (**W**: 97) £200
The Canal Walk, Landenstown
O 14 x 19", S, (**PI**: 143) £500

O'BRIEN, Dermod (1865-1945)
On the Thames below Goring
O 10 x 14", S, D, I, (**HI**: 94) £2,200
Trim Castle, County Meath
O 9.5 x 13.5", (**PI**: 93) £1,950
Harvest at Cahirmoyle
O 14 x 17", I, (**EII**: 310) £2,400
Classical Figure and doves
O 24 x 30", (**JII**: 123) £580

O'BRIEN, Geraldine (b.1922)
Still Life - Michelmas Daisies
O 26 x 32", S, (**JII**: 110) £1,700

O'BRIEN, Gretta (20th Century)
Wild Flowers, Co. Wicklow
O 16 x 20", S, (**GII**: 1411) £500
Wild Flowers
O 16 x 20", S, (**JII**: 224) £600
Through the Trees
O 16 x 24", (**JII**: 248) £600

O'BRIEN, Kitty Wilmer (1910-1982)
The Clock, Westport, County Mayo
O 22 x 28", (**PI**: 21) £4,800
Croagh Patrick, County Mayo
O 22 x 28", (**PI**: 46) £1,800
Mountjoy Square, Dublin
O 28 x 22", S, (**PI**: 128) £2,600

O'BROIN, Eamonn (20th Century)
A Hillside Stream with Trees and a Barn
O 14.5 x 11", S, I, (**EII**: 311) £320

O'CONNOR, James Arthur (1792-1841)
Auction Record: IR£30,000
The Gathering Storm (1826)
Oil 25 x 30 ins. S, D
James Adam & Bonhams, 10 December 1997, Lot 27
Wooded River Landscape with Man Rowing a Boat
O 8 x 11.5", S, (**D**: 111) £9,700
Sunset over a Rocky Wooded Valley with Figures
O 24 x 29", S, D, (**V**: 75) £29,000
Landscape with Figures beside a River
O 15 x 17.5", S, D, (**OI**: 242) £20,700
The Nut Gatherers
O 17 x 13", (**OI**: 245) £9,200
Figures on a Woodland Path - Twilight
O 8 x 10", S, D, (**PI**: 75) £3,100
O'CONNOR, Sean (20th Century)
The Lakes of Killarney
O 16 x 20", S, I, (**FII**: 209) £300
O'CONOR, Roderic (1860-1940)
New Auction Record: £276,500
Nature Morte aux Pommes
Oil 22 x 15 ins.
Sotheby's, 20th Century British Works of Art from the Hiscox Collection, 3 December 1998, Lot 1
Attic Interior
O 20 x 30", (**O**: 26) £20,000
Nature Morte aux Pommes
O 22 x 15", (**T**: 1) £276,500
Portrait Study of a Young Girl
O 22 x 18", (**EI**: 59) £4,800
Nude Study
D 8 x 14", (**EI**: 60) £670
Still Life with Tureen, Jug and Dish
O 18 x 22", (**NI**: 191) £205,000
Baigneuse a la Mer
O 39.5 x 32", (**OI**: 283) £111,500
Flowers
O 25.5 x 21", S, D, (**OI**: 291) £67,500
O'DEA, Mick (20th Century)
Dún Briste
A 32 x 40", (**G**: 237F) £700
O'DONNELL, Deirdre (20th Century)
Lake Landscape with Cottages
O 15.5 x 25", (**DII**: 42) £260
O'HALLORAN, James (20th Century)
Bantry Pier, Summer
O 11 x 13", (**EI**: 191) £560
Path through trees
O 10 x 8", S, D, (**LI**: 39) £480
Apple Blossom
O 16 x 11.5", S, I, (**VI**: 134) £300
Red Bedroom
O 19 x 15", S, (**JII**: 80) £1,100
Sunlit drawing room fireplace
O 10 x 12", S, I, (**JII**: 505) £825
O'HARA, Helen (1846-1919)
Cliffs, Co. Derry
W 12 x 10", S, I, (**NI**: 2) £1,955
The Young Fisherman
W 14 x 20.5", S, (**PI**: 165) £1,600
O'HARA, Maurice (20th Century)
Thatched Cottage, Co. Mayo
O 15.5 x 19", S, (**DII**: 54) £260
O'KEEFFE, Margaret (fl.1910-1930)
The Girl in the Scarlet Shawl
O 16 x 20", S, (**NI**: 113) £3,220
O'KEEFFE, Noelle (20th Century)
Sunflower
O 20.5 x 20", (**G**: 187) £420
O'KELLY, Aloysius (1851-c.1928)
Auction Record: IR£18,000
Old couple at the door of an inn c.1876/77
19 x 15 ins. S
James Adam, 13 December 1995, Lot 41
Cattle Grazing under Silver Birches
O 32 x 26", S, (**OI**: 305) £6,325
Concarneau
O 9 x 13", S, (**ZI**: 65) £3,000
O'MALLEY, Jane (20th Century)
New Years Day Painting, 1993
O 24 x 24", S, I, (**EI**: 224C) £500
O'MALLEY, Michael Augustine Power (1878-1946)
Unloading the Catch
O 19 x 30", (**V**: 70) £2,500
Afternoon Light
O 24 x 30", (**V**: 147) £2,400
Slea Head, Co. Kerry
O 24 x 30", S, (**NI**: 45) £2,070
O'MALLEY, Tony (b.1913)
Inscape Mozaga
O 36 x 48", (**G**: 189) £7,000
A Friend in Sweeney's Wood
M 9.5 x 14", (**G**: 237D) £950
St. Martins
W 7 x 10.5", S, D, I, (**W**: 98) £850
Earth Song, Spring 1983
O 42 x 24", S, D, I, (**EI**: 116) £5,200
Birdsong, April Walk 1969
O 13 x 8", S, D, I, (**EI**: 117) £1,900
Abstract Landscape
O 25 x 30", S, (**VI**: 77) £2,400
Lanzarote
M 12 x 16.5", S, D, (**VI**: 78) £1,700
View from a Window
M 13 x 19", S, D, (**VI**: 80) £1,000
Old Place in Ireland
W 9.5 x 20", I, (**ZI**: 32) £1,450
O'MEARA, Frank (1853-1888)
Reverie (Dreaming)
O 71 x 51", S, D, (**NI**: 189) £496,500
O'NEILL, Daniel (1920-1974)
New Auction Record: £62,000
Divorce and Departure
Oil 27 x 38 ins. S, I
Sotheby's, The Irish Sale, 21 May 1999, Lot 363
Rebecca
O 16 x 12", S, (**D**: 55) £6,000
Derelict Houses
O 20 x 24", (**D**: 78) £1,220
The Little River
O 18 x 24", S, (**F**: 306) £1,380
The Oriental
O 18.5 x 14.5", S, (**N**: 24) £7,475
Helen
O 24 x 18", S, (**N**: 27) £7,475
Travelling through Kerry
O 16 x 24", S, (**N**: 87) £8,625
Twilight
O 14 x 18", S, I, (**O**: 22) £3,800
The Fortress, Buncrana
O 23.5 x 35", S, I, (**O**: 30) £6,500
The Belfast Blitz
O 7 x 9", S, (**O**: 63) £1,000
Farewell Without Words
O 18 x 24", S, (**O**: 69) £6,000
The Road to Conlig
O 20 x 24", S, (**V**: 103) £4,000
Faust
O 13.5 x 17.5", S, I, (**V**: 120) £2,100
The Old Abbey, Donegal
O 20 x 24", S, (**V**: 167) £2,100
Helen
O 17 x 23.5", S, (**EI**: 38) £26,000
The Request
O 14 x 17", S, I, (**EI**: 56) £4,200
The Sea Horse
O 24 x 20", (**EI**: 168) £1,500
The Sunbather
O 18 x 20", S, (**EI**: 224K) £9,000
Indecision
O 34 x 39", S, I, (**HI**: 86) £11,000
The Wedding
O 20 x 28", (**NI**: 23) £35,600
Boy and Pegasus
O 24 x 20", S, (**NI**: 99) £8,050
Divorce and Departure
O 27 x 38", S, I, (**OI**: 363) £62,000
Horseman Pass By
O 20 x 27", S, I, (**OI**: 365) £29,900
The Meeting Place
O 18 x 24", S, I, (**OI**: 366) £3,680
The White Friar
O 14 x 18", S, (**OI**: 368) £3,680
Morning Light
O 10 x 14", S, I, (**OI**: 372) £10,925
A Last Look Back
O 19 x 29.5", S, (**OI**: 396) £27,600
Little River
O 18 x 24", S, (**PI**: 54) £6,200
The Astronomers
O 14 x 18", S, (**PI**: 150) £2,000
Ladies in a Landscape
O 5 x 9", S, D, I, (**VI**: 45) £4,000
The Salmon Leap, Bunbeg, Co. Donegal
O 19.5 x 23.5", S, (**VI**: 182) £2,600
Resting
O 13 x 17", S, (**ZI**: 53) £7,900
O'NEILL, Geraldine (20th Century)
The Artist in her Studio
O 43.5 x 71.5", (**G**: 190) £1,300
Lemon Sketch
O 17 x 11", S, I, (**EI**: 200) £300
O'NEILL, Mark (20th Century)
Green Walks
O 14 x 18", S, (**DII**: 79) £860
O'RYAN, Fergus (1911-1989)
The Mill at Athgarvan (1978)
O 20 x 24", S, (**D**: 72) £1,300
Cole's Lane, Dublin
W 11 x 15", S, (**O**: 129) £820
The Dodder at Milltown
O 12 x 17.5", S, (**V**: 3) £750
Minaun Cliffs from Keel, Achill
O 14.5 x 18", S, (**V**: 51A) £850
The Grange, Co. Dublin
O 12.5 x 15.5", S, (**W**: 37) £450
Summerhill, Dublin
O 24 x 20", S, (**W**: 92) £2,800
The Twelve Pins from Ballyrevick
O 10 x 18", S, (**HI**: 4) £1,400
Flowers
W 17 x 13", S, I, (**HI**: 116) £820
Old Dublin - View to Thomas Street
W 34.5 x 23.5", S, (**HI**: 118) £1,000
The Steep Street
O 21.5 x 14.5", S, (**OI**: 377) £1,725
Stacking the Turf in the Phoenix Park during the Emergency
O 27 x 32", S, (**VI**: 8) £2,000
Continental Town
O 19 x 23", S, (**VI**: 119) £920
The Mill Stream, Dartry
W 9 x 13", S, (**DII**: 9) £400
A View of Dublin Bay
O 15 x 23.5", S, I, (**EII**: 348) £550
A Sunny Beech Wood in a Wicklow Valley
O 13.5 x 17.5", S, (**EII**: 354) £550
Market Marrakesh
O 10.5 x 14", S, I, (**GII**: 1455) £750
O'SULLIVAN, Donal (20th Century)
Standing Figure
P 42 x 29", S, (**LI**: 93) £360
Problem Drawing III
D 14 x 16", S, I, (**DII**: 27) £320
O'SULLIVAN, Margaret (20th Century)
Sea Cave - Allihies (No. 2)
O 40.5 x 26", (**G**: 191) £670
O'SULLIVAN, Sean (1906-1964)
Portrait of Eamon de Valera
D 18 x 13.5", S, (**D**: 15) £1,900
Portrait of a young gentleman, seated
D 19 x 14.5", S, D, (**HI**: 108) £380
Cottage Interior
D 13 x 16", S, (**VI**: 99) £1,300
By the Fireside
D 11 x 15", S, D, (**VI**: 100) £1,400
Portrait of Kevin O'Sullivan, the artist's brother
P 22 x 16", S, (**ZI**: 15) £570
Study of a Young Boy Seated
D 12 x 9", S, (**DII**: 8) £360

ORPEN, Bea
A Village Road
W 6 x 9", S, (**ZI**: 2) £360
ORPEN, Sir William (1878-1931)
Auction Record: £716,500
A Mere Fracture: In the Newcomes, Fitzroy Street, The Fracture
Oil 39 x 37 ins. S, D
Christie's Irish Sale, 22 May 1998, Lot 21
The Wistful Gaze
W 13.5 x 10", S, (**V**: 56) £14,000
The Man from Aran (Self-Portrait); A Man from the Aran Islands
O 47 x 34", S, (**NI**: 24) £573,500
The Jockey; an illustrated letter to his wife, Grace
D 13 x 8", S, I, (**NI**: 25) £1,840
Kildare Street Dublin
D 13 x 8", I, (**NI**: 26) £1,035
An illustrated letter to his wife, Grace
D 13 x 8", S, I, (**NI**: 27) £1,955
An illustrated letter to his wife, Grace
D 13 x 8", S, I, (**NI**: 28) £1,380
Lane's Dinner
D 8 x 13", D, I, (**NI**: 29) £5,175
The Old Circus: The Three Musketeers
O 35 x 27", S, I, (**NI**: 30) £31,050
The Normandy Cider Press; The Cyder Press
O 21 x 30", S, (**NI**: 31) £62,000
OSBORNE, Walter Frederick (1859-1903)
Auction Record: £370,000
Beneath St. Jacques, Antwerp
Oil 26 x 23 ins. S, D
Christie's Irish Sale, 22 May 1998, Lot 156
Dorothy and Irene Falkiner
O 59 x 45", S, (**V**: 97) £355,000
Pastoral Landscape study with two Figures under the Tree and Cottage in the Distance
O 7 x 9", (**EI**: 46) £4,800
Portrait of Mrs Chadwyck-Healey and her Daughter
O 56 x 46", S, I, (**NI**: 173) £331,500
Portrait of Miss Armstrong
O 13 x 10", S, D, (**OI**: 293) £16,100
Portrait of the artist's mother reading
O 13 x 16", (**OI**: 297) £4,140
Portrait of Violet Osborne, painting
O 9 x 6", S, D, (**OI**: 304) £12,650
Walberswick
O 5.5 x 9", S, (**PI**: 94) £27,000
Cow Studies
D 10 x 14", S, (**VI**: 155) £820
OSBORNE, William
Auction Record: £16,000
Portrait of Mrs Thomas Conolly seated on a Chestnut Hunter
44 x 52 ins.
Christie's, 14 April 1992, Lot 82
PATTON, Eric (b.1925)
Lichens and Stones
O 30 x 36.5", (**G**: 193) £700
Fishing Boats
O 15.5 x 20", S, (**O**: 125) £700
Seascape
O 10 x 14", S, (**EI**: 125) £420
Fishing Boats, Ballinskelligs, Co. Kerry
O 16.5 x 19.5", S, I, (**EI**: 224B) £650
Coastal Landscape at Westport
O 20 x 24", S, (**VI**: 160) £400
Headland
O 16 x 12", S, (**ZI**: 81) £380
PEARSON, Peter (20th Century)
St Stephen's Green, Dublin
W 9 x 13.5", S, D, I, (**HI**: 11) £300
A View of Dun Laoghaire and Dublin Bay from Killiney Hill
O 10.5 x 20", S, D, (**HI**: 22) £1,200
Cork Harbour, Spike Island
O 10 x 15.5", S, (**LI**: 110A) £800
The Lagoon in Venice
O 7 x 5.5", S, (**LI**: 115A) £280
Liffey Evening - a Busy City Centre Scene
O 14.5 x 27", S, D, (**GII**: 1433) £700
PETTIGREW, Stanley (20th Century)
An Old Mill
O 12 x 16", S, (**D**: 134) £420
Wicklow Harbour
O 11.5 x 15", S, (**DII**: 16) £450
POTTER, George (20th Century)
Head of a Woman
M 13.5 x 9.5", S, (**LI**: 66) £220
POWER, Arthur (1891-1984)
The Hunter in Hiding
P 9 x 12.5", S, (**W**: 71) £200
PRAEGER, Sophia Rosamund (1867-1954)
The Dragon and the Three Bold Babes
W (2) 14 x 9", S, (**OI**: 307) £920
PROUD, Liam (20th Century)
The Woods at Ballycorus and Killiney Hill
O (2) 11.5 x 16", S, (**LI**: 112) £280
PURCELL, Niki (20th Century)
Follow the Red Road
O 30 x 36", (**G**: 197) £200
PURSER, Sarah (1848-1943)
Jane L'Estrange
D 9 x 5", (**G**: 196) £1,100
Sitting in the Garden (Portrait Painted in the Open Air)
O 36 x 28", S, I, (**O**: 29) £31,000
PYE, Patrick (b.1929)
Study of the Fishermen's Master
P 14 x 12", (**G**: 198) £700
Jacob's Dream - study for stained glass
M 7.5 x 5.5", S, (**W**: 61) £350
Still Life
M 25 x 20", S, I, (**EI**: 219) £920
RAE, Barbara (20th Century)
Caledon
Pr 35.5 x 23.5", (**G**: 200) £600
RAFFERTY, Phil (1919-1996)
Dragon Fly
M 14.5 x 21.5", (**G**: 201) £500
RAKOCZI, Basil (1908-1979)
Huntsman and the white stag
W 20 x 25", (**V**: 8) £950
Noah's Ark
W 11 x 16", S, (**V**: 26A) £1,000
Sailors
W 12 x 20", (**V**: 141) £1,300
Nature Morte aux Fruits
O 24 x 32", S, D, I, (**NI**: 89) £4,370
Connemara
O 20.5 x 29", S, (**OI**: 382) £3,450
Figure in a Landscape
M 6 x 13", S, D, I, (**VI**: 107) £520
Donkey and Turf Cart with Figures by a Monument
O 14 x 31", S, (**GII**: 1482) £1,200
Irish Fishing Harbour with Figures and Currach
O 14 x 31.5", S, (**GII**: 1483) £1,400
REID, Nano (1905-1981)
Auction Record: IR£4,800
Fishermen
Oil 24 x 48 ins. S
James Adam, 29 March 1995 Lot 36
Study of a Man Writing
D 14.5 x 18", S, (**QI**: 195) £862
REYNOLDS, Lee (20th Century)
Cityscape
O 47.5 x 60", S, (**LI**: 118) £310
RIBOULET, Eugene (1883-1972)
Still Life
O 28 x 21.5", S, (**VI**: 61) £570
RICE, Noreen (b.1936)
Abstract Composition
P 17 x 32", S, (**O**: 99) £400
Landscape with Goat
M 23 x 34", S, (**VI**: 31) £750
Birds and Insects
O 23 x 36", S, (**ZI**: 80) £400
RICHARDSON, H. Hughes
Ross Castle, Killarney
W 8 x 12", S, (**PI**: 179) £500
RIGNEY, P. (19th Century)
A Killarney Fair
O 22 x 35", S, (**O**: 39) £4,000
RIVERS, Elizabeth (20th Century)
Men with a Ladder
Pr (**G**: 204) £200
ROBERTS, Thomas (1748-1778)
Auction Record: £129,944
Wooden Landscape with Stags and Doe
44 x 60 ins. S & D 1774
Christie's (New York), 15 January 1988, Lot 46
ROBINSON, Markey (1918-1999)
Figures in Landscape
W 7.5 x 16", (**D**: 81) £950
Wed to the Sea
W 5 x 7.5", S, (**D**: 135) £280
Outside the Cathedral
W 26 x 32", S, (**O**: 120) £900
Still Life in a Landscape
W 13 x 21", S, (**O**: 121) £870
Three Trees
W 12 x 20", S, (**W**: 68) £500
The Joy of Peace
W 25 x 20", S, I, (**EI**: 139) £1,200
Moored Boat with Figure looking at the Sea
W 12 x 19", S, (**EI**: 140) £1,100
The Harbour Entrance, Honfleur (by Eugene Baboulene) [This is a print over-painted by Robinson]
W 25 x 31", (**EI**: 141) £1,900
Still Life, Harbour
W 24 x 21.5", S, (**EI**: 163) £1,300
Golden Autumn
W 12 x 27.5", S, (**EI**: 164) £800
Blue and Blue Shaded Trees
W 12 x 27.5", S, (**EI**: 181) £800
Still Life
O 15.5 x 4", (**EI**: 182) £620
Shawlies and Cottages
O 20 x 32", S, (**NI**: 194) £5,750
Men of the Road; and Turnip Seed
W & O (2) 13.5 x 23.5", S, I, (**NI**: 202) £10,580
Shawlies, Cottages and Sea
O (2) 5.5 x 12", S, (**NI**: 203) £2,300
Still Life with Flowers and Fruit
O 12.5 x 20", S, (**NI**: 204) £1,955
Achill Village
O 29.5 x 39", S, I, (**OI**: 397) £9,775
Harvest Time
O 15 x 26", S, (**PI**: 11) £11,000
Still Life
W 13.5 x 22", S, (**PI**: 18) £1,800
Sifting Corn
O 17 x 28", S, (**PI**: 31) £15,500
Circus Dancers
W 33 x 7", S, (**VI**: 29) £2,200
Still Life at a Window
W 40 x 20", S, (**VI**: 60) £2,800
Midsummer Day
W 8.5 x 19", S, (**VI**: 183G) £950
Gable end cottages
O 12 x 18", S, (**BII**) £640
Sailing Boats
O 10 x 24", S, (**BII**) £600
A Musical Evening with George Campbell
O 24 x 20", S, (**DII**: 12) £1,400
Gable End Walls at Dusk
O 7.5 x 20", S, (**DII**: 37) £800
A Forlorn Figure in a Lake; Mountain Landscape
O (2) 4 x 14", S, (**DII**: 38) £600
Celtic Warriors
W (2) 20 x 12.5", S, (**EII**: 320) £750
Haystacks by the Sea
O 10 x 15.5", (**JII**: 107) £525
Still Life - Cups, Bottles and Guitar
O 19 x 12", (**JII**: 126) £700
Figures on the West Coast
O 7 x 9.5", (**JII**: 226) £470
Turf stocking and figure in the West of Ireland
O 10 x 12", S, (**JII**: 232) £400
Circus Clown
O 19.5 x 12.5", S, (**JII**: 233) £850
Circus Clown
O 20 x 13", S, (**JII**: 237) £850

Fishing Boats - West of Ireland
12 x 19", S, (**JII**: 250) £1,300
Sailing Boat
O 8.5 x 11", S, (**JII**: 258) £900
The Clown
O 19.5 x 12", S, (**JII**: 440) £950
Near Merkesh, North Africa
5 x 9.5", S, I, (**JII**: 447) £300
Figures on a country path
O 5.5 x 13", (**JII**: 452) £420
Abstract
O 19.5 x 12", (**JII**: 458) £420
Still Life
O 20 x 13", S, (**JII**: 459) £570
Still Life - Fish
O 8.5 x 17.5", (**KII**: 652) £900
ROCHE,Tom (20th Century)
Strand Street
O S, (**W**: 108) £400
ROE, John William (19th Century)
Portrait of John Banim 1798-1842
O 8 x 7", (**OI**: 251) £1,265
ROSS, Helen (20th Century)
Children Skipping
O 17 x 19.5", S, (**EI**: 28) £750
ROTHSCHILD, Stephen (20th Century)
Untitled
M 19 x 21", (**G**: 203) £340
ROTHWELL, Richard (1800-1868)
A Mother and Child
O 40 x 34.5", (**NI**: 140) £6,900
RUSSELL, George (AE) (1867-1935)
Auction Record: £40,000
The Peat Gatherers
Oil 16 x 21 ins. S
Sotheby's Irish Sale, 21 May 1998, Lot 356
Muckish Mountain, Co. Donegal
O 21 x 32", S, (**D**: 32) £4,000
The Turf Cutter
O 21 x 32", S, (**V**: 40) £16,000
Forest interior with figures (Mid-summers night's dream)
O 14 x 18", S, (**V**: 94) £4,000
Twilight Landscape with Sheep
O 16 x 21", S, (**V**: 145) £2,000
On the Beach
O 21 x 32", S, (**NI**: 76) £13,800
Gifts of Heaven
O 15 x 20", S, (**NI**: 78) £2,070
The Sirens
O 21 x 32", S, (**OI**: 330) £13,800
Two Ladies on the Strand
O 16 x 21", S, (**OI**: 352) £4,830
A Peaceful Bathe
O 15 x 20", (**VI**: 15) £10,700
Three Children on a Beach
O 14 x 22", S, (**VI**: 48) £4,000
The Edge of the Lough
O 16 x 21", S, (**ZI**: 78) £1,900
Muckish Mountain with Village in Foreground
O 16.5 x 21.5", S, (**III**: 1219) £460
RYAN, Thomas (b.1929)
Trees at Mornington, Drogheda
O 12 x 11", S, (**D**: 38) £360
Portrait of Ken Dolan
O 20 x 16", S, D, I, (**D**: 66) £650
River Landscape with Bridge
O 13 x 16", S, (**D**: 71) £1,600
Pink Rose
O 6 x 8", S, (**O**: 112) £900
Cross of Jerusalem Rose
O 5.5 x 7.5", S, D, I, (**O**: 126) £700
Ryans Trees
O 20 x 24", S, (**V**: 57) £800
A Present from Kilkee
O 7 x 10", S, (**EI**: 220) £900
James's Street, Dublin
O 15.5 x 18", S, I, (**HI**: 8) £800
Alma Tadema Exhibition, Liverpool
W 5.5 x 5.5", S, D, I, (**LI**: 7) £360
A stroll on a country road
O 11.5 x 16", S, (**PI**: 12) £1,300

Markey ROBINSON, *Sifting Corn*, sold at James Adam & Bonhams, 26 May 1999 for £15,500

William SCOTT, *Figure and Still Life* (Orange Still Life) sold at Christie's London, 6 November 1998 for £79,600

Still life with willow pattern plate
O 14 x 18", S, (**PI**: 25) £2,500
Mary and Myles (1 year old)
D 20.5 x 15", S, (**PI**: 30) £750
Pool in the Phoenix Park
O 6 x 8", I, (**CII**) £800
Gathering Plums
O 12 x 10", S, (**GII**: 1445) £1,500
SADLER I, William (fl.1765-1788)
River Landscape with soldiers on a path near a cottage
O 11 x 17", (**OI**: 248) £1,725
Mountainous landscape with a view of a tower and figures in the foreground
O 8 x 12", (**OI**: 249) £2,300
SADLER II, William (c.1782-1839)
Auction Record: IR£25,000
Donnybrook Fair
21 x 35 ins.
Christie's (Dublin), 24 October 1988, Lot 25
Figures Crossing a Bridge in a Mountain Landscape
O 8.5 x 12", (**V**: 18) £2,200
Glendalough, Co. Wicklow
O 18 x 15", (**V**: 150) £3,000
A view of Dublin Bay with Kingstown Harbour in the foreground, the Hill of Howth in the distance, and the Pigeon House on the left
O 22.5 x 34", (**NI**: 145) £14,950
A view of the lower lake Killarney with the Eagle's Nest beyond
O 11.5 x 16", (**NI**: 147) £3,105
William III at the Battle of the Boyne
O 12 x 19", (**OI**: 250) £2,300
SALKELD, Cecil ffrench (1908-1968)
Music by Moonlight
O 23.5 x 18.5", S, (**HI**: 84) £1,600
Parting Lovers
O 24 x 20", S, D, (**VI**: 56) £4,500
Connemara - Beach Scene with Figures and Pony on a Hill
O 16 x 20", (**GII**: 1487) £1,900
Ballet - Ballerina looking in full length Mirror
O 20 x 16", S, D, I, (**GII**: 1488) £2,700

Glencree - Figures on a Road
O 13 x 9.5", (**III**: 1190) £1,300
Rock Temple Vishugram India
O 24 x 20", S, (**III**: 1207) £750
SANDERSON, Rosaleen (20th Century)
Tuscan Dancers
O 34.5 x 24.5", (**G**: 206) £380
SCHWATSCHKE, John (b.1943)
Rehearsal
O 30 x 35.5", (**G**: 208) £450
Thoughts of Second Marriage
O 23.5 x 20", S, I, (**VI**: 175) £700
SCOTT, Patrick (b.1920)
Gold Painting - 79
T 32 x 32", (**G**: 209) £3,000
Fount
Pr 23 x 23", S, (**O**: 123) £520
Distant Bog
T 24 x 30", (**W**: 58) £850
Bent Rainbow
O 72 x 72", S, D, I, (**LI**: 138) £2,000
SCOTT, William (1913-1989)
Auction Record: £117,000
Still Life
Oil 45 x 60 ins. S & D
Sotheby's, London, 18 June 1997, Lot 117
Eggs and Ivy Leaves
W 15 x 19.5", (**E**: 168) £27,600
Untitled
O 12 x 14", S, (**I**: 113) £9,775
Nile
O 20 x 20", (**I**: 114) £6,900
Black Circle
W 11 x 15", S, (**J**: 240) £5,980
Figure and Still Life (Orange Still Life)
O 48 x 60", (**J**: 241) £79,600
Ochre Still Life
O 36 x 41", (**S**: 81) £42,200
Composition with Blue and Grey
W 13 x 22", S, (**BI**: 196) £1,840
Head of a Girl
D 25 x 19", (**BI**: 204) £2,070
Still Life
W 11 x 15", S, (**DI**: 172) £8,050
Composition
W 7.5 x 9.5", S, D, (**DI**: 173) £2,875
Fish and Eggs
O 13 x 16", S, D, (**DI**: 174) £65,300
View of Enniskillen
W 16.5 x 20.5", S, I, (**HI**: 38) £2,600
Shapes
W 21.5 x 27.5", S, (**NI**: 98) £5,520
Table with Still Life, No.1
O 40 x 50", S, (**RI**: 78) £27,600
Still Life with Frying Pan 1952
O 22 x 26", S, (**SI**: 56) £26,450
Still Life
W 23 x 30", S, D, (**VI**: 144) £25,500
Blue and White Still Life
O 18 x 24", (**WI**: 104) £3,220
Five Blue Pears
O 16 x 20", (**WI**: 107) £21,850
Pears
Pr 19.5 x 25.5", S, I, (**LII**: 181) £1,955
Grapes
Pr 19.5 x 25", S, D, I, (**LII**: 182) £1,265
SCULLY, Harry (c.1863-1935)
A Quiet Harbour
W 5 x 8", S, D, (**D**: 58) £340
SEMPLE, Joseph (19th Century)
A Two Masted Sailing Vessel off a Lighthouse
O 20 x 31", S, D, (**OI**: 271) £1,725
SHACKLETON, Roger (1931-1987)
City Entrance
O 23 x 27", S, I, (**VI**: 42) £1,100
SHANNON, Sir James Jebusa (1862-1923)
In the Springtime
O 50 x 40", S, D, (**TI**: 28) £496,500
SHAWCROSS, Neil (20th Century)
Pink Chair
W 25 x 19", S, D, (**HI**: 92J) £950

SHEE, Sir Martin Archer (1769-1850)
Portrait of Dr Patrick Lynch
O 32.5 x 24", I, (**R**: 251) £2,070
SHELBOURNE, Anita (20th Century)
Winter Landscape
O 28 x 36", (**G**: 211) £1,000
SHERIDAN, Noel (b.1936)
Coastal Landscape
O 15 x 14.5", S, D, (**VI**: 59) £380
SHERIDAN, Vincent (20th Century)
Pretty Bird
Pr 26 x 33", (**G**: 212) £260
SHERRIN, Daniel (20th Century)
A Young Boy in a Country Path
O 38 x 24", S, (**ZI**: 51) £800
SINCLAIR, John (exh.1881-1923)
Gathering Peat
W 16 x 27", S, (**OI**: 281) £575
SKELTON, John (b.1923)
Aran Fisherman
O 15 x 22", S, (**ZI**: 31) £1,700
Sun & Shower, MacGillicuddy's Reeks, Co. Kerry
O 18 x 26", S, (**ZI**: 60) £340
Figures Under Trees in a landscape
W 12.5 x 17.5", S, (**EII**: 321) £200
SKERRETT, Pam (20th Century)
A Quiet Jar
W 22 x 15", S, (**ZI**: 86) £200
SLAUGHTER, Stephen (1697-1765)
Auction Record: £42,000
Ladies Gathering Fruit
48 x 39 ins.
Sotheby's, 19 November 1986, Lot 46
SLEATOR, James (1889-1950)
Auction Record: IR£18,000
A Dublin Interior
23 x 12 ins.
Christie's (Dublin), 12 December 1990, Lot 185
Still Life
O 19 x 24", (**O**: 5) £920
Female Nude in River Landscape
O 22 x 16", (**O**: 45) £2,300
Dick Devil
O 23 x 19.5", D, I, (**O**: 46) £1,200
A Head of a Man
O 7 x 9", (**O**: 76) £600
Chrysanthemums in a Vase
O 15 x 11", I, (**EI**: 76) £770
Self-Portrait with Hat
O 21 x 16.5", (**JI**: 14) £2,990
SLUIS, Pieter (20th Century)
La Toilette
O 19 x 15.5", S, (**O**: 128) £400
Figures
M 20 x 24", S, (**W**: 22) £200
Harmony
O 48 x 48", S, (**EI**: 205) £1,900
Still Life, Figure and Flowers
O 20.5 x 16", S, (**EI**: 206) £500
Figure holding a Plant
O 36 x 36", S, I, (**VI**: 67) £1,400
Dancing Girls
O 30 x 27", S, D, (**VI**: 140) £2,600
Circus Clown
O 19 x 16", S, (**VI**: 167) £970
The Musician
O 23 x 18", S, (**DII**: 73) £500
Abstract
W 16 x 22.5", S, (**DII**: 83) £480
SMITH, Blaise (20th Century)
Tadhg
O 24 x 20", (**G**: 215) £300
SMITH, Stephen Catterson (Junior) (1849-1912)
The Cameron Sisters
O 35 x 27", S, I, (**NI**: 182) £2,300
SOMERVILLE, Edith Oenone(1858-1949)
The Duke of Bronte's Garden, Taormina
O 13 x 21", S, (**EI**: 79) £750
I washes meself every morning whether I wants it or no - from 'A St. Patrick's Day Hunt'
D 8.5 x 6.5", I, (**PI**: 104) £280
Sunset over Lissard
O 9.5 x 10", (**ZI**: 27) £1,550
SOUTER, Camille (b.1929)
The Clown who makes Mistakes
O 22.5 x 24", S, (**O**: 96) £9,500
Snow in Mayo
O 7 x 11.5", S, I, (**EI**: 150) £4,800
Boxers
M 19 x 13", S, D, (**EI**: 224J) £6,500
Runway 5, Shannon Airport
A 18.5 x 24", S, (**QI**: 199) £6,900
Italian View
W & O 6.5 x 8", S, D, (**QI**: 206) £3,450
Abstract
W 12 x 18", S, D, I, (**QI**: 209) £4,025
Untitled
M 15.5 x 21", S, D, (**VI**: 70) £5,500
SPACKMAN, Basil (1895-1971)
Farm House
W 9.5 x 14.5", S, (**D**: 20) £220
SPILSBURY, Maria (1777-c.1823)
Samuel: Speak Lord for thy Servant Heareth
O 14 x 10" oval, S, (**OI**: 254) £1,725
SPODE, Samuel (fl.1825-1858)
'Foig-a-Ballagh' and 'Irish Birdcatcher'
O (2) 28 x 36", S, I, (**D**: 52) £26,000
Sultan and Lilla, two chestnut thoroughbreds standing in extensive landscapes
O (2) 20 x 24", S, (**PI**: 107) £10,000
STAPLES, Sir Robert Ponsonby, (1853-1943)
'Guilty or Not Guilty?'
O 44 x 59", S, (**NI**: 180) £20,700
At the Piano
W 9 x 11", S, D, I, (**NI**: 184) £2,760
Afternoon in the Park
O 20 x 24", S, (**PI**: 99) £16,000
STAPLETON, Rose (20th Century)
Molloy's Garden
O 20 x 16", (**G**: 217) £720
STEPHENSON, Desmond (1922-1963)
Still Life with Bottles
O 22 x 27", S, (**HI**: 18) £900
Wheatfield
O 11.5 x 19.5", S, (**HI**: 27) £850
Portrait of a Man
D 17.5 x 13", S, (**HI**: 114) £200
Landscape
O 16 x 20", (**JII**: 211) £575
Snow Glencree
O 15 x 22", S, (**JII**: 212) £800
STEYN, Stella (1907-1987)
Poster design for 'Long Winter Evenings'
C 29.5 x 20", (**F**: 240) £276
Avignon
W 4 x 3", (**CI**: 63) £253
Self Portrait with Palette
O 20 x 12", S, (**EI**: 51) £1,200
STOKES, Margaret (1916-1996)
Summers Night
O 12 x 16", S, (**O**: 59) £550
STOPFORD, Robert Lowe (1813-1898)
Cattle grazing, said to be Clew Bay, Ireland
W 18 x 27", S, D, (**OI**: 270) £1,035
STOPFORD, William Henry (1842-1890)
A View of the Blasket and Skellig Islands
W 20 x 28", S, (**PI**: 120) £1,400
STOUPE, Seamus (1872-1949)
Dun-na-Ngall
O 10 x 16", S, (**O**: 84) £400
STRONG, Rachel (20th Century)
Sailor, Monkey and Prostitute
A 24 x 30", S, (**W**: 115) £320
Nude Studies
A (2) 30 x 24", S, (**W**: 116) £250
Waiting
A 47 x 24", S, (**W**: 117) £300
STUART, Imogen (20th Century)
Mother and Child
Pr 31 x 25", (**G**: 218) £350
SUTTON, Ivan (20th Century)
Tall Ships, Dublin 1998
O 9 x 14.5", (**G**: 220) £1,200
The Drawing Room, Abbeyleix House
O 15 x 23", S, I, (**EI**: 131) £600
Outside the Oriel
O 28 x 32", S, (**LI**: 114) £1,500
SWANN, Lillian Bellingham
Early Morning
W 14 x 20.5", S, (**PI**: 173) £550
SWANZY, Mary (1882-1978)
Auction Record: £62,000
Woman with a White Bonnet
39 x 31.5 ins. S
Sotheby's, 16 May 1996, Lot 473
Portrait of a Young Girl holding a Muff
O 36 x 28", (**O**: 27) £6,200
Encounter in the Desert
O 12 x 9", S, (**O**: 67) £2,100
The Fisherboy with Sails
O 20 x 24", S, (**O**: 95A) £16,500
Continental Café
D 10 x 7.5", S, (**V**: 1) £900
Outdoor café scene, Czechoslovakia
D 6.5 x 10", (**W**: 72) £320
Snow Landscape, Slovakia
O 22 x 30", S, (**EI**: 75) £3,000
Pattern of Rooftops, Czechoslovakia
O 17 x 19", (**NI**: 4) £14,030
La Maison Blanche with Figures on the Lawn
O 16 x 14.5", (**NI**: 13) £14,950
Donegal
O 30 x 22", S, (**NI**: 15) £9,200
The Bridge
O 17 x 24", (**NI**: 19) £20,125
Cubist Landscape, Trees & Houses
O 13 x 18.5", (**VI**: 21) £7,500
Still Life - Fruit and Flowers
O 22 x 18", (**JII**: 118) £7,000
Ten Minute Pose
D 8 x 6.5", S, I, (**JII**: 222) £800
SWIFT, Patrick (1927-1983)
Landscape - study for 'Painting 74'
O 8 x 10", (**PI**: 133) £950
SWINEY, Eugene (20th Century)
Peasant Girl with a lamb in her hands
O 16 x 12", S, (**ZI**: 79) £700
TALLENTIRE, Anne (20th Century)
Harvest pattern (Muckish & Errigal)
O 15 x 30", S, (**W**: 104) £400
Evening Harbour
O 15 x 30", S, (**LI**: 95) £400
TALLON, Desmond (20th Century)
Gathering the Sheep
O 5 x 7", S, (**DII**: 20) £260
Slim Pickings - Donkeys in a Landscape
O 9.5 x 14", S, (**GII**: 1439) £320
TAYLOR, Maeve (20th Century)
Fishing at Derryinver, Renvyle
O 14 x 20", S, (**HI**: 96) £300
TAYLOR, Samuel C. (1870-1944)
Young Breton Girls on the Shore
O 13.5 x 9.5", (**O**: 47) £2,600
Set of 3 Views of Brittany
D (3) 12 x 9", 12 x 5.5", 8.5 x 7", (**O**: 91) £700
Views in Quimper, Brittany
D 11.5 x 8", I, (**EI**: 18) £340
Children, Brittany
O 10 x 14", (**VI**: 6) £1,700
TESKEY, Donald (20th Century)
Estuary II
O 15 x 22", (**G**: 222) £1,800
THOMPSON, Hugh (1860-1920)
Then her eyes caught sight
W 12 x 7", S, D, (**PI**: 103) £550
THONNES, Elke (20th Century)
Divided Attention
M 35.5 x 8", (**G**: 223) £450
TREACY, Liam (b.1934)
Boats in Mist
O 12 x 16", S, (**D**: 37) £350

The Sacristy
O 14 x 18", S, (O: 122) £950
The Flower Sellers - Duke Street
O 18 x 14", S, (V: 127) £900
Near Avoca
O S, (W: 103) £200
Snow at Avoca
O 14 x 18", S, (EI: 218) £720
Morning Shoppers
O 8 x 10", S, (HI: 2) £450
The Music Room
O 10 x 12", S, (HI: 53) £850
The Green Room
O 12 x 10", S, (LI: 106) £1,000
Cleggan Harbour
O 14 x 18", S, (PI: 169) £800
November Study
O 10 x 8", S, (ZI: 68) £400
Avoca in Winter
O 12 x 16", S, (III: 1217) £520
The harbour at Arklow
O 12 x 15", (JII: 81) £380
Near Avoca
O 14 x 18", S, (JII: 227) £280
Interior with red chair
O 11 x 13", S, (JII: 239) £575
Lock on the Canal
O 9.5 x 11.5", (JII: 253) £480
TUOHY, Patrick (1894-1930)
Portrait of Daniel Egan (& another)
O 41 x 33", (O: 44) £2,100
TURNER, Desmond (20th Century)
Achill Sound/ Beach in Achill
O 20 x 30", S, (D: 1) £550
Cottages in the West of Ireland
O 21 x 25", S, (JII: 108) £425
On Achill
O 20 x 24", (JII: 439) £440
West of Ireland Landscape
O 20 x 24", (JII: 441) £280
TYRRELL, Charles (b.1950)
Untitled 1997
O 54 x 54", (G: 227) £4,000
TYRRELL, Michael (20th Century)
Untitled
M 56 x 56", S, D, (LI: 137) £2,200
VALLELLY, John (b.1941)
Berber Musicians
W 14.5 x 18.5", S, (EI: 111) £1,100
VAN DER GRIJN, Eric (20th Century)
Painting 1 - 1981
O 31 x 31", S, D, I, (LI: 81) £280
Recess no. 15
O 30 x 30", S, I, (LI: 85) £400
VIALE, Patrick (20th Century)
Cornfield, Piemonte
O 16 x 12", (G: 228) £350
WADE, Jonathan (20th Century)
The Industrial Way
O 24 x 36", S, (ZI: 48) £800
WALKER, John Crampton (1890-1942)
A Spring Day, Caragh River,
Co. Kerry
O 18 x 24", S, I, (EI: 62) £800
WALMSLEY, Thomas (1763-1806)
Lake Scene (Possibly Killarney)
W 12 x 13", (EI: 144) £300
On the Dargle
O 22 x 32", (OI: 247) £3,450
A Farmer herding cattle in a winter landscape;
A Shepherd with sheep in a summer landscape
W (2) 11 x 15", I, (OI: 258A) £1,610
Bullock Castle, County Dublin
W 9.5 x 12", (PI: 43) £500
WALSH, Lorcan (20th Century)
The River Dodder
O 36 x 27", S, D, (W: 120) £460
Head I
A 12 x 8.5", S, (HI: 92G) £500
Head II
A 12 x 8.5", S, (HI: 92H) £600
Untitled - Head of a Man
A 24 x 20", S, D, (HI: 921) £480
WALSH, Wendy (20th Century)
A sprig of lily of the valley
W 12.5 x 12.5", S, D, (Q: 114) £1,700
Rosa "Narrow Water"
W 12 x 11", S, D, (W: 145) £440
WALSHE, Judith Caulfield (20th Century)
Dublin Street Scene
W 28 x 21", S, (LI: 12) £500
The Halfpenny Bridge, Dublin
W 19 x 20", S, (LI: 30) £360
The G.P.O., Dublin
W 18.5 x 20", S, (LI: 31) £320
Still Life - The Irish Times and Berries
W 17.5 x 23", S, (JII: 478) £1,050
WARREN, Barbara (b.1925)
Irelands Eye
O 24.5 x 28", (G: 231) £500
Paris Quayside
O 25 x 20", S, (O: 103) £1,000
Santa Eulalia
O 16 x 20", S, (JII: 450) £700
WATERWORTH, Anya (20th Century)
Untitled
O 12 x 16", (G: 230) £450
WATKINS, Bartholomew Colles (1833-1891)
The Gap of Dunloe, Killarney
O 10 x 13.5", S, D, (V: 6) £1,200
Murlough Bay and Fair Head, Coast of Antrim
O 13 x 20", S, (V: 68) £3,400
Peat Bog, Letterfrack, Connemara
O 28.5 x 44.5", S, (NI: 171) £21,850
Kylemore Lake, Connemara
O 29 x 46", S, D, I, (NI: 172) £11,500
WEBB, Kenneth (b.1927)
Autumn Forest
O 24 x 36", (G: 233) £10,000
Horn Head, Co. Donegal
O 15 x 36", S, (V: 161) £2,100
The Demesne, Carrickfergus
O 17 x 40", (W: 159A) £1,300
Last Day of Autumn
O 19 x 23", S, I, (EI: 202) £2,000
River Finn
O 11.5 x 15.5", S, (HI: 83) £460
The Twelve Bens
O 16 x 39.5", S, (HI: 110) £2,400
WHEATLEY, Francis (1747-1801)
Peasants drinking outside a Tavern, Ireland
W 5 x 7", S, (XI: 214) £276
WHELAN, Leo (1892-1956)
Old Man Seated in a Cottage Interior
O 15 x 12", S, I, (HI: 29) £2,100
Landscape with distant Mountain
O 9.5 x 14", (HI: 58) £1,500
Portrait of James Hicks
O 29 x 24", S, I, (FII: 218) £14,000
WILES, Frank (1889-1956)
Portfolio of Drawings
D various, (O: 95M) £750
WILKS, Maurice Canning (1911-1984)
New Auction Record: £9,775
Above Letterfrack, Co. Galway
O 30 x40 ins. S
Christie's London, The Irish Sale, 20 May 1999, Lot 36
On the Coast, Donegal
O 9.5 x 11.5", S, (D: 40) £1,300
Winter Evening, Lough Erne,
Co. Fermanagh
O 16 x 20", S, (D: 68) £5,000
Sunlit Day, Belfast Lough
W 9 x 12", S, (D: 119) £420
Trout Stream, Co. Antrim
O 16 x 20", S, (D: 125) £1,900
Landscape, Co. Galway
O 15.5 x 20", S, (D: 150) £2,900
Spring Morning, Kilkeel, Co. Down
O 15 x 19", S, I, (O: 64) £4,600
Stone and Hills, Inagh Valley, Connemara
O 13 x 16.5", S, I, (O: 68) £2,400
Sunshine and Rain & Incoming Tide
O (2) 10 x 12.5", (O: 83) £1,600
In the Inagh Valley - Connemara
O 16 x 20", S, I, (V: 5) £4,800
Connemara Landscape
O 12 x 16", S, (V: 95) £4,100
Antrim Coast at Drum-Na-Greer
O 16 x 30", S, I, (V: 109) £2,800
Showery weather, Dunfanaghy, Co. Donegal
O 16 x 20", S, (Z: 7) £1,955
Across Dublin Bay from Sutton
O 8 x 9.5", S, (EI: 4) £1,100
Landscape at Ballyconneely
O 8 x 9.5", S, (EI: 5) £1,000
Slieve Donard from Tyrella, Co. Down
O 16 x 20", S, I, (EI: 12) £3,500
Landscape, Connemara
O 20 x 24", S, I, (EI: 35) £2,300
Redbay Pier, Waterfoot, County Antrim
O 17 x 20", S, I, (EI: 177) £3,600
Silver Day Near Maam Cross, Connemara
O 18 x 22", S, (HI: 20A) £1,100
Ballintoy Harbour
W 10 x 14", S, (HI: 64) £610
Ballintoy, Co. Antrim
O 24 x 28", S, I, (NI: 32) £3,220
Harbour in Co. Donegal
O 20 x 24", S, (NI: 33) £3,450
Cushendun Bay, Co. Antrim
O 16 x 20", S, I, (NI: 34) £3,680
Boats at Low Tide
O 16 x 20", S, (NI: 35) £2,990
Above Letterfrack, Co. Galway
O 30 x 40", S, (NI: 36) £9,775
Cottages near Rosapenna, Co. Donegal
O 16 x 20", S, I, (NI: 38) £4,830
Reflections, Glenveagh, Co. Donegal
O 20 x 24", S, I, (NI: 39) £3,910
Antrim Stackyard
O 20 x 24", S, I, (NI: 40) £4,370
In Tollymore Park, Newcastle, Co. Down
O 18 x 24", S, I, (NI: 41) £2,530
Spring Day, Dun River, Co. Antrim
O 14 x 10", S, I, (NI: 108) £2,070
Cushendun, County Antrim
O 10 x 16", S, (PI: 8) £1,300
In the Rosses Country, County Donegal
O 25 x 30", S, (PI: 15) £6,200
Tyrella, County Down
O 10 x 16", S, (PI: 22) £1,800
Cottages at Roundstone, County Galway
O 16 x 20", S, (PI: 51) £3,600
Summer Day, Cushendun, County Antrim
O 25.5 x 30", S, (PI: 96) £7,200
In the Inagh Valley
O 20 x 24", S, (PI: 149) £3,600
Culdaff, County Donegal
O 16 x 20", S, (SI: 93) £4,025
Landscape, Maam Valley, Connemara
O 18 x 36", S, (VI: 4) £3,000
Bullock Harbour & Stephen's Green
D (2) 9 x 10" and 8 x 10", S, I, (VI: 120) £700
Approach to Inagh Valley
O 17 x 23", S, (AII) £2,850
Landscape Ballyconeelly, Connemara
O 20 x 24", S, (DII: 28) £2,000
A Half Length Portrait of a Lady
O 25 x 31", S, (DII: 53) £1,050
A Coastal Landscape in theWest
O 16 x 19", S, (EII: 298) £1,500
An Extensive Lake Landscape
O 16 x 31.5", S, I, (EII: 344) £1,300
On the Kerry Coast
O 15.5 x 19.5", S, (FII: 163) £7,500
Portrait of a Woman, seated
O 29.5 x 24.5", S, (FII: 204) £3,000
Near Bunbeg, Co. Donegal
O 20 x 26", S, (JII: 497) £5,400
WILLES, William (fl.1815-1849, d.1851)
The Mock Funeral
O 40 x 50", S, (NI: 156) £45,500

WILLIAMS, Alexander (1846-1930)
Auction Record: £5,800
When Boats Come Home, Skerries Beach
Oil
Christie's Glasgow, September 1991
Western Coastal Scene
O 10 x 7.5", S, (D: 7) £500
Lough Corrib and Long Range, Killarney
W (2) 10.5 x 18", S, (D: 19) £750
In the Vale of Avoca
W 9 x 17", S, I, (EI: 162) £380
Shipping off the Coast
O 7 x 9.5", S, (HI: 53A) £750
Wild Heather on the Achill Coast, Blacksod Bay, Co. Mayo
W 17 x 29", S, (NI: 185) £575
The Coast Road
O 24 x 42", S, (OI: 277) £4,370
Achill Island
O 9.5 x 17.5", S, (PI: 14) £1,500
Harvesters, Achill Sound, County Mayo
W 7 x 13.5", S, (PI: 158) £500
Wicklow Landscape
W 21 x 30", S, (ZI: 44) £430
Lake & Mountain Landscape
W 12 x 21", S, (ZI: 85) £360
Newport Bridge, Co. Mayo
W 6 x 16.5", S, (DII: 76) £440
Muckross Lake Killarney
W 9.5 x 17.5", S, I, (GII: 1441) £340
Castle Lough, Killarney
W 12 x 20", S, I, (JII: 514) £675
Isle of Anglesea
W 12 x 20", S, I, (JII: 515) £380
Salmon Pool from the bridge, Kylemore, Connemara
W 8 x 15", S, I, (MII: 14) £218

WILLIAMS, Lily (1874-1940)
Ernest Blythe and Mrs Blythe
O (2) 25 x 30", S, (VI: 153) £6,000
Enniskerry, Co. Wicklow
O 8 x 6", (III: 1160) £525
Cottage at Ticknock
O 6.5 x 9.5", S, (III: 1161) £775

WILLIAMS, Walter Heath (1835-1906)
Harvest Time
O 18 x 26", S, (O: 85) £800

WILLIAMSON, W.H. (19th Century)
Shipping Scene
O 18 x 24", S, (CII) £1,650

WOODS, Padraig (1893-1991)
Lakeside Cottage with Figure and Sheep outside
O 20 x 23", S, (EI: 64) £900

WYNNE, Gladys (1878-1968)
Lake and Mountain Landscape
W 10 x 14", S, (D: 109) £220
Band Stand, St. Stephens Green
W 9.5 x 13.5", S, (JII: 480) £1,200

WYNNE-JONES, Nancy (20th Century)
Wide Wicklow Landscape
A 16.5 x 21.5", (G: 116) £520

YEATS, Anne (b.1919)
The Overgrown Garden
O 22 x 15", S, (W: 78) £320
Still Life with Tangled Wool
O 20 x 27", S, I, (EI: 123) £800
Abstract Composition Collage
O 19 x 26", I, (EII: 307) £400
Cloth Painting Two
O 11 x 15", S, (GII: 1442) £280
Grey and brown strings
O 13 x 19", S, (JII: 256) £300

YEATS, Jack B. (1871-1957)
New Auction Record: £1,233,500
The Wild Ones
Oil 14 x 21 ins. S
Sotheby's, The Irish Sale, 21 May 1999, Lot 331
A Shop in a Sailor Town
Pr 6 x 8", (G: 236) £620
The Strand Races and The Start and the Finish
Pr (2) 5 x 17", (O: 32) £1,700

Maurice WILKS, *Portrait of a Woman*, sold at Hamilton Osborne King, 31 May 1999 for £3,000

A Son of the Claddagh
O 18 x 24", S, (O: 57) £210,000
The Forester
Pr 7 x 5", (O: 92A) £600
Galway Hooker
Pr 5.5 x 10", (O: 95) £500
Gallery Boys
W 4.5 x 6", S, D, I, (O: 95N) £3,000
The Clown among the People
O 18 x 24", S, (S: 74) £143,400
A Lift
O 9 x 14", S, (V: 20) £100,000
The Pirate
W 6 x 4.5", S, (V: 23) £5,600
Sailor and a Woman
W 5.5 x 5.5", S, (V: 26) £5,400
Business
O 18 x 24", S, (V: 31) £150,000
"His Greatest Feat - leaping the policeman's"
D 5.5 x 3.5", S, I, (V: 58) £1,500
Opening the Parcel
O 14 x 18", S, (V: 60) £90,000
A Side Walk of New York
W 14.5 x 10.5", S, (V: 61) £52,000
Man versus Horse
O 18 x 24", S, (V: 106) £300,000
Bacchus
W 12 x 9", S, (V: 116) £30,000
The Beachcomber
O 9 x 14", S, I, (V: 129) £29,000
The Post Car
Pr 9 x 11.5", (EI: 147) £220
The Hurley Player
Pr 8 x 5", (EI: 197) £280
The Strand Races, The Start & The Finish
Pr (2) 5 x 17", (EI: 198) £500
The Egoist
D 6 x 2", (HI: 12) £400
Between Cork and Kerry
O 9 x 14", S, (HI: 43) £35,000
Engravings
O 14 x 18", S, (HI: 60) £92,000
A series of twenty-four leaflets, entitled 'A Broadside'
Pr (24) 11 x 7.5", I, (NI: 124) £3,680
Illustration to 'Bucks Have at Ye All;
The Gallery Boys
W 4.5 x 6", S, I, (NI: 126) £6,325
Telling the Cards
W 10 x 14", S, (NI: 127) £11,730
Apples in our Orchard, Devon
W 5 x 7", S, D, I, (NI: 127A) £3,565
Singing 'My Dark Rosaleen'
O 18 x 24", S, I, (NI: 129) £293,000
A series of fourteen leaflets, entitled 'A Broad Sheet'
Pr (14) 20 x 15", I, (NI: 130) £6,670
By Streedagh Strand
O 9 x 14", S, (NI: 131) £26,450
On the Hazard
O 11.5 x 15", S, (NI: 132) £22,425
Old Walls
O 18 x 24", S, I, (NI: 133) £84,000
Portrait of Adeline Healy
D 6 x 5", S, D, (NI: 135) £920
Driftwood in a Cave
O 14 x 21", S, I, (NI: 136) £89,500
The Wild Ones
O 14 x 21", S, (OI: 331) £1,233,500
Sunday Evening in September
O 14 x 18", S, (OI: 332) £265,500
Let 'em go and take care of yourselves
O 24 x 36", S, (OI: 333) £551,500
An Outsider
W 13 x 9", S, D, I, (OI: 334) £8,625
The Crown and Anchor Man
D 6 x 3.5", S, (OI: 338) £4,140
From the Tram Top
O 9 x 14", S, I, (OI: 339) £122,500
A Patriot
W 14 x 6.5", (OI: 341) £14,950
That's Enough, Take Him Away
W 4.5 x 3", S, I, (OI: 342) £8,050
West Country Races
D 14.5 x 10", S, D, (OI: 343) £10,925
The Boxer
D 3 x 4.5", S, (OI: 344) £3,220
'How did you get here?' He asked
W 7 x 10", (OI: 345) £6,325
Those Others
O 24 x 36", S, I, (OI: 346) £331,500
Eyes
O 18 x 24", S, I, (OI: 350) £166,500
Osmunda Ferns in Creels with Fish
W 3 x 5", I, (OI: 354) £2,300
Man in a Court of Justice Reading
O 18 x 24", S, I, (OI: 355) £84,000
A Pair of Beauties
D (2) 5.5 x 4.5", S, (OI: 360) £3,680
Goose
W 3 x 5", (OI: 361) £2,530
A Roman Soldier and A Sailing Boat
D 4 x 7", (PI: 96A) £570
The First Away
O 14 x 21", S, (VI: 88) £135,000
Low Tide, The Drumcliffe River making its way to the Sea
O 14 x 21", S, (VI: 90) £50,000
The Strand Races, The Start and The Finish
Pr (2) 5 x 17", (VI: 179) £1,500
Dublin Quays
Pr 7 x 5", (VI: 180) £650
The Post Car
Pr 8 x 12", (VI: 181) £220

YEATS, John Butler (1839-1922)
Auction Record: IR£26,000
Portrait of Maire Nic Shiubhlaigh, The Abbey Actress
Gouache 19 x 15 ins. S
deVeres, 22 April 1998, Lot 33
Half length Portrait of John B Yeats
D 10 x 7", S, (ZI: 37) £1,800

YOUNG, Mabel (1890-1974)
Christmas Roses
O 12 x 14", S, (D: 137) £1,400
Mountainous Landscape
O 12 x 15.5", S, (GII: 1427) £400
Gweedore Bay, Co. Donegal, Coastal Scene
O 12 x 16", S, (GII: 1428) £360
The Swiss Alps
O 12 x 16", S, (III: 1187) £400
Still Life - Porcelain Vase with colourful flowers
O 12 x 16", S, (III: 1188) £850

Index to Irish Arts Review Yearbook Vol 16, 2000

Index of Advertisers in Irish Arts Review Yearbook 2000. Vol 16

PICTURE CREDITS FOR IRISH ARTS REVIEW YEARBOOK 2000

The numbers are those of the pages on which the photographs appear

Norman Parkinson Ltd: Front Cover; National Museums of Northern Ireland, Ulster Folk and Transport Museum (Figs 13 & 15) **39**; Bryan Rutledge, (Figs 2 & 3) **35, 37** (Figs 7, 8, 9, & 10) **38** (Fig 14) **39**, (Fig 16 & 17) **40**; Denis Mortell **62-72**; Anthony Hobbs, **94**; Norman Mc Grath Studio **99**, (Fig 7) **103**, **104-6**; Denis Mortell **110-19**; Denis Davison **132-38**; Denis Mortell **150**, **155**.